Creating a Web Site

Second Edition

THE MISSING MANUAL

*The book that
should have been
in the box*®

Creating a Web Site

Second Edition

Matthew MacDonald

POGUE PRESS™
O'REILLY®

Beijing · Cambridge · Farnham · Köln · Sebastopol · Tokyo

Creating a Web Site: The Missing Manual
by Matthew MacDonald

Published by O'Reilly Media, Inc., 1005 Gravenstein Highway North, Sebastopol, CA 95472.

O'Reilly books may be purchased for educational, business, or sales promotional use. Online editions are also available for most titles (*safari.oreilly.com*). For more information, contact our corporate/institutional sales department: (800) 998-9938 or *corporate@oreilly.com*.

Printing History:

October 2005:	First Edition.
December 2008:	Second Edition.

 This book uses RepKover™, a durable and flexible lay-flat binding.

ISBN: 978-0-596-52097-7
[M]

Table of Contents

Part Three: Connecting With Your Audience

Part Six: Appendixes

The Missing Credits

About the Author

Matthew MacDonald is an author and programmer extraordinaire. His books include *Excel 2007: The Missing Manual, Access 2007: The Missing Manual*, and over a dozen books about programming with the Microsoft .NET Framework. He's also the author of *Your Brain: The Missing Manual*, a quirky exploration into the odd and wondrous world of your squishy gray matter. In a dimly remembered past life, he studied English literature and theoretical physics.

About the Creative Team

Peter McKie (editor) is an editor at Missing Manuals. Having developed several failed Web sites prior to editing this book, he now sees where he went wrong. He lives in New York City where he hikes, kayaks, and canoes in the Hudson Highlands. A fan of old buildings, he's volunteered at Open House New York (*www. ohny.org*), a nonprofit that opens normally closed historic buildings to New Yorkers for free one weekend each year. Email: *pmckie@gmail.com*.

Nellie McKesson (production editor) lives in Jamaica Plain, Mass., and spends her spare time making t-shirts (*mattsaundersbynellie.etsy.com*) and playing music with her band Dr. & Mrs. Van Der Trampp (*http://myspace.com/drmrsvandertrampp*). Email: *nellie@oreilly.com*.

Alison O'Byrne (copy editor) has been a professional freelance editor for over six years. She lives with her family in Dublin, Ireland. Email: *alison@alhaus.com*. Web site: *www.alhaus.com*.

Ron Strauss (indexer) is a full-time freelance indexer specializing in IT. When not working, he moonlights as a concert violist and alternative medicine health consultant. Email: *rstrauss@mchsi.com*.

Tony Ruscoe (technical reviewer) is a web developer living in Sheffield, England. His first computer programs were written in Sinclair BASIC on his ZX Spectrum in the mid-1980s. He's been developing Web sites and Web applications using a variety of programming technologies and techniques since 1997. He currently maintains his personal Web site (*http://ruscoe.net*) and a site dedicated to researching his surname (*http://ruscoe.name*).

Megan Sorensen (technical reviewer) is an office manager working for a local community hospital. She lives with her husband and daughter in Santa Rosa, California. In her spare time she enjoys traveling, reading, and spending time with her family. Email: *briannmegan@gmail.com*.

Acknowledgments

No author could complete a book without a small army of helpful individuals. I'm deeply indebted to the whole Missing Manual team, especially my editor Peter McKie, who kept me on track with relatively gentle prodding, Dawn Frausto, who helped coordinate the entire process, and technical reviewers Tony Ruscoe and Megan Sorensen, who caught obscure mistakes and offered valuable suggestions. I also owe a hearty thanks to those who left their mark on the first edition of this book, including Sarah Milstein, Peter Meyers, and technical reviewers Jim Goodenough, Rhea Howard, and Mark Levitt. And, as always, I'm also deeply indebted to numerous others who've toiled behind the scenes indexing pages, drawing figures, and proofreading the final copy.

Finally, I'd never write any book without the support of my parents Nora and Paul, my extended parents Razia and Hamid, and my wife Faria. (And I'd write many more without the challenges of my two lovable daughters, Maya and Brenna.) Thanks everyone!

—Matthew MacDonald

The Missing Manual Series

Missing Manuals are witty, superbly written guides to computer products that don't come with printed manuals (which is just about all of them). Each book features a handcrafted index; cross-references to specific pages (not just chapters); and RepKover, a detached-spine binding that lets the book lie perfectly flat without the assistance of weights or cinder blocks.

Recent and upcoming titles include:

Access 2007: The Missing Manual by Matthew MacDonald

AppleScript: The Missing Manual by Adam Goldstein

AppleWorks 6: The Missing Manual by Jim Elferdink and David Reynolds

CSS: The Missing Manual by David Sawyer McFarland

Creating Web Sites: The Missing Manual by Matthew MacDonald

David Pogue's Digital Photography: The Missing Manual by David Pogue

Dreamweaver 8: The Missing Manual by David Sawyer McFarland

Dreamweaver CS3: The Missing Manual by David Sawyer McFarland

Dreamweaver CS4: The Missing Manual by David Sawyer McFarland

eBay: The Missing Manual by Nancy Conner

Excel 2003: The Missing Manual by Matthew MacDonald

Excel 2007: The Missing Manual by Matthew MacDonald

Facebook: The Missing Manual by E.A. Vander Veer

FileMaker Pro 8: The Missing Manual by Geoff Coffey and Susan Prosser

FileMaker Pro 9: The Missing Manual by Geoff Coffey and Susan Prosser

Flash 8: The Missing Manual by E.A. Vander Veer

Flash CS3: The Missing Manual by E.A. Vander Veer and Chris Grover

Flash CS4: The Missing Manual by Chris Grover with E.A. Vander Veer

FrontPage 2003: The Missing Manual by Jessica Mantaro

Google Apps: The Missing Manual by Nancy Conner

The Internet: The Missing Manual by David Pogue and J.D. Biersdorfer

iMovie 6 & iDVD: The Missing Manual by David Pogue

iMovie '08 & iDVD: The Missing Manual by David Pogue

iPhone: The Missing Manual by David Pogue

iPhoto '08: The Missing Manual by David Pogue

iPod: The Missing Manual, Sixth Edition by J.D. Biersdorfer

JavaScript: The Missing Manual by David Sawyer McFarland

Mac OS X: The Missing Manual, Tiger Edition by David Pogue

Mac OS X: The Missing Manual, Leopard Edition by David Pogue

Microsoft Project 2007: The Missing Manual by Bonnie Biafore

Office 2004 for Macintosh: The Missing Manual by Mark H. Walker and Franklin Tessler

Office 2007: The Missing Manual by Chris Grover, Matthew MacDonald, and E.A. Vander Veer

Office 2008 for Macintosh: The Missing Manual by Jim Elferdink

PCs: The Missing Manual by Andy Rathbone

Photoshop Elements 7: The Missing Manual by Barbara Brundage

Photoshop Elements 6 for Mac: The Missing Manual by Barbara Brundage

PowerPoint 2007: The Missing Manual by E.A. Vander Veer

QuickBase: The Missing Manual by Nancy Conner

QuickBooks 2008: The Missing Manual by Bonnie Biafore

Quicken 2008: The Missing Manual by Bonnie Biafore

Quicken 2009: The Missing Manual by Bonnie Biafore

QuickBooks 2009: The Missing Manual by Bonnie Biafore

Switching to the Mac: The Missing Manual, Tiger Edition by David Pogue and Adam Goldstein

Switching to the Mac: The Missing Manual, Leopard Edition by David Pogue

Wikipedia: The Missing Manual by John Broughton

Windows XP Home Edition: The Missing Manual, Second Edition by David Pogue

Windows XP Pro: The Missing Manual, Second Edition by David Pogue, Craig Zacker, and Linda Zacker

Windows Vista: The Missing Manual by David Pogue

Windows Vista for Starters: The Missing Manual by David Pogue

Word 2007: The Missing Manual by Chris Grover

Your Brain: The Missing Manual by Matthew MacDonald

Introduction

These days, it's all but impossible to find someone who *hasn't* heard of the Internet. Companies create Web sites before they make business plans. Ordinary people build obsessively detailed pages describing their celebrity-themed swizzle-stick collections. And political activists attack their opponents with gossip, pictures, and embarrassing videos. The Internet has even changed our language: *google* and *blog* are now verbs, for example, and social networking has nothing to do with face-to-face encounters.

Everyone wants their own piece of Web real estate. Unfortunately, building a Web site isn't as easy as it should be. Even though people have been building sites for years, Web site development has only become more complicated. That's because Web programmers have been busy creating new technologies and introducing new standards that add features, solve problems, and iron out earlier quirks. If you want to create a fresh, cutting-edge Web site (instead of one that looks as hokey as a 1960s yearbook portrait), you need to understand these different ingredients and how they fit together.

That's where this book comes in. Bookstore shelves are full of Web site design books written years ago. They don't cover the current techniques your site needs to distinguish itself, make money, and show up in search results. This book corrects those mistakes—it includes all the advice and guidance you need to build a modern Web site. With this book by your side, you'll learn how to:

- **Create Web pages.** XHTML (Extensible HyperText Markup Language) is the modern language of the Web, and the latest stage in the evolution of HTML. It's surprisingly easy to use but maddeningly inflexible—violate its strict syntax rules at your own peril. In this book, you'll learn how to write first-rate XHTML pages and get the most out of the language.

- **Make pages look beautiful using CSS (Cascading Style Sheets).** CSS picks up where XHTML leaves off, adding formatting muscle that can transform the drabbest of sites into a family of coordinated pages that look like they were professionally designed. Best of all, once you understand the *right* way to use CSS, you'll be able to apply a new look to your entire site by tweaking just a single file.

- **Put your Web site online.** The world's greatest Web site isn't much good if no one sees it. That's why you'll learn how to choose the best Web hosting company, pick a *domain name* (like *www.HotToTrotHorses.com*), and get your masterpiece online. Don't panic—there are plenty of cheap Web hosting companies ready to show off your site for pennies a day.

- **Attract visitors.** You'll learn how to make sure people can find your site using popular search engines and how to build an online community that encourages repeat visits with discussion boards.

- **Get rich (or at least earn some spare change).** The Web's a lynchpin of retail commerce, but even ordinary people can make money selling products (using convenient services like PayPal) or displaying ads (with Google). You'll learn how to get in on the action.

- **Pile on the frills.** Every Web site worth its salt boasts a few cool tricks. You'll learn how to dazzle visitors with cool buttons, slick menus, and other flashy elements, courtesy of JavaScript and Dynamic XHTML. You'll even learn how to (shudder) serenade visitors with background music.

What You Need to Get Started

This book assumes that you don't have anything more than a reasonably up-to-date computer and raw ambition. Although there are dozens of high-powered Web editing programs that can help you build a Web site, you *don't* need one to use this book. In fact, if you use a Web editor before you understand how Web sites work, you're liable to create more problems than you solve. That's because, as helpful as these programs are, they shield you from learning the principles of good site design—principles that can mean the difference between an attractive, easy-to-maintain Web creation and a disorganized design nightmare.

Once you master the basics, you're welcome to use a fancy Web-page editor like Microsoft Expression Web or Adobe Dreamweaver. You'll not only learn how these two leading programs work, you'll discover a few great free alternatives (in Chapter 4).

Note: Under no circumstances do you need to know anything about complex Web programming technologies like Java or ASP.NET. You also don't need to know anything about databases or XML. These topics are fascinating, but insanely difficult to implement without some solid programming experience. In this book, you'll learn how to create the best possible Web site without becoming a programmer. (You *will*, however, learn just enough about JavaScript to use many of the free samples you can find online.)

About This Book

No one owns the Web. As a result, no one is responsible for teaching you how to use it or how to build an online home for yourself. That's where this book comes in. If the Web *did* have an instruction manual—one that painstakingly details the basic ingredients, time-saving tricks, and impressive embellishments every site needs—this would be it.

Note: This book periodically recommends *other* books covering topics that are too specialized or diverse for a manual about creating Web sites. Careful readers may notice that not every one of these titles is published by Missing Manual parent O'Reilly Media. While we're happy to mention other Missing Manuals and books in the O'Reilly family, if there's a great book out there that doesn't happen to be published by O'Reilly, we'll still let you know about it.

Macintosh and Windows

One of the best things about the World Wide Web is that it truly is worldwide: Wherever you live, from Aruba to Zambia, the Web eagerly awaits your company. The same goes for whatever kind of computer you're using to develop your site. From an early-model Windows PC to the latest and greatest Mac, you can implement the tactics, tools, and tricks described in this book with pretty much whatever kind of computer you have. (Of course, a few programs favor one operating system over another, but you'll hear about these differences whenever they come up.) The good news is that this book is usable and suitable for owners of computers of all stripes.

About the Outline

This book is divided into five parts, each with several chapters:

- **Part One: Welcome to the Web.** In this part of the book, you'll start planning your Web site (Chapter 1). You'll learn the basics behind XHTML, the language of the Web (Chapter 2); and you'll put your page online with a reputable hosting company (Chapter 3). Finally, you'll look at how you can simplify your life by using Web-page editing software (Chapter 4).

- **Part Two: Building Better Web Pages.** This section shows you how to add essentials to your pages, like pictures, links, and tables. You'll learn your way around the CSS standard, which lets you specify fancy colors, fonts, and borders (Chapter 6). You'll master slick layouts (Chapters 9 and 10), and create an entire Web site made of linked pages.

- **Part Three: Connecting With Your Audience.** The third part of the book explains how to get your site noticed by search engines like Google (Chapter 11), and how to foster a community by making your site interactive with features like discussion boards (Chapter 12). Finally, you'll learn how to get on the path to Web riches by displaying ads or selling your own products (Chapter 13).

- **Part Four: Web Site Frills.** Now that you can create a professional, working Web site, why not deck it out with fancy features like glowing buttons and pop-out menus? You won't learn the brain-bending details of how to become a Java-Script programmer, but you'll learn enough to find great scripts online and to use them in your own creations. You'll also dabble with homemade movie clips and add an MP3 music player right inside an ordinary Web page.

- **Part Five: Blogs.** In this brief section, you'll take a look at *blogs* (short for *Web logs*) and the free software that helps you create them. Blogs are a type of Web page that consists of regular, dated postings—like an online journal. In recent years, blogs have become a self-publishing phenomenon and a great place to rant, rave, and spill company gossip.

At the end of this book, you'll find two appendixes. The first gives you a quick reference for XHTML. It explains the essential XHTML elements and points you to more detailed discussions in the various chapters of this book. The second appendix lists a pile of useful links culled from the chapters in this book, which can help you learn more, get free stuff (like pictures, Web software, and handy examples), and sign up for services (like Google's ad program and PayPal's shopping cart tools). Don't worry—you don't need to type these Web links into your browser by hand. It's all waiting for you on the Missing CD page for this book at *www.missingmanuals.com*.

About → These → Arrows

Throughout this book, you'll find sentences like this one: "To open a new window, choose File → New → Window." That's shorthand for a much longer instruction that directs you to open three menus in sequence, like this: "Open the File menu by clicking File in the menu bar. In the File menu, click New to open a second menu. In *that* menu, click Window to complete the process." Figure I-1 shows a closer look.

Downloadable Examples

This book includes a number of examples of Web page designs. Most of them are available for your downloading pleasure at *www.missingmanuals.com* (click the Missing CD page link, and then the link for this book; the files are organized by chapter). Playing with these files is a great way to learn more.

About MissingManuals.com

At *www.missingmanuals.com*, you'll find articles, tips, and updates to *Creating a Web Site: The Missing Manual.* In fact, we invite and encourage you to submit such corrections and updates yourself. In an effort to keep the book as up to date and accurate as possible, each time we print more copies of this book, we'll make any confirmed corrections you've suggested. We'll also note such changes on the Web

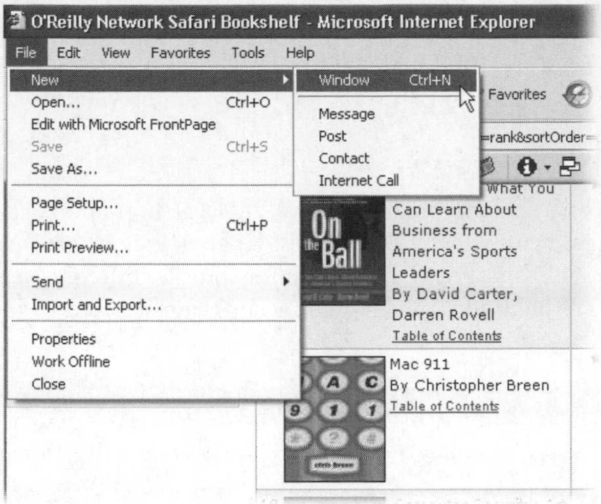

Figure I-1:
In this book, arrow notations help simplify folder and menu instructions. For example, "Choose File → New → Window" is a more compact way of saying "From the File menu, choose New; from the submenu that appears, choose Window," as shown here.

site, so that you can mark important corrections into your own copy of the book, if you like. (Go to *http://missingmanuals.com/feedback*, choose the book's name from the pop-up menu, and then click Go to see the changes.)

Also on our Feedback page, you can get expert answers to questions that come to you while reading this book, write a book review, and find groups for folks who share your interest in creating Web sites.

While you're there, sign up for our free monthly email newsletter. Click the "Sign Up for Our Newsletter" link in the left-hand column. You'll find out what's happening in Missing Manual land, meet the authors and editors, see bonus video and book excerpts, and so on.

We'd love to hear your suggestions for new books in the Missing Manual line. There's a place for that on MissingManuals.com, too. And while you're online, you can also register this book at *www.oreilly.com* (you can jump directly to the registration page by going here: *http://tinyurl.com/yo82k3*). Registering means that we can send you updates about this book, and you'll be eligible for special offers like discounts on future editions of *Creating a Web Site: The Missing Manual*.

Safari® Books Online

When you see a Safari® Books Online icon on the cover of your favorite technology book, it means the book is available online through the O'Reilly Network Safari Bookshelf.

Safari offers a solution that's better than e-Books. It's a virtual library that lets you easily search thousands of top tech books, cut and paste code samples, download chapters, and find quick answers when you need the most accurate, current information. Try it free at *http://safari.oreilly.com*.

Part One:
Welcome to the Web

1

Preparing for the Web

The Web's an exciting place. Every day, it processes millions of financial transactions, serves up late-breaking news and scandalous celebrity gossip, and provides a thriving meeting place for every type of community, from political anarchists to reality-show fans.

Since you're reading this book, you've probably decided to move in and join the Web. Congratulations! Just as you undertake some basic planning before you find a home in the real world, you also need to prepare before you make the move to your new online neighborhood. In this chapter, you'll get a good look at the Web and what it takes to establish your own site. You'll also learn how the Web works behind the scenes, and what ingredients you need to build your site.

Introducing the World Wide Web

Although it doesn't show its age, the Internet is older than you might think. The computer visionaries who created the Internet began developing the idea in the early 1960s. In 1969, the first transmission over the Internet took place, between a computer at the University of California at Los Angeles and one at the Stanford Research Institute. As far as pioneering moments go, it wasn't much to brag about—the computer crashed when it reached the G in the word "LOGIN." Still, the revolution was underway.

The early Internet was mostly traveled by academic and government types. It flourished as a tool for research and collaboration, letting scientists everywhere share information. In 1993 the first Web browser hit the scene. In the following years, the Internet was colonized by new types of people, including book shoppers, news junkies, hobbyists, and a lot of lonely computer programmers.

Tip: History buffs can follow the saga of the early Internet in much more detail at *www.isoc.org/internet/history* and *www.walthowe.com/navnet/history.html*.

Of course, the early Internet doesn't have much in common with today's Internet. In 1969, the Internet community consisted of four computers, all of which were beastly, complex machines that no one but a government lab or academic institution could love (or afford). In 1981, there were still fewer than 200 mainframe computers on the Internet, and most of the people using them were computer experts or scientists going about their day-to-day work. Today, well over one hundred million Web sites—and many more Web enthusiasts—are online. It's no wonder you're getting so much junk email.

FREQUENTLY ASKED QUESTION

The Web vs. the Internet

Is there a difference between the Web and the Internet?

Newscasters, politicians, and regular people often use these terms interchangeably. Technically, however, the concepts are different—and confusing them is likely to put computer techies and other self-respecting nerds on edge.

The *Internet* is a network of connected computers that spans the globe. These computers are connected together to share information, but there are a number of ways to do that, including emailing, instant messaging, transferring files through *FTP* (short for File Transfer Protocol), and downloading pirated Hollywood blockbusters through peer-to-peer programs (which of course you don't do). The *World Wide Web* is one of the many ways to exchange information across the Internet. And how does this information get exchanged? You guessed it—people use special programs called *Web browsers* to visit Web sites and Web pages spread across the globe.

Browsers

As you no doubt know, a Web browser is a piece of software that lets you navigate to and display Web pages. Without browsers, the Web would still exist, but you wouldn't be able to turn on your computer and take a look at it.

A browser is surprisingly simple—in fact, the bulk of its work consists of two tasks. First, it requests Web pages, which happens when you type in a Web site address (like *www.google.com*) or click a link in a Web page. The browser sends that request to a far-off computer called a *Web server*. A server is typically much more powerful than a home computer because it needs to handle multiple browser requests at the same time. The Web server heeds the request and sends back the contents of the desired Web page.

When the browser gets those contents, it puts its second skill into action and *renders*, or draws, the Web page. Technically, this means the browser converts the plain text it receives from the server into a display document based on formatting instructions embedded in the plain-text page. The end result is a graphically rich page with different typefaces, colors, and links. Figure 1-1 shows the process.

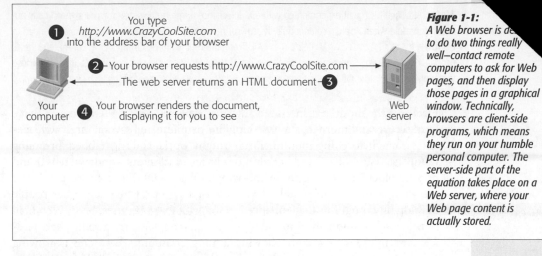

Figure 1-1:
A Web browser is de[signed] to do two things really [well]—contact remote computers to ask for Web pages, and then display those pages in a graphical window. Technically, browsers are client-side programs, which means they run on your humble personal computer. The server-side part of the equation takes place on a Web server, where your Web page content is actually stored.

Inside the figure:

1. You type *http://www.CrazyCoolSite.com* into the address bar of your browser

2. Your browser requests http://www.CrazyCoolSite.com

3. The web server returns an HTML document

4. Your browser renders the document, displaying it for you to see

Your computer

Web server

Choosing your Web browser

Depending on your personality type, choosing a Web browser is either a) a bore or b) an important expression of your character, individuality, and overall computer savvy. If you fall into the latter camp, you've probably already settled on a favorite browser. But if you're searching for something a little different, or you're curious to see what else is out there, the following quick overview sums up your options.

Even if you're not interested in changing your browser, it's a good idea to be familiar with the most common options out there. That's because when you design your Web site, you'll need to prepare for a wide audience of people with different browsers. To make sure your nifty graphics don't turn funky when viewed by other people, it's a good idea to test your own site on other computers, using other screen sizes, and with other Web browsers. At a bare minimum, all Web authors need a copy of Internet Explorer and Firefox, by far the most commonly used browsers today, so you can see what your hard work will look like to 95 percent of the world.

The following list describes the most popular browsers:

- **Internet Explorer** is the world's most used (and sometimes most reviled) Web browser. For better or worse, Internet Explorer sets the standard that other browsers need to follow. The clear advantage of using Internet Explorer (IE for short) is that you'll never run into a Web page you can't read—with a market share of near 80 percent, IE is simply too successful to ignore. The downside is that the developers at Microsoft have grown complacent, which means you're not likely to see dramatic innovations in future versions of IE. Success can also attract a little too much interest—if you use IE, unethical marketers have a bull's eye on your computer with the latest spyware (see the box on page 13).

  To download an updated version of Internet Explorer on a Windows computer, visit *www.microsoft.com/windows/ie*.

Although Microsoft experimented with a Mac version of Internet Explorer for years, they finally put
[t]o pasture when Apple created a built-in browser named Safari. That means Mac owners will need to
[vie]w a friend's PC to see what their pages look like in Internet Explorer. On their own computers, they'll
[pro]bly use Safari or Firefox. For an extensive list of Web browsers for Mac computers, including those
[that w]ork with the older OS 9 operating system, see *http://darrel.knutson.com/mac/www/browsers.html*.

[Fi]refox is the modern response to Internet Explorer—it's a Web browser that's lean, secure, and more than a little hip. Firefox pioneered several innovative features long before Internet Explorer caught up, including tabbed browsing (allowing visitors to view multiple Web pages in different window "tabs") and pop-up blocking (to stop those annoying pop-up ads). Firefox is still ahead of the game with their incredibly flexible *add-on* system, which lets other people develop tiny programs that enhance Firefox with extra features, like a Web mail notifier and thumbnails of the sites listed on a Google search results page. Firefox currently enjoys a cult following among computer geeks and a growing number of disillusioned Internet Explorer veterans. Best of all, Firefox is kept rigorously up-to-date by an army of volunteer programmers, including many who designed the original Netscape browser.

Give Firefox a go at *www.mozilla.org/products/firefox*.

- **Safari** is an Apple-designed browser that comes with current versions of the Mac OS X operating system. It's quick, elegant, and sports a set of useful features, like spell checking when you fill out online forms. Although Apple originally developed Safari for the exclusive use of Mac computers, they created a Windows incarnation in 2007. However, Safari is still far more popular on Mac computers.

Go on Safari at *www.apple.com/safari*.

- **Opera** is a slimmed down, easy-to-install browser that has existed for well over a decade, serving as an antidote to the bloated size and pointless frills of Internet Explorer. For years, Opera was held back by an unfortunate detail—if you wanted an ad-free version, you needed to pay. Today, Opera is available for free and is ad-free, too, just like the other browsers on this list. It has a small but loyal following, but runs a distant fourth in Web browser standings.

Check out Opera at *www.opera.com*.

- **Google Chrome** is the new kid on the block. At the time of this writing, the Google-built browser hadn't officially been released, but it's freely available to techno-nerds and other curious people. And although this newcomer is still short on a few features, it's already made significant strides toward its ultimate goal—becoming a sleek, lightweight browser that runs JavaScript (the snippets of code that power interactive Web pages) with blistering speed.

Experiment with Google Chrome at *www.google.com/chrome*.

- **Netscape Navigator** is one of the first Web pioneers, and was once a formidable challenger to Internet Explorer. But in early 2008, its developers finally pulled the plug. Although it's still the choice of a few nostalgic Web veterans, most former Netscape fans have moved on to Firefox.

To get antique versions of Netscape, go to *http://browser.netscape.com/releases*.

Tip: For current browser usage statistics, which estimate what percentage of people use each major browser, check out *http://en.wikipedia.org/wiki/Usage_share_of_web_browsers*. Browser usage statistics vary depending on what sites you examine and how you count the visitors, but at the time of this writing one reasonable estimate was: Internet Explorer (78%), Firefox (16%), Safari (3%), Opera (0.8%), and Netscape (0.06%). Just as important are browser *trends*, which show Firefox and Safari steadily creeping up in popularity at Internet Explorer's expense.

Along with the browsers listed above, there are some specialty niche browsers. One of these is Lynx, one of the earliest Web browsers and one that's changed the least. Lynx is an entirely text-based browser that's perfectly suited for terminals that don't support graphics. (You can sometimes find these beasts lurking about computer labs in universities and colleges.) Lynx also supports the visually impaired, who can use it in conjunction with a device that reads the text of a Web page aloud.

TROUBLESHOOTING MOMENT

Spyware: When Good Browsers Go Bad

Even though a Web browser is deceptively simple, many browsers are bloated up with plug-ins and extra frills, and some are even infected with (shudder) spyware. *Spyware* is among the most hideous forms of computer software you'll encounter. Essentially, a spyware program is an unwanted plug-in that attaches itself, leech-like, to your browser or operating system without your permission. It then harasses you with advertisements, or just bogs down your computer with unnecessary operations (like recording your surfing habits and sending them to a Big-Brother-like marketing company). Spyware thrives like a weed, particularly on the Windows operating system.

Spyware is notoriously difficult to remove. If you see the telltale signs—a sudden slowdown in Web access, Web page requests that get redirected to the wrong place, or pop-up ads that materialize out of nowhere, even when you aren't using your Web browser—you should have your computer checked out. The best remedy is a spyware removal tool that scans for delinquent programs and removes them, much like a virus scanner. Good bets include Spybot Search & Destroy (*www.safer-networking. org*), Microsoft's Windows Defender (*www.microsoft.com/ defender*), which is included with Windows Vista and available to download for Windows XP fans, and Lavasoft's Ad-Aware (*www.lavasoftusa.com/software/adaware*).

Web Servers

On the other end of the line, a Web server receives browser requests and sends back the correct Web page. For a busy Web site, this basic task can require a lot of work. As a result, Web servers tend to be industrial-strength computers. Even though the average Windows PC with the right setup can host a Web site, it's rarely worth the effort (see the box on this page). Instead, most people get another company to give them a little space on an existing Web server, usually for a monthly fee. In other words, you need to rent some space on the Web.

Often, you can rent this space from the same company you use for Internet access, or it may already be included with your Internet connection package for free. Alternatively, you can turn to a dedicated Web hosting company. Either way, you're going to take the Web sites you build and copy them to some far-off computer that will make sure your talents can be enjoyed by a worldwide audience.

In Chapter 3, you'll learn more about how a Web browser navigates the Web to find a specific Web page. But for now, keep focusing on the big picture so you can start planning your first Web site.

FREQUENTLY ASKED QUESTION

Becoming a Web Host

Can I run a Web server?

In theory, you definitely can. The Web was designed to be an open community, and no one is out to stop you. But in practice, it's not at all easy—no matter how many computer-savvy relatives you may have.

Several monumental challenges prevent all but the most ambitious people from running their own Web servers. The first is that you need to have a reliable computer that runs 24 hours a day. That computer also needs to run special Web hosting software that's able to serve up Web pages when browsers request them.

The next problem is that your computer requires a special type of connection to the Internet, called a *fixed IP address*.

The IP address is a number that identifies your computer on the Web. (*IP* stands for Internet Protocol, which is the super-successful standard that lays down the rules that govern how different devices communicate on a network.)

In order to have your computer run a Web site and make sure others can find it, you need to make sure your IP address is fixed—in other words, you need to lock it down so it's not constantly changing. Most ISPs (Internet Service Providers) randomly assign new IP addresses as they're needed and change them at a whim, which means most people can't use their computers to host a permanent Web site—at least not without special software. If you're still interested, you can call your ISP to ask if they provide a fixed IP address service, and at what cost.

Planning a Web Site

The last thing you need before you experience the joy of performing your first few Web creation tricks is to be buried under an avalanche of theory. However, every new Web site author can save time and effort by doing a little bit of planning before diving in to create a complete Web site. In the following sections, you'll consider some quick guidelines to get you on the right path.

Types of Sites

You don't have much chance of creating a successful Web site if you haven't decided what it's for. Some people have a very specific goal in mind (like getting hired for a job or promoting a book), while others are just planning to unleash their self-expression. Either way, take a look at the following list to get a handle on the different types of Web sites you might want to create:

- **Personal** sites are all about you. As the world gets more Web-savvy, it seems everyone is building online homes. Whether it's to share pictures of Junior with the relatives, chronicle a trip to Kuala Lumpur, or just post your latest thoughts and obsessions, it's no longer unusual to have a personal Web site. In fact, everyone from tweens to grandmothers is jumping in.

  If your plan is to create a personal Web site, think about what its format should be, and how you'll use it. Do you want to post regularly updated news tidbits in chronological format (in which case you might be interested in creating a blog, as covered in the bullet below)? Perhaps you want to create something more ambitious, like an online picture album or a site featuring your family's history. Either way, you should decide what you want your site to focus on before you start slapping pages together.

- **Blogs** (Figure 1-2) are personal Web sites organized like an online diary. The typical *blog* (short for Web logs) provides a list of entries in reverse chronological order, which means that whenever you visit the site, you see the latest news at the top of the page. These blogs are a great way to while away the hours and keep in touch with friends in far-off places. But before you choose this type of site, make sure you have plenty of free time. Nothing says "dead site" like a blog that hasn't been updated in eight months. By contrast, personal Web sites that aren't in a date-specific format can linger on quite happily without regular updates.

Figure 1-2:
Blogs are a great way to keep in touch, letting you share pictures and day-to-day reflections with an unlimited audience. If blogs satisfy your Web needs, you might not need to learn XHTML or add anything else to your Web site. Instead, skip straight to Chapter 17 to learn about the blogging services that make it easy.

If you just want to create a blog with minimum fuss, you can sacrifice your independence and join the masses on a Web site that offers free blog hosting, like Blogger (*www.blogger.com*). Alternatively, you can set out to create and host a blog on your own Web site. Either way, you'll probably create your blog entries using a specialized tool that dodges the complexities of Web page writing. If this sounds like your cup of tea, skip straight to Chapter 17.

Tip: Blogs aren't just for your personal life. They've become tremendously popular with computer geeks and IT workers as a way to share information and chat about a variety of topics, computer-related or otherwise. For example, Microsoft programmers and Google engineers use them to announce new products, discuss sought-after features, and generally muse about the future.

- **Résumé** sites can be powerful career-building tools. Rather than photocopy a suitcase full of paper résumés, why not send emails and distribute business cards that point to your online résumé? Best of all, with a little planning you can add more details to your résumé Web site, like links to companies where you've worked, online portfolio samples, and even background music playing "YMCA" (which is definitely not recommended).

- **Topical** sites focus on a particular subject that interests you. If you're more interested in building a Web site about your favorite music, art, books, food, political movement, or *American Idol* contestants than you are in talking about your own life, then a topical Web site is for you.

  Before you set out to create a topical Web site, consider whether other people with a similar interest will be interested in visiting your site, and take a look at existing sites on the topic. The best topical Web sites invite others with the same interest to join in. (If your Web site is really successful, you might want to use the techniques in Chapter 12 to let visitors talk to you and each other.) The worst Web sites present the same dozen links you can find anywhere else. Remember, the Web is drowning in information. The last thing it needs is another *Pamela Anderson Fan Emporium*.

- **Event** sites aren't designed to weather the years—instead, they revolve around a specific event. A common example is a wedding Web site. The event hosts create it to provide directions, background information, links to gift registries, and a few romantic photos. When the wedding is over, the Web site disappears—or morphs into something different (like a personal Web site chronicling the honeymoon). Other events that might be treated in a similar way include family reunions, costume parties, or do-it-yourself protest marches.

- **Promotion** sites are ideal when you want to show off your personally produced CD or hot-off-the-presses book. They're geared to get the word out about a specific item, whether it's handmade pottery or your own software. Sometimes, these Web sites evolve into small-business sites, where you actually sell your wares (see the "Small business" bullet on the next page).

- **Small business (or e-commerce)** sites show off the most successful use of the Web—selling everything from portable music players to prescription drugs. E-commerce sites are so widespread that it's hard to believe that when the Web was first created, making a buck was far from anyone's mind.

Creating a full-blown e-commerce site like Amazon.com or eBay is far beyond the abilities of a single person. These sites need the support of complex programs and computer-genius-level programming languages. But if you've come to the Web to make money, don't give up hope! Innovative companies like PayPal and Yahoo provide subscription services that can help you build shopping-cart-style Web sites and accept credit card payments. You can also host Google ads to rake in some cash. You'll learn about these great tricks in Chapter 13.

Understanding Your Audience

Once you pinpoint your Web site's *raison d'être*, you should have a better idea about who your visitors will be. Knowing and understanding your audience is crucial to making your Web site effective. (And don't even try to suggest you're creating a site just for yourself—if you were, there's no reason to put it on the Internet at all!)

Not only do you need to understand your audience, you also need to understand that audience's computer capabilities. Good Web designers avoid using fancy frills unless *everyone* can experience them. Nothing's more disappointing to a visitor than getting to a site rich with graphics, only to find that they can't enjoy them because their PC's underpowered. To avoid these letdowns and reach as many people as possible, you need to keep your visitors' computer capabilities in mind as you build and improve your pages.

Unfortunately, there's no single set of specifications you can use to develop your site, because everyone has a slightly different setup. The best strategy is to stick to widely accepted Web standards (a strategy you'll begin to explore in Chapter 2, when you meet XHTML) and try out your site on different computers (which can be time-consuming). Finally, to minimize the risk of incompatibilities, watch out for these common problem areas:

- **Computer monitors** aren't all created equal. Some computers use a smaller *screen resolution* (number of pixels), so they can't show as much content as others. If you create the perfect Web site for your wide-screen monitor, you might find that it's unbearably cramped (or even worse, partly amputated) on another screen.

- **Non-standard fonts** are another headache. Imagine you create a Web page for a rent-a-clown service using a font named FunnyKidzScript. When you check your page out on another computer that doesn't have that font, your text will revert to an automatic, no-frills typeface. At best, it's not what you intended; at worst, it's indecipherable.

- **Large pictures** are another trap that's easy to fall into if you're testing your site on a speedy computer with a fast Internet connection. When dial-up visitors try to see your work, they'll be stuck waiting for the goods, and might just give up. Fortunately, there's a lot you can do to slim down your graphics (which you'll learn in Chapter 7).

- **Plug-ins, media players, and browser-specific features** enliven your pages with animations, movies, and interactive features, but you need to treat them with caution. In the world of the Web, anything that limits how many visitors can enjoy your work is a danger. Steer clear of cutting-edge features that aren't widely supported.

The creators of the most popular Web sites have carefully considered all these issues. For example, think about the number of people whose computers won't let them buy a book on Amazon, make a bid on eBay, or conduct a search on Google. (Are you thinking of a number that's close to 0?)

It's been widely remarked that the average Web designer goes through three stages of maturity: 1) "I'm just learning, so I'll keep it simple;" 2) "I'm a Web guru, and I'll prove it by piling on the features;" 3) "I've been burned by browser compatibility problems, so I'll keep it simple."

The Lifespan of Your Site

The Web is a constantly changing place. Today's Web isn't the same as last year's—or even the Web of 15 seconds ago.

Here are two valuable truths about Web site lifetimes:

- **The best Web sites are constantly improving**. Their creators add support for new browser features, tweak their looks to match new style trends, and—most important of all—constantly add new content.

- **When a Web site stops changing, it's on life support**. Many great Web sites have crumbled through neglect.

Think about your favorite sites. Odds are, they change daily. A good Web site isn't one you consult once and then leave behind. It's a site you can bookmark, and then return to periodically. In a sense, a Web site is like a television channel. If you aren't adding new information, your site's showing reruns.

This problem poses a significant challenge. Making a Web site is hard enough, and keeping it up to date is even more challenging. Here are a few tips that can help you out:

- **Think in stages**. When you put your first Web site online, it won't be complete. Instead, think of it as version 1, and start planning a few changes for the next version. Bit by bit, and stage by stage, you can add everything you want your site to have.

- **Select the parts you can modify regularly, and leave the rest alone.** There's no way you can review and revise an entire Web site every week. Instead, your best strategy is to identify sections you want to change regularly. On a personal site, for example, you might put news on a separate page, and update just that page. On a small-business Web site, you might concentrate on the home page so you can advertise new products and upcoming specials.

- **Design a Web site that's easy to change.** This is the hardest principle to follow, because it requires not only planning, but a dash of hard-won experience. As you become a more experienced Web maven, you'll learn how to simplify your life by making your pages easier to update. One method is to start out by separating information into several pages, so you can add new content without needing to reorganize everything. Another technique is to use style sheets to separate page formatting from your content (see Chapter 6). That way, you can easily insert new material without having to reformat the content from scratch to make sure it matches the rest of your page.

Practice Good Design

Every year, hundreds of Web sites "win" awards for being abjectly awful. Sometimes, they have spinning globes and hot pink text on a lime green background. Other times, they have clunky navigation systems and grotesque flashing backgrounds. But no matter what the design sins, Web sites that are bad—hideously bad—are strangely common.

Maybe it's because creating a Web site really isn't that hard. Or maybe it's because we all have an impulse to play with color, texture, and sound, and sometimes newfangled Web tools encourage our ugliest instincts. For a glimpse at some of the all-too-familiar mistakes, go to *www.angelfire.com/super/badwebs* (see Figure 1-3). You can also visit *www.worstoftheweb.com*, which profiles new offenders every month.

This book won't teach you to become a professional Web designer. However, it *will* guide you in the time-honored art of Not Making Bad Web Sites. Throughout this book, you'll find helpful tips, suggestions, and warnings about usability and design. Look specifically for the "Design Time" boxes. In the meantime, here are a few general principles that can help make sure you never wind up on a worst-of-the-Web list (unless you absolutely want to).

- **Keep it simple (and don't annoy your visitors).** You can cram a lot of frills and goodies into a Web page. But unless they serve a purpose, just say no. You'll find that exercising restraint can make a few fancy touches seem witty and sophisticated. Adding a *lot* of fancy touches, on the other hand, can make your site seem heady and delusional. If you pare down the tricks, you'll make sure that your graphical glitz doesn't overshadow your site's content, and your visitors aren't driven away in annoyance.

Figure 1-3:
Here's a Web site that gets it all wrong— deliberately. With a combination of scrolling titles, a crazily blinking background, and unreadable text, www.angelfire.com/ super/badwebs *does a good job of demonstrating everything you should avoid in your own Web pages.*

- **Be consistent.** No matter how logical you think your Web site is, the majority of visitors probably won't think the same way. To cut down on the confusion, from one page to another, use similar organization, similar headings, similar graphics and links, a single navigation bar, and so on. These touches help make visitors feel right at home.

- **Know your audience.** Every type of Web site has its own unwritten conventions. You don't need to follow the same design in an e-commerce store as you do in a promotional page for an experimental electric harmonic band. To help decide what is and isn't suitable, check out lots of other sites that deal with the same sort of material as yours.

The Ingredients of a Web Site

The trickiest part of building a Web site is coordination. To get it right, you not only need the right tools, you also need to coordinate with other companies to get your Web site onto the World Wide Web and (optionally) to give it a catchy address like *www.StylinViolins.com*. In this section, you'll create a quick Web shopping list that maps out what you need—and tells you where you'll learn about it in the rest of this book.

- **Web pages.** Every Web site is made up of individual pages. To create a basic Web page, you need to understand XHTML (Extensible HyperText Markup Language), the modern language of the Web. You'll create your first Web page in the next chapter.

- **Web space.** Creating Web pages is fun, but to let other people take a look at them, you need to put them on a Web server. In Chapter 3, you'll consider your options for getting your first Web page online, either through a fee-based service or a free alternative.

- **A domain name.** There's a world of difference between the Web site address *www.inetConnections.com/Users/~jMallone012/web* and *www.JackieMallone.com*. You can get your own personalized *domain name*, if it's available. It's not free, but the cost is pretty small, about $10 or $15 per year. If you want to put your Web site address on a business card or a brochure for a small business, there's really no better choice than your own domain name. In Chapter 3, you'll learn how to buy one.

Note: The domain name is the first part of a Web address, which identifies the Web server that's storing and serving up your site. In the URL *www.ebay.com/help/index.html*, the domain name is *www.ebay.com*. You'll learn much more about domain names and URLs (short for Universal Resource Locator), and how they work, in Chapter 3.

- **Web design tools.** Creating Web pages from scratch is a great way to learn a new skill, but it's far too slow and painful to create a complete Web site that way. To get to the next level, you need to step up to a professional Web design tool. If you have a commercial program like Dreamweaver, you're in good hands. Even if you don't, there are many good free and shareware products that can help you out. Chapter 4 explains your options and helps you get started.

- **Hyperlinks.** On its own, a single Web page can only do so much. The real magic begins when you bind multiple pages together using links. Chapter 8 introduces the versatile hyperlink, which lets visitors move around your site.

- **Indispensable extras.** Once you master the basics of Web pages and Web sites, there's more ground to conquer. You can get your site listed in a search engine (Chapter 11), establish your own community forum (Chapter 12), and sell items (Chapter 13). Still hungry for more? Why not animate your page with a sprinkling of JavaScript code (Chapter 14), create eye-catching buttons (Chapter 15), and add audio and video (Chapter 16)? All these features take you beyond ordinary XHTML and put you on the road to becoming a genuine Web expert.

Creating Your First Page

Web pages are the basic unit of a Web site, and every Web site is a collection of one or more pages. The ideal Web page contains enough information to fill the width of a browser window, but not so much that readers need to scroll from morning until lunchtime to get to the page's end. In other words, the ideal page strikes a balance— it avoids the lonely feeling caused by too much white space, and the stress induced by an avalanche of information.

The best way to get a handle on what a Web page should hold is to look at your favorite sites. A news site like *www.nytimes.com* displays every news article on a separate page (and subdivides longer stories into several pages). At an e-commerce shop like *www.amazon.com*, every product has its own page. Similarly, a personal Web site like *www.MyUndyingLoveForPigTrotters.com* may be divided into separate Web pages with titles like "About Me," "Vacation Photos," "Résumé," and "Top Secret Recipes for Pig Parts."

For now, don't worry too much about how to divide your Web site into pages— that's a task you'll revisit in Chapter 8 when you start linking pages together. Instead, your first goal is to understand how a basic page works and how to create one of your own. In this chapter, you'll get a chance to build that first page. On the way, you'll learn the essential details of the most important standard in Web site design: XHTML.

The Anatomy of a Web Page

Web pages are written in *HTML* (HyperText Markup Language) or the closely related *XHTML* (Extensible HyperText Markup Language) standard. Essentially, HTML is the original language of the Web, while XHTML is the modernized version. It doesn't matter whether your Web page contains a series of text-only blog entries, a dozen pictures of your pet lemur, or a heavily formatted screenplay—odds are that, if you're looking at it in a browser, it's an HTML or XHTML page.

Note: In this book, you'll focus all your attention on XHTML, which is the latest and greatest Web markup language. However, most of what you'll learn applies equally well to the older HTML standard. For more information about how the two stack up, see the box on page 25.

XHTML plays a key role in Web pages—it tells a Web browser how to display the contents of a page. Although plenty of computer programs can format text (take Microsoft Word, for instance), it's almost impossible to find a single standard that every type of computer, operating system, and Web-enabled device supports. XHTML fills the gap by supplying information that any browser can interpret. These formatting details include special instructions (called *tags*) that tell a browser when to start a paragraph, italicize a word, or display a picture. To create your own Web pages, you need to learn to use this family of tags.

XHTML is such an important standard that you'll spend a good portion of this book digging through most of its features, frills, and shortcomings. Every Web page you build along the way will be a bona fide XHTML document.

Note: The XHTML standard doesn't have anything to do with the way a Web browser *accesses* a page on the Web. Instead, HTTP (HyperText Transport Protocol) is the low-level communication system that lets two computers exchange data over the Internet. If you were to apply the analogy of a phone conversation, the telephone line is HTTP, and the juicy tidbits of gossip you're exchanging with Aunt Martha are the XHTML documents.

Cracking Open an XHTML Document

On the inside, an XHTML page is actually nothing more than a plain-vanilla text file. That means that every Web page consists entirely of letters, numbers, and a few special characters (like spaces, punctuation, and everything else you can spot on your keyboard). This file is quite different from what you'd find if you cracked open a typical *binary file* on your computer. A binary file contains genuine computer language—a series of 0s and 1s. If another program is foolish enough to try and convert this binary information into text, you end up with gibberish.

To understand the difference between a text file and a binary file, take a look at Figure 2-1, which examines a traditional Word document under the microscope. Compare that with what you see in Figure 2-2, which dissects an XHTML document with the same content.

Why XHTML Beats HTML

Lots of people still use HTML. Why should I bother with its grown-up cousin, XHTML?

It's true that you can create equally snazzy pages using ordinary HTML. However, three good reasons to step up to XHTML are:

- **XHTML prevents you from developing nasty habits**. HTMI is a relatively lax standard that lets you make a variety of mistakes and be generally sloppy. XHTML isn't nearly as forgiving–it forces you to polish your pages and do things right the first time. (Incidentally, most browsers won't catch your XHTML mistakes. For that, you need an XHTML validation tool, like the online page checker described on page 49.)

- **XHTML helps you avoid browser compatibility issues.** When processing HTML pages, some browsers place a greater emphasis on backward compatibility than on standards compliance. For example, when Internet Explorer encounters an HTML page, it attempts to behave the same way earlier versions did 10 years ago, quirks and all. This ensures that really old Web pages will still display correctly, even if they rely on ancient browser bugs that have long

since been fixed. Unfortunately, different browsers have different idiosyncrasies, so they won't always display an HTML document in the same way. On the other hand, when browsers process an XHTML page, they follow the rules to the letter. This ensures that Web pages look the same (or as close as possible) on all browsers. That's why using the more rigorous XHTML standard is the way to go.

- **XHTML helps you fit in with your trendy Web designer friends.** Web design might not be a popularity contest, but it never hurts to speak the same language as your peers. That way, you have a better chance of learning from other people's pages and getting help when you run into trouble.

XHTML also has a number of benefits that appeal more to programmers than to Web site designers. For example, because XHTML is more consistent, it makes life easier for Web search engines and other types of automated tools that need to examine Web content. XHTML also makes it easier to design scaled-down Web browsers on specialized platforms, like cellphones, pocket computers, and even kitchen appliances.

To take a look at an XHTML document, all you need is an ordinary text editor, like Notepad, which is included on all Windows computers. To run Notepad, click the Start button, and then select All Programs → Accessories → Notepad (in Windows Vista) or Programs → Accessories → Notepad (in every other version of Windows). Choose File → Open, and then begin hunting around for the XHTML file you want. On the Mac, try TextEdit, which you can find at Applications → TextEdit. Choose File → Open, and then find the XHTML file. If you downloaded the companion content for this book (all of which you can find on the Missing CD page at *www.missingmanuals.com*), try opening the *popsicles.htm* file, which is shown in Figure 2-2.

Unfortunately, most text editors don't let you open a Web page directly from the Internet. To do that, they'd need to be able to send a request over the Internet to a Web server, which is a job best left to a Web browser. However, most browsers *do*

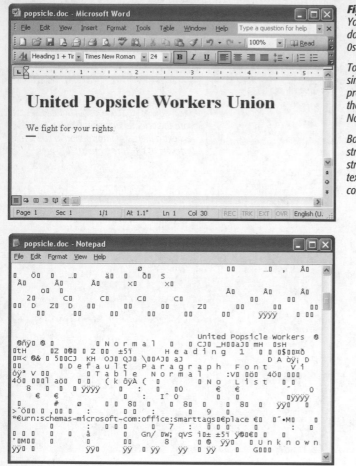

Figure 2-1:
*Your PC stores Word and most other
documents as binary files (consisting of just
0s and 1s).*

*Top: Even if your document looks relatively
simple in Word, it doesn't look nearly as
pretty when you bypass Word and open
the file in an ordinary text editor like
Notepad or TextEdit (bottom).*

*Bottom: Text editors usually convert a file's
string of 0s and 1s into a meaningless
stream of intimidating gibberish. The actual
text is there somewhere, but it's buried in
computer gobbledygook.*

give you the chance to look at the raw XHTML for a Web page. Here's what you
need to do:

1. **Open your preferred browser.**

2. **Navigate to the Web page you want to examine.**

3. **In your browser, look for a menu command that lets you view the source content of the Web page. In Internet Explorer (or Opera), select View → Source. In
Firefox and Netscape, use View → Page Source. In Safari, View → View Source
does the trick. Isn't diversity a wonderful thing?**

Once you make your selection, a new window appears showing you the XHTML
used to create the Web page. This window may represent a built-in text viewer
that's included with your browser, or it may just be Notepad or TextEdit. Either
way, you'll see the raw XHTML.

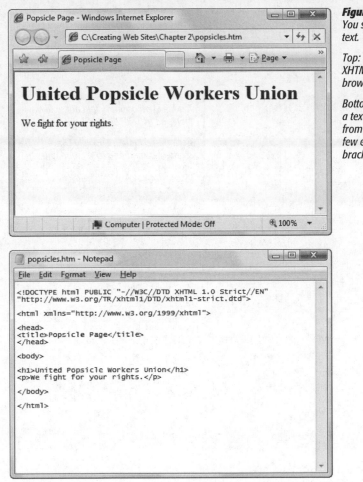

Figure 2-2:
*You store XHTML documents as ordinary
text.*

*Top: The Word document in rewritten as an
XHTML document and displayed in a Web
browser.*

*Bottom: When you display an XHTML file in
a text editor, you can easily spot all the text
from the original document, along with a
few extra pieces of information inside angle
brackets (<>). These are XHTML tags.*

Tip: Firefox has a handy feature that lets you home in on part of the XHTML in a complex page. Just
select the text you're interested in on the Web page, right-click it, and then choose View Selection Source.

Most Web pages are considerably more complex than the *popsicles.htm* example
shown in Figure 2-2, so you need to wade through many more XHTML tags. But
once you acclimate yourself to the jumble of information, you'll have an extremely
useful way to peer under the covers of any Web page. In fact, professional Web
developers often use this trick to check out the work of their competitors.

Creating Your Own XHTML Files

Here's one of the best-kept secrets of Web page writing: You don't need a live Web
site to start creating your own Web pages. That's because you can easily build and
test Web pages using only your own computer. In fact, you don't even need an
Internet connection.

Going Beyond XHTML

The creators of HTML designed it perfectly for putting research papers and other unchanging documents on the Web. They didn't envision a world of Internet auctions, e-commerce shops, or browser-based games. To add all these features to the modern Web browsing experience, crafty people have supplemented XHTML with some tricky workarounds. And although it's more than a little confusing to consider all the ways you can extend XHTML, doing so is the best way to really understand what's possible on your own Web site.

Here's an overview of the two most common ways to go beyond XHTML:

- **Embedded programs**. Most modern browsers support *Java applets*, small programs than run inside your Web browser and display information in a window inside a Web page. (To try one out and play some head-scratching Java Checkers against a computer opponent, go to *http://thinks.com/java/ checkers/checkers.htm*.) Internet Explorer can also host special tools called *ActiveX controls*. Both Java applets and ActiveX controls are miniature programs that you can use in a Web page (if a browser supports them), but neither is written in XHTML.

- **Browser plug-ins**. Browsers are designed to deal with XHTML, and they don't recognize other types of content. For example, browsers don't have the ability to interpret an Adobe PDF document, which is a specialized type of file that preserves the formatting of documents. However, depending on how your browser is configured, you may find that when you click a hyperlink that points to a PDF file, a PDF reader launches. The automatic launch happens if you installed a plug-in from Adobe that runs the Acrobat software (which displays PDF files). Another example of a common plug-in is Adobe Flash, which shows animations on a Web page. If you go to a page that includes a Flash animation and you don't have the plug-in, you'll be asked if you want to download it. (You'll use Flash to put a slick music player in your Web page in Chapter 16. In the meantime, check out *www.ferryhalim.com/orisinal* to play some of the best free Flash games around.)

Unfortunately, there's no surefire way to tell what extensions are at work on a particular page. In time, you'll learn to spot many of the telltale signs, because each type of content looks distinctly different.

The basic approach is simple:

1. **Fire up your favorite text editor.**

2. **Start writing XHTML content.**

   Of course, this part is a little tricky because you haven't explored the XHTML standard yet. Hang on—help is on the way in the following sections.

3. **When you finish your Web page, save the document (a simple File → Save usually does it).**

   By convention, XHTML documents typically have the file extension .htm or .html (which they inherit from the original HTML standard). For example, a typical XHTML file name is LimeGreenPyjamas.html. Strictly speaking, these extensions aren't necessary, because browsers are perfectly happy displaying Web pages with any file extension. You're free to choose any file extension you want for your Web pages. The only rule is that the file has to contain valid

XHTML content. However, using the .htm or .html file extensions is still a good idea; not only does it save confusion, it also helps your PC recognize that the file contains a Web page. For example, when you double-click a file with the .htm or .html extension, your PC automatically opens it in your Web browser.

For the record, there's no difference between .htm and .html—which one you use is just a matter of preference.

Note: It's also important to use the .htm or .html extension if you plan to upload your files to a Web server so other people can view them (which, of course, you do). Prickly Web servers may refuse to hand out pages that have nonstandard file extensions.

4. **To take a look at your work, open the file in a Web browser.**

If you use the extension .htm or .html, it's usually as easy as double-clicking the file. If not, you may need to type in the full file path in your Web browser's address bar, as shown in Figure 2-3.

Remember, when you compose your XHTML document in a text editor, you won't be able to see the formatted document. All you'll see is the plain text and the XHTML formatting instructions.

Tip: If you change and save the file *after* you open it in your Web browser, you can take a look at your recent changes by hitting the browser's Refresh button.

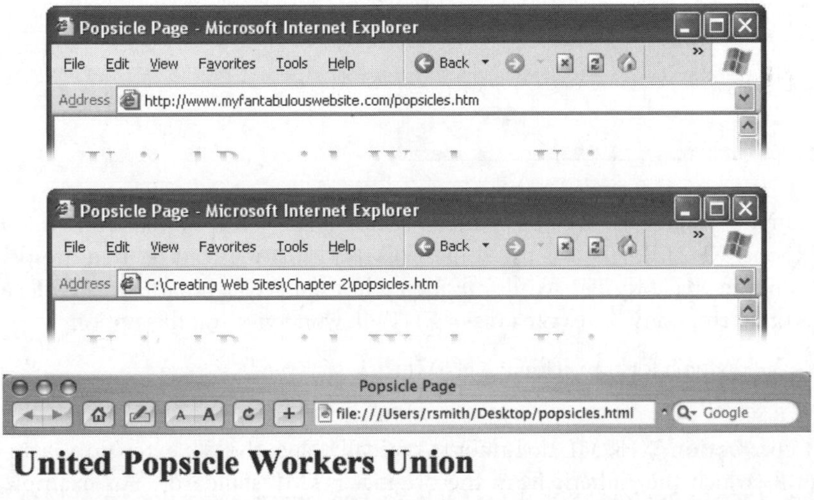

Figure 2-3:
A browser's address bar identifies where the current Web page is really located. If you see http://, it comes from a Web server on the Internet (top). If you're looking at a Web page on your own computer, you'll just see an ordinary file path (middle, showing a Windows file location in Internet Explorer), or you'll see a URL that starts with the prefix "file:///" (bottom, showing a Mac file location in Safari). Local addresses depend on the browser and operating system you're using.

The Document Type Definition

As you've already learned, Web browsers recognize two markup languages: old-school HTML and today's XHTML. When a browser examines a Web page, it needs to determine which language you wrote it in. To tell the browser what standard your page uses, you place something called a *document type definition* (DTD) at the very beginning of the page (see Figure 2-4). A DTD is also known as a *doctype*.

The doctype is cryptic code that looks like this:

```
<!DOCTYPE html PUBLIC "-//W3C//DTD XHTML 1.0 Strict//EN"
"http://www.w3.org/TR/xhtml1/DTD/xhtml1-strict.dtd">
```

This doctype specifies that the Web page uses the *strict* version of the XHTML 1.0 standard. This is the most common XHTML choice, and it's the doctype you'll see in most of the examples in this book.

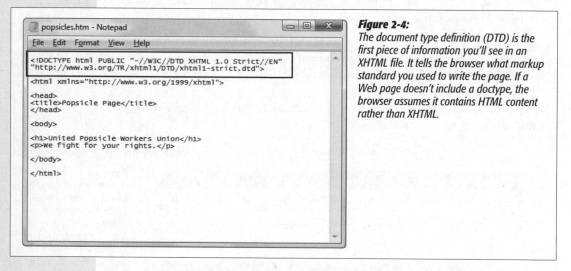

Figure 2-4:
The document type definition (DTD) is the first piece of information you'll see in an XHTML file. It tells the browser what markup standard you used to write the page. If a Web page doesn't include a doctype, the browser assumes it contains HTML content rather than XHTML.

Alternatively, you can use a watered-down version of XHTML 1.0 called *transitional*. Transitional XHTML lets you use some HTML formatting features that are being phased out in XHTML. The word *transitional* hints at the fact that this HTML support is only temporary. Later versions of XHTML won't give you this option.

Here's the doctype for transitional XHTML:

```
<!DOCTYPE html PUBLIC "-//W3C//DTD XHTML 1.0 Transitional//EN"
"http://www.w3.org/TR/xhtml1/DTD/xhtml1-transitional.dtd">
```

The best time to use transitional XHTML is when you're converting an old HTML page to XHTML, and you haven't yet met all the requirements of strict XHTML. Otherwise, strict XHTML is a better standard, because it keeps you on the high road of Web design. And don't worry about missing features. Serious Web designers don't need the cheap formatting hacks that HTML used—instead, they use a more powerful and better-organized *style sheet* standard, discussed in Chapter 6.

Tip: When looking at someone else's Web page, the doctype is the only reliable way for you to figure out if the page is written in HTML or XHTML.

At this point, you might wonder what happens if you create a Web page without a doctype. In this situation, the browser assumes you wrote your page in HTML. And because XHTML is really just a stricter form of HTML, the browser still displays your document successfully. However, all is not well. In many browsers, you'll also enter the dreaded *quirks mode*. For example, a missing doctype causes Internet Explorer to process your page in a way that's consistent with previous versions of Internet Explorer, but not with other browsers. As a result, the page looks subtly but annoyingly inconsistent on different browsers, often with differently sized text, inconsistent margins and borders, and improperly positioned content.

Tip: XHTML 1.0 strict and XHTML 1.0 transitional are the most commonly used types of XHTML, so you'll want to keep these two doctypes handy. The easiest option is to copy one from an existing Web page, and then paste it into any new Web pages you create.

UP TO SPEED

The Many Flavors of XHTML

XHTML 1.0 strict and XHTML 1.0 transitional aren't the only options for creating XHTML documents. Here are some other types of XHTML:

- **XHTML 1.0 Frameset.** This standard supports *frames*, a feature that lets you bring more than one Web page together in a single browser window. You'll learn how to use frames in Chapter 10.

- **XHTML 1.1.** This standard is a modest upgrade to XHTML, which removes the transitional and frameset options and improves the handling of East Asian languages. However, XHTML 1.1 is rarely used because of an obscure issue with the way Web servers transmit information. Essentially, when a Web server responds to a browser request, it tells the browser what type of information it's sending. When sending an HTML or XHTML 1.0 document, it tells the browser that the content type is *text/html*. When sending an XHTML 1.1 document, it tells the browser that the content is *application/xhtml+xml*. Unfortunately, even the latest versions of Internet Explorer don't support the *application/xhtml+xml* content type. Workarounds exist, but they're ugly.

- **XHTML Basic 1.1.** This standard defines a more limited version of XHTML 1.1 that's intended for less powerful Web devices (like mobile phones).

- **XHTML 2 and X/HTML 5.** These standards are locked in a duel to decide how XHTML will evolve. In one corner is the official XHTML 2 standard, which has been under development for more than 5 years. When it's finished, it will define a revised, streamlined version of XHTML that finally breaks compatibility with HTML. However, this radical new direction makes the software companies that build browsers nervous. They're also worried that XHTML 2 is more about documents than interactive Web programs. In response, they've started working on a revised version of XHTML that keeps closer compatibility with previous versions of XHTML and HTML. This competing standard is named X/HTML 5, because it builds on the last version of HTML, which is HTML 4.

To learn more about these other XHTML-based standards, check out the overview at *http://en.wikipedia.org/wiki/ XHTML*.

XHTML Tags

Now that you know how to peer into existing XHTML files and create your own, the next step is to understand what goes *inside* the average XHTML file. It all revolves around a single concept—*tags*.

XHTML tags are formatting instructions that tell a browser how to transform ordinary text into something that's visually appealing. If you were to take all the tags out of an XHTML document, the resulting Web page would consist of nothing more than plain, unformatted text.

What's in a Tag

You can recognize a tag by looking for angle brackets, two special characters that look like this: < >. To create a tag, you type XHTML code between the brackets. This code is for the browser's eyes only; Web visitors never see it (unless they use the View → Source trick to peek at the XHTML). Essentially, the code is an instruction that conveys information to the browser about how to format the text that follows.

For example, one simple tag is the <b> tag, which stands for "bold" (tag names are always lowercase). When a browser encounters this tag, it switches on boldface formatting, which affects all the text that follows. Here's an example:

    This text isn't bold. <b>This text is bold.

This isn't quite good enough for XHTML, though. The <b> tag is known as a *start tag*, which means it switches on some effect (in this case, bold lettering). To satisfy the rules of XHTML, though, every start tag needs a matching *end tag* that switches *off* the effect later in the document.

End tags are easy to recognize. They look the same as the start tag, except that they begin with a forward slash. They look like this </ instead of like this <. So the end tag for bold formatting is </b>. Here's an example:

    This isn't bold. <b>Pay attention!</b> Now we're back to normal.

Which the browser displays as:

This isn't bold. **Pay attention!** Now we're back to normal.

This example shows another important principle in how browsers work. They always process tags in order, based on where they show up in your text. To get the bold formatting in the right place, you need to make sure you position the <b> and </b> tags appropriately.

As you can see, the browser has a fairly simple job. It scans through an XHTML document, looking for tags and switching on and off various formatting settings. It takes everything else (everything that isn't a tag) and displays it in the Web browser window.

Note: Adding tags to plain-vanilla text is known as *marking up* a document, and the tags themselves are known as XHTML *markup*. When you look at raw XHTML, you may be interested in looking at the content (the text that's nestled between the tags), or the markup (the XHTML tags themselves).

Understanding Elements

As you've seen, tags come in pairs. When you use a start tag (like <b> for bold), you have to also include an end tag (like </b>). This combination of start and end tags and the text in between them makes up an XHTML *element*.

Here's the basic idea: elements are containers (see Figure 2-5). You place some content (like text) inside that container. For example, when you use the <b> and </b> tags, you create a container that applies bold formatting to the text in between. You place text inside the container to make that text appear boldfaced. As you create your Web pages, you'll wrap different pieces of text in different containers that do different things. If you think about elements this way, you'll never forget to include the end tag.

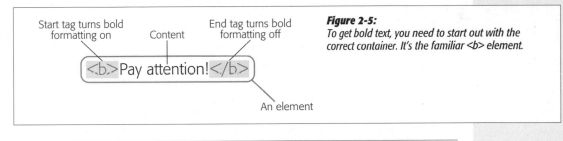

Start tag turns bold
formatting on

Content

End tag turns bold
formatting off

<b>Pay attention!</b>

An element

Figure 2-5:
To get bold text, you need to start out with the correct container. It's the familiar <b> element.

Note: When someone refers to the <b> *element*, it means the whole shebang–start tag, end tag, and the content inside. When someone refers to a <b> *tag*, it simply means the instruction that starts the element.

Of course, life wouldn't be much fun (and computer books wouldn't be nearly as thick) without exceptions. When you get right down to it, there are really *two* types of elements:

• **Container elements.** The container element is, by far, the most common type. Container elements apply formatting to the content nestled between the start and end tags.

• **Standalone elements.** Some tags don't come in pairs. These standalone elements don't turn formatting on or off. Instead, they *insert* something into a page, like an image. One example is the <br /> element, which inserts a line break in a page. Standalone elements include a slash character before the closing >, sort of like an opening and closing tag all rolled into one. This syntax is handy because it clearly indicates that you have a standalone element on your hands. Standalone elements are often called *empty* elements because there's no way to put any text inside them.

Figure 2-6 puts the two types of elements in perspective.

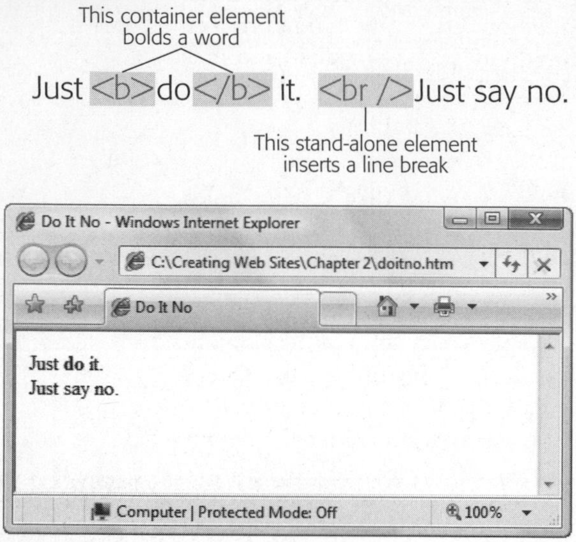

This container element
bolds a word

Just `<b>`do`</b>` it. `<br />`Just say no.

This stand-alone element
inserts a line break

Figure 2-6:
Top: This snippet of XHTML shows both a container element and a standalone element.

Bottom: The browser shows the resulting Web page.

Do It No - Windows Internet Explorer

C:\Creating Web Sites\Chapter 2\doitno.htm

Do It No

Just **do** it.
Just say no.

Computer | Protected Mode: Off   100%

Nesting Elements

In the previous example, you saw how to apply a simple `<b>` element for bold formatting. Between the `<b>` and `</b>` tags, you put text that you wanted to make bold. However, text isn't the only thing you can put between a start and end tag. You can also nest one element *inside* another. In fact, nesting elements is one of the basic building-block techniques of Web pages. Nesting lets you apply more detailed formatting instructions to text (for example it lets you create bold, italicized text) by piling all the elements you need in the same place. Nesting is also required for more complicated structures (like bulleted lists).

To see nesting in action, you need another element to work with. For the next example, consider both the familiar `<b>` element and the `<i>` element, which italicizes text.

The question is, what happens if you want to make a piece of text bold *and* italicized? XHTML doesn't include a single element for this purpose, so you need to combine the two. Here's an example:

```
This <b><i>word</i></b> has italic and bold formatting.
```

When the browser chews through this scrap of XHTML, it produces text that looks like this:

This ***word*** has italic and bold formatting.

Incidentally, it doesn't matter if you reverse the order of the `<i>` and `<b>` tags. The following XHTML produces exactly the same result.

```
This <i><b>word</b></i> has italic and bold formatting.
```

However, you should always make sure that you close tags in the *reverse* order from which you opened them. In other words, if you apply italic formatting and then bold formatting, you should always switch off bold formatting first, and then italic formatting. Here's an example that breaks this rule:

```
This <i><b>word</i></b> has italic and bold formatting.
```

Finally, it's worth noting that XHTML gives you many more complex ways to nest elements. For example, you can nest one element inside another, and then nest another element inside that one, and so on, indefinitely.

Note: If you're a graphic-design type, you're probably itching to get your hands on more powerful formatting elements to change alignment, spacing, and fonts. Unfortunately, in the Web world you can't always control everything you want. Chapter 5 has the lowdown, and Chapter 6 introduces the best solution, style sheets.

FREQUENTLY ASKED QUESTION

Telling a Browser to Ignore a Tag

What if I really do want the text "<b>" to appear on my Web page?

The tag system works great until you actually want to use an angle bracket (< or >) in your text. Then you're in a tricky position.

For example, imagine you want to write the following bit of text as proof of your remarkable insight:

```
The expression 5 < 2 is clearly false,
because 5 is bigger than 2.
```

When a browser reaches the less than (<) symbol, it becomes utterly bewildered. Its first instinct is to assume you're starting a tag, and the text following "2 is clearly false…" is part of a long tag name. Obviously, this isn't what you intended, and it's certain to confuse the browser.

To solve this problem, you need to replace angle brackets with the corresponding XHTML *character entity*. Character entities always begin with an ampersand (&) and end with a semicolon (;). The character entity for the less than symbol is < because the lt stands for "less than." Similarly, > is the character entity for the greater than symbol.

Here's the corrected example:

```
The expression 5 &lt; 2 is clearly false,
because 5 is bigger than 2.
```

In your text editor, this doesn't look like what you want. However, when the browser displays this document, it automatically changes the < into a < character, without confusing it with a tag. You'll learn more about character entities on page 132.

The XHTML Document

So far, you've been considering XHTML snippets—portions of a complete XHTML document. In this section, you'll learn how to put it all together and create your first genuine Web page.

The Basic Skeleton

To create a true XHTML document, you start out with three container elements: <html>, <head>, and <body>. These three elements work together to describe the basic structure of your page.

<html>
> This element wraps everything (other than the doctype) in your Web page.

<head>
> This element designates the *header* portion of your document. The header can include some optional information about your Web page, including the required title (which your browser displays in its title bar), optional search keywords, and an optional style sheet (which you'll learn about in Chapter 6).

<body>
> This element holds the meat of your Web page, including the actual content you want to display to the world.

There's only one right way to combine these three elements. Here's the correct arrangement of elements, with the doctype at the beginning of the page:

```
<!DOCTYPE html PUBLIC "-//W3C//DTD XHTML 1.0 Strict//EN"
"http://www.w3.org/TR/xhtml1/DTD/xhtml1-strict.dtd">

<html xmlns="http://www.w3.org/1999/xhtml">

<head>
...
</head>

<body>
...
</body>

</html>
```

Every Web page uses this basic framework. The ellipsis (…) shows where you insert additional information. The spaces between the lines aren't required— they're just there to help you see the element structure more easily.

You'll notice that the <html> start tag has an extra piece of information wedged inside of it. This is a known as the XHTML *namespace*, and it, like the doctype, is another non-negotiable part of the XHTML standard.

Once you have the XHTML skeleton in place, you need to add two more container elements to the mix. Every Web page requires a <title> element, which goes in the header section. Next, you need to create a container for text in the body section. One all-purpose text container is the <p> element, which represents a paragraph.

Here's a closer look at the elements you need to add:

<title>

> This element sets the title for your Web page. The title plays several roles. First, Web browsers display the title of the current Web page at the top of the window. Second, when a Web visitor bookmarks your page, the browser uses the title to label the bookmark in your Bookmark (or Favorites) menu. Third, when your page turns up in a Web search, the search engine usually displays this title as the first line in the search results, followed by a snippet of content from the page.

<p>

> This indicates a paragraph. Web browsers don't indent paragraphs, but they do add a little space between consecutive paragraphs to keep them separated.

Here's the Web page with these two new ingredients:

```
<!DOCTYPE html PUBLIC "-//W3C//DTD XHTML 1.0 Strict//EN"
"http://www.w3.org/TR/xhtml1/DTD/xhtml1-strict.dtd">

<html xmlns="http://www.w3.org/1999/xhtml">

<head>
<title>Everything I Know About Web Design</title>
</head>

<body>
<p></p>
</body>

</html>
```

If you open this document in a Web browser, you'll find that the page is still empty, but now the title appears (as shown in Figure 2-7).

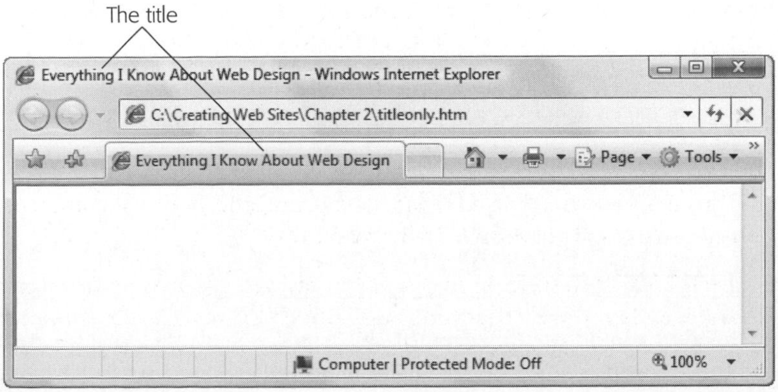

The title

Figure 2-7:
When a browser displays a Web page, it shows the page's title at the top of the window, with a little bit of extra text tacked on the end. If your browser uses tabbed browsing (as Internet Explorer does, shown here), the title also appears in the tab.

As it stands right now, this XHTML document is a good template for future pages. The basic structure is in place—you simply need to change the title and add some text.

Adding Content

You're finally ready to transform this XHTML skeleton into a real document by adding content. This detail is the most important, and it's the task you'll work on through most of this book.

For example, let's say you're writing a simple résumé page. Here's a very basic first go at it:

```
<!DOCTYPE html PUBLIC "-//W3C//DTD XHTML 1.0 Strict//EN"
"http://www.w3.org/TR/xhtml1/DTD/xhtml1-strict.dtd">

<html xmlns="http://www.w3.org/1999/xhtml">

<head>
<title>Hire Me!</title>
</head>
<body>
<p>I am Lee Park. Hire me for your company, because my work is <b>off the
hizzle</b>.</p>
</body>

</html>
```

This example highlights the modifications to the basic XHTML structure—a changed title and a single line of text. It uses a single <b> element inside the paragraph, just to dress up the page a little. Before you go any further, you may want to try creating this sample file in your own text editor (using the process you learned on page 25) and opening it in your favorite Web browser (see Figure 2-8).

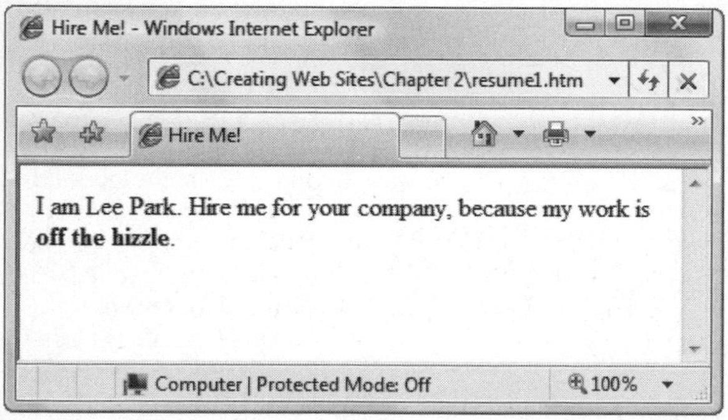

Figure 2-8:
Welcome to the Web. This page doesn't have much in the way of XHTML goodies (and it probably won't get Lee hired), but it does represent one of the simplest possible XHTML pages you can create.

You're now ready to build on this example by trying out all the XHTML tricks described in the following sections. Next up, you'll give Lee Park a better résumé.

Tip: Even if you have high-powered XHTML editing software like Dreamweaver, don't use it yet. To get started learning XHTML, it's best that you do it by hand so you understand every detail that's going into your Web page. Later on, when you've mastered the basics and are ready to create more sophisticated Web pages, you'll probably want to switch to other tools, as discussed in Chapter 4.

Structuring Text

As you start to create more detailed Web pages, you'll quickly discover that building a Web page isn't as straightforward as, say, creating a page in Microsoft Word. For example, you may decide to enhance the résumé page by creating a list of skills. Here's a reasonable first try:

```
<!DOCTYPE html PUBLIC "-//W3C//DTD XHTML 1.0 Strict//EN"
"http://www.w3.org/TR/xhtml1/DTD/xhtml1-strict.dtd">

<html xmlns="http://www.w3.org/1999/xhtml">

<head>
<title>Hire Me!</title>
</head>

<body>
<p>I am Lee Park. Hire me for your company, because my work is <b>off the
hizzle</b>.

My skills include:
*Fast typing (nearly 12 words/minute).
*Extraordinary pencil sharpening.
*Inventive excuse making.
*Negotiating with officers of the peace.</p>
</body>

</html>
```

The trouble appears when you open this seemingly innocent document in your Web browser (Figure 2-9).

The problem is that XHTML ignores extra white space. That includes tabs, line breaks, and extra spaces (anything more than one consecutive space). The first time this happens, you'll probably stare at your screen dumbfounded and wonder why Web browsers are designed this way. But it actually makes sense when you consider that XHTML needs to work as a *universal standard*.

Say you were to customize your hypothetical Web page (like the one shown in Figure 2-10) with the perfect spacing, indenting, and line width for *your* computer monitor. The problem is, it may not look as good on someone else's monitor.

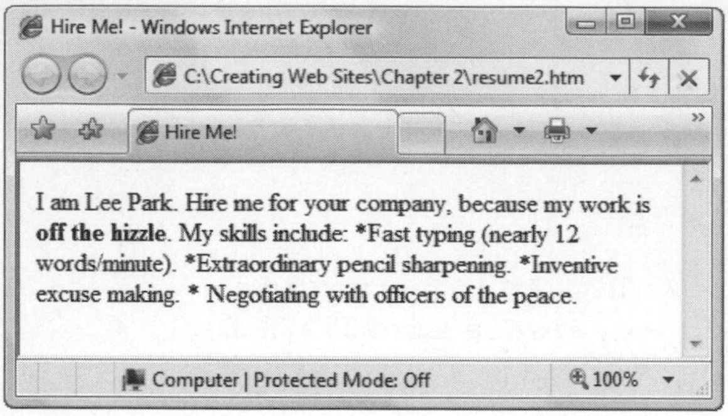

Figure 2-9:
XHTML disregards line breaks and consecutive spaces, so what appears as neatly organized text in your XHTML file can turn into a jumble of text when you display it in a browser.

For example, some of the text may scroll off the right side of the page, making it difficult to read. And different monitors are only part of the problem—today's Web pages need to work on different types of *devices*. Lee Park's future boss might view Parks' résumé on anything from the latest laptop to a fixed-width terminal to a Web-enabled cellphone.

To deal with this range of display options, XHTML uses elements to define the *structure* of your document. Instead of telling the browser, "Here's where you go to the next line and here's where you add four extra spaces," XHTML tells the browser, "Here are two complete paragraphs and here's a bulleted list." It's then up to the browser to display the page according to the instructions contained in your XHTML.

To correct the résumé example, you need to use more paragraph elements and two new container elements:

<ul>

Indicates the start of an unordered list. A list is the perfect way to detail Lee's skills.

<li>

Indicates an individual item in a bulleted list. Your browser indents each list item and, for sentences that go beyond a single line, properly indents subsequent lines so they align under the first. In addition, it precedes each list item with a bullet (•). You can only use the <li> element inside a list element like <ul>. In other words, every list item needs to be a part of a list.

Here's the corrected Web page (shown in Figure 2-10), with the structural elements highlighted in bold:

```
<!DOCTYPE html PUBLIC "-//W3C//DTD XHTML 1.0 Strict//EN"
"http://www.w3.org/TR/xhtml1/DTD/xhtml1-strict.dtd">

<html xmlns="http://www.w3.org/1999/xhtml">

<head>
<title>Hire Me!</title>
</head>
```

```
<body>
<p>I am Lee Park. Hire me for your company, because my work is <b>off the
hizzle</b>.</p>
<p>My skills include:</p>
<ul>
  <li>Fast typing (nearly 12 words/minute).</li>
  <li>Extraordinary pencil sharpening.</li>
  <li>Inventive excuse making.</li>
  <li>Negotiating with officers of the peace.</li>
</ul>
</body>

</html>
```

You can turn a browser's habit of ignoring line breaks to your advantage. To help make your XHTML documents more readable, add line breaks and spaces wherever you want. Web experts often use indentation to make the structure of nested elements easier to understand. In the résumé example, you can already see this trick in action. Notice how the list items (the lines starting with the <li> element) are indented. This has no effect on the browser, but it makes it easier for you to see the structure of the XHTML document, and to gauge how a browser will render it.

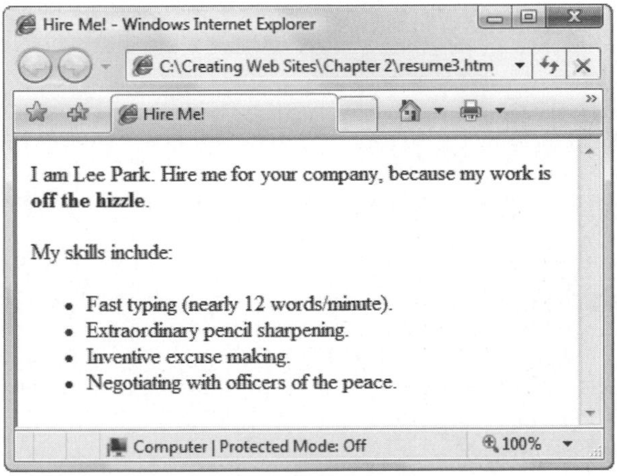

Figure 2-10:
With the right elements (as shown in the code earlier on this page), the browser understands the structure of your XHTML document, and knows how to display it.

Figure 2-11 analyzes the XHTML document using a *tree model*. The tree model is a handy way to get familiar with the anatomy of a Web page, because it shows the page's overall structure at a glance. However, as your Web pages get more complicated, they'll probably become too complex for a tree model diagram to be useful.

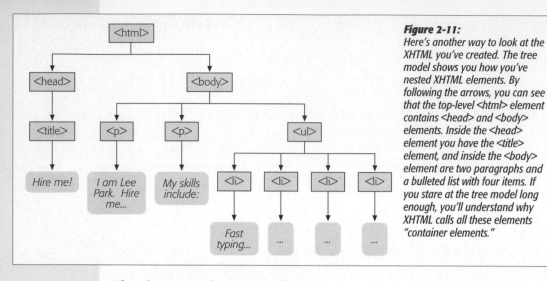

Figure 2-11:
Here's another way to look at the XHTML you've created. The tree model shows you how you've nested XHTML elements. By following the arrows, you can see that the top-level <html> element contains <head> and <body> elements. Inside the <head> element you have the <title> element, and inside the <body> element are two paragraphs and a bulleted list with four items. If you stare at the tree model long enough, you'll understand why XHTML calls all these elements "container elements."

If you're a masochist, you don't need to use any spaces. The previous example is exactly equivalent to the following much-less-readable XHTML document that omits white space entirely:

```
<!DOCTYPE html PUBLIC "-//W3C//DTD XHTML 1.0 Strict//EN"
"http://www.w3.org/TR/xhtml1/DTD/xhtml1-strict.dtd"><html xmlns="http://www.
w3.org/1999/xhtml"><html ="http://www.w3.org/1999/xhtml"><head><title>Hire
Me!</title></head><body><p>I am Lee Park. Hire me for your company, because
my work is <b>off the hizzle</b>.</p><p>My skills include:</p><ul><li>Fast
typing (nearly 12 words/minute).</li><li> Extraordinary pencil sharpening.</
li><li>Inventive excuse making.</li><li> Negotiating with officers of the
peace.</li></ul></body></html>
```

Of course, it's nearly impossible for a human to write XHTML like this without making a mistake.

Where Are All the Pictures?

Whether it's a stock chart, a logo for your underground garage band, or a doctored photo of your favorite celebrity, the Web would be a pretty drab place without pictures. So far, you've seen how to put text into an XHTML document, but what happens when you need an image?

Although it may seem surprising, you can't store a picture inside an XHTML file. There are plenty of good reasons why you wouldn't want to anyway—your Web page files would become really large, it would be hard to modify your pictures or do other things with them, and you'd have a fiendish time editing your pages in a text editor because the image data would make a mess. The solution is to store your pictures as separate files, and then *link* them to your XHTML document. This way, your browser pulls up the pictures and positions them exactly where you want them on your Web page.

Have Something to Hide?

When you're working with a complex Web page, you may want to temporarily remove an element or a section of content. This is a handy trick when you have a page that doesn't quite work right, and you want to try and find out which elements are causing the problem. One way to do this is with the good ol' fashioned cut-and-paste feature in your text editor. Cut the section you think may be troublesome, save the file, and then load it up in your browser. If the section is innocent, paste it back in place, and then re-save the file. Repeat this process until you find the culprit.

However, XHTML gives you a simpler solution—*comments*. With comments, you can leave the entire page intact. When you "comment out" a section of the page, XHTML ignores it.

You create an XHTML comment using the character sequence <!-- to mark the start of the comment, and the character sequence --> to mark the end. Your browser will ignore everything in between these two markers, whether it's content or tags. The comment markers can appear on the same line, or you can use them to hide an entire section of your XHTML document. However, don't try to nest one comment inside another, as that won't work.

Here's an example that hides two list items. When you open this document in your Web browser, the list will show only the last two items ("Inventive excuse making" and "Negotiating with officers of the peace").

```
<ul>
<!-- <li>Fast typing (nearly 12 words/
minute).
</li>
<li>Extraordinary pencil sharpening.</li>
-->
<li>Inventive excuse making.</li>
<li>Negotiating with officers of the
peace.</li>
</ul>
```

When you want to return the list to its original glory, just remove the comment markers.

The linking tool that performs this trick is the <img> element (short for "image"). The <img> element points to an image file, which the browser retrieves and inserts into the page. You can put the image file in the same folder as your Web page (which is the easiest option) or you can put it on a completely different Web site.

Although you'll learn everything you ever wanted to know about Web graphics in Chapter 7, it's worth considering a simple example right now. To try this out, you need a Web-ready image handy. (The most commonly supported image file types are JPEG, GIF, and PNG.) If you downloaded this book's companion content (from the Missing CD page at *www.missingmanuals.com*), you can use the sample picture *leepark.jpg*. Assuming you put this file in the same folder as your Web page file, you can display the image with the following image element:

```
<img src="leepark.jpg" alt="Lee Park Portrait" />
```

Like the <br /> element discussed earlier, the <img> element is a standalone element with no content. For that reason, it has a forward slash before its closing angle bracket. However, there's an obvious difference between the <br> element and the <img> element. Although <img> is a standalone element, it isn't self-sufficient. In order for the element to mean anything, you need to supply two more pieces of information: the name of the image file, and some alternate text, which is used in cases where your browser can't download or display the picture (see page 181). To incorporate this extra information into the image element, XHTML uses *attributes*. Attributes are extra pieces of information that appear *after* an element name, but before the closing > character.

The <img> example includes two attributes, separated by a space. Each attribute has two parts—a name (which tells the browser what the attribute does) and a value (a variable piece of information you supply). The name of the first <img> attribute is *src*, which is shorthand for "source"; it tells the browser where to get the image you want. In this example, the value of the src attribute is *leepark.jpg*, which is the name of the file with Lee Park's headshot.

The name of the second <img> attribute is *alt*, which is shorthand for "alternate text"; it tells a browser that you want it to show text if it can't display the image. Its value is the text you want to display, which is "Lee Park Portrait" in this case.

Once you've unraveled the image element, you're ready to use it in an XHTML document. Just place it inside an existing paragraph, wherever it makes sense.

```
<!DOCTYPE html PUBLIC "-//W3C//DTD XHTML 1.0 Strict//EN"
"http://www.w3.org/TR/xhtml1/DTD/xhtml1-strict.dtd">

<html xmlns="http://www.w3.org/1999/xhtml">

<head>
<title>Hire Me!</title>
</head>

<body>
<p>I am Lee Park. Hire me for your company, because my work is <b>off the
hizzle</b>.
<img src="leepark.jpg" alt="Lee Park Portrait" />
</p>
<p>My skills include:</p>
<ul>
  <li>Fast typing (nearly 12 words/minute).</li>
  <li>Extraordinary pencil sharpening.</li>
  <li>Inventive excuse making.</li>
  <li>Negotiating with officers of the peace.</li>
</ul>
</body>

</html>
```

Figure 2-12 shows exactly where the picture is displayed.

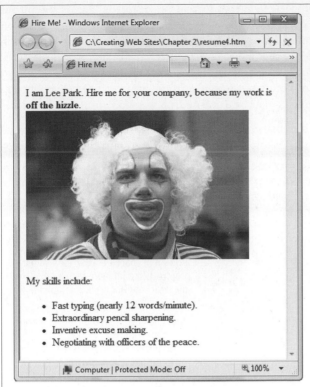

Figure 2-12:
Here's a Web page that embeds a picture, thanks to the linking power of the image element (shown on page 44). To display this document, a Web browser performs a separate request to retrieve the image file. As a result, your browser may display the text of the Web page before it downloads the graphic, depending on your connection speed.

Note: You'll learn many more tricks for Web graphics, including how to change their size and wrap text around them, in Chapter 7.

The 10 Most Important Elements (and a Few More)

You've now reached the point where you can create a basic XHTML document, and you're well on your way to XHTML mastery with several elements under your belt. You know the fundamentals—all that's left is to expand your knowledge by learning how to use more elements.

XHTML has a relatively small set of elements. In fact, there are just over 60 in all. You'll most likely use fewer than 25 on a regular basis.

Note: You can't define your own elements and use them in an XHTML document because Web browsers won't know how to interpret them.

Some elements, like the <p> element that formats a paragraph, are important for setting out the overall structure of a page. These are called *block-level elements*. You can place block-level elements directly inside the <body> section of your Web page or, sometimes, inside another block-level element. Table 2-1 provides a quick overview of some of the most fundamental block-level elements, several of which you've already seen. It also points out which of these are container elements and which are standalone elements. (As you learned on page 33, container elements require start and end tags, but standalone elements get by with just a single tag.)

Table 2-1. *Basic block-level elements.*

Element	Name	Type of Element	Description
<p>	Paragraph	Container	As your high school English teacher probably told you, the paragraph is the basic unit for organizing text. When you use more than one paragraph element in a row, a browser inserts a certain amount of space between the two paragraphs—just a bit more than a full blank line. Full details appear in Chapter 5.
<h1>,<h2>, <h3>,<h4>, <h5>,<h6>	Heading	Container	Heading elements are a good way to add structure to your Web page and make titles stand out. They display text in large, boldfaced letters. The lower the number, the larger the text, so <h1> produces the largest heading. By the time you get to <h5>, the heading has dwindled to the same size as normal-sized text, and <h6>, although bold, is actually smaller than normal text.
<hr>	Horizontal Line	Standalone	A horizontal line can help you separate one section of your Web page from another. The line automatically matches the width of the browser window. (Or, if you put the line inside another element, like a cell in a table, it takes on the width of its container.)
<ul>,<li>	Unordered List, List Item	Container	These elements let you build basic bulleted lists. The browser automatically puts individual list items on separate lines and indents each one. For a quick change of pace, you can substitute <ul> with <ol> to get an automatically *numbered* list instead of a bulleted list (ol stands for "ordered list").

Other elements are designed to deal with smaller structural details—for example, snippets of bold or italicized text, line breaks, links that lead to other Web pages, and images. These elements are called *inline elements*. You can't put inline elements directly inside the <body> section. Instead, they have to be nested *inside* a block-level element. Table 2-2 lists the most useful inline elements.

Table 2-2. *Basic inline elements*

Element	Name	Type	Description
<b>, <i>	Bold and Italic	Container	These two elements apply character styling—either bold or italic text. Some people use the more descriptive <strong> and <em> (for emphasis) elements, instead. They do exactly the same thing.
 	Line Break	Standalone	Sometimes, all you want is text separated by simple line breaks, not separate paragraphs. This keeps subsequent lines of text closer together than when you use a paragraph. You'll learn more about text layout in Chapter 5.
<img>	Image	Standalone	To display an image inside a Web page, use this element. Make sure you specify the *src* attribute to indicate the file name of the picture you want the browser to show.
<a>	Anchor	Container	The anchor element is the starting point for creating hyperlinks that let Web site visitors jump from one page to another. You'll learn about this indispensable element in Chapter 8.

To make the sample résumé look really respectable, use a few tricks from Table 2-1 and Table 2-2. Figure 2-13 shows this revised version of the Web page:

```
<!DOCTYPE html PUBLIC "-//W3C//DTD XHTML 1.0 Strict//EN"
"http://www.w3.org/TR/xhtml1/DTD/xhtml1-strict.dtd">

<html xmlns="http://www.w3.org/1999/xhtml">

<head>
  <title>Hire Me!</title>
</head>

<body>
  <h1>Hire Me!</h1>
  <p>I am Lee Park. Hire me for your company, because my work is <b>off the
hizzle</b>. As proof of my staggering computer skills and monumental work
ethic, please enjoy this electronic resume.</p>

  <h2>Indispensable Skills</h2>
  <p>My skills include:</p>
  <ul>
    <li>Fast typing (nearly 12 words/minute).</li>
    <li>Extraordinary pencil sharpening.</li>
    <li>Inventive excuse making.</li>
    <li>Negotiating with officers of the peace.</li>
```

```
    </ul>
    <p>And I also know XHTML!</p>

    <h2>Previous Work Experience</h2>
    <p>I have had a long and illustrious career in a variety of trades. Here
are
      some highlights:</p>
    <ul>
      <li>2005-2008 - Worked as a typist at <i>Flying Fingers</i></li>
      <li>2008-2009 - Performed cutting-edge Web design at <i>Riverdale
        Farm</i></li>
      <li>2009-2010 - Starred in Chapter 2 of <i>Creating Web Pages: The
        Missing Manual</i></li>
    </ul>

    <hr />
  </body>

</html>
```

Checking Your Pages for Errors

Even a Web designer with the best intentions can run afoul of the strict rules of XHTML. Although browsers really *should* catch these mistakes, virtually none of them do. Instead, they do their best to ignore mistakes and display flawed documents.

At first glance, this seems like a great design—after all, it smoothes over any minor slip-ups you might make. But there's a dark side to tolerating mistakes. In particular, this behavior makes it all too easy for serious errors to lurk undetected in your Web pages. What's a serious error? A problem that's harmless when you view the page in your favorite browser, but makes an embarrassing appearance when someone views the page in another browser; a mistake that goes undetected until you edit the code, exposing the mistake the next time your browser displays the page; or a problem that has no effect on page display but prevents an automated tool (like a search engine) from reading the page.

Fortunately, there's an easy way to catch problems like these. You can use a *validation tool* that reads through your Web page and checks to see if it meets the strict rules of XHTML. Validators can catch a number of problems that you've seen in this chapter, including:

- Missing mandatory elements (for example, the <title> element)

- A start tag without a matching end tag

- Incorrectly nested tags

- Incorrect capitalization (for example, <B> instead of <b>)

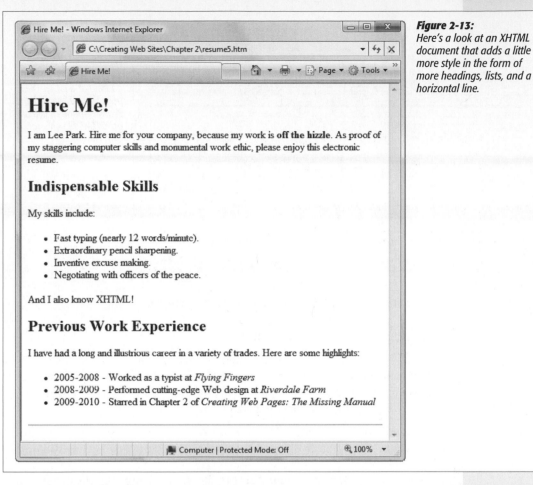

Figure 2-13:
Here's a look at an XHTML document that adds a little more style in the form of more headings, lists, and a horizontal line.

- Tags with missing attributes (for example, an <img> element without the src attribute)

- Elements or content in the wrong place (for example, text that's placed directly in the <body> section)

If you use a professional Web design tool like Dreamweaver, you can use its built-in error checker (Chapter 4 has the details). If you create pages by hand in a text editor, you can use a free online validation tool.

You can choose from plenty of validation tools, but most only validate pages that are already online. The validator at *www.validome.org* (shown in Figure 2-14) is a bit better—it lets you validate an online page or upload an XHTML document straight from your hard drive.

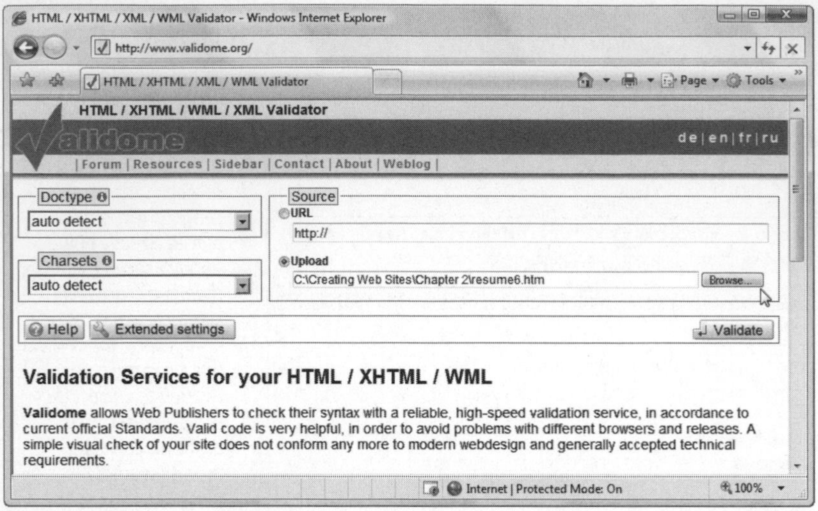

Figure 2-14:
The Web site www.validome.org gives you two options for validating XHTML. You can fill in the address of another Web page, or you can click the Browse button to call up an XHTML file on your own computer.

To validate a page at *www.validome.org*, follow these steps:

1. **Go to *www.validome.org*.**

2. **Click the Upload option to choose to validate a file from your computer.**

   On the other hand, if you want to validate a file that's already online, choose the URL option, enter a Web page address (like *http://www.MySloppySite.com/FlawedPage.html*), and then jump to step 5.

3. **Click the Browse button.**

   An Open dialog box appears.

4. **Browse to the location of your XHTML file, select it, and then click Open.**

   The file name appears in the text box, as shown in Figure 2-14.

   At this point, you can set other options, but you probably won't. It's best to leave the Doctype set to "auto detect"—that way, the validator will use the doctype specified in your Web page. Similarly, use "auto detect" for the Charsets option unless you have an XHTML page that's written in another language and the validator has trouble determining the correct character set.

5. **Click the Validate button.**

   Clicking the Validate button sends your XHTML page to the Validome Web server and, after a brief delay, the report appears. You'll see whether your document passed the validation check and, if it failed, what errors the validator detected (see Figure 2-15).

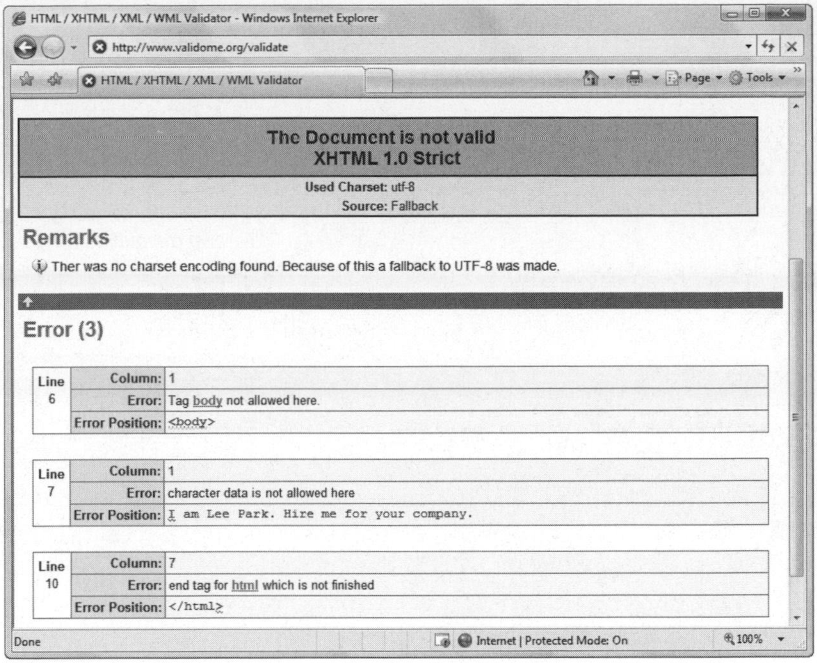

HTML / XHTML / XML / WML Validator - Windows Internet Explorer

http://www.validome.org/validate

HTML / XHTML / XML / WML Validator

Page ▼ Tools ▼

The Document is not valid
XHTML 1.0 Strict

Used Charset: utf-8
Source: Fallback

Remarks

Ther was no charset encoding found. Because of this a fallback to UTF-8 was made.

Error (3)

Line 6	Column:	1
	Error:	Tag body not allowed here.
	Error Position:	`<body>`

Line 7	Column:	1
	Error:	character data is not allowed here
	Error Position:	I am Lee Park. Hire me for your company.

Line 10	Column:	7
	Error:	end tag for html which is not finished
	Error Position:	`</html>`

Done   Internet | Protected Mode: On   100%

Figure 2-15:
The validator has discovered three errors in this file that stem from two mistakes. First, the page is missing the mandatory <header> section. Second, it contains text that's placed directly in the <body> section, rather than in a block-level element (like a paragraph). Incidentally, this file is still close enough to correct that most browsers will display it correctly, without warning you about the sloppy XHTML inside.

Putting Your Page on the Web

In the previous chapter you learned the basics of XHTML by creating a simple one-page résumé. There's a lot more you can do to perfect that page, but before going any further it's worth taking a look at one of the most important pieces of the Web puzzle—getting your pages online.

In this chapter, you start by taking a closer look at how Web servers work. Once you're armed with these high-tech nerd credentials, you'll be ready to search for your own *Web host*—the company that will let you park your site on its Web server. All you need to do is figure out your requirements, see which hosts offer what you need, and start comparison shopping.

How Web Hosting Works

As you learned in Chapter 1, the Web isn't stored on any single computer, and no company owns it. Instead, the individual pieces (Web sites) are scattered across millions of computers (Web servers). Only a subtle illusion makes all these Web sites seem to be part of a single environment. In reality, the Internet is just a set of standards that let independent computers talk to each other.

So how does your favorite browser navigate this tangled network of computers to find just the Web page you want? It's all in what's known as the *URL* (Uniform Resource Locator)—which is simply the Web site address you type into your browser, like *www.google.com*.

Understanding the URL

A URL consists of several pieces. Some of them are optional, because a browser or Web server can fill them in automatically. Others are required. Figure 3-1 dissects the URL *http://www.SellMyJunkForMillions.com/Buyers/listings.htm*.

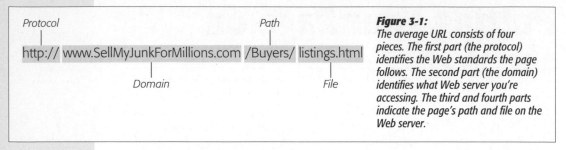

Protocol

Path

http:// www.SellMyJunkForMillions.com /Buyers/ listings.html

Domain

File

Figure 3-1:
The average URL consists of four pieces. The first part (the protocol) identifies the Web standards the page follows. The second part (the domain) identifies what Web server you're accessing. The third and fourth parts indicate the page's path and file on the Web server.

Web addresses pack a lot of information into a single line of text, including:

• **The protocol** indicates your chosen method of transmission—in other words, how your browser should communicate with the Web server. Web sites always use HTTP (HyperText Transport Protocol), which means the protocol portion of a URL is always *http://* or *https://*. (The latter establishes a super-secure connection over HTTP that encrypts sensitive information you type in, like credit card numbers or passwords.) In most browsers, you can get away without typing in this part of the URL. For example, when you type *www.google.com*, your browser automatically converts it to the full URL, *http://www.google.com*.

Note: Although http:// is the way to go when browsing the Web, depending on your browser, you may also use other protocols for other tasks. Common examples include *ftp://* (File Transfer Protocol) for uploading and downloading files and *file:///* for retrieving a file directly from your own computer's hard drive.

• **The domain** name identifies the Web server that hosts the site you want to see. By convention, server names usually start with *www* to identify them as *World Wide Web* servers. In addition, as you'll discover later in this chapter, friendly-seeming domain names like *www.google.com* or *www.Microsoft.com* are really just stand-ins for what your browser really needs to locate a server—namely, its numeric address.

• **The path** identifies the folder where the Web server stores the specific Web page you're looking for. This part of the URL can have as many levels as needed. For example, the path */MyFiles/Sales/2009/* refers to a MyFiles folder that contains a Sales folder that, in turn, contains a folder named 2009. Windows fans, take note—the slashes in the path portion of a URL are ordinary forward slashes, not the backward slashes used in Windows file paths (like *c:\MyFiles\Current*). This convention matches the file paths used by Unix-based computers, which were the first machines to host Web sites. It's also the convention used in modern Macintosh operating systems (OS X and later).

Note: Many browsers are smart enough to correct the common mistake of typing in the wrong type of slash. However, you shouldn't rely on this happening because similar laziness can break the Web pages you create. For example, if you use the <img> element to link to an image (as shown on page 44) and use the wrong type of slash, your picture won't appear.

- **The file name** is the last part of the path and it identifies the specific Web page you're requesting. Often, you can recognize it by the file extension .htm or .html, both of which stand for HTML, the forefather of XHTML.

Tip: Web pages often end with .htm or .html, but they don't need to. For example, if you look at a URL and see the strange extension *.blackpudding*, odds are you're still looking at an HTML or XHTML document. In most cases, browsers ignore an extension as long as the file contains information that a browser can interpret. However, just to keep yourself sane, this is one convention you shouldn't break.

- **The bookmark** (not be confused with the Web browser feature of the same name) is an optional part of a URL that identifies a specific position within a Web page. You can recognize a bookmark because it always starts with the number-sign character (#) and appears after a file name. For example, the URL *http://www.LousyDeals.com/index.html#New* includes the bookmark *#New*. When you click the URL, it takes you to the section of the index.html page where the page creator has placed the New bookmark. You'll learn how to place bookmarks on page 221.

- **The query string** is an optional part of a URL that some Web sites use to send extra information from one Web page to another. You can identify the query string because it starts with a question mark (?) and appears after a file name. To see a query string in action, go to *www.google.com* and perform a search for "pet platypus." When you click the Search button, you're directed to a URL like *http://www.google.ca/search?hl=en&q=pet+platypus&meta=*. This URL is a little tricky to analyze, but if you search for the question mark in the URL you'll discover that you're on a page named "search." The information to the right of the question mark indicates that you're executing an English-language search for pages that match both the "pet" and "platypus" keywords. When you request this URL, a specialized Google Web program analyzes this query string to determine what type of search it needs to perform.

Note: You won't use the query string in your own Web pages, because it's designed for heavy-duty Web programs like the one that powers Google. However, by understanding the query string, you get a bit of insight into how other Web sites work.

How Browsers Analyze a URL

Clearly, a URL packs a lot of information in one place. But how does a browser actually use the URL to fetch the Web page you want? To understand this, it helps to take a peek behind the scenes (see Figure 3-2).

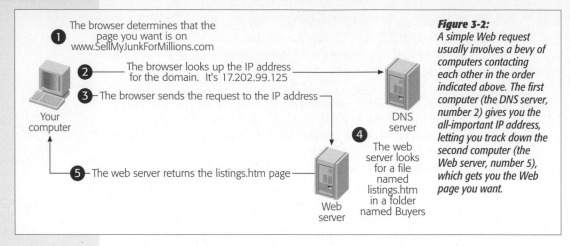

The browser determines that the
page you want is on
www.SellMyJunkForMillions.com ①

② The browser looks up the IP address
for the domain. It's 17.202.99.125

③ The browser sends the request to the IP address

Your
computer

DNS
server

④

The web
server looks
for a file
named
listings.htm
in a folder
named Buyers

⑤ The web server returns the listings.htm page

Web
server

Figure 3-2:
*A simple Web request
usually involves a bevy of
computers contacting
each other in the order
indicated above. The first
computer (the DNS server,
number 2) gives you the
all-important IP address,
letting you track down the
second computer (the
Web server, number 5),
which gets you the Web
page you want.*

The following list of steps shows a breakdown of what a browser does when you type *http://www.SellMyJunkForMillions.com/Buyers/listings.htm* into the address bar, and then press Enter:

1. **First, the browser needs to figure out what Web server to contact. It does this by extracting the domain name from the URL.**

   In this example, the domain name is *www.SellMyJunkForMillions.com.*

2. **To find the Web server named *www.SellMyJunkForMillions.com*, the browser needs to convert the domain name into a computer-friendly number called the *IP address.***

   Every computer on the Web—from Web servers to your PC—has its own unique IP address. To find the IP address for a Web server, the browser looks up the Web server's domain name in a giant catalog called the DNS (Domain Name Service).

   An IP address looks like a set of four numbers separated by periods (or, in techie speak, dots). For example, the *www.SellMyJunkForMillions.com* Web site may have the IP address 17.202.99.125.

Note: The DNS catalog isn't stored on your computer, so your browser actually needs to grab this information from the Internet. You can see the advantage of this approach. Under ordinary circumstances, a company's domain name will never change, because that's what customers use and remember. But an IP address may change, because a company could move its Web site from one server to another, for example. As long as the company remembers to update the DNS, this won't cause any disruption. Fortunately, you won't need to worry about managing the DNS yourself, because the company that hosts your site automatically handles it for you.

---

3. **The browser sends the page request to the Web server's now-retrieved IP address.**

   The actual route the message takes is difficult to predict. It may cross through a number of other Web servers on the way.

4. **When the server receives the request, it looks at the path and file name in the URL.**

   In this case, the Web server sees that the request is for a file named *listings.htm* in a folder named *Buyers*. It looks up that file, and then sends it back to the Web browser. If the file doesn't exist, it sends back an error message instead.

5. **Once the browser gets the XHTML page it's been waiting for (*listings.htm*), it displays that page for your viewing pleasure.**

The URL *http://www.SellMyJunkForMillions.com/Buyers/listings.htm* is a typical example. However, in the wild, you'll sometimes come across URLs that seem a lot simpler. For instance, consider *http://www.amazon.com*. It clearly specifies the domain name (*www.amazon.com*), but it doesn't include any information about the path or file name. So what's a Web browser to do?

When your URL doesn't include a file name, the browser just sends the request as is, and lets the Web server decide what to do. The Web server sees that you aren't requesting a specific file, and so it sends you the site's default Web page, which is often named *index.htm* or *index.html*. (However, a Web administrator can configure any Web page as the default.)

Now that you understand how URLs work, you're ready to integrate your own pages into the fabric of the Web. The first task is getting yourself a good domain name.

Domain Names

Shakespeare may have famously written "What's in a name? That which we call a rose/By any other name would smell as sweet." But he may not see things the same way if he had to type *www.thesweetsmellingredflowerwiththorns.biz* into his browser instead of *www.rose.com*. Short, snappy domain names attract attention and are easy to remember. Today, cheap personalized domain addresses are within the reach of every Web site creator. If you decide to get one of your own, it's worth taking the time to get it right.

Note: Valid domain names include only letters, numbers, and dashes.

Getting the Right Name

You'll find that most short, clever word combinations are no longer available as domain names. Even if they aren't in use, *domain squatters*—individuals who buy and hold popular names in hopes of selling them to desperate high bidders later—have long since laid claim to common names. Give up on *www.worldsbestchocolate.com*— it's gone. However, you may find success with names that are a little longer or

POWER USERS' CLINIC

Internet vs. Intranet

As you already know, the Internet is a huge network of computers that spans the globe. An *intranet* is a lot smaller—it's a network inside a specific company, organization, or home that joins together a much smaller number of computers. In fact, an intranet could have as few as two computers.

An intranet makes sense anytime you need to have a Web site that's only available to a small number of people in one location. For example, a company can use an intranet Web site to share marketing bulletins (or the latest office gossip). In your own home, you could use an intranet to let your housemates browse your Web creations from multiple computers. The only limitation is that a Web site on an intranet is only accessible to the computers on that network. Other Web visitors won't be able to see it.

Setting up a Web site for an intranet is easier than setting one up for the Internet because you don't need to register a domain name. Instead, you can use the network computer name. For example, if your computer has the network name "SuperServer," you could access a Web page with a URL like *http://SuperServer/MySite/MyPage.htm*.

To set up your own intranet, you need to start by setting up a local network, and then you need to make sure you have some Web hosting software. These tasks are outside the scope of this book, but if you're eager to give this do-it-yourself project a try, you'll need to start by setting up a home network. Check out *Home Networking: The Missing Manual* for complete instructions.

more specific (*www.worldsbestmilkchocolate.com*), use locations or the names of people (*www.bestvermontchocolate.com* or *www.anniesbestchocolate.com*), or introduce made-up words (*www.chocolatech.com*). All these domain names are available at the time of this writing.

There's no exact science to choosing a good domain name, but there's plenty of anecdotal evidence on names that don't work. Here are some mistakes to avoid:

- **Dashes.** It may be tempting to get exactly the domain name you want by adding extra characters, like dashes, between words. For example, you have no chance at getting *www.popularbusiness.com*, but *www.popular-business.com* is still there for the taking. Don't do it. For some reason, dashes seem to confuse everyone. People are likely to leave them out, confuse them with underscores, or have trouble finding the dash key on the keyboard.

- **Phrases that look confusing in lowercase.** Domain names aren't case-sensitive, and when you type a domain name into a browser, the browser converts everything to lowercase. The problem is that some phrases can blend together in lowercase, particularly if you have words that start with vowels. Take a look at what happens when the documentation company Prose Xact puts their business name into a lowercase domain name: *www.prosexact.com*. You get the picture.

Tip: Even though domain names don't distinguish case, that doesn't stop businesses from using capital letters in business cards, promotions, and marketing material to make the domain name more readable. Whether customers type *www.google.com* or *wWw.gOOgLE.cOm* into their browsers, they get to the same site.

- **Names that don't match your business**. It's a classic business mistake. You set up a flower shop in New York called Roses are Red. Unfortunately, the domain *www.rosesarered.com* is already taken so you go for the next best choice, *www.newyorkflorist.com*. Huh? What you've actually done is create two separate names, and a somewhat schizophrenic identity for your business. To avoid these problems, if you're starting a new business, try to choose your business name and your domain name at the same time so they match. If you already have a business name, settle on a URL that has an extra word or two, like *www.rosesaredflorist.com*. This name may not be as snappy as *www.newyorkflorist.com*, but it avoids the inevitable confusion of creating a whole new identity.

- **Settling for .org**. The last few letters of the domain (the part after the last period) is called the *top-level domain*. Everyone wants a .com address for their business, and as a result they're the hardest domain name to get. Of course, there are other top-level domains like .net, .org, .biz, and so on. The problem is, every Web visitor expects a .com. If you have the domain name *www.SuperShop.biz*, odds are someone will type in *www.SuperShop.com* while trying to find your site. That mistake can easily lead your fans to a competitor (or to a vastly inferior Web site). In other words, it's sometimes worth taking a second-choice name to get your first choice of a top-level domain (a .com).

Note: The top-level domain .org was originally intended for non-profit organizations. It's now available for anyone to use and abuse. However, if you're setting up a non-profit of your own, the .org domain may make more sense than .com and be almost as recognizable.

Domain name searches are an essential bit of prep work. Experiment—try to come up with as many variations and unusual name combinations as possible. Aim to record at least a dozen available name possibilities, so you can give yourself lots of choice. Once you've compiled the list, why not make a few late-night phone calls to pester friends and relatives for their first reactions?

In the time that's passed since the first edition of this book, it's become even harder to get a decent domain name. In the past, your only competition was other people planning to set up a Web site and unscrupulous domain name resellers looking to buy a hot name and flip it to someone for a big profit. But now, nefarious people buy just about any domain name at the drop of a hat, build a fly-by-night Web page filled with ads, and wait a few months to see if any unsuspecting Web traffic stumbles their way (this practice is called *domain tasting*). It's still possible to cook up a decent domain name, but you'll need a dash of compromise and all the creativity you've got.

Searching for a Name

Once you identify a few domain name ideas, it's time to start checking domain name availability. You can do this even if you haven't chosen a Web hosting company. In fact, the Web abounds with tools that let you check whether a domain name is available.

International Domain Names

Some domain names end with a country code. Should I get one?

A .com address is a Web site creator's best friend. Other top-level domains (.net, .org, .biz, and so on), generally aren't worth the trouble. However, there is one exception: regional domain names. If you can't get the .com you need, it just might make sense to go with a country-specific top-level domain like .us (USA) or .ca (Canada).

For example, if you're offering piano lessons in England, *www.pianolessons.co.uk* isn't a bad choice. But if you're planning to sell products to an international audience, *www.HotRetroRecords.co.uk* is likely to frighten away otherwise interested buyers, who may assume it's too much trouble to deal with a British seller.

There are special rules about who can register country-specific names. Due to these restrictions, many Web hosting companies can't sell certain country-specific domains. To search for domain names with a specific country code, use Google to find the right registrar. For example, to find a registrar for Australian domains, search for "Australian domain names."

Just about every Web hosting company provides its own version of a domain name search tool. Figure 3-3 shows an example from *www.domaindirect.com*.

When you perform a search and find an available domain name, the Web hosting company gives you the option to buy the name. But don't do anything yet, because you still need to find the best Web hosting company.

Tip: You may think you could see if a domain is free just by typing it into your Web browser. But this method of checking takes more time, and it doesn't give you a definitive result. Someone can buy a domain name without setting up a Web site, so even if you can't find a Web site using your browser, the domain may not be available.

Registering Your Name

After you find an available name, you probably want to wait to register it until you're ready to sign up for a Web hosting plan, too (which you'll read about in the next section). That's because most Web hosting companies offer free or discounted domain name registration when you rent space from them. In addition, doing both at once is the easiest way to set up your domain name, because the process automatically establishes a relationship between your domain name and your Web site.

However, there are cases where you may want to register a domain name separately from your Web hosting package. Here are some examples:

- You don't actually want to create a Web site right now, but you do want to register a name so no one else can grab it (a tactic known as *domain parking*). Sometime in the future, you may develop a Web site that uses that name.

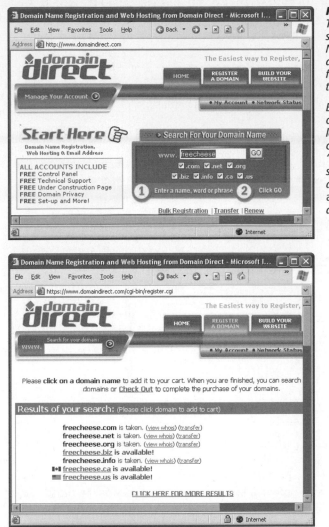

Figure 3-3:
Top: Using this free domain search tool, you can see if the domain name you want is available. Notice that you don't have to type in the www. at the start of the domain name, because the form's taken care of that for you (at the left of the box).

Bottom: The results aren't good. Your first choice, www.freecheese.com *is gone. All that's left are the less-catchy* www.freecheese.biz *and country-specific domains. You can click the "Click Here for More Results" link to have the search tool display related domains that are available (in this case, you'd find that* www.allfreecheese.com *and* www.bestfreecheese.com *are available).*

- You already have Web space, possibly through your ISP (Internet Service Provider). All you need to make your Web site seem more professional is to get a personalized domain name. This option can get a little tricky, and you may need to use a procedure called *domain forwarding* (which you'll read about in a moment).

- Your Web hosting company can't register the type of domain you want. This can happen if you need a domain name with a country-specific top-level domain.

If you don't fall into one of these special categories, skip ahead to the section "Getting Web Space" (page 67) to start searching for the right Web host. Otherwise, keep reading for more details about registering and managing a domain name on its own.

Note: All Web hosting companies let you register more than one domain for the same Web site. That means you can register both *www.FancyPants.com* and *www.FancyPants.org*, and have both these addresses point to the same Web site. Of course, you'll need to pay an extra domain name registration fee.

Domain parking

Domain parking (Figure 3-4) means you've registered a domain name but haven't yet purchased any other services, like renting Web storage space.

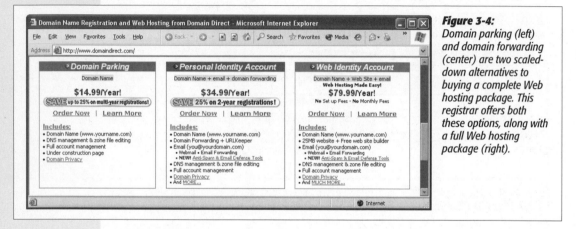

Figure 3-4:
Domain parking (left) and domain forwarding (center) are two scaled-down alternatives to buying a complete Web hosting package. This registrar offers both these options, along with a full Web hosting package (right).

Most people use domain parking to put a domain name away on reserve. In the increasingly crowded world of the Web, many people use it to protect their own names (for example, *www.samanthamalone.com*). Domain parking is also useful if you want to secure several potential business names you may use in the future.

Tip: If you do reserve a domain name, it's a good idea to do your research, and pick a company that you'd also like to use to host your Web site. You can switch domain names from one Web hosting firm to another, but it's a bit of a pain. Contact the Web host you're working with for specific instructions on how to pull this off.

The real appeal of domain parking is that it's cheap. You pay a nominal domain-name registration fee (as little as $5/year) and you get to keep the name for as long as you're willing to pay for it.

Domain forwarding

Domain forwarding lets you combine a personalized domain name with Web space you already have. For example, you may have free Web space through your ISP, your school, your job, from a free Web hosting service, or from a crazy uncle with a Web server in his basement. In these situations, you can save some money because you don't need to pay a company to host your Web site. However, you don't get to pick your domain name. For example, if you have Web space on an ISP, you might be stuck with a URL like *http://member.magicisp.com/members/personalwebspace/ ~henryj420/home*, which clearly isn't as catchy as *www.HenryTheFriendly.com*.

But take heart. Even if you get free Web hosting, you can still give your Web site a snappy URL. The trick is to buy the URL separately and use domain forwarding to point your brand-new URL to your existing Web site. In the previous example, for instance, you could buy the domain name *www.HenryTheFriendly.com* and use domain forwarding to point *www.HenryTheFriendly.com* to your Web space on *http://member.magicisp.com*.

Tip: Even if the URL from your ISP isn't as bad as in the example above, it's still a good idea to buy your own domain name. Here's why: If you use an ISP-provided URL and your ISP changes its configuration or you switch from one ISP to another, your Web visitors won't be able to find your site anymore. But if you use your own URL and domain forwarding, you simply need to update your domain-name settings to reflect your ISP's new configuration or your new ISP, All the while, your custom domain name keeps working. No one will even notice the change.

First you need to register a domain name that comes with forwarding as an included service (see Figure 3-4). Then you can log in and set the forwarding settings (see Figure 3-5).

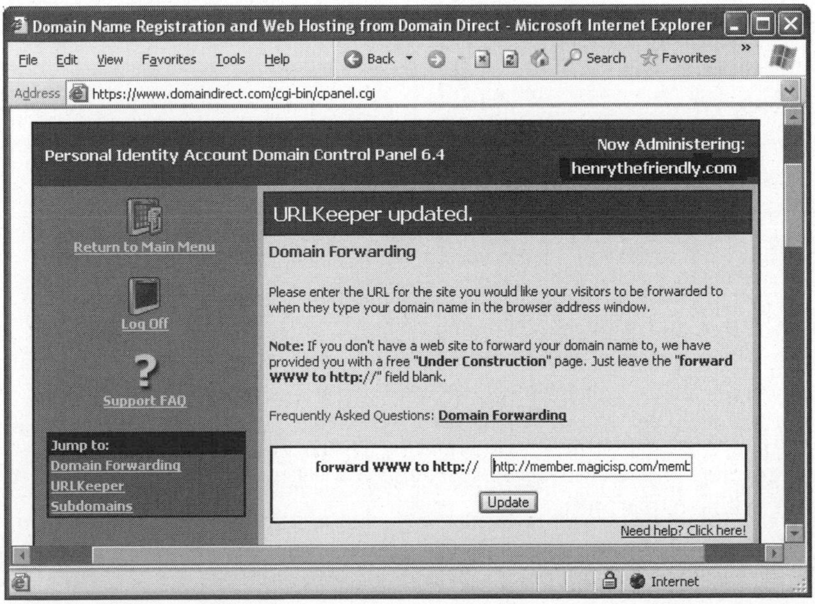

Figure 3-5:
Here, a domain forwarding service sends visitors who type in www. HenryTheFriendly.com *to a much more awkward URL where the Web site is actually located (bottom box). Usually, Web hosts implement domain forwarding in such a way that the browser address bar displays the original domain name even though the host sends visitors to a different site.*

With domain forwarding, many Web hosting firms give you the added ability to forward *subdomains*. Subdomains look like your domain name, but instead of starting with *www* they start with another word or phrase that you choose. For example, if you get a forwarding account for *www.PremiumPencils.com*, you could create a subdomain named *help.PremiumPencils.com* that goes to a customer support page or *resume.PremiumPencils.com* that gives visitors quick access to your electronic résumé (see Figure 3-6).

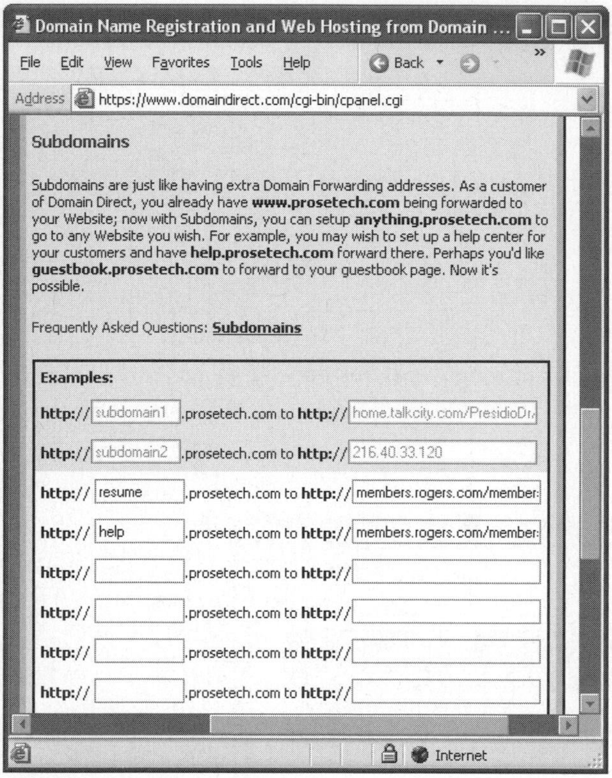

Figure 3-6:
Thanks to subdomains, you can provide easy access to several different pages on your site, or even to several different Web sites. All you need to do is forward each domain to a different URL, as shown here with the subdomains resume. prosetech.com and help.prosetech.com.

Domain forwarding can come in handy in other scenarios. Say you have an account with a hosting company and you want to use it to create several separate sites (like a personal site, a business site, a site for someone else in your family, and so on). Conceptually, it's easy—you just need to place each Web site in a separate folder. However, this tactic can muck up your URLs. If you have the business domain name *www.PremiumPencils.com* and you want to create a personal site for your upcoming marriage, you're stuck with something like *www.PremiumPencils. com/WeddingForDebbie*. A low-cost alternative is to buy a single Web hosting account and several domain names (like *www.PremiumPencils.com* and *www. DebbiesWedding.com*) with domain forwarding. Then set up domain forwarding, directing each domain name to the appropriate subfolder. Presto—your wedding guests will never know they're going to a subfolder on PremiumPencils.com, and they'll never be asked to stock up on office stationery, either.

A Host Here, a Domain There

Can I buy my domain name and Web space from different companies, and still make them work together?

The best approach is to get both from the same company, but that's not always possible. Maybe you bought your domain name before you set up your Web site and you don't want to pay the cost of transferring the domain. Or maybe you have a country-specific domain name (like *www.CunningPets.co.uk*) that your Web hosting company can't register.

To make this multiple-company tango work, you need some technical support from your Web hosting company. Contact their help desk and let them know what you plan to do. They can give you specific instructions, and they'll configure their name servers (more on what those are in a moment) to have the right information for your domain.

The next task is to change the registration information for your domain. Here are the steps you need to follow:

1. Find out the name of the *domain name servers (DNS servers)* at your Web hosting company. These are the computers that convert domain names into numeric IP addresses (page 56). The technical support staff can give you this information.

2. Go to the company where you registered the domain name and update your domain registration settings. Change the name server setting to match the name servers you found out about in step 1 (as shown in Figure 3-7).

Due to the way DNS servers work, the change can take 24 hours or more to take effect.

When you make this change, you're essentially saying that your Web hosting company is now responsible for giving out the IP address of your Web site. When someone types your domain name into a browser, the browser will contact the name server at your Web hosting company to get the IP address. From that point on, it's smooth sailing.

Once you modify your domain name registration, you still have the same two bills to pay. You'll pay your hosting fees to the Web hosting company and the yearly domain name registration fee to the company where you registered your domain name.

Free Domain Names

As you no doubt know, the Web is a great place for frugal shoppers. Not only can you score a great deal on a sporty iPod and a used sofa bed, you can also pick up a Web domain name for the princely sum of zero dollars. The trick is to register at a free subdomain service.

As you learned on page 34, subdomains are extensions that let you build on an existing domain name. A free subdomain service might own a domain like *www.net.tc* and let you register a subdomain like *www.acebusiness.net.tc*. Sure, the end portion of the domain (*.net.tc*) is a little awkward, but hey—it's free. Even better, it's much easier to get popular words in a subdomain than it is in a standalone domain name. For example, don't bother trying to scoop up *www.chocolates.com* or the .net, .org, .biz, .us, .ca versions of the name, as they're all taken. But if you head over to popular subdomain service *www.smartdots.com* (Figure 3-8), you can still register *www.chocolates.net.tc* without opening your wallet.

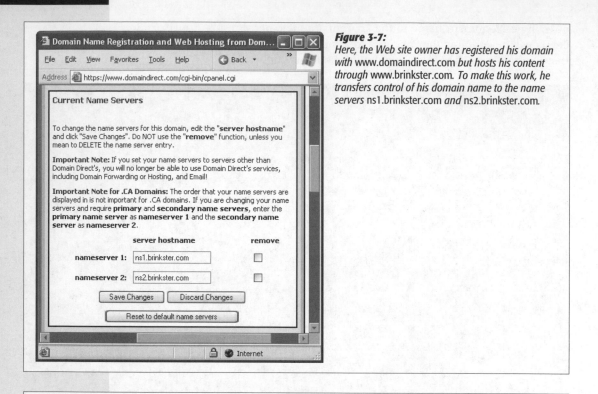

Figure 3-7:
Here, the Web site owner has registered his domain with www.domaindirect.com but hosts his content through www.brinkster.com. To make this work, he transfers control of his domain name to the name servers ns1.brinkster.com and ns2.brinkster.com.

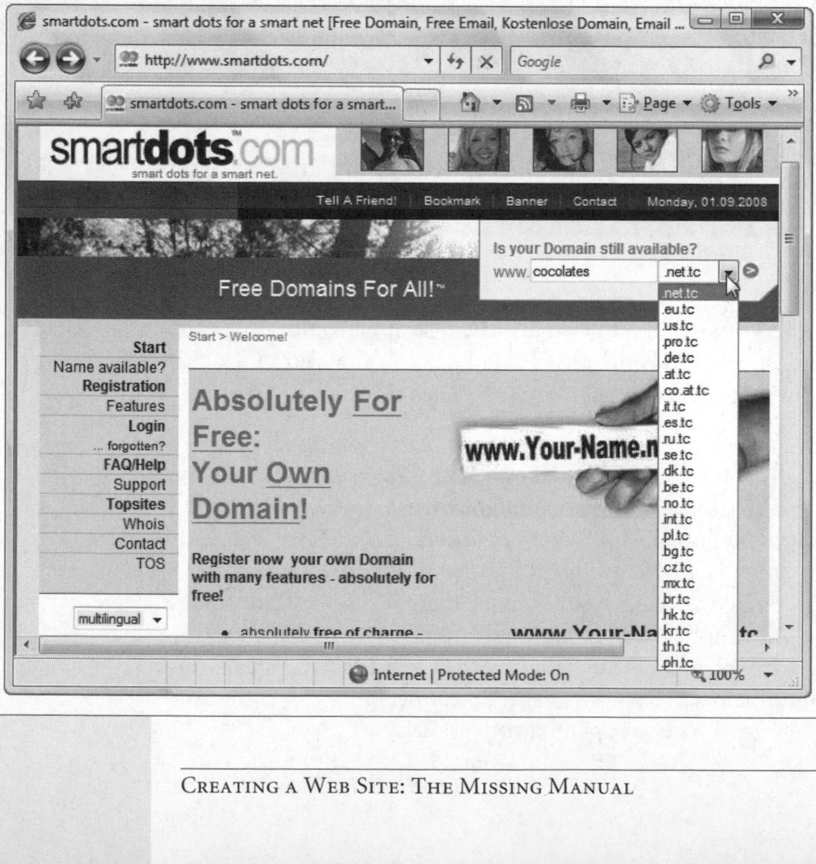

Figure 3-8:
At smartdots, you can register a free subdomain and point it to your real Web site. You can choose from several domain name roots, including the standard .net.tc, other domain names that suggest specific countries (like .us.tc and .uk.tc), and other domain names that suggest certain types of content (like .pro.tc, .shop.tc, and .edu.tc).

Getting Web Space

All you need to achieve Web superstardom is a domain name and a small amount of space on a Web server. There's no one-size-fits-all solution when it comes to finding a Web host. Instead, you choose the right hosting company based on your budget, what you want your Web site to be able to do, and your own capricious whims (let's face it—some Web hosting companies just have way cooler names than others).

Finding the right Web host can take a bit of searching, and it may require making a few phone calls or some browsing around the Web. Before you start tapping away, it helps to take a look at the big picture.

The Big Picture

Nowadays, Web hosting packages come in three main flavors:

- **Simplified Web site creation.** In this case, the Web hosting company offers special software that promises to help you create a Web site in two or three easy steps. These tools range from terrible to awful (see Figure 3-9). After all, if you're content to create the same cookie-cutter Web site as everyone else, you probably aren't interested in learning XHTML, and you wouldn't have picked up this book. Instead, go for standard Web site hosting and unleash your inner Web *artiste*.

Note: There's one case where simplified Web site creation makes sense—if all you want to do is create a *blog* (a personal site that consists of short, chronological postings about anything that interests you). Chapter 17 shows how you can create a blog on your own Web site, or how you can set one up at a free blogging host so you don't need to buy a domain name or pay for Web space.

- **Standard Web site hosting.** Here, you're given a slot of space on a Web server to manage as you see fit. You create your Web pages on your own computer, and then copy these files to the server so others can view them. This type of Web hosting is all you need to use this book.

- **Web program hosting.** This option makes sense if you're a programmer at heart, and you need a Web server that can run Web programs. Web programs do quite a few nifty tricks—they can perform complex calculations, read vast amounts of information from a database, and spit out made-to-measure XHTML on the fly. However, creating a Web program is far from easy. In this book, you'll focus on creating ordinary Web sites and using third-party services when you need more complex features, like an e-commerce shopping cart. That means Web program hosting is overkill.

Web hosting packages usually charge a monthly fee. For basic Web hosting, this fee starts at the reasonable sum of $5 to $10 per month. Of course, it can escalate quickly, depending on what features you want.

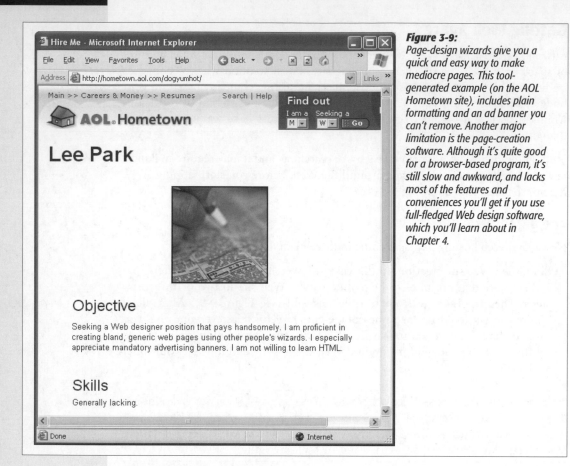

Figure 3-9:
Page-design wizards give you a quick and easy way to make mediocre pages. This tool-generated example (on the AOL Hometown site), includes plain formatting and an ad banner you can't remove. Another major limitation is the page-creation software. Although it's quite good for a browser-based program, it's still slow and awkward, and lacks most of the features and conveniences you'll get if you use full-fledged Web design software, which you'll learn about in Chapter 4.

Assessing Your Needs

Before you decide on a Web host, ask yourself one important question—what features do you need? Web hosts are quick to swamp their ads and Web sites with techie jargon, but they don't tell you which services are truly useful. Here's a quick overview that describes what Web hosts sell and what you need to know about each offering. If you'd like to keep track of which features you need, there's a Web host checklist you can fill out on page 70, or you can download it from the Missing CD page at *www.missingmanuals.com*.

- **Web space** is how much server space you're renting to store your Web site. Although XHTML pages are extremely small, you may need more space to fit in images or files you want others to download, like a video of your wedding. A modest site can easily survive with 20 MB (megabytes) of space, unless you're stuffing it full of pictures or videos. Most Web hosts throw in much more, knowing you'll probably never use it.

Note: For the numerically challenged, a gigabyte (GB) is the same as 1,024 megabytes (MB). To put that in perspective, today's hard drives can have 500 GB of space or more, enough room for tens of thousands of Web sites.

- **Bandwidth** (or Web traffic, as it's sometimes called) is the maximum amount of information you can deliver to anyone who visits your site in a month. Usually, you can make do with the lowest bandwidth your hosting company offers (with 1 GB being more than enough). For more information, see the box on page 71.

- **A domain name** is a custom Web site address, as in *www.HenryTheFriendly.com*. If you decide to get a personalized domain name, you don't necessarily need to get it from the same company that hosts your Web site. However, it does make life easier, and hosting companies often throw in one or more domain names at a discounted price when you sign up for a Web hosting plan.

- **Email addresses.** Odds are, you already have some of these. But you may want an email address that matches your Web site address, especially if you're paying for a customized domain name. For example, if you own *www.HenryThe-Friendly.com*, you'd probably like to use an email address like *Hank@HenryThe-Friendly.com*. Web hosting companies give you different options here—some may just forward the email to your everyday email address (which you'd need to supply them), while better packages give you a dedicated email inbox with plenty of space for receiving and storing messages.

- **Upload-ability.** How easy it is to transfer files to your Web server is another important detail. As you saw in the previous chapter, you can perfect your Web pages on your own computer before you upload them. But once your Web site is ready for prime time, you need a convenient way to copy all the files to your Web server. For greatest convenience, look for Web hosts that offer support for something called FTP (File Transfer Protocol), which lets you easily copy a number of files at once (for details, see page 80). Some Web hosts may also provide integration with popular Web design tools like Dreamweaver, letting you upload pages without leaving your Web editing program.

- **Server-side scripts** are miniature programs that can run on your Web site. They use one of a variety of programming frameworks, which have catchy acronyms like CGI, JSP, PHP, and ASP.NET. Although these features are powerful, they usually require programmer credentials. Occasionally, you might find a ready-made script that can perform a helpful task, like emailing you the information your Web visitors supply (page 347). But for the most part, server-side scripts and other types of Web server programming are beyond the scope of this book.

Note: Although this book doesn't cover server-side programs in depth, you'll learn about *client-side scripts* in Chapter 14; they run right inside Web site visitors' browsers, and are much more limited in ability than server-side scripts. Client-side scripts are commonly used for special effects like animated buttons. The nice thing about them is that even programming novices can drop a simple script into their Web pages and enjoy the benefits. But you don't need to worry about any of this right now, because unlike server-side scripts, client-side scripts don't require any special support from your Web hosting company.

- **Frills.** In an effort to woo you to their side, Web hosting companies often pack in a slew of frills. For example, sometimes they'll boast about their amazing, quick-and-easy Web site creation tools. Translation: they'll let you use a clumsy piece of software on their Web site to build yours. You'll end up with a cookie-cutter result and not much opportunity to express yourself. Steer clear of these pointless features. More usefully, a Web hosting company can provide Web site *statistics*—detailed information about how many visitors are flocking to your site on a daily or monthly basis. (In Chapter 11, you'll find out about a free visitor tracking tool that runs circles around what most Web hosts provide.)

A Web Host Checklist

✓ **Web space.** 20 MB is acceptable if you're getting free Web space from your ISP. If you're paying a monthly fee for Web space, you'll almost certainly get hundreds of megabytes or more. This is far more than you'll ever be able to use, even if you want to include photos, audio, or other large files. Many Web hosts offer gigabytes of space, knowing that almost no one has the time to upload that much information.

✓ **Bandwidth.** You don't need much. 1 GB works for most text-centric Web sites, but look for 5 GB or more if you want to provide large files or are expecting to create a popular Web destination. See the box on page 71 for tips that can help you estimate your bandwidth requirements.

✓ **Domain name.** This is your identity—*www.You.com*. Ideally, your Web host will throw in the domain name for free.

✓ **Email addresses.** These go with the domain name. Look for at least one POP mailbox. It's better to have five or more, because it lets you give separate email addresses to family members, or use them for different purposes. Also look for Web-based access to your email.

Note: POP stands for Post Office Protocol, an email standard your computer uses to communicate with an email server. When you have a POP email account, you're able to use desktop email programs like Microsoft Outlook and Thunderbird.

✓ **FTP access.** This lets you easily upload your files.

The Riddle of Bandwidth

Most Web hosting companies set their pricing, at least in part, on your Web space and bandwidth needs. This can be a problem, because the average Web site creator has no idea how to calculate these numbers. It's even harder to come up with realistic estimates.

Fortunately, you can save a lot of time and effort by understanding one dirty little secret: for the average personal or small-business Web site, you don't need much disk space or bandwidth. You can probably take the smallest amounts on offer from any Web hosting company and live quite happily. The only real exception is if your Web site is ridiculously popular, if you're showcasing a huge catalog of digital photos, or if you want to store extremely large files and let visitors download them.

If you still insist on calculating bandwidth, here's how it works. Let's say you've got a Web site with 100 relatively modest pages that are each about 50 KB (kilobytes) in size, including graphics. Right away, you can calculate your Web space requirement—it's 50 KB × 100, or about 5 MB.

To calculate the bandwidth, you need to make estimates about how many people will visit your site, and how much content they'll request over each visit. Suppose your site is doing well, and receives about 30 visitors in a day. Say an average visitor browses through 10 pages before leaving. In a day, your bandwidth usage is 30 visitors × 10 pages × 50 KB, or 15 MB. Over a 30-day month, that's 450 MB, still less than half of the 1 GB bare minimum that most Web hosting companies offer.

So why do Web hosting companies focus on Web space and bandwidth numbers? It's partly to satisfy large customers who really do have greater requirements, but it's also to confuse everyone else into buying more than they need.

Here's another scenario: you create a Web site and add links that let visitors download MP3 files of your underground all-percussion garage band. You give them a choice of three songs, each of which is a 4 MB MP3 file. Now the equation changes. Assuming your site gets a steady stream of 10 visitors a day, and assuming each visitor downloads all three songs, you've hit a bandwidth of 10 visitors × 3 songs × 4 MB, or 120 MB. Now your monthly bandwidth usage tops 3 GB. You're probably still in the clear, because many Web hosting companies offer 7 or 10 GB in their starter packages, but you'll want to pay more attention to the bandwidth number.

If bandwidth is important for you, you need to know what will happen if you surpass your bandwidth limit in a month. Some Web hosting companies cut your Web site off entirely (or just show your visitors an explanatory page saying the site is temporarily inactive). Others tack on extra fees. So ask.

✓ **Tech support.** The best companies provide 24-hour tech support, ideally through a toll-free number or a live chat feature that lets you ask a tech support person questions using your browser.

✓ **Server-side scripts**. Although Web server programming is too complex for most ordinary people, this feature gives you some room to grow. If your Web site supports a server-side programming technology (like CGI, ASP, or ASP.NET), you could conceivably take someone else's script and use it in your Web pages to carry out an advanced task, like collecting visitor information with a form (page 339).

✓ **FrontPage extensions.** If you create your Web site with Expression Web (the successor to FrontPage), you can use FrontPage server extensions to get a few extra frills. For example, FrontPage server extensions include server-side scripts that count the number of visitors to a certain page and let visitors upload files to the Web server.

Choosing Your Host

Now that you have your requirements in mind, it's time to start shopping for a Web host. The following sections take you through your options.

Your ISP (Internet Service Provider)

As you may have already realized, your ISP—the company that provides your access to the Internet—may have its own Web hosting services. In fact, these services are sometimes included in your subscription price, meaning you may already have a dedicated amount of Web space that you don't even know about. If you're in this situation, congratulations—you don't need to take any extra steps. If you're unsure, a quick call to your ISP will fill you in. Make sure you ask for "personal Web space," as many ISPs also provide large-scale Web hosting packages for a monthly fee.

Note: In some cases, your ISP may provide Web hosting that you decide not to use. For example, they may not give you enough space, or they may force you to use their limited Web site creation software (which is a definite drag). In these cases, you'll want to use one of the other Web hosting solutions described later.

Obviously, ISPs differ in whether or not they provide Web space. You're more likely to get a small amount of Web space if you have a high-speed broadband connection (cable or DSL) rather than a dial-up account. The space is always far smaller than what you receive from a Web hosting company, and it almost never includes a personal domain name (although you can purchase one separately).

Before continuing any further, it might be worth it to make a quick call to your ISP or visit their Web site to see if they provide Web hosting services.

Web hosting companies

Technically, any company that provides Web space is a Web host, but there's a class of companies that specialize in Web hosting and don't do anything else. You can find these companies all over the Internet, or in computer magazines. The disadvantage is that Web hosting companies always charge by the month. You won't get anything for free.

The sad truth is that it's almost impossible to research Web hosting companies online, because the Web is swamped with more advertisements for Web hosting than for cut-rate pharmaceuticals. Fortunately, there are many good choices.

Table 3-1 lists just a few good ones to get you started. If you're curious, be sure to check out these Web sites and start comparison shopping.

Table 3-1. *A few of the Internet's many Web hosting firms*

Name	URL
Brinkster	*www.brinkster.com*
DreamHost	*www.dreamhost.com*
GoDaddy	*www.godaddy.com*
HostGo	*www.hostgo.com*
Insider Hosting	*www.insiderhosting.com*
Pair Networks	*www.pair.com*
Sonic.net	*www.sonic.net*

It's quite difficult to find honest Web host reviews on the Web. Most Web sites that claim to review and rank Web hosts are simply advertising a few companies that pay for a recommendation. Popular computer magazines like PC World and PC Magazine haven't reviewed Web hosts in years, because a thorough analysis of even a fraction of the Web hosts that exist would require a massive amount of manpower. Their old reviews aren't much help either, because the quality of a Web hosting company can change quickly.

However, the Web isn't completely useless in your Web host hunt. You can get information about Web hosting companies from a Web discussion board where people like you chat with more experienced Web hosters. One of the best is WebHostingTalk, which you'll find at *http://tinyurl.com/5zffwp*. The WebHosting-Talk discussion board is particularly useful if you've narrowed your options down to just a few companies, and you'd like to ask a question or hear about other people's experiences. If you want to continue with still more research, check out *www. consumersearch.com/www/internet/web-hosting/review.html*, which does a respectable job of pointing out more discussion boards and a few Web sites with general Web hosting advice.

As you consider different Web hosting companies, you need to sort through a dizzying array of options on different Web sites. In the following sections, you'll learn how to dig through the marketing haze and find the important information on the Web sites of two Web hosting companies.

A Web host walkthrough (#1)

Figure 3-10 shows how you can assess the home page for the popular Web hosting company Aplus.Net. The company offers dedicated servers, standard Web hosting, domain name registration, and Web design services. All four options are designed to help you get online, but the Web hosting option is what you're really looking for.

Taming Long URLs with TinyURL

Keen eyes will notice that the URL mentioned above, the one that leads you to the WebHostingTalk forum, starts with the seemingly unrelated domain name *tinyurl.com*. That's because WebHostingTalk forum's URL has deliberately been shortened using TinyURL, a Web site that provides a free URL redirection service. TinyURL is a handy tool you can use whenever you come across a URL that's so impractically long or convoluted that you'd ordinarily have no chance of jotting it down, typing it in, or shouting it over the phone.

Here's how to use TinyURL. First, copy your awkwardly long URL. Then, head to the Web site *http://tinyurl.com*, type or paste the URL into the text box on the front page, and click Make TinyURL. You'll be rewarded with a much shorter URL that starts with *http://tinyurl.com*. In the previous example, TinyURL changed the ridiculously convoluted URL *http://www.webhostingtalk.com/forumdisplay.php?s=aa8768ada1bc5ddbd96e0578584cffce&f=1* to *http://tinyurl.com/5zffwp*.

Although this new URL doesn't mean anything, it's a heck of a lot shorter. Best of all, the tiny URL works just as well as the original one—type it into any browser and you'll get to the WebHostingTalk forum.

So how does this system work? When you type in a tiny URL, your browser takes you to the TinyURL Web site. TinyURL keeps a long list of all the whacked-out URLs people have given it as well as the new, shorter URLs it issues in their place. When you request a page, it looks up the tiny URL in that list, finds the original, long URL, and redirects your browser to the site you really want. But here's the neat part—the whole process unfolds so quickly that you'd have no idea it's taking place if you hadn't read this box.

Figure 3-10:
There's a lot of information packed into this page. Click the Web Hosting heading to find out about the hosting plans that Aplus offers (Figure 3-11). In the top-right corner of the page, you'll find toll-free numbers and a Chat Now button. Click this, and a chat window appears where you can type your question to an Aplus technician and get an immediate answer. If you're serious about signing up with Aplus, it's a good idea to give both these options a try so you can evaluate its technical support.

The dedicated server option is a premium form of Web hosting. It means that your Web site runs on its own server, a separate computer that doesn't host anyone else's site. This is primarily of interest to large business customers with high-powered sites that chew up computer resources. Most personal and small-business Web sites run on shared servers without any noticeable slowdown.

The domain name registration option is for people planning to reserve a name for future use. You'll get one as part of your Web hosting package when you sign up. And the Web design option is mainly of interest to XHTML-phobes. It lets you pay a Web design team to craft all the XHTML pages and graphics for your Web site. But where's the fun in that?

The choices don't end there. Figure 3-11 shows you the range of Web hosting plans you can choose from. As with most Web hosts, you can do perfectly well with the cheapest plan that Aplus provides. But there's another wrinkle—not only can you choose the type of plan, you can also pick the type of operating system used on the server where your Web site lives. Unless you're a programmer planning to create software that runs on the server, there's no reason to care what type of operating system runs on the server. Assuming the hosting company does its job and distributes the Web sites they host over multiple computers, your site will be just as fast and reliable on any operating system. Think about it this way: When was the last time you asked yourself what operating system runs eBay (Windows) or Amazon (Linux)?

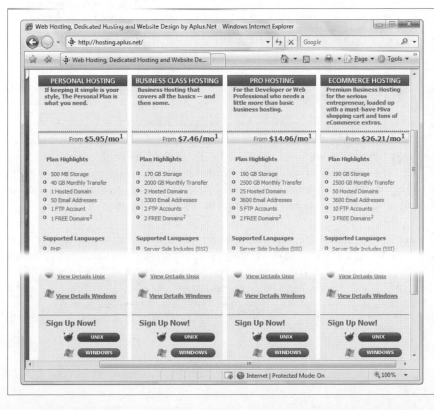

Figure 3-11:
At the end of your search, you've discovered that the cheapest option is currently $6/month for a 500 MB Web site with 40 GB of bandwidth. A free domain and 50 email addresses are thrown in for good measure, along with FTP support. The Supported Languages and Databases section has information that's tailored to computer programmers—if you're going code-free, you don't need to worry about it. Scroll down for the sign-up links.

A Web host walkthrough (#2)

Overall, the Aplus.Net search turned up a solid offer at a fair price. Discerning Web shoppers may be hoping to save a few dollars or get a little more space.

Figure 3-12 shows another Web hosting company—Brinkster. Brinkster's target audience includes personal Web site creators, small businesses, and developers, rather than large institutional customers. As a result, you just may find a better deal for your Web site.

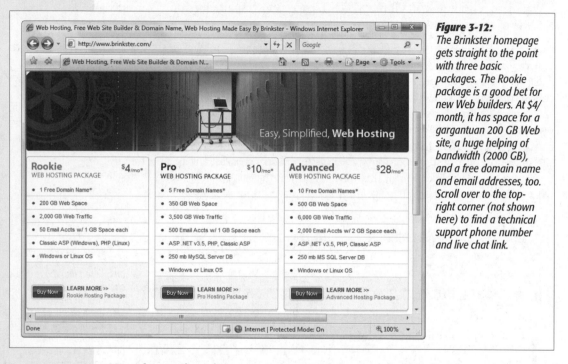

Figure 3-12:
The Brinkster homepage gets straight to the point with three basic packages. The Rookie package is a good bet for new Web builders. At $4/ month, it has space for a gargantuan 200 GB Web site, a huge helping of bandwidth (2000 GB), and a free domain name and email addresses, too. Scroll over to the top-right corner (not shown here) to find a technical support phone number and live chat link.

Now that you've taken a tour of two Web hosting company's sites, you're ready to evaluate some more. Or, if you're really impatient, you can set up your site using one of the hosting companies you've seen. It doesn't take anything more than a couple of mouse clicks, and you'll be online in only a few hours.

Tip: If your Web host is letting you down, don't panic. It's not too hard to switch hosts. The key thing to remember is when you change hosts, you're essentially abandoning one Web server and setting up shop on another. It's up to you to copy your Web pages to the new Web server—no one will do it for you. As long as you have a copy of your Web site on your personal computer (which you always should), this part is easy. If you're still a little skeptical of the company you choose, look for a 30-day, money-back guarantee.

Free Web Hosts

Not yet swayed by any of the hundreds of Web hosting companies on the Web? Not tempted by the offer of a little Web space from your ISP? If you're hoping to save a monthly fee at all cost, there is a solution, but it may not be worth the aggravation.

The Web has a significant number of free Web hosts. Free hosts are companies that give you a small parcel of Web space without charging anything. Sometimes it's because they hope to get you to upgrade to a cost-based service if you outgrow the strict limitations of the free package. Other times, they may just be interested in advertising revenue. That's because some free Web hosts force you to include an obnoxious ad banner at the top your Web pages.

Before you sign up for a free host, familiarize yourself with some of the headaches you can face:

- **Ad banners.** The worst free Web hosts force you to display their advertisements on your pages. If you'd like to crowd out your content with obnoxious credit card commercials, this is the way to go. Otherwise, move on to somewhere new. It's finally possible to find free Web hosts that don't impose the Curse of the Blinking Banner Ad, so don't settle for one that does.

- **Unreliability.** Free Web hosts may experience more down time, which means your Web site may periodically disappear from the Web. Or the Web servers the host uses may be bogged down by poor maintenance or other people's Web sites, causing your site to slow to a crawl.

- **Unpredictability.** Free Web hosts aren't the most stable companies. It's not unheard of for a Web host to go out of business, taking your site with it and forcing you to look for a new Web home in a hurry. Similarly, free hosts can change their requirements overnight, sometimes shifting from an ad-free Web haven to a blinking banner extravaganza without warning.

- **Usage limits.** Some free Web hosts force you to agree to a policy that limits the type of content you can put on your site. For example, you may be forbidden from running a business, selling ad space, or uploading certain types of files (like music, movies, or large downloads).

- **Limited tech support.** Many professional Web site operators say that what makes a good Web host isn't a huge expanse of free space or a ginormous bandwidth limit—it's the ability to get another human being on the phone at any hour to solve unexpected problems. Free Web hosts can't afford to hire a platoon of techies for customer service, so you'll be forced to wait for help—if you get it at all.

- **Awkward uploads.** Many free Web hosts lack support for easy FTP uploading (page 80). Without this convenience, you'll be forced to use a time-consuming upload page.

Despite all these possible problems, many thrifty wallet-watchers swear by their free Web hosts (and the $0/month price tag). If you have the time to experiment, and your business doesn't need rock-solid reliability and an immediate Web presence, you might want to try out a few. Check out *www.free-webhosts.com/user_reviews.php* for a huge catalog of free Web hosts, which painstakingly details the space they give you and the conditions they impose. You'll also find thousands of user reviews. However, keep in mind that some free Web hosts may pad the rankings with their own reviews, and any free Web host can suddenly change its offerings.

Tip: One thing that you don't get with a free Web host is a custom domain name. Although you can buy your domain name from another company and use domain name forwarding (page 62) for a few dollars a year, you can avoid any expense by opting for a subdomain from a free subdomain service, as explained on page 65.

Transferring Files

Once you sign up for Web hosting, you're ready to transfer some files to your Web space. To perform this test, you can use Lee Park's résumé from the previous chapter (which you can download from the Missing CD page at *www.missingmanuals. com*). The final version has the filename *resume5.htm*.

Browser-Based Uploading

Browser-based uploading is fairly easy, but it's not always convenient. The idea is that you go to a special Web page on your host's site where you specify the files on your hard drive that you want to transfer to the server. Many hosting companies provide both browser-based and FTP-based uploading. If you're using a budget plan or a free Web host, you may not have the FTP option at all. To perform browser-based uploading, follow these steps:

1. **Go to your Web hosting company's site.**

2. **Log in to your account with the user name and password you created when you signed up.**

    Usually you'll find a login box somewhere on the first page.

3. **Browse through the icons until you find the page for managing files.**

    Each Web hosting provider has its own slightly different site layout. Figure 3-13 shows what things look like at Brinkster.

4. **Specify the files you want to upload. You need to specify each file individually, by clicking the Browse button next to the text box.**

    For the résumé example to work properly, make sure you upload both the *resume5.htm* file and the linked picture, *leepark.jpg*, to the same place on your Web site.

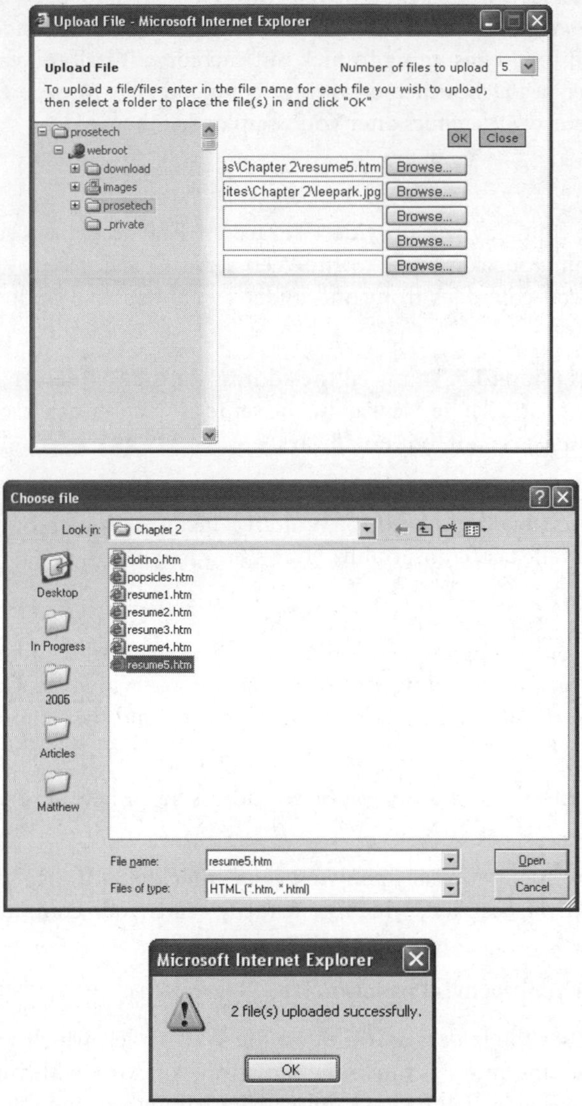

Figure 3-13:
Every Web hosting provider's site looks a little different, but you'll eventually find a set of text boxes that let you upload pages. These text boxes always work the same way. First you click the Browse button (top image), which shows an Open File dialog box (middle). Then you browse to the file you want, select it, and click Open. If you have several files to upload at once, repeat this process using different text boxes. When you've chosen all the files you want (or just run out of text boxes), click OK, and then wait until the files are copied and you get a confirmation message (bottom).

5. **Log out when you finish.**

Now you can test your work by entering your domain name followed by the Web page name. For example, if you uploaded the résumé example to your Web site *www.supersavvyworker.com*, try requesting *www.supersavvyworker.com/resume5. htm* in your browser. You don't need to wait—once you upload the file to your Web server, it's available almost instantly to any browser that requests it.

Unfortunately, the possibilities for mistakes with browser-based uploading are endless. The most common error occurs when you have a large number of files to copy at once. Not only is it time-consuming to pick out each one, it's all too easy to forget something. Other headaches include trying to upload files to different folders, or needing to rename or delete files after you've uploaded them.

FTP

Ideally, your Web hosting company will provide FTP access. FTP access lets you transfer groups of files from your computer to the Web server (or vice versa) in much the same way that you copy files from one folder to another in Windows Explorer or the Mac's Finder.

Before you can upload files using FTP, you need the address for the FTP server, as well as a user name and password. These are usually the same as the user name and password of your Web hosting account, but not always.

To upload files using FTP, you can use a standalone FTP program. However, in these modern times you probably don't need to. Windows includes its own built-in FTP browser that handles the task comfortably. Here's how it works:

1. **Open Windows Explorer.**

   There are many ways to open Windows Explorer, which lives in a slightly different part of the Start menu depending on your version of Windows. One approach that always works is to right-click the Start button, and then choose Explore.

2. **Type the FTP address into the Windows Explorer address bar. Make sure the URL starts with *ftp://*.**

   In other words, if you're trying to visit *ftp.myhost.com*, enter the URL *ftp://ftp.myhost.com*, not *http://ftp.myhost.com*, which incorrectly sends your computer off looking for Web pages.

3. **The next step is to enter your login information (see Figure 3-14).**

   Once you log in, you'll see the folders and files on the Web server, which you can copy, delete, rename, and move in much the same way you work with your local folders and files. Seeing as you haven't uploaded anything yet, the folder may be empty, or it may contain a generic *index.htm* file that shows an "under construction" message if someone happens to browse to it.

4. **The next step is to copy your files to the Web server. The easiest way to do this is to drag the files from another open window, and then drop them in the FTP window.**

   Figure 3-15 shows the steps you need to upload the résumé example.

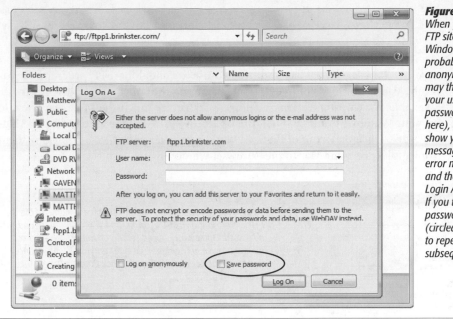

Figure 3-14:
When you first enter the FTP site address, Windows Explorer will probably try to log you in anonymously and fail. It may then prompt you for your user ID and password (as shown here), or it may just show you an error message. If you get an error message, click OK, and then select File → Login As from the menu. If you turn on the "Save password" checkbox (circled), you don't need to repeat this process on subsequent visits.

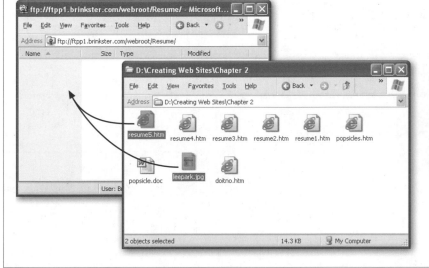

Figure 3-15:
To get Lee Park onto the Web, start by opening a window in your file system using Windows Explorer. Then browse to the appropriate folder on your computer. When you find the resume5. htm and leepark.jpg files you downloaded earlier, select them, and then drag them into the FTP window to start the uploading process.

Tip: Drag-and-drop isn't the only way to transfer files. You can use all the familiar Windows shortcuts, including the Cut, Copy, and Paste commands in the Edit menu, and the Ctrl+C (copy) and Ctrl+V (paste) keyboard shortcuts.

If you're working on a Mac, you need to use a standalone FTP program. Fortunately, you've got loads of free options, including the super-easy-to-use Rbrowser (available at *www.rbrowser.com*). Things work pretty much the same way they do for your Windows brethren. First, fire up Rbrowser. You'll be asked to log in (Figure 3-16). Once that's out of the way, you can transfer your files by dragging them from a folder on your Mac to the Rbrowser window.

Figure 3-16:
To log in to Rbrowser, you need to supply the name of the FTP server (in the Host/URL box), and your user name and password. Don't worry about setting an initial path—you can always browse to the right subfolder on your Web site once you make the connection. Finally, click Connect to seal the deal.

Power Tools

In Chapter 2, you built your first XHTML page with nothing but a text editor and a lot of nerve. This is how all Web-page whiz kids begin their careers. To really understand XHTML (and to establish your XHTML street cred), you need to start from scratch.

However, very few Web authors stick with plain text editors or use them to create anything other than simple test pages. That's because the average XHTML page is filled with tedious detail. If you have to write every paragraph, line break, and formatting tag by hand, you'll probably make a mistake somewhere along the way. Even if you don't err, it's hard to visualize a finished page when you spend all day staring at angle brackets. This is especially true when you tackle more complex pages, like those that introduce graphics or use multicolumn layouts.

There's a definite downside to outgrowing Notepad or TextEdit—namely, it can get expensive. Professional Web design tools can cost hundreds of dollars. At one point, software companies planned to include basic Web editors as a standard part of operating systems like Windows and Mac OS. In fact, some older versions of Windows shipped with a scaled-down Web editor called FrontPage Express, and Mac OS includes a severely truncated editor called iWeb, which limits you to ready-made templates and doesn't let you touch a line of XHTML. But if you want a full-featured Web page editor—one that catches your errors, helps you remember important XHTML elements, and lets you manage an entire site—you have to find one on your own. Fortunately, there are free alternatives for even the most cash-strapped Web designer.

In this chapter, you'll learn how Web page editors work and how to evaluate them to find the one that's right for you. You'll also tour some of the better free and shareware offerings currently out there. Most Web page editors are surprisingly similar, so this chapter helps you get started with your tool of choice, whether that's Adobe Dreamweaver, Microsoft Expression Web, or a nifty piece of freeware.

Choosing Your Tools

Tools like Notepad and TextEdit aren't all that bad for starting out. They keep page development simple, and they don't mess with your XHTML (as a word-processing program would). Seeing the result of your work is just a browser refresh away. So why are you destined to outgrow your favorite text editor? For a number of reasons, including:

- **Nobody's perfect**. With a text editor, it's just a matter of time before you make a mistake, like typing <b> instead of </b>. Unfortunately, you might not realize your mistake even when you view your page in a browser. Remember, some browsers compensate for some types of mistakes, while others don't. A good Web page editor can highlight faulty XHTML and help you correct it.

- **Edit-Save-Refresh. Repeat 1,000 times**. Text editors are convenient for small pages. But what if you're trying to size a picture perfectly, or line up a table column? You need to jump back and forth between your text editor and your Web browser, saving and refreshing your page each time. This process can literally take hours. With a good Web page editor, you get conveniences like drag-and-drop editing to fine-tune your pages—make a few adjustments, and your editor tweaks your XHTML appropriately. Editors also have a preview mode that lets you immediately see the effect of your XHTML edits on a Web page, with no browser required.

- **Help, I'm drowning in XHTML!** One of the nicest little frills in a Web page editor is color-coded XHTML. Color-coding makes those pesky tags stand out against a sea of text. Without this feature, you'd be cross-eyed in hours.

- **Just type <ul><li></li></ul>**. To create a bulleted list, of course. You haven't forgotten already, have you? The truth is, most Web authors don't memorize every XHTML element there is. With a Web editor, you don't need to. If you forget something, there's usually a help link or a menu command to compensate. Without a tool to guide you, you're on your own.

Of course, using a graphical Web page editor has its own risks. That's why you started out with a simple text editor, and why you'll spend a good portion of this book learning more about XHTML. If you don't understand XHTML properly, you can fall into a number of traps.

For example, you might use a slick Web page editor to apply fancy fonts to your text. Imagine your surprise when you look at that page on a PC that doesn't have those fonts installed. Your page reverts to an ugly or illegible typeface. (Chapter 6 has more about this problem.) Similarly, your editor can unwittingly lead you to insert elements that aren't supported by all browsers, or graphics that won't display properly on other computers. Finally, even with the best editor, you'll spend a significant amount of time looking at raw XHTML to see exactly what's going on, clean up a mess, or copy and paste useful bits to other pages.

Note: Web page editors are often called HTML editors. However, this is just a quirk of history, and virtually all Web page editors can build impeccable XHTML documents.

Types of Web Page Editors

Web page editors come in many flavors, but they all tend to fall into one of three categories:

- **Text-based** editors require you to work with the text and tags of raw XHTML. The difference between an ordinary text editor (like Notepad) and a text-based XHTML editor is convenience. Unlike Notepad or TextEdit, text-based XHTML editors usually include buttons to quickly insert common XHTML elements or element combinations, and a one-click way to save your file and open it in a separate browser window. Essentially, text-based XHTML editors are text editors with some useful Web-editing features stapled on top.

- **Split window** editors also make you write XHTML by hand. The difference is that a separate window shows the results of your work *as you type*. In other words, you get a live preview, which means you don't need to keep stopping to see what you've accomplished.

- **WYSIWYG** (What You See Is What You Get) editors work more like word processors. That means you don't need to write XHTML tags. Instead, you type in some text, format it, and insert pictures just as you would in a word-processing program. Behind the scenes, the WYSIWYG editor generates your XHTML markup.

Any of these editors makes a good replacement for a simple text editor. The type you choose depends mainly on how many features you want, how you prefer to work, and how much money you're willing to shell out. The best Web-editing programs blur the lines between these different types of editor, giving you the freedom to switch back and forth between XHTML and WYSIWYG views.

It's important to understand that no matter what type of Web page editor you use, you still need to know a fair bit about XHTML to get the results you want. Even if you have a WYSIWYG editor, you'll almost always want to fine-tune your markup by hand. Understanding XHTML's quirks lets you determine what you can and can't do—and what strategies you need to follow to get the most sophisticated results. Even in a WYSIWYG editor, you'll inevitably look at the XHTML underbelly of your Web pages.

Save As HTML

My word-processing/page layout/spreadsheet program has a feature for saving documents as Web pages. Should I use it?

Over the last decade, the Internet has become the hottest marketing buzzword around. Every computer program imaginable is desperate to boast about new Web features. For example, virtually every modern word processor has a feature for exporting your documents to HTML. Don't use it.

HTML export features don't work very well. Often, the problem is that the program takes a document designed for one medium (usually print) and tries to wedge it into another (the Web). But word processor documents just don't look like Web pages—they tend to have larger margins, fancier fonts, more text, more generous spacing around that text, no links, and a radically different layout.

Another problem is the fact that HTML export features often create wildly complex markup. You end up with an ungainly Web page that's nearly impossible to edit because it's choked with formatting details. (Dreamweaver even has a tool that aims to help you with the clean up. It's in the menu under Commands → Clean Up Word HTML.) And if you want to convert one of these pages into stricter, cleaner XHTML, you need to do it by hand.

The lesson? If you can, steer clear of the Save as HTML command. You're better off copying and pasting the contents of your document into an XHTML file as plain text, and then formatting it with XHTML tags on your own.

Finding a Free Web Page Editor

Unless you're one of the lucky few who already has a copy of a cutting-edge Web page editor like Expression Web or Dreamweaver, you're probably wondering how you can find a good piece of software for as little money as possible. After all, the Web's all about getting goodies for free. While you can't find an industrial-strength Dreamweaver clone for free, you *can* get a good basic editor without opening your wallet. Here's how:

- If you like to do your own research (always a good idea) and you don't mind installing several dozen programs on your computer until you find what you like, head to a top shareware site like *www.download.com*. To dig up some contenders, search for "HTML editor." (Even though most Web page editors turn out top-notch XHTML, they still go by their old description as HTML editors.)

Note: *Shareware*, as you no doubt already know, is software that's free to try, play with, and pass along to friends. If you like it, you're politely asked to pay for it (or not-so-politely locked out when the trial period ends). *Freeware* is software that has no cost at all—if you like it, it's yours! Usually, you won't get niceties like technical support. Some freeware is supported by donations. To make sure your shareware is virus- and spyware-free, download it from a reputable source like *www.download.com*.

- You can also browse a comprehensive list of Web page editors on Wikipedia at *http://en.wikipedia.org/wiki/Comparison_of_HTML_editors*. This list is noteworthy for the surprisingly thorough information it provides. For example, it details the price of each editor and the operating systems that editor supports. Most importantly, it points out which are free.

You'll quickly find out that there's a sea of free editors out there. Many have awkward and clunky button and menu arrangements. Some have outright errors. Finding one that's right for you might take a little time.

The following sections describe four worthwhile editors that don't cost a penny.

Nvu

Nvu (pronounced "n-view," as in "new view") is a nifty, lightweight editor that's supremely easy to use. Best of all, Nvu comes in a version for all three major operating systems: Windows, Mac, and Linux.

Nvu's creators used pieces of the Mozilla browser, godfather to the increasingly popular Firefox browser, when they developed this editor. Nvu's an open source project, which means that you can not only download and copy it for free, but you can, if you're a programmer type, browse through the source code and submit improvements. As a Web-head, you're most likely to fall in love with Nvu's multiple views, which let you make changes in either a text-only XHTML view or a slick WYSIWYG view that previews your pages (see Figure 4-1).

Nvu's key drawback is that its developers stopped working on it in 2006. Although Internet rumor has it that they're working on a replacement, nothing's on horizon right now, so don't expect bug fixes or enhancements. Confusingly, the developers named Nvu's last patched-up version KompoZer. You can download it at *www.kompozer.net*.

Amaya

Amaya is a Web page editor with real history. It's been around for more than a decade, with regular releases and updates continuing to this day. It helps that the World Wide Web Consortium, the heavyweight international standards organization that helped standardize the Web, has adopted Amaya. Like Nvu, Amaya supports the big three operating systems, which is a rare asset—most free Web page editors, including the two you'll learn about next, are for Windows PCs only. Amaya's options for viewing Web pages do Nvu one better (see Figure 4-2).

However, Amaya isn't as polished as a professional Web page editor, and finding the command you want in its cluttered menu and toolbars is often a chore. Still, for a free editor, it's hard to describe Amaya as anything other than a barn burner of a bargain. To give Amaya a whirl, go to *www.w3.org/Amaya*.

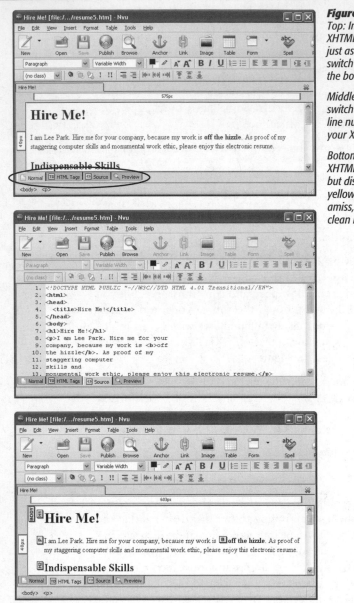

Figure 4-1:
Top: Instead of having to work with raw XHTML, Nvu's Normal view lets you format text just as you would in a word processor. To switch from one view to another, use the tabs at the bottom of the window (circled).

Middle: To fine-tune your XHTML markup, switch to the Source view. Nvu give you handy line numbers for reference, and color-codes your XHTML elements.

Bottom: Need something in between? The XHTML Tags view lets you edit formatted text, but displays your document's tags in floating yellow boxes. That way, if you find something amiss, you can switch to the Source view to clean it up.

HTML-Kit

HTML-Kit (*www.html-kit.com*) is a slightly eccentric Windows Web page editor with a screen layout that only Bill Gates' mother could love. On the plus side, HTML-Kit is 100 percent free, relatively reliable, and ridiculously customizable.

Unlike Nvu and Amaya, HTML-Kit doesn't provide a WYSIWYG editing mode. Instead, it has a split-preview editor, which means you can see a live preview of

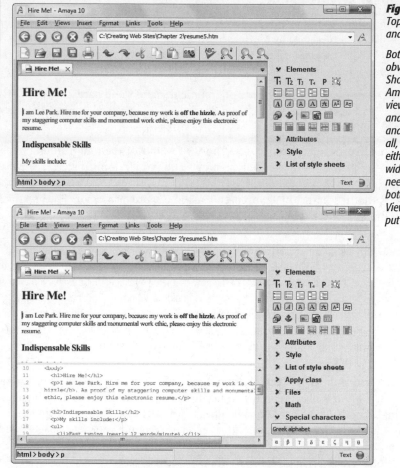

your XHTML document as you code it. For more HTML-Kit fun, check out the wide array of HTML-Kit plug-ins at *www.html-kit.com*, as long as you're not scared off by perplexing names like avwEncodeEmail and hkMakeOptionsList (see the Web site for slightly more helpful descriptions). One interesting plug-in is the XHTML reference found at *www.chami.com/html-kit/plugins/info/hkh_w3c_offline*. Once you install it, this plug-in gives you technical help on any XHTML element in HTML-Kit. Just put your cursor on an element (click it with your mouse or navigate to it with the arrow keys), and then press F1.

CoffeeCup Free HTML Editor

CoffeeCup Free HTML Editor is a scaled-down version of the full-blown Windows product of the same name (minus the word "Free"). The full version has both a text-only mode and a WYSIWYG mode, but the free version switches off the WYSIWYG mode. Get your copy at *www.coffeecup.com/free-editor*.

Professional XHTML Editors

Fed up with settling for a low-powered Web page editor and an editing environment that seems like it was designed by M. C. Escher? If you're ready to move on to a professional Web design package, take heart—your choice is surprisingly simple. That's because there are really only two top-tier Web page editors on the market today.

- **Adobe Dreamweaver** is the favorite of graphic designers and hard-core XHTML experts. It's packed with features and gives you fine-grained control of every XHTML ingredient.

- **Microsoft Expression Web** is a powerhouse revamp of the long-running Web editor Microsoft FrontPage. Start typing, and you'll immediately see why Expression Web is popular with XHTML novices. Its WYSIWYG mode is so seamless that it's hard to tell you aren't using a word processor. Features like automatic spell check duplicate what you find in Microsoft Word.

Note: Confusingly, Microsoft Expression Web has a distant cousin with most of the same features. It's named, in true long-winded Microsoft style, Microsoft Office SharePoint Designer. Like Expression Web, SharePoint Designer inherits the inner plumbing of the now-obsolete FrontPage. Unlike Expression Web, it has some optional features that work with Microsoft SharePoint, a Web-based program that big businesses use to share office documents and help employees collaborate. If you're buying a Microsoft Web page editor on your own dime, you'll almost certainly stick with Expression Web. But if you already have access to SharePoint Designer (say, through the company you work for), feel free to substitute it instead.

One of the reasons these products are so much better than their competitors is that they include a lot of tools you're sure to need once you start designing Web pages. For example, both let you create style sheets (an advanced feature you'll learn about in Chapter 6), resize images and drag them around your Web pages, and manage an entire Web site. Expression Web even includes a tool for generating fancy buttons. Another reason is that they're just so darned easy to use. Even though both come packed with sophisticated features, editing a simple XHTML file couldn't be easier.

In the past, Dreamweaver had a reputation for being complicated enough to scare away XHTML newbies. On the other hand, FrontPage (the predecessor to Expression Web) was known for being easy to use but possessed of a few bad habits—like inserting unnecessary elements into your code or relying on frills that worked only if your Web server supported the FrontPage server extensions. However, recent versions of both programs tackle these weaknesses. Now, Dreamweaver is virtually as easy to use as Expression Web, and Expression Web is almost as mature and well-rounded as Dreamweaver. In fact, common tasks in these two programs are surprisingly similar. The bottom line? You can't go wrong with either.

If you're still itching to be convinced, try a free 30-day trial of either product. Go to *www.microsoft.com/Expression/try-it* to get a free trial version of Expression Web, or to *www.adobe.com/products/dreamweaver* to download a working Dreamweaver demo. And, for an in-depth exploration of every Dreamweaver feature, check out *Dreamweaver CS4: The Missing Manual*.

Mid-Level XHTML Editors

A few years ago, there were a number of mid-level Web page editors in hot competition. Today, most have died out. The mid-level Web page editors that remain often aren't worth the expense. Instead, your best bet is to save up for one of the two leading-edge Web page editors—Adobe Dreamweaver or Microsoft Expression Web. Of the two, Expression Web is the more affordable (hovering around $250), while Dreamweaver commands a higher price because of its historical position as the tool-of-choice for professional Web developers (it's about $400). You may be able to find academic (or "student and teacher") editions of both programs at specialty retailers, like college campus computer stores. These editions are scaled down but still powerful, and they have a much lower price tag. You'll need to prove you're a student or starving academic to get in on the action.

Another option is to find a retailer that still offers copies of a slightly out-of-date version of Dreamweaver or Expression Web. For example, Amazon sellers often offer FrontPage 2003, which is the well-rounded predecessor to Expression Web, for little more than $100. Its core features work in much the same way as Expression Web, and you can get a lower-priced Expression Web upgrade when you decide to move on. However, there's a good case to be made for sticking with a free Web page editor until you're ready to move up to a more full-featured program.

Working with Your XHTML Editor

Once you choose a Web page editor, take it for a spin. In this section, you'll learn how to create a sample XHTML document and get it online, all without leaving the comfort of your editor.

Software companies have spent the last decade copying features from their competitors and as a result, common tasks in Expression Web, Dreamweaver, and many free Web page editors are startlingly similar. That means that no matter which program you use, the following sections will teach you the basics. Once you're comfortable with your editor, you can move on to the rest of the book and learn more about how XHTML works.

Note: Although future chapters won't lead you step by step through any of these Web page editors, look for boxes and tips that point out occasional shortcuts, tricks, and techniques for your favorite editor. The one exception is the keenly important page template feature that both Dreamweaver and Expression Web provide—you'll explore that in Chapter 10.

Starting Out

Here's what you need to do to get started with your editor of choice:

1. **Your first step is to launch the program by double-clicking the appropriate desktop icon or making a quick trip to the Start menu (in Windows PCs) or Finder → Applications (for Mac OS).**

   Your Web page editor appears.

2. **Some editors, including Nvu and Amaya, start you off with a tip of the day. If so, close this window to get to the main program.**

   You may also need to remove a few more distractions. Dreamweaver clutters your view with a pile of panels. Although these panels provide quick access to advanced features, you might want to shunt them out of the way when you're first getting started (see Figure 4-3). In Expression Web, you'll see similar panels latched onto either side of the main window. To close them, click the X in the top-right corner of each one. (You can get the panel back later by clicking it in the View of Task Panes menu.)

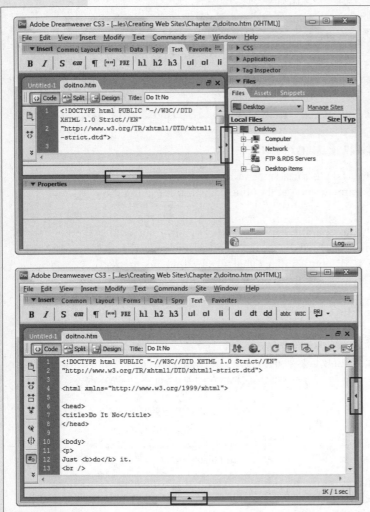

Figure 4-3:

Top: Dreamweaver is packed with features, many of which sit at your fingertips in specialized panels, which latch on to the right side and bottom of the main window. In this figure, you see the view that appears automatically when you open Dreamweaver. Until you learn the basics, you might find it helpful to push this clutter out of the way by clicking the arrows circled here. You can also hide all panels at once by choosing View → Hide Panels. (Choose View → Show Panels when you're psychologically ready for them to return.)

Bottom: In this figure, the panels are hidden, giving you more room to work with in the main window.

3. Now, choose File → Open, and then navigate to one of the XHTML file samples you worked on in Chapter 2 (also available on the Missing CD page at *www.missingmanuals.com*).

This step is easy—opening a document in a Web page editor is exactly the same as opening a document in any other self-respecting program.

Multiple Views

As you've already learned, you can look at an XHTML document in several ways, depending on whether you want the convenience of a word processor-like layout or the complete control of working directly with XHTML markup. Most Web page editors give you a choice and let you switch rapidly from one to the other. To switch views, you need to find a small series of buttons, usually displayed just above or just below the document you're working on. Figure 4-4 helps you spot these buttons. One exception is Amaya—it lacks these handy buttons, and forces you to travel to the Views menu to make the switch.

Most Web page editors start you out in a WYSIWYG view that shows formatted XHTML—in other words, an approximation of what a page will look like in a Web browser. When you switch to the XHTML code view, you see the real story—the familiar text-only display of color-coded tags and text. These views are the two staples of XHTML editing. However, the most useful choice just might be the split view, which shows both views at once. Most commonly, you'll use this view so you can edit XHTML tags and preview the results as you type. However, you can also work the other way, editing the WYSYWIG preview and seeing what XHTML tags your editor inserts, a great way to learn XHTML.

Some Web page editors give you interesting hybrid views. For example, Nvu has an HTML Tags view, which shows a formatted preview window with the corresponding XHTML elements floating in yellow boxes. To see what that looks like, flip back to Figure 4-1. In Amaya, you have two more specialized views. You can get an overview of the structure of your entire page using Views → Show Structure (see Figure 4-5), and you can review all the links to other Web pages (you'll learn how to link pages in Chapter 8) using Views → Show Links.

Creating a Web Page in Code View

The best way to understand how your Web page editor works is to create a new XHTML document. Begin by working in the code view, and try to replicate one of the resumes you developed in Chapter 2 (the one on page 40 is ideal).

Launch your program and follow these steps:

1. **Start by choosing File → New to create a new Web page.**

Some Web page editors start you out with a new, blank page, in which case you can skip the rest of these instructions. But most open some sort of New Document window that lets you choose the type of file you want to create.

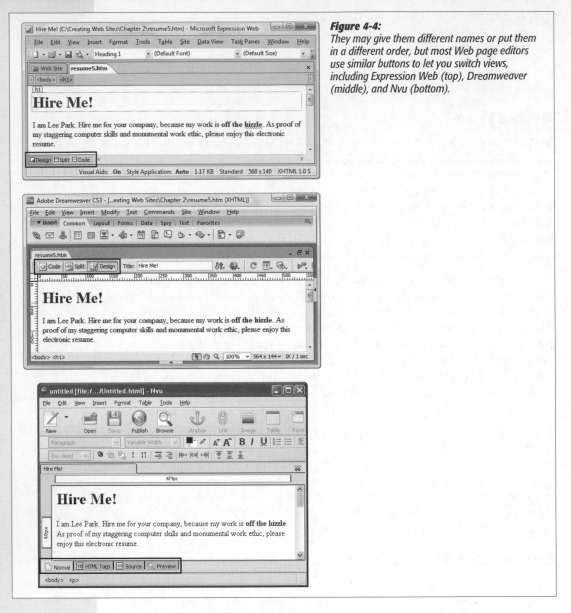

Figure 4-4:
They may give them different names or put them in a different order, but most Web page editors use similar buttons to let you switch views, including Expression Web (top), Dreamweaver (middle), and Nvu (bottom).

2. **Choose the type of page you want to create.**

Many Web editors give you a number of ready-made page designs you can use to get started. For example, in Dreamweaver and Expression Web, you can create Web pages with a variety of multicolumn layouts (more on that in Chapter 9). You're best off to avoid these until you've learned enough to create your own unique designs. For now, start with a blank, plain-vanilla XHTML page. In Dreamweaver, choose Blank Page. In Expression Web, choose the General group, and then pick HTML.

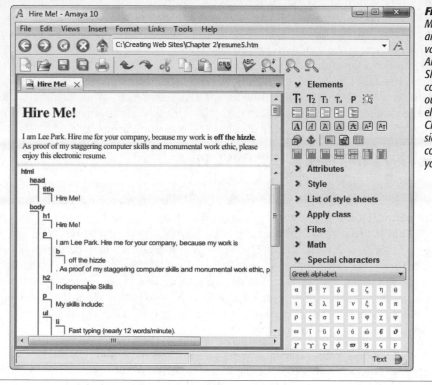

Figure 4-5:
*Many Web page editors
are packed full of
valuable extras. In
Amaya, the Views →
Show Structure
command gives you an
outline of all the
elements in your page.
Click any element in the
side panel to jump to the
corresponding place in
your Web page.*

Note: Even though virtually all Web page editors create ironclad XHTML markup, they often describe
your Web pages as HTML documents. Don't be confused. In their view, HTML is a catch-all term that
includes both old-style HTML and modern-day XHTML.

Many Web page editors also let you choose a doctype (page 30) for your new
Web page. In Dreamweaver, you can make your selection from the DocType list
in the New Document window. In Amaya, you use the similar Document Profile list in the New XHTML Document window. In Expression Web, you need
to take an extra step—first, click the Page Editor Options link in the New window, and then find the Document Type Declaration list in the Page Editor
Options window. Don't worry if you can't find the option you need in your
Web editor, because you can always edit the doctype by hand after you create
the page.

3. **Create the document.**

To make your selections official and actually create the document, click the
Create or OK button (depending on the program).

A blank document appears, showing a bare XHTML skeleton. In the XHTML
code view, you see the basic <html>, <head>, and <body> elements.

Make sure you're in XHTML Code view so you have complete control over the XHTML markup. Enter all the tags and text content for the résumé from beginning to end, just as though you were using Notepad or TextEdit. (You can pop back to Chapter 2 for a refresher on XHTML code-writing basics.) Along the way, you'll notice a few shortcuts. For example, when you start to type a tag in Expression Web or Dreamweaver, a drop-down menu appears with suggestions. You can choose a valid XHTML tag from the list, or just keep typing. Also, when you add the start tag for a container element (like <h1> for a heading), many Web editors automatically insert the end tag (like </h1>) so you won't forget it.

Creating a Web Page in WYSIWYG View

Creating and formatting a page in WYSIWYG view is a more interesting challenge, because you need to know where to find the various formatting options in your editor. Dreamweaver and Expression Web help you out by packing a fair bit of XHTML smarts right into their toolbars. To add an element in the WYSIWYG view, you first select the piece of text you want to format, and then click the appropriate toolbar button. You can then switch to the XHTML code view to verify that you got the result you expected. For example, to make text bold, select it and look for a toolbar button with the letter B. Clicking this button does the following behind the scenes (in your actual XHTML markup): inserts the <b> tag just before your selection and the </b> tag just after it.

Figure 4-6 shows you the most useful toolbar buttons in Nvu. But no matter what Web page editor you use, you need to spend a fair bit of time wandering through its toolbars and menus to find the most convenient way to get things done.

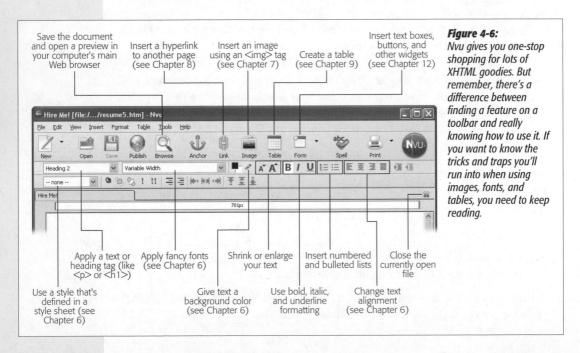

Save the document and open a preview in your computer's main Web browser

Insert a hyperlink to another page (see Chapter 8)

Insert an image using an <img> tag (see Chapter 7)

Create a table (see Chapter 9)

Insert text boxes, buttons, and other widgets (see Chapter 12)

Apply a text or heading tag (like <p> or <h1>)

Apply fancy fonts (see Chapter 6)

Shrink or enlarge your text

Insert numbered and bulleted lists

Close the currently open file

Use a style that's defined in a style sheet (see Chapter 6)

Give text a background color (see Chapter 6)

Use bold, italic, and underline formatting

Change text alignment (see Chapter 6)

Figure 4-6:
Nvu gives you one-stop shopping for lots of XHTML goodies. But remember, there's a difference between finding a feature on a toolbar and really knowing how to use it. If you want to know the tricks and traps you'll run into when using images, fonts, and tables, you need to keep reading.

Tip: It's up to you whether you want to write your Web pages in XHTML view or using the WYSIWYG pre-view mode. The WYSIWYG view is always quicker and more convenient at first, but it can leave you with a lot of XHTML to check and review, adding to future complications.

To practice your WYSIWYG editing, re-create one of the example pages from Chapter 2 (the mini-résumé you see on page 44 works best here). Instead of entering the tags by hand, however, enter the text and format it using the toolbar and menu options in your editor.

Create a new document as described above, and then follow these steps:

1. **Switch to WYSIWYG design view, and then type the title "Hire Me!"**

   The text appears at regular size.

2. **Select the text, and then find a toolbar or menu option that converts your text to a heading by adding the <h1> and </h1> tags.**

   To mark up the text, you need to get a bit more intimate with your Web page editor and its menu and toolbar options.

   In Expression Web, the quickest approach to apply a level-1 heading is to select Heading 1 from the drop-down Style list. In Dreamweaver, you have several worthwhile choices. You can use the shortcut key combination (Ctrl+1) for instant gratification; you can use the toolbar (as shown in Figure 4-7); or you can use the Properties window (choose Window → Properties if it isn't visible). In Amaya, you need to click the T1 icon in the toolbar-like panel that appears on the right side of the window. In Nvu, your only option is to choose Format → Paragraph → Heading 1, because this element didn't make it into Nvu's toolbar.

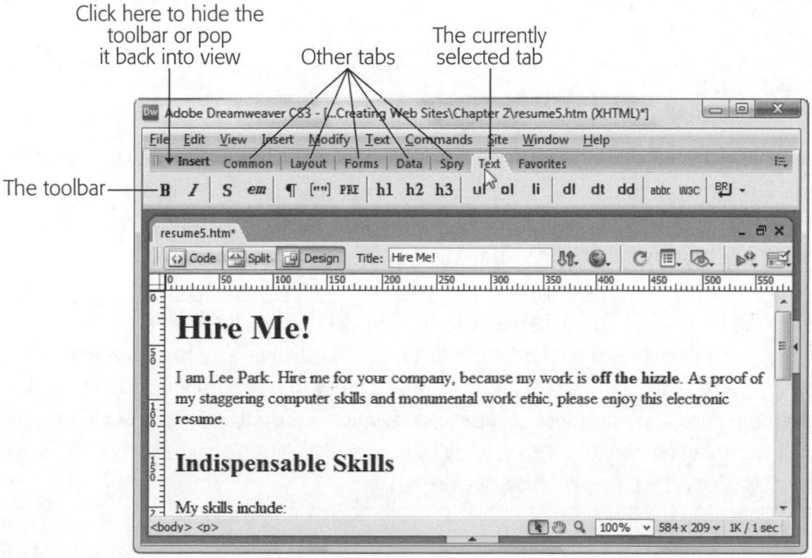

Click here to hide the toolbar or pop it back into view

Other tabs

The currently selected tab

The toolbar

Figure 4-7:
The Dreamweaver toolbar is actually several toolbars in one, organized by tabs. To see the buttons you want, click the appropriate tab. The Text tab (shown here) has buttons to apply bold and italic formatting, set different heading levels, and create numbered and unnumbered lists.

3. **Hit the Enter key to move to the next paragraph.**

   Your typeface reverts to normal, and you can begin typing the rest of the document. Your next challenge is creating the bulleted list. Expression Web, Dreamweaver, Nvu, and Amaya all have a button for bulleted lists in the toolbar, if you can ferret it out.

   It's easy to lose yourself in a thicket of tags. To make it easier to orient yourself, Expression Web, Dreamweaver, Nvu, and Amaya all include a quick element selector bar at the top or bottom of your document (Figure 4-8).

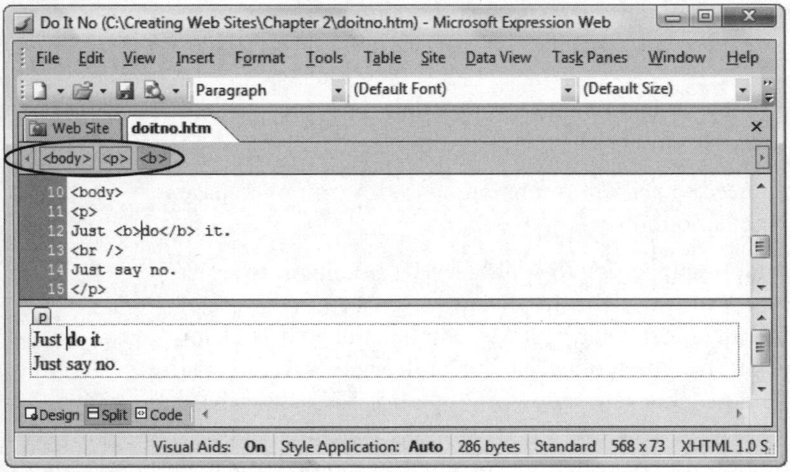

Figure 4-8:
The element selector (circled) is handy if you need to edit your XHTML. Once you scroll to the XHTML you want to edit in the page, double-check the element selector to confirm you're at the right spot. The selector lists all the elements in action at your current location. In this example, the cursor is positioned inside a <b> element (for bold formatting), which itself is placed inside a <p> (paragraph) element, which is nested inside the <body> element that wraps the content of the complete XHTML document. You can quickly select any one of these elements by clicking it in the bar.

4. **For a change of pace, try inserting a picture.**

   Nvu provides easy access with an Image button in the toolbar. Expression Web and Dreamweaver have similar buttons, but it's easier to head straight to the menu (choose Insert → Picture → From File in Expression Web or Insert → Image in Dreamweaver and Amaya).

Note: For this test, you should put the picture in the same directory as your Web page. Otherwise, some editors may add an <img> element that's linked to a specific location on your hard drive. This is a problem, because Web visitors can't access your hard drive, and so they won't see the picture. To double-check that everything's in order, look at the <img> element in XHTML view, and make sure the *src* attribute doesn't start with *file:///*. If it does, edit it by hand so that the src attribute just has the file name, like the <img> element you used in Chapter 2 (page 42).

---

5. When you're prompted to pick an image file, browse to the *leepark.jpg* sample, and then select it. (You can download this image from the Missing CD page at *www.missingmanuals.com*.)

The program adds the appropriate <img> element to your XHTML code. Once you insert the picture, you'll really start to appreciate the benefits of the WYSIWYG view. In all the Web page editors covered here, you can drag the picture to move it or drag the picture's borders to resize it.

Managing a Web Site

Most Web page editors don't limit you to working on a single Web page at a time. Expression Web, Dreamweaver, Nvu, and Amaya all give you the ability to load more than one document simultaneously and switch among them using tabs at the top of the document window (see Figure 4-9). This is particularly handy if you need to make the same change to a whole batch of pages, or if you want to cut a bit of content from one page and paste it into another.

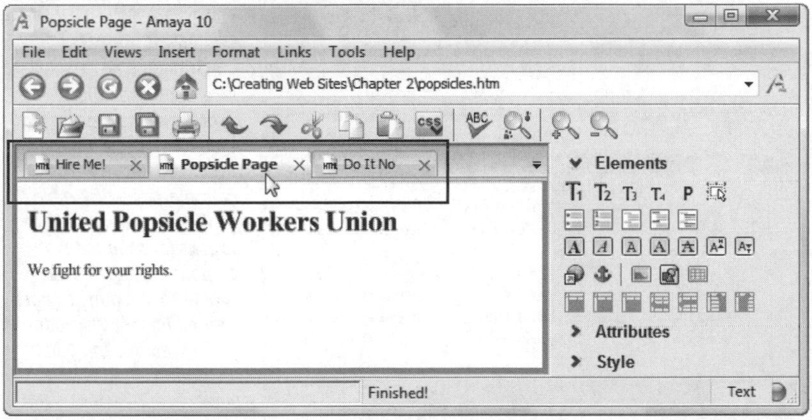

Figure 4-9:
With tabbed editing, your Web page editor creates a new tab each time you open a file. You can switch from one page to another by clicking the tabs in the tab strip, which usually sits above the top of the page (and underneath the editor's menus and toolbars). Here, Amaya has three Web pages open at once. To close a document, click the X on the right side of the tab.

Along with the ability to edit more than one Web page at once, many editors also let you manage your entire Web site. The following sections describe the process for Expression Web and Dreamweaver. In both cases, your first step is to define your site's folders and files so your editor knows just which documents make up your site.

Note: A Web site is simply a collection of one or more Web pages, along with any related files (like pictures). It's often useful to manage all these files together in a Web page editor. In some programs, creating a Web site also gets you access to advanced features, like templates, link checking, and Web site uploading.

Defining a site in Expression Web

To create a Web site in Expression Web, follow these steps:

1. **Select File → Open Site.**

   The Open Site dialog box appears. It looks like an ordinary Open File dialog box, except for one difference—it doesn't display a list of files. Instead, you see only folders.

2. **Browse to the folder you want to open, select it, and then click Open. You can download the Chapter 2 folder from the Missing CD page (*www. missingmanuals.com*) to get a ready-made folder and set of files (the résumé files you worked on earlier).**

   A Web Site tab appears with a list of all the files in your Web site (see Figure 4-10).

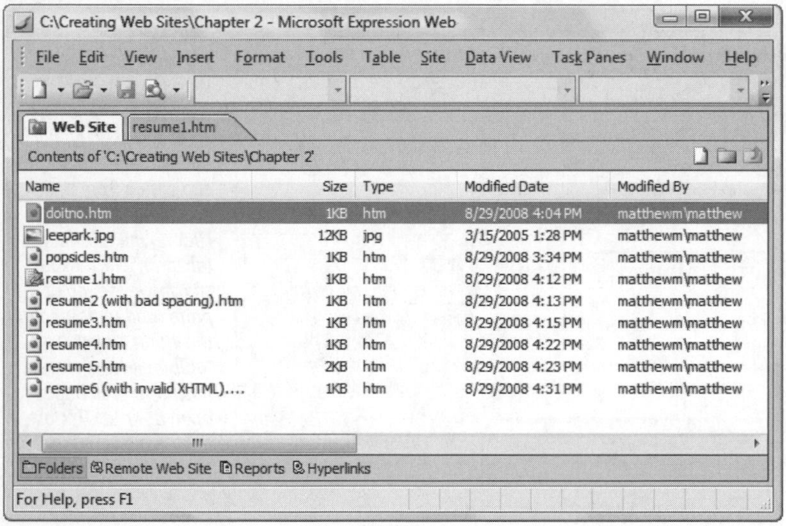

Figure 4-10:
When you access a folder in a Web site (here, it's a folder named C:\Creating Web Sites\Chapter 2), Expression Web adds a tab that displays all the files in that folder. You can do basic file management here—for example, right-click a file to pop open a menu with options for renaming or deleting it. You can also double-click a page to open it for editing. At the bottom of the Web Site tab you'll see buttons that let you publish your Web site, run a report, or check your links.

3. **Add the Expression Web metadata folders. To do so, choose Site → Site Settings, choose "Manage the Web site using hidden metadata files," and then click OK.**

   Many of Expression Web's site-management features require tracking information, which Expression Web stores in hidden subfolders. However, Expression Web doesn't create these folders automatically (unlike its predecessor, FrontPage). You need to opt in to get the program to generate them.

   The word *metadata* means "data *about* data." In other words, the metadata folders store data *about* the data in your Web site. If you're curious, you can see these subfolders in Windows Explorer—they have names like *_private*, *_vti_cnf*, and *_vti_pvt*. (Web trivia: The VTI acronym stands for Vermeer Technologies Inc.—the company that originally created FrontPage and sold it to Microsoft.)

These folders have several purposes. First, they keep track of what files you've uploaded to your Web server. That makes it incredible easy for you to update a Web site with Expression Web, because it transfers only changed files to your server, not the entire site. The folders also track information about your site's pages and resources, which helps with handy features like link checking (page 223) and templates (page 287).

Tip: Treat the metadata folders as a bit of behind-the-scenes plumbing. You need to have them for certain features, but once you create them you don't need to think about them again.

Uploading a site in Expression Web

One of Expression Web's most popular features is its support for updating a Web site without requiring a separate FTP program to transfer the files to your server. Before you can take advantage of this support, you need to follow the steps described above to tell Expression Web that your folder of Web pages represents a complete Web site. Then, you can update your site by following these steps:

1. **Choose File → Publish Site.**

   The first time you try to publish your site, Expression Web displays a Remote Web Site Properties dialog box. You use this window to set your FTP connection options, like the name of your FTP server (see Figure 4-11).

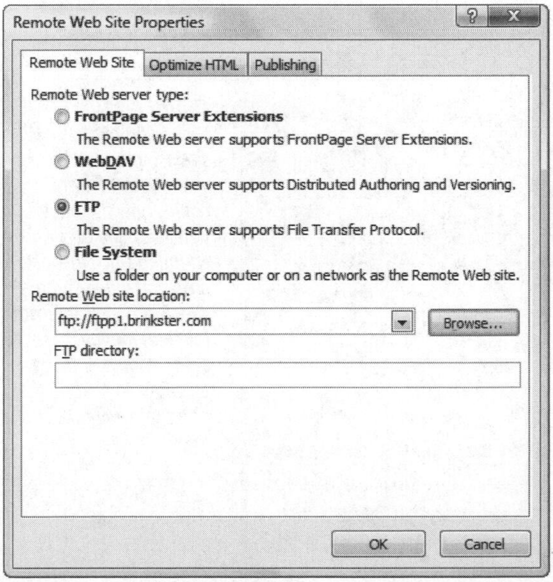

Figure 4-11:
Your Web hosting company should tell you the exact choices to make in the Remote Web Site Properties dialog box. Typically, you need the name of your FTP server, the directory (folder name) that belongs to your Web site on the server, and your FTP account name and password. You only need to complete this form once. If you're successful, Expression Web uses this information the next time you publish your Web site (though you'll have to type in your password each time).

2. **Fill in the information about how you want Expression Web to connect to your Web server, and then click OK.**

    You can also set some advanced options using the Publishing tab of this dialog box. Most usefully, you can set whether Expression Web uploads only changed or new pages (the standard setting), or always uploads everything in your copy of the site (the one stored on your PC).

3. **At this point, Expression Web may prompt you for a user name and password so it can access your FTP server. Enter the information, and then click OK.**

    Expression Web stores your user name for future use, but it's up to you to remember your password and supply it each time you connect.

    Once you're connected, Expression Web shows you a side-by-side file list that compares the contents of the Web site stored on your PC with that located on the server.

4. **To bring your Web server up to date, select the "Local to remote" option, and then click the Publish Web Site button. This starts the publishing process (see Figure 4-12).**

    The "Remote to local" option is handy if a file on your Web server is more recent than the copy on your own computer. This might happen if you edit the same Web site on more than one computer. The Synchronize option is like the "Remote to local" and "Local to remote" operations rolled into one. It examines each file and makes sure it updates any old versions on either your computer or the Web server.

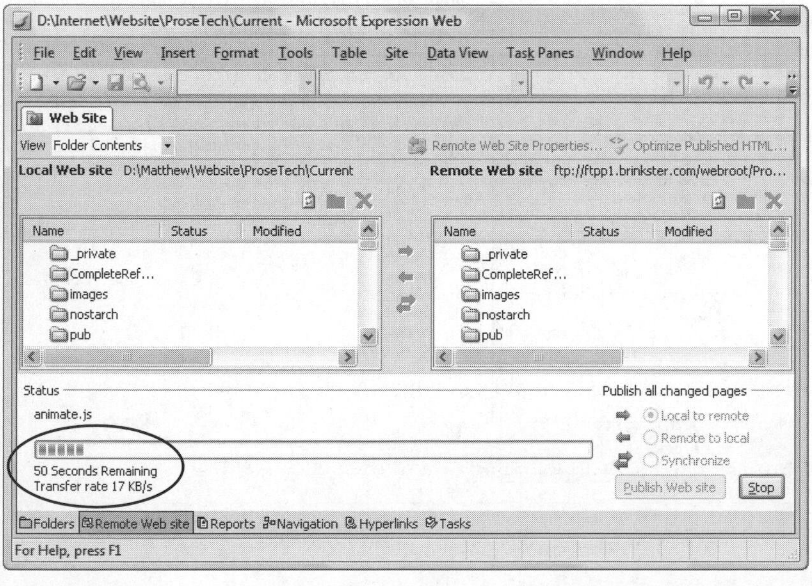

Figure 4-12:
When you publish a Web site, Expression Web scans your files and copies only the ones you've added or changed since the last time you published the site. A progress indicator (circled) identifies the file being copied and estimates how long the operation will take.

Defining a site in Dreamweaver

Dreamweaver gives you two different ways to work with a Web site. The simplest is to use the Files panel to look at the files in any folder on your computer (see Figure 4-13).

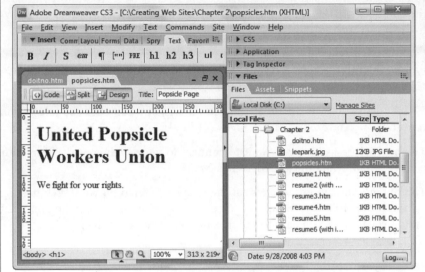

Figure 4-13:
You can browse all the files on your site without leaving Dreamweaver by using the Files panel.

Although using the Files panel is convenient, it's also limiting. The problem is that Dreamweaver doesn't have any way to tell what folders and files make up your Web site. To support Web site uploading and a few other tools, you may want to define a folder as a Web site. To do this, follow these steps:

1. **Click the Manage Sites link in the Files panel, or just select Site → Manage Sites.**

    Dreamweaver displays the Manage Sites dialog box, which lists all the Web sites you've configured so far. Initially, this list is empty.

2. **To define a new Web site, click the New button, and then choose Site.**

    Dreamweaver walks you through a Site Definition wizard that asks you several questions.

3. **Enter a descriptive Web site name, and then click Next.**

    The site name is just the name you use to keep track of your site. This name will also appear in the Files panel.

4. **Choose "No, I do not want to use a server technology", and then click Next.**

    A *server technology* is the framework on a Web server that runs complex Web programs like database searches. Because you aren't creating a full-blown program that runs on a Web server (you're creating ordinary XHTML files), you don't need this support.

5. **Choose "Edit local copies directly on my machine".**

   Some Web servers let you modify pages directly on the server. Even if you have this specialized support, it's always better to work with the files on your PC, and then upload them to the server. This gives you several advantages. First, you won't derail your Web site if you make a minor mistake. Second, you have a valuable backup if anything happens to your Web server. And third, you have the ability to experiment with changes and different designs that may take days to finish, without affecting the live version of your site.

6. **In the "Where on your computer do you want to store your files?" text box, type in the full file path for your Web site folder (usually something like *C:\ Creating Web Sites\Chapter 2*), and then click Next.**

   If you aren't sure where your Web site folder is, you can click the folder icon next to the text box to browse for it.

7. **The next step asks how you want to connect to your Web server. Fill in your connection information, and then click Next.**

   The option you choose depends on the support offered by your Web hosting company, but FTP is a common choice (see Figure 4-14). Depending on what option you choose, you have to supply a number of extra settings.

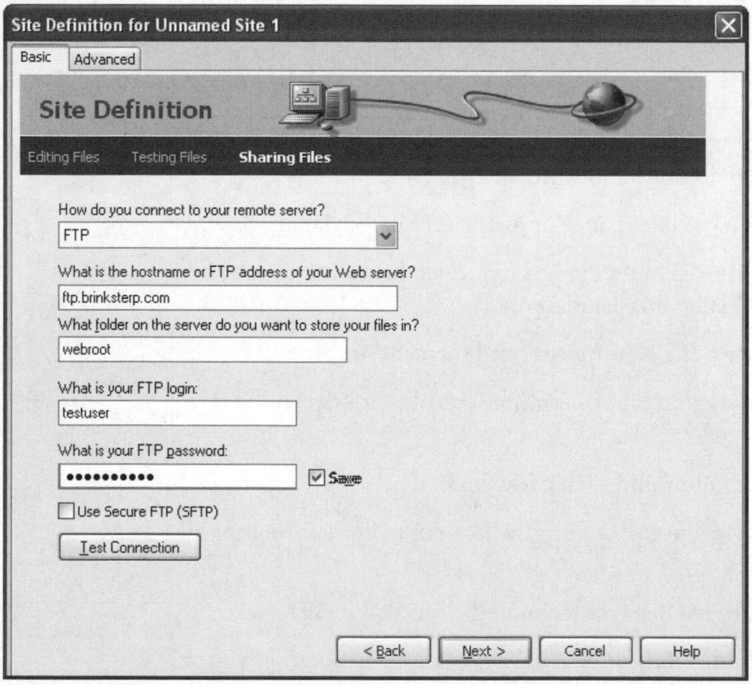

Figure 4-14:
In the "Sharing files" step of the Site Definition wizard, you choose how you want to transfer your files to the remote Web server that stores your Web site files. Usually, you send your files to a Web server using a communication method like FTP. However, if the Web server is part of a company network, you might be able to transfer your files just by copying them to the right folder on the network.

8. **Choose "Do not allow check in and check out", and then click Next.**

   Check in and *check out* features let you collaborate with a group of coworkers so you can each edit different parts of a Web site simultaneously. For information about this and other advanced Dreamweaver features, check out *Dreamweaver CS4: The Missing Manual*.

9. **The last step summarizes the information you entered. Click Done.**

   You return to the Manage Sites dialog box.

10. **Click Done.**

    You return to the Dreamweaver main window.

Uploading a site in Dreamweaver

Once you define your Web site, you'll see it in the Files panel, and you can browse your remote Web server for files, or transfer files back and forth from your PC to the server. Dreamweaver doesn't make things quite as intuitive as Expression Web, but it's still pretty convenient.

To transfer files from your local computer to your server, you use an operation that FTP jargon calls a *put*. It works like this:

1. **In the Files panel, choose your Web site from the drop-down menu at the top left.**

2. **Now, choose "Local view" from the drop-down menu at the top right.**

   The Files panel shows a list of the files on your computer (see Figure 4-15).

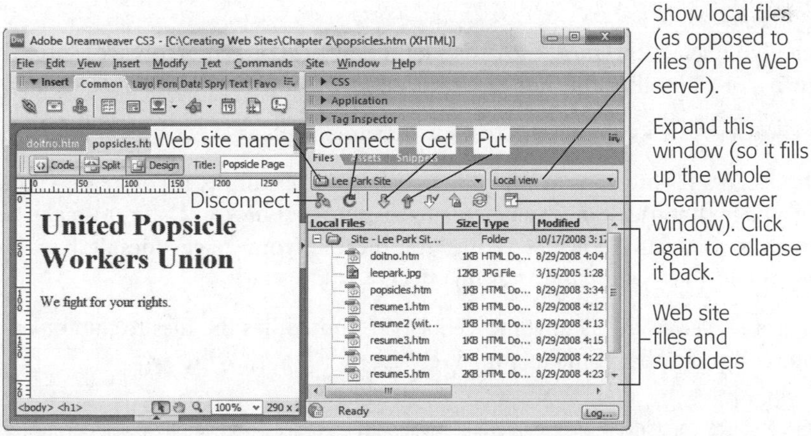

Figure 4-15:
This example shows the local view of the Lee Park site. The local view lists all the files in the Web site folder on your computer. Using the icons in this window, you can quickly transfer files to and from the remote server.

3. **Select the files you want to transfer to the Web server.**

   You can select multiple files by holding down Ctrl while you click each file's icon.

4. Once you select the files, click the Put arrow (the blue arrow icon pointing up), or right-click the files, and then choose Put from the drop-down menu.

Dreamweaver asks if you want to copy dependent files.

5. Choose Yes if you want to copy linked files. For example, if you're uploading a page that uses <img> elements to display graphics, you should click Yes to make sure Dreamweaver also uploads the graphics. If you don't have any dependent files, your choice has no effect.

Dreamweaver connects to your Web server and transfers the files.

To perform the reverse trick and transfer files from your Web server to your PC, you use a *get* operation. Follow these steps:

1. In the Files panel, choose your Web site from the drop-down menu at the top left.

2. Next, choose "Remote view" from the drop-down menu at the top right.

Dreamweaver doesn't automatically display the list of files on your Web server, because getting that list could take a little time. So you need to specifically ask Dreamweaver for an updated view of the files on the server, which you'll learn to do in the next step.

3. Click the refresh button, which looks like a circular arrow icon.

Dreamweaver connects to the Web server, retrieves the list of files on your site, and displays it.

4. Select the files you want to transfer to your computer.

You can select multiple files by holding down Ctrl while you click each file's name.

5. Once you select the files, click the Get arrow (the green arrow icon pointing down), or right-click the files, and then choose Get from the drop-down menu.

Dreamweaver asks if you want to copy dependent files.

6. Choose Yes if you want to copy linked files. For example, if you're downloading a page that uses <img> elements to display graphics, click Yes to make sure Dreamweaver also downloads the graphics. If your page doesn't have any dependent files, your choice has no effect.

Dreamweaver connects to your Web server and copies the files to the folder on your computer that contains your Web site.

Tip: Once you're comfortable with transferring small batches of files, you can try out the Synchronize button. It works like the Web site publishing feature in Expression Web. When you click it, Dreamweaver examines the Web page files on your PC, determines which ones you've updated, and transfers just those to the Web server.

Part Two: Building Better Web Pages

2

XHTML Text Elements

Getting text into a Web page is easy—you just open up an XHTML file, drop in your content, and add the occasional formatting tag. Unfortunately, getting text to look *exactly* the way you want it to is a completely different story.

One of the first things you'll notice when you start working on a Web site is how little control you have over your pages' final appearance. No matter how carefully you code your XHTML, you're at the mercy of your viewers' Web browsers and a dozen other details beyond your control. Under these conditions, writing a perfect page feels like trying to compose a 90-minute symphony with a triangle and a pair of castanets.

Faced with these limitations, what's an enterprising Web developer to do? The first step is to figure out just how much control you *do* have—to learn the XHTML commands you can use to structure your text into headings, paragraphs, lists, and more. That's the task you'll tackle in this chapter. The second step—which you won't dive into until the next chapter—is to use *style sheets*, powerful page-formatting instructions that let you change the appearance of individual Web pages or even your entire Web site.

Understanding Text and the Web

Sooner or later, every Web site creator discovers that designing for the Web is very different from designing something that's going to be printed. Before you can unleash your inner Web-page graphic designer, you need to clear a few conceptual hurdles.

Consider the difference between an XHTML page and a page created in a word processor. Word processing programs show you exactly how a document will look before you print it—you know how large your headlines will be, what font they're in, where your text wraps from one line to the next, and so on. If you see something you don't like, you change it using menus and formatting commands. Your word processor, in other words, gives you absolute control over every detail of your page.

The Web is a more freewheeling place. When you create an XHTML document, you have no idea how that Web page will appear on someone else's PC. That person may have set their browser to not show images, or they may display large type instead of standard-size characters, or they may have shrunk their browser window and tucked it away into a corner of their desktop. And visitors who access your site with a smartphone will get yet another—and completely different—view. In short, you can't control display details on the Web the way you can in print. But you *can* supply all the information a Web browser needs to present your pages properly. You do this by structuring your pages so that Web browsers treat your page elements consistently, regardless of your visitors' browser settings.

Note: XHTML is designed to avoid compatibility problems by giving you *less* control. Instead of letting you place every piece of content in an exact position on a page, XHTML forces you to use elements to shape the basic structure of your work (for example, to indicate paragraphs, headings, and lists). It's up to a Web browser to decide *how* to display these details on any given computer. In other words, XHTML is a compromise that sacrifices control for the sake of simplicity, flexibility, and compatibility.

Logical Structure vs. Physical Formatting

Before you start creating your Web pages with XHTML markup, you should understand one other concept—the difference between *structuring* a document (dividing its content into discrete components like headings, paragraphs, lists, and so on) and *formatting* a document (making those components look pretty by applying italics, changing the text size, adding color, and so on). Novice Web masters who don't understand this difference often end up formatting when they should be structuring, which leads to messy and difficult-to-maintain XHTML pages.

XHTML distinguishes between document structure and document formatting using two types of elements:

- **Logical elements** (sometimes called *idiomatic elements*) define the individual components that make up your Web page. They identify what in a page is a heading, a paragraph, a list, and so on. In other words, they tell you about the *structure* of your page. Logical elements don't, however, define the *format* of these components—what the components will look like once they're onscreen.

- **Physical elements** (sometimes called *typographic elements*) are all about formatting. Examples of physical elements include elements that apply italics, boldface, underlining, and different fonts to text. Physical elements don't tell you anything about the way your page is structured; instead, they tell browsers how to *format* the content in those pages.

You're already familiar with logical elements—you used them to organize the résumé document in Chapter 2, where logical elements defined the resume's heading, paragraphs, and bulleted list.

Chapter 2 also introduced physical elements. When you use physical elements, you specify the exact formatting you want your text to follow—in other words, you micromanage your Web page's appearance. It's like telling a browser: "Listen up. Put *this* word in italics, and put **that phrase** in bold face." Two of the most popular physical elements are the <b> (for bold) and <i> (for italics) elements.

Note: This book focuses on XHTML elements that are most widespread today. That means you'll learn about the most popular logical and physical elements, which makes it easier to carry on a conversation with other Web-heads.

Logical elements have ruled the markup roost since XHTML was invented. The creators of XHTML imagined a world where document writers didn't have to hassle with formatting content, particularly because different browsers would present the same document in different ways, depending on the capabilities of the reader's PC. Even better, logical elements let external programs analyze a page's XHTML. For example, someone could create an automated search program that scanned Web pages and extracted just the top-level headings to produce a barebones outline of the page. Or a program could browse Amazon.com to find only book reviews. Or one could create a junk-mail list by reading <address> elements. A comparable program that came across a Web page filled with nothing but physical elements wouldn't produce results nearly as interesting. After all, who cares how much of eBay's text is in boldface?

Note: The vision of a Web where elements indicate *what* a page contains (prices, size information, email addresses, and so on) rather than *how* it looks is called the *semantic Web*. According to the visionaries who first built the Internet, the semantic Web could usher in a golden age of information access and super-smart searching. Many of the same gurus are still at work planning the semantic Web. For a preview of the possible future, go to *http://logicerror.com/semanticWeb*.

CSS (Cascading Style Sheets)

All of this discussion about page structure raises a good question—if, in developing the "cleanest" pages possible, you're supposed to use elements just to set out the structure of your pages, what's left to make those pages look good? The XHTML powers-that-be could create more XHTML elements just for formatting, but that would force page creators to do more work, make XHTML more complicated, and choke the average Web page in a swamp of messy details about margins, colors, and alignment. Even worse, because every page would include both content and formatting instructions, it would be onerously hard to change the look of a site.

For example, say you want to give all your headings hot pink lettering. If XHTML had an element to specify text color, you'd need to include that element every time you placed a heading on a page. Now imagine that you later decide to go with a more refined dark purple heading. To change your Web site, you'd have to open and edit each and every one of your XHTML pages that had a heading. Consider how much easier life would be if you could link your headings to a formatting instruction in a central reference page. With this kind of setup, you could change the color of the headings across your entire site by simply changing the formatting instruction for headings in that central reference page.

That's the solution that XHTML experts finally hit on. They separated a document's structure—the elements that create headings, paragraphs, lists, and so on—from the formatting instructions, and placed each part in a separate file. Here's how it works. First of all, you create standard XHTML documents just like the ones you learned to create in Chapter 2. These documents include the same elements for headings, paragraphs, and lists that you learned about earlier. That's good news—it means you don't need to change your approach or throw out the basic elements you've already mastered.

Next, you create a separate document using a standard called CSS (Cascading Style Sheets). This separate document is called a *style sheet*, and it defines how browsers format the different elements in your XHTML document. For example, a style sheet might contain instructions like "make every heading bright red" or "give all paragraphs a 15-pixel left-hand margin."

There are many benefits to the style sheet system. First of all, you can reuse the same style sheet for all your Web pages. Because getting your formatting right can be a long and tedious chore, this is a major timesaver. Once you perfect your Web site's look and feel, you link your pages to this style sheet and they all take on that design (see Figure 5-1). Even better, when you're ready for a new look, you don't need to mess with your XHTML documents—just tweak your style sheet and every linked page gets an instant facelift.

Note: XHTML inherits a few formatting features from the original HTML standard, but these features aren't as powerful as style sheets, and they're a lot messier. Now that you're thinking with style sheets in mind, you're ready to steer clear of those headaches and concentrate on becoming comfortable with the staples of the XHTML diet—the elements for structuring text.

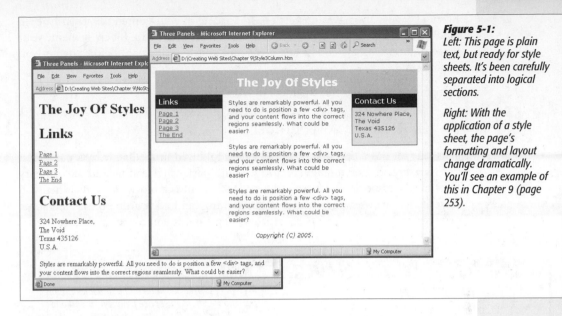

Figure 5-1:
Left: This page is plain text, but ready for style sheets. It's been carefully separated into logical sections.

Right: With the application of a style sheet, the page's formatting and layout change dramatically. You'll see an example of this in Chapter 9 (page 253).

XHTML Elements for Basic Text

As you learned in Chapter 2, there are two things you need to know about every new element you meet. To use the element correctly, without violating the rules of XHTML, you need to answer these two questions:

• **Is it a container element or a standalone element?**

• **Is it a block element or an inline element?**

The first question tells you something about the syntax you use when you add an element to a document. Container elements (like the <b> element that boldfaces text) require a start tag and an end tag, with the content sandwiched in between. Standalone elements (like the <img> element that inserts an image into a page) use a single, all-in-one tag. If standalone elements need additional information, like the location of an image file, you supply it using attributes.

The second question tells you something about *where* you can place an element. Block elements (like the <p> element) go inside the main <body> element or within other block elements. When you start building the overall structure of your Web page, you always begin with block elements. Inline elements (like the <img> element) have to go *inside* block elements. Inline elements don't make sense when they're on their own, floating free of any container.

Tip: To quickly check if an element is a container or standalone element, and to see if it's a block or inline element, check the XHTML reference in Appendix A.

Block elements also have an effect on the spacing of your content. Essentially, each block element defines a chunk of content. When you end a block element, your browser automatically adds a line break and a little extra space before the next bit of content.

For example, consider this fragment of XHTML:

```
<h1>Bread and Water</h1><p>This economical snack is really
all you need to sustain life.</p>
```

This snippet has a title in large, bold letters followed immediately by a paragraph of ordinary text. You might expect to see both parts (the heading and the ordinary text) on the same line. However, the <h1> element is a block element. When you close it, the browser does a little housecleaning, and adds a line break and some extra space. The paragraph text starts on a new line, as you can see in Figure 5-2.

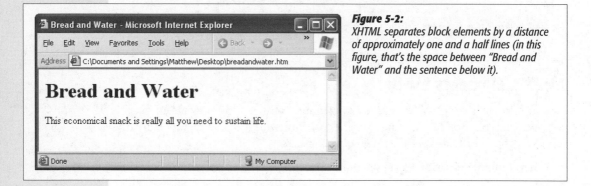

Figure 5-2:
XHTML separates block elements by a distance of approximately one and a half lines (in this figure, that's the space between "Bread and Water" and the sentence below it).

Tip: Block elements are nice because they make it easy to format a document. For example, the spaces that exist between block elements help ensure that one section of text doesn't run into another. However, there's also a clear downside. In some cases, you won't be happy with the automatic spacing between block elements. For example, for dense, information-laden pages, the standard spacing looks far too generous. To tighten up your text and shrink the spaces in between block elements, use style sheets to change the margin settings of your elements (page 163).

Now that you've learned about the basic types of elements, it's time to take a look through your element toolkit.

Paragraphs

You've already seen the basic paragraph element, <p>. It's a block element that defines a paragraph of text.

```
<p>It was the best of times, it was the worst of times...</p>
```

As you've no doubt noticed by now in your travels across the Internet, XHTML paragraphs aren't indented as they are in print media. That's just the way of the Web, although you can change this with style sheets (page 163). Figure 5-3 shows an example of paragraph elements in action.

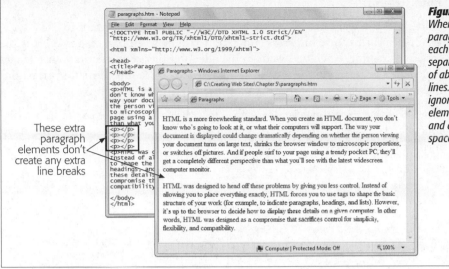

Figure 5-3:
When you put several paragraphs in a row, each paragraph is separated with a space of about one and a half lines. However, browsers ignore empty paragraph elements completely, and don't add any extra space for them.

These extra paragraph elements don't create any extra line breaks

You should get into the habit of thinking of the text in your Web pages as a series of paragraphs. In other words, before you type in any text, add the <p> and </p> tags to serve as a container. Most of the time, paragraphs are the first level of structure you add to a page.

Web browsers don't pay attention to *hard returns* (the line breaks you create when you hit the Enter key). That means you can space your text out over several lines as you type it in, and the browser still wraps it to fit the window. Technically, browsers treat line breaks (like the one you see at the end of this line) as a single space, and if it finds more than one space in a row, it ignores the extra ones. If you want to insert a *real* break between your lines, check out the next section.

UP TO SPEED

Getting More Space

The way that browsers ignore spaces can be exasperating. What if you really do want to add several spaces in a row? The trick is the nonbreaking space— —which is a special XHTML character entity (see page 132) that forces browsers to insert a space.

When a browser sees this entity, it interprets it as a space that it can't ignore. So if you create a paragraph like this:

- `<p>Hello   Bye</p>`

You end up with this text:

- `Hello   Bye`

Many Web editors automatically add nonbreaking spaces when you press the space key in Design view, which is why those spaces don't disappear. But try not to use nonbreaking spaces more than you need to. (If you really want indented paragraphs, you'll get a better solution with style sheets, which you'll learn about in Chapter 6.) And never, ever use spaces to try and align columns of text—that always ends badly, with the browser scrambling your attempts. Instead, use the layout features described in Chapter 9.

Line Breaks

Sometimes you want to start a new line of text, but you don't want to use a paragraph element because browsers add extra space between paragraphs. This is the case, for example, when you want to include a business address on your site and you want it to appear in the standard single-spaced three-line format. In situations like this, the standalone line break element <br /> comes in handy.

Line breaks are exceedingly simple—they tell a browser to move to the start of the following line (see Figure 5-4). They're inline elements, so you need to use them inside a block element, like a paragraph:

```
<p>This paragraph appears<br />
on two lines</p>
```

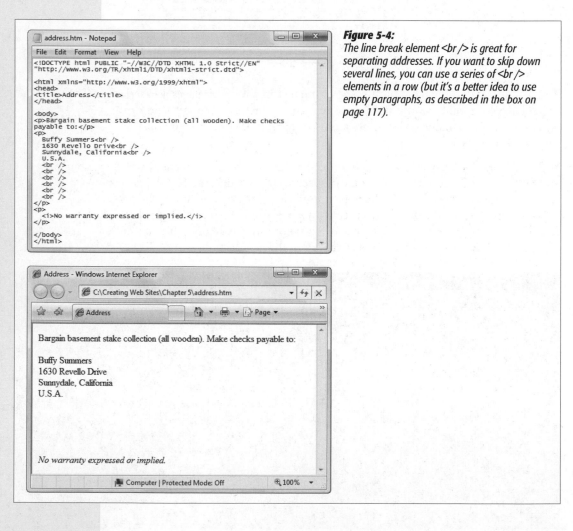

Figure 5-4:
The line break element <br /> is great for separating addresses. If you want to skip down several lines, you can use a series of <br /> elements in a row (but it's a better idea to use empty paragraphs, as described in the box on page 117).

Don't overuse line breaks. Remember, when you resize a browser window, the browser reformats your text to fit the available space. If you try to perfect your paragraphs with line breaks, you'll end up with pages that look bizarre at different browser window sizes. A good rule of thumb is to avoid line breaks in ordinary paragraphs. Instead, use them to force breaks in addresses, outlines, poems, and other types of text whose spacing you want to tightly control. Don't use them for bulleted or numbered lists, either—you'll learn about elements designed just for these lists on page 123.

In some cases, you want to *prevent* a line break, like when you want to keep the longish name of a company or a product on a single line. The solution is to use the nonbreaking space code (which looks like * *) instead of just hitting the space bar. The browser still displays a space when it gets to the   code, but it won't wrap the words on either side of it (see Figure 5-5).

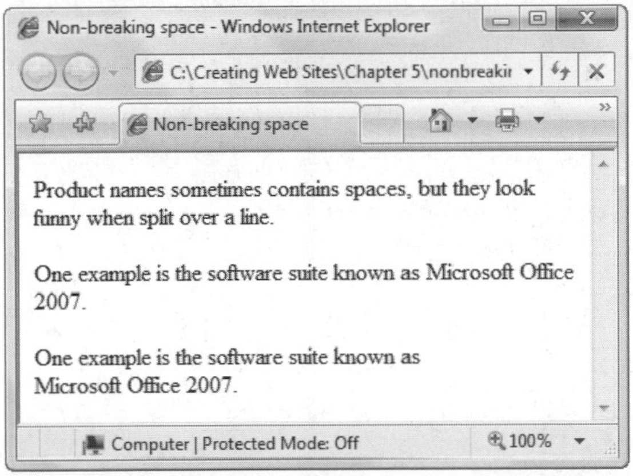

Figure 5-5:
Paragraphs 2 and 3 in this figure show how the   code affects line breaks. Paragraph 3 is actually coded as Microsoft Office 2007. As a result, the browser won't split this term.

HOW'D THEY DO THAT?

The Mystery of Empty Paragraphs

In Web authoring tools like Dreamweaver and Expression Web, if you're in Design view and you press Enter, the program creates a new paragraph. This seems a little counterintuitive, as you've seen that browsers normally ignore line breaks (see Figure 5-5).

The trick is that when you hit the Enter key, both programs insert a paragraph that contains a nonbreaking space. Here's what that creation looks like:

```
<p> </p>
```

This paragraph is still empty, but the browser won't ignore it because it includes the   code. Therefore, the browser gives it the same space as a single-line paragraph and bumps down the content underneath.

Incidentally, Dreamweaver and Expression Web do let you use more ordinary <br /> line break elements instead of empty paragraphs, even in Design view. To do this, press Shift+Enter instead of Enter.

Headings

Headings are section titles—for example, the word "Headings" just above this paragraph. Browsers display them in boldface at various sizes. The size depends on the *heading level*. XHTML supports six heading levels, starting at <h1> (the biggest) and dwindling down to <h6> (the smallest). Both <h5> and <h6> are actually smaller than regularly sized text, and Web developers don't use them too often. Figure 5-6 shows all the heading levels you can use.

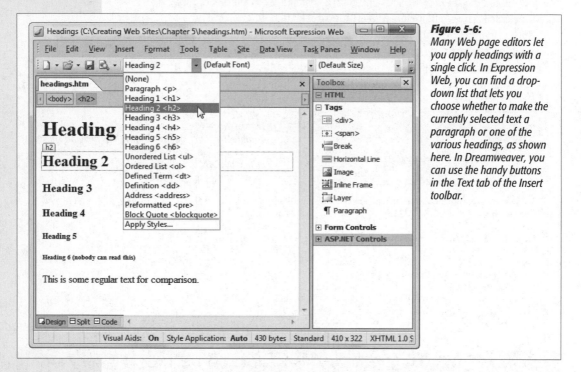

Figure 5-6:
Many Web page editors let you apply headings with a single click. In Expression Web, you can find a drop-down list that lets you choose whether to make the currently selected text a paragraph or one of the various headings, as shown here. In Dreamweaver, you can use the handy buttons in the Text tab of the Insert toolbar.

Headings aren't just useful for formatting—they also help define the hierarchy of your document. Big headings identify important topics, while smaller ones denote lesser issues related to that larger topic. To make sure your document makes sense, start with the largest headings (level 1) and work your way down. For instance, don't jump straight to a level-3 heading just because you like the way it looks.

Note: It's probably occurred to you that if everyone uses the same heading levels in the same order, the Web will become as bland as a bagel in a chain supermarket. Don't panic—it's not as bad as it seems. When you add style sheets into the mix, you'll see that you can completely change the look of any and every heading you use. So for now, stick to using the right levels in the correct order.

Horizontal Lines

Paragraphs and line breaks aren't the only way to separate sections of text. Another neat trick is the standalone <hr> element, which translates to "horizontal rule." A horizontal rule element adds a line that stretches from one side of its container to the other, separating everything above and below it.

Tip: Usually, you'll position a horizontal break between paragraphs, which means it will stretch from one side of a page to the other. However, you can also put a horizontal rule in a smaller container, like a single cell in a table, in which case it won't turn out nearly as big.

Horizontal rules are block elements, so you can stick them in between paragraphs (see Figure 5-7).

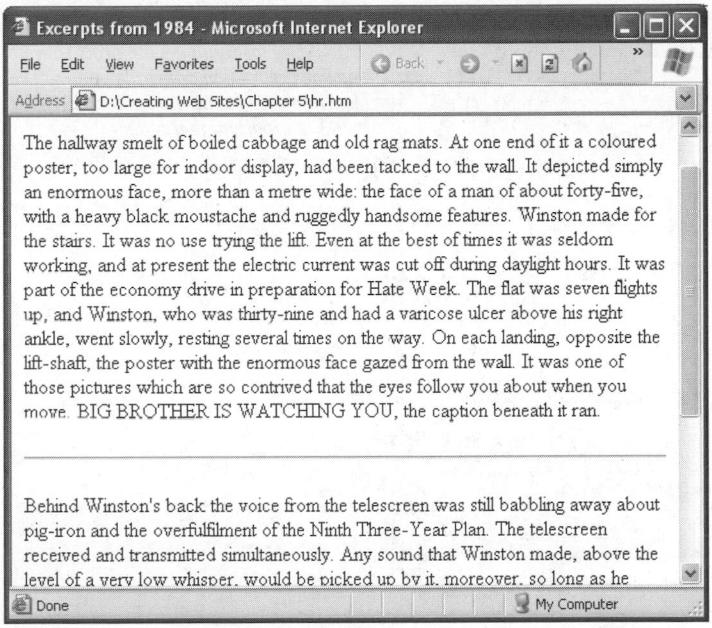

Figure 5-7:
In this example, two paragraphs have an <hr> element between them. The <hr> element inserts the solid line you see.

Preformatted Text

Preformatted text is a unique concept in XHTML that breaks the rules you've read about so far. As you've seen, Web browsers ignore multiple spaces and flow your text to fit the width of a browser window. Although you can change this to a certain extent by using line breaks and nonbreaking spaces, some types of content are still hard to deal with.

For example, imagine you want to display a bit of poetry. Using nonbreaking spaces to align the text is time-consuming and makes your XHTML markup difficult to read. The <pre> element gives you a better option. It tells your browser to re-create the text just as you entered it, including every space and line break, and it displays these details on-screen. Additionally, the browser puts all that text into a monospaced font (typically Courier). Figure 5-8 shows an example.

Note: In a *monospaced* font, every letter occupies the same amount of space. XHTML documents and books like this one use proportional fonts, where letters like W and M are much wider than l and i. Monospaced fonts are useful in preformatted text, because it lets you line up rows of text exactly. However, it doesn't look as polished.

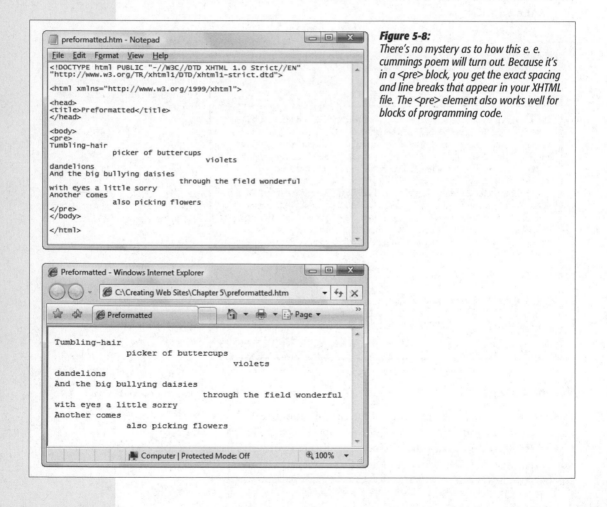

Figure 5-8:
There's no mystery as to how this e. e. cummings poem will turn out. Because it's in a <pre> block, you get the exact spacing and line breaks that appear in your XHTML file. The <pre> element also works well for blocks of programming code.

Quotes

It may be a rare Web page that spouts literary quotes, but the architects of XHTML created a block element named <blockquote> especially for long quotations. When you use this element, your browser indents text on the left and right edges.

Here's an example:

```
<p>Some words of wisdom from "A Tale of Two Cities":</p>

<blockquote>

<p>It was the best of times, it was the worst of times, it was the age of
wisdom, it was the age of foolishness, it was the epoch of belief, it was
the epoch of incredulity, it was the season of Light, it was the season of
Darkness, it was the spring of hope, it was the winter of despair, we had
everything before us, we had nothing before us, we were all going direct to
Heaven, we were all going direct the other way—in short, the period was so
far like the present period, that some of its noisiest authorities insisted
on its being received, for good or for evil, in the superlative degree of
comparison only.</p>

</blockquote>

<p>It's amazing what you can fit into one sentence.</p>
```

Figure 5-9 shows how this appears in the browser.

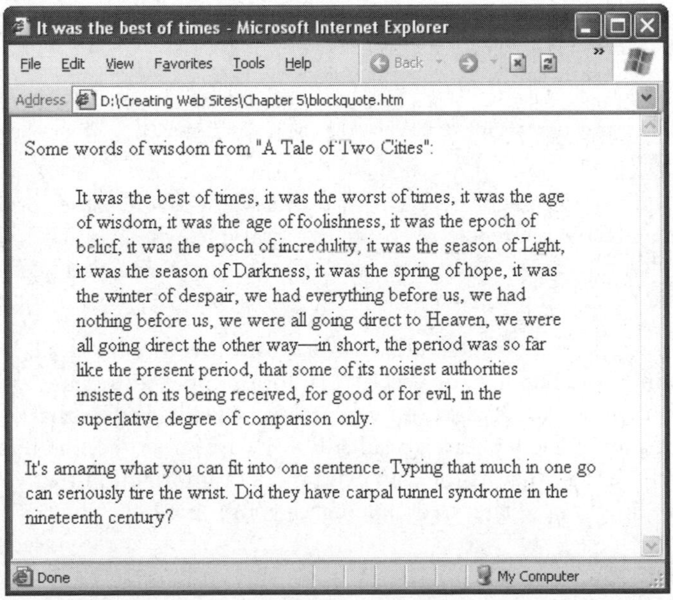

Figure 5-9:
Here, the <blockquote> element indents the middle paragraph.

Occasionally, people use the <blockquote> element purely for its formatting capability—they like the way it sets off text. Of course, this compromises the spirit of the element, and you'd be better off to use style sheets to achieve a similar effect. However, it's a fairly common technique, so it's more or less accepted.

The <blockquote> element is a block element, which means it always appears separately from other block elements, like paragraphs and headings. The <blockquote> has one further restriction—it can hold only other block elements, which means you need to put your content into paragraphs rather than simply type it in between the blockquote start and end tags.

If, instead of using a quote that runs a paragraph or longer, you want to include a simple one-line quote, XHTML's got you covered. It defines an inline element for short quotes that you can nest inside a block element. It's the <q> element, which stands for quotation:

```
<p>As Charles Dickens once wrote, <q>It was the best of times, it was the
worst of times</q>.</p>
```

Some browsers, like Firefox, add quotation marks around the text in a <q> element. Other browsers, like Internet Explorer, do nothing. If you want your quotation to stand out from the text around it in every browser, you might want to add some different formatting, like italics. You can do this by applying a style sheet rule (see Chapter 6).

And if you're dreaming of the semantic Web (see the box on page 111), you can add a URL that points to the source of your quote (assuming it's on the Web) using the *cite* attribute:

```
<p>As Charles Dickens once wrote, <q cite="http://www.literature.org/
authors/dickens-charles/two-cities">It was the best of times, it was the
worst of times</q>.</p>
```

Looking at this example, you might expect your browser to provide some sort of feature that takes you to the referenced Web site (for example, when you click the paragraph). But it doesn't. If you want your text to link to a reference, you need to investigate the anchor element in Chapter 8.

In fact, the information in the *cite* attribute won't appear on your page at all. It *is* available to programs that analyze your Web page—for example, automated programs that scan pages and compile a list of references, or a search engine that uses this information to provide better search results. But most of the time, the reference has little benefit, except that it stores an extra piece of information that you, the Web site creator, might need later to double-check your sources.

Divisions and Spans

The last block element you'll learn about—<div>—is one of the least interesting, at least at first glance. That's because, on its own, it doesn't actually *do* anything.

You use <div> to group together one or more block elements. That means you could group together several paragraphs, or a paragraph and a heading, and so on. Here's an example:

```
<div>
    <h1>...</h1>
    <p>...</p>
    <p>...</p>
</div>
<p>...</p>
```

Given the fact that <div> doesn't do anything, you're probably wondering why it exists. In turns out that the lowly <div> tag becomes a lot more interesting when you combine it with style sheets. That's because you can apply formatting commands directly to a <div> element. For example, if a <div> element contains three paragraphs, you can format all three paragraphs at once simply by formatting the <div> element.

The <div> element has an important relative—the <span> element. Like its cousin, the <span> element doesn't do anything on its own, but when you place it *inside* a block element and define its attributes in a style sheet, you can use it to format just a portion of a paragraph, which is very handy. Here's an example:

```
<p>In this paragraph, some of the text is wrapped in a span element. That
<span>gives you the ability</span> to format it in some fancy way later on.
</p>
```

You'll put the <div> and <span> elements to good use in later chapters.

XHTML Elements for Lists

Once you master XHTML's basic text elements, it's time to move on to XHTML's other set of elements for organizing text—list elements. XHTML lets you create three types of list:

• **Ordered lists** give each item in a list a sequential number (as in 1, 2, 3). They're handy when sequence is important, like when you list a series of steps that tell your relatives how to drive to your house.

• **Unordered lists** are also known as bulleted lists, because a bullet appears before each item in the list. To some degree, you can control what the bullet looks like. You're reading a bulleted list right now.

• **Definition lists** are handy for displaying terms followed by definitions or descriptions. For example, the dictionary is one huge definition list. In a definition list on a Web page, your browser left-aligns the terms and indents the definitions underneath them.

In the following sections you'll learn how to create all three types of list.

Webifying Your Text

As you learned earlier in this chapter, text on the Web isn't like text in print. But sometimes it's hard to shake old habits. Here are some unwritten rules that can help make sure you're making good use of text in your Web pages:

- **Split your text into small sections.** Web pages (and the viewers who read them) don't take kindly to long paragraphs.

- **Create short pages**. If a page is longer than two screenfuls, split it into two pages. Not only does this make your pages easier to read, it gives you more Web pages, which helps with the next point.

- **Divide your content into several pages.** The next step is to link these pages together (see Chapter 8). This gives readers the flexibility to choose what they want to read, and in what order.

- **Put your most important information in the first screenful.** This technique is called designing *above the fold*. The basic idea is to make sure there's something eye-catching or interesting for visitors to read without having to scroll down. (In the same way, well-designed newspapers give newsstand visitors something interesting to read without them having to flip over the folded broadsheet, hence the term "above the fold".)

- **Proofread, proofread, proofread.** Typos and bad grammar shatter your site's veneer of professionalism and Web-coolness.

- **Don't go wild with formatting until you understand style sheets**. If you break this rule, you'll leave a big mess that you'll only need to clean up later on.

Ordered Lists

In an ordered list, XHTML numbers each item consecutively, starting at some value (usually 1). The neat part about ordered lists in XHTML is that you don't need to supply the numbers. Instead, the browser automatically adds the appropriate number next to each list item (sort of like the autonumber feature in Microsoft Word). This is handy for two reasons. First, it lets you insert and remove list items without screwing up your numbering. Second, XHTML carefully aligns the numbers and list items, which isn't as easy if you do it on your own.

To create an ordered list, use <ol>, a block element (<ol> stands for "ordered list"). Then, inside the <ol> element, you place an <li> element for each item in the list (<li> stands for "list item").

For example, here's an ordered lists with three items:

```
<p>To wake up in the morning:</p>
<ol>
    <li>Rub eyes.</li>
    <li>Assume erect position.</li>
    <li>Turn on light.</li>
</ol>
```

In a browser, you'd see this:

> To wake up in the morning:

> 1.Rub eyes.

> 2.Assume erect position.

> 3.Turn on light.

XHTML inserts some space between the paragraph preceding the list and the list itself, as with all block elements. Next, it gives each list item a number.

Ordered lists get more interesting when you mix in the *start* and *type* attributes. The start attribute lets you start the list at a value other than 1. Here's an example that starts the counting at 5:

```
<p>To wake up in the morning:</p>
<ol start="5">
...
</ol>
```

This list will include the numbers 5, 6, and 7. Unfortunately, there's no way to count backward, or to automatically continue counting from a previous list elsewhere on a page.

You aren't limited to numbers in your ordered list, either. The *type* attribute lets you choose the style of numbering. You can use sequential letters and roman numerals, as described in Table 5-1. Figure 5-10 shows a few examples.

Table 5-1. *Types of ordered lists*

type Attribute	Description	Example
1	Numbers	1, 2, 3, 4…
a	Lowercase letters	a, b, c, d…
A	Uppercase letters	A, B, C, D…
i	Lowercase roman numerals	i, ii, iii, iv…
I	Uppercase roman numerals	I, II, III, IV…

Strict XHTML forbids both the *type* and *start* attributes. If you want to use these attributes, you need to stick an XHTML transitional doctype at the top of your Web page. Another option is to switch to styles (using CSS, the standard you'll pick up in Chapter 6). This is a partial solution, because CSS provides an alternative for the type attribute but not for the start attribute. When you use CSS, you can keep the XHTML strict doctype. Just remove the style attribute and replace it with the *list-style-type* CSS property (explained in Chapter 6).

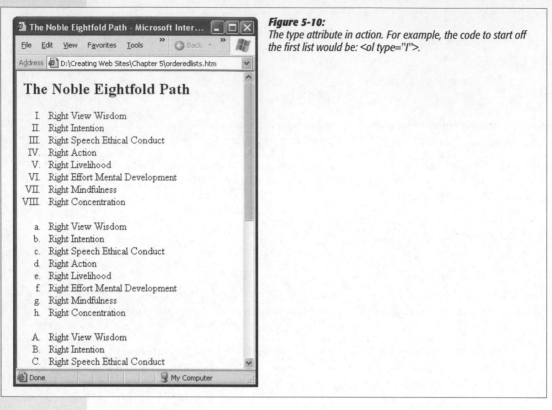

Figure 5-10:
The type attribute in action. For example, the code to start off the first list would be: <ol type="I">.

Unordered Lists

Unordered lists are similar to ordered lists except that they aren't consecutively numbered or lettered. The outer element is <ul>, and you wrap each item inside an <li> element. The browser indents each item in the list, and automatically draws the bullets.

The most interesting frill that comes with unordered lists is the *type* attribute, which lets you change the style of bullet. You can use *disc* (a black dot, which is automatic), *circle* (an empty circle), or *square* (a filled-in square). Figure 5-11 shows the different styles.

Once again, the type attribute is only suitable for XHTML 1.0 transitional—if you're going strict, you need to switch to the *list-style-type* style property.

Tip: Most Web page editors have handy links for quickly creating the different types of lists. In Dreamweaver, look for the "ul" and "ol" icons in the Text tab of the Insert toolbar.

Figure 5-11:
Three flavors of the same list.

Definition Lists

Definition lists are perfect for creating your own online glossary. Each list item actually has two parts—a term (which the browser doesn't indent) and a definition (which the browser indents underneath the term).

Definition lists use a slightly different tagging system than ordered and unordered lists. First, you wrap the whole list in a dictionary list element (<dl>). Then you wrap each term in a <dt> element (dictionary term), and each definition in a <dd> element (dictionary definition).

Here's an example:

```
<dl>
<dt>eat</dt>
<dd>To perform successively (and successfully) the functions of mastication,
humectation, and deglutition.</dd>
<dt>eavesdrop</dt>
<dd>Secretly to overhear a catalogue of the crimes and vices of another or
yourself.</dd>
<dt>economy</dt>
<dd>Purchasing the barrel of whiskey that you do not need for the price of
the cow that you cannot afford.</dd>
</dl>
```

In a browser you'd see this:

eat
> To perform successively (and successfully) the functions of mastication, humectation, and deglutition.

eavesdrop
> Secretly to overhear a catalogue of the crimes and vices of another or yourself.

economy
> Purchasing the barrel of whiskey that you do not need for the price of the cow that you cannot afford.

Nesting Lists

Lists work well on their own, but you can get even fancier by placing one complete list inside another. This technique is called *nesting* lists, and it lets you build multi-layered outlines and detailed sequences of instructions.

To nest a list, declare a new list inside an <li> element in an existing list. For example, the following daily to-do list has three levels:

```
<ul>
  <li>Monday
    <ol>
      <li>Plan schedule for week</li>
      <li>Complete Project X
        <ul style="square">
      <li>Preliminary Interview</li>
        <li>Wild Hypothesis</li>
        <li>Final Report</li>
      </ul>
      </li>
      <li>Abuse underlings</li>
    </ol>
  </li>
  <li>Tuesday
    <ol>
      <li>Revise schedule</li>
      <li>Procrastinate (time permitting). If necessary, put off
      procrastination until another day.</li>
    </ol>
  </li>
  <li>Wednesday
  ...
</ul>
```

> **Tip:** When using nested lists, it's a good idea to use indents in your XHTML document so you can see the different levels at a glance. Otherwise, you'll find it difficult to determine where each list item belongs.

In a nested list, the different list styles really start to become useful for distinguishing each level. Figure 5-12 shows the result of this example.

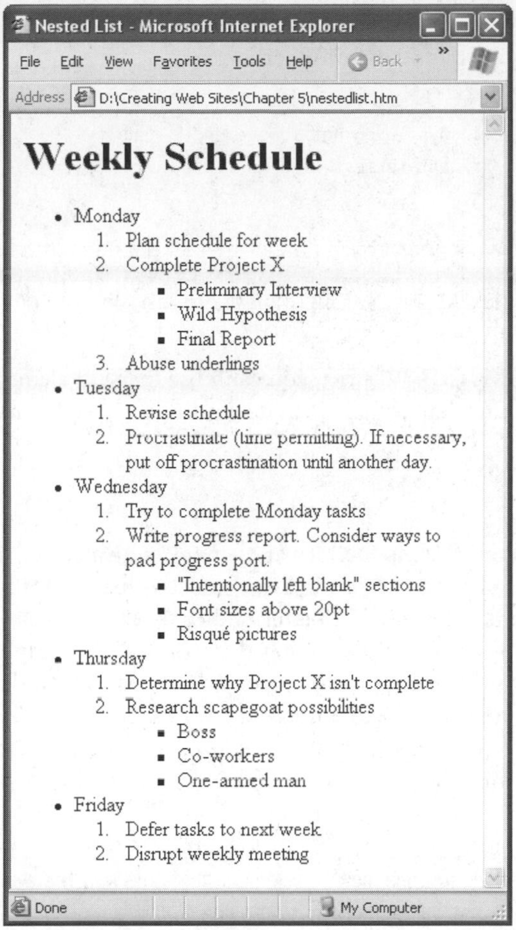

Figure 5-12:
In a nested list, browsers indent each subsequent list.
Although you aren't limited in the number of levels you can
use, you'll eventually run out of room and force your text up
against the right side of the page.

Inline Formatting

As you learned earlier in this chapter, it's best not to format XHTML too heavily.
To get maximum control and make it easy to update your Web site's look later on,
you should head straight to style sheets (as described in the next chapter). However, a few basic formatting elements are truly useful. You're certain to come
across them, and you'll probably want to use them in your own pages. These elements are all inline elements, so you use them inside a block element, like a paragraph, a heading, or a list.

Italics, Bold, and Underline

You've already seen the elements for bold (<b>) and italic (<i>) formatting in
Chapter 2. They're staples in XHTML, letting you quickly format snippets of text.

XHTML also has a <u> element for underlining text, but you can only use it in XHTML 1.0 transitional (page 30). Here's an example that uses all three elements—<i> for italics, <b> for bold, and <u> for underline:

```
<p
<b>Stop!</b> The mattress label says <u>do not remove under penalty
of law</u> and you <i>don't</i> want to mess with mattress companies.
</p>
```

A browser displays it like this:

> **Stop**! The mattress label says <u>do not remove under penalty of law</u> and you *don't* want to mess with mattress companies.

If you keep your pages clean with XHTML 1.0 strict, you can't use the <u> element. However, you can get exactly the same effect using text decorations in a style sheet. Page 155 shows you how.

Emphasis and Strong

The <em> element (for emphasized text) is the logical-element equivalent of the physical element <i>. These two elements have the same effect—they both italicize text. Philosophically, the <em> element is a better choice, because it's more generic. When you use <em>, you're simply indicating that you want to emphasize a piece of text, but you aren't saying *how* to emphasize it. Later on, you can use a style sheet to define just how browsers should emphasize it. Possibilities include making it a different color, a different font, or a different size. If you don't use a style sheet, the text inside the <em> element is set in italics, just as with the <i> element.

Note: Technically, you can use style sheets to redefine the <i> element in the same way. However, it seems confusing to have the <i> element do anything except apply italics. After all, that's its name.

The <strong> element is the logical-element equivalent of the physical element <b>. If you aren't using style sheets, this simply applies bold formatting to a piece of text. Overall, Web developers more commonly use the <i> and <b> elements over <em> and <strong>, but XHTML experts prefer the latter because they're more flexible.

Here's the previous example rewritten to use the <em> and <strong> elements:

```
<p>
<strong>Stop!</strong> The mattress label says <u>do not remove under penalty
of law</u> and you <em>don't</em> want to mess with mattress companies.
</p>
```

There's no logical-element equivalent for the <u> underline element, although you can always use one of the generic elements discussed earlier, like <span> in conjunction with the *text-decoration* style property (see page 155).

Subscript, Superscript, and Strikethrough

You can use the <sub> element for *subscript*—text that's smaller and placed at the bottom of the current line. The <sup> element is for *superscript*—smaller text at the top of the current line. Finally, wrapping text in a <strike> element tells a browser to cross it out, but you can use it only in XHTML 1.0 transitional. Figure 5-13 shows an example of all three.

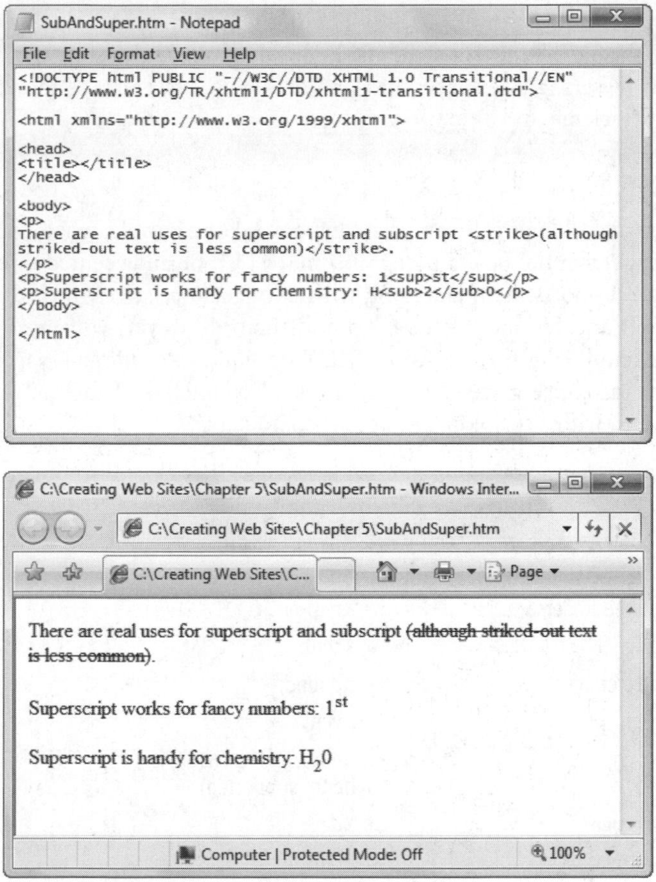

Figure 5-13:
Strikeout, superscript, and subscript tags in action.

Web designers who want to stay on the right side of XHTML law can still create crossed-out text. One alternative is to use the rare <del> element (which is meant to represent deleted text in a revised document). However, you can't trust that all browsers will format <del> the same way, and you really shouldn't use it for anything other than highlighting changes. A better approach is to use a style rule that applies the right text decoration, as explained on page 155.

Teletype

Text within a <tt> element appears in a fixed-width (monospaced) font, such as Courier. Programmers sometimes use it for snippets of code in a paragraph.

```
<p>To solve your problem, use the <tt>Fizzle( )</tt> function.</p>
```

Which shows up like this:

To solve your problem, use the `Fizzle( )` function.

Teletype text (or typewriter text) looks exactly like the text in a <pre> block (see page 119), but you should place <tt> text inside another block element. Unlike preformatted text, browsers ignore spaces and line breaks in <tt> text, as they do in every other XHTML element.

Special Characters

Not all characters are available directly on your keyboard. For example, what if you want to add a copyright symbol (©), a paragraph mark (¶), or an accented e (é)? Good news: XHTML supports them all, along with about 250 relatives, including mathematical symbols and Icelandic letters. To add them, however, you need to use some sleight of hand. The trick is to use *XHTML character entities*—special codes that browsers recognize as requests for unusual characters. Table 5-2 has some common options, with a sprinkling of accent characters.

Table 5-2. Common special characters

Character	Name of Character	What to Type
©	Copyright	&copy;
®	Registered trademark	&reg;
¢	Cent sign	&cent;
£	Pound sterling	&pound;
¥	Yen sign	&yen;
€	Euro sign	€ (but € is better supported)
°	Degree sign	&deg;
±	Plus or minus	&plusmn;
÷	Division sign	&divide;
×	Multiply sign	&times;
µ	Micro sign	&micro;
¼	Fraction one-fourth	&frac14;
½	Fraction one-half	&frac12;
¾	Fraction three-fourths	&frac34;
¶	Paragraph sign	&para;
§	Section sign	&sect;

Table 5-2. Common special characters (continued)

Character	Name of Character	What to Type
«	Left angle quote, guillemot left	«
»	Right angle quote, guillemot right	»
¡	Inverted exclamation	¡
¿	Inverted question mark	¿
æ	Small ae diphthong (ligature)	æ
ç	Small c, cedilla	ç
è	Small e, grave accent	è
é	Small e, acute accent	é
ê	Small e, circumflex accent	ê
ë	Small e, dieresis or umlaut mark	ë
ö	Small o, dieresis or umlaut mark	ö
É	Capital E, acute accent	É

Tip: The euro symbol is a relative newcomer to XHTML. Although you can use the character entity € you'll have the best support using the numeric code € because it works with older browsers.

XHTML character entities aren't just for non-English letters and exotic symbols. You also need them to deal with characters that have a special meaning according to the XHTML standard—namely angle brackets (< >) and the ampersand (&). You shouldn't enter these characters directly into a Web page because the browser will assume you're trying to give it a super-special instruction. Instead, you need to replace these characters with their equivalent character entity, as shown in Table 5-3.

Table 5-3. XHTML character entities

Character	Name of Character	What To Type
<	Left angle bracket	<
>	Right angle bracket	>
&	Ampersand	&
"	Double quotation mark	"

Strictly speaking, you don't need all these entities all of the time. For example, it's safe to insert ordinary quotation marks by typing them in from your keyboard—just don't put them inside attribute names. Similarly, browsers are usually intelligent enough to handle the ampersand (&) character appropriately, but it's better style to use the & code, so that there's no chance a browser will confuse the ampersand with another character entity. Finally, the character entities for the angle brackets are absolutely, utterly necessary.

Here's some flawed text that won't display correctly:

```
I love the greater than (>) and less than (<) symbols. Problem is, when I
type them my browser thinks I'm trying to use a tag.
```

And here's the corrected version, with XHTML character entities. When a browser processes and displays this text, it replaces the entities with the characters you really want.

```
I love the greater than (&gt;) and less than (&lt;) symbols. Problem is,
when I type them my browser thinks I'm trying to use a tag.
```

Most Web design tools insert the correct character entities as you type, as long as you're in Design view and not Code view.

Tip: To get a more comprehensive list of special characters and see how they look in your browser, check out *www.webmonkey.com/reference/Special_Characters*.

Non-English Languages

Although character entities work perfectly well, they can be a bit clumsy if you need to rely on them all the time. For example, consider the famous French phrase "We were given speech to hide our thoughts," shown here:

La parole nous a été donnée pour déguiser notre pensée.

Here's what it looks like with character entities replacing all the accented characters:

La parole nous a été donnée pour déguiser notre pensée.

French speakers would be unlikely to put up with this for long. Fortunately, there's a solution called *Unicode encoding*. Essentially, Unicode is a system that converts characters into the bytes that computers understand and can properly render. By using Unicode encoding, you can create accented characters just as easily as if they were keys on your keyboard.

So how does it work? First, you need a way to get the accented characters into your Web page. Here are some options:

• **Type it in.** Many non-English speakers will have the benefit of keyboards that include accented characters.

• **Use a utility.** In Windows, you can run a little utility called *charmap* (short for Character Map) that lets you pick from a range of special characters and copy your selected character to the clipboard so it's ready for pasting into another program. To run charmap, click Start → Run, type in charmap, and then hit Enter (in Windows Vista, click Start, and then type charmap into the search box).

- **Use your Web page editor.** Some Web page editors include their own built-in symbol pickers. In Expression Web, choose Insert → Symbol (see Figure 5-14). In Dreamweaver, you can use Insert → HTML → Special Characters → Other, but this process only inserts character entities, not Unicode characters. Though the end result is the same, your XHTML markup will still include a clutter of codes.

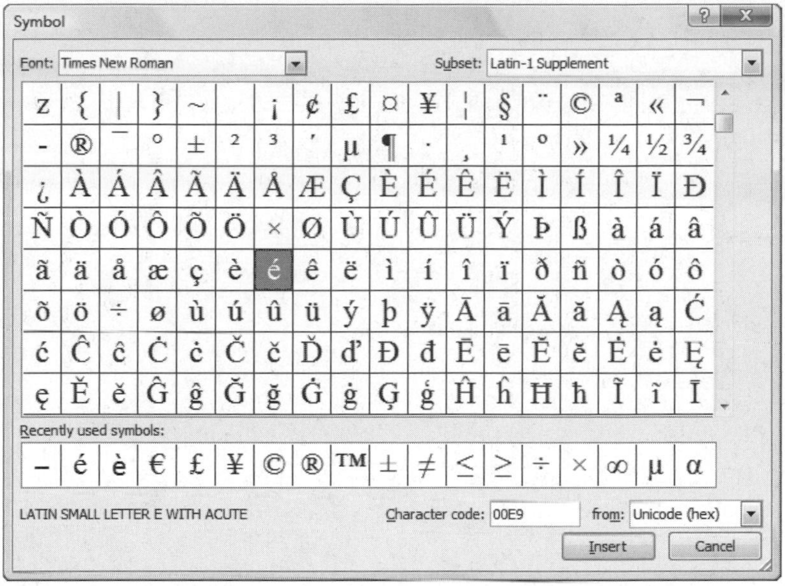

Figure 5-14:
Choose Insert → Symbol to see Expression Web's comprehensive list of special characters. When you pick one, Expression Web inserts the actual character, Unicode-style, not the cryptic character entity.

When using Unicode encoding, you need to make sure you save your Web page correctly. This won't be a problem if you use a professional Web page editor, which is smart enough to get it right the first time. But Unicode can trip up text editors. For example, in Windows Notepad, you need to choose File → Save As, and then pick UTF-8 from the Encoding list (see Figure 5-15). For the Mac's TextEdit, select Format → Make Plain Text, go to Preferences → Open and Save → Plain Text File Encoding → Saving Files, and then select Unicode (UTF-8) from the drop-down list. Every time you re-save your file thereafter, Notepad and TextEdit will encode it correctly.

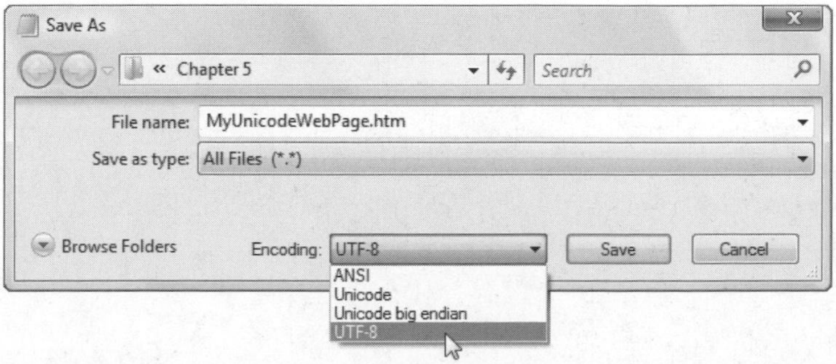

Figure 5-15:
UTF-8 is a slimmed down version of Unicode that saves space for normal characters. It's the overwhelming standard of the Web. However, you need to explicitly tell Notepad to use UTF-8 encoding when you save a Web page that includes special characters like accented letters.

Style Sheets

Last chapter, you learned XHTML's dirty little secret—it doesn't have much formatting muscle. If you want your Web pages to look sharp, you need to add style sheets into the mix.

A style sheet is a document filled with formatting rules. Browsers read these rules and apply them when they display Web pages. For example, a style sheet rule might say, "Make all the headings on this site bold and fuchsia, and draw a box around each one."

There are several reasons why you want to put formatting instructions in a style sheet instead of embedding them in a Web page. The most obvious is *reuse*. For example, thanks to style sheets, you can create a single rule to format level-3 headings, and every level-3 heading on every Web page on your site will reflect that rule. The second reason is that style sheets help you write tidy, readable, and manageable XHTML files. Because style sheets handle all your site's formatting, your XHTML document doesn't need to. All it needs to do is organize your pages into logical sections. (For a recap of the difference between structuring and formatting a Web page, refer to page 110.) And finally, style sheets give you more extensive formatting choices than those in XHTML alone. Using style sheets, you can control colors, borders, margins, alignment, and (to a limited degree) fonts.

You'll use style sheets throughout this book. In this chapter, you'll learn the basics of style sheets, and see how you can use them to create a variety of visual effects.

Style Sheet Basics

Style sheets use a standard that's officially known as *CSS* (Cascading Style Sheets). CSS is a system for defining style *rules*. These rules change the appearance of the elements in a Web page, tweaking details like color, font, size, borders, and placement.

When you use CSS in a Web page, a browser reads both the page's XHTML file and the style sheet rules. It then uses those rules to format the page. Figure 6-1 shows the process.

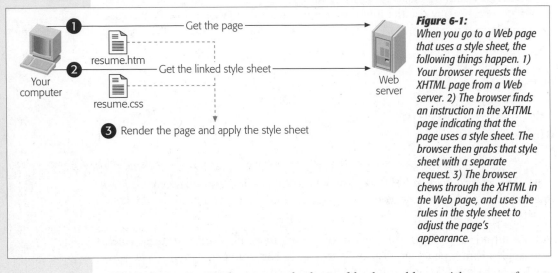

Figure 6-1:
When you go to a Web page that uses a style sheet, the following things happen. 1) Your browser requests the XHTML page from a Web server. 2) The browser finds an instruction in the XHTML page indicating that the page uses a style sheet. The browser then grabs that style sheet with a separate request. 3) The browser chews through the XHTML in the Web page, and uses the rules in the style sheet to adjust the page's appearance.

This system gives Web weavers the best of both worlds—a rich way to format pages and a way to avoid mucking up your XHTML document beyond recognition. In an ideal world, the XHTML document describes only the structure of your Web page (what's a header, what's a paragraph, what's a list, and so on), and the style sheet formats that Web page to give it its hot look.

The Three Types of Styles

Before you learn how to write CSS rules, you first have to think about *where* you're going to place those instructions. CSS gives you three ways to apply style sheets to a Web page:

- An **external style sheet** is one that's stored in a separate file. This is the most powerful approach, because it completely separates formatting rules from your XHTML pages. It also gives you an easy way to apply the same rules to many pages.

- An **internal style sheet** is embedded inside an XHTML document (it goes right inside the <head> section). You still have the benefit of separating the style information from the XHTML, and if you really want, you can cut and paste the embedded style sheet from one page to another (although it gets difficult to keep all those copies synchronized if you make changes later on). You use an internal style sheet if you want to give someone a complete Web page in a single file—for example, if you email someone your home page. You might also use an internal style sheet if you know that you aren't going to use any of its style rules on another page.

- An **inline style** is a way to insert style sheet language directly inside the start tag of an XHTML element. At first glance, this sounds suspicious. You already learned that it's a bad idea to embed formatting instructions inside a Web page, because formatting details tend to be long and unwieldy. That's true, but you might occasionally use the inline style approach to apply one-time formatting in a hurry. It's not all that clean or structured, but it does work.

These choices give you the flexibility to either follow the CSS philosophy wholeheartedly (with external style sheets), or to use the occasional compromise (with internal style sheets or inline styles). Because style sheet language is always the same, even if you use a "lazier" approach like internal style sheets, you can always cut-and-paste your way to an external style sheet when you're ready to get more structured.

UP TO SPEED

The "Other Way" to Format a Web Page

Style sheets aren't the only way to format a Web page—they're just the most capable tool. You've also got a few formatting options built right into the XHTML elements you learned about in Chapter 5. For example, you can change a page's background color or center text without touching a style sheet. For the most part, this book doesn't use these formatting options, for several good reasons:

- **They're patchy and incomplete.** Many style features, like paragraph indenting and borders, are missing—there are no XHTML formatting elements to achieve these effects. Even worse, the model isn't consistent—for example, you might be able to line up text in one type of element, but not the text contained in another type of element. This makes the model difficult to learn and remember.

- **They work only in XHTML 1.0 transitional**. As you learned earlier (page 30), transitional XHTML includes features that the official rulemakers of the XHTML standard—that'd be the good people who work at World Wide Web Consortium (W3C)—consider obsolete. If you use these old-school formatting features, your hard-core Web designer friends won't sit with you at restaurants.

- **They don't let you easily reuse formatting changes.** So after you reformat one page, you need to start all over again to fix the next page. And so on, and so on, and so on.

- **Why learn something you don't need?** Considering that style sheets have so much power and flexibility, and now that virtually every browser around—old and new—supports style sheets, it doesn't make sense to waste time with something you'll only outgrow.

Browser Support for CSS

Before you embrace style sheets, you need to make sure they work on all the browsers your site visitors use. That's not as easy to figure out as it should be. The first problem is that there's actually more than one version of the CSS standard—there's the original CSS1, the slightly improved CSS2, the corrected CSS2.1, and the still-developing CSS3. But the real problem is that browsers don't necessarily support the entire CSS standard no matter what version it is. And when they do, they don't always support it in exactly the same way. The discrepancies range from minor to troubling. As a result, in this book you'll focus on CSS1 and CSS2 properties known to be well-supported on all the major browsers (see below). You'll steer clear of CSS3, which is still too new to be useful. That said, don't forget to test your pages in a variety of browsers to be sure they look right.

As a basic rule of thumb, you can count on good all-around CSS1 support in Netscape Navigator 6, Internet Explorer 5, Opera 3.6, and any version of Firefox, Safari, or Google Chrome. In later versions of these browsers, CSS support gets more consistent and more comprehensive, with added features from CSS2 and even CSS3.

People who've used the Web for a few years may still remember an earlier generation of browsers, namely Netscape 4.x and Internet Explorer 4.x. Both of these browsers are unreliable when it comes to the fancier features of CSS. However, you're unlikely to run into them outside of a museum. If you're in doubt, take a look at some recent statistics to see which browsers people use online (page 13).

If you're still concerned about whether a specific browser version supports a specific CSS feature, see the box on page below.

FREQUENTLY ASKED QUESTION

A Browser Compatibility Reference

How can I tell if a particular browser supports a CSS feature?

If you're a hard-core Web maven, you may be interested in one of the Web browser compatibility charts for CSS available on the Web. Two good resources are *www.webdevout. net/browser-support-css* and *www.quirksmode.org/css/ contents.html*. These charts specify which browsers support which CSS features.

But chart-reader beware: These tables include many rarely used or new and poorly supported features. For example, you probably don't care that virtually no browser supports the *pitch-range* property, used in conjunction with text-reading devices. Unfortunately, the CSS charts can cause panic in those who don't know the standards. However, they can be handy if you need to check out support for a potentially risky feature.

The Anatomy of a Rule

Style sheets contain just one thing: *rules*. Each rule is a formatting instruction that applies to a part of your Web page. A style sheet can contain a single rule, or it can hold dozens (or even hundreds) of them.

Here's a simple rule that tells a browser to display all <h1> headings in blue:

```
h1 { color: blue }
```

CSS rules don't look like anything you've seen in XHTML markup, but you'll have no trouble with them once you realize that three ingredients make up every rule: *selectors*, *properties*, and *values*. Here's the format that every rule follows:

```
selector { property: value }
```

And here's what each part means:

- The **selector** identifies the type of content you want to format. A browser then hunts down all the parts of a Web page that match the selector. For now, you'll concentrate on selectors that match every occurrence of a specific page element, like a heading. But later in this chapter (page 171), you'll learn to create more sophisticated selectors that act only on specific sections of your page.

- The **property** identifies the type of formatting you want to apply. Here's where you choose whether you want to change colors, fonts, alignment, or something else.

- The **value** sets a value for the property defined above. This is where you bring it all home. For example, if your property is color, the value could be light blue or a queasy green.

Of course, it's rarely enough to format just one property. Usually, you want to format several properties at the same time. You can do this with style sheets by creating a rule like this:

```
h1 { text-align: center;
   color: black; }
```

This example changes the color of *and* centers the text inside an <h1> element. That's why style rules use the funny curly braces { and }—so you can put as many formatting instructions inside them as you want. You separate one property from the next using a semicolon (;). It's up to you whether to include a semicolon at the end of the last property. Although it's not necessary, Web-heads often do so to make it easy to add another property onto the end of a rule when needed.

Note: As in an XHTML file, CSS files let you use spacing and line breaks pretty much wherever you want. However, people often put each formatting instruction on a separate line (as in the example above) to make style sheets easy to read.

Conversely, you might want to create a single formatting instruction that affects several different elements. For example, imagine you want to make sure that the first three heading levels, h1 to h3, all have blue letters. Rather than writing three separate rules, you can create a selector that includes all three elements, separated by commas. Here's an example:

```
h1, h2, h3 { color: blue }
```

Believe it or not, selectors, properties, and values are the essence of CSS. Once you understand these three ingredients, you're on your way to style sheet expertise.

Here are a few side effects of the style sheet system that you might not yet realize:

- A single rule can format a whole bunch of XHTML. When you implement a rule for the kind of selectors listed above (called *type selectors*), that rule applies to every one of those elements. So when you specify blue h1 headings as in the example above, every h1 element in your page becomes blue.

- It's up to you to decide how much of your content you want to format. You can fine-tune every XHTML element on your Web page, or you can write rules that affect only a single element, using the techniques you'll find at the end of this chapter (page 171).

- You can create two different rules for the same element. For example, you could create a rule that changes the font of every heading level (<h1>, <h2>, <h3>, and so on), and then add another rule that changes the color of just <h1> elements. Just make sure you don't try to set the same property multiple times with conflicting values, or the results will be difficult to predict.

- Some elements have built-in style rules. For example, browsers always display text that appears in a <b> element as boldfaced, even when the style sheet doesn't include a rule to do so. Similarly, browsers display text in an <h1> heading in a large font, with no style sheet rule necessary. But you can override any or all of these built-in rules using custom style rules. For example, you could explicitly set the font size of an <h1> heading so that it appears *smaller* than normal text. Similarly, you can take the underline off of a link, make the <b> element italicize text instead of bolding it, and so on.

Don't worry about memorizing the kind of properties and values you can specify. Later in this chapter, after you see how style sheets work, you'll get acquainted with all the formatting instructions you can use.

Applying a Style Sheet

Now it's time to see style sheets in action. Before you go any further, dig up the *resume.htm* file you worked on in Chapter 2 (it's also available from the Missing CD page at *www.missingmanuals.com*). You'll use it to test out a new style sheet. Follow these steps:

1. **First, create the style sheet. You do this by creating a new file in any text editor, like Notepad or TextEdit.**

   Creating a style sheet is no different from creating an XHTML page—it's all text. Many XHTML editors have built-in support for style sheets (see the box on page 145 for more information).

2. **Type the following rule into your style sheet:**

```
h1 { color: fuchsia }
```

This rule instructs your browser to display all <h1> elements in bright fuchsia lettering.

3. **Save the style sheet with the name *resume.css*.**

Like an XHTML document, a style sheet can have just about any file name. However, as a matter of convention, style sheets almost always use the extension .css. For this example, make sure you save the style sheet in the same folder as your XHTML page.

4. **Next, open the *resume.htm* file.**

If you don't have the *resume.htm* file handy, you can test this style sheet with any XHTML file that has at least one <h1> element.

5. **Add the <link> element to your XHTML file.**

The <link> element points your browser to the style sheet you wrote for your pages. You have to place the <link> element in the <head> section of your XHTML page. Here's the revised <head> section of *resume.htm* with the <link> element added:

```
<head>
  <link rel="stylesheet" type="text/css" href="resume.css" />
  <title>Hire Me!</title>
</head>
```

The link element includes three details. The *rel* attribute indicates that the link points to a style sheet. The *type* attribute describes how you encoded the document. You should copy both these attributes exactly as shown above, as they never change. The *href* attribute is the important bit—it identifies the location of your style sheet ("href" stands for hypertext reference). Assuming you put your style sheet in the same folder as your XHTML file, all you need to supply is the file name. (If you put these two files in different folders, you need to specify the location of the .css file using the file path notation system you'll learn about on page 171.)

6. **Save the XHTML file, and open it in a browser.**

Here's what happens. Your browser begins processing the XHTML document and finds the <link> element, which tells it to find an associated style sheet and apply all its rules. The browser then reads the first (and only, in this case) rule in the style sheet. To apply this rule, it starts by analyzing the selector, which targets all <h1> elements. Then it finds all the <h1> elements on the XHTML page and applies the fuchsia formatting.

The style sheet in this example isn't terribly impressive. In fact, it probably seems like a lot of work to simply get a pink heading. However, once you've got this basic model in place, you can quickly take advantage of it. For example, you could edit the style sheet to change the font of your *resume.htm* headings. Or, you could add rules to format other parts of the document. Simply save the new style sheet, and then refresh the Web page to see the effect of the changed or added rules.

To see this at work, change the *resume.css* style sheet so that it has these rules:

```
body {
    font-family: Verdana,Arial,sans-serif;
    font-size: 83%;
}

h1 {
    border-style: double;
    color: fuchsia;
    text-align: center;
}

h2 {
    color: fuchsia;
    margin-bottom: 0px;
    font-size: .100%;
}

li {
    font-style: italic;
}

p {
    margin-top: 2px;
}
```

These rules change the font for the entire document (through the <body> element rule), tweak the two heading levels, italicize the list items, and shave off some of the spacing between paragraphs. Although you won't recognize all these rules at first, the overall model (content in the Web page, formatting in the style sheet) is the same as in the earlier resume example. Figure 6-2 shows the result.

Internal style sheets

The *resume.css* example demonstrates an external style sheet. External style sheets are everybody's favorite way to use CSS because they let you link a single lovingly crafted style sheet to as many Web pages as you want. However, sometimes you're not working on an entire Web site, and you'd be happy with a solution that's a little less ambitious.

Figure 6-2:
Left: By now, you can recognize a plain-vanilla Web page.

Right: A style sheet revamps the entire page.

Creating Style Sheets with Web Page Editors

Some Web Page editors, like Dreamweaver and Expression Web, have handy features for editing style sheets. To try them out, start by opening an existing style sheet or creating a new one. To create a style sheet in Expression Web, choose File → New → CSS. To create a style sheet in Dreamweaver, choose File → New, pick CSS in the Page Type list, and then click Create.

So far, you won't see anything to get excited about. But life gets interesting when you start to *edit* your style sheet. As you type, your Web page editor pops up a list of possible style properties and values (see Figure 6-3). If you dig deeper, you'll find that both Web editors have windows that let you build styles by pointing and clicking, as well as convenient shortcuts for applying styles to your Web page elements.

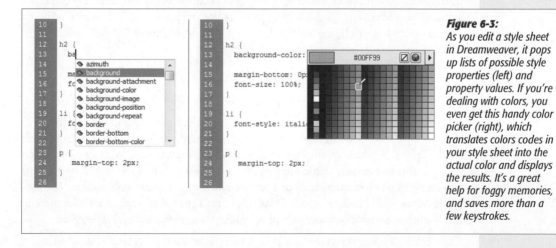

Figure 6-3:
As you edit a style sheet in Dreamweaver, it pops up lists of possible style properties (left) and property values. If you're dealing with colors, you even get this handy color picker (right), which translates colors codes in your style sheet into the actual color and displays the results. It's a great help for foggy memories, and saves more than a few keystrokes.

CHAPTER 6: STYLE SHEETS

An internal style sheet is one that, rather than being linked, is *embedded* in the <head> area of your Web page. Yes, it bulks up your pages and forces you to give each page a separate style sheet. But sometimes the convenience of having just one file that contains your page *and* its style rules makes this approach worthwhile.

To change the earlier example so that it uses an internal style sheet, remove the <link> element from your XHTML markup and add the style rules in a <style> element inside the <head> section of the page, as shown here:

```
<head>
  <title>Hire Me!</title>
  <style type="text/css">
     h1 { color: fuchsia }
  </style>
</head>
```

Inline styles

If you want to avoid writing a style sheet altogether, you can use yet another approach. Inline styles let you insert the property and value portion of a style sheet rule right into the start tag for an XHTML element. You don't need to specify the selector because browsers understand that you want to format only the element where you add the rule.

Here's how you use an inline style to format a single heading:

```
<h1 style="color: fuchsia">Hire Me!</h1>
```

The rule above affects only the h1 element where you added it; any other <h1> headings in the page are unchanged.

Unlike internal and external style sheets, inline styles don't require the *type="text/css"* attribute, which tells browsers that you're using CSS as your style language. For the most part, this missing detail is harmless, because every browser ever created assumes you're using CSS. However, to meet the strict rules of XHTML, you really should specify your choice of style language by adding the following <meta> element to the <head> section of your Web page:

```
<meta http-equiv="Content-Style-Type" content="text/css" />
```

You can pop this element into place right after the <title> element.

Inline styles may seem appealing at first, because they're clear and straightforward. You define the formatting information exactly where you want to use it. But if you try to format a whole Web page this way, you'll realize why Web developers go easy on this technique. Quite simply, the average CSS formatting rule is long. If you need to put it alongside your content and copy it each time you use the element, you quickly end up with a Web page that's mangled beyond all recognition. For example, consider a more complex heading that needs several style rules:

```
<h1 style="border-style: double; color: fuchsia; text-align: center">Hire
Me!</h1>
```

Even if this happens only once in a document, it's already becoming a loose and baggy monstrosity. So try to avoid inline styles if you can.

WORD TO THE WISE

Boosting Style Sheet Speed

External style sheets are more efficient on Web sites because of the way browsers use *caching*. Caching is a performance-improving technique where browsers store a copy of some downloaded information on your computer so they don't need to download it again.

When a browser loads a Web page that links to a style sheet, it makes a separate request for that style sheet, as shown back in Figure 6-1. However, if the browser loads another page that uses the *same* style sheet, it's intelligent enough to realize that it already has the right .css file on hand. As a result, it doesn't make the request. Instead, it uses the cached copy of the style sheet, which makes the Web page load a little bit faster. (Of course, browsers only cache things for so long. If you go to the same site tomorrow, the browser will have to re-request the style sheet.)

If you embed the style sheet in each of your Web pages, the browser always downloads the full page with the duplicate copy of the style sheet. It has no way of knowing that you're using the same set of rules over and over again. Although this probably won't make a huge difference in page-download time, it could start to add up for a Web site with lots of pages. Speed is just one more reason Web veterans prefer external style sheets.

The Cascade

By now, you might be wondering what the "cascading" part of "cascading style sheets" means. It refers to the way browsers decide which rules take precedence when you've got multiple sets of rules.

For example, if an external style sheet indicates that <h1> headings should have blue letters, and then you apply bold formatting with an inline style, you'll end up with the sum of both changes: a blue-lettered, bold-faced heading. It's not as clear what happens if the rules conflict, however. For example, if one rule specifies blue text while another mandates red, which color setting wins?

To determine the answer, you need to consult the following list to find out which rule has highest priority. This list indicates the steps a browser follows when applying styles. The steps toward the bottom are the most powerful: the browser implements them after it applies the steps at the top, and they override any earlier formatting.

1. Browser's standard settings

2. External style sheet

3. Internal style sheet (inside the <head> element)

4. Inline style (inside an XHTML element)

So, if an external style sheet conflicts with an internal style sheet, the internal style sheet wins.

Based on this, you might think that you can use this cascading behavior to your advantage by defining general rules in external style sheets, and then overriding them with the occasional exception using inline styles. In fact, you can, but there's a much better option. Rather than format individual elements with inline style properties, you can use class selectors to format specific parts of a page (see page 171 for details), as you'll see later in this chapter.

Note: The "cascading" in cascading style sheets is a little misleading, because in most cases you won't use more than one type of style sheet (for the simple reason that it can quickly get confusing). Most Web *artistes* favor external style sheets primarily and exclusively.

Inheritance

Along with the idea of cascading styles, there's another closely related concept—style *inheritance*. To understand style inheritance, you need to remember that in XHTML documents, one element can contain other elements. Remember the unordered list element (<ul>)? It contained list item elements (<li>). Similarly, a <p> paragraph element can contain character formatting elements like <b> and <i>, and the <body> element contains the whole document.

Thanks to inheritance, when you apply formatting instructions to an element that contains *other* elements, that formatting rule applies to *every one of those other elements*. For example, if you set a <body> element to the font Verdana (as in the résumé style sheet shown earlier), every element inside that <body> element, including all the headings, paragraphs, lists, and so on, gets the Verdana font.

Note: Elements inherit most, but not all, style properties. For example, elements never inherit margin settings from another element. Look for the "Can Be Inherited" column in each table in this chapter to see whether a property setting can be passed from one element to another through inheritance.

However, there's a trick. Sometimes, formatting rules may overlap. In such a case, the most specific rule—that is, the one hierarchically closest to the element—wins. For example, settings you specify for an <h1> element will override settings you specified for a <body> element for all level-1 headings. Or consider this style sheet:

```
body {
  color: black;
  text-align: center;
}

ul {
  color: fuschia;
  font-style: italic;
}
```

```
li {
  color: red;
  font-weight: bold;
}
```

These rules overlap. In a typical document (see Figure 6-4) you put an <li> (list item) inside a list element like <ul>, which in turn exists inside the <body> element. In this case, the text for each item in the list will be red, because the <li> rule overrides the <ul> and <body> rules that kick in first.

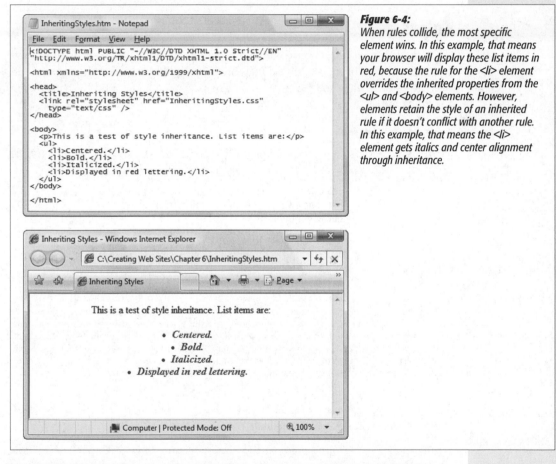

Figure 6-4:
When rules collide, the most specific element wins. In this example, that means your browser will display these list items in red, because the rule for the <li> element overrides the inherited properties from the <ul> and <body> elements. However, elements retain the style of an inherited rule if it doesn't conflict with another rule. In this example, that means the <li> element gets italics and center alignment through inheritance.

Crafty style sheet designers can use this behavior to their advantage. For example, you might apply a font to the <body> element so that everything in your Web page—headings, paragraph text, lists, and so on—has the same font. Then, you can judiciously override this font for a few elements by applying element-specific formatting rules.

Tip: Although you probably won't see cascading styles in action very often, you'll almost certainly use style inheritance.

Now that you've learned how style sheets work, you're ready to start with the hard part—learning about the dozens of different formatting properties you can change. The following sections group the key style properties into categories.

Note: In this chapter, you won't learn about every CSS property. For example, there are some properties that apply primarily to pictures and layout. You'll learn about those properties in later chapters.

Colors

It isn't difficult to inject some color into your Web pages. Style sheet rules have two color-related properties, listed in Table 6-1. You'll learn about the types of values you can use when setting colors (color names, color codes, and RGB values) in the following sections.

Table 6-1. Color properties

Property	Description	Common Values	Can Be Inherited?
color	The color of the text. This is a handy way to make headings or emphasized text stand out.	A color name, color code, or RGB color value.	Yes
background-color	The color behind the text, for just that element.	A color name, color code, or RGB color value. You can also use the word "transparent".	No[a]

[a] The background-color style property doesn't use inheritance (page 148). This means that if you give the <body> section of a page a blue background color and you place a heading on the page, the heading doesn't inherit the blue background. However, there's a trick. If you don't explicitly assign a background color to an element, its color is transparent. This means the color of the containing element shows through, which has the same effect as inheritance. So the heading in this example still ends up with the appearance of a blue background.

The *color* property is easy to understand—it's the color of your text. The *background-color* property is a little more unusual.

If you apply a background color to the <body> element of a Web page, the whole page adopts that color, as you might expect. However, if you specify a background color for an individual element, like a heading, the results are a bit stranger. That's because CSS treats each element as though it's enclosed in an invisible rectangle. When you apply a background color to an element, CSS applies that color to just that rectangle.

For example, the following style sheet applies different background colors to the page, headings, paragraphs, and any bold text:

```
body {
  background-color: yellow;
}

h1 {
  color: white;
  background-color: blue;
}

p {
  background-color: lime;
}

b {
  background-color: white;
}
```

Figure 6-5 shows the result.

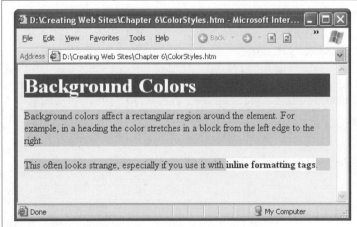

Figure 6-5:
If you apply a background color to an element like <h1>, it colors just that line. If you use it on an inline element like <b> or <span>, it affects only the words in that element. Both results look odd—it's a little like someone went wild with a highlighter. A better choice is to apply a background color to the whole page by specifying it in the <body> element, or to tint just a large box-like portion of the page, using a container element like <div>.

Specifying a Color

The trick to using color is finding the code that indicates the exact shade of electric blue you love. You can go about this in several ways. First of all, you can indicate your color choice with a plain English name, as you've seen in the examples so far. Unfortunately, this system only works with a small set of 16 colors (aqua, black, blue, fuchsia, gray, green, lime, maroon, navy, olive, purple, red, silver, teal, white, and yellow). Some browsers accept other names, but none of these names are guaranteed to be widely supported, so it's best to use another approach. CSS gives you two more options: hexadecimal color values and RGB (or *red-green-blue*) values.

Hexadecimal color values

With *hexadecimal color values* you use a strange-looking code that starts with a number sign (#). Technically, hexadecimal color values are made up of three numbers that represent the amount of red, green, and blue that go into creating a color. (You can create any color by combining various amounts of these three primary colors.) However, the hexadecimal color value combines these three ingredients into an arcane code that's perfectly understandable to computers, but utterly baroque to normal people.

You'll find hexadecimal color notation kicking around the Web a lot, because it's the original format for specifying colors under HTML. However, it's about as intuitive as reading the 0s and 1s that power your computer.

Here's an example:

```
body {
    background-color: #E0E0E0
}
```

Even a computer nerd can't tell that #E0E0E0 applies a light gray background. To figure out the code you need for your favorite color, check out the "Finding the Right Color" section further down this page.

RGB color values

The other approach to specifying color values is to use RGB values. According to this more logical approach, you simply specify how much red, green, and blue you want to "mix in" to create your final color. Each component takes a number from 0 to 255. For example, a color that's composed of red, green, and blue, each set to 255, appears white; on the other hand, all those values set to 0 generates black.

Here's an example of a nice lime color:

```
body {
    background-color: rgb(177,255,20)
}
```

Finding the Right Color

Style sheets can handle absolutely any color you can imagine. But how do you find the color code for the perfect shade of sunset orange (or dead salmon) you need?

Sadly, there's no way this black-and-white book can show you your choices. But there *are* a lot of excellent color-picking programs online. For example, try *www. colorpicker.com*, where all you need to do is click a picture to preview the color you want (and to see its hexadecimal code). Or try *www.colorschemer.com/online.html*, where you can find groups of colors that complement each other, which is helpful

Web-Safe Colors

Will the colors I pick show up on other computers?

Decades ago, when color became the latest fad in Web pages, the computing world was very different. The average PC couldn't handle a wide variety of colors. Many computers could display a relatively small set of 256 colors, and had to deal with other colors by *dithering*, a dubious process that combines little dots of several colors to simulate a different color, leading to an unattractive speckled effect. To avoid dithering, Web designers came up with a standard called *Web-safe colors*, which identifies 216 colors that any PC can reliably replicate. Even better, they look almost exactly the same on every computer.

But the world has changed, and you'd be hard pressed to find a computer that can't display at least 65,000 colors (a standard called 16-bit color, or *high color*). Most support a staggering 16.7 million colors (a standard called 24-bit color, or *true color*). In fact, even very small devices (like cell phones and palmtop computers) support every color a Web designer will ever need.

So here's the bottom line: in the 21st century, it's safe for Web designers to finally forget about Web-safe colors. However, it's still a good idea to check out your Web pages and color preferences on a variety of computers. That's because different monitors don't always reproduce the colors exactly—some tend to tint colors unexpectedly, and Windows computers tend to produce darker colors than their Macintosh counterparts (even when using the same monitor). Pick colors carefully, because a color combination that looks great on your PC can look nauseating (or worse, be illegible) on someone else's.

for creating Web sites that look professionally designed. If you use a Web design tool like Expression Web or Dreamweaver, you have an even easier choice—the program's built-in color-picking smarts, as shown back in Figure 6-3.

Note: The RGB system lets you pick any of 16.7 million colors, which means that no color-picking Web site will actually show you every single possible RGB color code (if they do, make sure you don't hit the Print button; even with 10 colors per line, you'd wind up with thousands of pages). Instead, most sites limit you to a representative sampling of colors. This works, because many colors are so similar that they're nearly impossible to distinguish by eye.

The RGB color standard is also alive and well in many computer programs. For example, if you see a color you love in a professional graphics program like Photoshop (or even in a not-so-professional graphics program, like Windows Paint), odds are there's a way to get the red, green, and blue values for that color. This gives you a great way to match the text in your Web page with a color in a picture. Now that's a trick that will please even the strictest interior designer.

Fonts

Using the CSS font properties, you can choose a font family, font weight (its boldness setting), and font size (see Table 6-2). Be prepared, however, for a bit of Web-style uncertainty, as this is one case where life isn't as easy as it seems.

DESIGN TIME

Making Color Look Good

Nothing beats black text on a white background for creating crisp, clean, easy-to-read Web pages with real presence. This black-and-white combination also works best for pages that have a lot of colorful pictures. It's no accident that almost every top Web site, from news sites (*www.cnn.com*) to search engines (*www.google.com*) to e-commerce shops (*www.amazon.com*) and auction houses (*www.ebay.com*), use the winning combination of black on white.

But what if you're just too colorful a person to leave your Web page in plain black and white? The best advice is to follow the golden rule of color: *use restraint*. Unless you're creating a sixties revival site or a Led Zeppelin tribute page, you don't want your pages to run wild with color. Here are some ways to inject a splash of color without letting it take over your Web page:

- **Go monochrome**. That means use black, white, and one other dark color. Use the new color to emphasize an important design element, like sub-headings in an article. For example, the *Time* magazine Web site once used its trademark red for headlines (although now it favors a sleeker black-and-white combination).

- **Use lightly shaded backgrounds**. Sometimes, a faint wash of color in the background is all you need to perk up a site. For example, a gentle tan or gold can suggest elegance or sophistication (see the Harvard library site at *http://lib.harvard.edu*). Or light pinks and yellows can get shoppers ready to buy sleepwear and other feminine accoutrements at Victoria's Secret (*www.victoriassecret.com*).

- **Use color in a box**. Web designers frequently use shaded boxes to highlight important areas of a Web page (see Wikipedia at *http://en.wikipedia.org*). You'll learn how to create boxes later in this chapter.

- **Be careful about using white text**. White text on a black or dark blue background can be striking—and strikingly hard to read. The rule of thumb is to avoid it unless you're trying to make your Web site seem futuristic, alternative, or gloomy. (And even if you do fall into one of these categories, you might still get a stronger effect with a white background and a few well-chosen graphics with splashy electric colors.)

Table 6-2. Font properties

Property	Description	Common Values	Can Be Inherited?
font-family	A list of font names. The browser scans through the list until it finds a font that's on your visitor's PC. If doesn't find a supported font, it uses the standard font it always uses.	A font name (like Verdana, Times, or Arial) or a generic font-family name: serif, sans-serif, monospace.	Yes
font-size	Sets the size of the font.	A specific size, or one of these values: xx-small, x-small, small, medium, large, x-large, xx-large, smaller, larger.	Yes
font-weight	Sets the weight of the font (how bold it appears).	normal, bold, bolder, lighter	Yes
font-style	Lets you apply italic formatting.	normal, italic	Yes

Table 6-2. Font properties (continued)

Property	Description	Common Values	Can Be Inherited?
font-variant	Lets you apply small caps, which turns lowercase letters into smaller capitals (LIKE THIS).	normal, small-caps	Yes
text-decoration	Applies a few miscellaneous text changes, like underlining and strikeout. Technically speaking, these aren't part of the font (the browser adds these).	none, underline, overline, line-through	Yes
text-transform	Transforms text so that it's all capitals or all lowercase.	none, uppercase, lowercase	Yes

Although most CSS font properties are straightforward, the *font-family* property has a nasty surprise—it doesn't always work. The inescapable problem you face is that no two computers have the same set of fonts installed, so the fonts you use to design your Web page won't necessarily be the fonts your visitors have installed on their PCs. A simple way to solve this problem is to create browsers that automatically download fonts they don't have, but this would be a Web nightmare. First, automatic downloads could swamp the average computer's hard drive with thousands of (potentially low-quality) fonts. Second, it would infuriate the software companies who sell fonts. (Fonts aren't free, and so wantonly copying them from one computer to another isn't kosher.)

There may be practical solutions to these problems, but, unfortunately, browser companies and the people who set Web standards have never agreed on any. As a result, any font settings you specify are just recommendations. If a PC doesn't have the font you request, the browser reverts to the standard font it uses whenever it's on a site that doesn't have special font instructions.

Given that caveat, you're probably wondering why you should bother configuring font choices at all. Well, here's one bit of good news. Instead of requesting a font and blindly hoping that it's available to a browser, you can create a list of *font preferences*. That way, the browser tries to match your first choice and, if it fails, your second choice, and so on. At the end of this list, you should use one of the few standard fonts that almost all PCs support in some variation. You'll see this technique at work in the next section.

Specifying a Font

To select a font, you use the *font-family* attribute. Here's an example that changes the font of an entire page:

```
body {
    font-family: Arial;
}
```

DESIGN TIME

Graphical Text

The only guaranteed cure for font woes is *graphical text*. With graphical text, you don't type your content into an XHTML file. Instead, you perfect it in a drawing program, save it as a picture, and then display the *picture* of that text on your page using the <img> element.

Graphical text is clearly unsuitable for large amounts of text. First of all, it's an image and images require more bytes of storage space than text, so it bloats the size of your Web page horribly. It's also much less flexible. For example, graphical text can't adjust itself to fit the width of a browser window or take into account your visitors' browser preference settings. There's also no way for a visitor to search an image for specific words (or for a Web search engine to figure out what's on your site).

However, graphical text is commonly used for Web page menus, buttons, and headings, where these issues aren't nearly as important. Sometimes, graphical text isn't obvious. For example, you may never have noticed that the section headings on your favorite online newspaper are actually images. To figure out if a Web site uses graphical text or the real deal, try to select the text with your mouse. If you can't, the text is really a picture.

You'll learn how to use graphics (including graphical text) in Chapter 7.

Arial is a *sans-serif* font found on just about every modern PC, including those running Windows, Mac OS, Unix, and Linux operating systems. (See Figure 6-6 for more about the difference between serif and sans-serif fonts.)

Figure 6-6:
Serif fonts use adornments, or serifs, that make them easier to read in print. This book uses a serif font, for example. If you look closely at the letter "S" in the body text, you'll see tiny curlicues in the top-right and bottom-left corners. On the other hand, sans-serif fonts have a spare, streamlined look. They can make pages seem less bookish, less formal, more modern, and colder.

To be safe, when you create a font list, always end it with a generic font-family name. Every PC supports generic fonts under the font-family names serif, sans-serif, and monospace.

Here's the modified rule:

```
body {
    font-family: Arial, sans-serif;
}
```

At this point, you might be tempted to get a little creative with this rule by adding support for a less common sans-serif format. Here's an example:

```
body {
    font-family: Eras, Arial, sans-serif;
}
```

If Eras is relatively similar to Arial, this technique might not be a problem. But if it's significantly different, it's a bad idea.

The first problem is that by using a nonstandard font, you're creating a Web page whose appearance may vary dramatically depending on the fonts installed on your visitor's PC. Whenever pages vary, it becomes more difficult to really tweak them to perfection because you don't know exactly how they'll appear elsewhere. Different fonts take up different amounts of space, and if text grows or shrinks, the layout of other elements (like pictures) changes, too. Besides, is it really that pleasant to read KidzzFunScript or SnoopDawg font for long periods of time?

A more insidious problem happens if a visitor's computer has a font with the same name that looks completely different. Even worse, browsers may access an online database of fonts to try and find a similar font that's already installed. This approach can quickly get ugly. At worst, either of these problems can lead to illegible text.

Tip: Most Web page editors won't warn you when you apply a nonstandard font, so be on your guard. If your font isn't one of a small set of widely distributed Web fonts (more on those in a moment), you shouldn't use it.

Finding the Right Font

To make sure your Web page displays correctly, you should use a standard font that's widely available. But just what are these standard fonts? Unfortunately, Web experts aren't always in consensus.

If you want to be really conservative, you won't go wrong with any of these fonts:

- Times
- Arial
- Helvetica
- Courier

Of course, all these fonts are insanely boring. If you want to take more risk, you can use one of the following fonts, found on almost all Windows and Mac computers (but not necessarily on other operating systems, like Unix):

- Verdana
- Georgia
- Tahoma

- Comic Sans MS

- Arial Black

- Impact

To compare these different fonts, see Figure 6-7.

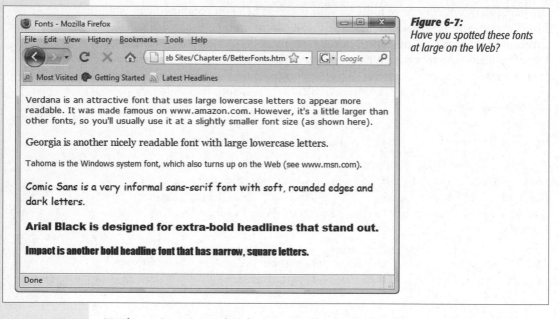

Figure 6-7:
Have you spotted these fonts at large on the Web?

Verdana, Georgia, and Tahoma can all help give your Web pages a more up-to-date look. However, the characters in Verdana and Tahoma start off a bit large, so you usually need to ratchet them down a notch in size (a technique described in the next section).

For a good discussion of fonts, the platforms that reliably support them, and the pros and cons of each font family (some fonts look nice onscreen, for example, but they generate lousy printouts) see *http://web.mit.edu/jmorzins/www/fonts.html* and *www.upsdell.com/BrowserNews/res_fontsamp.htm*.

Font Sizes

Once you sort out the thorny issue of choosing a font, you may also want to change its size. It's important that you select a text size that's readable and looks good. Resist the urge to shrink or enlarge text to suit your personal preferences. Instead, aim to match the standard text size you see on other popular Web sites.

Despite what you might expect, you don't have complete control over the size of the fonts on your Web pages. Most site visitors use browsers that let them scale font sizes up or down, either to fit more text on-screen or, more commonly, to make text easy to read on a high-resolution monitor. In Internet Explorer and Firefox, you find these options in the View → Text Size menu.

A browser's font-size settings don't completely override the size you've set in your Web page, however. Instead, they tweak it up or down. For example, if you choose to use a large font size on your Web page (which corresponds to a setting of about 15 points in a word processor) and a visitor using Internet Explorer selects View → Text Size → Larger, the text size grows about 20 percent, to 18 points.

The fact that your visitors have this kind of control is another reason you shouldn't use particularly small or large fonts on your pages. When you combine them with browser preferences, a size that's a little on the large size could become gargantuan, and text that's slightly small could turn unreadable. The best defense for these problems is to test your Web page with different browsers *and* different font size preferences.

As you'll discover in the following sections, you can set font sizes in several ways.

Keyword sizing

The simplest way to specify the size of your text is to use one of the size values listed previously in Table 6-2. For example, to create a really big heading and ridiculously small text, you can use these two rules:

```
body {
   font-size: xx-small;
}
h1 {
   font-size: xx-large;
}
```

These size keywords are often called *absolute sizes*, because they apply an exact size to text. Exactly what size, you ask? Well, that's where it gets a bit complicated. These size details aren't set in stone—different browsers are free to interpret them in different ways. The basic rule of thumb is that the font size *medium* corresponds to a browser's standard text size, which is the size it uses (12 points) if a Web site doesn't specify a text size. Every time you go up a level, you add about 20 percent in size. (For math geeks, that means that every time you go down a level, you lose about 17 percent.)

The standard font size for most browsers is 12 points (although text at this size typically appears smaller on Macs than on Windows PCs). That means *large* text measures approximately 15 points, *x-large* text is 18 points, and *xx-large* text is 27 points.

Figure 6-8 shows the basic sizes you can choose from.

Note: When using size keywords, make sure your Web page specifies an XHTML doctype. If you don't, Internet Explorer renders your page in the dreaded "quirks" mode, which makes your text one size larger than it should be. As a result, your page won't look the same in Internet Explorer as it does in other browsers, like Firefox.

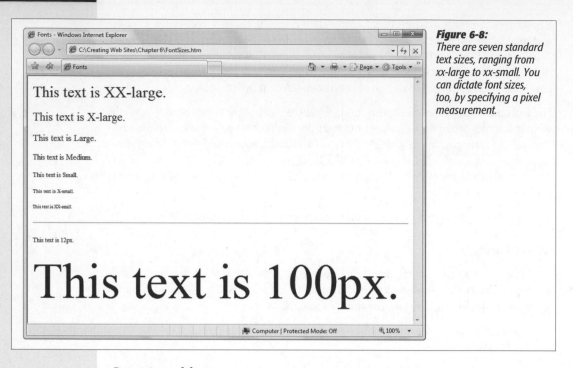

Figure 6-8:
There are seven standard
text sizes, ranging from
xx-large to xx-small. You
can dictate font sizes,
too, by specifying a pixel
measurement.

Percentage sizing

Another font-size option is to use percentage sizes instead of size keywords. For example, if you want to make sure your text appears normal size, use this rule:

```
body {
    font-size: 100%;
}
```

And if you want to make your text smaller, use something like this:

```
body {
    font-family: Verdana,Arial,sans-serif;
    font-size: 83%;
}
```

This displays text at 83 percent of its standard size. It doesn't matter whether the standard size is considered *small* (Internet Explorer) or *medium* (most other browsers). This particular example creates nicely readable text with the Verdana font.

It's just as easy to upsize text:

```
h1 {
    font-size: 120%;
}
```

But keep in mind that 100 percent always refers to the standard size of normal *paragraph* text, not the standard size of the element you're styling, like an h1 heading. So if you create a heading with text sized at 120 percent, your heading is going to be only a little bigger than normal paragraph text, which is actually quite a bit smaller than the normal size of an <h1> heading.

Using percentage sizes is the safest, most reliable way to size text. Not only does it provide consistent results across all browsers, it also works in conjunction with the browser size preferences described earlier.

Relative sizing

Another approach for setting font size is to use one of two *relative size* values—"larger" or "smaller". This is a bit confusing, because as you learned in the last section, absolute sizes are already relative—they're all based on the browser setting for standard text.

The difference is that relative size settings are influenced by the font of the element that contains them. The easiest way to understand how this works is to consider the following style sheet, which has two rules:

```
body {
  font-size: xx-small;
}

b {
  font-size: larger;
}
```

The first rule applies an absolute *xx-small* size to the whole page. If your page includes a <b> element, the text inside *inherits* the xx-small size (see page 148 for a recap of inheritance), and then the second style rule steps it up one notch, to x-small.

Now consider what happens if you edit the body text style above to use a larger font, like this:

```
body {
  font-size: x-small;
}
```

Now all bold text will be one level up from *x-small*, which is *small*.

The only limit to the two relative sizes is that they can step up or down only one level. However, you can get around this limitation by using font numbers. For example, a size of +2 is a relative size that increments a font two levels. Here's an example:

```
body {
  font-size: x-small;
}
```

```
b {
   font-size: +2;
}
```

Now the bold text becomes *medium* text, because *medium* is two levels up from *x-small*.

Relative sizes are a little trickier to get used to than absolute sizes. You're most likely to use them if you have a style sheet with a lot of different sizes. For example, you might use a relative size for bold text if you want to make sure bold text is always a little bit bigger than the text around it. If you were to use an absolute size instead, the bold text would appear large in relation to small-sized paragraph text, but it wouldn't stand out in a large-sized heading.

Note: When you use absolute or relative sizes, you create flexible pages. If a visitor ratchets up the text size using his browser's preferences, the browser resizes all your other fonts proportionately.

Pixel sizing

Most of the time, you should rely on absolute and relative sizing for text. However, if you want to have more control, you can customize your font size precisely by specifying a *pixel size*. Pixel sizes can range wildly, with 12 pixels and 14 pixels being about normal for body text. To specify a pixel size, use the number immediately followed by the letters *px*, as shown here:

```
body {
   font-size: 11px;
}
h1 {
   font-size: 24px;
}
```

Note: Don't put a space between the number and the letters "px". If you do, your rule may work in Internet Explorer but it will thoroughly confuse other browsers.

As always, you need to test, refine, and retest your font choice to get the sizes right. Some fonts look bigger than others, and require smaller sizes. Other fonts work well at larger sizes, but become less legible as you scale them down in size.

Web purists avoid using exact sizes because they're horribly inflexible in Internet Explorer. For example, if a near-sighted visitor has upped the text size settings in Internet Explorer, this adjustment won't have any effect on a page that uses pixel sizing. (For some reason, other browsers don't suffer from this problem—they're able to resize pages even if you use pixel sizes.) As a result, using pixel sizes is a quick shortcut to inconsistent results. By using them, you could inadvertently lock out certain audiences or create pages that visitors find difficult to read or navigate on certain types of browsers. It just goes to show that in the Web world there's a price to be paid for getting complete control over formatting.

Text Alignment and Spacing

CSS includes a great many properties for controlling how text appears on a Web page. If you've ever wondered how to indent paragraphs, space out lines, or center a title, these are the tools you need.

Table 6-3 has the details on all your alignment options.

Table 6-3. *Alignment and spacing properties*

Property	Description	Common Values	Can Be Inherited?
text-align	Lines text up on one or both edges of a page.	left, right, center, justify	Yes
text-indent	Indents the first line of text (typically in a paragraph).	A pixel value (indicating the amount to indent) or percentage of the width of the containing element.	Yes
margin	Sets the spacing added around the outside of a block element (page 113). You can also use the similar properties margin-bottom, margin-left, margin-right, and margin-top to change the margin on just one side.	A pixel value or percentage indicating the amount of space to add around the element.	No
padding	Sets the spacing added around the inside of a block element. Has the same effect as margin, unless you have an element with a border or background color.	A pixel value or percentage indicating the amount of space to add around the element.	No
word-spacing	Sets the space between words.	A pixel value or percentage.	Yes
letter-spacing	Sets the space between letters.	A pixel value or percentage.	Yes
line-height	Sets the space between lines.	A pixel value or percentage. You can also use a multiple (for example, use 2 for double-spacing).	Yes
white-space	Tells the browser how to deal with spaces in your text.	normal, pre, nowrap	Yes

For example, if you want to create a page that has indented paragraphs (as a novel or newspaper does), use this style sheet rule:

```
p {
    text-indent: 20px
}
```

In the following sections, you'll see examples that use the alignment and margin properties.

Alignment

Ordinarily, all text in a Web page lines up on the left side of the browser window. Using the *text-align* property, you can center text, line it up on the right edge, or justify it. Figure 6-9 shows your options.

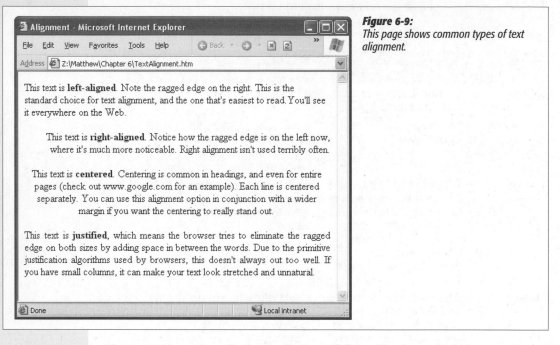

Figure 6-9:
This page shows common types of text alignment.

The most interesting alignment choice is full justification, which formats text so that it appears flush with both the left and right margins of a page, like the text in this book. You specify full justification with the *justify* setting. Originally, printers preferred full justification because it crams more words onto each page, reducing a book's page count and, therefore, its printing cost. These days, it's a way of life. Many people feel that text with full justification looks neater and cleaner than text with a ragged edge, even though tests show plain, unjustified text is easier to read.

Justification doesn't work as well in the Web world as in print. A key problem is a lack of word-splitting rules, which split long words into syllables, hyphenate them, and extend them over two lines. Browsers use a relatively simplistic method to justify text. Essentially, they add words to a line one at a time, until no more words can fit, at which point they add extra spacing between the words to pad the line to its full length. By comparison, the best page layout systems for print analyze an entire paragraph and find the optimum justification strategy that best satisfies every line. In problematic cases, a skilled typesetter may need to step in and adjust the line breaking manually. Compared to this approach, Web browsers are irredeemably primitive, as you can see in Figure 6-10.

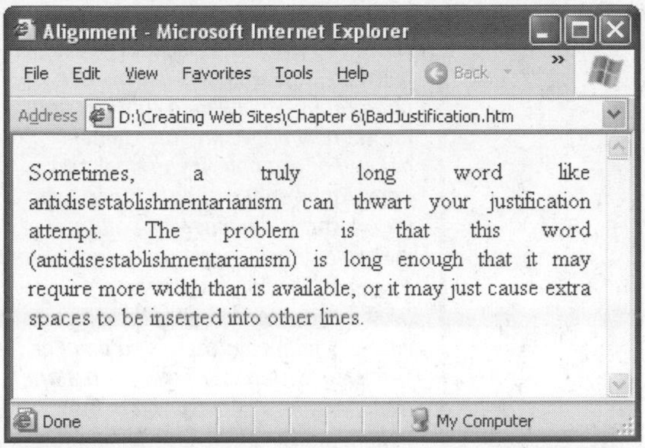

Figure 6-10:
If you decide to use full justification on a Web page, make sure you use fairly wide paragraphs. Otherwise, you'll quickly wind up with gaps and rivers of white space. Few Web sites use justification.

Spacing

To adjust the spacing around any element, use the *margin* property. For example, here's a rule that adds a fixed spacing of 8 pixels to all sides of a paragraph:

```
p {
  margin: 8px;
}
```

This particular rule doesn't have much effect, because 8 pixels is the standard margin that Web browsers apply around block elements on all sides. The 8-pixel margin ensures a basic bit of breathing space. However, if you want to create dense pages of information, this space allowance can be a bit too generous. Therefore, many Web site developers look for ways to slim down the margins a little bit.

One common trick is to close the gap between headings and the text that follows them. Here's an example that puts this into action using inline styles:

```
<h2 style="margin-bottom: 0px">This heading has no bottom margin</h2>
<p style="margin-top: 0px">This paragraph has no top margin.</p>
```

You'll notice that this style rule uses the more targeted *margin-top* and *margin-bottom* properties to home in on just one margin. You can also use *margin-left* and *margin-right* to set side margins. Figure 6-11 compares some different margin choices.

If you're daring, you can even use *negative* margins. Taken to its extreme, this can cause two elements to overlap. However, a better approach for overlapping elements is absolute positioning, a style trick you'll pick up on page 253.

Note: Unlike most other CSS properties, margin settings are never inherited. That means if you change the margins of one element, other elements inside that element aren't affected.

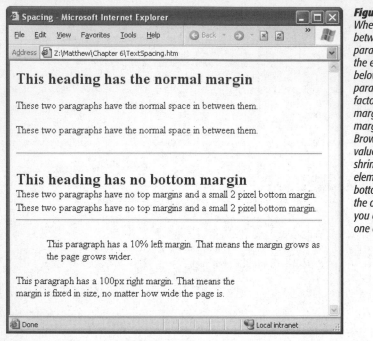

Figure 6-11:
When you want to change the spacing between page elements like headers and paragraphs, you need to consider both the element above and the element below. For example, if you stack two paragraphs on top of each other, two factors come into play—the bottom margin of the top paragraph, and the top margin of the bottom paragraph. Browsers use the larger of these two values. That means there's no point in shrinking the top margin of the bottom element unless you also shrink the bottom margin of the top element. On the other hand, if you want more space, you only need to increase the margin of one of the two elements.

White Space

As you learned in earlier chapters, XHTML has a quirky way of dealing with spaces. If you put several blank spaces in a row, XHTML treats that first space as a single space character, and ignores the others. That makes it easy for you to write clear XHTML markup because you can add spaces wherever you like without worrying about it affecting your Web page.

You've already learned about two ways to change how browsers deal with spaces: the   character entity (page 117) and the <pre> element (page 119). You can replace both of these workarounds with the *white-space* style sheet property.

First, consider the   character entity. It has two purposes—it lets you insert spaces that a browser won't ignore, and it prevents the browser from wrapping a line in the middle of a company name or some other important term. Here's an example of the latter technique:

```
<p>You can trust the discretion of
Hush Hush Private Plumbers</p>
```

This works (the page displays the text *Hush Hush Private Plumbers* and doesn't wrap the company name to a second line), but it makes the markup hard to read. Here's the style-sheet equivalent with the *white-space* property set to *nowrap*:

```
<p>You can trust the discretion of
<span style="white-space: nowrap">Hush Hush Private Plumbers</span></p>
```

To make this trick work, your XHTML needs to wrap the company name in a container that applies the formatting. The <span> element (page 123) is a good choice, because it doesn't apply any formatting except what you explicitly add.

Now, consider the <pre> element, which tells a browser to pay attention to every space in the content inside. On page 119, you saw how you could use the <pre> element to give the correct spacing to an e. e. cummings poem. You can get the same effect by setting the *white-space* property of an element (say, a <div>, <span>, or <p> element) to *pre*:

```
<p style="white-space: pre">Your browser won't   ignore   these
              s   p   a   c   e   s   .</p>
```

When you use the *pre* value for the *white-space* property, the browser displays all spaces, tabs, and hard returns (the line breaks you create when you hit the Enter key). But unlike the <pre> element, the *pre* value of the *white-space* property doesn't change the text font. If you want to use a fixed-width font like Courier to space your letters and spaces proportionally, you need to add a *font-family* property (page 154).

Borders

The last group of style sheet properties you'll learn about in this chapter lets you add borders to your Web page (Figure 6-12). Borders are a great way to separate small pieces or entire blocks of content.

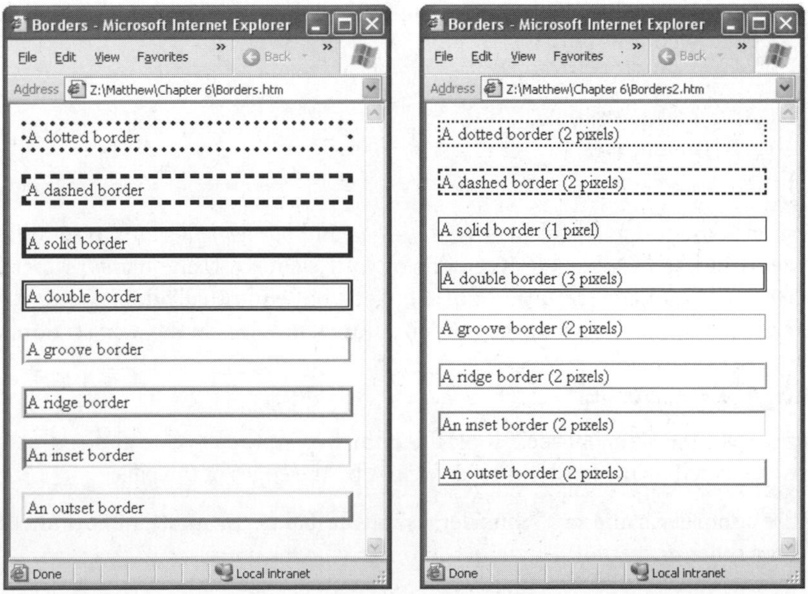

Figure 6-12:
Left: The basic border styles look a bit old-fashioned in today's sleek Web.

Right: Shrink these borders down to one or two pixels, and they blend in much better.

Table 6-4 lists the three key border properties.

Table 6-4. *Border properties*

Property	Description	Common Values	Can Be Inherited?
border-width	Sets the thickness of the border line. Usually, you'll want to pare this down.	A pixel width.	No
border-style	Browsers have eight built-in border styles. The border style determines what the border looks like.	none, dotted, dashed, solid, double, groove, ridge, inset, outset	No
border-color	The color of the border.	A color name, hexadecimal color code, or RGB value (see page 151).	No

Basic Borders

The first choice you make when you create a border is the style you want it to have. You can use a dashed or dotted line, a groove or a ridge, or just a normal thin hairline (which often looks best). Here's a rule that creates a dashed border:

```
p {
    border-style: dashed;
}
```

To make a border look respectable, you need to reduce the border width. The standard border width is almost always too clunky. You should reduce it to one or two pixels, depending on the border style:

```
p {
    border-style: dashed;
    border-width: 2px;
}
```

You can also use properties like *border-top-style* and *border-left-width* to set different styles, width, and colors for every side of your element. Using many properties at once can occasionally create an unusual effect, but you usually don't need to get this detailed. Instead, check out the border optimization tips in the next section.

Making Better Borders

In Figure 6-12 the actual borders look fine, but they're too close to the text inside the boxes formed by the borderlines, as well as by the edges of the page.

To make a border stand out, consider using the *border* property in conjunction with three other properties:

• **background-color** (page 151) applies a background color to your element. When used in conjunction with a border, it makes your element look like a floating box, much like a sidebar in a magazine article.

- **margin** (page 163) lets you set the spacing between your border box and the rest of your page. Increase the margin so that your boxes aren't crowded up against the rest of the page's content or the sides of a browser window.

- **padding** works like the *margin* property, but it sets spacing *inside* your element, between the edges of the box and the actual content within it. Increase the padding so that there's a good amount of space between a border and your box text. Figure 6-13 shows the difference between margin and padding.

Here's an example of a paragraph that looks like a shaded box:

```
p {
    background-color: #FDF5E6;
    margin: 20px;
    padding: 20px;
    border-style: solid;
    border-width: 1px;
}
```

Figure 6-13 shows how the *margin, padding,* and *background-color* properties change an ordinary paragraph into a shaded box.

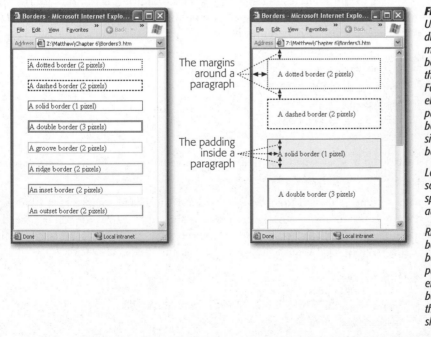

Figure 6-13:
Usually, you can't tell the difference between margins and padding, because you can't see the edges of the element. For example, a <p> element displays a paragraph in an invisible box, but you won't see its sides. When you add a border, this changes.

Left: These boxes have some extra margin spacing, but no additional padding.

Right: The result is much better when you increase both the margin and padding. For added effect, throw in a light background color (like the solid border box shown here).

Using Borders to Separate Sections

In Chapter 5 (page 119), you learned about the unremarkable <hr> element, which gives you a quick and easy way to separate one section of text from another with a horizontal line. With style sheets, you get several more ways to create attractive separators.

The first line of attack is to style the <hr> element itself. You can use the *width* property to shrink the separator horizontally. You specify width in terms of the percentage of a line's full span. For example, here's a half-width line centered on a page:

```
hr {
    width: 50%;
}
```

You can also thicken the line by using the *height* property and supplying a thickness in pixels. Here's a thick line:

```
hr {
    height: 5px;
}
```

For a variety of more interesting effects, you can bring borders into the mix. For example, here's a rule that thickens the horizontal line, applies the *double border* style, and adopts a modern light gray color:

```
hr {
    height: 3px;
    border-top-width: 3px;
    border-top-style: double;
    border-top-color: #D8D8D8;
}
```

This gives you a quick way to revitalize all your separators. However, if you aren't already using the <hr> element, you don't need to start now.

Another option is to bind the horizontal line to another element, like a heading. For example, the following <h1> element adds a grooved line at the top of a heading. The *margin* property sets the space between the line and previous element, while the padding sets the space between the line and the heading text:

```
h1 {
    margin-top: 30px;
    margin-bottom: 20px;
    padding-top: 10px;
    border-top-width: 2px;
    border-top-style: groove;
}
```

Figure 6-14 shows both of these examples.

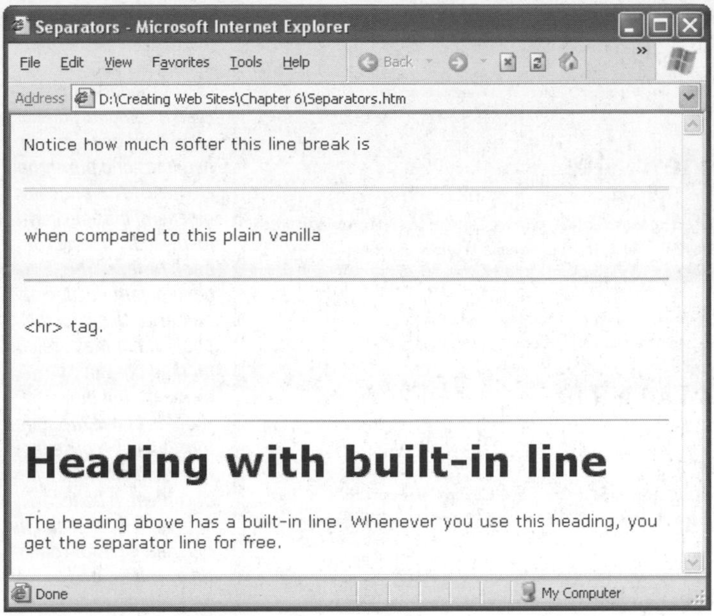

Figure 6-14:
This document includes (from top to bottom), a customized <hr> line, a normal <hr> separator, and an <h1> heading with a top border.

Class Selectors

So far, you've seen how formatting rules apply to every occurrence of a specific XHTML element (except when you use an inline style). The selectors in these universal styles are known as *type selectors*.

Type selectors are powerful, but not that flexible. Sometimes you need a little more flexibility to modify subsections or small portions of an XHTML document. Fortunately, style sheets have the perfect solution with *class selectors*.

Class selectors are one of the most practical style sheet tricks around. They let you separate your rules from your elements, and use them wherever you please. The basic idea is that you carve your Web page content into conceptual groups, or *classes*. Once you take this step, you can apply different formatting rules to each class. The trick is to choose where you want to use each class in your Web page. For example, you might have two identical <h1> headings, but assign them to unique classes so you can format each heading differently.

For a more detailed example, consider the page shown in Figure 6-15. In the following sections, you'll work with this example to apply class-based style rules.

Creating Class Rules

To use classes, you begin by mentally dividing your page into different kinds of content. In this case, it makes sense to create a specialized class for book reviews and an author byline.

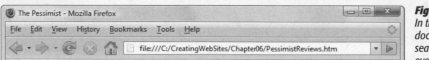

Figure 6-15:
In the average XHTML document, you have a sea of similar elements— even a complex page often boils down to just headings and paragraph elements. This page has a general introduction followed by a series of book reviews. The general introduction, the author credits, and the book summaries are all marked up with <p> elements, but they shouldn't have the same formatting because they represent different types of content. A better approach is to format the different types of content (title, author, and description) in different ways.

To create a class-specific rule, you use a two-part name, like this:

```
p.review {
   ...
}
```

The first part of the name indicates the element that the rule applies to—in this case, the paragraph element. The second part (the part after the period) is the class name. You can choose whatever class name you want, as long as you stick to letters, digits, and dashes, and make sure that the first character is always a letter.

The point of the class name is to provide a succinct description of the type of content you want to format. In this example, the class name is *review*, because you're going to apply this style to all the paragraphs that are book reviews.

Tip: Good class names describe the *function* of the class rather than its appearance. For example, *WarningNote* is a good class name, while *BoldRedArialBox* isn't. The problem with the latter is that it won't make sense if you decide to change the formatting of your warning note box (for example, giving it red lettering).

So how does a browser know when to apply a rule that uses a class selector? It turns out that browsers never apply class rules automatically. You have to add the class names in your XHTML file to the element you want formatted. Here's an example that applies the review class to a paragraph:

```
<p class="review">The actual review would go right here.</p>
```

As long as the class name in the element matches a class name in the style sheet, the browser applies the formatting. If the browser can't find a style with a matching class name, nothing happens.

Note: Class rules work *in addition* to any other rules. For example, if you create a rule for the <p> element, that rule applies to all paragraphs, including those that are part of a specialized class. However, if the class rule conflicts with any other rules, the class rule wins.

Here's the complete style sheet you might use to format the book review page:

```
/* Set the font for the whole page. */
body {
  font-family: Georgia,serif;
}

/* Set some standard margins for paragraphs. */
p
{
  margin-top: 2px;
  margin-bottom: 6px;
}

/* Format the heading with a background color. */
h1 {
  background-color: #FDF5E6;
  padding: 20px;
  text-align: center;
}

/* Make the bylines small and italicized. */
p.byline {
  font-size: 65%;
  font-style: italic;
  border-bottom-style: outset;
  border-bottom-width: 1px;
  margin-bottom: 5px;
  margin-top: 0px;
}
```

```
/* Make book reviews a little smaller, and justified. */
p.review {
  font-size: 83%;
  text-align: justify;
}

/* Make the review headings blue. */
h2.review {
  font-size: 100%;
  color: blue;
  margin-bottom: 0px;
}
```

This style sheet includes three type selector rules. The first formats the <body> element, thereby applying the same font to the whole Web page. The second gives every <p> element the same margins, and the third changes the alignment and background color of <h1> headings. Next, the style sheet defines two new paragraph classes—one for the author byline, and one for the review text. Lastly, the sheet creates a class for the review headings.

This example also introduces another feature—CSS comments. CSS comments don't look like XHTML comments. They always start with the characters /* and end with the characters */. Comments let you document what each class represents. Without comments, it's all too easy to forget what each style rule does in a complicated style sheet.

And here's the XHTML markup that uses the classes defined in the above style sheet. (To save space, most of the text is left out, but the essential structure is there.)

```
<!DOCTYPE html PUBLIC "-//W3C//DTD XHTML 1.0 Strict//EN"
"http://www.w3.org/TR/xhtml1/DTD/xhtml1-strict.dtd">

<html xmlns="http://www.w3.org/1999/xhtml">

<head>
  <link rel="stylesheet" href="PessimistReviews1.css"
  type="text/css" />
  <title>The Pessimist</title>
</head>

<body>

  <h1>The Pessimist's Review Site</h1>
  <p>...</p>
  <p>...</p>
  <h2 class="review">How To Lose Friends and Fail in Life</h2>
  <p class="byline">Chris Chu</p>
  <p class="review">...</p>
```

```
<h2 class="review">Europe 2009: Great Places to Miss</h2>
<p class="byline">Antonio Cervantes</p>
<p class="review">...</p>


</body>
</html>
```

Figure 6-16 shows the result.

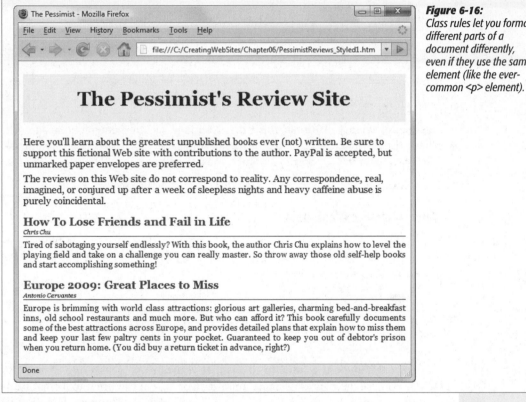

Figure 6-16:
Class rules let you format different parts of a document differently, even if they use the same element (like the ever-common <p> element).

Note: Creating style sheets is an art and takes a fair bit of practice. To make the best use of them, you need to become comfortable with class rules. Not only do class rules give you complete flexibility, they also help you think in a more logical, structured way about your Web pages.

Saving Work with the <div> Element

It can get tedious applying the class attribute to every element you want to format in your Web page. Fortunately, there's a great shortcut, courtesy of the <div> element.

You may remember the <div> element from the previous chapter (page 122). It's a block element that lets you group together arbitrary sections of your Web page.

You can group as many elements with the <div> element as you want, including headings, paragraphs, lists, and more.

Thanks to style sheet inheritance (page 148), if you apply a class name to a <div> element, inheritance automatically applies the defined style to all the nested elements. That means you can change this:

```
<p class="review">...</p>
<p class="review">...</p>
<p class="review">...</p>
```

To this:

```
<div class="review">
  <p>...</p>
  <p>...</p>
  <p>...</p>
</div>
```

Essentially, when you format this <div> element, all the paragraphs inside of it inherit that format. And although there are some style properties (like margin and padding) that don't support inheritance, most do. Figure 6-17 shows this example.

The <div> element is a great way to save loads of time. Web experts use it regularly.

More Generic Class Rules

You can also create a rule that has a class name but doesn't specify a type of element. All you need to do is leave the first part of the selector (the portion before the period) blank. Here's an example:

```
.emphasize {
  color: red;
  font-weight: bolder;
}
```

The great thing about a rule like this is that you can use it with *any* element, so long as you use the right class name. In other words, you can use it to format paragraphs, headings, lists, and more with bold, red lettering. The class name in this example reflects its more general-purpose use. Instead of indicating the type of *content*, it indicates the type of *formatting*.

Most Web designers use both element-specific class rules, and more generic class rules that don't specify an element. Although you could stick exclusively with generic rules, if you know that you'll use a certain set of formatting options only with a specific type of element, it's good to clearly indicate this fact with an element-specific class rule. That way, you won't forget the purpose of the rule when you edit your style sheet later on.

Figure 6-17:
In this example, the XHTML markup wraps each review in a <div> element. The <div> element applies a background color and some borders, separating the reviews from the rest of the page. Techniques like these can help organize dense pages with lots of information.

Note: There are still a few more advanced types of selectors you haven't considered yet. For example, you can use selectors that target certain types of elements when they appear inside another, specific element. Selectors like these are useful when you start using your style sheet mojo to create sophisticated page layouts, and you'll learn about them in Chapter 9.

Creating a Style Sheet for Your Entire Web Site

Class rules aren't just useful for separating different types of content. They're also handy if you want to define rules for your entire site in a single style sheet.

In a typical Web site, you'll have pages or groups of pages you want to format differently. For example, you might have a page with your résumé, several pages chronicling your trip to Guadeloupe, and another group of pages that make up an online photo gallery. Rather than create three style sheets, you can create a single style sheet that handles everything. The trick is to use different class names for each section. In other words, you'll create a résumé class, a trip diary class, and a photo gallery class. Here's a basic outline of this approach:

```
/* Used for the resume pages. */
p.resume { ... }
h1.resume { ... }
h2.resume { ... }
...
/* Used for the trip diary pages. */
p.trip { ... }
h1.trip { ... }
h2.trip { ... }
...
/* Used for the online photo gallery. */
p.gallery { ... }
h1.gallery { ... }
h2.gallery { ... }
...
```

Obviously, each page will use only a few of these rules. However, it's often easier to maintain your site when you keep your styles together in one place.

Adding Graphics

It's safe to say that the creators of the Internet never imagined it would look the way it does today—thick with pictures, ads, and animated graphics. They designed a meeting place for leading academic minds; we ended up with something closer to a Sri Lankan bazaar. But no one's complaining, because the Web would be an awfully drab place without graphics.

In this chapter, you'll master the art of Web images. You'll learn how to add graphics to a Web page and to position them perfectly. You'll also consider what it takes to prepare pictures for the Web—or to find good alternatives online.

Understanding Images

To understand how images work on the Web, you need to know two things:

- They don't reside in your XHTML files. Instead, you store each one as a separate file.

- To display pictures on a page, you use the <img> element in your XHTML document.

You'll use images throughout your site, even in spots where you might think ordinary text would work just fine (see Figure 7-1).

Tip: If you can't tell whether a piece of content on a page is a graphic, try right-clicking it. If it's an image, browsers like Internet Explorer and Firefox give you a Save Picture As option in a pop-up menu.

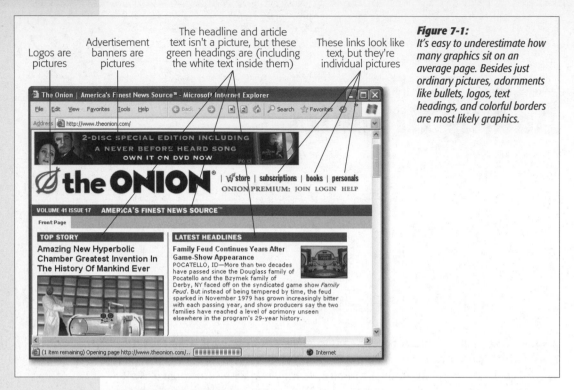

Logos are pictures

Advertisement banners are pictures

The headline and article text isn't a picture, but these green headings are (including the white text inside them)

These links look like text, but they're individual pictures

Figure 7-1:
It's easy to underestimate how many graphics sit on an average page. Besides just ordinary pictures, adornments like bullets, logos, text headings, and colorful borders are most likely graphics.

The <img> Element

Pictures appear on your Web pages courtesy of the <img> element, which tells a browser where to find them. For example, here's an <img> element that displays the file named *photo01.jpg*:

```
<img src="photo01.jpg" />
```

Pictures are standalone elements (page 33), which means you don't need to include separate start and end tags in the element. Instead, you include the slash (/) character at the end of the tag, just before the closing angle bracket.

Pictures are also inline elements (page 46), which means you put them *inside* other block elements, like paragraphs:

```
<p><img src="photo01.jpg" /></p>
```

When a browser reads this <img> element, it sends out a request for the *photo01.jpg* file. Once it retrieves it, the browser inserts the file into the Web page where you put the <img> element. If the image file is large or the Internet connection is slow, you might actually see this two-stage process take place, because smaller page components, like text, will appear before the image does.

Tip: You'll usually want to organize your site's many files by putting images in a subfolder of the folder
that holds your Web pages. You'll learn how to do this in Chapter 8.

Although it may seem surprising, the <img> element is the only piece of XHTML you
need to display a picture. But to get the results you want, you need to understand a
few more issues, including how to use alternate text, modify the size of your images,
choose a file format, and align your images with other content on a page.

Alternate Text

Although a browser can display an <img> element as long as it has a *src* attribute,
the rules of XHTML demand a little more. Technically, you also need to provide
an *alt* attribute, which represents the alternate text a browser displays if it can't display the image itself. Here's an example:

```
<img src="photo01.jpg"
  alt="There's no picture, so all you get is this alternate text." />
```

Alternate text proves useful not only in the above circumstance, but in several
other cases as well, like when:

- A browser doesn't support images (this is understandably rare these days).

- A Web visitor switches off his browser's ability to display pictures to save time
  (this isn't terribly common today, either).

- A browser requests a picture, but can't find it. (Perhaps you forgot to copy it to
  your Web server?)

- The visitor is viewing-impaired and uses a *screen-reading* program (a program
  that "speaks" text, including the words in an alt tag).

- A search engine (like Google) analyzes a page and all its content so it can index
  the content in a search catalog.

The last two reasons are the most important. Web experts always use meaningful
text when they write alt descriptions to ensure that screen readers and search
engines interpret the corresponding pictures correctly.

These days, many sites use alternate text for a completely different purpose—as a
pop-up message that appears when you move your mouse over a picture (see
Figure 7-2). The message might caption the picture rather than describe it, or it
might be a humorous remark.

This behavior is a little controversial, because it defeats the true purpose of alternate text. If you want non-descriptive pop-up text like that shown in Figure 7-2,
there's a better solution: the *title* attribute. After all, XHTML's creators designed
the title attribute exclusively for this purpose. Here's an example:

```
<img src="bullhero.jpg" alt="A flying bull-headed superhero."
  title="A flying bull-headed superhero." />
```

CHAPTER 7: ADDING GRAPHICS

If you specify a title attribute, browsers use it as the pop-up text. But if you *don't* specify one, different browsers react differently. Internet Explorer uses the alt text instead. Firefox uses the correct approach, and doesn't show any pop-up text at all.

Figure 7-2:
Left: For this <img> element to work, you have to put the file it points to in the same folder as the Web page. Otherwise, you'll see the dreaded broken image link icon.

Middle: The alternate text helps a bit–use it to explain what your visitor should have seen.

Right: In many browsers, if you don't specify a title, the alternate text becomes pop-up text if the picture appears, which can be confusing.

Picture Size

When you start thinking about the size of your images, remember that the word *size* has two possible meanings: it can refer to the dimensions of the picture (how much screen space it takes up on a Web page), or it can signify the picture's file size (the number of bytes required to store it). To Web page creators, both measures are important.

Picture dimensions are noteworthy because they determine how much screen real estate an image occupies. Web graphics are measured in units called pixels. A pixel represents one tiny dot on a PC screen (see the discussion on page 232). Fixed units like inches and centimeters aren't useful in the Web world because you never know how large your visitor's monitor is, and therefore how many pixels it can cram in. (Page 230 has a detailed discussion of screen size and how to design your pages to satisfy the largest number of potential viewers.)

File size is also important because it determines how long it takes to send a picture over the Internet to a browser. Large pictures can slow down a Web site significantly, especially if you have multiple pictures on a page and your visitor is struggling with a slow Internet connection. If you're not careful, impatient people might give up and go somewhere else. (To understand file size and how you can control it, you need to understand the different image file formats Web browsers use, a topic discussed in the next section.)

Interestingly, the <img> element lets you resize a picture through its optional height and width attributes. Consider this element:

```
<img src="photo01.jpg" alt="An explicitly sized picture" width="100"
height="150" />
```

In this line of code, you give the picture a width of 100 pixels and a height of 150 pixels. If this doesn't match the real dimensions of your source picture, browsers stretch and otherwise mangle the image until it fits the size you set (see Figure 7-3).

Figure 7-3:
Never use the height and width attributes to resize a picture, because the results are almost always unsatisfying. Enlarged pictures are jagged, shrunken pictures are blurry, and if you change the ratio of height to width (as with the top-right and bottom images shown here), browsers squash pictures out of their normal proportions.

Note: Approach height and width attributes with extreme caution. Sometimes, novice Web authors use them to make *thumbnails*, small versions of large pictures. But using the height and width attributes to scale down a large picture comes with a performance penalty—namely, the browser still needs to download the original, larger image, even though it displays it at a smaller size. On the other hand, if you create thumbnails in a graphics editor like Photoshop, you can save them with smaller file sizes, ensuring that your pages download much speedier.

Many Web page designers leave out image height and width attributes. However, experienced Web developers sometimes add them using the *same* dimensions as the actual picture. As odd as this sounds, there are a couple of good reasons to do so.

First, when you include image size attributes, browsers know how large a picture is and can start laying out a page even as the graphic downloads (see Figure 7-2, left). On the other hand, if you don't include the height and width attributes, the browser won't know the dimensions of the picture until it's fully downloaded, at which point it has to rearrange the content. This is potentially distracting if your visitors have slow connections and they've already started reading the page.

The second reason to use size attributes is because they control the size of the picture box. If a browser can't download an unsized image for some reason, it displays a picture box just big enough to show a tiny error icon and any alternate text. In a complex Web page, that might mess up the alignment of other parts of your page.

So should you use the height and width attributes? It's up to you, but they're probably more trouble than they're worth for the average Web site. If you use them, you need to make sure to update them if you change the size of your picture, which quickly gets tedious.

Note: Many XHTML editors, like Expression Web, automatically add the height and width attributes when you insert a picture.

File Formats for Graphics

Browsers can't display every type of image. In fact, they're limited to just a few image formats, including:

- **GIF** (pronounced "jif" or "gif") format is suitable for graphics with a very small number of colors (like simple logos or clip art). It gives terrible results if you use it to display photos.

- **JPEG** (pronounced "jay-peg") format is suitable for photos that can tolerate some loss of quality. (As you'll learn in a moment, the JPEG format shrinks down, or compresses, an image's file size so that it downloads more quickly.) JPEG doesn't work well if your picture contains text or line art.

- **PNG** (pronounced "ping") format is suitable for all kinds of images, but old browsers don't support it, and it doesn't always compress as well as JPEG.

All of these formats are known as bitmap or *raster* graphics, because they represent pictures as a grid of dots. Browsers don't support *vector* graphics, which represent pictures as mathematically rendered shapes.

Raster graphics generally have much larger file sizes than vector graphics. For that reason, Web designers spend a lot of time worrying about *compression*—reducing the amount of disk space an image takes up. Web page graphics use two types of compression: *lossy*, which compresses files to a greater degree than its alternative but also reduces image quality; and *lossless*, which preserves image quality but doesn't compress as much. For full details, see the box on page 187. Table 7-1 gives you a quick overview of the different image formats.

Table 7-1. *Image file formats for the Web*

Format	Type of Compression	Maximum Colors	Best Suited For:
GIF	Lossless	8-bit color (256 colors)	Logos, graphical text, and diagrams with line art
JPEG	Lossy	24-bit (16.7 million colors)	Photos
PNG-8	Lossless	8-bit color (256 colors)	Rarely used, since it's similar to GIF but with less browser support
PNG-24	Lossless	24-bit (16.7 million colors)	Images that would normally be GIF files, but need more colors

---

Tip: Some browsers give you a few more options, but you're better off steering away from them to ensure widest browser compatibility. For example, Internet Explorer supports bitmaps (image files that end with the .bmp file name extension). Don't ever use them—not only will they confuse other browsers, they're also ridiculously large because they don't support compression.

You'll probably end up using different file formats throughout your site, depending on what kind of image you want to display (photo, illustration, graphical text, and so on). Each format occupies its own niche (see Figure 7-4). The following sections help you decide when to use each format.

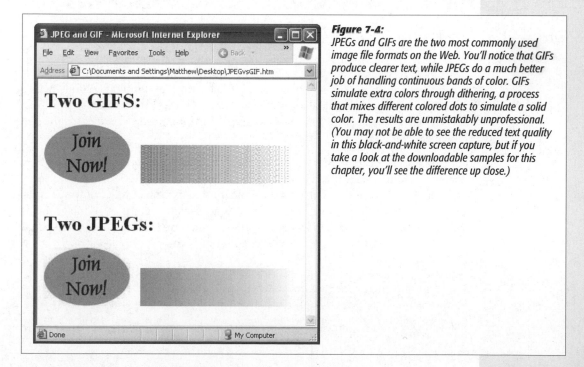

Figure 7-4:
JPEGs and GIFs are the two most commonly used image file formats on the Web. You'll notice that GIFs produce clearer text, while JPEGs do a much better job of handling continuous bands of color. GIFs simulate extra colors through dithering, a process that mixes different colored dots to simulate a solid color. The results are unmistakably unprofessional. (You may not be able to see the reduced text quality in this black-and-white screen capture, but if you take a look at the downloadable samples for this chapter, you'll see the difference up close.)

Typical File Sizes for Images

How much disk space does a typical picture occupy?

There's no single answer to this question, because it depends on several factors, including the dimensions of the picture, the file format you use, the amount of compression you apply, and how well the picture responds to compression techniques. However, here are a few basic things to keep in mind.

The file size of a typical Web site logo is vanishingly small. Amazon's small logo (about 150 × 50 pixels) has a file size of a paltry 2 kilobytes (KB), less than the size of most other site logos. Google's signature logo banner clocks in nearly as tiny, at 10 KB. Both are GIF files.

A picture can take up much more disk space. A small news picture in an article on the *New York Times* Web site rarely uses more than 20 KB. A typical eBayer includes a picture of her product that's 30 KB to 150 KB. At this size, the picture usually takes up a larger portion of your browser window. However, that's nothing compared to the size the picture would be if you weren't using compression. For example, even a low-end 1-megapixel camera can take a raw, uncompressed picture of about 3,000 KB. In a Web page, you might compress this to 300 KB or less by using the JPEG file format with a lower quality level.

Of course, the important number is how long it takes a Web visitor to download a page that has a picture in it. Obviously, this depends on the speed of the visitor's Internet connection—a broadband connection won't blink while grabbing a huge graphic, while someone with a dial-up modem can only get about 5 KB each second, meaning it takes about 20 seconds to see all of a 100 KB eBay photo. In Internet time, 20 seconds is a lifetime.

The best advice for keeping your pictures small is to crop them to the right dimensions, use the right image format, and try lowering the quality level of JPEGs to get better compression.

Compression

In Web graphics, space is a key concern. You may have tons of storage space on your Web server, but large files take more time to send across the Internet, which means your visitors will experience some frustrating, toe-tapping seconds before your page appears. To make a graphics-heavy Web site run smoothly—and these days, what Web site *doesn't* have lots of graphics?—you need to pare down the size of your pictures.

Of course, it's not quite that simple. JPEGs give you the best compression, but they throw out some image detail in the process (see the box on page 187). As you compress a JPEG image, you introduce various problems collectively known as *compression artifacts*. The most common artifacts are blocky regions of an image, halos around edges, and a general blurriness. Some pictures exhibit these flaws more than others, depending on the image's amount of detail.

Tip: Most graphics programs let you choose how much you compress a picture, and many even let you preview the result before you save anything.

Figure 7-5 shows the effect of compression settings on a small section of a picture of a church.

100% Quality, 984 KB

75% Quality, 298 KB

50% Quality, 247 KB

15% Quality, 231 KB

Figure 7-5:
Compression can work—up to a point. In this example, cutting the quality factor from 100 percent to 75 percent shaves the file size of the picture to one-third without compromising its appearance. Reducing the quality further doesn't save much more disk space, and introduces a raft of compression artifacts. Note that the file sizes listed are for the whole picture, which is much bigger than the small portion shown here.

UP TO SPEED

How Compression Works in JPEG, GIF, and PNG Files

All three of the common Web image formats use *compression* to shrink picture information. However, the type of compression you get with each format differs significantly.

The GIF and PNG formats support *lossless compression*, which means there's no *loss* of any information from your picture. Lossless compression uses a variety of techniques to perform its space-shrinking magic—for example, it might find a repeating pattern in the file, and replace each occurrence of it with a short abbreviation. When the browser decompresses your file, it gets all the original image data back.

The JPEG format uses *lossy compression*, which means that some information about your picture is discarded, or *lost*. As a result, your picture's quality diminishes, and there's no way to get it back to its original tip-top shape. However, the JPEG format is crafty, and it tries to trick your eye by discarding information that doesn't harm the picture that much. For example, it might convert slightly different colors to the same color, or replace fine details with smoothed-out blobs, because the human eye isn't that sensitive to small changes in color and shape. Usually, the overall result is a picture that looks softer and (depending how much compression you use) more blurry. On the other hand, the size-shrinking results you get with lossy compression are more dramatic than those offered by lossless compression.

Choosing the right image format

It's important to learn which format to use for a given task. To help you decide, walk through the following series of questions.

Is your picture a hefty photo or does it have fine gradations of color?

> **YES:** JPEG is the best choice for cutting large, finely detailed pictures down to size. Depending on the graphics program you use, you may be able to choose how much compression you want to apply.

Does your picture have sharp edges, text, or does it contain clip art images? Does it use 256 colors or less?

> **YES:** GIF is your format—it compresses pictures without creating blurred edges around text and shapes (the way JPEG files often do). However, keep a watch on your file size, because GIFs don't compress as well as JPEGs.

Does your picture have sharp edges and need more than 256 colors?

> **YES:** PNG is the best answer here. It supports full color, gives you lossless compression, and you don't lose any detail. However, there are two caveats. First, old browsers don't support some PNG features (like semi-transparency). Second, PNG files can sometimes end up being bigger than they should be. The problem is that even though PNG offers good compression, not all graphics programs take advantage of it. So check your file sizes to make sure you aren't getting a raw deal.

Does your picture include a transparent area?

> **YES:** Use GIF. Although PNG supports transparency (and even goes further, with support for partially transparent areas), support for this feature is sketchy in many browsers. But think twice before you use transparency—the next section explains the problems you'll face.

Putting Pictures on Colored Backgrounds

Graphics editing programs always store image files as rectangles, even when the image itself isn't rectangular. For example, if you create a smiley face graphic, your editing program saves that round illustration on a white, rectangular background.

If your page background is white as well, this doesn't pose a problem because the image background blends in with the rest of your page. But if your page has a different background color (page 150), you'll run into the graphical clunkiness shown in Figure 7-6.

Web designers came up with two solutions to this problem. One nifty idea is to use transparency, a feature that GIF graphics support (as do PNG graphics, but not all browsers support PNG transparency). The basic idea is that your graphic contains *transparent pixels*—pixels that don't have any color at all. When a browser comes across these, it doesn't paint anything. Instead, it lets the background of the page show through. To make part of an image see-through, you define a transparent color using your graphics program. In the example above, for instance, you'd set the white background of your smiley face graphic as the transparent color.

UP TO SPEED

Graphics Programs

It's up to you to choose the format for your image files. Most good graphics programs (like Macromedia Fireworks and Adobe Photoshop) save your documents in a specialized file format that lets you perform advanced editing procedures. Photoshop, for example, saves files in the .psd format. When you're ready to put your picture on a Web page, you save a copy of the .psd file in a *different* format, one specially designed for the Web, like JPEG or GIF. Usually, you do so by choosing File → Save As from the program's menu (although sometimes it's something a little different, like File → Export or File → Save For Web).

As a rule of thumb, you always need at least two versions of every picture you create—a copy in the original format your graphics program uses, and a copy in the GIF, JPEG, or PNG format you use on your Web site. You need to keep the original file so you can make changes whenever necessary, and to make sure the image quality for future versions of the picture are as high as possible.

Once you choose your Web format, your graphics program gives you a number of other options that let you customize details like the compression level. At higher compression levels, your image file is smaller but of lower quality. Some really simple image editors (like the Paint program that ships with Windows) don't let you tweak these settings, so you're stuck with the program's built-in settings.

Graphics programs usually come in two basic flavors—*image editors*, which let you retouch pictures and apply funky effects to graphics, and *drawing programs*, which let you create your own illustrations by assembling shapes and text. Adobe Photoshop (and its lower-priced, less powerful sibling, Photoshop Elements), Corel PHOTO-PAINT, and Corel Paint Shop Pro are well-known image editors. Adobe Illustrator, CorelDRAW, and Macromedia FreeHand are popular drawing programs. Which type of tool you use depends on what you're trying to do. If you're editing pictures of the office party to cut out an embarrassing moment, an image editor makes sense. If you're creating a logo for your newly launched cookie company, you need a drawing program.

If you don't have the luxury of getting a professional graphics program, you can hunt for one on a shareware site like *www.download.com*. Two popular free image editors are GIMP (*www.gimp.org*), which supports all the major operating systems, and Paint.NET (*www.getpaint.net*), which is Windows only.

 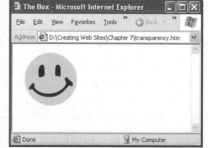

Figure 7-6:
Left: With a non-white background, the white box around your picture is glaringly obvious.

Right: But when you place the picture on a page with a white background, the smiley face blends right in.

Although transparency seems like a handy way to make sure your image always has the correct background, in practice, it rarely looks good. The problem you usually see is a jagged edge where the colored pixels of your picture end and the Web page background begins (see Figure 7-7).

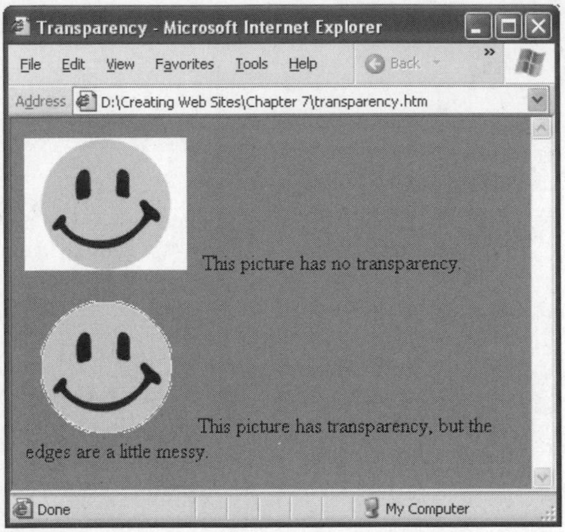

Figure 7-7:
The picture at the bottom of this page uses transparency, but the result—a jagged edge around the smiley face—is less than stellar. To smooth this edge, graphics programs use a sophisticated technique called anti-aliasing, which blends the picture color with the background color. Web browsers can't perform this feat, so the edges they make aren't nearly as smooth.

The best solution is to use the correct background color when you create your Web graphic. In other words, when you draw your smiley-face image, give it the same background color as your Web page. Your graphics program can then perform anti-aliasing, a technology that smoothes an image's jagged edges to make them look nice. That way, the image edges blend in well with the background, and when you display the image on your Web page, it fits right in.

The only limitation with this approach is its lack of flexibility. If you change your Web page color, you need to edit all your graphics. Sadly, this is the price of creating polished Web graphics.

Images and Styles

The <img> element supports a few optional attributes you can use to control an image's alignment and borders. But in the modern world, these attributes are obsolete, and you won't use them in this book. Instead, you'll learn the best way to position images—with style sheet rules.

The following sections describe your image-alignment options, and help you practice some of the style sheet smarts you picked up last chapter.

Inline Images in Text

If you don't take any extra steps, a browser inserts every image right into the flow of XHTML text. It lines up the bottom of a graphic with the baseline of the text that surrounds it, as shown in Figure 7-8. (The baseline is the imaginary line on which a line of text sits.)

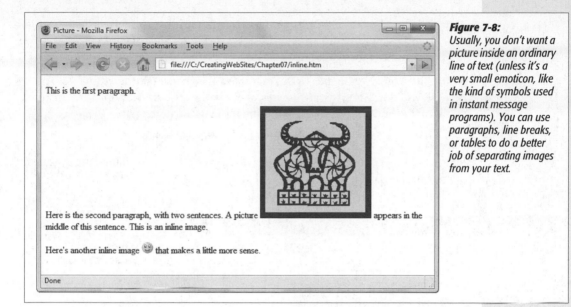

Figure 7-8:
Usually, you don't want a picture inside an ordinary line of text (unless it's a very small emoticon, like the kind of symbols used in instant message programs). You can use paragraphs, line breaks, or tables to do a better job of separating images from your text.

You can change the vertical alignment of text using the vertical-align property. Specify a value of top, middle, or bottom, depending on whether you want to line the picture up with the top, middle, or bottom of the line of text.

Here's an example of an inline style that uses the vertical-align property to line a picture up with the top of the line of text.

```
<img src="happy.gif" alt="Happy Face" style="vertical-align: top" />
```

This technique is worthwhile if you're trying to line up a very small picture, like a fancy bullet. But it doesn't work very well with large images. That's because no matter which vertical-align option you choose, only one line of text can appear alongside the picture (as you can see in Figure 7-8). If you want to create floating pictures with wrapped text, see page 192.

Borders

In Chapter 6, you considered style properties that let you add and modify borders around boxes of text. It should come as no surprise that you can use these borders just as easily around images.

For example, here's a style that applies a thin, grooved border to all sides of an image:

```
img.BorderedImage {
   border-style: groove;
   border-width: 3px;
}
```

As with all style sheet rules, you need to place the rule in an internal style sheet in the current Web page or in an external style sheet that your page uses (see page 138 for a discussion of the difference).

Notice that you give the style in this example a class name (BorderedImage). That's because you don't want your browser to apply the style to every picture. Instead, you want to choose when to apply it using the class attribute:

```
<img src="food.jpg" alt="A Meal" class="BorderedImage" />
```

Figure 7-9 shows the basic border styles. Remember, you can change the thickness of any border to get a very different look.

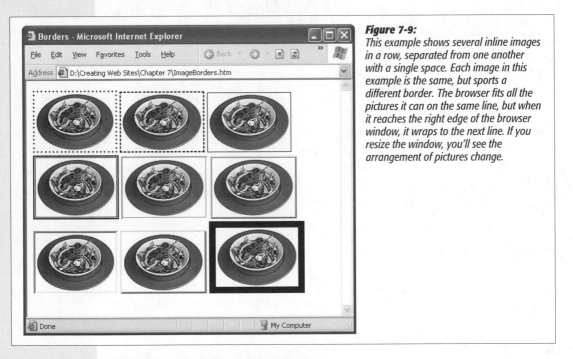

Figure 7-9:
This example shows several inline images in a row, separated from one another with a single space. Each image in this example is the same, but sports a different border. The browser fits all the pictures it can on the same line, but when it reaches the right edge of the browser window, it wraps to the next line. If you resize the window, you'll see the arrangement of pictures change.

Wrapping Text Around an Image

Using inline images is the simplest way to add pictures to your pages, but they have a downside: they pop up in the middle of text. To prevent this from happening, you can separate your pictures and text using paragraph elements (<p>), line breaks (<br />), horizontal rules (<hr>), and other divisions. You might decide, for example, to put a picture between two paragraphs of text, like this:

```
<p>This paragraph is before the picture.</p>
<p><img src="food.jpg" alt="A Meal" /></p>
<p>This paragraph is after the picture.</p>
```

Inline images are locked into place. They never move anywhere you don't expect.

Sometimes, however, you want a different effect. Instead of separating images and text, you want to put them *alongside* each other. For example, you may want your text to wrap *around* one side of a picture.

Images that have text wrapped on one side or the other are called *floating* images, because they float next to an expanse of text (see Figure 7-10). You create floating images using a CSS property named *float*. You set the value of the float property to either left or right, which lines up the image on either the left or right edge of the text.

```
img.FloatLeft {
  float: left;
}
```

Notice that this example uses a class name. You probably don't want every image on your Web page to float, so it's always a good idea to use a class name. Here's an <img> using the above class, followed by some text:

```
<p>
  <img src="food.jpg" alt="A Meal" class="FloatLeft" />
  If you place a floating image at the beginning of a paragraph,
  it floats in the top-left corner, with the text wrapped along
  the right edge.
</p>
```

When you set the float attribute, it makes sense to adjust the image's margin settings at the same time, so you have a little breathing room between your image and the surrounding text:

```
img.FloatLeft {
  float: left;
  margin: 10px;
}
```

Figure 7-10 shows several floating images.

Tip: To get floating text to work the way you want, always put the <img> element just *before* the text that should wrap around the image.

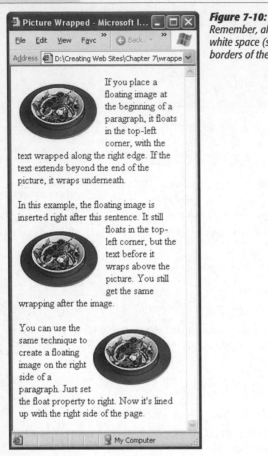

Figure 7-10:
Remember, all image files are really rectangles that include the surrounding white space (see Figure 7-6). As a result, the browser wraps text around the borders of these invisible squares.

Wrapping text can get a little tricky, because the results you get depend on the width of the browser window. For example, you might think your text is long enough to wrap around a graphic, but in a wide window that might take up just a few short lines, letting the rest of the page's content bump into your floating graphic, which isn't what you want (see Figure 7-11). To prevent this from happening, you can put your images in different containers, which is like having different cells in a table. Alternatively, you can manually stop your browser from wrapping text at any point using the *clear* property in a line break (<br />) element:

```
<br style="clear: both;" />
```

Place this line at the end of the wrapped paragraph, like so:

```
<p>
   <img src="food.jpg" alt="A Meal" class="FloatLeft" />
   Here is a paragraph with a floating image.
   <br style="clear: both;" />
</p>
```

```
<p>
  <img src="food.jpg" alt="A Meal" class="FloatLeft" />
  This should be a separate paragraph with another
  floating picture.
</p>
```

The clear property in a <br> element tells your browser to stop wrapping text, ensuring that the next paragraph starts after the floating picture (see Figure 7-11).

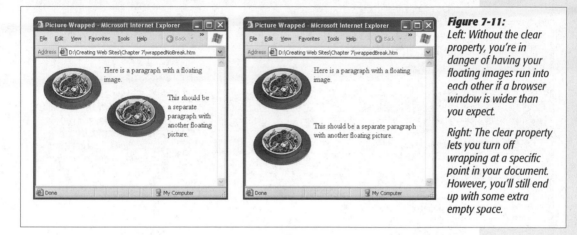

Figure 7-11:
Left: Without the clear property, you're in danger of having your floating images run into each other if a browser window is wider than you expect.

Right: The clear property lets you turn off wrapping at a specific point in your document. However, you'll still end up with some extra empty space.

Based on these examples, you might think that the *float* property sends a picture to the left or right side of a page, but that's not exactly what happens. Remember, in CSS, XHTML treats each element on a page as a container. When you create a floating image, the image actually goes to the left or right side of its container. In the previous examples, this means that the image goes to the left or right side of a paragraph, because the containing element is a paragraph.

In the example above, the paragraph took up the full width of the page. But that doesn't have to be the case. You can use style rules to put a paragraph into a padded note box to get a completely different effect.

To try this out, you need to wrap the image and the paragraph in a <div> element, like this:

```
<div class="Box">
  <p>
    <img src="food.jpg" alt="A Meal" class="FloatLeft" />
    <b>But Wait!</b> A tip box can interrupt the discussion
    to let you know just how good mixed veggies can taste.
    Of course, this tip box is really just an ordinary paragraph with
    the right border and margin style properties.
  </p>
</div>
```

You can then apply a fancy border to the <div> element through a style rule:

```
div.Box {
    margin-top: 20px;
    margin-bottom: 10px;
    margin-left: 70px;
    margin-right: 70px;
    padding: 5px;
    border-style: dotted;
    border-width: 2px
}
```

Figure 7-12 shows the result.

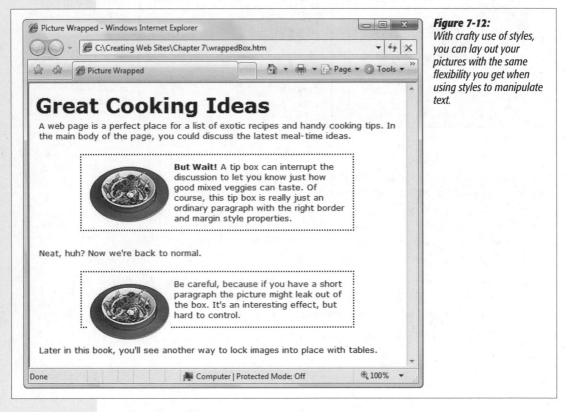

Figure 7-12:
With crafty use of styles, you can lay out your pictures with the same flexibility you get when using styles to manipulate text.

Adding Captions

Another nice touch is to caption your pictures above or below an image. You can do this easily with inline images—just put a line of text immediately above or after the picture, separated by a line break. It's not so easy with a floating image, however. In this case, you need to have your image *and* the caption float in the same way.

As it happens, the solution is quite easy. You simply take the *FloatLeft* style rule shown earlier and change the name from *img.FloatLeft* to *.FloatLeft* so you can use the rule with *any* element:

```
.FloatLeft {
  float: left;
  margin: 10px;
}
```

Next, you wrap the <img> element and your text into a <span> element. You can then make the entire <span> element float, by using the *FloatLeft* style rule:

```
<span class="FloatLeft">
    <img src="planetree.jpg" alt="Plane Tree" />
    <br />
    <i>The bark of a plane tree</i>
</span>
```

Figure 7-13 shows the result.

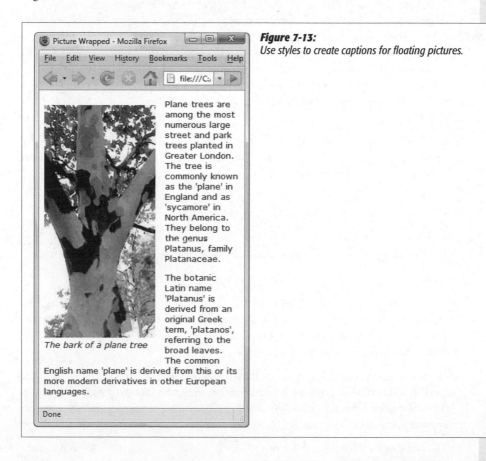

Figure 7-13:
Use styles to create captions for floating pictures.

Note: The reason you use a <span> element in this example instead of a <div> element is because you can put a <span> element *inside* other block elements, like a paragraph. In other words, by using a <span> element, you can easily put your floating picture-and-caption container inside one of your paragraphs.

Background Images

CSS makes it possible to use an image as a page background, which is a particularly handy way to create "themed" Web sites. For example, you could use light parchment paper as a background if you're developing a literary site. A *Buffy* fan site might put a dark cemetery image to good use. Some people find the effect a little distracting, but it's worth considering if you want to add a really dramatic touch and you can restrain yourself from going overboard.

Tip: Background images can make your Web site seem tacky. Be wary of using them for a résumé page or a professional business site. On the other hand, if you want to go a little kitschy, have fun!

Web designers almost always choose to *tile* background images, which means the browser copies a small picture over and over again until the image fills the window (see Figure 7-14). You can't use a single image to fill a browser window because you have no way of knowing how wide and tall to make it, given people's variable browser settings. Even if you did have visitors' exact screen measurements, you'd need to create an image so ridiculously large that it would take an impractically long time to download.

To create a tiled background, use the *background-image* style property. Your first step is to apply this property to the <body> element, so that you tile the whole page. Next, you need to provide the file name of the image using the form *url('filename')*, as shown here:

```
body {
   background-image: url('stones.jpg');
}
```

This takes the image *stones.jpg* and tiles it across a page to create your background.

Keep these points in mind when you create a tiled background:

- Make your background light, so the text displayed on top of it remains legible. (If you really have to go dark, you can use white, bold text so that it stands out. But don't do this unless you're creating a Web site for a trendy new band or you're opening a gothic clothing store.)

- Set the page's background color to match the image. For example, if you have a dark background picture with white text, make the background color black. That way, if a browser can't download the background image, visitors can still see the text.

- Use small tiles to reduce the amount of time your visitors need to wait before they can see the page.

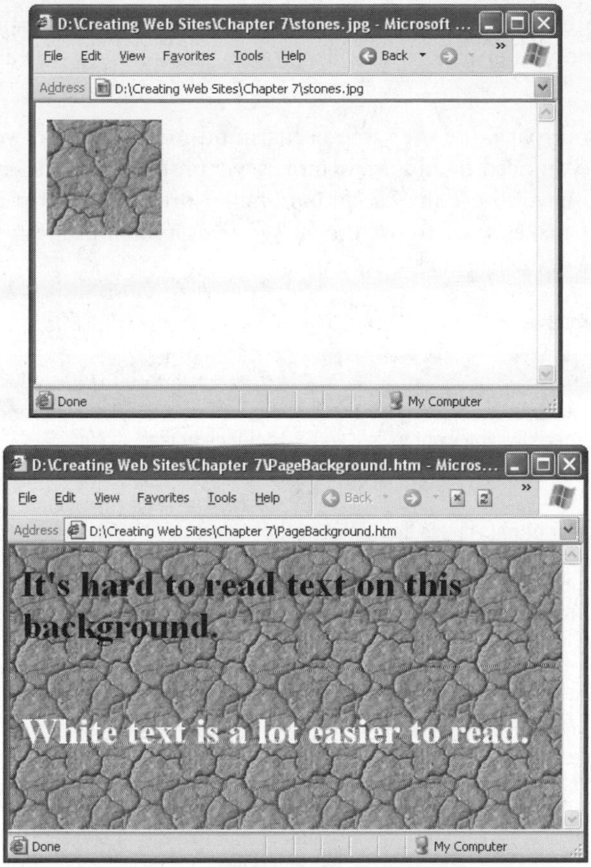

Figure 7-14:
Left: A small tile graphic with a stony pattern.

Right: Using style sheets, you can tile this graphic over the whole page. In a good tiled image, the edges line up to create the illusion of a seamless larger picture.

- If your tiled image has an irregular pattern, make sure the edges line up. The left edge should continue the right edge, and the top edge should continue the bottom edge. Otherwise, when the browser tiles your image, you'll see lines where it stitches the tiles together.

Tip: The Web is full of common background images, like stars, blue skies and clouds, fabric and stone textures, fires, dizzying geometric patterns, borders, and much more. You can find these by searching Google for "backgrounds," or head straight to top sites like *www.grsites.com/textures* (with over 5,000 backgrounds indexed by dominant color), *www.backgroundcity.com*, and *www.backgroundsarchive.com*.

Background "watermarks"

Most Web sites tile a picture to create a background image, but that's not your only option. You can also take a single image and place it at a specific position on your page. Think, for example, of a spy site whose background image faintly reads "Top Secret and Confidential."

An inconspicuous single-image background like this is called a *watermark*. (The name stems from the process used to place a translucent logo on paper saturated with water.) To make a good watermark, use a background picture that's pale and unobtrusive.

To add a watermark to your page, use the same background-image property you learned about above. But you need to add a few more style properties to the mix (see Table 7-2). First, you have to use the *background-repeat* property to turn off tiling. At the same time, it makes sense to use the *background-position* property to align your picture to a side of the page or to its center.

Table 7-2. *Background image properties*

Property	Description	Common Values	Can Be Inherited
background-image	The image file you want to use as your page background.	A URL pointing to the image file, as in *url('mypig.jpg')*.	No[a]
background-repeat	Whether or not you tile the image to fill the page; you can turn off tiling altogether, or turn it off in one dimension (so that images tile vertically but not horizontally, for example).	repeat, repeat-x, repeat-y, no-repeat	No
background-position	Where you want to place the image. Use this only if you *aren't* tiling the image.	top left, top center, top right, center left, center, center right, bottom left, bottom center, bottom right	No
background-attachment	Whether you want to fix the image (or tiles) in place when the page is scrolled.	scroll, fixed	No

[a] Background pictures aren't inherited (see page 148). However, if you don't explicitly assign a background color to an element, it's given a transparent background, which means the background of the containing element will show through.

Here's an example that places a picture in the center of a Web page:

```
body {
   background-image: url('smiley.jpg');
   background-repeat: no-repeat;
   background-position: center;
}
```

Note: The center of your document isn't necessarily the center of your browser window. If you position your image in the center of a long Web page, you won't see it until you scroll down.

You can also turn off an image's ability to scroll along with the rest of a page to get the rather odd effect of an image that's fixed in place (see Figure 7-15). For example, use this style to create a background image that sits squarely in the center of a window:

```
body {
   background-image: url('smiley.gif');
   background-repeat: no-repeat;
   background-position: center;
   background-attachment: fixed;
}
```

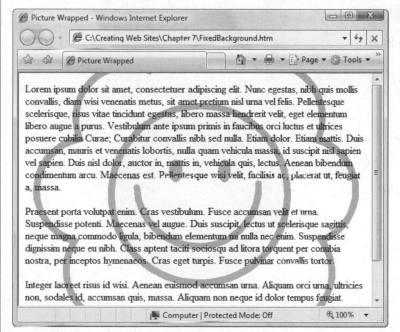

Figure 7-15:
This staring smiley face remains perpetually in the center of the window, even when you scroll up or down. It's a little creepy.

Techniques with Graphics

Now that you've mastered the <img> element, it's time to learn a few tricks of the trade. In the following sections, you'll tour three common techniques that Web developers everywhere use to create more polished pages.

Graphical Text

In Chapter 6, you learned that using exotic fonts on Web pages can be risky, since you don't know which typefaces your visitors has. Although there's no way to get around this problem when you've got large blocks of text, enterprising Web *artists* commonly put text for headings, buttons, and logos into picture files. That way, they get *complete* control of what the text looks like.

Here's a high-level look at what you do to create small pictures with text:

1. **Fire up your favorite image editor or drawing program.**

   Figure 7-16 shows an example with Adobe Illustrator.

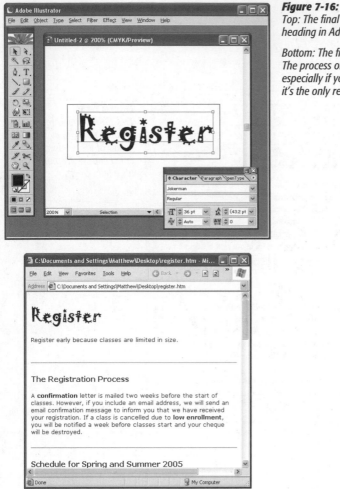

Figure 7-16:
Top: The final touches being made to a single-word heading in Adobe Illustrator.

Bottom: The final picture as it appears on a Web page. The process of creating graphical text can be tedious, especially if you have a lot of headings to generate. But it's the only reliable way to bring funky fonts to the Web.

2. **Use a background color that matches your Web page.**

   In some programs, the easiest way to fill a section with color is to draw a shape (like a rectangle), and then give it the proper fill color.

3. **Choose your font, and then type the text over the background color.**

4. **Cut your image down to size.**

   Ideally, you want to make the image as small as possible without clipping off any text.

5. Save your picture.

GIF is the best format choice, but you'll need PNG if the image has more than 256 colors. Don't use JPEG, or your text will have blurred edges.

Note: Web designers often turn graphical text into clickable buttons that take you from one page to another. You'll learn more about links in Chapter 8, and you'll find out how to make fancy graphical buttons in Chapter 15.

Backgrounds for Other Elements

You don't need to apply a background to a whole page. Instead, you can bind a background to a single paragraph or, more usefully, to a <div> element, creating the same effect as a sidebar in a magazine. Usually, you want to add a border around this element to separate it from the rest of your Web page. You might also need to change the color of the foreground text so it's legible (for example, white shows up better than black on dark backgrounds).

Here's an example of a background image you can use with any container element:

```
.pie {
  background-image: url('pie.jpg');
  margin-top: 20px;
  margin-bottom: 10px;
  margin-left: 70px;
  margin-right: 70px;
  padding: 10px;
  border-style: double;
  border-width: 3px;
  color: white;
  background-color: black;
  font-size: large;
  font-weight: bold;
  font-family: Verdana,sans-serif;
}
```

This style specifies a background image, sets the margins and borders, and chooses background and foreground colors to match.

Here's a <div> element that uses this style:

```
<div class="pie">
  <p>Hungry for some pie?</p>
</div>
```

Figure 7-17 shows the result.

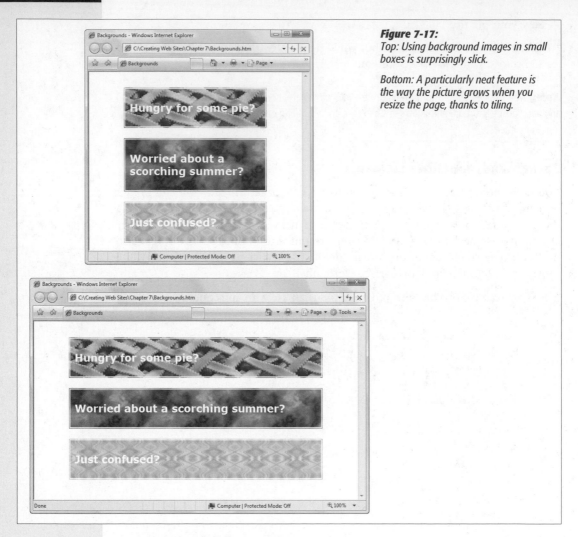

Figure 7-17:
Top: Using background images in small boxes is surprisingly slick.

Bottom: A particularly neat feature is the way the picture grows when you resize the page, thanks to tiling.

Graphical Bullets in a List

In Chapter 5, you learned how to use the <ul> element to create a bulleted list. However, you were limited to a small set of predefined bullet styles. If you look around the Web, you'll see more interesting examples of bulleted lists, including some that use tiny pictures as custom bullets.

You can add custom bullets by hand using the <img> element, but there's an easier option. You can use the *list-style-image* property to set a bullet image. Here's an example that uses a picture named 3Dball.gif:

```
ul {
    list-style-image: url('3Dball.gif');
}
```

Once you create this style rule and put it in your style sheet, your browser automatically applies it to an ordinary bulleted list like this one:

```
<ul>
  <li>Are hard to miss</li>
  <li>Help compensate for feelings of inadequacy</li>
  <li>Look so darned cool</li>
  <li>Remind people of boring PowerPoint presentations</li>
</ul>
```

Figure 7-18 shows the result.

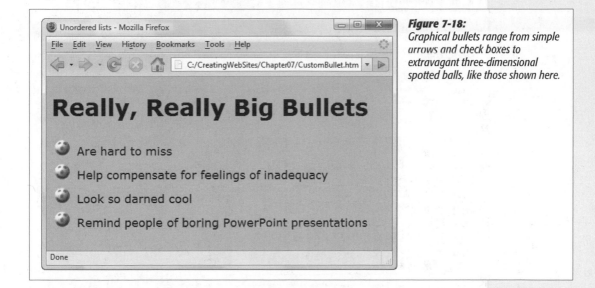

Figure 7-18:
Graphical bullets range from simple arrows and check boxes to extravagant three-dimensional spotted balls, like those shown here.

Finding Free Art

The Web is awash in graphics. In fact, finding a Web page that isn't chock full of images is about as unusual as spotting Bill Gates in a dollar store. But how do you generate all the pictures you need for a graphically rich site? Do you really need to spend hours in a drawing program fine-tuning every picture you want? The answer depends on exactly what type of pictures you need, of course, but you'll be happy to hear that the Web is a great resource for ready-to-use pictures.

It's not hard to locate pictures on the Web. In fact, you can even use a handy Google tool to search for graphics on a specific subject (type *http://images.google.com* into your browser and search away). Unfortunately, *finding* an image usually isn't good enough. To use it without worrying about a nefarious lawyer tracking you down, you also need the *rights* to use the picture. If you get lucky, a Web site owner might grant you permission to use a graphic after you send a quick email. But that's the exception rather than the rule.

Fortunately, photo enthusiasts have set up community sites where they post their pictures for the world to see—and on some of these sites, you can search for and reuse anything you want, for free. One of the most remarkable is Stock.XCHNG (pronounced "stock exchange," after *stock photography*, the name for the vast catalogues of reusable pictures that graphic designers collect). To visit Stock.XCHNG, go to *http://sxc.hu*. Figure 7-19 shows a Stock.XCHNG search in progress.

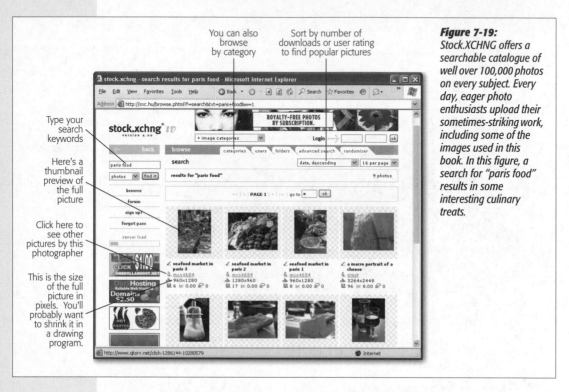

You can also browse by category

Sort by number of downloads or user rating to find popular pictures

Figure 7-19:
Stock.XCHNG offers a searchable catalogue of well over 100,000 photos on every subject. Every day, eager photo enthusiasts upload their sometimes-striking work, including some of the images used in this book. In this figure, a search for "paris food" results in some interesting culinary treats.

Type your search keywords

Here's a thumbnail preview of the full picture

Click here to see other pictures by this photographer

This is the size of the full picture in pixels. You'll probably want to shrink it in a drawing program.

If you can't find the picture you want at Stock.XCHNG, you may never find it—at least not without going to a commercial site, like iStockPhoto (*www.istockphoto. com*), Fotolia (*www.fotolia.com*), or Dreamstime (*www.dreamstime.com*), all of which charge a few dollars for royalty-free images. But if you'd like to look at some other no-pay alternatives, check out the article on finding free photographs at *www.masternewmedia.org/where_to_find_free_images_and_visuals*.

Tip: A lot of so-called "free" clip art sites are choked with ads and subscription demands. However, if you have a copy of Microsoft Office, you can download free clip art straight from the Office Online Web site. You'll need to open this clip art with a graphics program, and then save it in a Web image format (like JPEG or GIF), but it's a small price to pay for access to a large, free clip art connection. Head to *http:// office.microsoft.com/clipart* to start searching.

CHAPTER 8

Linking Pages

So far in this book, you've worked on individual Web pages. While creating a single page is a crucial first step in building a Web site, sooner or later you'll want to wire several pages together so a Web trekker can easily jump from one to the next. After all, linking is what the Web's all about.

It's astoundingly easy to create links—officially called *hyperlinks*—between pages. In fact, all it takes is a single new element: the *anchor* element. Once you master this bit of XHTML lingo, you're ready to start organizing your pages into separate folders and transforming your humble collection of standalone documents into a full-fledged site.

Understanding the Anchor

In XHTML, you use the anchor element, <a>, to create a link. When a visitor clicks that link, the browser loads another page.

The anchor element is a straightforward container element. It looks like this:

```
<a>...</a>
```

You put the content that a visitor clicks inside the anchor element:

```
<a>Click Me</a>
```

The problem with the above link is that it doesn't *point* anywhere. To turn it into a fully functioning link, you need to supply the URL of the destination page using an *href* attribute (which stands for *hypertext reference*). For example, if you want a link to take a reader to a page named *LinkedPage.htm*, you create this link:

```
<a href="LinkedPage.htm">Click Me</a>
```

For this link to work, the *LinkedPage.htm* file has to reside in the same folder as the Web page that contains the link. You'll learn how to better organize your site by sorting pages into different subfolders on page 212.

Tip: To create a link to a page in Expression Web, select the text you want to make clickable, and then hit Ctrl+K. Browse to the correct page, and Expression Web creates the link. To pull off the same trick in Dreamweaver, select the text and press Ctrl+L.

The anchor tag is an inline element (page 46)—it fits inside any other block element. That means that it's completely acceptable to make a link out of just a few words in an otherwise ordinary paragraph, like this:

```
<p>
    When you're alone and life is making you lonely<br />
    You can always go <a href="Downtown.htm">downtown</a>
</p>
```

Figure 8-1 shows this link example in action.

Figure 8-1:
If you don't take any other steps to customize an anchor element, its text appears in a browser with the familiar underline and blue lettering. When you move your mouse over a hyperlink, your mouse pointer turns into a hand. You can't tell by looking at a link whether it works or not—if the link points to a non-existing page, you'll get an error only after you click it.

Internal and External Links

Links can shuffle you from one page to another within the same Web site, or they can transport you to a completely different site on a far-off server. You use a different type of link in each case:

- **Internal links** point to other pages on your Web site. They can also point to other types of resources on your site, as you'll see below.

- **External links** point to pages (or resources) on other Web sites.

For example, say you have two files on your site, a biography page and an address page. If you want visitors to go from your bio page (*MyBio.htm*) to your address

HOW'D THEY DO THAT

Changing Link Colors with Style Sheets

Virtually everyone born since the year 1900 instinctively understands that blue underlined text is there to be clicked. But what if blue links are at odds with the overall look of your site? Thanks to style sheets, you don't need to play by the rules.

Based on what you learned about CSS in Chapter 6, you can quickly build a style sheet rule that changes the text color of all the link-producing anchor tags on your site. Here's an example:

```
a {
    color: fuchsia;
}
```

But watch out: making this change creates two problems. First, custom link colors change the way links work. Ordinarily, when you click a link, it turns purplish red to show that you've visited the page. Custom links, however, never change color—they retain their hue even after you click them. Web visitors who depend on the blue-to-red reminder may not appreciate your artistic flair. Second, if you apply a rule to all anchor tags, that rule will affect any bookmarks in your page. Ordinarily, bookmarks are invisible page markers (see page 221), but if you change the anchor color, your bookmarked text will also change color. This probably isn't the behavior you want.

A better way to create colorful links is to use another style sheet trick: *pseudo-selectors*. Pseudo-selectors are specialized versions of the selectors you learned about earlier. They rely on details that a browser tracks behind the scenes. For example, ordinary selectors apply rules indiscriminately to a given element, like an anchor tag. But pseudo-selectors apply rules to elements that meet certain criteria, in this case to links that are either clicked or unclicked.

Pseudo-selectors are a mid-range CSS feature, which means they don't work on very old browsers like Internet Explorer 4 and Netscape 4.

Four pseudo-selectors help you format links. They are *:link* (for links that point to virgin ground), *:visited* (for links a reader has already visited), *:active* (the color a link turns as a reader clicks it, before releasing the mouse button), and *:hover* (the color a link turns when a reader moves the mouse over it). As you can see, pseudo-selectors always start with a colon (:).

Here's a style rule that uses pseudo-selectors to create a misleading page—one where visited links are blue and unvisited links are red:

```
a:link {
  color: red;
}
a:visited {
  color: blue;
}
```

If you want to apply these rules to some, but not all, your links, you can use a class name with the pseudo-selector rule:

```
a.BackwardLink:link {
  color: red;
}
a.BackwardLink:visited {
  color: blue;
}
```

Now an anchor element needs to specify the class name to display your new style, as shown here:

```
<a class="BackwardLink" href="...">...</a>
```

page (*ContactMe.htm*), you create an internal link. Whether you store both files in the same folder or in different folders, they're part of the same Web site on the same Web server, so an internal link's the way to go.

On the other hand, if you want visitors to go from your Favorite Books page (*FavBooks.htm*) to a page on Amazon.com (*www.amazon.com*), you need an external link. Clicking an external link transports the reader out of your Web site and on to a new site, located elsewhere on the Web.

When you create an internal link, you should always use a *relative URL*, which tells browsers the location of the target page *relative to the current folder*. In other words, it gives your browser instructions on how to find the new folder by telling it to move down into or up from the current folder. (Moving *down into* a folder means moving from the current folder into a subfolder. Moving *up from* a folder is the reverse—you travel from a subfolder up into the parent folder, the one that *contains* the current subfolder.)

All the examples you've seen so far use relative URLs. For example, imagine you go to this page:

```
http://www.GothicGardenCenter.com/Sales/Products.htm
```

Say the text on the *Products.htm* page includes a sentence with this relative link to *Flowers.htm*:

```
Would you like to learn more about our purple
<a href="Flowers.htm">hydrangeas</a>?
```

If you click this link, your browser automatically assumes that you stored *Flowers. htm* in the same location as *Products.htm*, and, behind the scenes, it fills in the rest of the URL. That means the browser actually requests this page:

```
http://www.GothicGardenCenter.com/Sales/Flowers.htm
```

XHTML gives you another linking option, called an *absolute URL*, which defines a URL in its entirety, including the domain name, folder, and page. If you convert the URL above to an absolute URL, it looks like this:

```
Would you like to learn more about our purple <a href=
"http://www.GothicGardenCenter.com/Sales/Flowers.htm">hydrangeas</a>?
```

So which approach should you use? Deciding is easy. There are exactly two rules to keep in mind:

• **If you're creating an external link, you *have to* use an absolute URL.** In this situation, a relative URL just won't work. For example, imagine you want to link to the page *home.html* on Amazon's Web site. If you create a relative link, the browser assumes that *home.html* refers to a file of that name on *your* Web site. Clicking the link won't take your visitors where you want them to go (and may not take them anywhere at all, if you don't have a file named *home.html* on your site).

• **If you're creating an internal link, you really, really should use a relative URL.** Technically, either type of link works for internal pages. But relative URLs have several advantages. First, they're shorter and make your XHTML more readable and easier to maintain. More importantly, relative links are flexible. You can rearrange your Web site, put all your files into a different folder, or even change your site's domain name without breaking relative links.

One of the nicest parts about relative links is that you can test them on your own computer and they'll work the exact same way as they would online. For example, imagine you've developed the site *www.GothicGardenCenter.com* on your PC and you store it inside the folder *C:\MyWebSite* (that'd be *Macintosh HD/MyWebSite*, in Macintosh-ese). If you click the relative link that leads from the *Products.htm* page to the *Flowers.htm* page, the browser looks for the target page in the *C:\MyWebSite* (*Macintosh HD/MyWebSite*) folder.

Once you polish your work to perfection, you upload the site to your Web server, which has the domain name *www.GothicGardenCenter.com*. Because you used relative links, you don't need to change anything. When you click a link, the browser requests the corresponding page in *www.GothicGardenCenter.com*. If you decide to buy a new, shorter domain name like *www.GGC.com* and move your Web site there, the links still keep on working.

Note: Internet Explorer has a security quirk that appears when you test pages with external links. If you load a page from your hard drive, and then click a link that points somewhere out on the big bad Web, Internet Explorer opens a completely new window to display the target page. That's because the security rules that govern Web pages on your hard drive are looser than those that restrict Web pages on the Internet, so Internet Explorer doesn't dare let them near each other. This quirk disappears once you upload your pages to the Web.

FREQUENTLY ASKED QUESTION

Navigating and Frames

How do I create a link that opens a page in a new browser window?

When visitors click external links, you might not want to let them get away from your site that easily. Web developers use a common trick that opens external pages in separate browser windows (or in a new tab, depending on the browser's settings). This way, your site remains open in the visitor's original window, ensuring the visitor won't forget about you.

To make this work, you need to set another attribute in the anchor element—the *target*. Here's how:

```
<a href="LinkedPage.htm" target="_blank">
Click Me</a>
```

The target attribute names the frame where a browser should display the destination page (you'll learn more about frames in Chapter 10). The value *_blank* indicates that the link should load the page in a new, empty browser window.

Before you start adding the target attribute to all your anchors, it's important to recognize two drawbacks with this technique:

- **It breaks strict validation.** The target attribute isn't allowed in XHTML 1.0 strict. If you want to use it, you should change your doctype to XHTML 1.0 transitional (page 30). Other, clumsier workarounds are possible—for example, Web designers sometimes use JavaScript (see Chapter 14) to open a new window when visitors click a link. The target feature may also reappear in a future version of CSS.

- **It may not always work.** Some vigilant *pop-up blockers* intercept this type of link and prevent the new window from appearing altogether. (Pop-up blockers are standalone programs or browser features designed to prevent annoying pop-up ads from appearing.) Internet Explorer 6 (and later) includes its own pop-up blocker, but its standard settings allow links that use the *target="_blank"* attribute.

Some people love the new-window feature, while others think it's an immensely annoying and disruptive act of Web site intervention. If you use it, apply it sparingly on the occasional link.

Relative Links and Folders

So far, all the relative link examples you've seen have assumed that both the *source page* (the one that contains the link) and the *target page* (the destination you arrive at when you click the link) are in the same folder. There's no reason to be quite this strict. In fact, your Web site will be a whole lot better organized if you store groups of related pages in *separate* folders.

Consider the Web site shown in Figure 8-2.

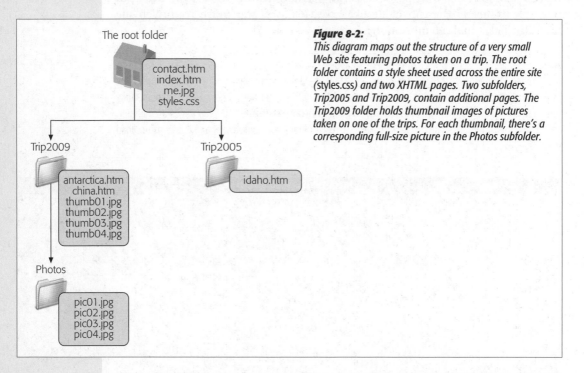

Figure 8-2:
This diagram maps out the structure of a very small Web site featuring photos taken on a trip. The root folder contains a style sheet used across the entire site (styles.css) and two XHTML pages. Two subfolders, Trip2005 and Trip2009, contain additional pages. The Trip2009 folder holds thumbnail images of pictures taken on one of the trips. For each thumbnail, there's a corresponding full-size picture in the Photos subfolder.

Note: The root folder is the starting point of your Web site—it contains all your other site files and folders. Most sites include a page with the name *index.htm* or *index.html* in the root folder. This is known as the *default page*. If a browser sends a request to your Web site domain without supplying a file name, the Web server sends back the default page. For example, requesting *www.TripToRemember.com* automatically returns the default page *www.TripToRemember.com/index.htm*.

This site uses a variety of relative links. For example, imagine you need to create a link from the *index.htm* page to the *contact.htm* page. Both pages are in the same folder, so all you need is a relative link:

```
<a href="contact.htm">About Me</a>
```

You can also create more interesting links that move from one folder to another, which you'll learn how to do in the following sections.

Tip: If you'd like to try out this sample Web site, you'll find all the site's files on the Missing CD page at *www.missingmanuals.com*. Thanks to the magic of relative links, all the links will work no matter where on your computer (PC or Mac) you save the files, so long as you keep the same subfolders.

Moving down into a subfolder

Say you want to create a relative link that jumps from an *index.htm* page to a page called *antarctica.htm*, which you've put in a folder named Trip2009. When you write the relative link that points to *antarctica.htm*, you need to include the name of the Trip2009 subfolder, like this:

```
See pictures from <a href="Trip2009/antarctica.htm">Antarctica</a>
```

This link gives the browser two instructions—first to go into the subfolder Trip2009, and then to get the page *antarctica.htm*. In the link, you separate the folder name ("Trip2009") and the file name ("antarctica.htm") with a slash character (/). Figure 8-3 shows both sides of this equation.

Interestingly, you can use relative paths in other XHTML elements, too, like the <style> element and the <img> element. For example, imagine you want to display the picture *photo01.jpg* on the page *index.htm*. This picture is two subfolders away, in a folder called Photos, which is inside Trip2009. But that doesn't stop you from pointing to it in your <img> element:

```
<img src="Trip2009/Photos/photo01.jpg" alt="A polar bear" />
```

Using this technique, you can dig even deeper into subfolders of subfolders of subfolders. All you need to do is add the folder name and a slash character for each subfolder, in order.

But remember, relative links are always *relative to the current page*. If you want to display the same picture, *photo01.jpg*, in the *antarctica.htm* page, the <img> element above won't work, because the *antarctica.htm* page is actually in the Trip2009 folder. (Take a look back at Figure 8-2 if you need a visual reminder of the site structure.) From the Trip2009 folder, you only need to go down one level, so you need this link:

```
<img src="Photos/photo01.jpg" alt="A polar bear" />
```

By now, you've probably realized that the important detail lies not in how many folders you have on your site, but in how you organize the subfolders. Remember, a relative link always starts out from the *current* folder, and works it way up or down to the folder holding the target page.

Tip: Once you start using subfolders, you shouldn't change any of their names or move them around. That said, many Web page editors (like Expression Web) are crafty enough to help you out if you do make these changes. When you rearrange pages or rename folders inside these programs, they adjust your relative links. It's yet another reason to think about getting a full-featured Web page editor.

Figure 8-3:
Using a relative link, you can jump from the main index.htm page (top) to a page with picture thumbnails (bottom). Each picture is itself a link—visitors click it to see a larger-sized version of the photo.

Moving up into a parent folder

The next challenge you'll face is going *up* a folder level. To do this, use the character sequence ../ (two periods and a slash). For example, to add a link in the *antarctica. htm* page that brings the reader back to the *index.htm* page, you'd write a link that looks like this:

```
Go <a href="../index.htm">back</a>
```

And as you've probably guessed by now, you can use this command twice in a row to jump up two levels. For example, if you have a page in the Photos folder that leads to the home page, you need this link to get back there:

```
Go <a href="../../index.htm">back</a>
```

For a more interesting feat, you can combine both of these tricks to create a relative link that travels up one or more levels, and then travels down a different path. For example, you need this sort of link to jump from the *antarctica.htm* page in the Trip2009 folder to the *idaho.htm* page in the Trip2005 folder:

```
See what happened in <a href="../Trip2005/idaho.htm">Idaho</a>
```

This link moves up one level to the root folder, and then back down one level to the Trip2005 folder. You follow the same process when you browse folders to find files on your computer.

Moving to the root folder

The only problem with the relative links you've seen so far is that they're difficult to maintain if you ever reorganize your Web site. For example, imagine you have a Web page in the root directory of your site. Say you want to feature an image on that page that's stored in the *images* subfolder. You use this link:

```
<img src="images/flower.gif" alt="A flower" />
```

But then, a little later on, you decide your Web page really belongs in *another* spot—a subfolder named Plant—so you move it there. The problem is that this relative link now points to *plant/images/flower.gif*, which doesn't exist—the Images folder isn't a subfolder in Plants, it's a subfolder in your site's root folder. As a result, your browser displays a broken link icon.

There are a few possible workarounds. In programs like Expression Web, when you drag a file to a new location, the XHTML editor updates all the relative links automatically, saving you the hassle. Another approach is to try to keep related files in the same folder, so you always move them as a unit. However, there's a third approach, called *root-relative* links.

So far, the relative links you've seen have been *document-relative*, because you specify the location of the target page relative to the current document. *Root-relative* links point to a target page *relative to your Web site's root folder*.

Root-relative links always start with the slash (/) character (which indicates the root folder). Here's the <img> element for *flower.gif* with a root-relative link:

```
<img src="/images/flower.gif" alt="A flower" />
```

The remarkable thing about this link is that it works no matter where you put the Web page that contains it. For example, if you copy this page to the Plant subfolder, the link still works, because the first slash tells your browser to start at the root folder.

The only trick to using root-relative folders is that you need to keep the real root of your Web site in mind. When using a root-relative link, the browser follows a simple procedure to figure out where to go. First, it strips all the path and file name information out of the current page address, so that only the domain name is left.

Then it adds the root-relative link to the end of the domain name. So if the link to *flower.gif* appears on this page:

```
http://www.jumboplants.com/horticulture/plants/annuals.htm
```

The browser strips away the */horticulture/plants/annuals.htm* portion, adds the relative link you supplied in the *src* attribute (*/images/flower.gif*), and looks for the picture here:

```
http://www.jumboplants.com/images/flower.gif
```

This makes perfect sense. But consider what happens if you don't have your own domain name. In this case, your pages are probably stuck in a subfolder on another Web server. Here's an example:

```
http://www.superISP.com/~user9212/horticulture/plants/annuals.htm
```

In this case, the domain name part of the URL is *http://www.superISP.com*, but for all practical purposes, the root of your Web site is your personal folder, *~user9212*. That means you need to add this detail into all your root-relative links. So to get the result you want with the *flower.gif* picture, you need to use this messier root-relative link:

```
<img src="/~user9212/images/flower.gif" alt="A flower" />
```

Now the browser keeps just the domain name part of the URL (*http://www. superISP.com*) and adds the relative part of the path, starting with your personal folder (*/~user9212*).

Linking to Other Types of Content

Most of the links you write will point to bona fide XHTML Web pages. But that's not your only option. You can link directly to other types of files as well. The only catch is that it's up to the browser to decide what to do when someone clicks a link that points to a different type of file.

Here are some common examples:

- **You can link to a JPEG, GIF, or PNG image file (page 184).** When visitors click a link like this, the browser displays the image in a browser window without any other content. Web sites often use this approach to let visitors take a close-up look at large graphics. For example, the Trip2009 Web site in the previous section has a page chock full of small image thumbnails. Click one of those, and the full-size image appears.

- **You can link to a specialized type of file, like a PDF file, a Microsoft Office document, or an audio file (like a WAV or an MP3 file).** When you use this technique, you're taking a bit of a risk. These links rely on a browser having a plug-in that recognizes the file type, or on your visitors having a suitable program installed on his PC. If the computer doesn't have the right software, the only thing your visitors will be able to do is download the file (see the next point), where it will sit like an inert binary blob. However, if a browser has the right plug-in, a small miracle happens. The PDF, Office, or audio file opens up right inside the browser window, as though it were a Web page!

The Rules for URLs

The rules for correctly writing a URL in an anchor element are fairly strict, and there are a few common mistakes that creep into even the best Web pages. Here are some pointers to help you avoid these headaches:

- When you create an absolute URL, you have to start it with its protocol (usually http://). You don't need to follow this rule when typing a URL into a browser, however. For example, if you type *www.google.com*, most browsers are intelligent enough to assume the http:// part. However, in an XHTML document, it's mandatory.

- Don't mix up the backslash (\) and the ordinary forward slash (/). Windows uses the backslash in file paths (like *C:\Windows\win.ini*). In the Web world, the forward slash separates subfolders (as in *http://www.ebay.com/Help/index.html*). Once again, many browsers tolerate backslash confusion, but the same mistake in an anchor element breaks your links.

- Don't ever use file paths instead of a URL. It's possible to create a URL that points to a file on your computer using the *file* protocol (as in *file:///C:/Temp/myPage.htm*). However, this link won't work on anyone else's computer, because they won't have the same file on their hard drive. Sometimes, design tools like Expression Web may insert one of these so-called local URLs (for example, if you drag and drop a picture file into your Web page). Be vigilant—check all your links to make sure this doesn't happen.

- Don't use spaces or special characters in your file or folder names, even if these special characters are allowed. For example, it's perfectly acceptable to put a space in a file name (like *My Photos.htm*), but in order to request this page, the browser needs to translate the space into a special character code (*My%20Photos.htm*). To prevent this confusion, steer clear of anything that isn't a number, letter, dash (–), or underscore (_).

- **You can link to a file you want others to download.** If a link points to a file of a specialized type and the browser doesn't have the proper plug-in, visitors get a choice: They can ignore the content altogether, open it using another program on their computer, or save it on their PC. This is a handy way to distribute large files (like a ZIP file featuring your personal philosophy of planetary motion).

- **You can create a link that starts a new email message.** It's easy to build a link that fires up your visitors' favorite email program and helps them send a message to you. Page 337 has all the details.

Image Links and Image Maps

It's worth pointing out that you can also turn images into links. The trick is to put an <img> element inside an anchor element (<a>), like this:

```
<a href="LinkedPage.htm"><img src="MyPic.gif" alt="My Picture" /></a>
```

XHTML adds a thick blue border to pictures to indicate they're clickable. Usually, you want to turn this clunky-looking border off using the style sheet border properties described on page 167. When a visitor hovers her cursor over a linked picture, the cursor changes to a hand.

In some cases, you might want to create distinct clickable regions, called hotspots, *inside* a picture. For example, consider Figure 8-4.

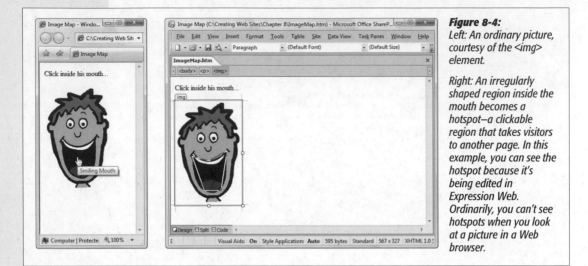

Figure 8-4:
Left: An ordinary picture, courtesy of the <img> element.

Right: An irregularly shaped region inside the mouth becomes a hotspot—a clickable region that takes visitors to another page. In this example, you can see the hotspot because it's being edited in Expression Web. Ordinarily, you can't see hotspots when you look at a picture in a Web browser.

To add a hotspot to a picture, you start by creating an *image map* using the <map> element. This part's easy—all you do is choose a unique name for your image map so you can refer to it later on:

```
<map id="FaceMap" name="FaceMap">
</map>
```

Note: If you noticed that the <map> element uses two attributes that duplicate the same information (*id* and *name*), you're correct. Although in theory just the id attribute should do the trick, you need to keep the name attribute there to ensure compatibility with a wide range of browsers.

Then you need to define each hotspot, which you do inside the <map> element, between its start and end tags. You can add as many hotspots as you want, although they shouldn't overlap. (If they do, the one that's defined first takes precedence.)

To define each hotspot in an image, you add an <area> element. The area element identifies three important details: the target page a visitor goes to after clicking the hotspot (the *href* attribute), the shape of the hotspot (the *shape* attribute), and the exact dimensions of the shape (the *cords* attribute). Much like an image, the <area> element requires an alt attribute with some alternate text that describes the image map to search engines and ancient text-only browsers.

Here's a sample <area> element:

```
<area href="MyPage.htm" shape="rect" coords="5,5,95,195" alt="A clickable
rectangle" />
```

This hotspot defines a rectangular region. When visitors click it, they go to *MyPage.htm*.

The *shape* attribute supports three types of shape, each of which corresponds to a different value for the attribute. You can use circles (*circle*), rectangles (*rect*), and multi-edged shapes (*poly*). Once you choose your shape, you need to supply the coordinates, which are a bit trickier to interpret. To understand hotspot coordinates, you first need to understand how browsers measure pictures (see Figure 8-5).

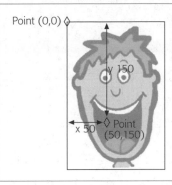

Figure 8-5:
Browsers designate the top-left corner in a picture as point (0, 0). As you move down the picture, the y-coordinate (the second number) gets bigger. For example, the point (0, 100) is at the left edge of the picture, 100 pixels from the top. As you move to the right, the x-coordinate gets bigger. That means the point (100, 0) is at the top of a picture, 100 pixels from the left edge.

You enter image map coordinates as a list of numbers separated by commas. For a circle, list the coordinates in this order: center point (x-coordinate), center point (y-coordinate), radius. For any other shape, supply the corners in order as a series of x-y coordinates, like this: x1, y1, x2, y2, and so on. For a polygon, you supply every point. For a rectangle, you only need two points—the top-left corner, and the bottom-right corner.

You define the rectangle mentioned earlier by these two points: (5, 5) at the top-left and (95, 195) at the bottom right. You define the more complex polygon that represents the mouth region in Figure 8-4 like this:

```
<area href="MyPage.htm" shape="poly" alt="Smiling Mouth"
coords="38, 122, 76, 132, 116, 110, 102, 198, 65, 197" />
```

In other words, your browser creates this shape by drawing lines between these five points: (38, 122), (76, 132), (116, 110), (102, 198), and (65, 197).

Tip: Getting coordinates correct is tricky. Many Web page editors, like Expression Web and Dreamweaver, have built-in hotspot editors that let you create an image map by dragging shapes over your picture, which is a lot easier than trying to guess the correct values. To use this tool in Dreamweaver, select a picture, and then look for the three hotspot icons (circle, square, and polygon) in the Properties panel. In Expression Web, you use similar icons in the Picture toolbar. If the Picture toolbar isn't visible, right-click the picture, and then select Show Pictures Toolbar.

Once you perfect all your hotspots, there's one step left: to apply the hotspots to the image by adding the *usemap* attribute to your <img> element. The *usemap* attribute is the same as the name of the image map, but it starts with the number-sign character (#), which tells browsers that you've defined an image map for the picture on the current page:

```
<img src="face.gif" usemap="#FaceMap" alt="Smiling Face" />
```

Here's the complete XHTML for the mouth hotspot example:

```
<!DOCTYPE html PUBLIC "-//W3C//DTD XHTML 1.0 Strict//EN"
"http://www.w3.org/TR/xhtml1/DTD/xhtml1-strict.dtd">

<html xmlns="http://www.w3.org/1999/xhtml">

<head>
  <title>Image Map</title>
  <style type="text/css">
    img {
      border-style: none;
    }
  </style>
</head>

<body>
  <p>Click inside his mouth...</p>
  <p>
    <map id="FaceMap" name="FaceMap">
      <area href="http://edcp.org/factsheets/handfoot.html" shape="poly"
      coords="38, 122, 76, 132, 116, 110, 102, 198, 65, 197" alt="Smiling
Mouth" />
    </map>
    <img src="face.gif" usemap="#FaceMap" alt="Smiling Face" />
  </p>
</body>

</html>
```

The hotspots you create are invisible (unless you draw lines on your picture to indicate where they are). When visitors hover over them, their mouse pointers change to a hand. Clicking a hotspot has the same effect as clicking an ordinary <a> link—visitors get transported to a new page.

Note: It's tempting to use image maps to create links in all kinds of graphics, including buttons you may custom-design in an image editor. Hold off for a bit. Sophisticated Web sites like yours can go many steps further with menus and buttons, but to implement these nifty tricks you need the JavaScript know-how you'll learn in Chapters 14 and 15.

Adding Bookmarks

Most links lead from one page to another. When you make the jump to a new page, the browser plunks you down at the very top of the page. But you can also create links to specific parts of a page. This is particularly useful if you create long, scrolling pages and you want to direct your visitors' attention to a particular passage.

You can create links to another position on the *current* page (see Figure 8-6), or to a specific place in *another* Web page. The place you send your reader is technically called a *fragment*.

Creating a link that points to a fragment is a two-step process. First, you need to identify that fragment. Imagine you want to send a visitor to the third level-3 heading in a Web page named *sales.htm*. To make this work, you need to embed a marker just before that level-3 heading. XHTML calls this marker a *bookmark*.

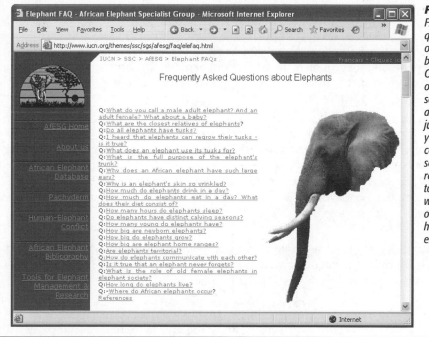

Figure 8-6:
FAQ (frequently asked questions) pages are one of the best examples of bookmarks at work. Often, an entire FAQ is one long page, with a series of bookmark links at the top that let you jump to just the topic you're interested in. You could break a FAQ into separate pages, but readers wouldn't be able to scan through the whole list of questions in order, and they wouldn't have a way to print the entire document at once.

To create a bookmark, you use the <a> anchor element, but with a twist: You don't supply an *href* attribute, because bookmarks don't actually lead anywhere—they simply identify fragments. What you *do* supply is a *name* attribute, which gives your bookmark a descriptive name. It's up to you whether you put any text inside an anchor—technically you don't need to, but most people find it easier to lock a bookmark to a specific word or title on the target page.

Here's an example:

```
...
<h3><a name="Canaries">Pet Canaries</a></h3>
<p>Pet canary sales have plummeted in the developed world, due in large part
to currency fluctuations and other macroeconomic forces.</p>
...
```

In this example, you create a bookmark named Canaries that drops visitors at the heading "Pet Canaries."

Once you create a bookmark, you can write a URL that points to it. The trick is to add the bookmark information to the end of the URL. To do this, you add the number-sign symbol (#), followed by the bookmark name.

For example, to send a reader to a bookmark named Canaries in the *sales.htm* page, here's the link you use:

```
Learn about recent developments in <a href="sales.htm#Canaries">canary
sales</a>.
```

When you click this link, the browser heads to the *sales.htm* page and scrolls down the page until it encounters the Canaries bookmark, The browser then displays, at the very top of the browser window, the text that starts with the heading "Pet Canaries."

Tip: If your bookmark is near the bottom of a page, a browser might not be able to scroll the bookmark all the way to the top of its window. Instead, the bookmarked section will appear somewhere in the middle of the browser window. This happens because the browser hits the bottom of the page, and can't scroll down any further. If you think there's some potential for confusion (perhaps because you have several bookmarked sections close to each other at the bottom of a page), you can add a few <br /> elements at the end of your document, which lets the browser scroll down farther.

Sometimes you want to create a link that points to a bookmark in your *current* page. In this case, you don't need to specify a page name at all. Just start with the number sign, followed by the bookmark name:

```
Jump to the <a href="#Canaries">canary</a> section.
```

Using bookmarks effectively is an art. Resist the urge to overcrowd your pages with links that direct readers to relatively small sections of content. Only use bookmarks to tame large pages that take several screenfuls of scrolling.

When Good Links Go Bad

Now that you've learned all the ways to build links, it's a good time to consider what can go wrong. Links that go to pages on the same site can break when you rename or move files or folders. Links to other Web sites are particularly fragile—they can break at any time, without warning. You won't know that anything's gone wrong until you click the link and get a "Page Not Found" error message.

Broken links are so common that Web developers have coined a term to describe how Web sites gradually lose their linking abilities: *link rot*. Sadly, you can upload a perfectly working Web site today and return a few months later to find that many of its external links have died off. They point to Web sites that no longer exist, have moved, or been rearranged.

Link rot is an insidious problem because it reduces visitor confidence in your site. They see a page that promises to lead them to other interesting resources, but when they click one of the links, they're disappointed. Experienced visitors won't stay long at a site that's suffering from an advanced case of link rot—they'll assume you haven't updated your site in a while and move on to a snazzier site somewhere else.

So how can you reduce the problem of broken links? First, you should rigorously test all your internal links—the ones that point to pages within your own site. Check for minor errors that can stop a link from working, and travel every path at least once. Leading Web page editors include built-in tools that automate this drudgery.

External links pose a different challenge. You can't create iron-clad external links, because link destinations are beyond your control and can change at any time. You could reduce the number of external links you include in your Web site to minimize the problem, but that isn't a very satisfying solution. Part of the beauty of the Web is the way a single click can take you from a comprehensive rock discography to a memorabilia site with hand-painted Elvis office supplies. As long as you want to connect your Web site to the rest of the world, you need to include external links. A better solution is to test your Web site regularly with a *link validator*, which walks through every one of your pages and checks each link to make sure it still leads somewhere.

In the following sections, you'll take a quick look at Web site management and link validators.

Site Management

Dreamweaver, Expression Web, and many other Web page editors include site management tools that let you see your entire Web site at a glance. In most cases, you need to specifically define a site to take advantage of these features (a process described on page 99). Once you do, you get a bird's eye view of everything it holds (see Figure 8-7).

In many ways, looking at the contents of your Web site folders isn't as interesting as studying the web of links that bind your pages together. Many Web page editors give you the ability to get an at-a-glance look at where all your links lead (see Figure 8-8).

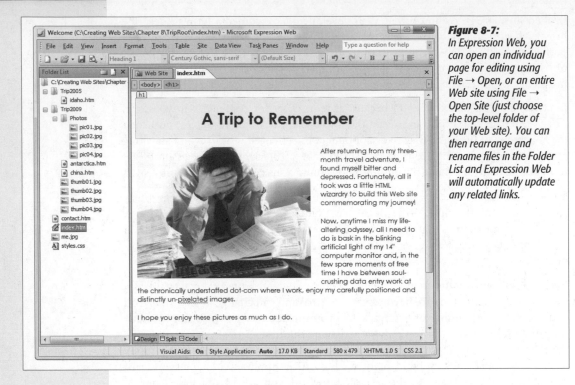

Figure 8-7:
In Expression Web, you can open an individual page for editing using File → Open, or an entire Web site using File → Open Site (just choose the top-level folder of your Web site). You can then rearrange and rename files in the Folder List and Expression Web will automatically update any related links.

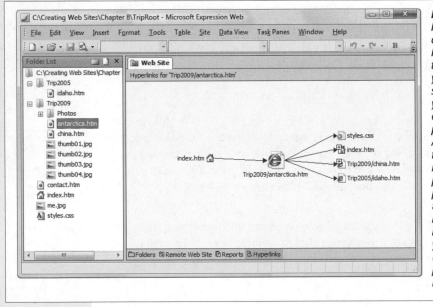

Figure 8-8:
In Expression Web, choose Tools → Hyperlinks, and you'll see this view, which shows you how the currently selected page fits into your Web site. In this example, the current page is antarctica.htm. *Arrows pointing away from* antarctica.htm *represent links on that page that lead to other pages. Arrows pointing to* antarctica.htm *represent links in other pages that lead to* antarctica.htm. *If you click one of the plus (+) boxes next to another page, you'll see all the links for that page, too.*

Note: Expression Web's hyperlink viewer is one of the features that requires hidden metadata folders (page 100). If you open the hyperlink viewer and select a file but don't see any links, you probably haven't added the metadata folders yet. To get them, choose Site → Site Settings, turn on the "Manage the Web site using hidden metadata files" setting, and then click OK.

Link Checkers

A *link checker* is an automated tool that scans through one or more of your Web pages. It tests each link it finds by trying to retrieve the target page (the page a link points to). Depending on the tool and the type of validation you're doing, link checkers might only scan internal links, or they might branch out to follow every link in every page until they've tested every link on your site.

Programs like Expression Web and Dreamweaver include sophisticated link checkers, and they're great for digging through your site and finding problems. In Dreamweaver, use the command Site → Check Links Sitewide to check links. In Expression Web, you can use a similar feature by choosing Site → Reports → Problems → Hyperlinks.

The link checkers built into these Web page editors work on the copy of your Web site stored on your PC. That's the best way to keep watch for errors as you're developing your site, but it's no help once your site's out in the wild. For example, it won't catch mistakes like a link to a file on your hard drive or to a file you forgot to upload to the Web server.

To get the final word on your Web site's links, you might want to try a free online link checker. The World Wide Web Consortium provides a solid choice at *http://validator.w3.org/checklink*. To start your free online link check, follow these steps:

1. **Go to *http://validator.w3.org/checklink*.**

   This takes you to the W3C Link Checker utility.

2. **In the text box, enter the full URL of the page you want to check.**

   If your Web site has a default page like *index.htm*, you can type in just the domain name without explicitly supplying a file name.

3. **Choose the options you want to apply (Figure 8-9).**

   Select "Summary only" if you want the checker to omit the detailed list of steps it takes as it examines each page. It's best to leave this option turned off so you can better understand exactly what pages the link checker examines.

   Select "Hide redirects" if you want the checker to ignore instructions that would redirect it to another page (page 227). Usually, redirects indicate that your link still works, but also that you should updated it to point to a new page.

   The "Don't send the Accept-header" option prevents a link checker from telling a Web site its language preferences. This setting only matters if you're creating a multilingual Web site, which is beyond the scope of this book.

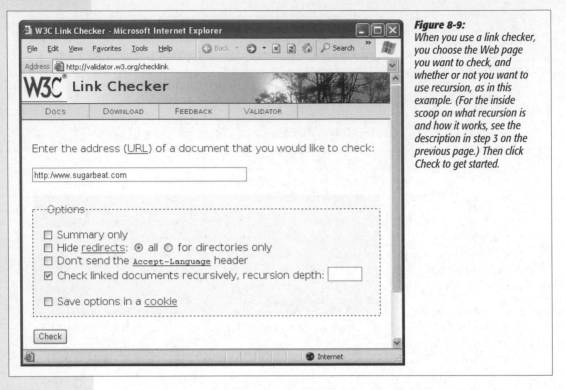

Figure 8-9:
*When you use a link checker,
you choose the Web page
you want to check, and
whether or not you want to
use recursion, as in this
example. (For the inside
scoop on what recursion is
and how it works, see the
description in step 3 on the
previous page.) Then click
Check to get started.*

The "Check linked documents recursively" option validates links using recursion. If you don't use this option, the validator simply checks every link in the page you specify, and makes sure it points to a live Web page. If you use recursion, the validator checks all the links in the current page, and then *follows* each internal link on your site. For example, if you have a link that points to a page named *info.htm*, the link checker first verifies that *info.htm* exists. Then it finds all the internal links in *info.htm* and starts testing *them*. In fact, if *info.htm* links to yet another internal page (like *contact.htm*), the link checker branches out to that page and starts checking *its* links as well. The link checker is smart enough to avoid checking the same page twice, so it doesn't waste time checking links it has already validated.

Note: Link checkers don't use recursion on external links. That means that if you start your link checker on the home page of your Web site, it follows the links to get to every other page on your site, but won't go any further. Still, recursion's a great way to drill through all the links in your site in one go.

If you want to limit recursion (perhaps because you have a lot of pages and you don't need to check them all), you can supply a "recursion depth," which specifies the maximum number of levels the checker digs down. For example, with a recursion depth of 1, the checker follows only the first set of links it encounters. If you don't supply a recursion depth, the checker checks everything.

4. Select "Save options in a cookie" if you want your browser to remember the link-checker settings you specify.

   If you use this option, the next time you use the link checker, your browser fills in the checkboxes using your previous settings.

5. Click "Check to start checking links."

   The link checker shows a report that lists each link it checks (Figure 8-10). It updates this report as it works. If you use recursion, you'll see the link checker branch out from one page to another. The report adds a separate section for each page.

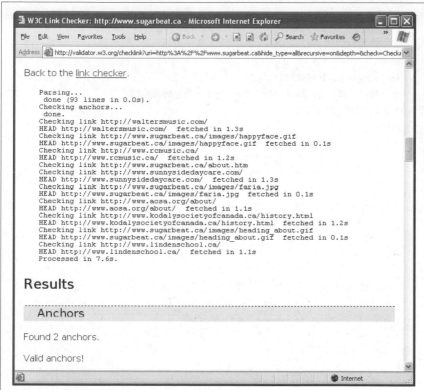

Figure 8-10:
The link checker's final report shows a list of links found in anchors and images. The checker highlights links that lead to dead ends in red, and flags those that may need attention in yellow. One example of potential problem links are redirected links. Although they still work, they may be out of date and might not last for long.

Using Redirects

To be a good Web citizen, you need to respect people who link to your site. That means that once you create your site and it becomes popular, try to avoid tinkering with page and folder names. Making a minor change could disrupt someone else's link, making it difficult for return visitors to get back to your site.

Some Web experts handle this problem using *redirects*. When they rearrange their sites, they keep all the old files, removing the content from them and replacing the old pages with a *redirect*—a special instruction that tells browsers to automatically navigate to a new page. The advantages of redirects are twofold: they prevent broken links, and they don't lock you into the old structure of your site if you decide to make a change.

To create a redirect, you need to add a special <meta> element to the <head> portion of your Web page. This element indicates the new destination using an absolute URL, and lists the number of seconds a browser should wait before performing the redirect. Here's an example:

```
<!DOCTYPE html PUBLIC "-//W3C//DTD XHTML 1.0 Strict//EN"
"http://www.w3.org/TR/xhtml1/DTD/xhtml1-strict.dtd">

<html xmlns="http://www.w3.org/1999/xhtml">

<head>
  <meta http-equiv="REFRESH"
  content="10; URL=http://www.mysite.com/homepage.htm" />
  <title>Redirect</title>
</head>

<body>
  <h1>The page you want has moved</h1>
  <p>
    Please update your bookmarks. The new home page is
    <a href=" http://www.mysite.com/homepage.htm">
    http://www.mysite.com/homepage.htm</a>.
  </p>
  <p>
    You should be redirected to the new site in 10 seconds. Click
    <a href=" http://www.mysite.com/homepage.htm">
    here</a> to visit the new page immediately.
  </p>
</body>
</html>
```

To adapt this page for your own purposes, change the number of seconds (currently at 10) and the redirect URL. When a browser loads this page, it shows the temporary page for the indicated number of seconds, and then automatically requests the new page.

Redirect pages really serve two purposes. They keep your pages working when you change your site's structure, and they inform Web visitors that the link is obsolete. That's where the time delay comes in—it provides a few seconds to notify visitors that they're entering the site the wrong way. Many sites keep their redirect pages around for a relatively short amount of time (for example, a year), after which they remove the page altogether.

Page Layout Tools

When engineers first created HTML, they focused on delivering basic information: the score in yesterday's ball game, the price of coffee beans in Colombia, the dance steps for the Electric Slide. As strange as it seems, no one thought layout tools were that important. Fortunately, a few pioneering Web designers recognized the problem and set out to rescue the Web from the scientists who invented it. These Web-heads invented a number of clever workarounds that gave the HTML universe a much-needed blast of pizzazz.

The best known of these tactics is the *invisible table*. Using an invisible table, you can align content, pictures, and headings within an invisible grid. It's impossible to overstate how important invisible tables were in the early days of the Web—they almost single-handedly saved Web fans from a world of drab, plain-text pages. But now that styles are on the scene, invisible tables are starting to outgrow their usefulness. Although Web sites still use them, many Web developers find they're just too awkward to manage.

Today, invisible-table-based layout is slowly but surely giving way to *style-based layout*. Style-based layouts use CSS positioning rules to place panels, columns, and pictures in specific spots on a Web page. When you use style-based layouts, your XHTML markup is easier to understand, and you have less trouble replicating your design across multiple pages. With a little planning, you can even create pages that you can completely rearrange without touching a line of XHTML—all you need to do is modify a linked style sheet. (See Chapter 6 for all the details on how to get started working with style sheets.)

In this chapter, you'll learn how to use both table-based and style-based layouts. But first, you need to take a step back, consider the challenges that await you, and learn why layout on the Web isn't as straightforward as you might expect.

Note: Overall, style-based layout is the most elegant, and neatly structured, approach to page design—it's the wave of the future. You can still find examples of table-based layout, thanks to its compatibility with old browsers and its usefulness in a few special scenarios where style-based design is unnaturally difficult. And you can't ignore tables altogether—you still need them for laying out dense grids of information.

The Challenge of Screen Space

When you design a page for print, you take into account the physical size of your final document. You'd use much larger text on a poster than on a business card, for example. But in the world of the Web, this system breaks down, because users can set their monitors to all kinds of screen resolutions, and resize their browser windows to all sorts of different dimensions. These details affect how much screen real estate your Web pages have to work with. The higher the resolution and the bigger a browser window, the more of your content fits on-screen. This raises a dilemma—how do you make sure your pages look their best when you don't know your visitors' screen settings?

Web designers use two basic layout strategies to deal with this issue:

- **Go for flexibility with proportional sizing.** With proportional sizing, your layout expands or shrinks to fit the available space in a browser window. For example, if you create a proportionally sized Web page with a fixed menu bar and a variable content area, the menu bar always stays at the same width, while the content area grows or contracts to fit the browser window, no matter how big or small that window gets. If you're in doubt, proportional sizing is the way to go, because it ensures that your Web pages will conform to any size browser window.

- **Pick a reasonable fixed size.** Sometimes, too much flexibility can cause its own problems. For example, if you shrink a proportionally sized page to extremely small dimensions, some page elements might get bumped into odd positions. If you have a complex layout with lots of graphics and floating elements, the result can be a bit of a mess. On the other hand, extremely large windows can cause their own problems. For example, if you stretch a proportionally size page to fit the full width of a widescreen monitor, you might end up with extremely long lines of text that are hard to read. The solution is to use fixed-width pages that look good at a range of browser settings.

Generally, proportional sizing is the safest approach to page design. After all, if your Web site looks less than perfect in a browser window that's extremely small or extremely big, you can count on a visitor to resize it to something more reasonable.

That said, there are plenty of professional sites that use fixed sizes, including news-papers like the *New York Times* (*www.nytimes.com*)—see Figure 9-1. If you opt for the fixed-width solution, you need to figure out what that width should be. Of course, you have no way of knowing the two most important factors affecting that decision—the size of a visitor's browser window and his screen resolution. The fact is, you'll probably never know the browser window setting, but you *can* take advantage of anecdotal evidence for screen resolution. Nearly half of all people use larger 1024×768 displays, and most of the rest (nearly 40%) use higher resolutions—often widescreen resolutions like 1280×800. For this reason, your Web page should look brilliant at a width of about 1,000 pixels. This is the roughly the amount of browser real estate your page gets when a visitor uses a resolution of 1024×768 and sets his browser window to fill the whole screen. If you go with a fixed layout, follow this 1,000-pixel guideline and make sure all your content fits comfortably at this size, with no scrolling required. The *New York Times* article (Figure 9-1) provides a good model.

In this chapter, you'll learn how to put both of these layout strategies to work.

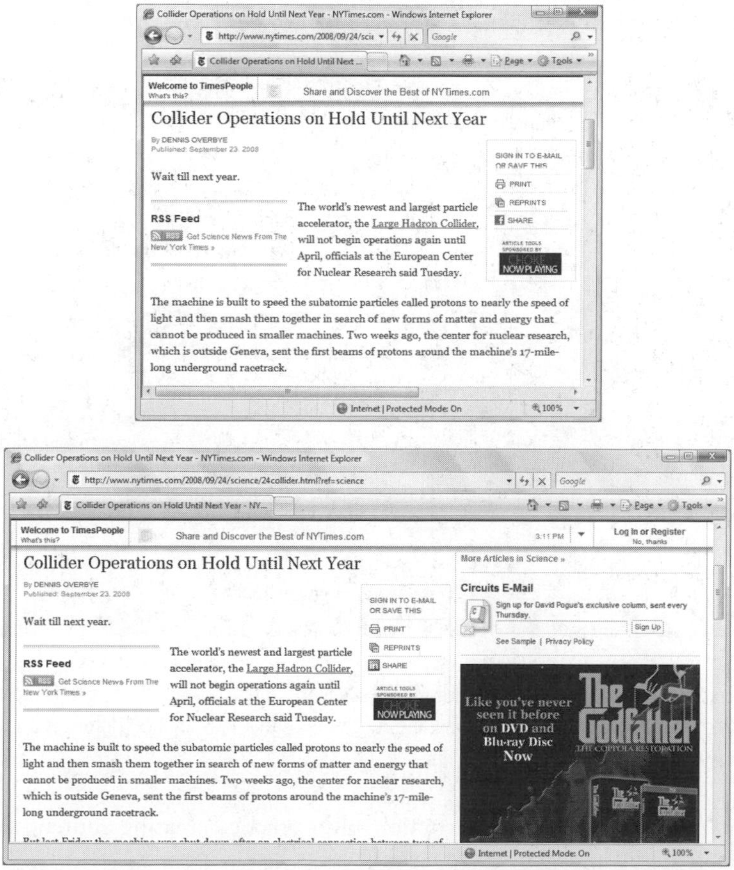

Figure 9-1:
Top: To read this article without scrolling, you need a window that's about 600 pixels wide, which is a comfortable fit for an 800×600–pixel monitor.

Bottom: Widen the window to about 1,000 pixels and you see frills like videos, ads, a search box, and a list of popular articles. If you make the window any wider, all you see is blank space on the right side. Almost all news sites use this kind of page design to deal with variable window sizes.

Testing Different Page Sizes

No matter which layout strategy you choose, you should test your pages at a variety of browser sizes to make sure your visitors see the best side of your work.

Fortunately, many Web page editors let you open pages in a range of browser window sizes. For example, in Expression Web you can choose File → Preview in Browser, which has options for common window sizes. And some Web browsers have add-ons that do the same thing. For example, Firefox fans can use the Web Developer toolbar (*http://addons.mozilla.org/en-US/firefox/addon/60*), which adds a menu packed full of handy Web design tools, including an option to quickly change the size of the browser window.

This raises an obvious question—at what window sizes should you test your pages? Web research companies estimate that just under 10% of all people use cramped 800×600 resolution computer monitors. That means these people can't make their browser any wider than 800 pixels, so you should make sure your pages look acceptable at this width. In other words, maybe folks whose monitors are set to 800×600 resolution will have to scroll a bit (up or down, or left or right) to see your page, but for the most part they'll be able to see everything you want them to, so long as they size the browser window to fill up the whole screen.

UP TO SPEED

Understanding Resolution

A resolution of 1024×768 means that a monitor displays a grid of pixels that's 1,024 pixels wide and 768 pixels high. A pixel is the smallest unit of measurement on a monitor, and is otherwise known as a "dot." In other words, a resolution of 1024×768 gives programs 786,432 pixels to play with, while a mediocre 800 x 600 resolution offers only 480,000 pixels. Clearly, higher resolutions can display a lot more content.

It's important to realize screen resolution isn't directly related to the size of your monitor. In other words, a 17-inch monitor can have a higher resolution (and show more information) than a 19-inch monitor. However, it makes sense for larger monitors to use higher resolutions. That's because, on a small monitor, high resolutions look cramped and text can be hard to read.

To get some perspective, you might want to figure out what screen resolution you're using—or even change it. To do so in Windows Vista, right-click the desktop, choose Personalize, click Display Settings, and then adjust the resolution using the handy slider. In earlier versions of Windows, you can find the same settings when you right-click the desktop and select Properties → Settings. In Mac OS X, click System Preferences → Displays, and select from the list of resolutions.

Note: Remember, people with large monitors won't necessarily size their browser window to fill up the entire screen. After all, it's hard to read really long lines of text.) For that reason, 1,000 pixels is a good assumption for the average width of a browser window.

Now it's time to put your two layout options into practice creating content-rich pages using table-based and style-based layouts.

Tables

A table is a grid of cells built of rows and columns. Originally, designers used tables to (predictably) display tables of information. But crafty Web developers quickly discovered that *invisible* tables offered a perfect way to lay out content in a variety of new ways (see Figure 9-2).

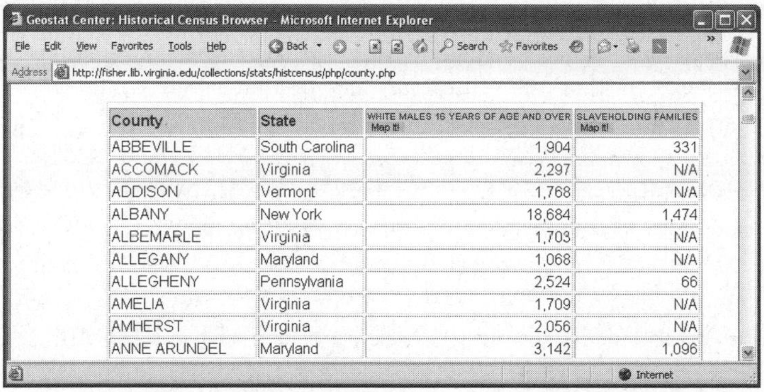

Figure 9-2:
Top: This detailed census information from 1790 makes perfect sense in an ordinary table.

Bottom: A combination of invisible tables (technically, tables with no borders) gives you all the underpinning you need for this headache-inspiring, multi-columned newspaper view.

In the following sections, you'll explore how to create tables using XHTML.

The Anatomy of a Table

You can whip up a table with just a few new XHTML elements:

- **<table>** wraps the whole shebang. It's the starting point for every table.

- **<tr>** represents a single table row. Every table element (<table>) contains a series of one or more <tr> elements.

- **<td>** represents a table cell (it stands for table data). For each cell you want in a row, you add one <td> element. You put the text (or numbers, or <img> elements, or pretty much any XHTML you like) that you want to appear in that cell inside the <td> element. If you put text in the cell, it gets displayed in the same font as ordinary body text.

- **<th>** is an optional table element you use when you want to define a column heading. You can use a <th> element instead of a <td> element any time, although it usually makes the most sense in the first row of a table. Browsers format the text inside the <th> element in almost the same way as text in a <td> element, except that they automatically boldface and center the text (unless you apply different formatting rules with a style sheet).

Note: There are a few other table-specific elements, but they've fallen by the wayside. These elements, which designers no longer need or that browsers don't universally support, include <thead>, <tbody>, <tfoot>, and <caption> elements.

Figure 9-3 shows a table at its simplest. Here's a portion of the XHTML used to create that table:

```
<table>
  <tr>
    <th>Rank</th>
    <th>Name</th>
    <th>Population</th>
  </tr>
  <tr>
    <td>1</td>
    <td>Rome</td>
    <td>450,000</td>
  </tr>
  <tr>
    <td>2</td>
    <td>Luoyang (Honan), China</td>
    <td>420,000</td>
  </tr>
  <tr>
    <td>3</td>
    <td>Seleucia (on the Tigris), Iraq</td>
    <td>250,000</td>
  </tr>
  ...
</table>
```

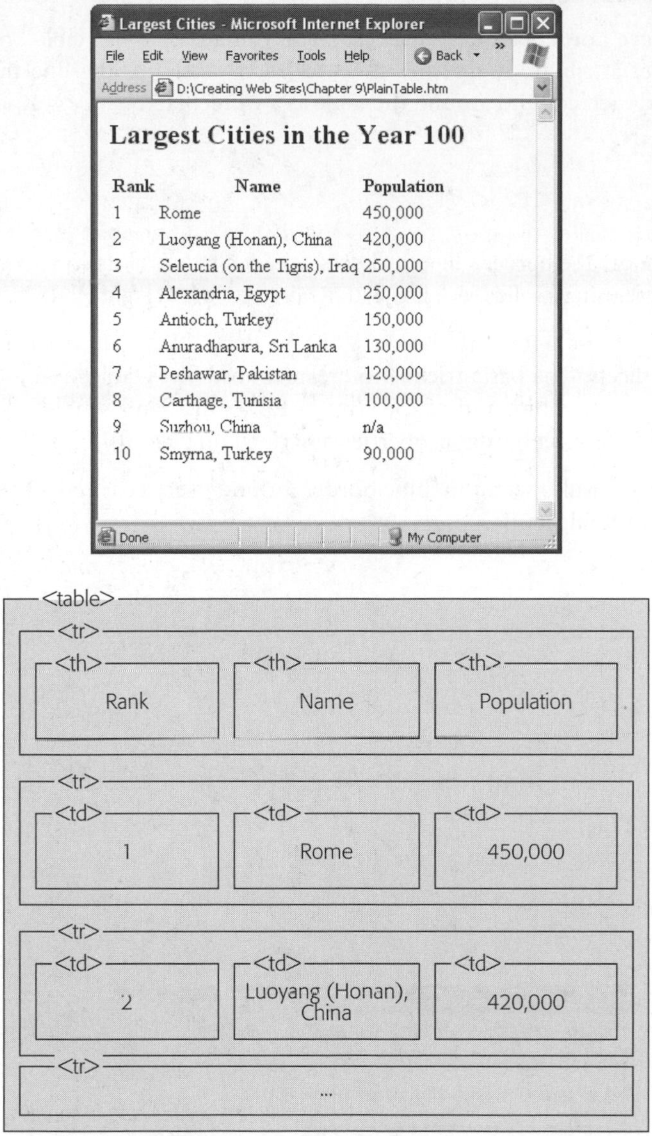

Figure 9-3:
Top: This basic table doesn't have any borders thanks to a style sheet rule, but you'll still spot the signature sign that you're looking at a table: text lined up neatly in rows and columns.

Bottom: This behind-the-scenes look at the XHTML powering the table above shows the <table>, <tr>, <th>, and <td> elements for the first three rows.

The markup for this table uses indented table elements to help you see the structure of the table. Indenting table elements like this is always a good idea, as it helps you spot mismatched tags. In this example, the only content in the <td> elements is ordinary text. But you can put other XHTML elements in cells, too, including hyperlinks (the <a> element) and images (the <img> element).

Tip: You might be able to avoid writing tables by hand, as most Web design tools include their own table editors that let you point and click your way to success. These table-creation features are similar to those you find in a word processor.

Formatting Table Borders

Traditional tables have borders around each cell. You can adjust those table borders using the *border* attribute. It specifies the width (in pixels) of the line that browsers add around each cell and around the table as a whole. Here's an example:

```
<table border="1">
  ...
</table>
```

Although you can choose the border's line thickness, you can't control its style. Most browsers outline a table using a solid black line with a raised edge (see Figure 9-4).

Don't feel limited by these automatic borders. If you don't like them, there's a work-around: style sheets. The basic trick is to create a borderless table, and then apply a border to some combination of the <tr>, <td>, <th>, and <table> elements. You can find style sheet border properties described on page 167.

The following style sheet rules set a thin blue border around every cell, and a thick blue border around the table itself:

```
table {
   border-width: 3px;
   border-style: solid;
   border-color: blue;
}
td, th {
   border-width: 1px;
   border-style: solid;
   border-color: blue;
}
```

Figure 9-4 shows the result. 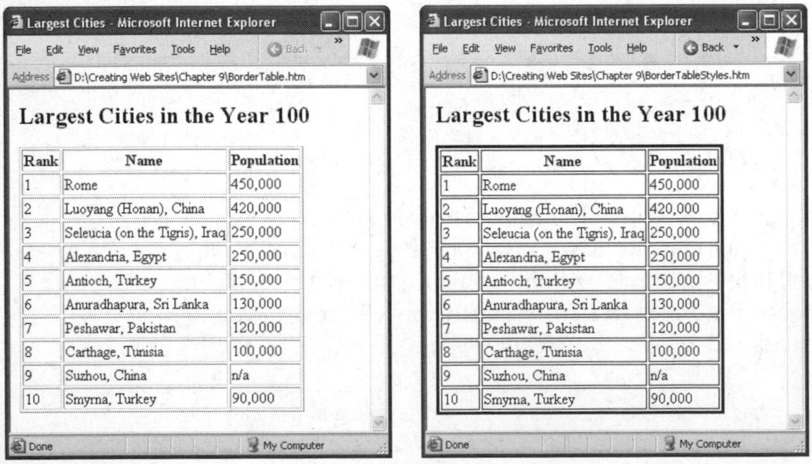

Figure 9-4:
Left: A standard XHTML table border with a thickness of 1 pixel.

Right: A custom border using style rules.

CREATING A WEB SITE: THE MISSING MANUAL

Tip: Borders aren't the only style sheet feature you can apply to table cells. You can also change a cell's text font and text alignment (page 153), its padding and margins (page 163), and the colors it uses (page 151). You can even set a background image for an individual cell or the whole table using the background-image property (page 198). And if you want to apply style rules to individual cells (rather than to the table as a whole), you just need to use class names (page 171).

There's one hiccup to watch for when you create tables with borders. If the table includes empty cells, they'll appear "collapsed," which means they won't get any borders at all (see Figure 9-5).

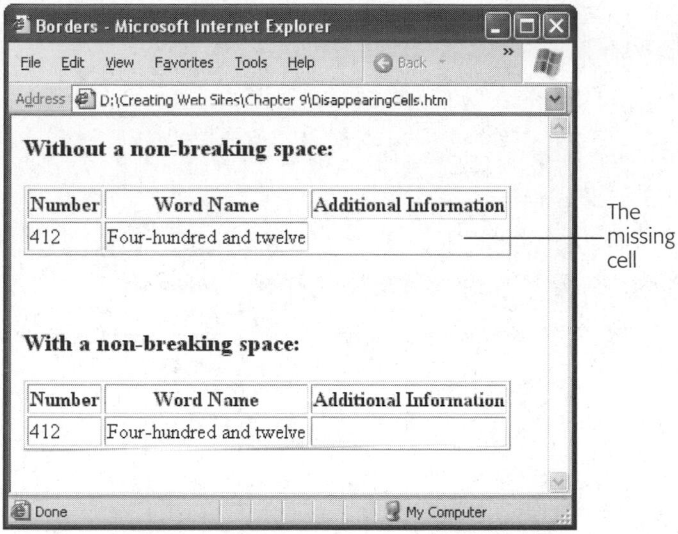

Figure 9-5:
If you don't include a non-breaking space, you'll lose the borders around empty cells.

To prevent cells from collapsing, add a single non-breaking space to them:

```
<td> </td>
```

The browser won't display this space, but it will ensure that your borders stay put.

Cell Spans

Tables support *spanning*, a feature that lets a single cell stretch out over several columns or rows. Think of spanning as XHTML's version of the Merge Cells feature in Microsoft Word and Excel.

Spanned cells let you tweak your tables in all kinds of funky ways. You can, for example, specify a *column span* to stretch a cell over two or more columns. Just add a *colspan* attribute to the <td> element you want to extend, and specify the total number of columns you want to skip.

Here's an example that stretches a cell over two columns, so that the cell ends up occupying the space of two full cells:

```
<table>
  <tr>
    <td>Column 1</td>
    <td>Column 2</td>
    <td>Column 3</td>
    <td>Column 4</td>
  </tr>
  <tr>
    <td> </td>
    <td colspan="2">Look out, this cell spans two columns!</td>
    <td> </td>
  </tr>
  ...
</table>
```

Figure 9-6 shows this trick in action.

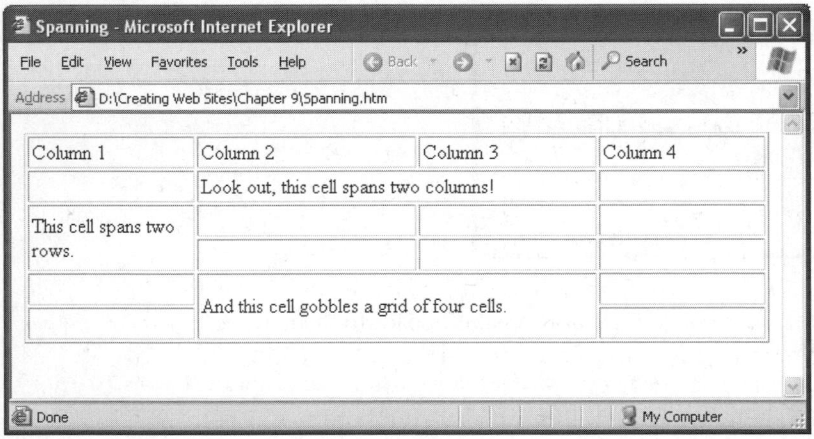

Figure 9-6:
A table with row spanning and column spanning run amok.

To make sure your table doesn't get mangled, you need to keep track of the total number of columns you have to work with in each row. In the previous example, the first row starts off by defining four basic columns:

```
<tr>
  <td>Column 1</td>
  <td>Column 2</td>
  <td>Column 3</td>
  <td>Column 4</td>
</tr>
```

In the next row, the second column extends over the third column, thanks to column spanning (see the markup below). As a result, the third <td> element actually represents the *fourth* column. That means you need only three <td> elements to fill up the full width of the table:

```
<tr>
  <!-- This fills column 1 -->
  <td> </td>

  <!-- This fills columns 2 and 3 -->
  <td colspan="2">Look out, this cell spans two columns!</td>

  <!-- This fills column 4 -->
  <td> </td>
</tr>
```

This same principle applies to *row spanning* and the *rowspan* attribute. In the following example, the first cell in the row leaks through to the second row:

```
<tr>
  <td rowspan="2">This cell spans two rows.</td>
  <td> </td>
  <td> </td>
  <td> </td>
</tr>
```

In the next row, the cell from above already occupies the first cell, so the first <td> element you declare actually applies to the second column. All in all, therefore, this row needs only three <td> elements:

```
<tr>
  <td> </td>
  <td> </td>
  <td> </td>
</tr>
```

If you miscount and add too many cells to a row, you end up with an extra column at the end of your table.

Tip: Many Web page editors let you create spans by joining cells. In Dreamweaver and Expression Web, select a group of cells, right-click them, and then select Merge Cells.

Sizing and Aligning Tables

If you don't explicitly set the size of a table, it gets as wide as necessary to display all its columns, and each column grows just wide enough to fit the longest line of text (or to accommodate any other content you've added, like a picture by adding an <img> element). However, there's one additional rule—the table can't grow wider than the browser window. Once a table reaches the full width of the current window, the browser starts wrapping the text inside each column, so that the table grows taller as you pile in more content.

Tip: Need more space inside your table? Style rules can make it easy. To add more space between the cell content and its borders, increase the padding property for the <td> and <tr> elements. To add more space between the cell borders and any adjacent cells, up the margin width for the <td> and <tr> elements. Page 163 has more on adjusting these dimensions.

In most cases, you want to explicitly set the width of your table and its individual columns. When you do so, the table respects these dimensions and wraps text to accommodate those widths. Once again, style sheets provide the best approach. All you do is set height and width properties, as explained in the next section.

Sizing a table

You have two choices when you specify table dimensions:

- **Relative sizing** sizes a table in sync with the dimensions of a browser window. You supply the percentage of the window you want the table to fill.

- **Absolute sizing** uses pixel measurements to set the exact size of a table.

The following style sheet rule ensures that this table always occupies the full width of a browser window:

```
table {
  width: 100%;
}
```

A browser sizes this table *in relation to* the size of the browser window.

This rule limits the table to half the width of the current window:

```
table {
  width: 50%;
}
```

Either way, the table dynamically resizes as you resize the browser window.

Note: In the examples you've seen so far, all the tables have been plopped directly into the <body> section of a page. This is a common design, but it's not the only possibility—alternatively, you can put a table inside some other container element. If you use a relative width for this table, its width is proportional to the size of its container. So if you set the table width to 50%, it takes half the width of its container, no matter how big or how small it is. To try this out, put your table in a cell inside another table (a trick described on page 247) or in a <div> element that uses a fixed width (page 253).

If you use exact pixel widths, the table dimensions never change. For example, the following rule creates a table that's a generous 500 pixels wide:

```
table.Cities {
  width: 500px;
}
```

Because you create this table with a specific width, you should only use it for content that justifies that width. To prevent your browser from applying this style to every table it encounters (because the table's size may not suit every type of content), you give it a class name, like Cities in the example above. To display this specific table, you cite the table class in your XHTML document:

```
<table class="Cities">
   ...
</table>
```

In addition to specifying the width of a table, you can also set its height. Usually, you set the height using an absolute size, as shown here:

```
table.Cities {
   height: 500px;
}
```

That's because, if you set a table height as a percentage of a browser window, it creates a strange (and rarely seen) effect—the table grows taller and shorter as you lengthen or shorten your browser window.

There's one important caveat to table sizing. Although you can make a table as large as you want (even if it stretches beyond the borders of a browser window), you don't have the same ability to shrink a table. If you specify a table size that's smaller than the minimum size the table needs to display your content, the table appears at this minimum size (see Figure 9-7).

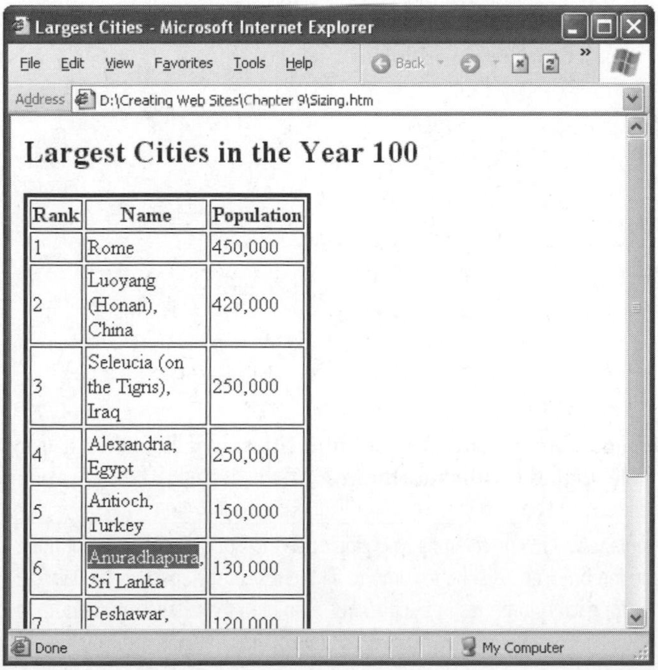

Figure 9-7:
In this example, the XHTML called for a table width of 1 pixel. But the browser doesn't shrink the table down that far because the content influences the table's minimum size. In this table, the city name Anuradhapura is the longest un-splittable value, so the browser uses that name to determine the width of the column. If you really want to ratchet the size down another notch, try shrinking the text by applying a smaller font size.

Sizing a column

Now that you know how to size a table, you probably want to know what your browser does if a table has more than enough space for its content. Once a table reaches its minimum size (just large enough to fit all its data), your browser distributes any extra space proportionately, so that every column width increases by the same amount.

Of course, this isn't necessarily what you want. You might want to create a wide descriptive column paired with a narrow column of densely packed text. Or you might want to set columns to a specific size so that all your pages look uniform, even if the content differs.

To set a column's size, you use the *width* property in conjunction with the <td> and <th> elements. Once again, you can do this proportionately, using a percentage, or exactly, using a pixel width. However, proportional sizing has a slightly different effect when you use it with columns. Earlier, when you used a percentage value for table width, you sized the entire table relative to the width of the page. In that example, you had a table width of 50%, which means the table occupied 50 percent of the full width of the page. But when you use a percentage value to set a *column* width, you're defining the percentage of the *table* width that the column should occupy. So when you set a column width of 50%, the column takes up 50 percent of the *table*.

When you size columns, you need to create a style rule for each one, giving it a unique class name (page 171). That's because each column is potentially a different width—you can't just write a single style rule that applies to every column, unless you want them all to have exactly the same width.

The following style rules set different widths for each column of the table you saw in Figure 9-7.

```
th.Rank {
   width: 10%;
}
th.Name {
   width: 80%;
}
th.Population {
   width: 10%;
}
```

In this example, the class names match the column titles, which makes it easy to keep track of which rule applies to which column.

Tip: When you use percentage widths for columns, you don't need to specify values for all three columns. If you leave one out, the browser sizes that column to fill the rest of the space in the table. If you do decide to include widths for each column (as in the previous example), make sure they add up to 100 percent to avoid confusion. Otherwise, the browser will override one of your settings, and you won't know how your table will actually appear.

For these rules to take effect, you need to apply them to the corresponding cells:

```
<table class="Cities">
  <tr>
    <th class="Rank">Rank</th>
    <th class="Name">Name</th>
    <th class="Population">Population</th>
  </tr>
  <tr>
    <td>1</td>
    <td>Rome</td>
    <td>450,000</td>
  </tr>
  ...
</table>
```

Notice that you specify widths only for the column elements in the first row (the ones that contain the cell headers in this example). You could apply the rule to every row, but there's really no point. When the browser builds a table, it scans the whole table structure to determine the required size, based on the cell content and any explicit width settings. If you apply a different width to more than one cell in the same column, the browser simply uses the largest value.

Tip: It's a good idea to size your table by applying style rules to the first row. This makes your XHTML more readable, because it's immediately obvious what the dimensions of your table are.

Sizing a row

You can size a row just as easily as you size a column. The best approach is to use the *height* property in the <tr> attribute, as shown here:

```
tr.TallRow {
  height: 100px;
}
```

Once again, XHTML lets you use either percentages or pixel values. When you resize a row, you affect every cell in every column of that row. However, you're free to make each row in the table a different height, using the techniques just described.

Organizing a Page with Tables

So far, the tables you've seen have been fairly typical grids of information. But on many Web sites, tables play another role—they organize pages into separate regions of content.

One of the most common Web site designs is to divide a page into two or three columns. The column on the left typically holds navigation buttons or other links.

The column in the middle takes up the most space and includes the main content for the page. The column on the right, if present, displays additional information, like an advertisement or another set of links. Figure 9-8 shows how it all breaks down.

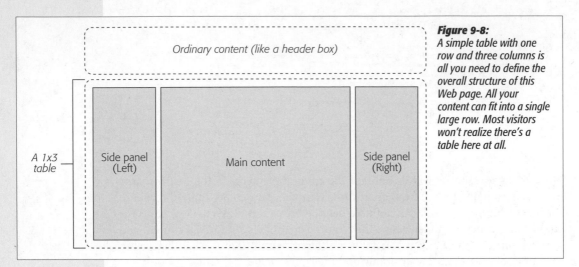

A 1x3 table

Ordinary content (like a header box)

Side panel (Left)

Main content

Side panel (Right)

Figure 9-8:
A simple table with one row and three columns is all you need to define the overall structure of this Web page. All your content can fit into a single large row. Most visitors won't realize there's a table here at all.

To make this design work, you need to consider several details:

- **Vertical text alignment**. Ordinarily, browsers position row content in the center of the row, between the top and bottom edge. This isn't what you want in tall rows, and it's a particularly bad choice for any row that's more than a screenful high. For example, if you have a set of navigation links in the left-most column and that column extends below the bottom of the screen, your vertically centered links could fall below the bottom of the screen, too. To ensure this doesn't happen, you want to have your browser put the content in each cell at the top of the table, so it sits at the top of your page, immediately visible.

- **Borders**. If you decide to use borders, you'll want them only on *some* edges to emphasize the separation of content. You won't want them around every cell or around the entire table. In many cases, you'll do away with borders altogether and use different background colors or images to separate the sections of a page.

- **Sizing**. Typically, you set a specific width for the left and right side panels. The middle panel needs to command the most space. If you leave its width unspecified, it can grow as visitors enlarge their browser windows or as they switch to widescreen monitors.

Figure 9-9 gives you a taste of what a finished page that uses a table to lay out the page might look like. You can see the entire page with the downloadable content for this chapter (go to *www.missingmanuals.com*, and then click the Missing CD link).

The table in this example is relatively simple because you keep and maintain all its formatting and sizing details separately, in a style sheet. Therefore, all you need to

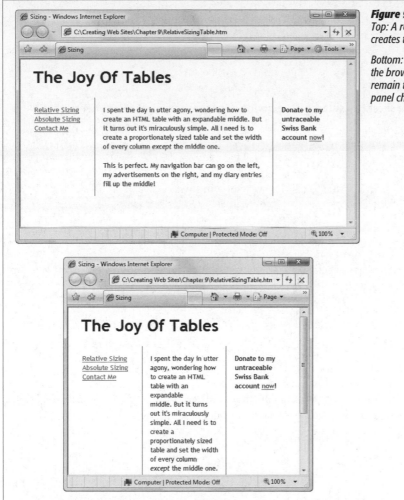

Figure 9-9:
Top: A relatively easy-to-make table creates this attractive page layout.

Bottom: When you shrink the size of the browser window, the side panels remain the same size; only the middle panel changes.

do is create an ordinary table with one row and three columns. You then map each column to a different style using a class name:

```
<table>
  <tr>
    <td class="Left">
      <a href="RelativeSizing.htm">Relative Sizing</a><br />
      <a href="AbsoluteSizing.htm">Absolute Sizing</a><br />
      <a href="mailto:no-one">Contact Me</a><br />
    </td>
    <td class="Middle">
      I spent the day in utter agony, wondering how
      to create a table with an expandable middle...
    </td>
```

```
    <td class="Right">
      Donate to my untraceable Swiss Bank account
      <a href="http://www.paypal.org">now</a>!
    </td>
  </tr>
</table>
```

The style sheet rules start by specifying a font for the whole document:

```
body {
  font-family: Trebuchet MS, serif;
}
```

Next, you size the table to fill the browser window:

```
table {
  width: 100%;
}
```

Then you give every cell some standard settings for text alignment, font size, and padding (to provide a little extra space between the column border and the text):

```
td {
  font-size: x-small;
  padding: 15px;
  vertical-align: top;
}
```

Finally, you set the widths and borders with column-specific rules. Here are the two rules that give the side panels fixed, 100-pixel widths:

```
td.Left {
  width: 100px;
}
td.Right {
 width: 100px;
 font-weight: bold;
}
```

Next up is the style sheet rule for the middle column. Unlike the side columns, the middle column doesn't have an explicit width. Instead, the browser sizes it to fit whatever space remains. This style sheet rule also gives the middle column left and right borders to separate it from the side panels:

```
td.Middle {
  border-left-width: 1px;
  border-right-width: 1px;
  border-top-width: 0px;
  border-bottom-width: 0px;
  border-style: solid;
  border-color: blue;
}
```

CREATING A WEB SITE: THE MISSING MANUAL

There's one last detail you might want to change in the above style sheet. This example uses proportional sizing for the table, which lets the middle panel grow and shrink as visitors resize their browser window. Although this is the most flexible option, in dense, graphics-rich Web sites where you've precisely positioned text, images, sidebars, and other content, you may need absolute sizing to preserve your carefully crafted layout. (For more about this issue, see page 230.)

You can convert the above example to use absolute sizing by changing the style rule that applies to the <table> element, as shown here:

```
table {
  width: 600px;
}
```

This sets the table width at 600 pixels. The left and right panels are still 100 pixels wide, so the middle column gets whatever's left—in this case, 400 pixels (based on a total width of 600 pixels, minus 100 pixels for each panel). Figure 9-10 shows the difference.

Nested Tables

In sophisticated Web sites, the show doesn't end with a single table. Instead, site creators put tables *inside* other tables, which they then put inside yet more tables. For example, you might create a basic three-column setup using one table, and then divide the right column into a series of distinct ads using a second table. When you put one table inside another like this, you create a *nested table*.

Building nested tables is easy, although it can be a little difficult to keep track of everything. The trick is to define a table inside one of the cells in an existing table. For example, if you have this table with three columns:

```
<table>
  <tr>
    <td class="Left">...</td>
    <td class="Middle">...</td>
    <td class="Right">...</td>
  </tr>
</table>
```

You can slide a table right into the <td> tags for the third column:

```
<table>
  <tr>
    <td class="Left">...</td>
    <td class="Middle">...</td>
    <td class="Right">
      <table>
        <tr>...</tr>
        <tr>...</tr>
      </table>
    </td>
  </tr>
</table>
```

Resizing all the parts of these two tables can get confusing. It's easiest to size the nested table using a relative width of 100 percent. That way, the nested table expands or shrinks based on the width of the column it's in.

Style-Based Layout

Although the table-based approach to page layout seems perfect at first, it has a few frustrating quirks. One of the most daunting is that once you perfect your table-based layout, you need to painstakingly copy the exact table structure to every

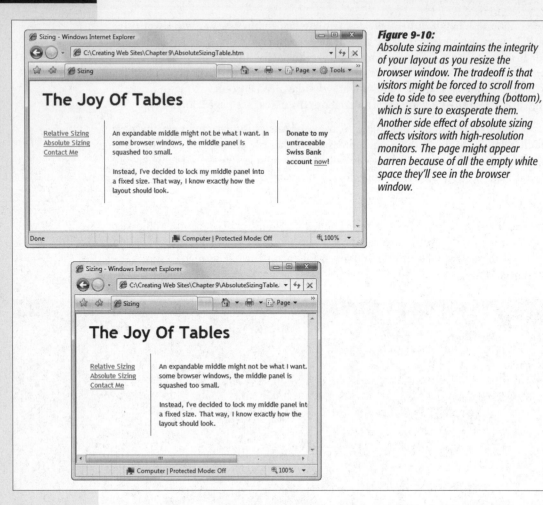

Figure 9-10:
Absolute sizing maintains the integrity of your layout as you resize the browser window. The tradeoff is that visitors might be forced to scroll from side to side to see everything (bottom), which is sure to exasperate them. Another side effect of absolute sizing affects visitors with high-resolution monitors. The page might appear barren because of all the empty white space they'll see in the browser window.

other page on your site. That's tedious work, and tables are notorious for going haywire if a single tag goes missing. Even worse, what happens once you copy your table-based layout into a hundred different pages and then decide you want to improve it with a minor change?

In the early, lawless days of the Web, tables went unchallenged. But once styles appeared, leading Web designers began to explore new layout options. For most Web-heads, style-based layout takes a little bit longer to grasp, but causes fewer long-term headaches. Here are some of its benefits:

• The XHTML is cleaner and easier to read.

• Ideally, you store all the style information in a separate style sheet, which means you can apply it to multiple pages with little effort.

• When you modify the style sheet, you reconfigure the layout of every linked page in one (immensely gratifying) step.

You've already taken your first tentative steps toward style-sheet nirvana by learning about style-based layout for boxed text and floating images in Chapter 7. You can apply that same idea to full pages. But before you go any further, it's a good idea to consider a few more style sheet features that make style-based layouts possible.

Structuring Pages with the <div> Element

Before you start placing elements in specific positions on a page, you need a way to bundle related content into a single, neat package. In the table-based layout examples above, that package was the table cell. When you use style-based table layout, that package is the <div> element—the all-purpose container described on page 122.

Imagine you want to create a box that has several links on the left side of your page. Positioning each link in that column is as much fun as peeling grapes. By using the <div> element, you can group everything together:

```
<div class="Menu">
  <a href="...">Home Page</a>
  <a href="...">Buy Our Products</a>
  <a href="...">File a Lawsuit</a>
  ...
</div>
```

Whenever you create a <div> element, you should choose a class name that describes the type of content it contains (like Menu, Header, AdBar, and so on). Later on, you can create a style rule that positions this <div> element and sets its font, colors, and borders.

Remember, a <div> element doesn't have any built-in formatting. In fact, on its own, it doesn't do anything at all. The magic happens when you combine your <div> element with a style sheet rule.

Even Better Selectors

In Chapter 6, you learned about different *selectors*, the part of a style sheet rule that identifies what you want to format, such as a paragraph, heading, or list item. The most common type of selectors are *type* selectors, which format every occurrence of a specific XHTML element, and *class* selectors, which format every element that uses the same class name. As it turns out, you can target content even more specifically in a couple of ways.

Contextual selectors

A *contextual selector* is stricter than an ordinary type selector. Whereas a type selector matches an element, a contextual selector matches an element *inside another element*. To understand the difference, take a look at this type selector:

```
b {
  color: red;
}
```

This selector formats all bold text in red. But what if you want to work only on bold text that appears inside a bulleted list? You can do that using the following contextual type selector, which finds unordered list elements (<ul>) and then hunts for bold elements inside of them. If it finds any, it makes the bold text red:

```
ul b {
  color: red;
}
```

To create a contextual type selector, you simply put a space between the two elements.

Contextual selectors are useful, but thinking through the different possibilities for combining elements can get a little dizzying. You'll see the real benefit of a contextual selector when you use one to match a specific type of element inside a specific type of *class*.

For example, imagine you want to change the look of all the links in the menu panel above. The menu panel is a <div> element with the class name Menu. Here's the rule you need:

```
div.Menu a {
  color: red;
}
```

The first part of this selector finds all the <div> elements in your page. The second part limits those matches to <div> elements with the class name Menu—which is exactly one. The third and final part of the selector locates the <a> elements inside the menu panel. The end result is that every anchor in the menu panel will have red lettering, while the anchors in the rest of the page are left alone.

This technique is a wildly popular way to define different formatting rules for different sections of a page. It also makes a particularly nice fit with the CSS-based layout techniques you'll learn about next.

id selectors

There's one other type of selector you need to know about: the *id selector*. It's a lot like the class selectors you've used until now. Like a class selector, the id selector lets you pick a descriptive name for your rule. But instead of separating the element and descriptive names with a period (.), you separate the element name from the id name with a number-sign character (#), as shown here:

```
div#Menu {
  border-width: 2px;
  border-style: solid;
}
```

This example defines a rule named Menu that applies only to <div> elements.

As with class rules, browsers don't apply id rules unless you specifically tell them to in your XHTML. However, instead of switching on the rules with a *class* attribute, you do so with the *id* attribute.

For example, here's a <div> element that uses the Menu style:

```
<div id="Menu">...</div>
```

At this point, you're probably wondering what the point of all this is—after all, the id selector seems almost exactly the same as the class selector. The only difference you've seen so far is in the name of the attribute that links an element to a style rule (it's id instead of class) and the number sign.

But there's one more restriction: You can assign an id element to only *one* element in a page. In other words, if you define an id selector to format a menu, you can use the menu id selector only once in that page. This restriction doesn't apply to classes, which you can use as many times as you like.

Web designers like the id selector because it's clearer than a class selector. By their very nature, id selectors can refer to one and only one element on a page. For example, if a page has a menu id selector, or a navigation bar id selector, the designer knows that there's only one menu or navigation bar on that page. The id attribute clearly communicates this fact. Of course, the reason you need to understand id attributes is because you frequently see them in the wild (for example, you'll find them in the *www.csszengarden.com* examples shown later in Figure 9-13). Now that you know they're just a version of class attributes, you won't have any trouble understanding how they work.

Incidentally, you can use id selectors in all the same ways as other selectors. That means you can combine id selectors with other selectors using a comma (,) or you can create contextual selectors like the one shown here, which acts only on anchors inside a <div> menu:

```
div#Menu a {
  color: red;
}
```

Floating Boxes

Most of the example pages in previous chapters used *relative positioning* to place objects on a page, which is the original XHTML model. When you use relative positioning, your browser orders page elements based on where they appear in an XHTML document. If you have one <div> element followed by another in your XHTML markup, the browser positions the second <div> element below the first one.

To get richer layouts—for example, to create any of the pages you see in Figure 9-11—you need more flexibility in positioning content. One option is a *floating layout*, which you used to make pictures float in Chapter 7. A floating layout works just as readily with <div> elements as it did with those <img> elements, with one exception—you need to supply a width for the <div> element.

Note: When you float an image, browsers automatically make the floating box as wide as the image. When you float a <div> element with text inside, it's up to you to choose how wide you want it.

Here's an example that defines a box that floats on the right side of some text:

```
.Float {
    float: right;
    width: 150px;
    background-color: red;
    border-width: 2px;
    border-style: solid;
    border-color: black;
    padding: 10px;
    margin: 8px;
    font-weight: bold;
    color: white;
}
```

With floating content, text outside the floating content wraps around the edges of it (see Figure 9-11).

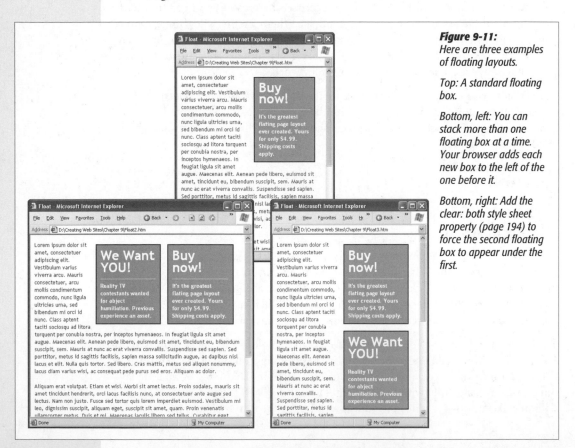

Figure 9-11:
Here are three examples of floating layouts.

Top: A standard floating box.

Bottom, left: You can stack more than one floating box at a time. Your browser adds each new box to the left of the one before it.

Bottom, right: Add the clear: both style sheet property (page 194) to force the second floating box to appear under the first.

Absolute Positioning

Style sheets also let you place elements at fixed locations on a page, with no wrapping involved. This is handy when you want to create multi-columned pages (see Figure 9-12).

To use absolute positioning, set the position property of your <div> element to *absolute*. Then, set the location of your <div> element using a combination of the *top, left, right*, and *bottom* properties.

The following style rule defines a panel that's 150 pixels wide and positioned along the left side of a page. The left edge of the box is 10 pixels from the edge of the browser window, and the top edge of the box is 70 pixels from the top of the browser window:

```
.LeftPanel {
  position: absolute;
  top: 70px;
  left: 10px;
  width: 150px;
}
```

It's just as easy to create a fixed panel on the right side of a page. Just use the top and right position properties to place the box relative to the right edge of the browser window:

```
.RightPanel {
  position: absolute;
  top: 70px;
  right: 10px;
  width: 150px;
}
```

The final step is to define the content section that sits between these two panels. You can't use absolute positioning for this, because you don't know how large the browser window will be. Fortunately, you don't need to—all you need to do is specify how far from the left and right edges of the browser window the center panel should sit. For example, the left panel you defined above measures 150 pixels wide and sits 10 pixels from the left edge of the browser window. That means your center panel needs a left margin of 160 pixels (*150+10*). It needs to accommodate the right panel in the same way. It's customary to tack on extra pixel to each margin to make sure your panels don't overlap, making the final style sheet rule:

```
.CenterPanel {
  margin-left: 161px;
  margin-right: 161px;
}
```

Once you define the sections of your page, you can insert content into them using <div> elements. Because your style sheet places <div> elements precisely on a page, it doesn't matter how you order the <div> elements in your XHTML document. For example, you might want to define the content for your left and right panels, and *then* your center panel. The point is, the order in which you lay down your <div> elements in your XHTML markup doesn't matter. Here's an example:

```
<div class="LeftPanel">
  <h1>Links</h1>
  <a href="...">Page 1</a><br />
  <a href="...">Page 2</a><br />
  ...
</div>

<div class="RightPanel">
  <h1>Contact Us</h1>
  ...
</div>

<div class="CenterPanel">
  Styles are remarkably powerful. All you need to do is position
  a few &lt;div&gt; elements, and your content flows...
</div>
```

Figure 9-12 shows the results.

The remarkable part about this example is that your XHTML document is free of messy formatting details. Instead, it's a small miracle of clarity, with content divided into several easy-to-understand sections. If you created the same layout using invisible tables, your XHTML document would be cluttered with table elements, making it more difficult to interpret. And if you save your styles into an external style sheet (page 138), you can start building a second page using the same layout without spending any time puzzling out the correct formatting.

To use style-based layouts, begin by planning each page as a collection of separate regions. Then put each region into a <div> element with a unique class name, even if you don't intend to apply style sheet rules for these sections yet. Finally, write the style sheet rules that position and format each <div> element. This is the most time-consuming part of your markup to write, but it's time well spent—you can tweak your formatting rules at any time without disturbing your content. Figure 9-13 shows a Web site that takes this concept to the extreme.

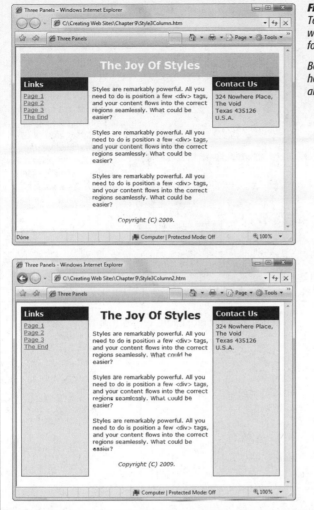

Figure 9-12:
Top: This page uses a three-panel style sheet layout, with a few more refinements (like fine-tuned borders, fonts, and background colors).

Bottom: Another variation of the same design sets the height of the side panels to 90 percent, so they always fill up a browser window.

Layering

It may have occurred to you that you need to position elements carefully when you use absolute positioning to make sure you don't overlap one element with another. Interestingly, advanced Web pages sometimes deliberately overlap elements to create dramatic effects. For example, you might create a logo by overlapping two words, or create a heading by partially overlapping a picture. These tricks use overlapping *layers*.

When you use overlapping layers, you need to tell your browser which element goes on top. You do this through a simple number called the *z-index*. Browsers put elements with a high z-index in front of elements with a lower z-index.

Figure 9-13:
One page, dozens of different looks. The Web site www.csszengarden. com shows the holy grail of style-based formatting: a page you can thoroughly reformat and rearrange just by editing or switching the style sheet it uses. Best of all, you can download the XHTML for this page and dozens of sample style sheets to try it out for yourself.

For example, here are two elements positioned absolutely so that they overlap:

```
.Back {
  z-index: 0;
  position: absolute;
  top: 10px;
  left: 10px;
  width: 150px;
  height: 100px;
  background-color: orange;
  border-style: dotted;
  border-width: 1px;
}

.Front {
  z-index: 1;
  position: absolute;
  top: 50px;
  left: 50px;
  width: 230px;
  height: 180px;
  font: xx-large;
  border-style: dotted;
  border-width: 1px;
}
```

The first class (Back) defines an orange background square. The second class (Front) defines a large font for text. You set the elements' z-indexes so that the browser superimposes the Front box (which has a z-index of 1) over the Back box (which has a z-index of 0). In the example above, the XHTML code adds a dotted border around both elements to make it easier to see how the boxes overlap on a page.

Note: The actual value of a z-index isn't important, the only important characteristic is how it compares to other z-indexes. For example, if you have two elements with z-indexes of 48 and 100, you'll get the same effect as two elements with z-indexes of 0 and 1—the second element overlaps the first. If two or more elements have the same z-index, the one that's first in the XHTML gets shoved underneath those that come later.

In your XHTML, you need to create both boxes with <div> elements. It also makes sense to supply some text for the Front box:

```
<div class="Back">
</div>

<div class="Front">
  This text is on top.
</div>
```

Load this page in a browser and you'll see a block of text that stretches over part of the orange box and out into empty space (see Figure 9-14, left).

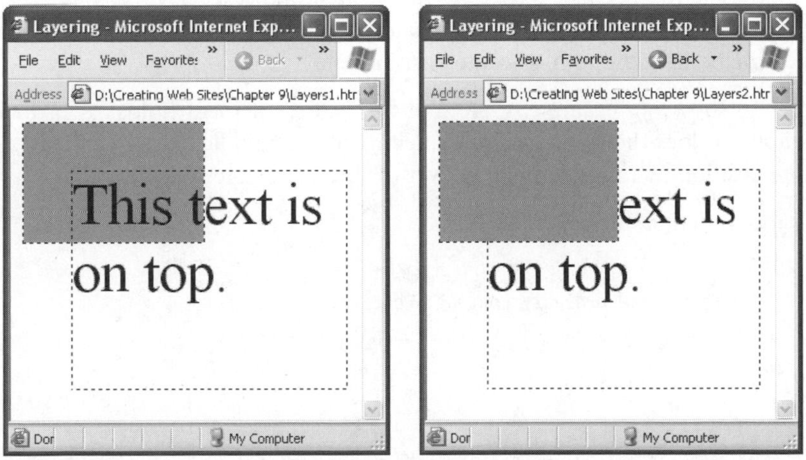

Figure 9-14:
Left: The colored box has the lower z-index.

Right: The colored box has the higher z-index, and obscures the text.

You can reverse the z-index to change the example:

```
.Back {
  z-index: 1;
  ...
}
```

```
.Front {
  z-index: 0;
  ...
}
```

Combining Absolute and Relative Positioning

Style sheet experts know that they don't need to stick to just absolute or relative positioning—they can get the best of both worlds with a little careful planning.

To understand how this technique works, you need to know the following style-sheet secret: When you use absolute positioning, your browser interprets the coordinates relative to the *container*. As you saw in several examples earlier, when you put a <div> element in the <body> section of a page, your browser positions that element in relation to the page. Set the <div> element's left coordinate to 10 pixels, and your browser positions the element 10 pixels from the left edge of the page. But here's a nifty experiment—try placing the same <div> element inside another element, like a table cell. Now your browser positions the <div> element 10 pixels from the left edge of the table cell, *no matter where you place that table cell on the page*. It's as if the <div> element exists in its own private world—and that's the world of the container it's in, not the world of the main page.

So how can you use this understanding to your advantage? One technique is to use absolute positioning to create a special effect, like text superimposed on a photo. To try this out, create a page with several <div> elements. But don't use absolute positioning—instead, let these <div> elements fit themselves into the page one after the other, the normal Web way. In the first and last <div> elements, add ordinary content (text, pictures, and whatever else you like). But in the middle <div> element, let loose with absolute positioning.

Figure 9-15 shows an example. Here, the first <div> element holds an ordinary paragraph, as does the third <div> element. But the middle <div> element uses absolute positioning to add white text over the picture of a tombstone.

Here's the content of the page:

```
<div>
  <p>Here is some ordinary content. Whatever you put here
  bumps the grave stone box further down the page.</p>
</div>

<div class="GraveContainer">
  <img class="GraveImage" alt="Tombstone" src="tombstone.jpg" />
  <p class="GraveText">Fatal error.<br />Please reboot.</p>
</div>

<div>
  <p>Here is some more ordinary content.</p>
</div>
```

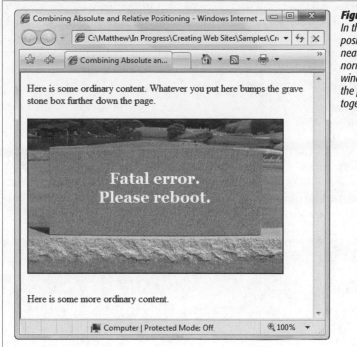

Figure 9-15:
In this page, the middle section uses absolute positioning to place text over a picture. The neat part is that the rest of page is perfectly normal, and even if you shrink the browser window (thereby bumping the picture down the page), the text and picture stay locked together.

The middle <div> element uses three style rules to apply all the style properties this example needs. The GraveImage and GraveText rules turn on the absolute positioning:

```
img.GraveImage {
  position: absolute;
  left: 10px;
}

p.GraveText {
  position: absolute;
  top: 150px;
  left: 120px;
  color: white;
  font-size: x-large;
  font-weight: bold;
  text-align: center;
}
```

The GraveContainer rule sizes the <div> element. Ordinarily, a <div> element enlarges itself to fit its contents. But when you use absolute positioning, the <div> element no longer knows how big it should be, and it shrinks itself down to nothing. Here's the rule that gives the <div> element the correct height, and ensures that the subsequent content in the page (the third <div> element with the final paragraph) appears in the right place:

```
div.GraveContainer {
  height: 250px;
}
```

As a general rule, you should use relative positioning to make sure a page's layout is as flexible and adaptable as possible. But as you see in this example, it's perfectly reasonable to use a <div> element to section off smaller regions that use absolute positioning—in fact, doing so gives you the chance to add some nifty effects.

DESIGN TIME

Become a Style Sheet Expert

Style sheets are one of the hottest topics in Web development today. The Web buzzes with discussion groups, articles, and tutorials that show you how to create slick style-powered designs. If you want to become a style aficionado, there's still quite a bit to learn, including the ins and outs of browser quirks, workarounds for style sheet limitations, and innovative ways to combine graphics and text. Here are a few of the best resources:

- **Style sheet basics**. Is your style sheet expertise a little wobbly? Brush up with the tutorials at *www.w3schools.com/css*. And check to make sure you aren't making any mistakes by using the CSS validator at *http://jigsaw.w3.org/css-validator*.

- **Style sheet examples (the barebones)**. See some of the basic style sheet designs (like two- and three-column layouts) at the Layout Reservoir (*www.bluerobot.com/web/layouts*) and Glish (*http://glish.com/css*), along with handy links to other good online resources.

- **Style sheet examples (full-featured)**. See the dozens of different ways you can format the same XHTML document. This small miracle of CSS design (see Figure 9-13) is at *www.csszengarden.com*. There's even a book tie-in named *The Zen of CSS Design* (Peachpit Press) that discusses some of the more exotic examples.

- **Advanced style sheet resources**. Planning to become a cutting-edge Web designer? Check out the legendary books by Eric Meyer, like *Eric Meyer on CSS* (New Riders Press), and stop by the Web site at *www.westciv.com/style_master/house*.

Multipart Pages

As you start to build bigger and more elaborate Web sites, you'll no doubt discover one of the royal pains of Web site design: getting a common ingredient to appear on every page.

For example, you might decide to add a menu of links that lets visitors jump from one section of your site to another. You can place these links in a table or a <div> element (two techniques shown in Chapter 9) to get them in the right position on a page, but either way there's a problem—you need to do a fair bit of copying and pasting to display the menu on every page of your site. If you're not careful, one page can end up with a slightly different version of the same menu. And when you decide to make a change to the menu, you'll face the nightmare of updating every one of your pages. Web creators who try this approach don't get out much on the weekend.

There's no simple solution to this problem, but crafty Web designers can use a variety of techniques to get around it:

- **Server-side includes.** A server-side include is a command that injects the contents of one XHTML file inside another. This lets you carefully separate a block of XHTML content (for example, a menu) and reuse it in multiple pages. However, there's a significant caveat—the XHTML standard doesn't support server-side includes on its own, so you can use this feature only if you have the right type of Web server.

- **Frames.** Frames are a sometimes-controversial XHTML feature that let you display more than one Web page in the same browser window. Although frames work well and have been used for years, they're distinctly unpopular today thanks to a variety of minor quirks (discussed on page 267).

- **Page templates.** Some high-powered Web page editors (namely, Expression Web and Dreamweaver) include a page template feature. You begin by creating a template that defines the structure of your Web pages and includes the repeating content you want to appear on every page (like a menu or a header). Then you use that template to create all your site pages. Here's the neat part: when you update the template, your Web page editor automatically updates all the pages that use that template.

In this chapter, you'll see how you can use these techniques to tame large Web sites, and you'll consider their risks and rewards.

Understanding Multipart Pages

By this point, you've amassed a solid toolkit of tactics and tricks for building Web pages. You learned to polish your pages with modern fonts and colors, gussy them up with a trendy layout, and add images and links to the mix. However, as you apply these techniques to a complete Web site, you'll run into some new challenges.

One of the first hurdles you face when you go from one Web page to a dozen or more is how to make them all consistent. Consistent formatting is relatively easy—as long as you carefully plan the structure of your Web site and use an external style sheet (see Chapter 6), you can apply a common look and feel to as many pages as you want.

But style sheets have their limits. They can't help you if you need to have the same *content* in more than one page. That's a problem, because modern Web sites have specific elements that repeat on every page, like a header and a set of navigation buttons (see Figure 10-1).

So how do Web designers create multipart pages? For large sites, individually pasting the same bit of XHTML into every page just isn't an option—it would be a management disaster. But popular Web sites don't seem to have a problem dealing with repeated content. No matter what product you view on Amazon, for example, you see the familiar tabbed search bar at the top. No matter what vacation you check out in Expedia, you keep the same set of navigation tabs. That's because Amazon and Expedia, like almost all of the Web's hugest and most popular sites, are actually *Web applications*. When you request a page from one of these sites, a custom-tuned piece of software creates the right XHTML page on the fly.

For example, when you view a product on Amazon, a Web application reads the product information out of a gargantuan database, transforms it into an XHTML page, and tops it off with the latest version of the search bar. Your browser displays the end result as a single page. This technique avoids the hassle of maintaining the same content (in this case, the search bar) in thousands of different files.

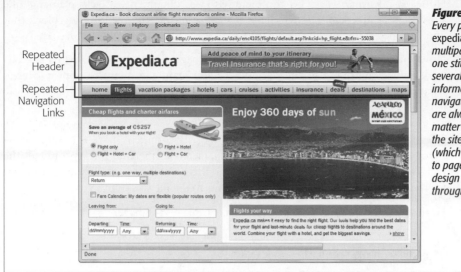

Repeated
Header

Repeated
Navigation
Links

Figure 10-1:
*Every page on www.
expedia.com is a
multipart page. Each
one stitches together
several pieces of
information, including
navigation tabs (which
are always the same, no
matter where you go on
the site) and content
(which varies from page
to page). This sort of
design crops up on sites
throughout the Web.*

Although Web applications offer an elegant solution for creating multipart pages, it's a dead end for the casual Web-head. To build and maintain a Web application of your own, you'd need top-shelf programming skills and a team of IT experts to help you out. So unless you're ready to start a new career as a hard-core code jockey, you need to compromise.

Note: Don't rush off to pick up a degree in computer science just yet. Programming is a completely different cup of tea than writing XHTML. Unless you have a lot of time to spare for removing cryptic errors from computer code (a process known as debugging) and even more time to put them there in the first place (politely known as programming), you're better off using the techniques described in this chapter.

Server-Side Includes

Even though you can't write a Web application on your own, you *can* borrow a few tricks from the Web applications model—if your Web host supports them. The simplest example is a technology called *server-side includes* (SSIs), which is a scaled-down version of the XHTML-assembling trick used on sites like Amazon and Expedia.

Essentially, a server-side include is an instruction that tells a Web server to insert the contents of one XHTML file into another. For example, imagine you want to use the same menu on several pages. You would begin by saving the menu as a separate file, which you could name *menu.htm*. Here are its contents:

```
<h1>Menu</h1>
<a href="...">Page 1</a><br />
<a href="...">Page 2</a><br />
<a href="...">Page 3</a><br />
<a href="...">The End</a>
```

Notice that *menu.htm* isn't a complete XHTML document. It lacks elements like <html>, <head>, and <body>. That's because *menu.htm* is a building block that you'll embed inside other, full-fledged XHTML pages.

Now you're ready to use the menu in a Web page. To do that, you add a specialized *include* command to the page where you want the menu to appear. Here's what it looks like:

```
<!--#include file="menu.htm" -->
```

The include command disguises itself as an XHTML comment (page 43) using the <!-- characters at the beginning and the --> characters at the end. But its core tells the real story. The number sign (#) indicates that this command is actually an instruction for the Web server, and the file attribute points to the file you want to use.

Here's the include command at work in a complete Web page:

```
<!DOCTYPE html PUBLIC "-//W3C//DTD XHTML 1.0 Strict//EN"
"http://www.w3.org/TR/xhtml1/DTD/xhtml1-strict.dtd">

<html xmlns="http://www.w3.org/1999/xhtml">
<head>
  <title>Server-Side Include Test</title>
  <link rel="stylesheet" href="styles.css" type="text/css" />
</head>

<body>
  <div class="Header">
    <h1>Templates Rule!</h1>
  </div>

  <div class="MenuPanel">
    <!--#include file="menu.htm" -->
  </div>

  <div class="Content">
    <p>This is the welcome page. Just above this text is the handy menu
    for this site.</p>
  </div>
</body>
</html>
```

When you request this page, the Web server scans through it, looking for instructions. When it finds the include command, it retrieves the specified file and inserts its contents into that position on the page. It then sends the final, processed file to you. In the current example, that means your Web browser receives a Web page that actually looks like this (see Figure 10-2):

```
<!DOCTYPE html PUBLIC "-//W3C//DTD XHTML 1.0 Strict//EN"
"http://www.w3.org/TR/xhtml1/DTD/xhtml1-strict.dtd">

<html xmlns="http://www.w3.org/1999/xhtml">
<head>
  <title>Server-Side Include Test</title>
  <link rel="stylesheet" href="styles.css" type="text/css" />
</head>

<body>
  <div class="Header">
    <h1>Welcome to a Multipart Page</h1>
  </div>

  <div class="MenuPanel">
    <h1>Menu</h1>
    <a href="...">Page 1</a><br />
    <a href="...">Page 2</a><br />
    <a href="...">Page 3</a><br />
    <a href="...">The End</a>
  </div>

  <div class="ContentPanel">
    <p>This is the welcome page. Just to the left of this text is the
    handy menu for this site.</p>
  </div>
</body>
</html>
```

The advantage to this technique is obvious. You can add the include command to as many Web pages as you want, and still keep just one copy of your menu. That lets you edit your menu easily, and ensures that all your pages have the same version of the menu.

If this discussion sounds a bit too good to be true—well, it is. You may face a number of complications:

• **Web server support.** Not all Web servers support server-side includes. To get the lowdown, contact your Web hosting company.

• **Page types.** For a server-side include to work, the Web server has to process your page and search for include instructions every time a browser requests a page. That happens automatically, but only if you use the right page type. You can't give your pages the .htm or .html extensions; instead, you need to use .shtm or .shtml (on an Apache Web server), or .asp or .aspx (on a Microsoft IIS Web server). Once again, contact your Web hosting company for details.

Figure 10-2:
Although this page looks normal enough, it takes some magic to make it work. Just before the Web server sends this page to your browser, it reads the menu links from a separate file and inserts them into the page.

Welcome.shtm

Menu.htm

- **Design difficulties.** Server-side includes only come into effect when there's a Web server at work. If you open a Web page that's stored on your hard drive, your browser ignores the include instruction and you won't see the menu at all. That makes it difficult to test your site without uploading it to a live Web server. Dreamweaver gives you partial relief—if you open a Web page that uses server-side includes, you'll see the contents of the included files in Dreamweaver's design window while you edit the page.

If you know your Web host supports server-side includes and you aren't fazed by the design difficulties, why not give them a whirl? And if they still don't suit you, you have two other compromises to consider: frames (up next) and page templates (at the end of this chapter).

Note: Because the include command masquerades as an XHTML comment, it won't cause a problem if you put pages with include instructions on a Web server that doesn't support server-side includes. The server simply ignores the SSIs.

Frame Basics

Frames work by carving a browser window into two or more regions, or *frames*. Once you split a window this way, you can display a different Web page in each frame.

There are two obvious differences between frames and server-side includes. First, frames do their work in a browser, not on a Web server. That means they don't need any special Web server support. Second, frames bring together distinct Web pages, not just chunks of XHTML content. Each frame holds a complete XHTML document you can look at either in a frame, alongside other pages, or on its own.

The Frames Controversy

Are there reasons to avoid frames?

The Web developer community has been steadily moving away from frames for several years. Although they're still alive and well in small- and medium-sized Web sites, you're unlikely to see them turn up in a large-scale site like eBay or Amazon.

Some of the reasons that frames have a bad reputation are historical—for example, ancient browsers didn't support them that well, and Web newbies used them in all the wrong ways. However, frames also have a few quirks of their own.

Here are the reasons that top-level Web professionals look like they've just bit into a lemon when you tell them you're thinking about using frames:

- **Search engine confusion**. In a frames page, each frame displays a separate XHTML file. This has the potential to confuse search engines, because they examine each of these files separately. That means they might have trouble interpreting what one file is about because related content sits in a separate file, which is meant to be displayed by its side. Or the search engine might index just one file from a frames page instead of the entire frameset. In this case, people who follow the search engine link will wind up seeing this content page without the frames or any of the other, related files. These idiosyncrasies aren't the end of the world, but they aren't ideal.

- **Frame abuse**. Some Stone Age Web developers used frames to keep part of their Web site visible when a visitor clicked on an external link. The effect is like an ad bar that never goes away. This leech-like use of frames is universally despised and almost completely expunged from today's Internet.

- **Accessibility and Compatibility**. While frames will probably never disappear from the Web completely, designers are slowly phasing them out because they cause problems for people with disabilities (who often use screen-reading devices) and people who do their browsing with small Web-enabled devices (like cellphones). XHTML 1.0 transitional supports frames, but XHTML 1.0 strict and XHTML 1.1 don't.

- **Less-effective URLs**. You can't bookmark a frames page anywhere but at the initial page. As you navigate through a site that uses framed pages, the content within the frames changes, but the URL doesn't—it still reflects the frameset page. Therefore, there's no way to supply visitors or friends with a URL that goes straight to a page of interest—they need to go to the main frameset page and click their way through. You'll learn more about this issue on page 281.

Creating a Frames Page

The first step in using frames is to create a *frameset* document, which are the instructions that define the number and location of the frames you want in a browser window, and what page should appear in each one of those frames.

A frameset page is a special type of XHTML document. Like all XHTML documents, it starts with a doctype. But frameset pages use a specialized doctype you haven't seen yet:

```
<!DOCTYPE html PUBLIC "-//W3C//DTD XHTML 1.0 Frameset//EN"
"http://www.w3.org/TR/xhtml1/DTD/xhtml1-frameset.dtd">
```

After the doctype, the frameset page uses the standard <html> element. It includes a <head> section, where you define a title for the page, but it doesn't continue with the familiar <body> element, where you usually put the content of a page. Instead, it introduces a new ingredient: a <frameset> element that divides the page into separate frames:

```
<!DOCTYPE html PUBLIC "-//W3C//DTD XHTML 1.0 Frameset//EN"
"http://www.w3.org/TR/xhtml1/DTD/xhtml1-frameset.dtd">

<html xmlns="http://www.w3.org/1999/xhtml">
<head>
  <title>A Sample Frames Page</title>
</head>

<frameset>...</frameset>
</html>
```

The information inside your <frameset> element is the heart of your frameset page. It tells a browser how to split the window into separate columns or rows, with each column or row becoming a distinct frame. The <frameset> element also sets the size of each frame.

If you split the window into columns, you have to define the width of each using the *cols* attribute. You can set the width as a percentage of the total window space, or as a fixed number of pixels. Here's an example that splits a page into two equal columns:

```
<frameset cols="50%,50%">
   ...
</frameset>
```

If you carve the window into rows, you use the *rows* attribute. Here's an example that creates three rows using a percentage value to set their relative sizes, with the middle one being the largest:

```
<frameset rows="25%,50%,25%">
   ...
</frameset>
```

Figure 10-3 shows what this example looks like in a browser.

In addition to percentage values, you can define the size of each column or row using an exact pixel size. Here's a three-column page where the left and right columns are always 100 pixels wide:

```
<frameset cols="100,*,100">
   ...
</frameset>
```

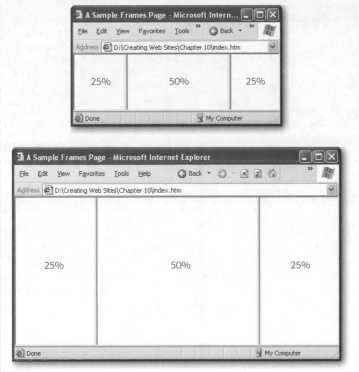

Figure 10-3:
These browser windows use the same frameset, with a 25/50/25 percent split among the frames. Because the frameset page specifies frame sizes using a percent value (rather than an exact pixel size), the browser resizes all the frames proportionately when a visitor stretches the browser window.

This example introduces another nifty trick—using the asterisk (*). It tells your browser to make that frame occupy any remaining space on a Web page. For example, if this browser window is 800 pixels wide, you have two 100-pixel columns on the flanks and a 600-pixel column in the leftover space. Figure 10-4 shows what this looks like.

Note: If you specify fixed pixel sizes for every row or column, the browser gives them the requested size and then checks to see if there's more space left over in the window. If so, the browser expands all your frames proportionately. This probably isn't the effect you want, so it's a good idea to use the asterisk to give all the extra space to a specific frame.

As you probably figured out by now, frames always occupy rectangular regions of a browser window. There's no way to create frames with fancy shapes. That doesn't mean you can't create the *illusion* of a shaped frame, however. All you do is use the background-image property discussed in Chapter 7 (page 198) to show some sort of shaped or curved picture as the background for one of the pages in your frameset. Figure 10-5 shows an example.

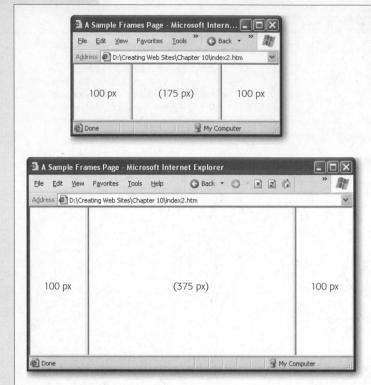

Figure 10-4:
In this example, the frameset has a fixed 100-pixel frame on either side, and a middle frame that gets the remaining space. When a visitor resizes the browser window, only the middle frame widens.

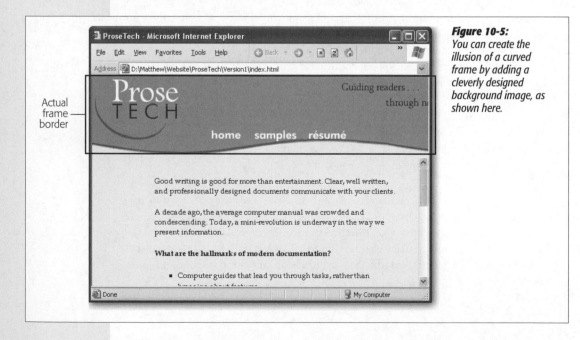

Figure 10-5:
You can create the illusion of a curved frame by adding a cleverly designed background image, as shown here.

Putting Documents in a Frameset

Splitting a window into frames is a good first step, but to see some actual content on your pages, you need to identify the *source* of the content you want to put in each frame.

To define a frame source, you add one <frame> element for each column or row your frameset includes. You add these elements inside the <frameset> element, keeping the same order you used to list the columns (left to right) or rows (top to bottom).

Here's the basic skeleton of a page with two frames:

```
<frameset cols="30%,*">
  <frame />
  <frame />
</frameset>
```

To link a Web page to a frame, you set various attributes of the <frame> element. The most important are *src* (which is the file name of the Web page you want to display in that frame) and *name* (which gives the frame a descriptive title so you can use it later in your links). Here's a typical example of a complete frameset page:

```
<!DOCTYPE html PUBLIC "-//W3C//DTD XHTML 1.0 Frameset//EN"
"http://www.w3.org/TR/xhtml1/DTD/xhtml1-frameset.dtd">

<html xmlns="http://www.w3.org/1999/xhtml">
<head>
  <title>A Sample Frames Page</title>
</head>

<frameset cols="30%,*">
  <frame name="Menu" src="menu.htm" />
  <frame name="Main" src="welcome.htm" />
</frameset>
</html>
```

In this case, it's likely you'll always put the Menu frame on the left (that is, as the first frame listed) to display the navigation links in *menu.htm* page. On the other hand, you'll use the Main frame on the right (the second frame listed) to show all kinds of content. Initially, the Main frame displays a welcome page, but that will change as a reader clicks links and moves through your site. That's why the frame name and the XHTML file name don't match.

Tip: When you supply the source for a frame, you follow all the same rules you do when identifying the source for an image or hyperlink. That means you include just the file name if the file is in the same folder as the current page, or you can use a relative or absolute path (see page 210).

To try out this example, save the frameset page using the file name *index.htm*.

Tip: Many Web servers treat *index.htm* as the entry point of your Web site. That means they send it to the browser automatically if they receive a request that doesn't specify a page. See page 57 for more information.

Next, create the *menu.htm* and *welcome.htm* pages. All the *menu.htm* page needs is a simple list of links, as shown here:

```
<!DOCTYPE html PUBLIC "-//W3C//DTD XHTML 1.0 Strict//EN"
"http://www.w3.org/TR/xhtml1/DTD/xhtml1-strict.dtd">

<html xmlns="http://www.w3.org/1999/xhtml">
<head>
  <title></title>
</head>

<body>
  <p>
    <a href="welcome.htm">Welcome</a><br />
    <a href="page1.htm">Page 1</a><br />
    <a href="page2.htm">Page 2</a><br />
    <a href="page3.htm">Page 3</a>
  </p>
</body>
</html>
```

When a browser displays frames, it displays the title of the *frameset* page at the top of the browser window, ignoring the titles of the pages that appear within the frames. That means that the titles in the *menu.htm* and *welcome.htm* pages never appear. You still need to include <title> elements, however, because they're a required part of XHTML. Additionally, this title information sometimes appears in search engine listings.

Note: In the examples in this chapter, the <title> element is left blank if it won't appear in a browser. That way, you can quickly sort out which titles are most important.

The *welcome.htm* page shows some straightforward content:

```
<!DOCTYPE html PUBLIC "-//W3C//DTD XHTML 1.0 Strict//EN"
"http://www.w3.org/TR/xhtml1/DTD/xhtml1-strict.dtd">

<html xmlns="http://www.w3.org/1999/xhtml">
<head>
  <title></title>
</head>

<body>
```

```
<h1>Welcome</h1>
<p>This simple welcome page shows how two frames can be joined in happy
matrimony. On the left is a menu with a set of links.
Over here on the right, there's a heading and an ordinary paragraph,
which makes up a content page.</p>
</body>
</html>
```

As always, you could use styles to make these two pieces look a lot more impressive (see Chapter 6 for more on styles). However, these pages are enough to give you an idea of how this frames business works. Assuming that all the pages are in the same folder, you'll see a single integrated window when you request *index.htm* (see Figure 10-6).

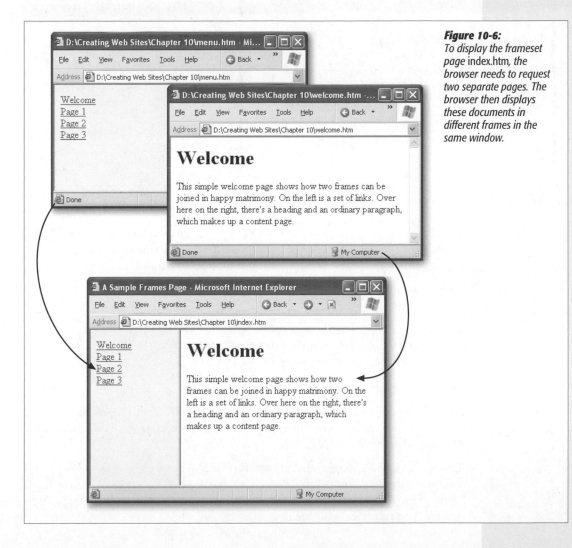

Figure 10-6:
To display the frameset page index.htm, the browser needs to request two separate pages. The browser then displays these documents in different frames in the same window.

Note: High-powered Web page editors like Expression Web and Dreamweaver provide tools that make it easier to work with frames. For example, you can edit all the pages that belong to a frameset in one window.

Targeting Frames

There's actually a small but important flaw in the frameset shown in the previous example. When you click one of the navigation links, the target page of the link opens in the frame where the link appears (see Figure 10-7).

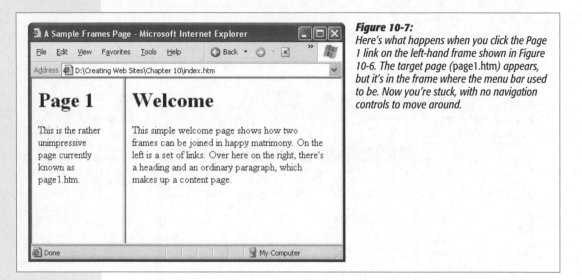

Figure 10-7:
Here's what happens when you click the Page 1 link on the left-hand frame shown in Figure 10-6. The target page (page1.htm) appears, but it's in the frame where the menu bar used to be. Now you're stuck, with no navigation controls to move around.

To correct this problem, you need to change your links so that they explicitly tell the browser to open a target page in the Main frame. To take care of this, you add the *target* attribute to the <a> element, and supply the name of the target frame.

Here's how you rewrite the *menu.htm* page to target your links:

```
<a href="welcome.htm" target="Main">Welcome</a><br />
<a href="page1.htm" target="Main">Page 1</a><br />
<a href="page2.htm" target="Main">Page 2</a><br />
<a href="page3.htm" target="Main">Page 3</a>
```

Figure 10-8 shows the corrected behavior.

There's one other change you need to make. XHTML strict doesn't support the target attribute, so you need to make sure your Web page uses the doctype for XHTML 1.0 transitional (page 30).

Rather than add the target attribute to every link in your page, it would be nice if there were a way to automatically assign a target frame to every one of those links. Fortunately, XHTML makes this easy with the <base> element. Using the <base> element, you can rewrite the menu page as follows.

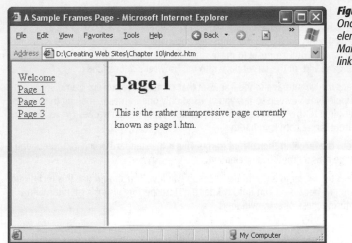

Figure 10-8:
Once you add the target attribute to the <a> element, the menu links send pages to the Main frame on the right, keeping the menu links visible at all times.

```
<!DOCTYPE html PUBLIC "-//W3C//DTD XHTML 1.0 Transitional//EN"
"http://www.w3.org/TR/xhtml1/DTD/xhtml1-transitional.dtd">

<html xmlns="http://www.w3.org/1999/xhtml">
<head>
  <base target="Main" />
  <title></title>
</head>

<body>
  <p>
    <a href="welcome.htm">Welcome</a><br />
    <a href="page1.htm">Page 1</a><br />
    <a href="page2.htm">Page 2</a><br />
    <a href="page3.htm">Page 3</a>
  </p>
</body>
</html>
```

In all, XHTML defines four target names. You can use these names instead of the name of an actual frame, either in individual links or with the <base> element. For example, you can use the *_blank* target to open a new page in a pop-up window, as shown here:

```
<a href="contact.htm" target="_blank">Welcome</a>
```

Table 10-1 lists XHTML's target names.

Table 10-1. *Reserved target names*

Name	Description
_top	Opens the target page in the "top" level of a window. That means the browser clears away your frameset to make room for the new document. It's equivalent to typing the URL of the target page into the browser's address box.
_parent	Opens the target page in the frameset that contains the current frame. In the examples you've seen so far, you've used only one frameset, making this name equivalent to the _top target. But if you start using nested frames (page 282) the _parent target comes in handy.
_self	Opens the target in the current frame. This is the standard behavior, unless you change it using the <base> element.
_blank	Opens the target in a brand-new pop-up window. You should use this technique sparingly, because it can quickly litter the unsuspecting visitor's monitor with a confusing mess of extra windows.

Building Better Frames Pages

So far, you've learned enough about frames to create a Web site that sports a never-changing navigation bar (like the one shown in Figure 10-8). In this section, you'll learn about a few refinements that help you make sure your frames look respectable, as well as a way to create more complex site structures using nested frames.

Frame Borders and Resizing

When you create a basic frameset, browsers add a thick gray bar between each frame. Web visitors can drag this bar to resize your frames at will, potentially scrambling your content (see Figure 10-9).

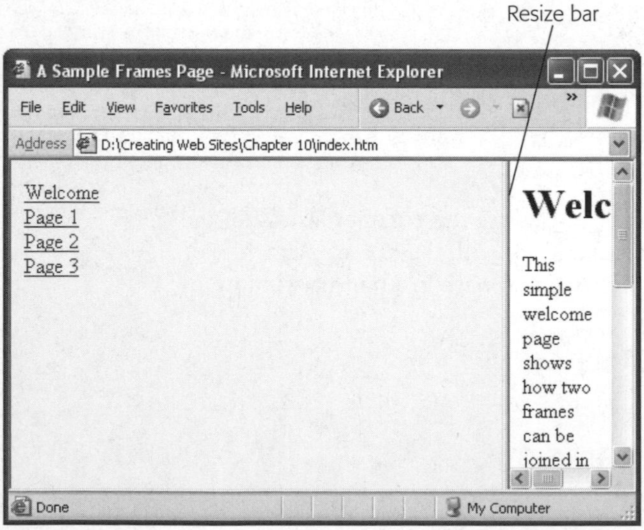

Resize bar

Figure 10-9:
Resizable frames give your Web visitors too much control.

Although you may find resizable frames occasionally useful, few Web sites use them. Most lock frames in place with the *noresize* attribute. That way, *you* decide what the page looks like—and stays like. You need to apply the *noresize* attribute to each <frame> element, like so:

```
<frame noresize="noresize" ... />
```

Many Web pages go even further and hide the ugly gray bar altogether by adding a *frameborder* attribute to each <frame> element. You need to add a number to the *frameborder* attribute that represents the width of the bar (in pixels). Set this number to 0 and the border disappears, so the page blends into one seamless whole:

```
<frame noresize="noresize" frameborder="0" ... />
```

Here's a cleaned-up version of the frameset shown earlier (Figure 10-10 shows the result):

```
<!DOCTYPE html PUBLIC "-//W3C//DTD XHTML 1.0 Frameset//EN"
"http://www.w3.org/TR/xhtml1/DTD/xhtml1-frameset.dtd">

<html xmlns="http://www.w3.org/1999/xhtml">
<head>
  <title>A Sample Frames Page</title>
</head>

<frameset cols="30%,*">
  <frame name="Menu" src="menu.htm" frameborder="0" noresize="noresize" />
  <frame name="Main" src="welcome.htm" frameborder="0" noresize="noresize" />
</frameset>
</html>
```

Figure 10-10:
This frameset page might as well be an ordinary Web page—the only indication that there are two pages involved is that each page uses a different background color. You could change this so they blend together completely, or you could use styles to add a fancier border.

Scrolling

Frames have one unmistakable feature—the scroll bar. When the content of one page grows larger than the size of its frame, scrollbars appear. But what makes this scrolling feature different from that in an ordinary Web page is the fact that you can scroll each frame *independently*, as shown in Figure 10-11.

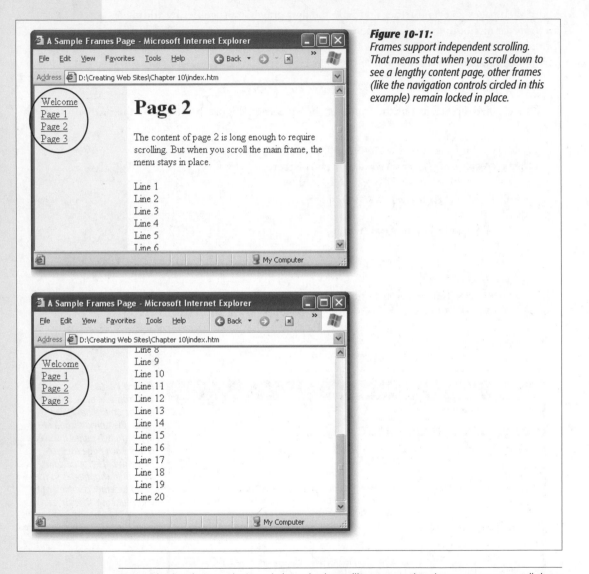

Figure 10-11:
Frames support independent scrolling. That means that when you scroll down to see a lengthy content page, other frames (like the navigation controls circled in this example) remain locked in place.

Note: The fact that you *don't* see independently scrolling page sections is one way you can tell that a Web site like Amazon *isn't* designed using frames. When you scroll a page on the Amazon Web site, everything—content, menu, and header sections—scrolls as part of the same page.

To prevent confusion, it's a good idea to keep as little text as possible in non-content frames (like menu panels) so your page doesn't display more than one set of scrollbars, which can confuse the hardiest Web fan.

Alternatively, you can change the scrolling behavior of a frame using the *scrolling* attribute. The standard setting, *auto* (which you get automatically if you don't include the scrolling attribute), shows scrollbars only when your page needs them. Your other options are *no* (to never show scrollbars, and prevent scrolling) or *yes* (to always show them).

Here's an example that turns off scrolling for the menu frame:

```
<frame name="Menu" src="menu.htm" noresize="noresize" scrolling="no" />
```

Figure 10-12 shows the difference.

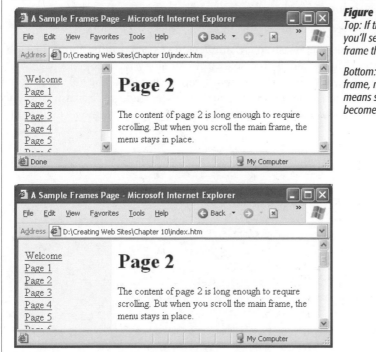

Figure 10-12:
Top: If the browser window is small enough, you'll see two sets of scrollbars, one for each frame that can't accommodate its content.

Bottom: When you turn off scrolling in a frame, no scrollbars appear, even if that means some content gets chopped off or becomes completely inaccessible.

Note: Resist the temptation to turn off scrolling, because visitors might need it if their browser window is very small. Ideally, you should test your Web site at the minimum expected browser window size (see page 230 for a discussion about screen resolution and page layout) and ensure that, at this size, only the main content page needs a scrollbar. The only time you may want to turn off scrolling is when you show a small frame for a navigation bar or a page banner.

Handling Browsers That Don't Support Frames

Occasionally, you might find a browser that doesn't support frames. Here are some examples when you can't count on frame support:

- The browser is really old. This is incredibly rare today. (Netscape's supported frames since version 2.) For that reason, you can ignore this concern.

- It's a mobile browser, like those used on small devices like smartphones. Of course, if you want to support these devices, you need to design your site with these small screens and limited display powers in mind.

- The Web visitor is viewing-impaired and uses a text-to-speech program (which "speaks" the text on a Web page). To make the page accessible to screen readers, use the <noframes> technique described below.

Framesets have a built-in mechanism to accommodate these situations. You put a <noframes> element inside the <frameset> element. Inside the <noframes> element, you add content that appears if a browser doesn't support frames.

For example, consider the two-frame example you've been reading about throughout this chapter. It uses frames to display a menu alongside a content page. At a bare minimum, browsers that don't support frames should still be able to read the content pages one at a time, in an ordinary browser window. The easiest way to serve up these individual pages is to provide an ordinary link to the *menu.htm* file, as shown here:

```
<!DOCTYPE html PUBLIC "-//W3C//DTD XHTML 1.0 Frameset//EN"
"http://www.w3.org/TR/xhtml1/DTD/xhtml1-frameset.dtd">

<html xmlns="http://www.w3.org/1999/xhtml">
<head>
  <title>A 3-Part Frames Page</title>
</head>

<frameset rows="80,*">
  <frame frameborder="0" name="Header" src="header.htm" />
  <frameset cols="100,*">
    <frame frameborder="0" name="Menu" src="menu.htm" />
    <frame frameborder="0" name="Main" src="welcome.htm" />
  </frameset>

  <noframes>
   <body>
    <h1>Your Browser Does Not Support Frames</h1>
```

```
      <p>
        Click <a href="menu.htm">here</a> to go to the menu.
      </p>
    </body>
  </noframes>
</frameset>
</html>
```

Notice that the <noframes> section picks up where the rest of the XHTML document leaves off—with the <body> element that defines the start of the XHTML content.

Now, when you look at the page in a browser that lacks frames support, you'll see a warning message and a link to the menu. You can click through to the menu, and then continue to each content page. The solution isn't perfect (for example, to move from a content page back to the menu, you need to click your browser's Back button), but it does provide a rudimentary way to use your site's menu as a way to link to other pages. An alternate approach is to copy the full menu content directly into the <noframes> section, so you don't need to click an extra link.

Tip: It's also a good idea to add content to the <noframes> section so any search engine that stumbles across your page can find out more about the page, increasing the likelihood that the engine will catalogue and search the rest of your site. Chapter 11 discusses search engines and how they find your Web site in more detail (page 316).

Better URLs for Framesets

There's no law against requesting a frameset page. You can type its URL into your browser window or link to it in the same way you link to any page. But frameset pages are a lot less flexible than ordinary Web pages, because they combine several pages into one URL. To understand the problem they can create, consider this example.

When you head to a frameset page (say, *index.htm*), your browser requests the initial page for each frame. For example, the browser might request *navbar.htm* to get a menu and *start.htm* to display a start page. When you start clicking links in the navigation bar, the browser performs the nifty little trick you saw earlier—it keeps the same frame layout, but loads new Web pages into one of the frames. For example, if you click Contact Us, the link might swap the *start.htm* page for *contact.htm*.

But here's the problem: The URL in the browser window never changes. No matter what page you're looking at, the URL still reflects the name of the initial frameset page (*index.htm*). That means that there's no way to bookmark individual site pages so you can directly request, say, the frameset with the *contact.htm* page displayed. Instead, you have to type *index.htm* into your browser, which takes you to the initial set of frames (with *start.htm* displayed), and then click your way through to *contact.htm*.

Note: The limitation discussed in this section actually doesn't apply to the Favorites feature in Internet Explorer. That's because IE is crafty enough to store information about what page it should load into each frame, so it can restore the exact arrangement of frames. However, this limitation does apply to other browsers like Firefox. More significantly, it applies if you need to type the URL in by hand, send it in an email message, or provide a link from another Web site.

You might think you could solve this problem by requesting *contact.htm* directly. But that would get you the *contact.htm* page only, *not* the frameset page. As a result, you wouldn't see the content in other frames, like the ever-so-important navigation bar.

One way around this problem is to create extra frameset pages. For example, if you want a way to get back to the *contact.htm* page, you could create a frameset page named *contact_frames.htm*. This frameset page would use the exact same frameset as *index.htm*, with one minor difference. Instead of loading the *start.htm* page initially, it would load the *contact.htm* page. If you want to point someone to the Contact Us page, just use *contact_frames.htm*. Think of it as a back door that gives visitors direct access to the pages on your site. The only problem with this approach is that you need to create a lot of extra frameset pages—as much as one for every page of content. If you decide to change your layout later on, you're stuck with a lot of updating.

Note: A more advanced approach is to add JavaScript code to each page. The idea is that each content page should check to see if it's part of a frameset page when a browser displays it. If it isn't, the content page should send the reader back to the frameset page, with specific instructions about what frames to load. If you want to experiment with this more complex approach, work through the JavaScript section in Chapter 14, and then read the solution at *http://javascript.about.com/library/blframe.htm*.

Nested Framesets

As you get more comfortable with frames, you may begin to plan more ambitious layouts. Sooner or later, you'll want to divide and subdivide your browser window with wild abandon. The good news is that this isn't that difficult to do—you simply need to *nest* one set of frames inside another.

Imagine you want to divide a page into two rows, and put the header information in the top row. Then, you want to subdivide the remaining content into two columns, featuring a menu in one and a content page in the other. Figure 10-13 shows the result of this kind of slicing and dicing.

In such a case, you need two framesets. The outer frameset defines the two rows, and the inner one splits one of those rows into two columns. Here's the complete markup for the page:

```
<!DOCTYPE html PUBLIC "-//W3C//DTD XHTML 1.0 Frameset//EN"
"http://www.w3.org/TR/xhtml1/DTD/xhtml1-frameset.dtd">

<html xmlns="http://www.w3.org/1999/xhtml">
```

Figure 10-13:
This page uses three frames. The Header frame is always 80 pixels high and the Menu frame is always 100 pixels wide. The main content page (where it says "Welcome") expands to fill whatever space is left over.

```
<head>
  <title>A 3-Part Frames Page</title>
</head>

<frameset rows="80,*">
  <frame name="Header" src="header.htm" frameborder="0" />
  <frameset cols="100,*">
    <frame name="Menu" src="menu.htm" noresize="noresize" frameborder="0" />
    <frame name="Main" src="welcome.htm" noresize="noresize"
      frameborder="0" />
  </frameset>
</frameset>
</html>
```

The only challenge in writing nested framesets is determining the correct order for dividing your page. If you reverse the nesting in this example (so you split the window into columns first, and *then* into rows), you'll end up with a very different result:

```
<!DOCTYPE html PUBLIC "-//W3C//DTD XHTML 1.0 Frameset//EN"
"http://www.w3.org/TR/xhtml1/DTD/xhtml1-frameset.dtd">

<html xmlns="http://www.w3.org/1999/xhtml">
<head>
  <title>A 3-Part Frames Page</title>
</head>

<frameset cols="100,*">
  <frame name="Menu" src="menu.htm" noresize="noresize" frameborder="0" />
  <frameset rows="80,*">
```

```
      <frame name="Header" src="header.htm" frameborder="0" />
      <frame name="Main" src="welcome.htm" noresize="noresize"
        frameborder="0" />
    </frameset>
  </frameset>
</html>
```

Figure 10-14 shows this reorganized version.

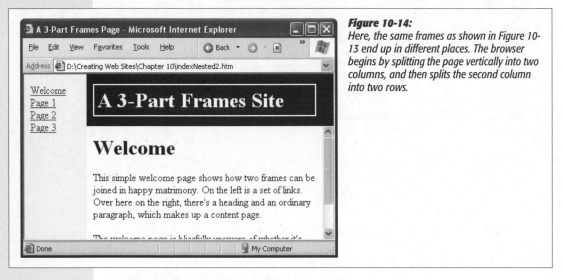

Another Way to Nest Frames

You'll run into one limitation if you define all your frames in a single page. To understand what it is, it helps to consider a new example.

Figure 10-15 shows a page divided into a typical layout of three frames: a header at the top, a topic panel at the left, and a content region on the right. However, the way you use these frames differs from previous examples. If you click one of the topic links on the left, you jump to a different portion of the *current* page. If you click one of the header links at the top, you navigate to a whole new page with a different set of topics.

Tip: Topic links are a great way to break down large pages and make them easier to navigate on the Web. Add these links to your pages by using bookmarks (as described on page 221).

The problem that this example presents is that every time a reader clicks a new link in the header, you need to replace *both* of the frames underneath. That's because you need to load a new content page *and* a new list of topic links. Unfortunately, if you implement this design using a single frameset, that isn't possible. Every time you click a link in the header, you can change only a single frame.

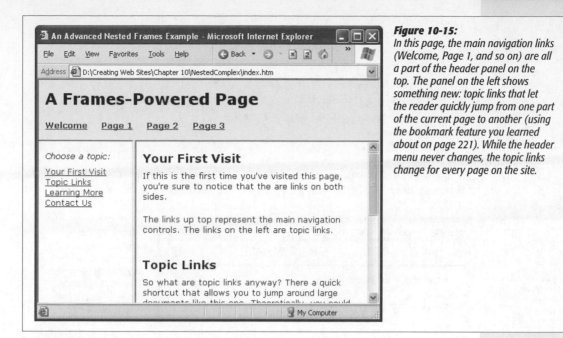

Figure 10-15:
*In this page, the main navigation links
(Welcome, Page 1, and so on) are all
a part of the header panel on the
top. The panel on the left shows
something new: topic links that let
the reader quickly jump from one part
of the current page to another (using
the bookmark feature you learned
about on page 221). While the header
menu never changes, the topic links
change for every page on the site.*

The workaround is to create more than one frameset page. The first frameset is
index.htm, which defines the overall structure of the site. It simply splits the page
into a Header frame and another frame underneath, as shown here:

```
<!DOCTYPE html PUBLIC "-//W3C//DTD XHTML 1.0 Frameset//EN"
"http://www.w3.org/TR/xhtml1/DTD/xhtml1-frameset.dtd">

<html xmlns="http://www.w3.org/1999/xhtml">
<head>
  <title>An Advanced Nested Frames Example</title>
</head>

<frameset rows="94,*">
  <frame name="Header" scrolling="no" src="header.htm"
   noresize="noresize" frameborder="0" />
  <frame name="Main" src="welcome_frame.htm" frameborder="0" />
</frameset>
</html>
```

The trick here is that the frame underneath points to *another* frameset document,
named *welcome_frame.htm*. The *welcome_frame.htm* file then splits the page with
frames *again*, this time into two columns:

```
<!DOCTYPE html PUBLIC "-//W3C//DTD XHTML 1.0 Frameset//EN"
"http://www.w3.org/TR/xhtml1/DTD/xhtml1-frameset.dtd">

<html xmlns="http://www.w3.org/1999/xhtml">
```

```
<head>
  <title></title>
</head>

<frameset cols="150,*">
  <frame name="TopicLinks" src="welcome_topics.htm" scrolling="no" />
  <frame name="Content" src="welcome.htm" />
</frameset>
</html>
```

The frame on the left, TopicLinks, holds the topic links. The frame on the right, Content, holds the actual text for your site (see Figure 10-16).

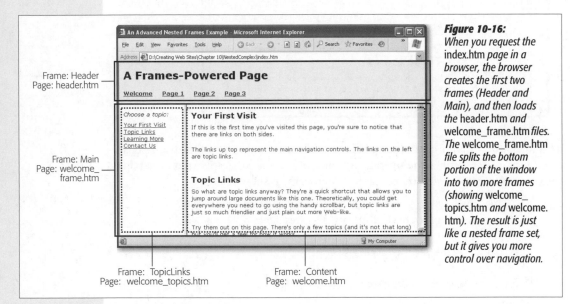

Figure 10-16:
When you request the index.htm *page in a browser, the browser creates the first two frames (Header and Main), and then loads the* header.htm *and* welcome_frame.htm *files. The* welcome_frame.htm *file splits the bottom portion of the window into two more frames (showing* welcome_topics.htm *and* welcome.htm*). The result is just like a nested frame set, but it gives you more control over navigation.*

Frame: Header
Page: header.htm

Frame: Main
Page: welcome_
frame.htm

Frame: TopicLinks
Page: welcome_topics.htm

Frame: Content
Page: welcome.htm

For this model to work, you need to create a frameset page for every content page. That's the messy bit. For example, when a reader clicks the Page 1 link, the browser replaces the bottom frame with the *page1_frame.htm* page. Here's the link you'd put in the *header.htm* document:

```
<a href="page1_frame.htm" target="Main">Page 1</a>
```

The *page1_frame.htm* document looks exactly the same as *welcome_frame.htm*, because it defines the same two column frames, in exactly the same positions. The only difference is that the source changes to point to a new topic page and a new content page, as shown here:

```
<!DOCTYPE html PUBLIC "-//W3C//DTD XHTML 1.0 Frameset//EN"
"http://www.w3.org/TR/xhtml1/DTD/xhtml1-frameset.dtd">

<html xmlns="http://www.w3.org/1999/xhtml">
```

```
<head>
  <title></title>
</head>

<frameset cols="150,*">
  <frame name="TopicLinks" src="page1_topics.htm" scrolling="no" />
  <frame name="Content" src="page1.htm" />
</frameset>
</html>
```

That's all you need to make this example work. As you can see, by creating more than one frameset, you buy yourself oodles more flexibility. However, this approach requires some extra effort. To use this solution, you need a frameset page, a topic page, and a content page for each link in your header. Sadly, there's no way to dodge this work.

Page Templates

Web designers often need to put the same content on a whole batch of pages. So far, you've seen two ways to approach this challenge: server-side includes and frames. Both approaches have their weaknesses, but for many small-scale Web creators, these problems don't matter. That's because the alternative (making a separate copy of the repeated content on each page) is a surefire way to fry the last few neurons of your overworked brain.

However, Web designers who own one of the two premiere Web design tools—Microsoft Expression Web or Adobe Dreamweaver—have one more option. They can create a *page template* that sets out the structure of their site pages, and then reuse that template relentlessly. The technique is similar to server-side includes, but instead of having a Web server do the work, you're giving the task to your Web page editing program. That means you don't need to worry about mistakes or Web server compatibility. You also don't need to mess around with frame borders, scroll bars, or the target attribute. For all these reasons, page templates might just be the perfect compromise for small- or medium-sized Web sites.

Before you get started with page templates, it's time to face a few drawbacks:

- **More time.** Every time you change a page template, your Web design tool needs to update all the pages that use the template. For this reason, page templates aren't a great idea for huge Web sites, because the updating process takes too long.

- **More fragile.** As you'll see, the page template system is based on a few secret comments you bury in your XHTML pages. Unfortunately, it's all too easy to accidentally delete or move one of these comments and break the link between a page and its template. When using page templates, you need to edit your pages with extra caution.

- **Nonstandard.** Page templates work differently in Expression Web and Dreamweaver. If you use page templates to craft the perfect Web site in Expression Web, you can't switch your site over to Dreamweaver—at least not without a painstaking conversion process that you have to carry out by hand.

If you're willing to put up with these shortcomings to create true multipart pages, keep reading.

Understanding Page Templates

The page template system in Expression Web and Dreamweaver is surprisingly similar. Here are the ground rules:

- You begin by creating a page template. Oddly enough, the page template in both programs uses a file extension of .dwt. In Dreamweaver, that stands for Dreamweaver Web Template. In Expression Web, it's short for Dynamic Web Template.

- The page template is an ordinary XHTML page you use as the basis for every other page on your site. The content you put inside the template becomes *fixed content*—it's passed along to every page that uses the template, where it's unchangeable. If you pop a menu bar into the page template, every page gets that exact menu bar. No page can modify it.

- Along with fixed, unchangeable content, the page template includes *editable regions*—places where you insert each page's unique content. To create one of these editable regions, you use specialized XHTML comments. Although the comments look similar in Expression Web and Dreamweaver, they aren't exactly the same, so you can't reuse a page template from one program with the other.

- Once you perfect your page template, you can create the individual site pages that use it. These pages acquire all the fixed content from the page template and supply new content for each editable section in the page. The specialized comments always remain in place. They let your Web page editor update the page when the template changes.

To really understand how Dynamic Web Templates work, you need to see them in the context of a complete page. Figure 10-17 shows a suitable candidate—a simple multipart page that shares a header and menu. It closely resembles the server-side include example you saw at the beginning of this chapter (page 263).

In the following sections, you'll build the page template for the example shown in Figure 10-18, and create the four pages that use it.

Creating a New Page Template

Although you can turn any existing page into a page template, it's often easiest to let your Web page editor start you out with an example.

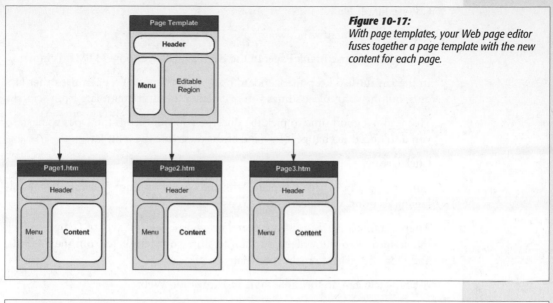

Figure 10-17:
With page templates, your Web page editor fuses together a page template with the new content for each page.

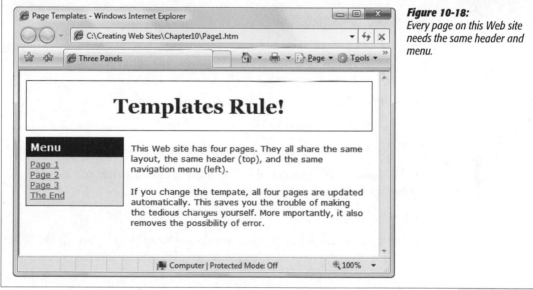

Figure 10-18:
Every page on this Web site needs the same header and menu.

Here's how you do that in Dreamweaver:

1. **Before getting started, make sure you define your Web site, as described on page 103.**

   Dreamweaver always puts page templates in a Templates subfolder inside your Web site folder. If you don't define a Web site, you'll still be able to create a page template, but you won't be able to apply it to other pages, which makes it relatively useless.

2. **Choose File → New.**

   The New Document window appears.

3. **On the left, choose Blank Page. In the Page Type list, choose HTML Template.**

   In the Layout list, keep the standard option of <none>. You can use other layouts, but this example assumes you're creating the entire template from scratch.

   This is also a good time to pick the doctype you want from the DocType list, so you don't need to change it by hand after you create the template.

4. **Click Create.**

   This creates a new page template, with the bare minimum markup. In the following sections, you'll learn how to customize it.

   After you finish perfecting your template, choose File → Save As Template. Pick the defined Web site where you want to store your template from the Site lists, and then click Save to make it official.

Here's how you can do the same thing in Expression Web:

1. **Before getting started, make sure you create Expression Web's hidden metadata folders (page 100).**

   Expression Web uses these folders to store details about the Web pages in your site. For example, it keeps track of all the pages that use a given template, which lets it update these pages when you change the template.

2. **Choose File → New.**

   The New window appears.

3. **In the first list, choose Page. In the second list, choose Dynamic Web Template.**

   At this point, you can click the Page Editor Options link to set additional options, including the automatic doctype.

4. **Click OK.**

   You start out with a page template named something like *Untitled_1.dwt*. When you save it (by choosing File → Save) you can pick a better name.

You now have a brand-new page template. Currently, it's little more than a basic XHTML skeleton. To turn it into something useful, you need to understand a bit more about how page templates work.

The Anatomy of a Page Template

Page templates are completely ordinary XHTML pages. The magic happens through specialized comments. Although these look like ordinary XHTML comments (page 43), they actually carve the page into separate, editable regions.

As you already learned, the content in your page template is fixed. When you create a new page that uses that template, you can't change the fixed content. The comments in the template identify editable sections where you can insert new content. These comments come in pairs, so the first one defines the start of an editable region, while the second one demarcates its end. Here's a comment pair in a Dreamweaver template:

```
<!-- TemplateBeginEditable name="body" -->
...
<!-- TemplateEndEditable -->
```

And here's the same thing in an Expression Web template:

```
<!-- #BeginEditable "body" -->
...
<!-- #EndEditable -->
```

There are two things to notice here. First, comments begin with the standard comment indicator *<!--*followed by a specific command (like *TemplateBeginEditable* or *#BeginEditable*). That's how your Web page editor recognizes that the comment is actually a template instruction. Second, you can see that the comments give your editable region a name. In both these examples, the region is named "body".

Tip: Because templates use comments, they're a bit fragile. Seemingly minor changes, like deleting one of the comments in a pair, changing a section name, or rearranging comments in the wrong order, can cause problems. At worst, your Web page editor will become so confused that updating the template will cause it to erase part of your page. To avoid issues like these, always make a backup of your Web site before you begin editing it, especially when page templates are involved.

Now that you understand the comment system, you can create a page template for the page shown in Figure 10-18. In this example, the header and navigation bar are fixed, unchangeable elements. The content region is the portion that appears under the header and just to the right of the menu bar.

Here's the Dreamweaver version of the page template:

```
<!DOCTYPE html PUBLIC "-//W3C//DTD XHTML 1.0 Strict//EN"
"http://www.w3.org/TR/xhtml1/DTD/xhtml1-strict.dtd">

<html xmlns="http://www.w3.org/1999/xhtml">
<head>
  <!-- TemplateBeginEditable name="title" -->
  <title></title>
  <!-- TemplateEndEditable -->

  <link rel="stylesheet" href="styles.css" type="text/css" />
</head>
```

```
<body>
  <div class="Header">
    <h1>Templates Rule!</h1>
  </div>

  <div class="MenuPanel">
    <h1>Menu</h1>
    <p
      <a href="">Page 1</a><br />
      <a href="">Page 2</a><br />
      <a href="">Page 3</a><br />
      <a href="">The End</a>
    </p>
  </div>

  <!-- TemplateBeginEditable name="content" -->
  <div class="ContentPanel">
  </div>
  <!-- TemplateEndEditable -->

</body>
</html>
```

And here's the Expression Web equivalent:

```
<!DOCTYPE html PUBLIC "-//W3C//DTD XHTML 1.0 Strict//EN"
"http://www.w3.org/TR/xhtml1/DTD/xhtml1-strict.dtd">

<html xmlns="http://www.w3.org/1999/xhtml">
<head>
  <!-- #BeginEditable "title" -->
  <title></title>
  <!-- #EndEditable -->

  <link rel="stylesheet" href="styles.css" type="text/css" />
</head>

<body>
  <div class="Header">
    <h1>Templates Rule!</h1>
  </div>

  <div class="MenuPanel">
    <h1>Menu</h1>
```

```
    <p>
      <a href="">Page 1</a><br />
      <a href="">Page 2</a><br />
      <a href="">Page 3</a><br />
      <a href="">The End</a>
    </p>
  </div>

  <!-- #BeginEditable "content" -->
  <div class="ContentPanel">
  </div>
  <!-- #EndEditable -->

</body>
</html>
```

Notice that there are actually *two* editable regions in this example. One is for the content that will appear to the right of the menu panel. The other is for the title that appears at the top of the browser window. Thanks to this detail, you don't have to give all your pages the same title.

You'll also notice that both editable regions include some content (like the tags for the <title> element or a <div> element). When you create a page that uses this template, you start out with these elements in your editable regions. However, you're free to change or replace them with something completely different.

Using a Page Template

Once you finish your template, you're ready to put it into action. The process is similar in both programs. Here's how it goes down in Dreamweaver:

1. **Choose File → New.**

   The New Document window appears.

2. **On the left of the New Document window, choose Page From Template. Then, in the Site list, choose your Web site.**

   You'll see a list of all the templates in the Templates folder of your Web site.

3. **Select the template you want, and then click Create.**

   Make sure you keep the "Update page when template changes" checkbox selected. This way, when you change your template, Dreamweaver updates all the pages that use the template.

And here's the same task in Expression Web:

1. **Choose File → New.**

   The New window appears.

2. **In the first list, choose General. In the second list, choose "Create from Dynamic Web Template". Then click OK.**

   The Attach Dynamic Web Template window appears.

3. **Browse to the .dwt file you created in the previous section, select it, and then click Open.**

In your new page, you'll see the combined markup, including the fixed content and the editable regions. However, you won't be able to change the fixed content. Dreamweaver displays the XHTML for the fixed content in light gray. Expression Web highlights it with a yellow background. Either way, the editable content regions clearly stand out from the fixed content. And both programs make it even more distinct in Design view, as shown in Figure 10-19.

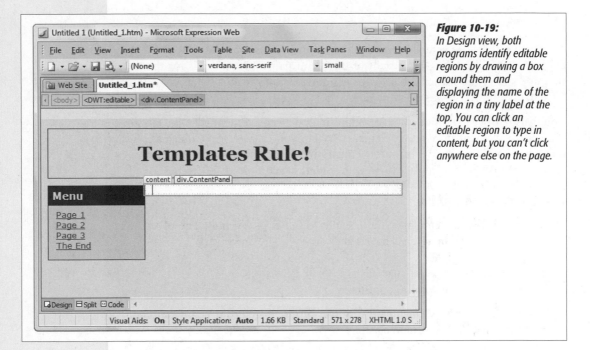

Figure 10-19:
In Design view, both programs identify editable regions by drawing a box around them and displaying the name of the region in a tiny label at the top. You can click an editable region to type in content, but you can't click anywhere else on the page.

To create the page shown in Figure 10-18, you simply add a title and a couple of paragraphs of text in the editable content region. Here's the finished page in Dreamweaver, with the new additions highlighted:

```
<!DOCTYPE html PUBLIC "-//W3C//DTD XHTML 1.0 Strict//EN"
"http://www.w3.org/TR/xhtml1/DTD/xhtml1-strict.dtd">

<html xmlns="http://www.w3.org/1999/xhtml">
<!-- InstanceBegin template="/Templates/PageTemplate.dwt"
codeOutsideHTMLIsLocked="false" -->
```

```
<head>
  <!-- InstanceBeginEditable name="title" -->
  <title>Page Templates</title>
  <!-- InstanceEndEditable -->

  <link rel="stylesheet" href="styles.css" type="text/css" />
</head>

<body>
  <div class="Header">
    <h1>Templates Rule!</h1>
  </div>

  <div class="MenuPanel">
    <h1>Menu</h1>
    <p>
      <a href="">Page 1</a><br />
      <a href="">Page 2</a><br />
      <a href="">Page 3</a><br />
      <a href="">The End</a>
    </p>
  </div>

  <!-- InstanceBeginEditable name="content" -->
  <div class="ContentPanel">
    <p> This Web site has four pages. They all share the same layout,
    the same header (top), and the same navigation menu (left).</p>
    ...
  </div>
  <!-- InstanceEndEditable -->

</body>

<!-- InstanceEnd --></html>
```

When you use a template to build individual pages in Dreamweaver, your new page gets comments that are slightly different from those in the original page. For example, Dreamweaver replaces the TemplateBeginEditable instruction with an InstanceBeginEditable command.

In Expression Web, the new page gets exactly the same comments as the original template, as shown here:

```
<!DOCTYPE html PUBLIC "-//W3C//DTD XHTML 1.0 Strict//EN"
"http://www.w3.org/TR/xhtml1/DTD/xhtml1-strict.dtd">

<html xmlns="http://www.w3.org/1999/xhtml">
```

```
<!-- #BeginTemplate "PageTemplate.dwt" -->
<head>
  <!-- #BeginEditable "title" -->
  <title>Page Templates</title>
  <!-- #EndEditable -->

  <link rel="stylesheet" href="styles.css" type="text/css" />
</head>

<body>
  <div class="Header">
    <h1>Templates Rule!</h1>
  </div>

  <div class="MenuPanel">
    <h1>Menu</h1>
    <p>
      <a href="">Page 1</a><br />
      <a href="">Page 2</a><br />
      <a href="">Page 3</a><br />
      <a href="">The End</a>
    </p>
  </div>

  <!-- #BeginEditable "content" -->
  <div class="ContentPanel">
    <p> This Web site has four pages. They all share the same layout,
    the same header (top), and the same navigation menu (left).</p>
    ...
  </div>
  <!-- #EndEditable -->

</body>
<!-- #EndTemplate -->
</html>
```

This example shows just a single page. You see the real advantages when you create dozens of pages based on a template. In every case, to create a new page, you need do nothing more than set a title and add a bit of content.

But you'll see the biggest benefit when you change the original page template. For example, imagine you modify your original template to use a spiffy new graphic for its header:

```
<div class="Header">
  <img src="TemplatesRule.jpeg" alt="Templates Rule!" />
</div>
```

Once you save your changes, your Web page editor asks if you want to apply the changes to all the linked pages in the current Web site. Say yes and the editor quickly and quietly opens all the pages that use the template and updates them with the new content. The result is an instant facelift for all the pages on your site (see Figure 10-20).

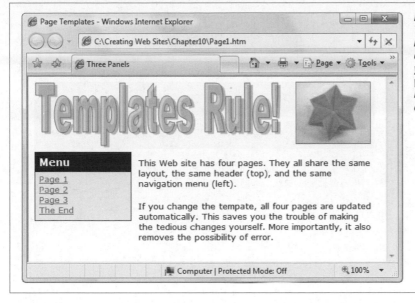

Figure 10-20:
This header graphic really makes your Web pages stand out. But the best part is that you never cracked open page1.htm to add this graphic. Instead, your Web page editor did the updating for you.

Tip: Although this chapter gives you a solid overview of the page template system, you may need to consider other subtleties. For example, you may make changes to a page template so dramatic that the edited template becomes incompatible with the pages that currently use it. Or, you might want to rewire an existing page to use a different template. To learn about the finer points of page templates, consult a dedicated resource for your Web editor of choice. Dreamweaver fans can pick up a copy of *Dreamweaver CS4: The Missing Manual*. Expression Web-ers can check out a free e-book dedicated to the topic of templates at *http://any-expression.com/expression-web/ebooks/expression-web-dwt-ebook.htm*.

Part Three: Connecting With Your Audience

3

Attracting Visitors

Over the past 10 chapters, you've polished your Web designing mettle and learned how to build a variety of sleek pages. Now it's time to shift to an entirely different role and become a Web site *promoter*.

The best Web site in the world won't do you much good if it's sitting out there all by its lonesome self. For your site to flourish, you need to find the best way to attract visitors—and keep them flocking back for more. In this chapter, you'll learn some valuable tricks for promoting your site. You'll also see how search engines work, how to make sure they regularly index your site, and how to work your way up the rankings of search results. Lastly, you'll learn to gauge the success of your site with visitor tracking, and you'll use a powerful free service called Google Analytics to learn some of your visitors' deepest secrets (like where they live, what browsers they use, and which of your Web pages they find absolutely unbearable). Before you know it, you'll be more popular than chocolate ice cream.

Your Web Site Promotion Plan

Before you plunge into the world of Web site promotion, you need a plan. So grab a pencil and plenty of paper, and get ready to jot down your ideas for global Web site domination (fiendish cackling is optional).

Although all Webmasters have their own tactics, it's generally agreed that the best way to market a Web site is to follow these steps:

1. **Build a truly great Web site.**

   If you start promoting your site before there's anything to see, you're wasting your effort (and probably burning a few bridges). Nothing says "never come back" like an empty Web site with an "under construction" message.

2. **See step 1.**

   If in doubt, keep polishing and perfecting your site. Fancy graphics aren't the key concern here—the most important detail is whether you have some genuinely useful content. Ask yourself—if you were browsing the Web, would you stop to take a look at this site? Make sure you've taken the time to add the kinds of add-on features that will keep visitors coming back. One great option: include a discussion forum (see the next chapter for more details on how to do so).

3. **Share links with friends and like-minded sites.**

   This step is all about building community. Contrary to what you might expect, this sort of small-scale, word-of-mouth promotion might bring more traffic to your site than high-powered search engines like Google.

4. **Perfect your site's meta elements.**

   Meta elements contain hidden words that convey important information about your site's content, like a site description. Search engines use them as one way to determine what your Web site's all about.

5. **Submit your Web site to Internet directories.**

   Like search engines, directories help visitors find Web sites. The difference between directories and search engines is that directories are generally smaller catalogs put together by humans, rather than huge sprawling text indexes amassed by computers.

6. **Submit your Web site to Internet search engines.**

   Now you're ready for the big time. Once you submit your Web site to Web heavyweights like Google and Yahoo, it officially enters the public eye. However, it takes time to climb up the rankings and get spotted.

7. **Figure out what happened.**

   To assess the successes and failures of your strategy, you need to measure some vital statistics—how many people visit your site, how long they're staying, and how many visitors come back for more. To take stock, you need to crack open tools like hit counters and server logs.

Throughout this chapter, you'll tackle these steps, get some new ideas, and build up a collection of promotion strategies.

Spreading the Word

Some of the most effective promotion you can do doesn't involve any high-tech XHTML wonkery, but instead amounts to variations on the theme of good old-fashioned advertising.

The first step is to find other Web sites like yours. If you create a topic-oriented site—your musings on, say, golf, fine jewelry, or jeweled golf clubs—similar sites make up your virtual neighborhood. They're part of a larger online community to which you now belong. So why not introduce yourself? Strike up a *reciprocal link* relationship (see the next section).

On the other hand, if you're creating a business site, similar sites are, obviously, your competitors. As a result, you're unlikely to share links. However, it's a great idea to Google your competition. You'll probably find service sites—business directories, news sites, content sitcs, and so on—that link to these competitors. Once you find these service sites, you can publicize your site there as well.

Reciprocal Links

A reciprocal link is a link-trading agreement. The concept is simple. You find a Web site with similar content and strike a bargain: Link to my site, and I'll link to yours. Reciprocal links are an important thread in the underlying fabric of the Web. If you're not sure where to start searching for potential link buddies, pay a visit to Google and use the *link*: operator (as explained in Figure 11-1) to see who's linking to sites similar to yours. (You can get an even more powerful link viewer as part of the Google Webmaster Tools, described on page 319.)

Reciprocal links only work if there's a logical connection between the two sites. For example, if you create the Web site *www.ChocolateSculptures.com*, it probably makes sense to exchange links with *www.101ChocolateRecipes.com*. But *www.Homer-SimpsonForPresident.com* is a far stretch, no matter how much traffic it gets.

Topic isn't the only consideration in link exchanges. You should also look for sites that *feel* professional. If a similarly themed site is choked with ads, barren of content, formatted with fuchsia text on a black background, and was last updated circa 1998, keep looking.

Once you find a site you want to exchange links with, dig around on the site for the Webmaster's email address. Send a message explaining that you love *www.101ChocolateRecipes.com*, and plan to link to it from your site, *www.ChocolateSculptures.com*. Then, gently suggest that you think your Web site would be of great interest to *www.101ChocolateRecipes.com* readers.

Tip: Reciprocal linking can require a little finesse. It's best to look for sites that complement yours, but don't necessarily compete with it. You'll also have more luck if you approach Web peers, sites of similar quality or with a similar amount of traffic to yours.

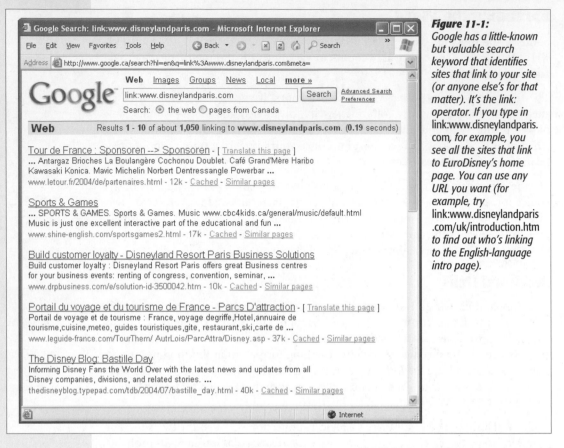

Figure 11-1:
Google has a little-known but valuable search keyword that identifies sites that link to your site (or anyone else's for that matter). It's the link: operator. If you type in link:www.disneylandparis. com, for example, you see all the sites that link to EuroDisney's home page. You can use any URL you want (for example, try link:www.disneylandparis .com/uk/introduction.htm to find out who's linking to the English-language intro page).

Once you enter into a link agreement—even if it's just an informal exchange of emails—remember to keep your end of the deal. Don't remove the link from your site without letting the other Webmaster know about the change. It's also a good idea to keep checking on the other site to make sure your link remains prominent. If it disappears, don't fly into an Othellian rage—just send a polite email asking where it went or why it disappeared.

Reciprocal links are also a good way to start working your way up search engine rankings (see page 318). That's because one of the criteria Google takes into account when it determines how to order the results of a Web search is how many other sites link to yours. The more popular you are, the more likely you'll climb up the list.

Note: There are some companies that sell reciprocal link services. The basic idea is that they try to pair up different Web sites (for a fee) in a link-sharing agreement. Don't fall for it. Your traffic might increase, but the visitors you get won't really be interested in the content of your site, and they won't hang around for long.

Web Rings

A Web ring is similar to a reciprocal link, but instead of sharing a link between two partners, it binds a *group* of Web sites together.

For example, imagine you create a brilliant new site featuring reality TV trivia. To get more exposure, you can join a Web ring dedicated to reality TV. You agree to put a block of XHTML on your site that advertises the ring and lets your visitors go to other sites in it. As payback, you become another stop within the ring (see Figure 11-2). Web rings are almost exclusively the province of topic-based sites.

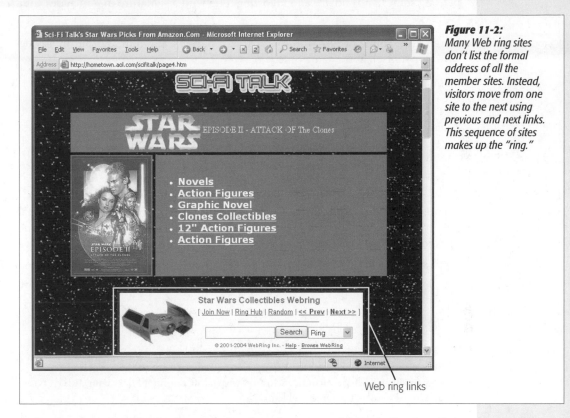

Figure 11-2:
Many Web ring sites don't list the formal address of all the member sites. Instead, visitors move from one site to the next using previous and next links. This sequence of sites makes up the "ring."

Web ring links

Sadly, the majority of Web rings consist of gaudy, amateurish Web disasters. Pair up with these nightmares and your site will be deemed guilty by association. However, with a little research, you may find a higher-quality ring. Maybe. To search for one, use Google (enter the topic followed by the words "Web ring").

Note: The biggest disadvantage to Web rings is that they usually require you to add a fairly ugly set of links to your page. Before you sign up, carefully evaluate whether the extra traffic is worth it, and travel to all the other sites in the ring to see if they're of similar quality. If you're in a ring with low-quality sites, it can hurt your reputation.

Shameless Self-Promotion

To get your Web site listed on many of the Web's most popular sites, you need to fork over some cold, hard cash. However, some of the best advertising doesn't cost anything. The trick is to look for sites where you can promote *and* contribute at the same time.

For example, if you create the Web site *www.HotComputerTricks.com*, why not answer a few questions on a computing newsgroup or discussion board? It's considered tactless to openly promote your site, but there's nothing wrong with dispensing some handy advice and following it up with a signature that includes your URL.

Here's an example of how you can answer a poster's question and put in a good word for yourself at the same time:

> Jim,
>
> The problem is that most hard drives will fail when submerged in water. Hence, your fishing computer idea won't work.
>
> Sasha Mednick
>
> www.HotComputerTricks.com

An answer posting is much better than sending an email directly to the original poster because on a popular site hundreds of computer aficionados with the same question will read your posting. If even a few decide to check out your site, you've made great progress.

If you're very careful, you might even get away with something that's a little more explicit:

> Jim,
>
> The problem is that most hard drives will fail when submerged in water. Hence, your fishing computer idea won't work. However, you might want to check out my homemade hard-drive vacuum enclosure (www.HotComputerTricks.com), which I developed to solve the same problem.
>
> Sasha Mednick
>
> www.HotComputerTricks.com

Warning: This maneuver requires a very light touch. The rule of thumb is that your message should be well-intentioned. Only direct someone to your site if there really is something specific there that addresses the question.

Some sites let you post tips, reviews, or articles. If that's the case, you can use a variation of the technique above. Remember, dispense useful advice, and then follow it up with a byline at the end of your message. For example, if you submit a free article that describes how to create your groundbreaking vacuum enclosure, end it with this:

> Sasha Mednick is a computer genius who runs the first-rate computing Web site www.HotComputerTricks.com.

Promotion always works best if you believe in your product. So make sure there's some relevant high-quality content on your site before you boast about it. Don't ever send someone to your site based on some content you plan to add (someday).

Tip: If you're a business trying to promote a product, you'll get further if you recruit other people to help you spread the word. One excellent idea is to look for influential *bloggers*—people who create Web sites with the personal posting format you'll learn about in Chapter 17. For example, if you're trying to sell a new type of fluffy toddler towel pajamas, hunt down popular people with blogs about parenting. Then, offer them some free pajamas if they'll offer their thoughts in a blog review. This sort of word-of-mouth promotion can be dramatically more successful in the wide-reaching communities of the Web than it is in the ordinary offline world.

Return Visitors

Attracting fresh faces is a critical part of Web site promotion, but novice Webmasters often forget something equally important—return visitors. For a Web site to become truly popular, it needs to attract visitors who return again and again. Many a Web site creator would do better to spend less time trying to attract new visitors and more time trying to keep the current flock.

If you're a marketer, you know that a customer who comes back to the same store three or four times is a lot more likely to make a purchase than someone who's there on a first visit. These regulars are also more likely to get excited and recruit their friends to come and take a look. This infectious enthusiasm can lead more and more people to your Web site's virtual doorstep. The phenomenon is so common it has a name: the *traffic virus*.

Note: Return visitors are the ultimate measuring stick of Web site success. If you can't interest someone enough to come back again, your Web site's just not fulfilling its destiny.

So how does your Web site become a favorite stopping point for Web travelers? The old Internet adage says it all—*content is king*. Your site needs to be chock full of fascinating must-read information. Just as important, this information needs to change regularly and noticeably. If you update information once a month, your Web site barely has a pulse. But if you update it two or more times a week, you're ready to flourish.

Never underestimate the importance of regular updates. It takes weeks and months of up-to-date information to create a return visitor. However, one dry spell—say, three months without changing anything more than the color of your buttons— doesn't just stop attracting newcomers, it can kill off your current roster of return visitors. That's because savvy visitors immediately realize when a Web site's gone stale. They have much the same sensation you feel when you pull out a once-attractive pastry from the fridge and find it's as hard as igneous rock. You know what happens next—it's time to toss the pastry away, clear out the Web site bookmarks, and move on.

Tip: Signs of a stale site include old-fashioned formatting, broken links, and references to old events (like a Spice Girls CD release party or a technical analysis of why Florida condos are an ironclad investment).

The other way to encourage return visitors is to build a *community*. Discussion forums, promotional events, and newsletters are like glue. They encourage visitors to feel like they're participating in your site and sharing your Web space. If you get this right, hordes of visitors will move in and never want to leave. You'll learn specific techniques for community-building in the next chapter.

GEM IN THE ROUGH

Favorite Icons

One of your first challenges in promoting your site is getting visitors to add your site to their browser bookmarks. However, that's not enough to guarantee a return visit. Your Web site also needs to be fascinating enough to beckon from the bookmark menu, tempting visitors to come back. If you're a typical Web traveler, you regularly visit only about five percent of the sites you bookmark.

One way to make your site stand out from the crowd is to change the icon that appears in visitors' bookmarks or favorites menu (an icon technically called a *favicon*). This technique is browser-specific, but it works reliably in most versions of Internet Explorer, Firefox, and Safari. The illustration in this box shows the favicons for Google and Amazon.

To create a favicon, add an icon file to the top-level folder of your Web site, and make sure you name it *favicon.ico*. The best approach is to use a dedicated icon editor, because it lets you create both a 16-pixel × 16-pixel icon and

a larger 32-pixel × 32-pixel icon in the same file. Browsers use the smaller icon in their bookmark menus, and Windows PCs display the larger version when visitors drag the favicon to their desktop (Macs don't support the desktop-icon feature). If you don't have an icon editor, just create a bitmap (a .bmp file) that's exactly 16 pixels wide and 16 pixels high. To get an icon editor, visit a shareware site like *www.download.com*.

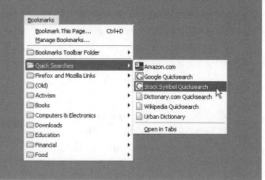

Adding Meta Elements

Meta elements give you a way to add descriptive information to your Web pages, which is important because some Web search engines rely on these elements to help visitors find your site. Figure 11-3 explains how it all works.

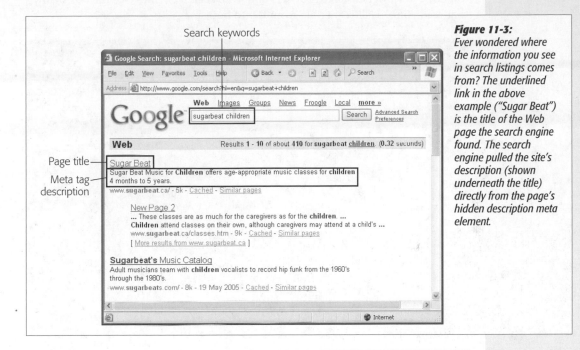

Figure 11-3:
Ever wondered where the information you see in search listings comes from? The underlined link in the above example ("Sugar Beat") is the title of the Web page the search engine found. The search engine pulled the site's description (shown underneath the title) directly from the page's hidden description meta element.

Note: Fun fact for etymologists and geeks alike: the term "meta element" means "elements *about*," as in "elements that provide information *about* your Web page."

You put all meta elements in the <head> section of a page. Here's a sample meta element that assigns a description to a Web page:

```
<!DOCTYPE html PUBLIC "-//W3C//DTD XHTML 1.0 Strict//EN"
"http://www.w3.org/TR/xhtml1/DTD/xhtml1-strict.dtd">

<html xmlns="http://www.w3.org/1999/xhtml">
<head>
  <meta name="description"
    content="Noodletastic offers custom noodle dishes made to order." />
  <title>Noodletastic</title>
</head>

<body>...</body>

</html>
```

All meta elements look more or less the same. The element name is <meta>, the *name* attribute indicates the type of meta element it is, and the *content* attribute supplies the relevant information.

Meta elements don't show up when your page appears in a browser. They're intended for programs, like browsers and Web search engines (see the box below), that read your XHTML markup from top to bottom.

How Web Search Engines Work

A Web search engine like Google has three pieces. The first is an automated program that roams the Web, downloading everything it finds. This program (often known by more picturesque names like *spider, robot,* or *crawler*) eventually stumbles across your Web site and copies its contents.

The second piece is an indexer that chews through Web pages and extracts a bunch of meaningful information, including a Web page's title, description, and keywords. The indexer also records a great deal of more esoteric data. For example, a search engine like Google keeps track of the words that crop up the most often on a page, what other sites link to your page, and so on. The indexer inserts all this digested information into a giant catalog (technically, a *database*).

The final piece of the search engine is the part you're probably most familiar with—the front-end, or search page. You enter the keywords you're hunting for, and the search engine scans its catalog looking for suitable pages. Different engines have different ways of ranking pages, but the basic idea is that the search engine attempts to make sure the most relevant and popular pages turn up early in the search results. A search engine like Google doesn't rank Web sites individually. That is, there's no such thing as the world's most popular Web page (in the eyes of Google). Instead, Google ranks pages in terms of how they stack up against whatever search keywords a visitor enters. That means that a slightly different search (say, "green tea health" instead of just "green tea") could get you a completely different set of results.

In theory, there's no limit to the types of information you can put inside a meta element. For example, some Web page editing programs insert meta elements that say its software built your pages (don't worry; once you understand meta elements, you'll recognize this harmless fingerprint and you can easily remove it). Another Web page might use a meta element to record the name of the Web designers who created it, or the last time you updated the page.

Some meta elements are more important than others, because search engines heed them. In the following sections, you'll learn about two of these: the *description* and *keywords* meta elements. These details, in conjunction with the <title> element, constitute the basic information that a search engine needs to gather about your page.

The Description Meta Element

The description of your page is probably the easiest meta element to come up with. You simply write a few sentences that distill the content of your site into a few plain phrases. Here's an example:

```
<meta name="description" content="Sugar Beat Music for Children offers age-
appropriate music classes for children 4 months to 5 years old." />
```

Although you can stuff a lot of information into your description, it's a good idea to limit it to a couple of focused sentences that total no more than around 50 words. Some search engines home in on the description text, while others rely more heavily on the text in the page. Even if your description appears on a search results page, readers see only the first part of it, followed by an ellipsis (…) where it gets cut off.

Tip: The *description* meta element gives search engines some key information. You should include it in every page you create.

The Keyword Meta Element

Your keyword meta element should contain a list of about 25 words or phrases that represent your Web site. Separate each word in the list by a comma. Here's an example:

```
<meta name="keywords" content="sugarbeat, sugar, beat, music, children,
musical, classes, movement, babies, infants, kids, child, creative" />
```

The keyword list is a great place to add important terms (like "horseback riding"), alternate spellings ("horse back riding"), synonyms or related words ("equestrian"), and even common misspellings ("ecquestrian"). Keywords aren't case-sensitive.

Unfortunately, there's a huge caveat. Most search engines don't use the keyword list any longer. That's because it was notorious for abuses (many a Web master stuffed his keyword list full of hundreds of words, some only tangentially related to what was actually on the site). Search engines like Google take a more direct approach—they look at all the words in your Web page, and pay special attention to words that appear more often, appear in headings, and so on. Most Web experts argue that the keyword list has outlived its usefulness, and many don't bother adding it to their pages at all.

Keyword Tricks

Can I make my Web site more popular by adding hidden keywords?

There are quite a few unwholesome tricks that crafty Web weavers use to game the search engine system (or at least try). For example, they might add a huge number of keywords, but hide the text so it isn't visible on the page (white text on a white background is one oddball option, but there are other style-sheet tricks). Another technique is to create pages that aren't really a part of your Web site, but that you store on your server. You can fill these pages with repeating keyword text. To implement this trick, you use a little Java-Script code to make sure real people who accidentally arrive at the page are directed to the entry point of your Web site, while search engines get to feast on the keywords (JavaScript is discussed in Chapter 14).

As seductive as some of these tricks may seem to lonely Web sites (and their owners), the best advice is to avoid them altogether. The first problem is that they pose a new set of headaches and technical challenges, which can waste hours of your day. But more significantly, search engines learn about these tricks almost as fast as Web developers invent them. If a search engine catches you using these tricks, it may ban your site completely, relegating it to the dustbin of the Web.

If you're still tempted, keep this in mind: Many of these tricks just don't work. In the early days of the Web, primitive search engines gave a site more weight based on the number of times a keyword cropped up, but modern search engines like Google use much more sophisticated page-ranking systems. A huge load of keywords probably won't move you up the search list one iota.

Directories and Search Engines

Now that you're well on your way to perfecting and popularizing your site, it's time to start looking at the second level of Internet promotion—search engines. Getting your Web site into the most important search engine catalogs is a key step in publicizing it. Working your way up the rankings so Web searchers are likely to find you takes more work, and monopolizes the late-night hours of many a Webmaster.

Directories

Directories are searchable site listings with a difference: humans, not programs, create them. That means a small army of workers painstakingly puts together a collection of sites, neatly sorted into categories. The advantage of directories is that they're well-organized. A couple of clicks can get you a complete list of California regional newspapers, for example. The unquestioned disadvantage is that directories are dramatically smaller than *full-text search* catalogs. That means directories aren't very useful for those in search of a piece of elusive information that doesn't easily fall into a category, like a list of the English language's most commonly misspelled words. Over the years, as the Web's ballooned in size, directories have become increasingly specialized, and full-text search tools like Google and Yahoo have become the most common way that people hunt for information.

So, given that directories are just the unattractive cousins of full-text search engines, why do you need to worry about them? Two reasons. First, some Web visitors still use directories, even if they don't use them as often as they do full-text search engines. Second, some search engines (including Google) pay attention to directory listings, and tend to rank sites higher if they turn up in certain directories. Getting into the right directories can help you start to move up the results list in a full-text search. And just like college, getting into a directory requires that you submit an application, which you'll learn about next.

The Open Directory Project

The most important directory to submit your site to is the Open Directory Project (ODP) at *http://dmoz.org*. The ODP is a huge, long-standing Web site directory staffed entirely by thousands of volunteer editors who review submissions in countless categories. The ODP isn't the most popular Web directory (that honor currently goes to the Yahoo directory), but other search engines use it behind the scenes. In fact, Google bases its own directory service (*http://directory.google.com*) on the ODP.

Before submitting to the ODP, take the time to make sure you do it right. An incorrect submission could result in your Web site not getting listed at all. You can find a complete description of the rules at *http://dmoz.org/add.html*, but here are the key requirements:

- Don't submit your site more than once.

- Don't submit your site to more than one category.

- Don't submit more than one page or section of your site (unless you have a really good reason, like the separate sections are notably different).

- Don't submit sites that contain "illegal" content. By the OPD's definition, this is more accurately described as unsavory content, like pornography, libelous content, or material that advocates illegal activity—you know who you are.

- Clean up any broken links, outdated information, or any other red flags that might suggest to an editor that your site isn't here for the long term.

- When you submit your site, describe it carefully and accurately. Don't promote it. In other words "Ketchup Masters is a manufacturer of gourmet ketchup" is acceptable. "Ketchup Masters is the best food-oriented site on the Web—the Louisville Times says you can't miss it!" isn't.

- Don't submit an incomplete site. Your "under construction" page won't get listed.

The next step is to spend some time at the *http://dmoz.org* site, until you find the single best category for your site (see Figure 11-4).

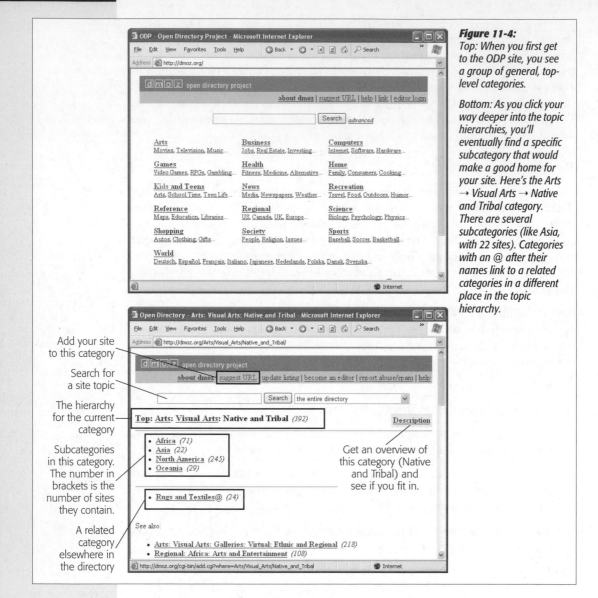

Figure 11-4:

Top: When you first get to the ODP site, you see a group of general, top-level categories.

Bottom: As you click your way deeper into the topic hierarchies, you'll eventually find a specific subcategory that would make a good home for your site. Here's the Arts → Visual Arts → Native and Tribal category. There are several subcategories (like Asia, with 22 sites). Categories with an @ after their names link to a related categories in a different place in the topic hierarchy.

Once you do so, click the "suggest URL" link at the top of the page and fill out the submission form (see Figure 11-5). The form asks for your URL, the title of your site, a brief description, and your email address.

Note: If you have some free time on your hands, you can offer to help edit a site category—just click the "become an editor" link. And even if you don't have editorial aspirations, why not check out the editor guidelines at *http://dmoz.org/guidelines* to get a better idea of what's going on in the mind of ODP editors, and how they evaluate your site submission?

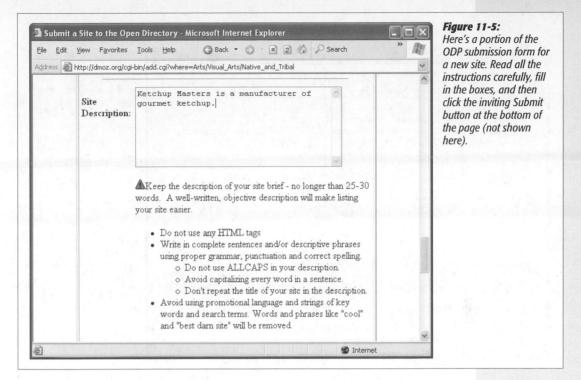

Once you submit your site, there's nothing to do but wait (and submit your site to the other directories and search engines discussed in this chapter). If two or three weeks pass without your site appearing in the listing and you haven't received an email describing any problems with it, try submitting your site again. If that still doesn't work, it's time to contact the category editor. Write a polite email asking why your site wasn't added to the listings, and include the date of your submission(s) and the name, URL, and description of your site. You can find the email address for the category editor at the very bottom of the category page (see Figure 11-6).

The Yahoo directory

ODP is a great starting point, but it isn't the only directory on the block. The other heavyweight is the Yahoo directory (*http://dir.yahoo.com*). Unfortunately, getting your site into the Yahoo directory takes considerably more work.

First, there's the issue of cost. If you've created a non-commercial site, you can probably get in free, but it may take persistence, emails, multiple submissions, and a bit of luck. If you've created a commercial site (one whose primary purpose is to make money) and you want to register it in the U.S. Yahoo directory, you need to pay an annual fee of several hundred dollars. And in the ultimate case of adding insult to injury, you won't get your money back if Yahoo rejects your site.

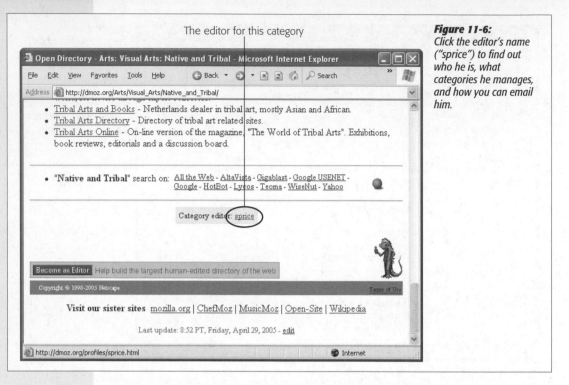

Figure 11-6:
Click the editor's name ("sprice") to find out who he is, what categories he manages, and how you can email him.

The editor for this category

Open Directory - Arts: Visual Arts: Native and Tribal - Microsoft Internet Explorer

File   Edit   View   Favorites   Tools   Help   Back ▾   ▾ ⊗ ▯ ⌂   🔍 Search

Address   http://dmoz.org/Arts/Visual_Arts/Native_and_Tribal/

- <u>Tribal Arts and Books</u> - Netherlands dealer in tribal art, mostly Asian and African.
- <u>Tribal Arts Directory</u> - Directory of tribal art related sites.
- <u>Tribal Arts Online</u> - On-line version of the magazine, "The World of Tribal Arts". Exhibitions, book reviews, editorials and a discussion board.

- **"Native and Tribal"** search on: <u>All the Web</u> - <u>AltaVista</u> - <u>Gigablast</u> - <u>Google USENET</u> -
  <u>Google</u> - <u>HotBot</u> - <u>Lycos</u> - <u>Teoma</u> - <u>WiseNut</u> - <u>Yahoo</u>

Category editor: <u>sprice</u>

Become an Editor Help build the largest human-edited directory of the web

Copyright © 1998-2005 Netscape   Terms of Use

Visit our sister sites <u>mozilla.org</u> | <u>ChefMoz</u> | <u>MusicMoz</u> | <u>Open-Site</u> | <u>Wikipedia</u>

Last update: 8:52 PT, Friday, April 29, 2005 - <u>edit</u>

http://dmoz.org/profiles/sprice.html   Internet

To get started, you can review Yahoo's official submission guidelines at *http://help. yahoo.com/l/us/yahoo/directory/suggest/listings-03.html*. However, you'll be much happier with the *unofficial* write-up at *www.apromotionguide.com/yahoo.html*, which discusses your free and for-fee options, and explains what the cryptic rejection emails Yahoo sends out really mean. And if you have a commercial Web site, or you just don't want to suffer through the slow and unreliable free registration process, you'll need to use the Yahoo Directory Submit service (formerly called Yahoo Express), which is described at *https://ecom.yahoo.com/dir/submit/intro*.

Once you're done with directories (or just ready to move on), it's time to take a look at full-text search engines.

Search Engines

For most people, search engines are the one and only tool for finding information on the Web. If you want the average person to find your site, you need to make sure it's in the most popular search engine catalogs, and turns up as one of the results in relevant searches. This task is harder than it seems, because the Web is full of millions of sites jockeying for position. To get noticed, you need to spend time developing your site and enhancing its visibility. You also need to understand how search engines rank pages (see the box below for an example).

The undisputed king of Web search engines is Google (*www.google.com*). Not only
is it far and away the Web's most popular search engine, it also powers other
search engines (usually without being credited). Google performs an amazing
amount of work—every day it chews through hundreds of millions of search
requests.

Tip: For more information about search engines, including who's on top and who owns who, check out
www.searchengineland.com.

It's not too difficult to get Google to notice your site. By the time your site's about
a month old, Google will probably have stumbled across it at least once, usually by
following a link from another site or from the ODP. As described in the box above,
Google takes outside links into consideration when sizing up a site, so the more
sites that link to you, the more likely you are to turn up in someone's search
results.

If you're impatient or you think Google's passing you by, you can introduce yourself
directly using the submission form at *www.google.com/addurl* (see Figure 11-7).
Most popular search engines include a submission form like this. Just make sure
you keep track of where you've submitted, so you don't inadvertently submit your
site to the same search engine more than once.

Figure 11-7:
*You can safely skip the
comments section on this
page but make sure to
include the http:// prefix
at the start of your Web
page's URL.*

UP TO SPEED

How Google's PageRank Works

Google uses a rating system called *PageRank* to size up different Web pages. Google doesn't use PageRank to *find* search results; instead, it uses it to *order* them. When you execute a search with Google, it pulls out all the sites that match your search keywords. Then it orders the results according to the PageRank of each page.

The basic idea behind the PageRank system is that the value of your Web site is determined by the community of other Web sites that link to it. There are a few golden rules:

- The more sites that link to you, the better.

- A link from a more popular site (a site with a high PageRank) is more valuable than a link from a less popular site.

- The more links a site has, the less each link is worth. In other words, if someone links to your site and just

a handful of other sites, that link is valuable. If someone links to your site and *hundreds* of other sites, the link's value is diluted.

Although Google regularly fine-tunes its secret PageRank recipe, Web experts spend hours trying to deconstruct it. For some fascinating reading, you can learn more about how PageRank works (loosely) at *www.akamarketing.com/ google-ranking-tips.html* and *www.markhorrell.com/seo/ pagerank.html*. Google co-founders Sergey Brin and Larry Page describe the original formulation of PageRank in an academic paper by at *http://infolab.stanford.edu/ ~backrub/google.html*.

For way more information about Google and its internal workings, check out *Google: The Missing Manual*.

Rising up in the rankings

You'll soon discover that it's not difficult to get into Google's index. But you might find it exceedingly hard to get noticed. For example, suppose you've submitted the site *www.SamMenzesHomemadePasta.com*. To see if you're in Google, try an extremely specific search that targets just your site, like "Sam Menzes Homemade Pasta." This should definitely lead to your doorstep. Now, try searching for just "Homemade Pasta." Odds are, you won't turn up in the top 10, or even the top 100.

So how do you create a site that the casual searcher's likely to find? There's no easy answer. Just remember that the secret to getting a good search ranking is having a good PageRank, and getting a good PageRank is all about connections. To stand out, your Web site needs to share links with other leading sites in your category.

If you want to delve into the nitty-gritty of *search engine optimization* (known to Webmasters as SEO), consider becoming a regular reader of *www.webmasterworld. com* and *www.searchengineland.com*. You'll find articles and forums where Webmasters discuss the good, bad, and downright seedy tricks you can try to get noticed.

Tip: It's possible to get too obsessed with search engine rankings. Here's a good rule of thumb—don't spend more time trying to improve your search engine ranking than you do improving your Web site. In the long term, the only way to gain real popularity is to become one of the best sites on the block.

The Google Webmaster Tools

If you're feeling a bit in the dark about how your Web site rates with Google, you'll be happy to know that Google has a service that can help you out. It's called the Google Webmaster Tools, and you can sign up your site for free at *www.google. com/webmasters/tools.*

Note: Before you can actually use the Google Webmaster Tools, you need to prove you own the site. To do this, Google asks you to upload a small file (a task that only a site owner can perform). Once Google finishes verifying your site, you can remove this file.

The Google Webmaster Tools let you look at your Web site through the eyes of Google. It divides its features into several sections. When you sign up, here's what you see:

- **Overview.** This section tells you whether Google has visited your site, and whether it's successfully added your site to its index. You'll also find links to help documents that explain how Google sizes up a Web site and how you can climb the rankings.

- **Diagnostics.** This section warns you about any problems Google has encountered, like incorrect metadata (page 309) or pages that it couldn't access (and therefore couldn't index).

- **Statistics.** This section provides information about the searches that lead Googlers from the search engine to your Web site. For example, you might find out that people reach your pet food site after searching for "san francisco doggie treats." You can get even more detailed statistics using the Google Analytics tracking service described on page 324.

- **Links.** This section is most notable for its external link viewer, which shows you what Web sites link to yours. It's like a super-powered version of the *link:* search operator that you learned about on page 304.

- **Sitemaps.** This section helps you build a *sitemap*—a special file that describes the structure of your site and the files in it. You can submit your sitemap to Google and other search engines so they know what to index. This is particularly useful if you have pages that Google might ordinarily miss, like standalone pages (those not linked to other pages).

- **Tools.** This section lets you tweak a few miscellaneous Google settings (for example, how often it examines your site for new content). It also lets you create and analyze *robots.txt* files, which you can use to hide a portion of your site from nosy search engines, as explained on page 321.

Most serious Web designers eventually check out their Web sites with the Google Webmaster Tools. If nothing else, you can use it to make sure everything is running smoothly—in other words, that Google can access your site, that its automated search robots return frequently to check for new content, and that the robots review all the pages you have to offer.

Google AdWords

As a Web-head, you've no doubt seen several lifetimes' worth of flashing messages, gaudy banners, and invasive pop-ups, all trying to sell you some hideously awful products. It probably comes as no surprise to learn that these types of ads aren't the way to promote your site—in fact, they're more likely to alienate people than entice them. However, there are respectable paid placements that can get your site in front of the right readers, at the right time, and with the right amount of tact. One of the best is AdWords (*http://adwords.google.com*), Google's insanely flexible advertising system.

The idea behind AdWords is that you create text ads that Google shows alongside its regular search results (see Figure 11-8). The neat part is that Google doesn't show the ads indiscriminately. Instead, you choose the search keywords you want your ad associated with.

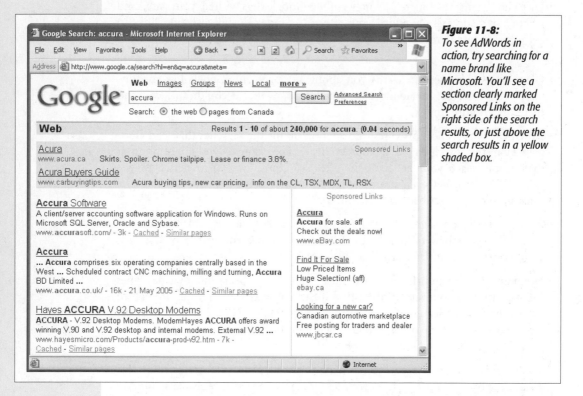

Figure 11-8:
To see AdWords in action, try searching for a name brand like Microsoft. You'll see a section clearly marked Sponsored Links on the right side of the search results, or just above the search results in a yellow shaded box.

The nice (and slightly confusing) part about AdWords is that you *bid* for the keywords you want to use. For example, you might tell Google you're willing to pay 25 cents for the keyword "food." Google takes this into consideration with everyone else's bids, and displays the higher bidders' ads more often. But Google isn't out to rip anyone off, and it charges you only the going rate for your keyword, regardless of how much you told Google you're willing to pay. And Google doesn't charge you anything to simply display your ad on a search results page. It charges you only when someone clicks on your ad to get to your site.

By this point, you might be getting a little nervous. Given the fact that Google handles hundreds of millions of searches a day, isn't it possible for a measly one-cent bid to quickly put you and your site into bankruptcy? Fortunately, Google's got the solution for this, too. You just tell Google how much you're willing to pay per day. Once you hit your limit, Google stops showing your ad.

Interestingly, the bid amount isn't the only factor that determines how often your ad appears. Popularity is also important. If Google shows your ad over and over again and it never gets a click, Google realizes that your ad just isn't working, and lets you know that with an automatic email message. It may then start showing your ad significantly less often, or stop showing it altogether, until you improve it.

AdWords can be competitive. To have a chance against all the AdWords sharks, you need to know how much a click is worth to your site. For example, if you sell monogrammed socks, you need to know what percentage of visitors actually *buy* something (the *conversion rate*) and how much they're likely to spend. A typical cost-per-click hovers around 75 cents, but there's a wide range. At last measure, the word *free* topped the cost-per-click charts at $2.26, while the keyword combination *llama care* could be had for a song—a mere 5 cents. (And in recent history, law firms have bid "mesothelioma"—an asbestos-related cancer that could become the basis of a class-action lawsuit—up close to $100.) Before you sign up with AdWords, it's a good idea to conduct some serious research to find out the recent prices of the keywords you want to use.

Note: You can learn more about AdWords from *Google: The Missing Manual*, which includes a whole chapter on it, or on Google's AdWords site (*http://adwords.google.com*). For a change of pace, go to *www.iterature.com/adwords* for a story about an artist's attempt to use AdWords to distribute poetry, and why it failed.

Hiding from search engines

In rare situations, you might create a page that you *don't* want to turn up in a search result. The most common reason is because you've posted some information that you want to share with only a few friends, like the latest Amazon e-coupons. If Google indexes your site, thousands of visitors could come your way, sucking up your bandwidth for the rest of the month. Another reason may be that you're posting something semi-private that you don't want other people to stumble across, like a story about how you stole a dozen staplers from your boss. If you fall into the latter category, be very cautious. Keeping search engines away is the least of your problems—once a site's on the Web, it *will* be discovered. And once it's discovered, it won't ever go away (see the box on page 323).

But you can do at least one thing to minimize your site's visibility or, possibly, keep it off search engines altogether. To understand how this procedure works, recall that search engines do their work in several stages. In the first stage, a robot program crawls across the Web, downloading sites. You can tell this robot to not index your site, or to ignore a portion of it, in several ways (not all search engines respect these rules, but most—including Google—do).

To keep a robot away from a single page, add the *robots* meta element to the page. Use the content value *noindex*, as shown here:

```
<meta name="robots" content="noindex" />
```

Remember, like all meta elements, you place this one in the <head> section of your XHTML document.

Alternatively, you can use *nofollow* to tell robots to index the current page, but not to follow any of its links:

```
<meta name="robots" content="nofollow" />
```

If you want to block larger portions of your site, you're better off creating a specialized file called *robots.txt*, and placing it in the top-level folder of your site. The robot will check this file before it goes any further. The content inside the *robots.txt* file sets the rules.

If you want to stop a robot from indexing any part of your site, add this to the *robots.txt* file:

```
User-Agent: *
Disallow: /
```

The User-Agent part identifies the type of robot you're addressing, and an asterisk represents all robots. The Disallow part indicates what part of the Web site is off limits; a single forward slash represent the whole site.

To rope off just the Photos subfolder on your site, use this (making sure to match the capitalization of the folder name exactly):

```
User-Agent: *
Disallow: /Photos
```

To stop a robot from indexing certain types of content (like images), use this:

```
User-Agent: *
Disallow: /*.gif
Disallow: /*.jpeg
```

As this example shows, you can put as many Disallow rules as you want in the *robots.txt* file, one after the other.

Remember, the *robots.txt* file is just a set of *guidelines* for search engine robots, it's not a form of access control. In other words, it's similar to posting a "No Flyers" sign on your mailbox—it works only as long as advertisers choose to heed it.

Tip: You can learn much more about robots, including how to tell when they visit your site and how to restrict the robots coming from specific search engines, at *www.robotstxt.org*.

Web Permanence

You've probably heard a lot of talk about the ever-changing nature of the Web. Maybe you're worried that the links you create today will lead to dead sites or missing pages tomorrow. Well, there's actually a much different issue taking shape—old site copies that just won't go away.

Once you put your work on the Web, you've lost control of it forever. The corollary to this sobering thought is: Always make sure you aren't posting something that's illegal, infringes on copyright, is personally embarrassing, or could get you fired. Because once you put this material out on the Web, it may never go away.

For example, imagine you accidentally reveal your company's trade secret for carrot-flavored chewing gum. A few weeks later, an excited customer links to your site. You realize your mistake, and pull the pages off your Web server. But have you really contained the problem?

Assuming the Google robot has visited your site recently (which is more than likely), Google now has a copy of your old Web site. Even worse, people can get this *cached* (saved) copy from Google if they know about the *cache*

keyword. For example, if the offending page's URL is *www.GumLover.com/newProduct.htm*, a savvy Googler can get the old copy of your page using the search "cache:www.GumLover.com/newProduct.htm." (Less savvy visitors might still stumble onto a cached page by clicking the Cached link that appears after each search result in Google's listings.) Believe it or not, this trick's been used before to get accidentally leaked information, ranging from gossip to software license keys.

You can try to get your page out of Google's cache as quickly as possible using the remove URL feature at *www.google.com/webmasters/tools/removals*. But even if this works, you're probably starting to see the problem—there's no way to know how many search engines have made copies of your work. Interested people who notice that you pulled down information will hit these search engines and copy the details to their own sites, making it pretty near impossible to eliminate the lingering traces of your mistake. There are even catalogs dedicated to preserving old Web sites for posterity (see the Wayback Machine at *www.archive.org*).

Tracking Visitors

As a Web site owner, you'll try a lot of different tactics to promote your site. Naturally, some will work while others won't—and you need to keep the good strategies and prune those that fail. To do this successfully, you need a way to assess how your Web site is performing.

Almost every Web hosting company (except free Web hosts) gives you some way to track the number of visitors to your site (see Figure 11-9). Ask your hosting company how to use these tools. Usually, you need to log on to a "control panel" or "my account" section of your Web host's site. You'll see a variety of options there—look for an icon labeled "site counters" or "Web traffic."

With more high-end hosting services, you often have more options for viewing your site's traffic statistics. Some hosts provide the raw *Web server logs*, which store detailed, blow-by-blow information about every one of your visitors. This information includes the time a visitor came, their IP addresses (page 56), their browser type, what site referred them to you, whether they ran into an error, what pages

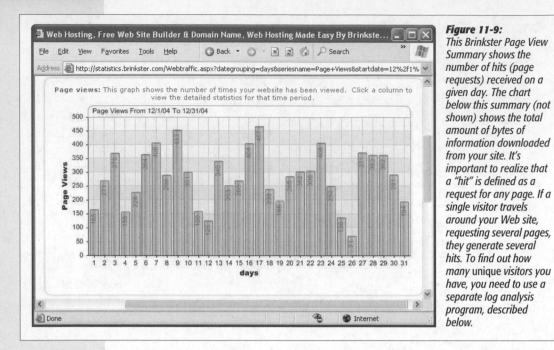

Figure 11-9:
This Brinkster Page View Summary shows the number of hits (page requests) received on a given day. The chart below this summary (not shown) shows the total amount of bytes of information downloaded from your site. It's important to realize that a "hit" is defined as a request for any page. If a single visitor travels around your Web site, requesting several pages, they generate several hits. To find out how many unique *visitors you have, you need to use a separate log analysis program, described below.*

they ignored, what pages they loved, and so on. To make sense of this information, you need to feed it into a high-powered program that performs *log analysis*. These programs are often complex and expensive. An equally powerful but much more convenient approach is to use the Google Analytics tracking service, described next.

Understanding Google Analytics

In 2005, Google purchased Urchin, one of the premium Web tracking companies. They transformed it into *Google Analytics* and abolished its hefty $500/month price tag, making it free for everyone. Today, Google Analytics just might be the best way to see what's happening on any Web site, whether you're building a three-page site about dancing hamsters or a massive compendium of movie reviews.

Google Analytics is refreshingly simple. Unlike other log analysis tools, it doesn't ask you to provide server logs or other low-level information. Instead, it tracks all the information you need *on its own*. It stores this information indefinitely, and lets you analyze it any time with a range of snazzy Web reports.

To use Google Analytics, you need to add a small snippet of JavaScript code to every Web page you want to track (usually, that's every page on your site). Once you get the JavaScript code in place, everything works seamlessly. When a visitor heads to a page on your site, the browser sends a record of the request to Google's army of monster Web servers, which store it for later analysis. The visitor doesn't see the Google Analytics stuff. Figure 11-10 shows you how it works.

Note: Remember, JavaScript is a type of mini-program that runs inside a browser. Virtually every Web browser in existence supports it. Chapter 14 provides a JavaScript introduction.

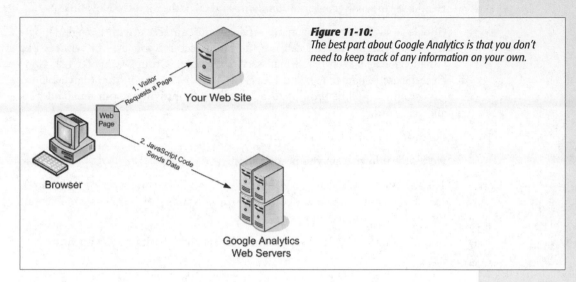

Figure 11-10:
The best part about Google Analytics is that you don't need to keep track of any information on your own.

Using this system, Google Analytics collects two kinds of information:

• **Information about your visitors' browsers and computers.** Whenever a browser requests a page, it supplies a basic set of information. This information includes the type of browser it is, the features it supports, and the IP address of the computer it connects through (an *IP address* is a numeric code that uniquely identifies a computer on the Internet). These details don't include the information you really want—for example, there's no way to find out personal details like names or addresses. However, Google uses other browser information to infer additional details. For example, using the IP address, it can make an educated guess about your visitor's geographic location.

• **Visitor tracking.** Thanks to its sophisticated tracking system, Google Analytics can determine more interesting information about a visitor's patterns. Ordinarily, if a visitor requests two separate Web pages from the same site, there's no way to establish whether those requests came from the same person. However, Google uses a *cookie* (a small packet of data stored on a visitor's computer) to uniquely identify each visitor. As a result, when visitors click links and move from page to page, Google can determine their navigation path, the amount of time they spend on each page, and whether they return later.

Google Analytics wouldn't be nearly as useful if it were up to you to make sense of all this information. But as you'll see, Google not only tracks these details, it provides reports that help you figure out what the data really means. You generate the reports using a handy Web screen menu, and you can print them out or download the data and use it in another program, like Excel, to do further analysis.

Signing Up for Google Analytics

Signing up for Google Analytics is easy:

1. **Head over to** *www.google.com/analytics* **and click the Sign Up Now link.**

   Google Analytics is one of many services you can access with a single Google account. That means you can use the same account you use for services like Gmail (Google's Web-based mail service), Google Groups (Chapter 12), Google AdSense (Chapter 13), and Blogger (Chapter 17). If you don't have a Google account, you'll be prompted to create one by providing your email address and password.

2. **Fill in the information about your Web site.**

   Here's the information you need to supply:

   The URL for the Web site you want track (for example, *www.supermagicalpotatoes. co.uk*). A Google Analytics account can track as many Web sites as you like, but for now start with just one.

   Your time zone. This lets Google Analytics synchronize its clock with yours.

3. **Click Finish.**

   When you finish the sign-in process, Google gives you a box with the Java-Script code you need to start tracking visits (see Figure 11-11). The next section tells you how to add that code to your pages.

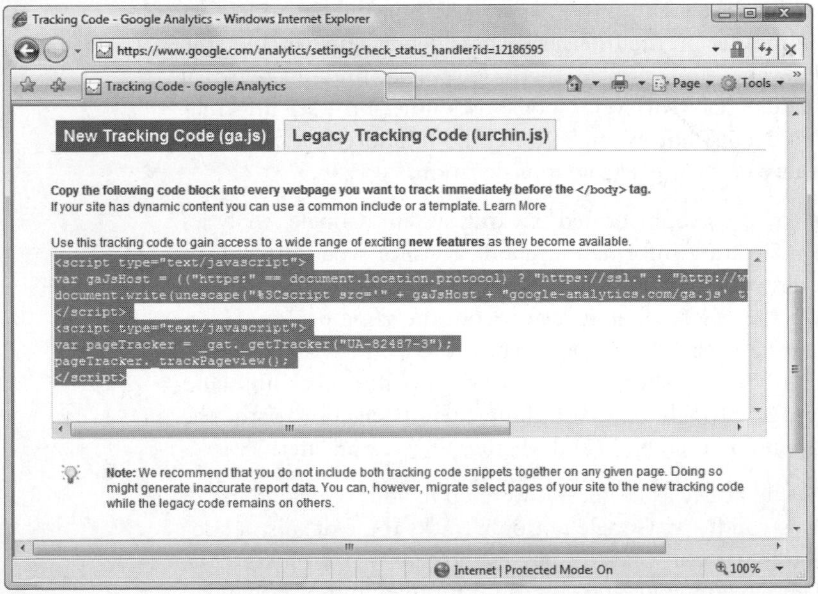

Figure 11-11:
The Google Analytics code is lean and concise, requiring just a few lines. That's because it links to a file on Google's Web servers to get the real tracking code. Select all the code displayed, and then copy it to your clipboard (you do this in most browsers by right-clicking the selected text, and then choosing Copy).

4. **Click Finish to complete the process.**

Google sends you to the main management page for Google Analytics.

5. **Add the tracking code to your Web pages.**

When you add Google's script code to a page, put it at the very end of the `<body>` section, just before the closing `</body>` tag. Here's an example of where it fits in a typical Web page:

```
<!DOCTYPE html PUBLIC "-//W3C//DTD XHTML 1.0 Strict//EN"
"http://www.w3.org/TR/xhtml1/DTD/xhtml1-strict.dtd">

<html xmlns="http://www.w3.org/1999/xhtml">
<head>
  <title>Welcome</title>
</head>

<body>
  ...

  <!-- Put the analytics code here. -->
</body>
</html>
```

Tip: For best results, copy the tracking code to every Web page in your site. The only exception is for frames-based sites. If you have one, don't copy the tracking code to the pages used for navigation bars, headers, and other non-content regions. There's generally no point in recording requests for these elements, because your site displays them automatically.

---

6. **Upload the new version of your Web pages.**

Once you change all your pages, make sure to upload them to your Web server. Only then can Google Analytics start tracking visits. The tracking features won't work when you run the pages from your own computer's hard drive.

Now, it's a waiting game. Within 24 hours, Google Analytics has enough information about recent visitors to provide its detailed reports.

Examining your Web Traffic

As a registered Google Analytics user, you can log in to read reports and make sure everything's running smoothly. If you haven't already done so, now's the time to head to *www.google.com/analytics*.

When you first log in, you see the Analytics Settings page shown in Figure 11-12. Using this page, you can add new Web sites you want to track or configure existing ones. You can also get a little guidance from a list of help topics that appears on the side.

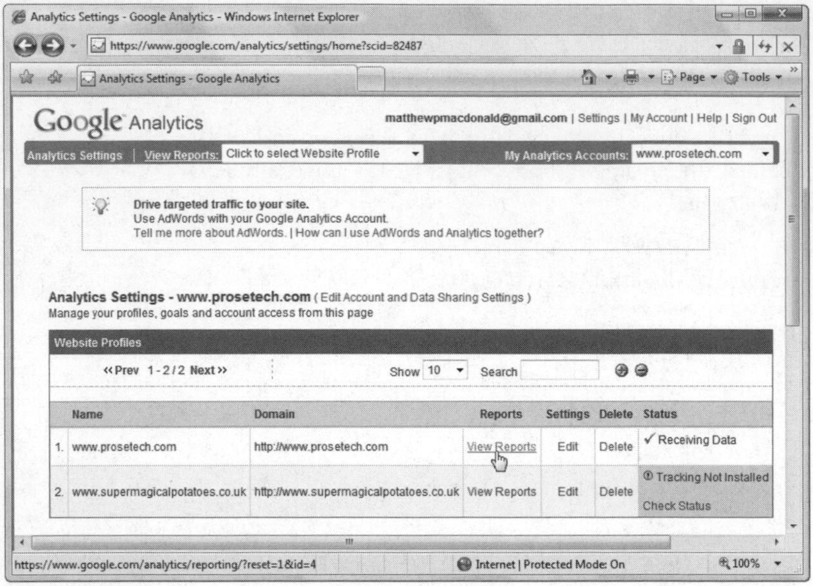

Figure 11-12:
This sample account tracks two Web sites, but only one is successfully collecting data. You can use the View Reports link to start reviewing reports, the Edit link to change the information you supplied for your Web site, and the Delete link to remove your profile altogether.

To determine whether your Web site's tracking code is working, check the Status column in the Website Profiles list. Here's how to interpret the different status values your site might have:

- **Receiving Data** indicates that all's well. Your visitors are going from page to page under the watchful eye of Google Analytics.

- **Waiting For Data** indicates that Google's JavaScript code is running on your pages, but the information isn't available for reporting yet. Usually, you see this for the first 6 to 12 hours after you register a new site.

- **Tracking Data Not Installed** indicates that Google isn't collecting any information. This could be because you need to wait for visitors to hit your site, or it could suggest you haven't inserted the correct JavaScript tracking code.

If you see Receiving Data, congratulations—you're reports are ready and waiting. Click the View Reports link next to your Web site to continue on to the Dashboard (Figure 11-13).

The information that appears in the Dashboard can be a little overwhelming. To give you a better sense of what's going on, the following sections break down the key points, one chart at a time.

Graph of Visits

The graph of visits at the top of the page (Figure 11-14) shows the day-by-day popularity of your site over the last month. This count doesn't say anything about how many pages the average visitor browsed, or how long visitors lingered. It simply

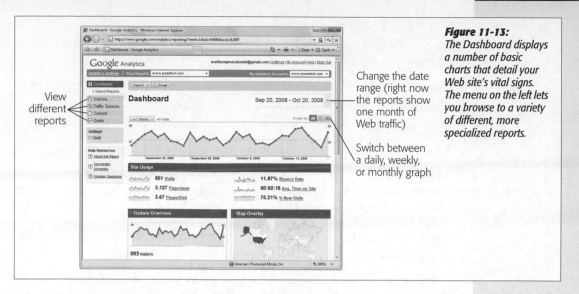

View different reports

Change the date range (right now the reports show one month of Web traffic)

Switch between a daily, weekly, or monthly graph

Figure 11-13:
The Dashboard displays a number of basic charts that detail your Web site's vital signs. The menu on the left lets you browse to a variety of different, more specialized reports.

records how many different people visited your site. Using this chart, you can get a quick sense of the overall uptrend or downtrend of your Web traffic, and you can see if it rises on certain days of the week or around specific dates.

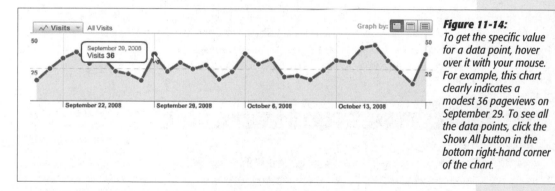

Figure 11-14:
To get the specific value for a data point, hover over it with your mouse. For example, this chart clearly indicates a modest 36 pageviews on September 29. To see all the data points, click the Show All button in the bottom right-hand corner of the chart.

With a few clicks, you can change this chart to show *pageviews*, the count of how many Web pages all your visitors viewed. For example, if an eager shopper visits your Banana Painting e-commerce store, checks out several enticing products, and completes a purchase, Google Analytics might record close to a dozen pageviews but only a single visit. The number of pageviews is always equal to or greater than the number of visits—after all, each visit includes at least one pageview. To see pageviews, click the down arrow next to the word Visits in the top-left corner of the chart, and then choose Pageviews from the list of options.

Tip: Remember, you can look at the data Google Analytics collects over a different range of dates using the date box in the top-left corner of the Dashboard, as identified in Figure 11-13.

Site Usage

The Site Usage section (Figure 11-15) is crammed with key statistics. Details include:

- The total number of visits in the selected date range (initially, it's the month leading up to the current day).

- The total number of pageviews.

- The average number of pages that a visitor reads before leaving your site.

- The bounce rate. A *bounce* occurs when a visitor views only one page—in other words, they get to your site through a specific page, and then depart without browsing any further. A bounce rate of 11% tells you that 11% percent of your visitors leave immediately after they arrive. Bounces are keenly important to Web masters because they indicate potential lost visitors. If you can identify what's causing a big bounce, you can capture a few more visitors.

- The average time a visitor spends on your site before browsing elsewhere.

- The percentage of new visits. For example, a rate of 75% indicates that 25% of your traffic is repeat business, and 75% are new visitors. Both types of visitor are important to keep your Web site healthy.

Note: There are some types of repeat visitors that Google won't correctly identify. For example, if a repeat visitor uses a different computer, a different browser, or logs into their computer with a different user name, they'll appear to be a new visitor. For these reasons, the number of repeat visitors may be slightly underreported.

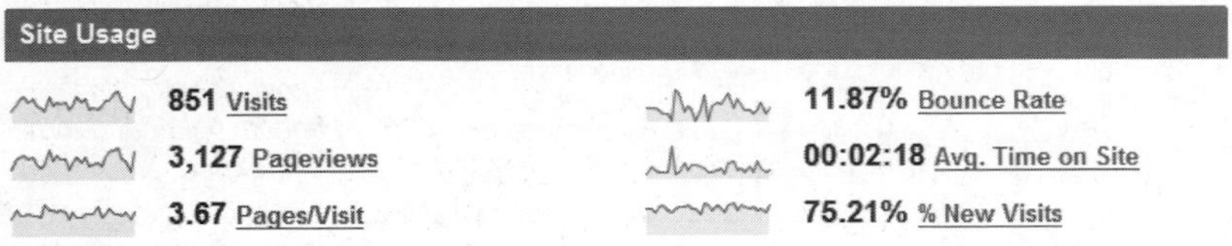

Site Usage	
851 Visits	**11.87%** Bounce Rate
3,127 Pageviews	**00:02:18** Avg. Time on Site
3.67 Pages/Visit	**75.21%** % New Visits

Figure 11-15:
The Site Usage numbers are the most important indicator of your site's Web health. You can click any of these stats to see a separate report with more detail.

Map Overlay

The Map Overlay section gives a fascinating look at where your visitors are located on the globe. Google Analytics divides the map into countries, and colors them different shades of green—the darker the color, the more popular your Web site in that country.

The Map Overlay gets even more interesting if you use the City view shown in Figure 11-16. To use the City view, click the "view report" link under the Map Overlay on the Dashboard. A new page appears with a larger version of the map and a detailed breakdown in a table underneath. Look for the Detail Level box at the top of the table, and then change the selection in this box from Country/Territory to City.

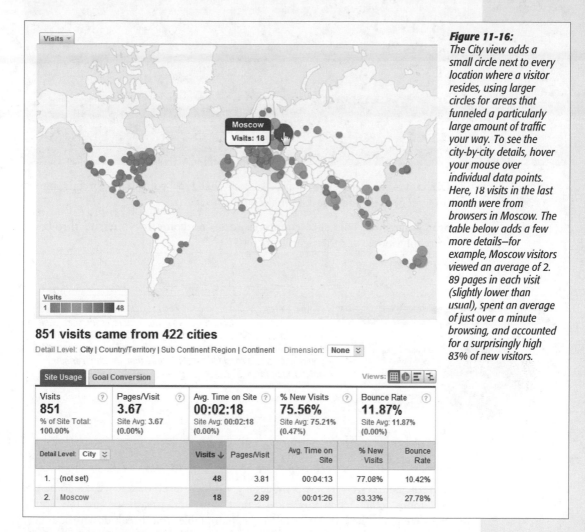

Figure 11-16:
The City view adds a small circle next to every location where a visitor resides, using larger circles for areas that funneled a particularly large amount of traffic your way. To see the city-by-city details, hover your mouse over individual data points. Here, 18 visits in the last month were from browsers in Moscow. The table below adds a few more details—for example, Moscow visitors viewed an average of 2. 89 pages in each visit (slightly lower than usual), spent an average of just over a minute browsing, and accounted for a surprisingly high 83% of new visitors.

Traffic Sources Overview

The Traffic Sources Overview is a pie chart identifying how visitors get to your site. It has three slices:

- **Referring Sites.** This slice counts visitors that arrive through Web sites that link to yours.

- **Direct Traffic.** This slice counts visitors that type your URL directly into a browser or use a bookmark to make a return visit.

- **Search Engines.** This slice counts visitors who come to your site through a search in Google or other search engine.

Figure 11-17 shows a closer look.

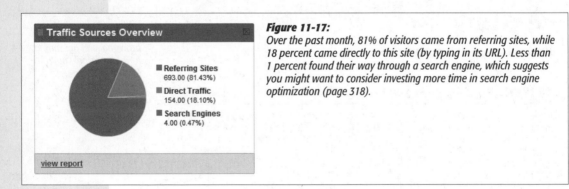

Figure 11-17:
Over the past month, 81% of visitors came from referring sites, while 18 percent came directly to this site (by typing in its URL). Less than 1 percent found their way through a search engine, which suggests you might want to consider investing more time in search engine optimization (page 318).

The Traffic Sources Overview provides a good high-level look at what's going on. To get more details, click the "view report" link underneath, or use the Traffic Sources menu on the left. You can then explore tables that break down the Referring Sites and Search Engines slices. For the Referring Sites slice, you see exactly which Web sites send you traffic, which is a great tool for quickly identifying your most successful Web partnerships. For the Search Engines slice, you can review the search keywords that lead to your site, which lets you determine what your visitors are looking for (and possibly diagnose why they left unhappy).

Content Overview

As every Web master knows, all pages aren't created equal. Some might command tremendous interest while others languish ignored. The Content Overview section lists top-performing pages (Figure 11-18).

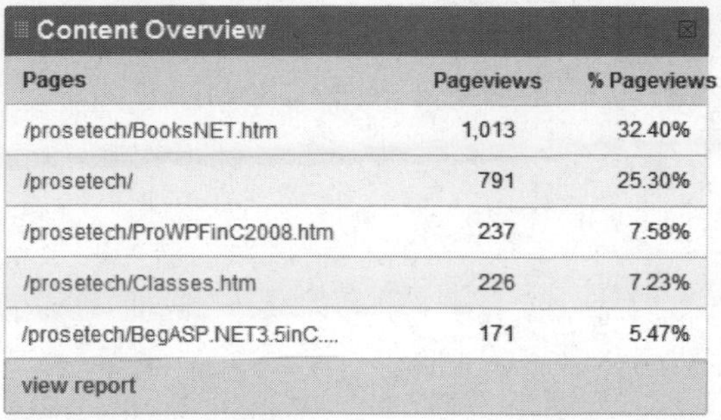

Content Overview		⊠
Pages	**Pageviews**	**% Pageviews**
/prosetech/BooksNET.htm	1,013	32.40%
/prosetech/	791	25.30%
/prosetech/ProWPFinC2008.htm	237	7.58%
/prosetech/Classes.htm	226	7.23%
/prosetech/BegASP.NET3.5inC....	171	5.47%
view report		

Figure 11-18:
In this site, BooksNET.htm is the clear winner of the Most Popular Page award, with 32 percent of the total Web site traffic.

However, it's not enough to simply determine which pages your visitors view the most. Some pages are extra important because of their ability to *attract* visitors. For example, the page of Member Photos on your International Nudist site might attract large volumes of visitors who then stick around to check out your personalized coffee cups, clothing, and memorabilia. A good reporting tool also shows you where visitors *enter* your site, so you know what pages are the attention-getters that lure traffic. Almost as important are the pages that mark the end of a visit. They may indicate a problem, like a page that's extremely large, doesn't work correctly in some browsers, or just plain irritates people. To get this sort of detailed information in Google Analytics, click the "view report" button in the bottom of the Content Overview section, or use the Content menu on the left side of the page.

Note: There are many more reports you can explore in Google Analytics, and many more ways to slice and dice its results to come up with conclusions about your Web traffic. In fact, entire books have been written about the fine art of analyzing Web site performance. However, the five charts explained above get you started with great insight into how your Web site is doing.

CHAPTER 12

Letting Visitors Talk to You (and Each Other)

The Web is the crowded home of several million people, so when you put your Web site online, it doesn't just drop into a vacuum. Instead, it takes center stage in front of an audience that's always interested, often opinionated, and occasionally irritable.

For your site to really fit in with the rest of the Web, you need to interact with your visitors. The idea of dialogue—back-and-forth communication between peers—is hard-wired into the Internet's DNA. Heated discussion flows over all sorts of different channels, and includes insightful postings on discussion groups, scathing reviews on Amazon, shout-outs on Web site guestbooks, daily blog entries, email notes, instant messages, chat rooms, and much more. Online discussions never stop—they just billow across the globe like giant clouds of hot air.

In this chapter, you'll learn to connect with your audience using basic tools like your email inbox, and to incorporate the often-rollicking world of Web-based groups and discussion forums into your site.

Transforming a Site into a Community

The Web sites you've created so far are lonely affairs. Visitors can come and look around, but there isn't any way for them to really participate. If the Web were a one-way medium, like cable television or newspapers, this wouldn't be a problem. But the Internet is all about *community*, which means you need to let your visitors react, respond, and (occasionally) harass you.

Talking the Talk

Community is so important to the Web that ubergeeks have their own catchy jargon to describe the process of people meeting up online. Here are some popular terms so you won't feel left out of the discussion:

- A **netizen** is an active, responsible citizen of the Internet—someone who takes Web community as seriously as life in the real world.

- **Flaming** is a blistering exchange of insults on a public forum. If you post your personal theory about how an alien race created the human species on a discussion group about evolution, you're sure to be flamed.

- **Trolling** is the act of enticing people to flame you, either to make them look ridiculous or just for sport. For example, if you ask for donations for your "Michael Moore for President" campaign on a Web site for young Republicans, you're trolling.

- **Blogging** is the practice of posting regular, dated entries on a special kind of Web site (called a *blog*— short for "Web log"). Blogs can contain anything from detailed technical articles to rambling, random thoughts. Often, bloggers let other people add comments to their blog entries, which lets blogs become another forum for community interaction. You'll learn about blogs in Chapter 17.

How do you start transforming your Web site into a Web community? The first trick is to change your perspective, so that you plan your Web site as a meeting place instead of just a place to vent your (admittedly brilliant) thoughts. Here are a few tips to help you get in the right frame of mind:

- **Clearly define the purpose of your site**. For example, the description "www. BronteRevival.com is dedicated to bringing Charlotte Bronte fans together to discuss and promote her work" is more community-oriented than "www. BronteRevival.com contains information and criticism of Charlotte Bronte's work." The first sentence describes what the site aims to do, while the second reflects what it contains, thereby limiting its scope. Once you define a single-sentence description, you can use it in your description meta element (page 310) or in a mission statement on your home page.

- **Build gathering places**. No one wants to hang around a collection of links and static text. Jazz up your site with discussion forums or chat boards, where your visitors can kick up their heels. You'll learn how to get these bits in place later in this chapter.

- **Give your visitors different roles**. Successful community sites recognize different levels of contribution. At one extreme, the right people can grow into leadership roles and even coordinate events, newsletters, discussion groups, or portions of your site. At the other extreme are visitors who are happiest lurking in the background, watching what others do. There are different ways to recognize individual contributions—some sites use a personal feedback rating system that adds gold stars (or some other sort of icon) next to a person's name. Another approach is to give certain visitors more power, like the ability to manage members in a Google group (page 357).

- **Advertise new content before and after you add it.** To get visitors coming back again and again, you need lots of new content. But new content on its own isn't enough—you need to build up visitors' expectation of new content so they know enough to return, and you need to clearly highlight the new material so they can find it once they do. To help this work smoothly, try adding links on your first page that lead to newly added content, along with a quick line or two about upcoming content you plan to add and concrete information about when it'll be there.

- **Introduce regular events.** It's hard to force yourself to update your site regularly—and even when you do, visitors have no way of knowing when there's something that makes a return visit worthwhile. Why not help everyone keep track of what's going on by promoting regular events (like a news section you update weekly or a promotional drawing that happens on a set date)?

- **Create feedback loops.** It's a law of the Web—good sites keep getting better, while bad sites magnify their mistakes. To help your site get on the right track, make sure there's a way for visitors to tell you what they like. Then, spend the bulk of your time strengthening what works and tossing out what doesn't.

Now that you have your Web site good-citizenship philosophy straight, it's time to learn how to build the ingredients every Web community needs.

POWER USERS' CLINIC

Planning for the Future

The techniques you learn about in this chapter will help you start and manage a small Web community. However, keeping up with all the tools you need to use takes effort, and as your site starts to grow, you might not have the time to manage mailing lists by hand or keep track of your visitors.

All large communities on the Web are supported with some type of nifty software that can manage these tasks. Only a small fraction of Web site creators build their own software. Most buy an existing program.

You won't learn about full-fledged community software in this chapter (aside from some free solutions for setting up forums). However, you can take your search online to hunt down professional software.

Helping Visitors Email You

The first step in audience participation is letting your visitors email you. This is a small-scale interaction, because it's exclusively between two people (you and one visitor) and the conversation is private. Later on in this chapter you'll learn how to expand the discussion to include a whole gaggle of Web browsers.

Mailto Links

Unlike the standard-issue hyperlinks you learned about back in Chapter 8, there's one special type of link you haven't seen yet—the *mailto* link. When you click a mailto link, your browser starts your email program and begins creating a message. It's still up to you to actually send the message, but the mailto link can get the process started with a boilerplate subject line and body text.

Note: The mailto link is a great way to get feedback from others, but for it to work, visitors have to have an email program installed and configured on their PC. Alternatively, if your visitors use Firefox they can get by with an email add-on (see page 12) that supports a Web-based email service like Gmail.

To create a mailto link, you specify a path that starts with the word *mailto*, followed by a colon (:) and your email address. Here's an example:

```
<a href="mailto:me@myplace.com">Email Me</a>
```

Most browsers also let you supply text for the message's subject line and body. When someone clicks the mailto link, the new message loads this information, ready for sending (or editing).

To supply the subject line and body text, you have to use a slightly wonky syntax that follows these rules:

- Put a question mark after the email address.

- To declare the subject line, add *subject=* followed by the subject text.

- If you want to define some body text, add the character sequence *&* after your subject text, and then type *body=* followed by the body text.

- Replace characters that could cause problems with specialized codes. Letters, numbers, and the period are all fine, but most other punctuation isn't. For example, you have to replace every space in the subject and body text with the character sequence *%20*. This gets quite tedious and makes your message hard to read after you compose it, but this step ensures that the mailto link works in every browser. The easiest way to prepare your message text is to visit a page like *http://meyerweb.com/eric/tools/dencoder*, which adds the code for you. Simply enter your message text into the provided text box, and then click Encode to replace potentially problematic codes with the appropriate ones.

Confused? The easiest way to grasp these rules is to take a look at a couple of examples. First, here's a mailto link that includes the subject text "Automatic Email":

```
<a href="mailto:me@myplace.com?subject=Automatic%20Email">
Email Me</a>
```

And here's a link that includes both subject text and body text:

```
<a href=
"mailto:me@myplace.com?subject=Automatic%20Email&amp;body=
  I%20love%20your%20site.">Email Me</a>
```

When you click this link, you'll probably see some sort of warning message informing you that the Web page is about to open your email program and asking your permission (the exact message depends on your browser and operating system). If you agree, you see an email form pop up, like the one shown in Figure 12-1.

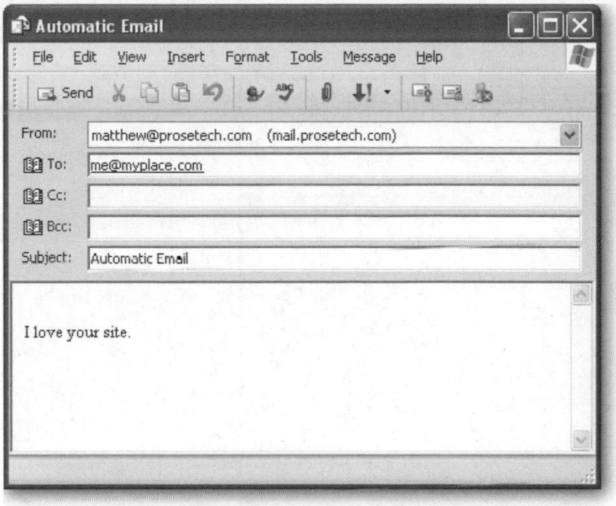

Figure 12-1:
When you click a mailto link, your browser creates an email message (as shown here). It fills in the recipient, subject, and body according to information in the link, although whoever's clicked the link can change these details (or close the window without clicking Send). The actual email window differs depending on the email program installed on the Web visitor's computer. This example shows the message window from Microsoft Outlook.

XHTML Forms

XHTML forms is a corner of the XHTML standard you haven't explored yet. It defines elements you can use to create graphical components that go into forms, like text boxes, buttons, checkboxes, and lists. Visitors interact with these components, which are commonly called *controls,* to answer questions and provide information. Figure 12-2 shows an example of an XHTML form in action.

Note: XHTML forms are also known as HTML forms, because they were first introduced as an add-on for HTML. The XHTML version has relatively few changes—it's just tweaked up with the stricter syntax rules of XHTML, which forbid improperly nested elements, require lowercase tag names, and so on.

XHTML forms are an indispensable technology for many Web sites, but you probably won't get much mileage out of them. That's because they're best suited for high-powered Web applications, not the smaller-scale Web sites you're creating.

For example, consider the account creation form shown in Figure 12-2. Once a visitor fills out all the details and clicks the Submit button at the bottom of the page, the browser does something special—it collects this information and patches it together into one long piece of text. Then it sends the information back to the server. That's where the Web application comes in. It examines the submitted data,

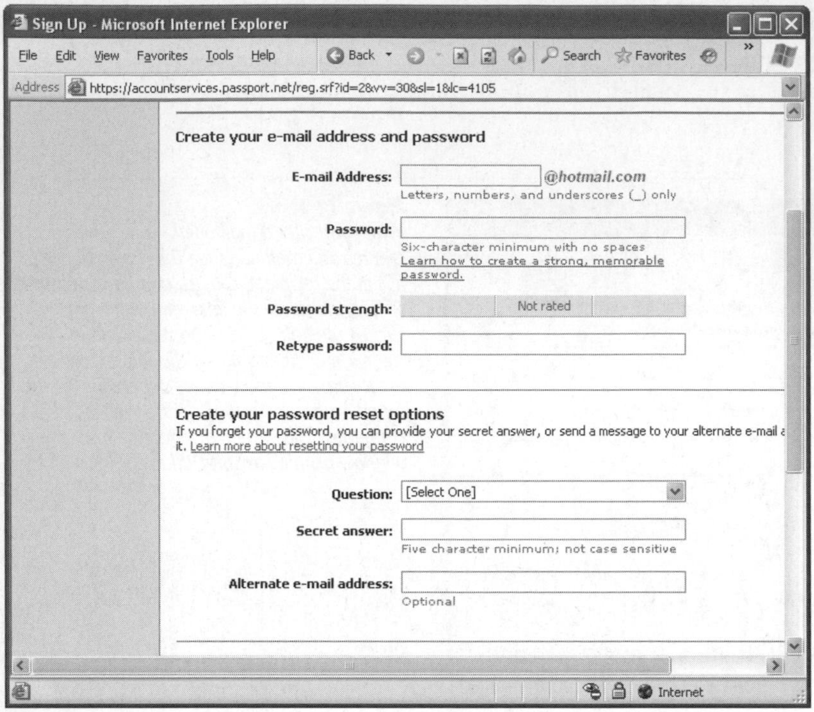

Figure 12-2:
Before Microsoft will grant you a Hotmail account, you need to submit some seriously detailed information. The text boxes, lists, and buttons you use are all part of an XHTML form.

chews through it, and then carries out some sort of action. This action might involve storing the information in a database or sending back another page with different XHTML (for example, an error message if the application detects a problem).

Forms are the basic building block of highly dynamic Web sites, but if you're not a Web programmer, you probably won't use forms all that often. Even so, there's still a way to use them to collect information. You can configure the forms on your site to email you. In other words, when someone clicks the Submit button on your form, the form won't send the collected data to a Web application—it sends *you* the information in an email message. If you use this technique, you'll need to sift through the emails yourself (which can be a major chore if you get hundreds of messages a day), but you'll have a valuable channel for visitor feedback.

Form basics

Every XHTML form starts out with a <form> element. The <form> element is a container element (page 33), and everything inside is automatically deemed to be part of your form.

```
<form>
    ...
</form>
```

POWER USERS' CLINIC

Becoming a Programmer

Want to unleash forms throughout your site and become a hard-core programmer? It's not easy going, but it can open up a lot of options for a stylin' site. The first task is to choose the programming framework you want to use. Here are some options:

- **JavaScript** is a simplified way to program for the Web. On its own, it's not enough to power most professional Web sites, because it runs only inside a browser (not on a Web server). But it's a good way to start out with a kind of programmer's training wheels. You get a basic introduction to JavaScript in Chapter 14, and you'll create a JavaScript-powered form on page 434.

- **CGI** (Common Gateway Interface) is the favorite of Internet traditionalists. It's a thorny but widely adopted standard that's been around since the dawn of the Internet. CGI isn't for the faint of heart, because it requires jargon-filled languages like C and Perl. If you aren't familiar with these languages, you might still be able to download a CGI script file from the Web and get it working for you. Head over to *www.cgi101.com/book* to dip a toe into CGI.

- **ASP** (Active Server Pages) and ASP.NET (a newer and far more ambitious version) are Microsoft technologies that are a good fit for people familiar with friendly programming languages like Visual Basic. You can learn some ASP basics at *www.w3schools.com/asp*, or tackle the more complex but much more capable ASP.NET at *www.w3schools.com/aspnet*, with which you can build everything from a joke-a-day message to industrial-strength e-commerce shops.

Form elements are also block elements (page 113), which means you put them directly in the <body> section of a page. When you create a form, your browser adds a little bit of space and starts you off on a new line.

What goes inside your form element? You can put ordinary XHTML content (like paragraphs of text) inside or outside a form element—it really doesn't matter. But you should always put form controls (those graphical components like buttons, text boxes, and lists) *inside* a form element. Otherwise, you won't have any way to capture the information a visitor enters into the form.

To create controls, you use yet another set of XHTML elements. Here's the weird part—most form controls use the *exact same* element. That element is named <input>, and it represents information you want to get *from* the visitor. You choose the type of input control by using a *type* attribute. For example, to create a checkbox, you use the *checkbox* type:

```
<input type="checkbox" />
```

To create a text box (where a visitor types in whatever text he wants), you use the text attribute:

```
<input type="text" />
```

To create a complete form, you mix and match <input> elements with ordinary XHTML:

```
<!DOCTYPE html PUBLIC "-//W3C//DTD XHTML 1.0 Strict//EN"
"http://www.w3.org/TR/xhtml1/DTD/xhtml1-strict.dtd">

<html xmlns="http://www.w3.org/1999/xhtml">
<head>
  <title>A Form-idable Test</title>
</head>

<body>
  <form>
    <p>
      First Name: <input type="text" />
      <br />
      Last Name: <input type="text" />
      <br />
      Email Address: <input type="text" />
      <br /><br />
      <input type="checkbox" />Add me to your mailing list
    </p>
  </form>
</body>
</html>
```

Figure 12-3 shows the page this creates.

Figure 12-3:
This very basic XHTML form brings together four controls: three text boxes and one checkbox. Everything else is just ordinary XHTML content. To make the page look nicer (and align it more neatly), you can use all the tricks you learned in previous chapters, including tables and styles. But one thing's still missing: a way for your visitor to actually send you the form's info. You'll learn how to fix that shortcoming below.

Every <input> element also supports a *value* attribute, which you usually use to set the initial state of a control. For example, if you want to put some text inside a text box when a page first appears, you could use this markup:

```
<input type="text" value="Enter the first name here" />
```

Checkboxes are a little different. You can start them off so that they're turned on by adding the *checked="checked"* attribute, as shown here:

```
<input type="checkbox" checked="checked" />
```

Not all controls use the <input> element. In fact, there are two notable exceptions. You use the <textarea> element to grab large amounts of text that span more than one line (don't ask why XHTML uses a new element for this purpose—it's largely for historical reasons). You use the <select> element to create a list from which a visitor selects items. Table 12-1 lists all of the most common controls.

Table 12-1. *XHTML form controls*

Control	XHTML Element	Description
Single-line Text Box	`<input type="text" />` `<input type="password" />`	Shows a text box where visitors can type in text. If you use the password type, the browser won't display the text. Instead, visitors see an asterisk (*) or a bullet (•) in place of each letter as they type in their password, hiding it from prying eyes.
Multi-line Text Box	`<textarea>...</textarea>`	Shows a large text box that can fit multiple lines of text.
Checkbox	`<input type="checkbox" />`	Shows a checkbox you can turn on or off.
Option Button	`<input type="radio" />`	Shows a radio button (a circle you can turn on or off). Usually, you have a group of radio buttons next to each other, in which case the visitor can select only one.

Button	`<input type="submit" />`
	`<input type="image" />`
	`<input type="reset" />`
	`<input type="button" />`
		Shows the standard clickable button. A *submit* button always gathers up the form data and sends it to its destination. An *image* button does the same thing, but lets you display a clickable picture instead of the standard text-on-a-button. A *reset* button clears the visitor's selections and text from all the input controls. A "button" button doesn't do anything unless you add some JavaScript code (Chapter 14).

List	`<select>...</select>`	Shows a list where your visitor can select one or more items. You add an <option> element for each item in the list.

Mailing a form

Right now, the only problem with the form in Figure 12-3 is that it doesn't actually do anything. You need a way for the form to send its data to you. To do that, you need to take two steps. First, you need to add a Submit button so a visitor can signal that he's completed the form. Use the *value* attribute to set the text that appears inside this button.

```
<input type="submit" value="OK" />
```

Next, you modify the <form> element so that it uses a *mailto* link to mail the form's data to an address you specify:

```
<form action="mailto:myaccount@HelloThere.com"
 method="post" enctype="text/plain" >
```

Note: Using mailto in a form is a riskier proposition than using it in a link. Depending on the browser and email program your Web visitors use, it might not work. And when it does work, it's more than likely to irritate your visitors with one or more warning messages. For better results, build a form you love, and then try mailing it with a server script or using a free form service, as described on page 348.

Finally, you need a way to uniquely identify each control. Otherwise, you won't be able to identify the type of information (first name, last name, and so on) your visitor typed in. The solution is to give each control a name with the *name* attribute.

Here's the revised form:

```
<form action="mailto:myaccount@HelloThere.com"
 method="post" enctype="text/plain">
  <p>
    First Name: <input type="text" name="FirstName" />
    <br />
    Last Name: <input type="text" name="LastName" />
    <br />
    Email Address: <input type="text" name="Email" />
    <br /><br />
    <input type="checkbox" checked="checked" name="MailCheck" />
    Add me to your mailing list<br />
    <br />
    <input type="submit" value="OK" />
  </p>
</form>
```

Now, say a visitor fills out the form with the information shown in Figure 12-4.

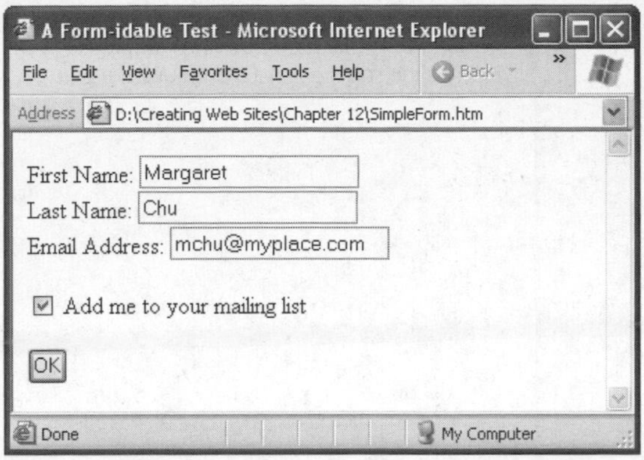

Figure 12-4:
A form with some visitor-supplied information.

When she clicks OK, the form puts the information in an email message and sends it to you. Here's the content of the email you receive:

```
FirstName=Margaret
LastName=Chu
Email=mchu@myplace.com
MailCheck=on
```

All this email contains is a list of *name-value pairs*. The *name* (on the left side of the equal sign) identifies the control. The *value* (on the right side) indicates the value your visitor supplied. As you can see, it could take a lot of work to read all these emails and record these details if you have a popular Web site. A nicer, but far more complex, approach is to have some sort of program that understands this type of message, and uses the information in it to carry out a desired set of actions automatically.

Tip: When a visitor submits a form, you might want to display a confirmation message or send her to a follow-up Web page. You do this by reacting to the form's onsubmit event using JavaScript, which will make a lot more sense once you tackle Chapter 14. For now, check out this example that redirects a visitor to a page named thanks.htm after she submits a form. You can use this code in your form—just modify the page name.

```
<form action="mailto:myaccount@HelloThere.com" method="post"
enctype="text/plain" onsubmit="location.href='thanks.htm'">
```

Creating a more complex form

In the previous example, you learned to collect information with text boxes and check boxes. But as you saw in Table 12-1, there's a whole toolkit of form controls waiting for you to crack open. In the following example, you'll learn about two new ingredients, which let you create a set of radio buttons and a drop-down list (see Figure 12-5).

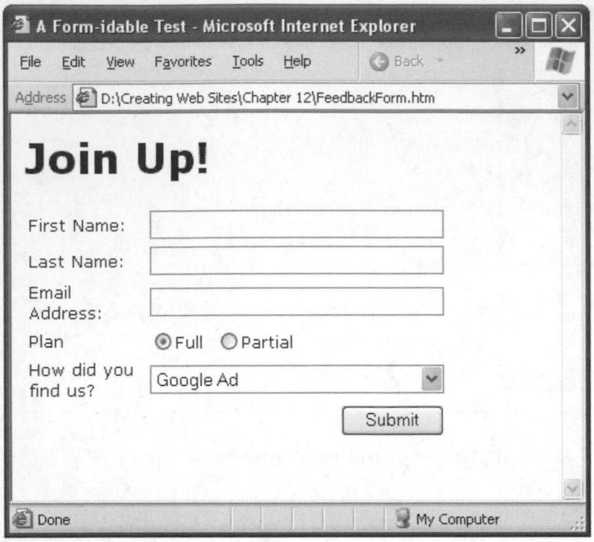

Figure 12-5:
This form aligns its controls neatly, and features a radio button selection and a drop-down menu.

First up are the two radio buttons that allow the form-filler to choose the plan type. To create them, you need two instances of the *radio* type of <input> element. Here's the XHTML that makes it happen:

```
<input type="radio" name="Plan" value="Full" checked="checked" />Full
<input type="radio" name="Plan" value="Part" />Partial
```

The trick is to make sure you give every radio button in a related group the same name. That way, your browser knows they belong together, and when a visitor clicks one option, the others remain unselected. You also need to give every radio button a unique value. That's how you tell, when you receive the form results, which option the visitor selected. For example, if someone clicks the Full option, and then clicks the button to submit the form, this is the line you see in the emailed data:

```
Plan=Full
```

To add a selectable drop-down menu, use the <select> element to create the list (and choose a name for it), and then add an <option> element to define each item in the list (and give it a unique value). Here's the XHTML:

```
<select name="PromoSource">
  <option value="Ad">Google Ad</option>
  <option value="Search">Google Search</option>
  <option value="Psychic">Uncanny Psychic Intuition</option>
  <option value="Luck">Bad Luck</option>
</select>
```

Now, if someone selects the first option, the email message contains this line:

```
PromoSource=Ad
```

Note: You can switch your menu from its drop-down appearance to a large list box using the *size* attribute. For example, if you write <select size="3"> you create a scrollable list box of three items at once. If you want to allow multiple selections, add the attribute *multiple="multiple"*. Now, a visitor can select several items at once by holding down the Ctrl key (or ⌘, if she's using a Mac). For more low-level form details, check out *www.w3schools.com/html/html_forms.asp*.

The last interesting detail about the form shown in Figure 12-5 is that it uses tables and styles to neaten up its appearance. Various style rules set the fonts and sizes of the different controls. (See the downloadable content for this chapter—available from the Missing CD page at *www.missingmanuals.com*—to take a look at the details.) Additionally, style rules put each item inside a separate table row so they all line up neatly. The table has two columns. The leftmost column holds the information prompts, and the rightmost column has the control.

Here's the first part of the table structure:

```
<table>
  <tr>
    <td>First Name:</td>
    <td><input type="text" name="FirstName" /></td>
  </tr>
  <tr>
    <td>Last Name:</td>
    <td><input type="text" name="LastName" /></td>
  </tr>
  <tr>
    <td>Email Address:</td>
    <td><input type="text" name="Email" /></td>
  </tr>
  ...
</table>
```

The table technique is a handy way to rein in sprawling forms.

More reliable forms with server scripts

Now that you've mastered the XHTML forms standard, you're ready to improve the slightly wonky submission method of the previous examples. Instead of using mailto forms, you can use a more reliable *server script*.

A server script is a miniature program that runs on a Web server. It's not a full Web application like those that power Web sites like Amazon and eBay. Instead, it consists of a few brief processing instructions embedded in your Web page alongside your XHTML, or stored in a separate file on your site. For example, for the email form submission example above, you can add a script that uses the Web server to send the email message. This server script approach has numerous advantages—for example, it works even if your visitor doesn't have an email program installed, and it hides your email address so spammers can't find it by looking at the XHTML for your Web page.

Adding a server script is easy. In most cases, you can keep your Web form the way it is, and just add a block of code in the right place. The problem is that different Web hosts support different scripting languages, and some might lock down certain features. So what's an ordinary Web weaver to do?

- **Ready-made scripts.** First, check with your Web host. Search its online help (or ask a support person) for a server script that can email a form. If you find one, it'll have instructions on how to paste the code into your Web page. If this approach turns up an answer, your work is done.

- **Scripts on the Web.** If you can't find a ready-made script, check with your Web host again—this time to find out if they support a server scripting language, and what that language is. Then you can use Google to hunt down a suitable script. For example, the tool at *www.tele-pro.co.uk/scripts/contact_form* creates scripts for popular scripting languages including ASP, PHP, and Perl. All you need to do is enter the names of all your input controls, pick a scripting language, and then click Finish. You'll get a new script to upload to your Web site, and you'll need to modify the *action* attribute of your <form> element to match. For example, if you create a script for ASP, you have to upload a file named *contact.asp*, and then set *action="contact.asp"* on your <form> element. This tells your Web server to run the *contact.asp* code when a visitor submits the form. Fortunately, you don't need to write that code yourself, or even understand how it works.

- **Form submission services.** Finally, if your Web host doesn't support server scripts, or you just don't want to wrestle with headaches a programmer would normally handle, you can use a free *form submission service*. Essentially, this service runs your form on its Web servers, but emails *you* the data. Good form submission services are free, but the companies that provide them usually offer more feature-filled counterparts that come with a price tag. You can find decent options at *www.emailmeform.com* and *www.response-o-matic.com*.

Adding Forums and Groups to Your Site

In the early days of the Internet, Web sites weren't at the heart of the action. Instead, the most interesting and lively interactions took place on a mammoth collection of online bulletin boards called *Usenet*. Sadly, Usenet fell into decline as the Web grew, spam became pervasive, and slick graphical sites became the norm. More recently, Google bought the collection of Usenet groups, which is experiencing a small renaissance as a part of Google Groups (see *http://groups.google.com*).

Although Usenet isn't ever going to recapture the limelight, different types of discussion forums are still ragingly popular. But instead of subject-based, administrator-moderated groups controlled by a single organization, forums crop up as a bonus feature on all sorts of Web sites. Here are some examples:

- Technology vendors large and small use them to provide community support and spread information. For example, Microsoft veterans and newbies exchange Microsoft Office tips on the boards at *www.microsoft.com/office/community/ en-us/flyoutoverview.mspx.*

- Topic sites use them to host rollicking discussions. For example, you can tear reality TV to shreds on the popular *http://survivorsucks.yuku.com* or register your Microsoft Office frustration at *www.officefrustration.com.*

- Individuals use them to provide technical support and get feedback. For example, popular computer book author Jesse Liberty helps readers with questions about his technical books at *http://forums.delphiforums.com/JLTechSupport.*

One of the best parts about forums is that they drive themselves. Once you get the right ingredients in place, a forum can succeed without you having to intervene. Think of forums as a dinner party that you host, and all you need to do is get the conversation started before making a polite retreat. And if you use forums to answer technical questions, you can reduce your workload immensely. For example, on many forums the emphasis is on customers or experts helping each other. That means forum members share information, advice, and answers, and you only need to step in to clear up a long-running debate.

Although discussion forums are wildly popular, they come in many flavors. All the examples in the previous list run on different software. Some of it's free, other options cost money, and still others are developed by hand by Web site programmers and aren't for sale to the public.

To create your own groups, you have a few choices. You could purchase an expensive product, install it on your own in-house Web server, and have complete control over everything: what your discussion pages look like, who gets to post messages (or not), and so on. This approach makes sense for a gargantuan company like American Express, but it doesn't fit the bill for a small- to medium-sized site. Instead, you'll probably want to use an online service provided by another company. In this scenario, you link to the other company's Web server, which hosts the forum. The only catch? Usually, most companies that provide discussion forums sell advertising space. That means that as you read messages in the group, you're likely to see some ads on the sidelines.

In the following sections, you'll learn to create a forum with one of the most capable discussion forum tools around, Google Groups.

About Google Groups

Google Groups is a thriving community of discussion forums. Although it hasn't been around as long as some other forum hosts, it includes a collection of useful features that rivals any of its competitors. And, of course, it's all free.

Here are some important details about Google Groups:

- When you create a group, you get a unique, easy-to-remember URL. That's the group address, and it never changes (unless you update it yourself).

- Group members can search through group postings with some of the best search tools on the planet. For bragging rights, nothing rivals the catalog of searchable Usenet content that Google has acquired, which ranges back to 1981.

- The group creator (you) controls who can and can't post. If the group gets busy, you can give other members some or all of your management powers.

- Google manages the registration process itself. That means you don't need to manually add and remove group members (although you can, if you like).

- Each group member can choose whether to read group messages online, or receive them in regular emails that Google sends automatically.

- Google's page layout is a frazzled Web browser's dream. It's easy to search posts, see all the replies to a post at a glance, bookmark the posts you want to follow, and more.

- Although Google displays ads in the corners of your group windows, it does its best to choose relevant ad content. For example, if the most common topic in a group is favorite DVDs, you're likely to see ads that promote Blu-ray DVD players and mail-order movie clubs.

You can learn more about Google Groups at *http://groups.google.com/googlegroups/ overview.html*.

Creating a Group

To create a new Google Group, follow these steps:

1. **Head on over to** *http://groups.google.com*. **Look for a link inviting new members to join, and then click it.**

   You need to register (with a valid email address and password) before you can create a group. You can use your Google account if you have one. Once you complete the process and activated your account, you're ready to return to the group setup page.

2. **Click the "Create a group" link to get started.**

3. When asked, log in with your user name and password. The "Create a group" page appears, as shown in Figure 12-6.

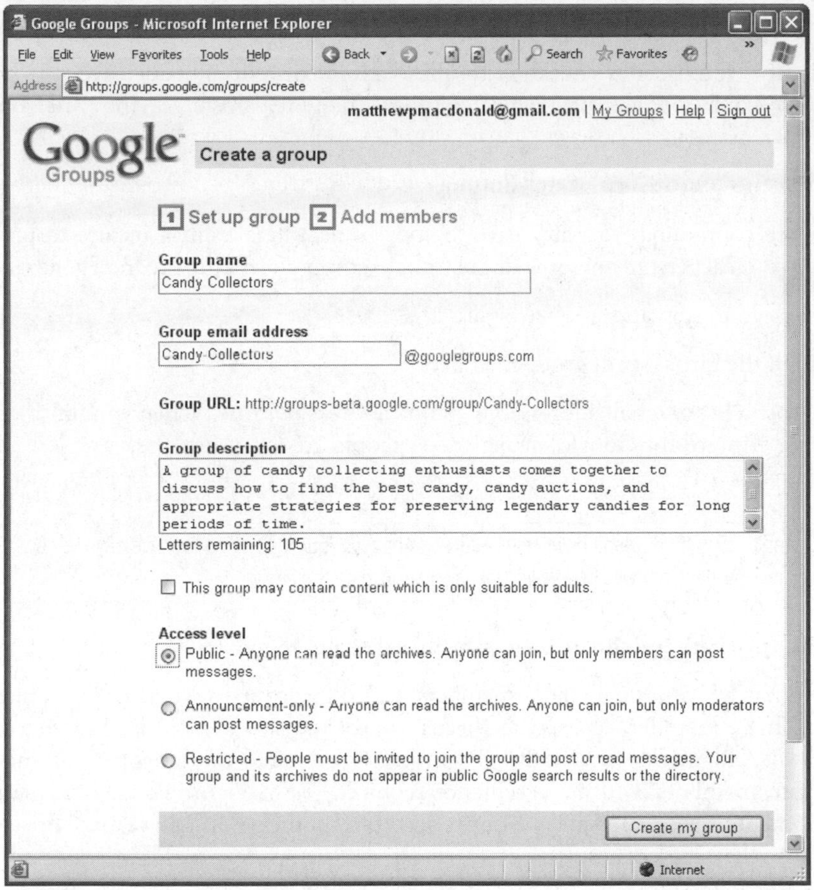

Figure 12-6:
Creating a Google group takes two steps. In the first, you define all the basic information about your group, including its name and email address.

4. Fill in all the information for your group.

The *group name* identifies your group, like *Candy Collectors*.

The *group email address* is a version of the name and it works as an email address or URL. You can't use spaces, but *Candy-Collectors* and *CandyCollectors* work. The email address also becomes part of the group URL, so make sure it's memorable.

The *group description* explains what the group's all about, using two or three sentences.

The *access level* indicates who's allowed to post. If you want to create a completely open group that accepts all comers, choose *Public*, which makes sense for most Web groups. Anyone who stumbles across your group can join at will, without your intervention. If you want to use the group solely as a place to post your own musings, choose *Announcements-only*. However, you're probably better off to put these announcements right on your Web site instead of in a group. Finally, if you want to micromanage who you let in, choose *Restricted*. That way, the only people allowed to join are those you specifically invite.

Finally, you'll see a checkbox to allow adult content. If you leave this box unchecked, Google automatically blocks naughty posts, saving you some embarrassment.

5. **Click the "Create my group" button.**

    Before continuing, you may have to copy some letters from a picture to prove you're a real person, not some sort of Google-group-generating program gone wild.

    The second step appears (see Figure 12-7).

6. **Fill in the initial set of group members.**

    Supply a list of email addresses, with one address per line. When you finish creating the group, Google emails these people to tell them they can join the group.

Note: Don't worry if you don't have email addresses handy. You don't need to invite anyone now. You can return to this page to invite people later on, after you create the group.

---

7. **Choose whether to invite or add the initial group members.**

    Ordinarily, you invite new members to your group by email. To actually become a member, each invitee needs to visit the site and opt in. But you can click "Add members directly" if you prefer to make these people automatic group members, with no acceptance required (as in Figure 12-7). Either way, recipients need to create a Google account (if they don't have one already) before they can post messages.

8. **If you invite members, set the subscription option.**

    If you add rather than invite people, you see a section named "Email subscription options." This lets you choose how these new members will interact with the group over email. (You don't get to make this choice if you're merely inviting new members. Instead, they'll get to pick their subscription option when they join the group.)

    The subscription options include:

    No email. Group members have to read the group posts in a browser, by visiting the group site.

    Send email for each message. Google sends every post to every group member. This is a bad idea unless it's a quiet discussion group.

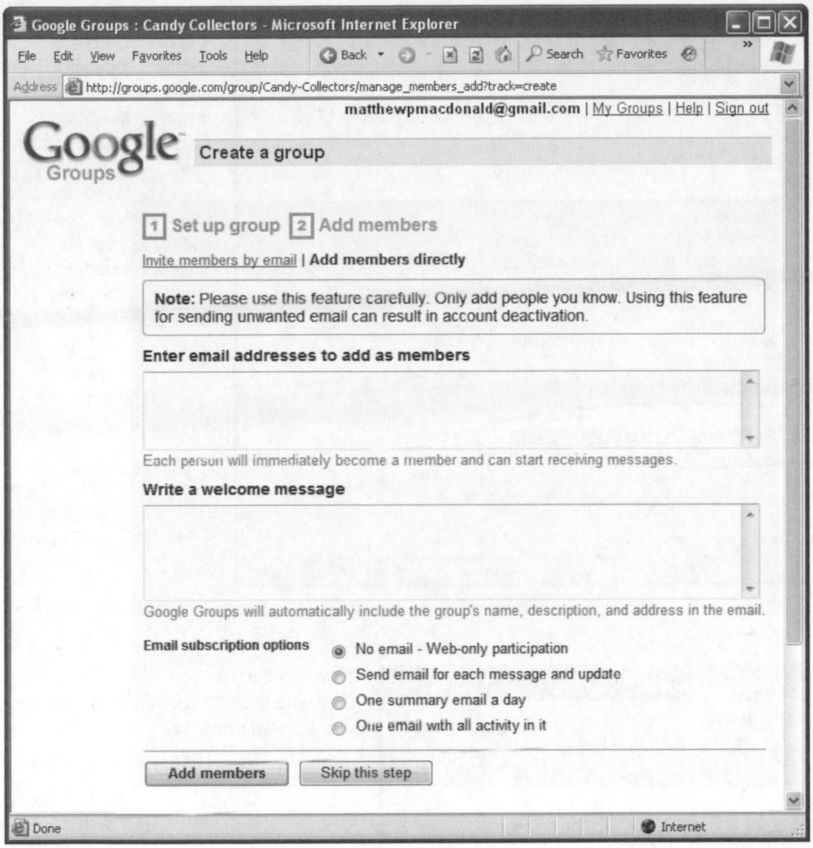

Figure 12-7:
In the second step, you choose your initial group members. Remember, if you create a public group, new people can join at any time through Google.

One summary email a day. Group members receive one email message per day (as long as there's at least one new post). This message contains a list of new message titles, with a link to the full text next to each one. This option is a handy way to stay on top of group activity, and keep an eye out for interesting posts.

One email with all activity. Group members receive all the new content once per day in a single gargantuan email. This option won't clutter an email inbox as much as receiving each message separately, but in a busy group it results in long emails that make for impractical browsing.

No matter what subscriber type you choose, group members can change this setting to match their personal preference later on.

9. **Enter a welcome message, and then click Done.**

   Google creates the group, and shows you a summary (Figure 12-8). Sometime shortly thereafter, it sends welcome messages to the initial set of group members to let them know you've created the group (see Figure 12-9).

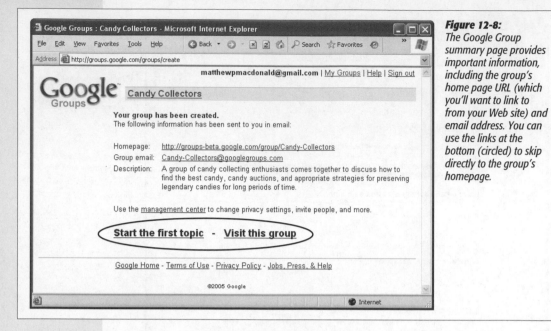

Figure 12-8:
The Google Group summary page provides important information, including the group's home page URL (which you'll want to link to from your Web site) and email address. You can use the links at the bottom (circled) to skip directly to the group's homepage.

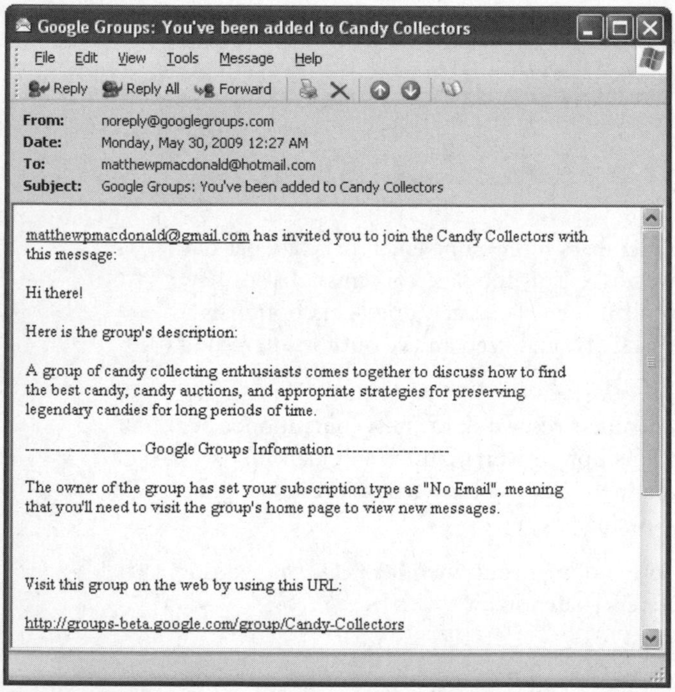

Figure 12-9:
Welcome aboard! You're a new member of a Google group.

Participating in a Group

When you first head over to your group, you'll find that it's awfully barren. To get the discussion started, why not post the first topic?

Google gives you two ways to post a topic. You can add a topic right from the Web page by clicking the "Start a new topic" link. Or, if you're really in a hurry, you can simply send an email message to the group email address. Google then converts the message into a group topic (Figure 12-10).

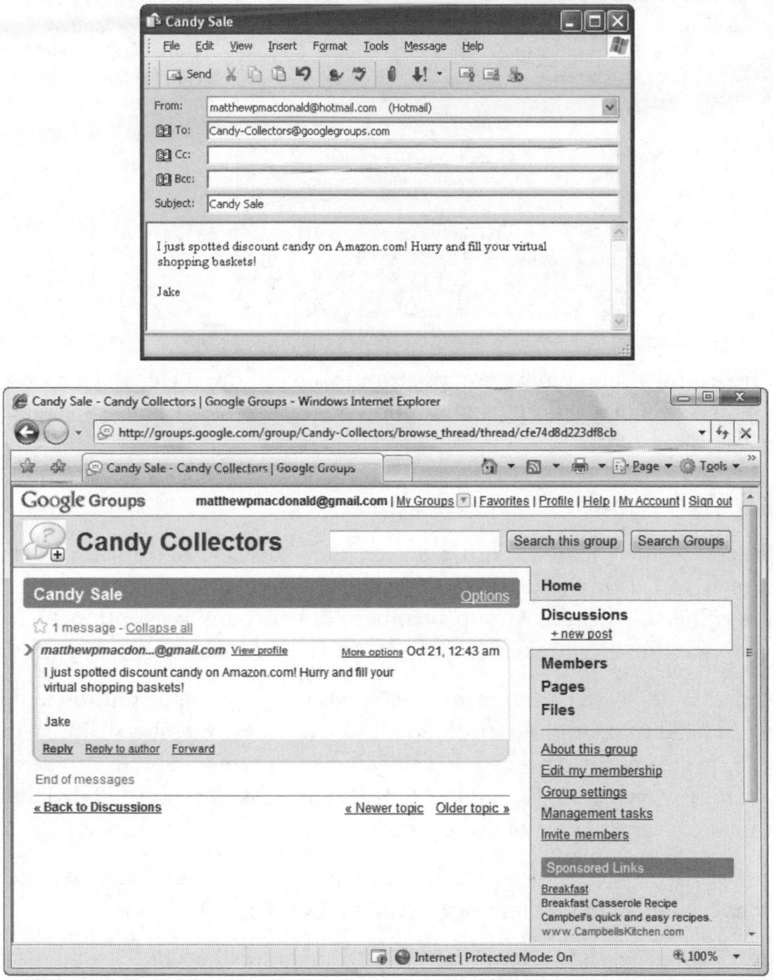

Figure 12-10:
Top: This email is about to be sent to a Google group.

Bottom: Once Google Groups receives the email, it becomes an ordinary posting (shown here). You can click "View profile" to learn more about the message poster or "More options" to reply, forward, or remove the message (assuming you're the group owner). Interestingly, even with a single topic, Google's already picked out an ad for the group (shown on the bottom right). As people use your group, Google refines the types of ads it uses, based on which ones get the most clicks from group members.

Of course, discussions are all about back-and-forth exchanges. Once someone posts a message, you can read it, and then click the Reply link to post a response. Google *threads* posts and replies, which means it groups them together so you can easily see what message goes with what topic (see Figure 12-11).

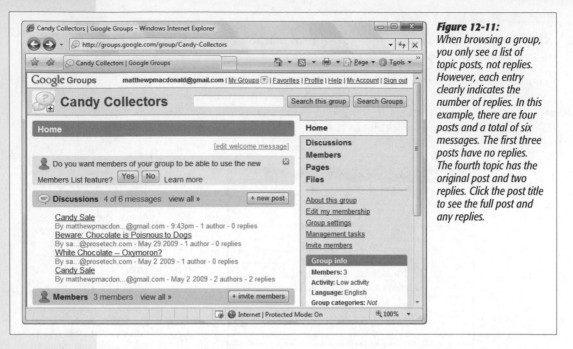

Figure 12-11:
*When browsing a group,
you only see a list of
topic posts, not replies.
However, each entry
clearly indicates the
number of replies. In this
example, there are four
posts and a total of six
messages. The first three
posts have no replies.
The fourth topic has the
original post and two
replies. Click the post title
to see the full post and
any replies.*

You now have a fully functioning group. From this point on, the challenge isn't in using the group, it's in attracting enough interesting people so that it becomes a lively community.

Managing Your Group

When ordinary group members visit a group, they have the option to post new messages, reply to existing ones, or change their delivery settings (by clicking the "Edit my membership" link). Group members can use this last option to have group messages automatically emailed to them or to see a summary of group activity.

On the other hand, when the group *creator* visits the group, additional links appear. If you head to your group page, you'll see an "Invite members" link, which lets you send welcome messages to a new batch of groupies. You'll also see the "Group settings" (Figure 12-12) and "Management tasks" (Figure 12-13) links, which let you take control of a lot more.

The "Group settings" section is chock full of options you can set, organized into a few subgroups. Here's a quick rundown of what they offer:

• **General.** This page shows basic group information, like your group name, description, URL, and email address. You can click the Edit button to change these details.

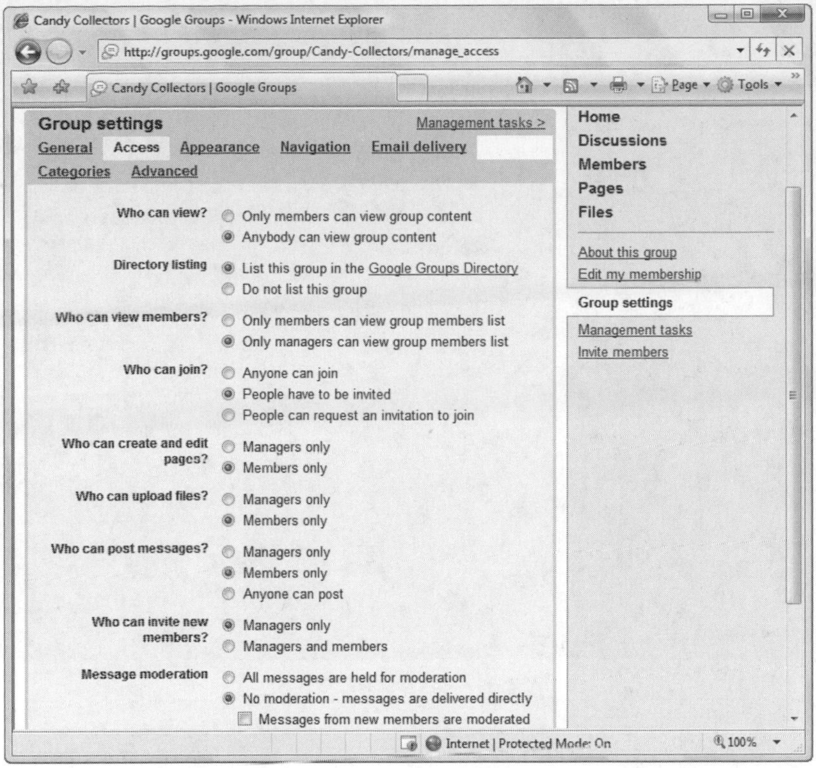

Figure 12-12:
When you click "Group settings," you see this page, which lets you set everything from your group's color scheme to restrictions that limit different types of group members. The settings here are far more detailed than those you saw when you created the group.

- **Access.** These settings let you define who can perform various tasks. For example, you can control who can read and create posts (anybody, or only group members), who's allowed to invite new members (just you, or any group member), and who's allowed to join. This last option is the most interesting. You can allow everyone, restrict the group to just people you invite, or force strangers to apply for group membership. If you use the last choice, anyone can apply to join, but you have the chance to review the application and give the final vote of acceptance or refusal. You can even tell Google to give hopeful applicants a specific question. You can then review their answers to determine whether they're group-worthy. Lastly, you can use the Access settings to turn on *moderated messages*. With moderated messages, Google sends every new message to you before it posts it. Messages won't appear until you give them a thumbs-up (and if you don't, they never reach the group). Only use moderated messages if you have a lot of spare time.

- **Appearance.** If you want your group to stand out from the crowd, you can use these options to give your group site different fonts and a snazzy color scheme.

- **Navigation.** This section lets you hide some of the links shown on the main group page. For example, if you don't want to let group members upload and share files, you can remove the Files link.

Group Restrictions

Should I restrict people from joining my group or posting messages?

It's tempting to force group members to apply to your group, but resist the ego trip. On the Web, people are impatient and easily distracted. If you place barriers in the way of potential group members, they may just walk away.

On the other hand, there are some cases where restricted group membership makes a lot of sense. Two examples are when you want to discuss semi-secret information, like company strategies, or if you're afraid your topic might attract the wrong kind of crowd. For example, if you set up a group called Software-Piracy to discuss the social implications of software piracy, you might find yourself deluged with requests for the latest versions of stolen software. As a general rule, restrictions make sense only if you use them to maintain group quality control.

The same holds true for message moderation. Most healthy online communities are self-regulating. If a member inadvertently offends the general community, others will correct him or her; if it's deliberate, most will eventually ignore the provocation. You might need to step in occasionally to ban a member, but screening every message is overkill. It also adds a huge amount of extra work for you, and severely cramps the dynamic of your group, because a new message won't appear until you have the chance to review it, which will usually be several hours after the poster wrote it. For fans of the Web who expect instant gratification, this isn't good news.

You'll find the settings for restricting people and moderating messages in the "Group settings" page, in the Access section.

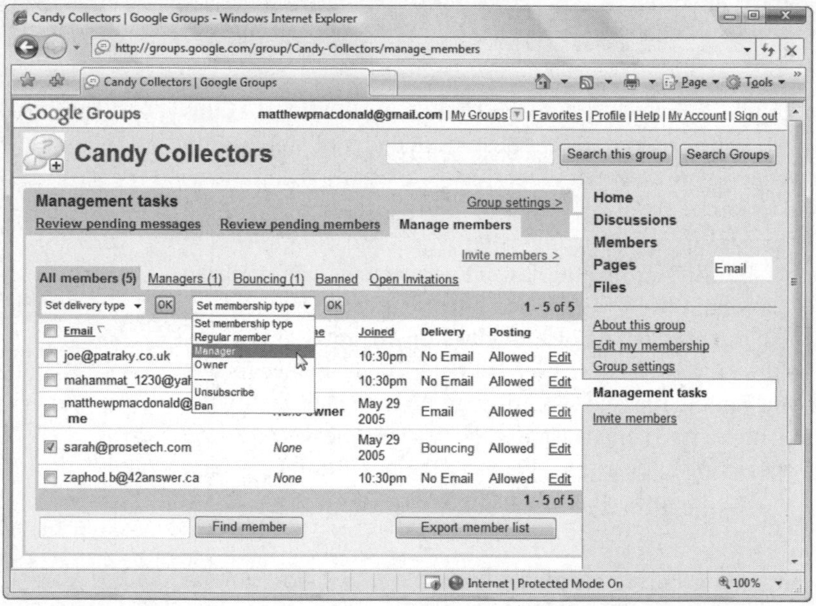

Figure 12-13:
Here, the group member Sarah has been selected (note the checkmark on the left). Using the drop-down lists at the top, you can quickly change her message delivery options or assign her a different access level. In this example, she's about to be made into a manager, giving her the ability to remove posts, invite new members, and change group settings (but not delete the entire group). Other options include Unsubscribe, which would remove her from the group, and Ban, which would remove her with extreme prejudice, so she would never be allowed to rejoin.

- **Email delivery.** If some of your group members receive messages by email, you can use these settings to tweak the footer text and control what happens if a member replies to an emailed posting. Ordinarily, the reply is posted alongside the original message for the whole group to see, but you can choose to direct replies to just the original poster or to the group owner (you).

- **Categories.** Here, you can define a category for your group (like People → Relationships or Health → Addictions). Once you do so, it's easier for Google searchers to stumble across your group.

- **Advanced.** This section lets you perform some low-level administrative tasks, like setting up a group that's stored on another server, or deleting your group altogether.

While the "Group tasks" link presents you with a wide range of settings, the "Management tasks" link focuses on a single concept—dealing with group members. Using the "Management tasks" page, you can review the full list of group members, see who hasn't responded to a group invitation, ban troublemaking posters, and give other members managerial powers (see Figure 12-13).

GEM IN THE ROUGH

Social Networking

It can be tough to build a group from scratch. That's why an increasing number of Web dwellers don't try to do it alone. Instead, they bring their audience to an existing community—one that's set up around a social networking site. And when it comes to social networking, no company is better known than Facebook.

Facebook began as a way for college students to keep in touch with each other. In only a few years, it mushroomed into a social site where millions of ordinary people track down everyone from long-lost loves to faintly remembered high-school acquaintances. Recently, it's been making strides as a business tool—one with both unique advantages and limitations.

To control the chaos, Facebook limits how people interact. You can't view someone else's Facebook profile unless you sign up with Facebook. And even then, you'll probably be locked out unless that person accepts you as a "friend." Restrictions like these limit the ways people can interact (and the ways a business can promote itself). But it also makes it easier for you to communicate with contacts once you establish a relationship, without being lost in the clamor of the Internet.

If you're already a Facebook fan, here's what you can do to bring it into your Web site promotion:

- **Make friends.** If you're running a business, add your business contacts. If you're planning a new community, hook up with others in the field. If you don't make connections and pump up your friend list, you'll find that Facebook is a very lonely place.

- **Join a group.** Use the search box to hunt for groups that relate to your interests or business. Join them. And then keep looking. As with most things in Facebook, more is more.

- **Create your own group.** If you have a cause of your own or a business to promote, you'll need to create a group for it. The advantage of a Facebook group is that it's wired into the Facebook community—so when you post a message, your Facebook followers are sure to notice.

To learn far more about Facebook and hone your promotional strategies, check out *Facebook: The Missing Manual*.

CHAPTER 13

Making Money with Your Site

If it's not for sale on the Web, it's probably not for sale at all. It's no secret that the Internet is a global bazaar with more merchandise than a decade's worth of garage sales. Visitors generate huge amounts of traffic hunting for travel discounts, discussing hot deals, and scouring eBay for bargains. So how can you get your share of Web capital?

One obvious option is to sell a real, tangible product. The Internet abounds with specialty shops hawking art, jewelry, and handmade goods. But even if you have a product ready to sell, you still need a few specialized tools to transform your corner of the Web into a bustling e-commerce storefront. For example, you'll probably want a virtual *shopping cart*, which lets visitors collect items they want to buy as they browse. And when they finally head for the virtual checkout counter, you need a secure way to accept their cash—usually by way of a credit card transaction. In this chapter, you'll learn how to get both these features using PayPal's merchant tools.

Even if you aren't looking for a place to unload your hand-crafted fishbone pencils, your Web site can still help fatten your wallet. In fact, just about any Web site can become profitable, either by selling ad space or by recommending other companies' products. In this chapter, you'll consider how to use two of the Web's most popular *affiliate programs*—Google AdSense and Amazon Associates—to collect some spare cash.

Note: Not a U.S. citizen? Don't worry—all the money-making ideas in this chapter rely on companies that provide services worldwide. Google, Amazon, and PayPal let you rake in the cash no matter what country you live in.

Money-Making the Web Way

The Web offers many paths to fiduciary gain. Here are some of the most popular ways Web sites make money:

- **Donations**. It sounds crazy, but some Web sites badger visitors for spare change. Donations might work if your site provides some truly valuable and unique content (see Figure 13-1). Otherwise, don't bother. Don't be seduced by logic like "If 1,000 visitors come to my site and every one pays just 10 cents…" They won't. However, if you still want to add a Donate button to your Web pages, you can use a payment service like PayPal, discussed later in this chapter.

Figure 13-1:
Sites that offer free software programs are some of the most likely to ask for a handout. Here, Paint.NET begs for spare change. But even the best Web sites have trouble making real money this way. Paint.NET hedges its bets by selling ad space elsewhere on its site.

- **Advertisements**. The most popular way to make money on the Web is by selling small pieces of Web-page real estate. Unfortunately, it's also a great way to exasperate your visitors, especially if the ads are distracting, unrelated to your site, or simply take up too much space. Not long ago, ads were the worst thing you could do to Web pages. Fortunately, in the 21st century, monitors are bigger, and companies like Google provide targeted, unobtrusive ads that fit right in with the rest of your site.

- **Affiliate Programs**. Rather than plastering ads across your site, why not put in a good word for a company you really believe in? Many affiliate programs give you a commission for referring customers to their sites. For example, if you review gourmet cookbooks, why not include links to the books on Amazon's Web site? If an interested reader buys a book, Amazon's associate program forks over a few dollars.

- **Sell Stuff.** If you have your own products to sell, the Web is the perfect medium, since the cost to set up shop online is much less than it is in the real world. You can build a slick store, complete with product pictures and a shopping cart, with surprisingly little work.

- **Pay-for-content.** If you have really great content, you can ask for cash *before* letting your visitors into your site. Warning: This is even harder to pull off than asking for donations, because visitors need to take a huge leap of faith. It's a technique used by established media companies like the *Wall Street Journal* and by hucksters promising secret ways to conquer the real estate market or to get free camcorders.

Note: Pay-for-content is the only money-making scheme you won't learn to pull off in this chapter. That's because in order for it to work, you need a way to *authenticate* visitors—in other words, you need to be able to identify visitors to tell whether they've paid you or not. This needs some heavy-duty programming (or a pay service from another company).

Google AdSense

Even if you don't have any products to sell, you still have one valuable asset: the attention of your visitors. The good news is there are a huge number of companies ready to pay for it.

Some of these companies pay you a minuscule fee every time someone visits one of your pages that carries one of their ads, while others pay you only when a reader actually clicks an ad, or when a visitor both clicks an ad *and* buys something. Fortunately, you don't need to waste hours checking out all these options, because Google has an advertising program that handily beats just about every other system out there.

The program is called Google AdSense, and it requires you to display small, text-only advertisements on your pages. You sign up, set aside some space on one or more pages, and paste in some Google-supplied XHTML (see Figure 13-2). Google takes care of the rest, filling in that space with a group of ads every time someone requests your page.

Just displaying Google AdSense ads doesn't get you anything, but whenever a visitor *clicks* one of the ad links, you earn a few cents. When your total reaches $100, Google mails you a check or sends the cash straight to your bank account.

There's no way to know for sure how much money an individual AdSense click is worth. That's because Google advertisers compete by bidding for different keywords (see page 320) and keyword prices can fluctuate over time. Google *does* let you know how much your clicks were worth (in total) when it pays you. A typical click nets you about 10 cents, but per-click prices often range from a few pennies to several dollars.

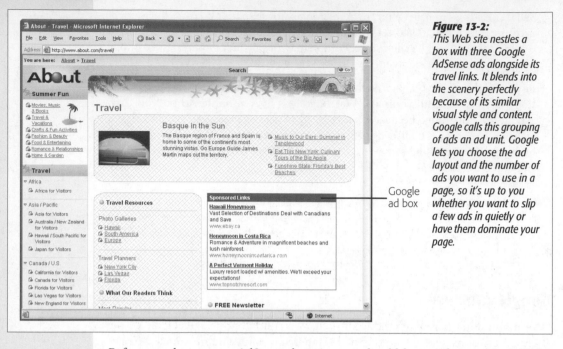

Figure 13-2:
This Web site nestles a box with three Google AdSense ads alongside its travel links. It blends into the scenery perfectly because of its similar visual style and content. Google calls this grouping of ads an ad unit. Google lets you choose the ad layout and the number of ads you want to use in a page, so it's up to you whether you want to slip a few ads in quietly or have them dominate your page.

Google ad box

Before you become an AdSense devotee, you should know what makes AdSense different from other ad programs. Here are some of its top advantages:

- **AdSense ads are relevant.** Google automatically scans your site and picks ads based on your site's content. That means that if you have a site devoted to *SpongeBob SquarePants*, Google provides ads hawking SpongeBob DVDs, inflatable dolls, and birthday gear. Using content-based ads is far, far better than aggravating your visitors with offers for completely unrelated products, like high-tech spy cameras. Even better from a profit perspective, these "targeted" ads dramatically increase the chance that a visitor will click an ad and generate a click-through fee. And if you're worried about a competitor's site turning up in an advertisement, you can tell Google to filter it out.

- **AdSense ads blend in with the scenery.** Google gives you a wide range of layout and color options for its ads. This ensures that the ads you place on your page match the design and slick color scheme of your site.

- **Google provides fair payment.** As you learned in Chapter 11 (page 320), Google charges advertisers different amounts of money for different keywords. Some advertising providers would just swallow the extra money and pay their members the same amount for any click-through. Not Google. It pays you according to the current value of the keyword, which guarantees that you always get a competitive rate.

- **There are no start-up charges.** The AdSense program is free to join.

Tip: Don't try to cheat AdSense. Devious Web developers have tried to game the system by clicking their own ads over and over again, or even firing up automated programs to do it for them. The problem is that Google uses various techniques to spot suspicious usage patterns. If it sees a ridiculous number of clicks over a short period of time all originating from the same computer, it's likely to spot the deception and ban your site outright.

Signing Up for AdSense

You can learn much more about the specifics of Google's ad program by visiting *www.google.com/adsense*. There's also a great, not-too-detailed walkthrough at *www.google.com/services/adsense_tour*.

When you're ready to get started with AdSense, follow these steps:

1. **On the AdSense homepage (*www.google.com/adsense*), click the Sign Up Now button.**

   Google starts gathering account information (Figure 13-3). First, type in your site URL and identify its language. Next, indicate whether you're applying as an individual or as a registered business. This determines the kind of tax information Google needs to collect. Registered businesses based in the U.S. need an EIN (Employer Identification Number). U.S. citizens applying as individuals need to give Google an SSN (Social Security Number). Citizens of other countries may need to apply for a U.S. TIN (Taxpayer Identification Number)—see *www.google.com/adsense/taxinfo* for the lowdown.

Note: Google won't pay you until it gets the tax details it needs. To help make the process less painful, it guides you to the correct form and lets you submit it online. However, Google won't prompt you for tax information until it has collected at least $10 in advertising revenue.

   Finally, fill in your name, address, and phone number.

   Along the way, you need to tick the checkboxes next to several disclaimers, vouching that you won't click your own ads, place ads on pornographic sites, and so on.

2. **Once you finish, click Submit Information.**

   The next page summarizes all the information you supplied.

3. **If you already have a Google account, choose "I have an email and password I already use with Google services." Otherwise, choose "I do not use these other services."**

   Google provides a dizzying number of online services. To prevent you from having to track dozens of passwords, it's a good idea to group them all under one Google account. If you already have a Google account, you need to fill in your email address and current password. If you don't, you need to fill in your email address and choose a password.

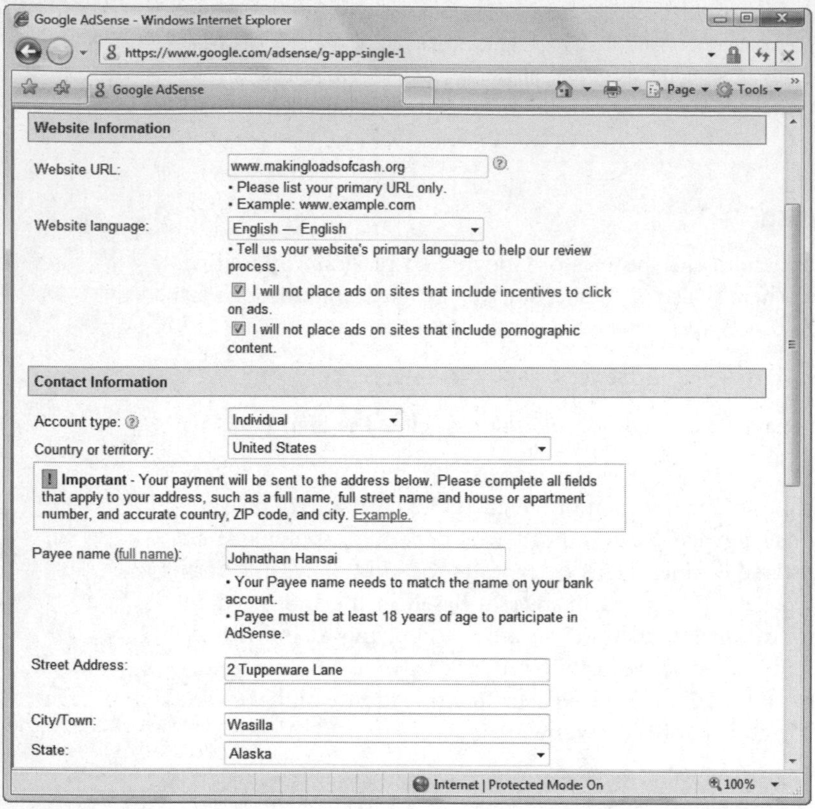

Figure 13-3:
Google AdSense collects all the information it needs, from Web site details to your address, in a single page.

4. **Click Continue to finish the process.**

   Now you need to wait for Google to contact you by email to confirm your account. This involves two steps. First, Google sends you an email confirmation message almost immediately. This message contains a link you need to click to confirm your email address. However, this still doesn't finish the job.

   Someone at Google needs to take a quick look at your site to confirm that it really exists and that it isn't promoting illegal activity (for example, offering pirated copies of Windows Vista). Once they do this, which usually takes a couple of days, you'll get a second email message confirming that Google has activated your account.

Creating an Ad

Now that you have an AdSense account, you're ready to generate some ads and put them on your site. Go to *www.google.com/adsense*, and log in with your email address and Google password. You'll see Google's AdSense page (see Figure 13-4), divided into four sections by tabs at the top.

UP TO SPEED

AdSense Rules

Google enforces a handful of rules that your Web site has to follow to be a part of AdSense. Many are common sense, but it's still worth taking a quick look at them.

- You can't put the Google ads in email messages or pop-up windows—the temptation for spammers to abuse the system is just too great.

- You can't put ads on pages that don't feature any "real" content. This includes error, login, registration, welcome, and under-construction pages. You definitely can't create pages that include nothing but ads.

- You can't try to obscure parts of an ad (for example, by placing other elements over them using a style sheet). The entire content of an ad needs to be visible.

- You can't click your own ads. You also can't use programs that do this for you. Finally, you can't entice your visitors to click your links using threats or incentives.

- Your Web site can't include excessive profanity, copyrighted material, pornography, content about hacking hi-tech security systems, advocacy for illegal drugs, hate speech, or anything related to gambling.

For the full AdSense policy, visit *www.google.com/adsense/policies*.

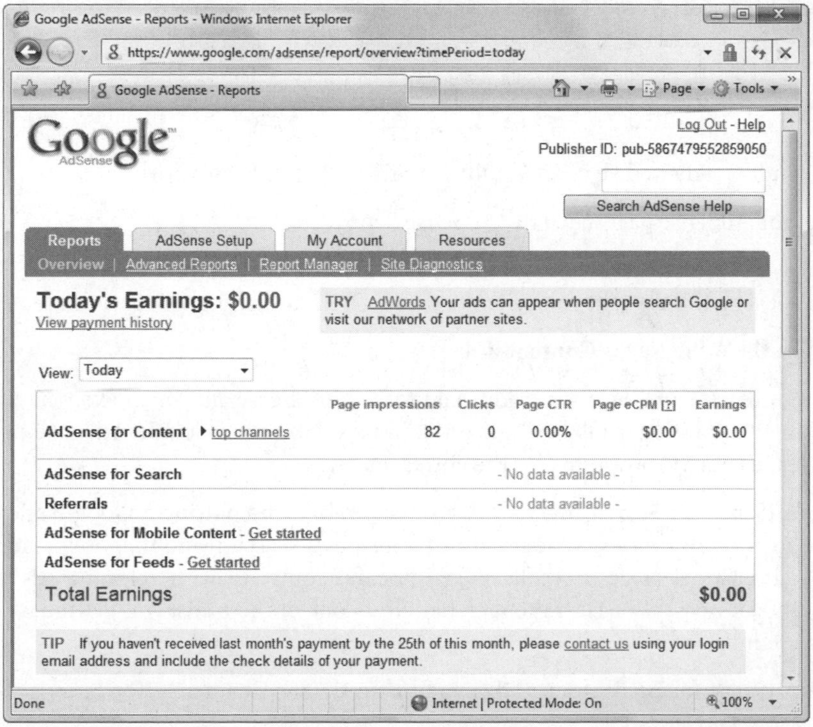

Figure 13-4:
Google divides its AdSense page into several tabs. Initially, you begin at the Reports tab, where you can survey a day-by-day breakdown of the money you've made.

These sections include:

- **Reports.** Reports help you assess the performance of your ads. You'll see a summary of the money you made today and over the last week. To get more detailed information, click a report link, like "This month, by day," which gives you your earnings for the current month, totaled by day. (Google won't tell you what each individual click was worth, or which particular ad caught a reader's eye.) You can also view a payment history that records each check Google mailed to you (click the "View payment history" link).

- **AdSense Setup.** This is your starting point for generating AdSense ads—it's where you specify the display format for your ads and get the XHTML markup to insert into your Web pages. You can also access some advanced features, like filtering out ads from specific Web sites.

- **My Account.** This tab lets you update most of the information you supplied when you registered, including your mailing address and tax information.

- **Resources.** This tab has links to other useful information and tools. For example, you can browse the AdSense blog, chat with others in AdSense's help forum, or read through some inspiring success stories and optimization tips.

Note: Before you can generate the right ad unit, you need to have a basic idea of where you plan to put your ads. Consider whether you want a vertical or horizontal strip of ads, and try to assess how wide or long that bar should be. You can skip ahead to Figure 13-6 to see a preview of some of your layout options.

Now you're ready to dive in and build your first ad unit. Here's how:

1. **On the AdSense page, click the AdSense Setup tab.**

   You see several clickable subcategories, including the automatic selection, Get Ads. Using this subtab, you generate the XHTML code for a Google ad unit.

2. **Click the AdSense for Content link.**

   AdSense for Content is the traditional form of AdSense ad, which lets you earn money by placing small text ads on your site. However, Google AdSense provides several other options for the entrepreneur:

   - **AdSense for Search** invites you to make money by putting a Google search box on your pages. When a visitor executes a search using this box, a standard Google search results page appears, complete with relevant ads (as shown on page 364). If the searcher clicks one of these ads, you get the usual commission.

   - **AdSense for Feeds** inserts ads in a blog feed. (See Chapter 17 for more about blogs and feeds.)

- **Video Units** let you show movies on your Web page with small embedded ads at the bottom of the playback window. You choose a category of movie (or let Google choose one based on your page's content), and then add a video window to your page. When a visitor plays a movie, ads appear underneath, and if the video watcher clicks one, you earn your usual commission. The Video Units service uses YouTube, which you'll learn about in Chapter 16.

- **AdSense for Mobile Content** appeals to people who build tiny Web sites for the browsers in mobile phones. It's the mobile equivalent of AdSense for Content.

Note: Google is constantly tweaking and refining the types of ads it offers. Don't be surprised if you find even more types of ad formats available than those described here when you check out the AdSense program.

---

3. **Choose the type of ad you want to create—either an ad unit or a link unit—and then click Continue.**

Google shows you a preview of each type of ad (Figure 13-5).

An *ad unit* is a group of one or more ads, complete with descriptive text or (optionally) images. When visitors click an ad, they wind up at the advertiser's Web site and you get paid.

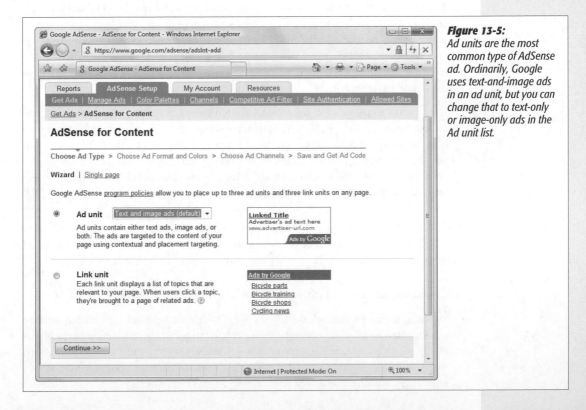

Figure 13-5:
Ad units are the most common type of AdSense ad. Ordinarily, Google uses text-and-image ads in an ad unit, but you can change that to text-only or image-only ads in the Ad unit list.

A *link unit* is a slim box of links with no descriptive text. The box has the title "Ads by Google" and the links are one- or two-word entries, like "Digital Cameras" or "Consumer Electronics." If a visitor clicks one of these links, Google serves up a new page filled with ads for products in that category. If your visitor clicks one of these ads, you get paid.

If you create an ad unit, you can choose whether you want to use text ads, image ads, or both (the default). Generally, image ads stand out more than text ads. However, you need to balance two conflicting goals—the desire to make money by attracting clicks with eye-catching ads, and the desire to minimize distraction on your page by choosing less obtrusive ads.

4. **Choose the ad layout in the Format section.**

Google always packages AdSense ads in boxes. Each box includes several ads. The ad format you choose determines whether you'll get a vertical stack of ads or a horizontal row. It also determines how many ads you see at once (from one to five).

It's difficult to picture what different ad layouts really look like. To orient yourself, click the Ad Formats link, which opens a window with an example of every layout option (see Figure 13-6, bottom). Using this page, you can find the format that best suits your site.

5. **Choose a color palette (this step is optional).**

The *color palette* sets the colors Google uses for the ad unit's text, background, and border. Google has preset palettes, with names that rival those in designer paint lines ("Mother Earth" and "Fresh Mint" are two). As you choose the palette you want, Google previews the result in a small ad at the bottom-left of the page. To see the effect on your entire ad box, click the "Preview this AdSense unit" link underneath.

If you want to make sure your colors match the ones on your Web site, you can adjust them. For example, you might want the ad box's border or background color to blend in with the background on your page. To change the colors of an ad unit, modify the color codes in the boxes underneath the list of color palettes. If you want to reuse a custom color scheme later, click the "Edit palettes" link, name the scheme, and then save it.

Tip: Usually, you choose background and text colors that match the colors you already use on your Web page. If you don't change the standard colors, your ad box will have the same background color as your Web page, and no border. For some advice on how to choose custom XHTML colors, see page 152.

---

6. **Choose an alternate ad (this step is optional). Then, click Continue.**

When you first put an ad unit on a page, Google doesn't yet know what ads are a good match for your content, so it temporarily uses alternate content. Ordinarily, Google uses public service ads—messages from nonprofit organizations like Unicef. Not long thereafter, Google's text-sniffing software pays a visit to your page, and the real ads materialize within a couple of days.

Figure 13-6:
Top: Google AdSense has layout options for virtually any Web site. This example (top) uses a 300-×250-pixel rectangle, which holds four ads, one on top of the other. Of course, the only way you'll know how many ads fit in a layout is by clicking "Ad Formats" (circled) to see Google's sample (bottom).

If you don't want to put up with generic ads, you can display alternate content. You have two options—you can choose an alternate color, in which case Google uses a block of color without any ad content. The idea is that you use a color that matches the background of your page, so the "ad" disappears entirely. Your second option is to specify a URL for a page you want to use. Until the real ads are ready, that content appears on your page.

Tip: Alternate ads probably aren't worth the trouble. It's better to use the generic ads, because the ad layout is the same, which makes it easy to place the ad in the right place and get an idea of what it looks like alongside the rest of your content.

7. **Choose a channel (this step is optional). Then, click Continue.**

If you generate a half-dozen ads and scatter them on different pages through-out your site, you don't know which ones are making you money. Google's report shows you only the total number of clicks for all the pages on your site. Many site owners want more detail about which ads are working. Enter Google's *channels* feature.

To track the performance of different ads, you place each ad in a separate, vir-tual "channel." Google then lets you create reports that compare each channel so you can tell which performs best.

To create a new channel, click the "Add new channel" link, which pops open a window asking you to name the channel. Once you create a channel, you can apply it to your current ad by clicking the tiny "add" link next to the channel name (Figure 13-7). (By the same token, click "remove" to stop tracking an ad.)

Tip: Channels are a great way to try out different ad strategies, and see which ad formats and place-ments have the most success coaxing clicks out of your visitors. You can add multiple ads to the same channel to track them as a group, or you can create a separate channel for each ad.

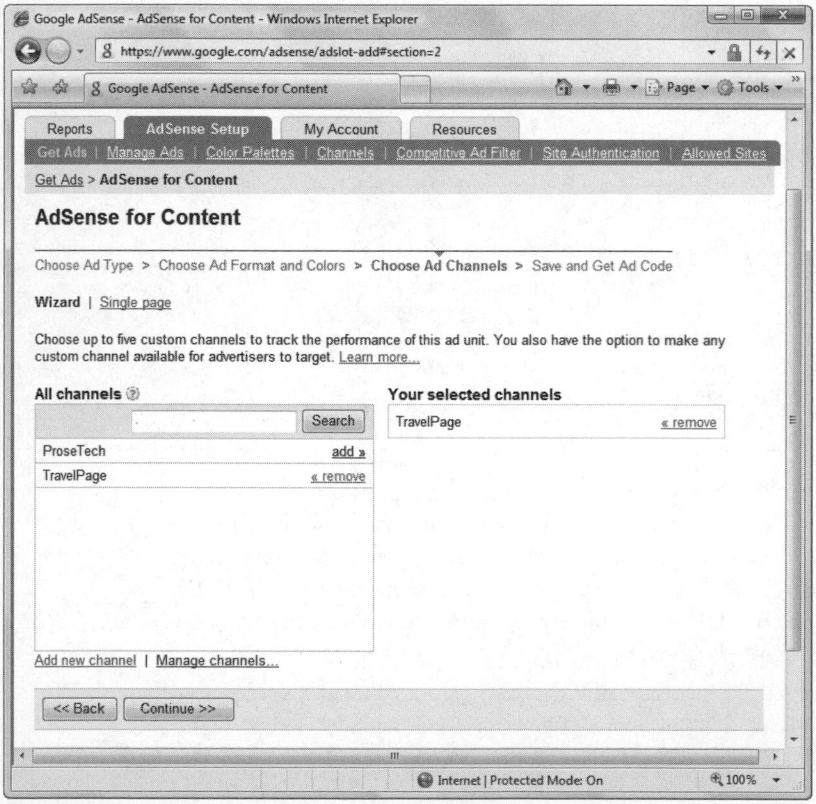

Figure 13-7:
This AdSense account has two different channels. The current block of ads (the one in the process of being created) uses the TravelPage channel.

8. **Choose a name for your AdSense unit, and then click "Submit and Get Code".**

   This name identifies your ad unit. That way, you can log in to AdSense, call up the ad unit by name, and modify the unit, instead of rebuilding it from scratch. To try this out, click the AdSense Setup tab, and then click Manage Ads underneath. Most changes—say, altering the ad box color scheme—take effect immediately. However, if you want to change the format of your ad box, you need to get new code and paste it into your pages, because the size of your ad unit will change.

9. **Copy your ad code.**

   The final page has your complete, customized ad unit code (see Figure 13-8). Click in the text box to select it, right-click the selection, and then choose Copy. You're now ready to paste the code into one or more Web pages, as described in the next section.

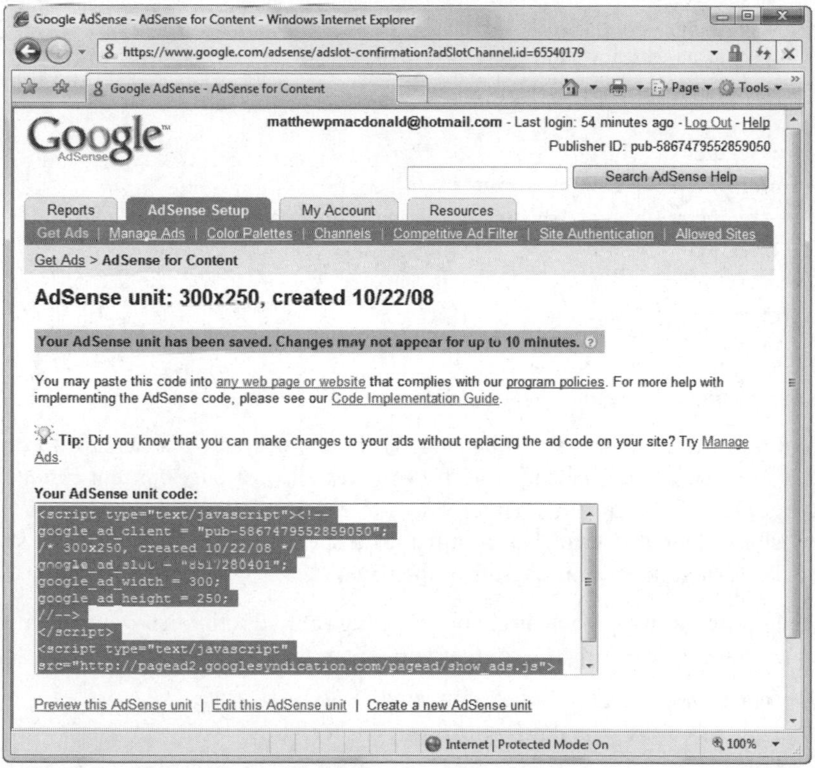

Figure 13-8:
The ad unit doesn't consist of XHTML elements—instead, it's JavaScript code (which you'll learn about in Chapter 14). Google uses a script because it needs to be able to generate blocks of ads dynamically, according to the preferences you choose. Whenever a visitor requests your page, the ad script runs, communicates with the Google Web servers, and asks for a set of ads. The server looks up relevant ads, applies your layout and color options, and then sends the final block of XHTML back to the script so it can insert the ads into your page.

Placing Ads in Your Web Pages

Once you generate an ad script, you're ready to pop it into your Web page. Horizontal strips are the easiest to position. You simply paste the entire script right where you want it to appear.

Here's an example that places ads at the bottom of a page:

```
<!DOCTYPE html PUBLIC "-//W3C//DTD XHTML 1.0 Strict//EN"
"http://www.w3.org/TR/xhtml1/DTD/xhtml1-strict.dtd">

<html xmlns="http://www.w3.org/1999/xhtml">
<head>...</head>
<body>
  <h1>A Trip to Remember</h1>
  <p><img src="me.jpg" alt="Me" class="floatLeft" />
  After returning from my three-month travel adventure ...</p>
  <p>I hope you enjoy these pictures as much as I do.</p>
  <p>See pictures from ...</p>

  <script type="text/javascript"><!--
   google_ad_client = "pub-5876479552859050";
   google_ad_slot = "8247622134";
   google_ad_width = 728;
   google_ad_height = 90;
   //-->
  </script>
  <script type="text/javascript"
   src="http://pagead2.googlesyndication.com/pagead/show_ads.js">
  </script>

</body>
</html>
```

Figure 13-9 shows the result.

Positioning vertical ad strips requires a little more work, but it's easy to do once you learn the trick. The challenge is to flow the rest of your page content *beside* the vertical ad. As you learned in Chapter 9, two techniques help you do this. You can use invisible tables and lock the ad unit into a specific cell, or you can use style sheet rules to float the ads on the side of the page.

To use the style sheet approach, begin by wrapping your ad script in a <div> element. Here's an example featuring the content you saw in Figure 13-9:

```
<!DOCTYPE html PUBLIC "-//W3C//DTD XHTML 1.0 Strict//EN"
"http://www.w3.org/TR/xhtml1/DTD/xhtml1-strict.dtd">

<html xmlns="http://www.w3.org/1999/xhtml">
<head>...</head>
<body>
  <div class="floatRight">
    <h1>A Trip to Remember</h1>
```

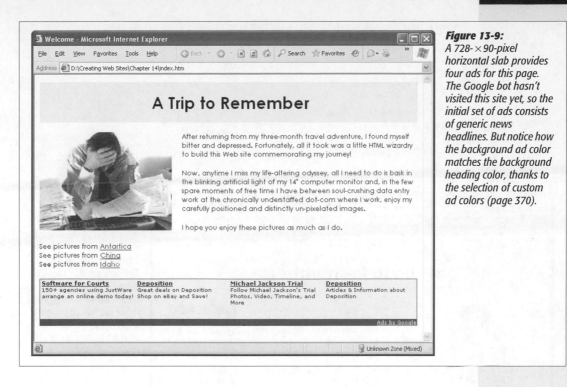

Figure 13-9:
A 728- × 90-pixel horizontal slab provides four ads for this page. The Google bot hasn't visited this site yet, so the initial set of ads consists of generic news headlines. But notice how the background ad color matches the background heading color, thanks to the selection of custom ad colors (page 370).

```
<script type="text/javascript"><!--
  google_ad_client = "pub-5876479552859050";
  google_ad_slot = "4493177655";
  google_ad_width = 120;
  google_ad_height = 240;
  //-->
</script>
<script type="text/javascript"
  src="http://pagead2.googlesyndication.com/pagead/show_ads.js">
</script>
</div>

<p><img src="me.jpg" alt="Me" class="floatLeft" />
  After returning from my three-month travel adventure ...</p>
<p>I hope you enjoy these pictures as much as I do.</p>
<p>See pictures from ...</p>
</body>
</html>
```

Notice that the <div> element (which has no formatting on its own), uses the style sheet class *floatRight*. In your style sheet, you use the rule below to make the <div> section float using the *float* attribute (see page 193):

```
.floatRight {
  float: right;
  margin-left: 20px;
}
```

Figure 13-10 shows the result.

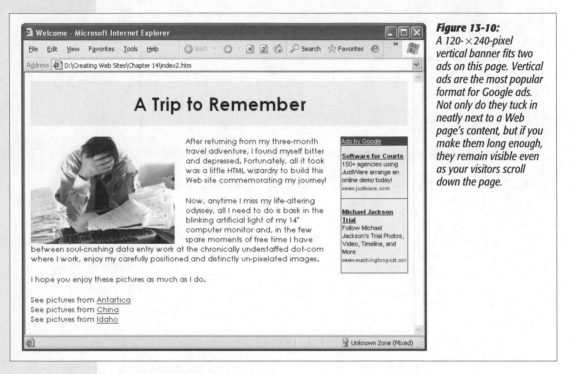

Figure 13-10:
A 120- × 240-pixel vertical banner fits two ads on this page. Vertical ads are the most popular format for Google ads. Not only do they tuck in neatly next to a Web page's content, but if you make them long enough, they remain visible even as your visitors scroll down the page.

Google-Powered Searches

Google gives you another way to please your visitors (and earn some cash in the process). You can add a search box to your pages, letting visitors launch Google queries right from your site. Even better, you get the earnings for any ads they click in the search results—a feature Google calls (rather unimaginatively) AdSense for Search.

Once you have an AdSense account, it's easy to add a Google search box to your site:

1. **Log in to your AdSense account, click the AdSense Setup tab, and then click the AdSense for Search link.**

   An introductory page appears. On the right, you can play a two-minute video to get an overview of AdSense straight from the people at Google. Or, click the Get Started button to dive right into the process.

How AdSense Creates Targeted Ads

Every time you serve up a Web page that contains Google ads, the AdSense script sends a message to the Google Web server asking for ads. This message includes your ad preference information and your unique client ID. (Your client ID is something like *pub-5876479552359052*; you can see it in the script code.)

The first time Google receives this request, it realizes that it hasn't examined your page yet, and it doesn't know what types of ads are best suited for it. So Google sends you a block of generic ads (or sends back your alternate content, if you choose that feature, as described on page 370). Google also adds your page to a list of pages it needs to visit. Sometime in the next couple of days, the Google bot heads over to your site and analyzes its content. From that point forward, you'll see ads based on the content of your page.

If 48 hours pass and you still aren't getting targeted ads, there could be a problem. One of the most common mistakes is putting ads on pages that don't have much text, in which case Google can't figure out what your site is really all about. Remember, Google only considers a single page—the one with the ad unit—when it checks out your site. Another potential problem happens if you put your ad in an inaccessible page. For example, the Google bot can't get to any page that's not on the Internet—pages on your personal computer or a local network just won't cut it. Likewise with password-protected pages. Some Web sites block robots through exclusion rules (see page 321), which stops the Google bot cold.

2. **Choose the search type.**

   Choose "The entire Web" to create a search box that uses the familiar Google search engine we all know and love.

   Choose "Only sites I select" to restrict the search to a limited set of sites. You can use this feature to limit searches to your site only.

   If you want to provide both options (searching the entire Web and searching just your Web site), follow the above instructions twice to create two different search boxes. But be careful you don't wind up confusing your visitors.

3. **If you choose to limit the search, fill in a list of searchable sites in the "Selected sites" box (Figure 13-11).**

   You can enter individual pages (as in *http://www.ChocolateMysteries.com/recipe01.html*), or use an asterisk to represent all the pages in a folder or on a Web site (as in *http://www.ChocolateMysteries.com/**), which is more common. If you need to enter multiple URLs, put them on separate lines in the box.

Note: Even when you choose to limit searches to your Web site, Google still uses its standard, centralized catalog of Web pages--it just limits the results it displays to the pages from your site. If Google doesn't have your pages in its catalog (either because you just created the site or because Google doesn't know your site exists), these pages won't turn up in any searches, no matter how you customize your search box. For a refresher about getting Google to notice you, see page 316.

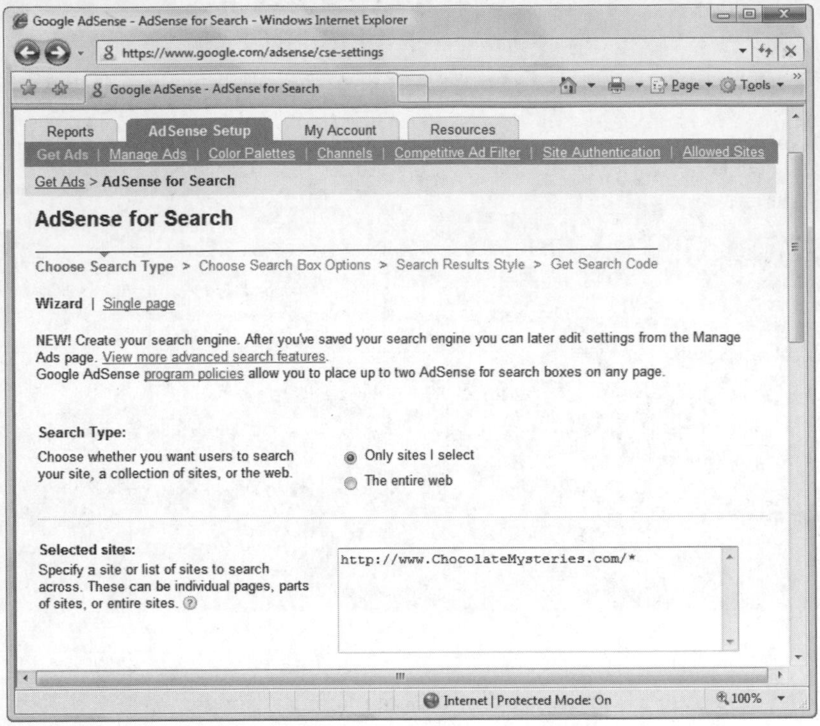

Figure 13-11:
Usually, when you pick "Only sites I select," you enter just one site in the "Selected sites" box—yours. That way, visitors can hunt for one of your pages without being seduced by another site on the Web. For example, if you have dozens of pages of travel stories, a visitor could home in on the page they want by searching for "funny story about rubber chicken in Peru."

4. **Fill in the Optional Keywords box.**

   AdSense for Search automatically adds any keywords you include here to your visitors' searches. This gives you a way to design a search box that's targeted to certain types of content. For example, if your site is all about golf, you might include the keyword *golf*. That way, if a visitor searches for *tiger*, the search returns pages about Tiger Woods, not the African savannah.

5. **Tweak the other settings on the page, if they apply to you. Then click Continue to move on.**

   These settings include your Web site's language and geographic location. As you probably know, Google has country-specific pages that can tweak search results, providing them in different languages or giving priority to local sites.

   You can also place your search box in a specific channel, which is useful if you want to track the ad dollars you make from this box. See page 372 for more information about channels.

   Finally, if you want to filter out profanity and sexual content from the search results, choose the SafeSearch option. You'll find SafeSearch useful in two situations. First, it's de rigueur for sites that provide children's content. Second, it's handy if your Web site deals in a topic that shares some keywords with adult-only sites. For example, if you're creating a breast cancer awareness page, you don't want searches for "breast exam" to dig up the wrong goods.

6. **Tailor the appearance of the Google search box, and then click Continue.**

There's not a lot to change here. You can change the size of the search box and the placement of the Google logo.

7. **Choose how Google displays the search results.**

Choose "Open results on Google in the same window" to replace the current page with Google's standard search results page.

Choose "Open results on Google in a new window" to pop open a new browser window with the search results. Pop-up windows are usually annoying to Web visitors, but this technique is handy if you want to make sure your Web site sticks around on your visitor's desktop.

Choose "Open results within my own site" to keep your visitors on your Web site, and show the search results alongside your content. This is everyone's favorite option, but it requires slightly more work because you need to create two pages—one with the search box, and one that holds the search results. Google gives you some markup to place on each page. If you want to use this option, you need to supply the URL for your search results page (for example, *http://www.ChocolateMysteries.com/searchresults.html*). Don't worry if you haven't created this page yet—you can create and upload it when you finish creating the search box. You also need to tell Google how wide the search results should be. The standard option is 800 pixels, which is a good choice if you don't plan to pad the sides of your page with extra content (like ads or a menu bar). If you have other content you want to show on the page, you can place it above the search results.

8. **Choose a color palette, and then click Continue.**

Choose a color palette for the search results page. This way, the search results can blend in with the color scheme on the rest of your site. This feature is almost the same as the color palettes for AdSense ad units (page 370).

9. **Supply a name, and then click Submit and Get Code.**

The name lets you log in later, tweak your search box settings, and get new code without starting from scratch.

10. **Copy your search box.**

The final setup page includes the markup for your complete, customized search box (see Figure 13-12) in a <form> element. (Page 339 has more about forms in XHTML.) As with the AdSense code, you can copy this XHTML and paste it into any Web page.

If you choose to use a search results page on your own site, you'll get a second box with the markup you need to add to your search results page. This consists of a <div> element and some JavaScript code. It works in much the same way as the AdSense code—you simply place the <div> element where you want the search results to appear.

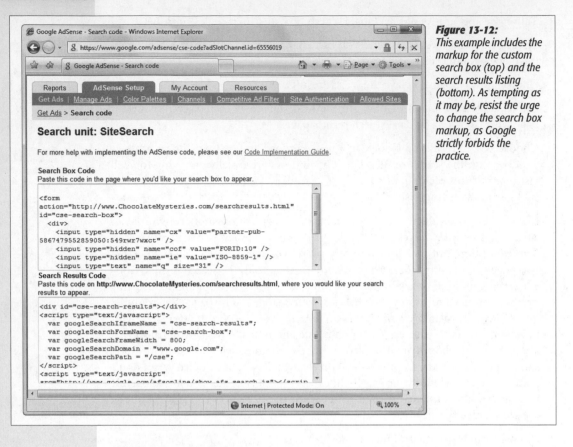

Figure 13-12:
This example includes the markup for the custom search box (top) and the search results listing (bottom). As tempting as it may be, resist the urge to change the search box markup, as Google strictly forbids the practice.

Amazon Associates

As popular as ads are with Web site owners, they have one serious drawback—they clutter up your pages. Once you perfect a design with carefully chosen pictures and style sheets, you might not want to insert someone else's ad. And although Google ads aren't as visually distracting as other types of ads, like animated banners or pop-up windows, they still chew up valuable screen space. If you can't bear to disturb your Web page masterpieces, you might be interested in a subtler affiliate program.

Amazon Associates is the Web's longest-running affiliate program. If you have a personal site with a "favorite books" page, or if you just refer to the odd book here and there, you might be able to make some extra money by signing up.

The basic idea behind the Amazon Associates program is that you provide links to book pages and other product pages on Amazon's Web site. For example, if you write a blurb about a great recipe you tried, you could add a link that, when a reader clicks it, goes to the Amazon page that sells the cookbook you're quoting. The link itself is a nice feature for your site, since it provides visitors with more relevant information. But the best part is what happens if a visitor decides to buy the book. You wind up making a healthy commission of 4 percent of the book's sale price.

Tip: Amazon commissions aren't just for books. You can provide links to pretty much everything for sale on Amazon (excluding items sold by other retailers, like Target and Office Depot). But there are limits to how much you can make on non-book items. For example, with personal computers, you're capped at a maximum $25 commission per item. These rules change from time to time, so make sure you scour the Amazon Associates Web site carefully to get the lowdown.

Signing Up As an Associate

Signing up for the Amazon Associates program is even easier than joining AdSense. Just follow these steps:

1. **Go to** *http://affiliate-program.amazon.com,* **click the "Join now" button, and then log in with your Amazon email and password.**

   To join the associates program, you need to be an Amazon customer. If you aren't, click "I am a new customer" to create an account.

2. **Enter your personal information and your Web site information**

   For your personal information, you need to supply your name, address, and telephone number.

   For your Web site information, you need to supply a Web site name, URL, and brief description (see Figure 13-13).

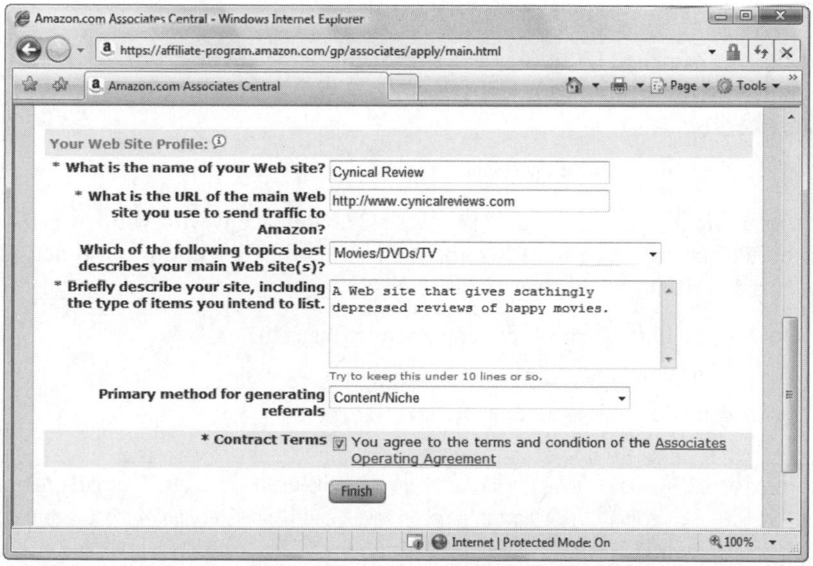

Figure 13-13:
To become an Amazon associate, you need to supply some basic information about your site. Don't skip over this step, because someone from Amazon will take a quick look at your site before it approves you for the program.

3. **Click Finish to submit your application.**

   Shortly after you submit your application, you'll get a confirmation message that approves you on a trial basis. This email also supplies you with your unique associate ID. This number is important, because it's the single piece of information you need to add to all your Amazon links to start earning commissions. You can now use the associate tools at *http://associates.amazon.com* (see the next section).

   In a couple of days, when someone at Amazon verifies your site and confirms that it doesn't run afoul of the law, you'll get a second email message confirming that you're in for good.

4. **If you'd like to tell Amazon how to pay you right now, click Specify Payment Method Now.**

   You can choose your preferred form of payment even before Amazon officially accepts you into its program. Your choices include check, Amazon gift certificate, or direct deposit to a U.S. bank account. Amazon doesn't send checks until you make at least $100, and it charges you a $15 processing fee. Other payment types kick in once you reach $10, and they don't involve any fees.

Generating Associate Links

Once you have your associate ID, which Amazon provides in its confirmation email, you can create *associate links*, the hyperlinks that send your visitors to Amazon. The trick is formatting the URL in the right way.

You add your associate ID to the very end of the associate link. For example, the first email Amazon sends includes an example of the associate link to its homepage. It looks like this:

```
http://www.amazon.com?tag=prosetech-22
```

In this example, the associate ID is *prosetech-22*. (Replace it with your own ID to create a link for your Web site.) If someone follows this link and buys something, you earn a 4 percent commission.

Here's how you could use this link in an anchor (page 207):

```
Visit <a href="http://www.amazon.com?tag=prosetech-22">
Amazon</a> and help me save up to buy a Ferrari.
```

Tip: Amazon encourages you to advertise the fact that you're an Amazon associate. If you'd like to boast, Amazon provides a collection of ready-made Amazon logos and banners at *http://associates.amazon. com/gp/associates/network/build-links/banner/main.html*. You can add these to your site, and even put them in anchor elements to transform them into associate links. (You have to be an Amazon associate to view the banner page.)

Product links

You get better commissions with links that lead directly to a specific product. Amazon supports several associate link formats, and here's one of the simplest:

```
http://www.amazon.com/dp/ASIN/?tag=AssociateID
```

And here's a specific example:

```
http://www.amazon.com/dp/0141181265/?tag=prosetech-22
```

In this link, you customized two details, the ASIN (Amazon Standard Item Number) and the associate ID. The ASIN is 0141181265 (which leads to the book *Finnegans Wake*) and the associate ID is *prosetech-22*. Figure 13-14 shows you where to find an ASIN.

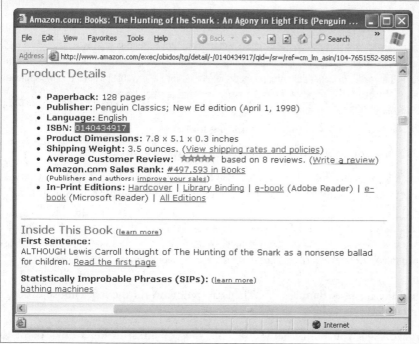

Figure 13-14:
Every item in the Amazon catalog has a unique ASIN, which you can find in the Product Details section on the page for that product. For books, the ASIN is the same as the ISBN (highlighted), which is an industry-standard book ID number.

Here's an example of a complete link:

```
The development of the modern personal computer was first presaged in Joyce's
<a href="http://www.amazon.com/dp/0141181265/?tag=prosetech-22">
Finnegans Wake</a>.
```

That's all you need.

Note: If one of your Web site visitors follows a link to a specific Amazon product, but then goes on to buy something completely different, it's all good. You still get the same 4 percent commission.

Advanced links

Amazon has a set of specialized tools that help you generate links. Using these tools, you can create a range of snazzy links. Your options include:

- Links with thumbnail pictures.
- Links to product categories (like *equestrian magazines* or *bestselling kitchen gadgets*).
- Ad banners that advertise a specific Amazon department.
- Amazon search boxes that let visitors perform their own queries.

Even if you don't want these fancier links (and if your life isn't dedicated to selling books, you probably don't), there's still good reason to build links with the tools Amazon provides: They create links that have built-in tracking, so you can determine how many people see each link.

Note: Amazon tracking is very clever. Essentially, Amazon embeds a tiny one-pixel image alongside each link. If someone requests a page that contains one of these links, the browser automatically fetches the invisible picture from Amazon. When Amazon gets the request for the invisible picture, it knows someone is looking at the link, and it records a single *impression* in its tracking database.

Here's how you use Amazon's link-building tools:

1. **Go to *http://affiliate-program.amazon.com* and log in.**

   This takes you to the Associates Central home page, which gives you a variety of reports for checking your progress to date, as well as tools for building links.

Tip: For detailed information about the more ambitious things you can do with Amazon Associates, click the Get Started Now button. You can also get invaluable advice from other associates by visiting the discussion forums—look for the Discussion Boards link at the bottom of the menu bar on the left.

---

2. **Click the Links & Banners tab. Then, in the menu on the left, choose Product Links.**

   Amazon lets you build many different types of links. Product links point to individual items on Amazon's site. They're generally the most useful one for your site. But if you plan to go Amazon-crazy, feel free to explore all the other types of links.

3. **In the search box, type the ASIN for your product, and then click Go.**

   If you don't know the ASIN, select what you think is the most appropriate category, and then type in the product name. When you click Go, Amazon searches for the product and lists the results (see Figure 13-15).

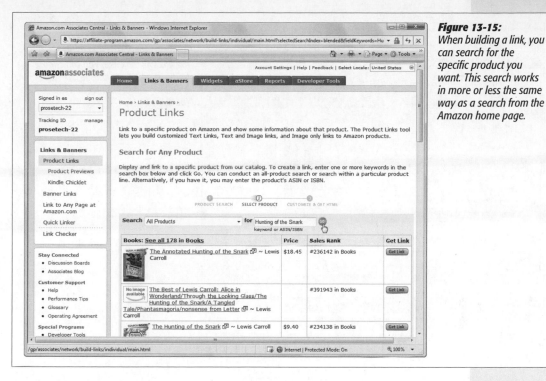

Figure 13-15:
When building a link, you can search for the specific product you want. This search works in more or less the same way as a search from the Amazon home page.

4. **Click the Get Link button next to the product you want to link to.**

   You'll see a page that shows you the product and previews the link you're about to create.

5. **Choose the link type and customize its appearance.**

   You can configure your product link to be as fancy or as simple as you want (see Figure 13-16). To create a text link, choose Text Only as the link type. Otherwise, you'll get a more detailed box that includes a product picture and price.

   You can choose whether your page opens the link in a new browser window, how big the image is, what price information the product box includes, and what colors it uses.

   Once you finish, copy the XHTML from Amazon's text box and paste it in any Web page on your site.

When you create a text link, Amazon generates an anchor element that looks fairly complex. (As described earlier, the anchor element contains an <img> element for an invisible picture that lets Amazon track how many times it displays the link.)

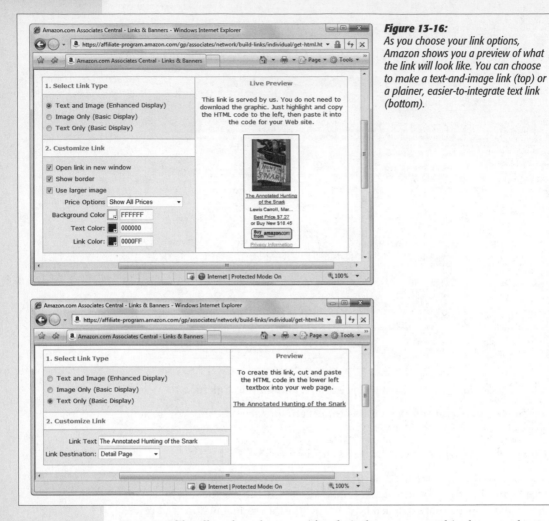

Figure 13-16:
As you choose your link options, Amazon shows you a preview of what the link will look like. You can choose to make a text-and-image link (top) or a plainer, easier-to-integrate text link (bottom).

However, like all anchor elements, it's relatively easy to put this element where you want it. Just pop it into an existing paragraph, like this:

```
<p>Lewis Carroll's work as a mathematician may have driven him insane,
as his famous book
<a href="http://www.amazon.com/exec/obidos/...">The Hunting of the Snark</a>
<img src="http://www.assoc-amazon.com/..." width="1" height="1" />
attests.</p>
```

Note: *Amazon puts the full title of the book inside the anchor element. This title might be a little longer than you intend, because it might include information about the edition or a byline. If so, just cut it down to the title you want to use.*

Amazon sends you monthly emails to let you know how your much you're earning. But if you can't stand the suspense, you can log in to Amazon Associates any time. Click the Reports tab (Figure 13-17) to get detailed information on how much you're earning per day, week, month, or quarter.

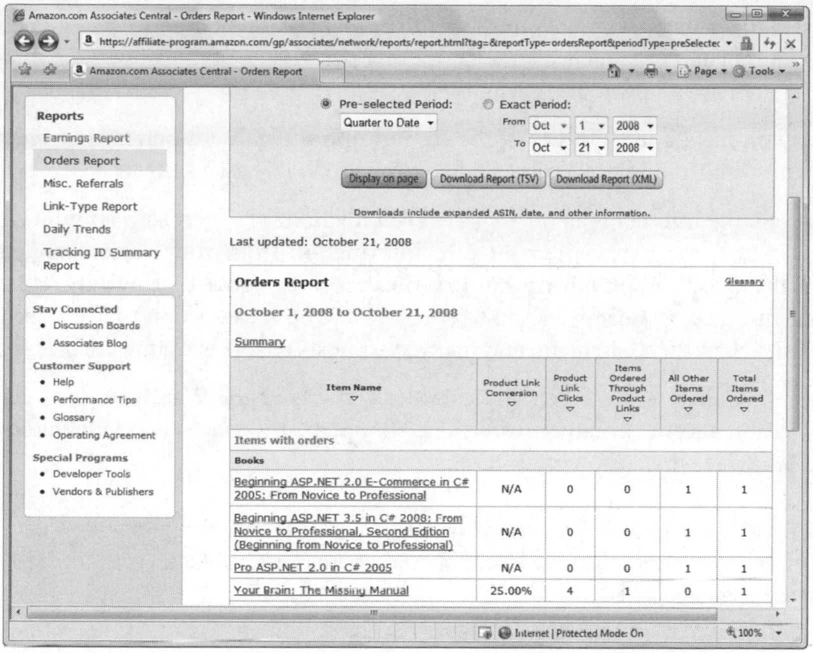

Figure 13-17:
Amazon provides many different types of reports. To get a fascinating look at what items your visitors are buying, click the Orders Report link in the menu on the left.

PayPal Merchant Tools

Unless your Web site is wildly popular, ads and other affiliate programs will net you only spare change. If you have all-consuming dreams of Web riches, you need to actually sell something.

You don't need to go far to run into self-made Internet commerce kingpins. A surprisingly large number of people have made their living with creative products. Examples include t-shirts with political catchphrases, empty bottles of wine with Titanic labels, and collectable toys from a relative's basement. Your path to a thriving e-business might involve little more than buying tin spoons from Honest Ed's and decorating them with macramé.

But no matter how good your goods are, you need a way to sell vast quantities easily and conveniently. Very few people will go through the hassle of mailing you a personal check. However, if they can make an impulse purchase with a credit card, your odds of making a sale improve significantly.

Accepting credit cards isn't the easiest thing in the world to do. An e-business can do so in two ways:

- **Open a merchant account with a bank.** This is the traditional way to accept credit cards. Requirements vary from country to country, but you may need a business plan, an accountant, and some up-front capital.

- **Use a third-party service.** A number of companies accept credit card payments on your behalf in exchange for a flat fee or a percentage of the sale. In this chapter, you'll learn how to use one of the best—PayPal.

Unless you have a large business, the second option is always better. The reason has to do with the additional risks that accompany Web-based sales.

First of all, the Internet is an open place. Even if you have a merchant account, you need a *secure* way to accept credit card information from your customers. That means the credit card number needs to be *encrypted* (scrambled using a secret key) so that Internet eavesdroppers can't get it. Most Web masters don't have a secure server sitting in their basement, and many Web hosts charge extra for the privilege.

Another problem is that when you conduct a sale over the Web, you don't have any way to collect a signature from the e-shopper. This makes you vulnerable to *chargebacks* (see the box on page 389).

Note: PayPal is a staggeringly large Internet company that offers its payment services in well over 100 countries, and has more than 100 million account members worldwide. PayPal was established in 1998 and purchased by eBay in 2002.

Signing Up with PayPal

Once you sign up with PayPal, you can accept payments from customers across the globe. Here's how you go about it:

1. **Head to the PayPal Web site (*www.paypal.com*). Click the Sign Up link on the home page.**

   This sends you to the Sign Up Web page.

2. **Choose your country and language.**

3. **Choose the type of account you want to create (Personal, Premier, or Business), and then click the Get Started button in the corresponding box.**

   A *personal account* is ideal if you want to use PayPal to buy items on sites like eBay using your credit card or with funds from your bank account. You can also accept payments from other people, without having to pay any fees. However, there's a significant catch—credit card payments aren't supported. In order to do business with you, your customers need to already have money in their PayPal accounts (which they get by selling something and receiving a PayPal payment, or by transferring money from a linked bank account).

Understanding Chargebacks

What's a chargeback?

A chargeback happens when a buyer asks their credit card company to remove a charge from their account. The buyer may claim that the seller didn't live up to their end of the agreement, or claim that they never made the purchase in the first place. A chargeback can occur weeks or months after an item is purchased.

From the buyer's point of view, a chargeback is relatively easy. They simply phone the credit card company and reverse the transaction. The money you made is deducted from your account, even though you've already shipped the product. If you want to dispute the buyer's claim, you're in the unenviable position of trying to convince a monolithic credit card company to take your side. Many small businesses don't dispute chargebacks at all, because the process is too difficult, expensive, and unsuccessful.

However, when you use a third-party service, the odds tilt in your favor. If the buyer asks for a chargeback, the chargeback is made against the third-party company that accepted the payment (like PayPal), not you. And even though PayPal isn't as large as the average multinational bank, it's still a major customer of most credit card companies, which means it has significant clout to fight a chargeback.

The end result is that buyers are less likely to charge back items to PayPal. And if they do, PayPal gives you the chance to dispute the chargeback. PayPal even lets you contact the buyer to see if there's a simple misunderstanding (for example, to check whether you sent the item to the wrong address). And if you're really paranoid, you can use PayPal's Seller Protection Policy which, if you take a few additional steps (like retaining proof of delivery), insures you for up to a $5,000 loss. For more information about how PayPal handles chargebacks, check out *www.paypal.com/chargeback*. To learn about PayPal's seller protection, refer to *www.paypal.com/SellerProtection*.

A *premier account* is the best way to run a small business. You get the ability to send money (great if you crave a rare movie poster on eBay) and accept any type of payment that PayPal supports, including credit cards and bank account debit cards. You also get to use PayPal's e-commerce tools. However, you'll be charged a fee for every payment you receive, which varies by volume but ranges from 1.9 percent to 2.9 percent of the payment's total value (with a minimum fee of 30 cents). That means that on a $25 sale, PayPal takes about $1 off the top. If you accept payments in another currency, you surrender an extra 2.5 percent. To get the full scoop and to see the most current rates, refer to *www.paypal.com/fees*.

A *business account* is almost identical to a premier account, except that it supports multiple logins. This is the best choice if you have a large business with employees who need to access your PayPal account to help you manage your site.

4. **The next page collects typical account details. Enter your email address and choose a password. Then fill in your name, postal address, and phone number.**

   Make your password complex—you don't want a malicious hacker guessing it and using your PayPal account to go on an electronic buying binge.

Tip: As a general rule of thumb, guard your PayPal account information the same way you guard your bank PIN. If you're really paranoid, don't use your PayPal account to buy items on other Web sites, and don't use your credit card to do so either.

5. **Finally, click Agree and Create Account to complete the process.**

   PayPal sends you an email confirmation immediately. Once you click the link in the message, PayPal activates your account, and you can start creating PayPal buttons and shopping carts to collect payments.

Accepting Payments

PayPal makes it ridiculously easy to create e-commerce Web pages. One way is to add a Buy Now button to any Web page on your site. Here's how:

1. **Head to *www.paypal.com*, and sign in.**

   Once you sign in, you can access several tabs crammed with goodies.

   Use My Account to update your account information, see what recent transactions you've made, check your balance, and request a withdrawal.

   Use Send Money to email someone cash (which you need to supply from a real-world bank account or credit card), and Request Money to send a buyer an email asking for payment.

   Use the Merchant Services tab to build buttons you can add to your Web pages.

   Use Auction Tools to specify PayPal as the form of payment for things you sell on eBay. (eBay is still one of the most popular places to set up an e-business.)

   Use the Products & Services tab to learn about various PayPal services.

2. **Click the Merchant Services tab.**

   Scroll down the page, and you see a variety of tools for collecting money, as explained in Figure 13-18.

3. **Click the "Buy Now button" link.**

   PayPal displays a page where you configure your Buy Now button's appearance and set the price of your product (Figure 13-19).

4. **Give your item a name and, if you want to keep track of it, a product code. Then supply the price and currency.**

   Don't worry about locking out international visitors when you set your currency. Credit card companies are happy to charge Canadian customers in U.S. dollars, U.S. customers in euros, and European customers in rupees. Just choose the currency you think your buyers expect to see.

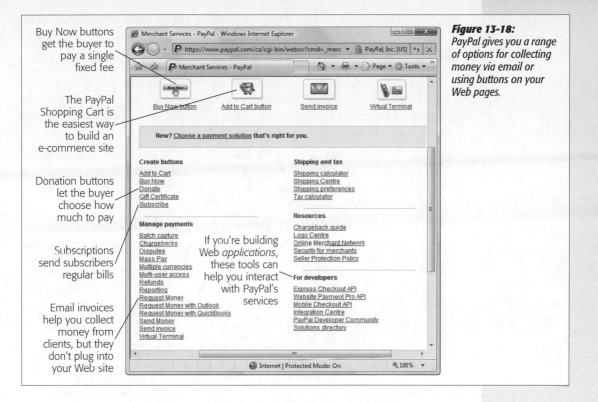

Figure 13-18:
*PayPal gives you a range
of options for collecting
money via email or
using buttons on your
Web pages.*

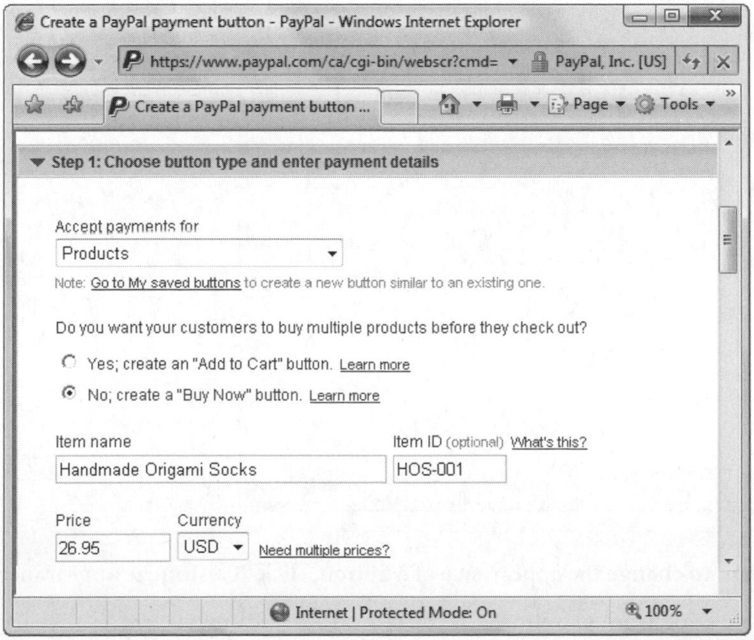

Buy Now buttons
get the buyer to
pay a single
fixed fee

The PayPal
Shopping Cart is
the easiest way
to build an
e-commerce site

Donation buttons
let the buyer
choose how
much to pay

Subscriptions
send subscribers
regular bills

Email invoices
help you collect
money from
clients, but they
don't plug into
your Web site

If you're building
Web *applications*,
these tools can
help you interact
with PayPal's
services

Figure 13-19:
The basics of a Buy Now button.

5. **If you want to give buyers different options, fill in the information in the "Customize button" box.**

You can collect extra buying information from your buyers in three nifty ways:

Choose "Add drop-down menu with price/option." This lets you give buyers a list of options, each with a different price (see Figure 13-20). For example, you could let a buyer choose between a plain, premium, or organic tin of hamster food.

Choose "Add drop-down menu without prices." This also gives your buyers a list of options, but without changing the product's price. For example, you could use a list like this to let buyers choose the color of the embroidered undergarments they're about to buy.

Choose "Add text field." This adds a text box where buyers can type in anything. Use this if you need to collect information that varies, like the name your buyer wants engraved on a magnetic screwdriver.

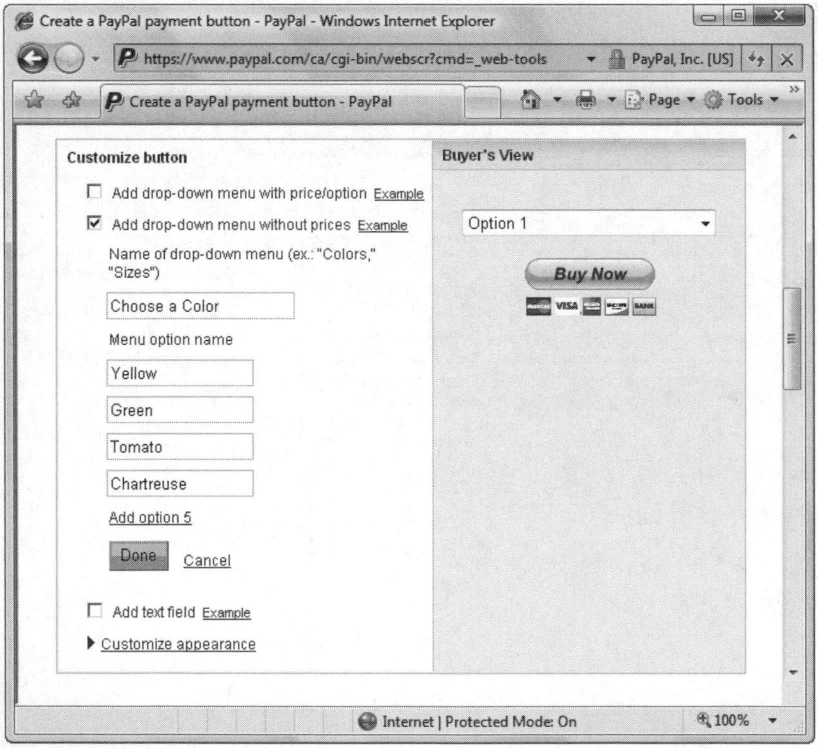

Figure 13-20:
With a drop-down list of options, you can collect additional information about the type of product your visitor wants. This is useful if you offer the same item in multiple sizes or colors (as shown here). To add another color to the list, click the "Add option" link under the current values.

6. **If you want to change the appearance of a button, click "Customize appearance."**

PayPal gives you limited options for the button's size and text.

The standard Buy Now button is perfectly usable, but a little plain. If you've created a nicer button (see Chapter 15 for tips) and uploaded it to your site, supply the URL for the image here. (You can always change the XHTML that PayPal generates if you want to use a different button picture later on.)

7. **Scroll down and fill in any additional options you want.**

PayPal gives you a heap of extra possibilities. You can add a flat surcharge for shipping and a percentage for sales tax. You can get PayPal to track how many items you have in stock, and stop selling your product when it's sold out—all you do is fill in the number of items you currently have.

And PayPal has an entire section of advanced possibilities, like whether you need a buyer's address (PayPal assumes you do), if you want your customers to fill in additional comments with their payments (ordinarily, they can't), and where PayPal should send visitors after they complete or cancel a payment (you can send shoppers to a specific URL on your site, rather than to PayPal's generic pages).

8. **Click Create Button.**

You'll see a text box with the markup for your customized Buy Now button, which you copy and paste into your Web page.

When you create a Buy Now button, PayPal puts everything inside a <form> element (explained on page 339). If you haven't used encryption, you might be able to figure out what's going on inside your form.

Here's an example of a button for a pair of handmade origami socks based on the last few steps above:

```
<form action="https://www.paypal.com/cgi-bin/webscr" method="post">
  <input type="hidden" name="cmd" value="_s-xclick" />
  <input type="hidden" name="hosted_button_id" value="633788" />
  <table>
    <tr><td>
      <input type="hidden" name="on0" value="Choose a Color" />
       Choose a Color</td></tr><tr><td>
      <select name="os0">
        <option value="Yellow">Yellow</option>
        <option value="Green">Green</option>
        <option value="Tomato">Tomato</option>
        <option value="Chartreuse">Chartreuse</option>
      </select>
    </td></tr>
  </table>
  <input type="image" border="0" name="submit" alt=""
   src="https://www.paypal.com/en_US/i/btn/btn_buynowCC_LG.gif" />
  <img src="https://www.paypal.com/en_US/i/scr/pixel.gif" alt=""
   width="1" height="1" />
</form>
```

If you added any option fields, you'll see <select> and <option> elements that define the relevant list boxes (page 343). The form also includes the Buy Now button. Clicking it sends the form to PayPal. You can change the button's *src* attribute (bolded in the listing above) to point to a different image file. After the code for the Buy Now button is an invisible image that lets PayPal track how many times visitors view the page that includes the button. Amazon Associates provides this same service; see page 384 for a description.

Tip: As long as you don't tamper with the <input> fields and you keep everything inside the <form> elements, you can tweak the markup PayPal creates for you. For example, you can add other elements into the form, or apply style sheet formatting. Or you might want to remove the invisible table (represented by the <table>, <tr>, and <td> elements) that PayPal uses to organize your button and your option fields to get a different layout.

So what happens when a shopper clicks the Buy Now button and submits this form? The action attribute in the very first line of the above code tells the story. When someone clicks the button, the browser sends the buyer's information to PayPal using the action URL (*https://www.paypal.com/cgi-bin/webscr*). The browser uses a secure channel to prevent Internet eavesdroppers—that's why the URL starts with "https" instead of "http."

Notice that this form doesn't include key pieces of information, like the product name or price. That's a safety measure designed to prevent troublemakers from tampering with the markup in your Web page to attempt to pay you less than you or your products are worth. When PayPal receives the form data, it retrieves the hidden ID value (633788 in the example above), and then looks that ID up in its giant, private database of buttons to identify the relevant product, price, and seller (you).

In fact, the PayPal markup doesn't provide any information about the item you're selling. You put the item name, picture, description, and price into your Web page (probably before the Buy Now button). Here's an example:

```
<html>
<head>...</head>

<body>
  <h1>Handmade Origami Socks</h1>
  <p><img src="origami.jpg" alt="Handmade Origami Socks" class="float">
  You've waited and they're finally here. Order your own
  pair of origami socks for only $26.95 and get them in time
  for the holidays. What better way to show your loved ones how
  poor your gift giving judgement really is?</p>
  <form action="https://www.paypal.com/cgi-bin/webscr" method="post">
    ...
  </form>
</body>
</html>
```

Note: Unfortunately, at the time of this writing, PayPal buttons use ordinary HTML that's not quite up to the stricter standards of XHTML. Although this is sure to change in the future, you can give PayPal a helping hand by cleaning up its markup. Often, the changes involve little more than making sure empty elements like <input> are closed properly (they should end with the characters /> rather than just >). Or, leave it the way it is and rest assured that it will still work in any Web browser, even if it gives your XHTML validator indigestion.

Figure 13-21 shows the result. This example displays the standard PayPal ordering page, but you can customize it with your own logo (see the next section).

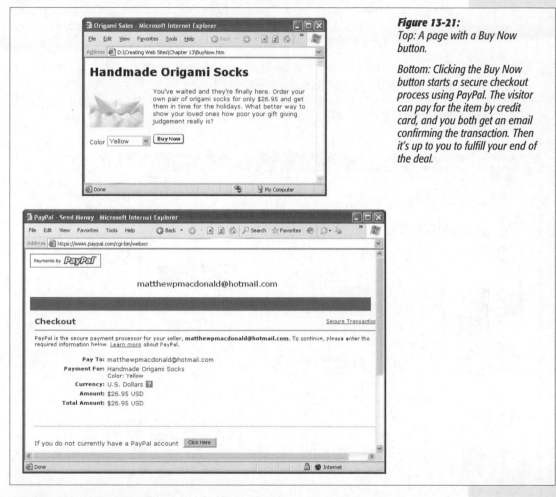

Figure 13-21:
Top: A page with a Buy Now button.

Bottom: Clicking the Buy Now button starts a secure checkout process using PayPal. The visitor can pay for the item by credit card, and you both get an email confirming the transaction. Then it's up to you to fulfill your end of the deal.

Building a Shopping Cart

PayPal's Buy Now button gives you a great way to make a quick sale. But if you dream about a Web e-commerce empire, you need to create a store where visitors can collect several items at once and pay for them all at the same time. To give your buyers this kind of convenience, you need a shopping cart, which is a staple of e-commerce Web sites. The good news is that you don't need to program your own cart—instead, you can use PayPal's prebuilt shopping cart service, which integrates smoothly into your Web site.

Creating a PayPal shopping cart is remarkably similar to creating a Buy Now button (so if you haven't tried that, you might want to play around with it before you go any further). The basic idea is that you create a separate Add To Cart button for each item you sell. You'll get many of the same options you saw when you created a Buy Now button—for example, you can set a price, product code, shipping charges, and so on. The difference is that when visitors click an Add To Cart button, PayPal doesn't send them straight to a checkout page. Instead, it displays a shopping cart page in a new window. Visitors can keep shopping until they have everything they want. Then they click a Checkout button to complete their purchase.

To show how this works, the following example uses the page shown in Figure 13-22 as a starting point. This example also shows a great use of style-based layout. Check out the downloadable samples—available from the Missing CD page at *www.missingmanuals.com*—to try it out for yourself.

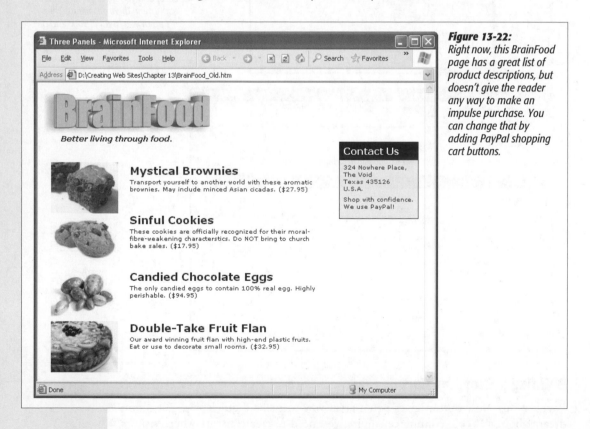

Figure 13-22:
Right now, this BrainFood page has a great list of product descriptions, but doesn't give the reader any way to make an impulse purchase. You can change that by adding PayPal shopping cart buttons.

Creating a custom page style

Before you create your shopping cart, there's an extra step you can take to really personalize your payment page. If you're happy with the PayPal standard, feel free to skip straight to the next section. But if you'd like to have your company logo appear on the shopping cart pages, keep reading.

1. **If you're not already there, head to** *www.paypal.com,* **and sign in.**

2. **Select the My Account tab, and then click the Profile link just underneath.**

   You'll see a page with a slew of information about your preferences, grouped into three main categories: Account Information (who you are and where you live), Financial Information (your bank, credit card, and payment history information), and Selling Preferences (extra options you can use with PayPal's merchant services). In this case, you're interested in the Selling Preferences section.

3. **In the Selling Preferences section, click the Custom Payment Pages link.**

   This takes you to the Custom Payment Page Styles page, where you can set up new page styles or edit existing ones.

4. **Click Add to create a new page style.**

   You start off with only a single page style—the PayPal standard, which sports a basic PayPal logo.

5. **Supply information for your page style.**

   Type a descriptive title into the Page Style Name box to help you remember which style is which.

   Use the Header Image URL to point to a picture on your Web site. This picture is the logo you want to show at the top left of the PayPal shopping cart page. You can use an image up to 750 pixels wide by 90 pixels high.

Note: Because PayPal's shopping cart page is a secure page, when you use a custom logo, the shopper may get a message informing them that there are some insecure items on the page (namely, your picture). If you want to avoid this message, talk to your Web hosting company about putting your picture on a secure (https) server.

   The settings for Header Background Color, Header Border Color, and Background Color let you specify page colors with color codes (see page 152). This part is optional—leave it out if you're happy with the standard white.

6. **Click Save to store your page style.**

   Before you commit, you can click Preview to take a sneak peek at what the PayPal payment page looks like.

7. **Select your new page style, and then click Make Primary.**

   Now all your customers will see your customized checkout page.

Generating the shopping cart buttons

You're ready to build the buttons that add items to an e-shopper's cart. Here's how:

1. If you're not already there, head to *www.paypal.com* and sign in.

2. Click Merchant Services, and then click the "Add to Cart button" link.

   PayPal displays a page where you configure the Add To Cart button for a single item.

3. Give your item a name and, if you want to keep track of it, a product code. Then supply the price, currency, and any other relevant information.

   These settings are exactly the same as for a Buy Now button.

4. Click Create Button.

   You'll see a text box with the markup for your customized Add To Cart button. Copy it out of the text box and paste it into your Web page. But remember, this Add To Cart code applies to a single, specific product. If you have more than one item on a page (as in the BrainFood example), you need to generate multiple buttons. To do so, click "Create similar button" and head back to step 3. When you finish generating all the buttons you need and copying each one into your page, continue with the next step.

5. Create a View Cart button.

   Your shopping cart solution wouldn't be complete without a button that lets shoppers see what's in their carts (and then head to the virtual checkout counter). To create one, click the "Create a View Cart button" link.

   You have virtually no options for the View Cart button, as its purpose is pretty straightforward. PayPal lets you use the standard View Cart button or supply a URL that points to a button picture of your own design. Once you make your selection, click Create Button, and then copy the markup into your page along with all the other buttons. Figure 13-23 shows the final result.

Withdrawing Your Money

PayPal safely stashes all your payments in your PayPal account (which is like a virtual bank account). You can see the balance any time. Just log in and click the My Account tab.

If you earn a small amount of money, you may be happy leaving it with PayPal so you can buy other stuff on Web sites like eBay and *www.buy.com*. But if you're raking in significant dough, you'll want to transfer some of it to the real world.

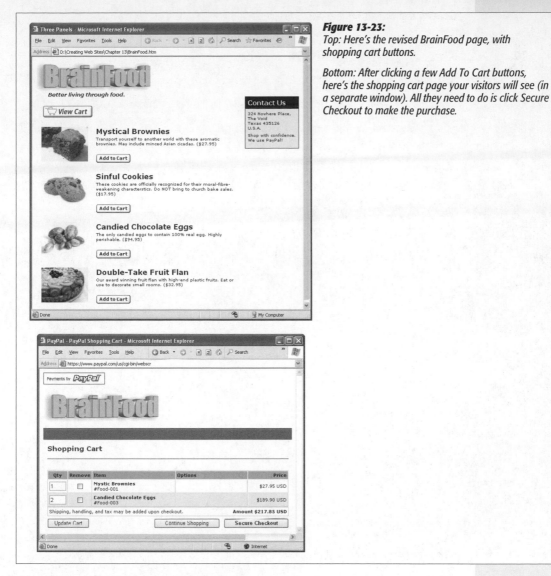

Figure 13-23:

Top: Here's the revised BrainFood page, with shopping cart buttons.

Bottom: After clicking a few Add To Cart buttons, here's the shopping cart page your visitors will see (in a separate window). All they need to do is click Secure Checkout to make the purchase.

The most common approach is to send money to your bank account. To do this, you need to give PayPal your bank account information. PayPal waives its transfer fee as long as your withdrawal meets a certain minimum (like $150). However, your bank may apply an electronic transaction fee. Depending on the country you live in, PayPal may offer other withdrawal options, too. For example, it may let you transfer money to a debit card or a credit card.

To get started with any of these approaches, log in, click the My Account tab, click the Withdraw link just underneath, and then follow the instructions there.

Part Four:
Web Site Frills

4

JavaScript: Adding Interactivity

JavaScript is a simplified programming language designed to beef up XHTML pages with interactive features. It gives you just enough programming muscle to add some fancy effects, but not enough to cause serious damage if your code goes wonky. JavaScript is perfect for creating pop-up windows, marquee-style scrolling text, and buttons that light up when visitors mouse over them. On the other hand, JavaScript can't help you build a hot e-commerce storefront; for that, you need the PayPal tools described in Chapter 13.

The goal of this chapter isn't to teach you all the details of JavaScript—instead, it's to give you enough background so you can find great JavaScript code online, understand it well enough to make basic changes, and then paste it into your pages to get the results you want. Since the Web has dozens of JavaScript sites offering thousands of ready-made scripts for free, these basic skills can come in very handy.

Understanding JavaScript

The JavaScript language has a long history—it first hit the scene with the Netscape Navigator 2 browser in 1995, and Internet Explorer jumped on the bandwagon by adding JavaScript compatibility to IE version 3. Today, all modern browsers support JavaScript, and it's become wildly popular as a result. However, some justifiably paranoid Web visitors turn off JavaScript compatibility because malicious developers have, on occasion, used JavaScript-fueled agents to attack computers with pop-up ads and other types of browser annoyances. That means that the best rule of thumb with JavaScript is to use it to improve your pages, but make sure your page still works (even if it doesn't look quite as nice) for people who disable it.

Note: JavaScript is thoroughly different from the Java language (although the code sometimes looks similar, because they share some syntax rules). Sun Microsystems developed Java, and it's a full-fledged programming language, every bit as powerful—and complicated—as C++, C#, and Visual Basic.

So what can JavaScript do?

- It can dynamically insert new content into a Web page or modify an existing XHTML element. For example, you can display a personalized message to your visitors ("Hello, Joe!") or make titles grow and shrink perpetually (an example of which is shown on page 424).

- JavaScript can gather information about the current date, your visitor's browser, or the content your visitors type into forms. You can display any of this information on a page or use it to make decisions about what your page does next. For example, you could stop visitors from going any further on your site until they type in an email address.

- JavaScript can react to events that take place in a browser. For example, you can write code that runs when a page finishes loading or when a visitor clicks a picture.

It's just as important to understand what JavaScript *can't* do. JavaScript code is *sandboxed*, which means a browser locks your page into a carefully controlled place in memory (known as a sandbox) so it can't access anything on your visitor's computer. This design, which is necessary to ensure good security, effectively prevents JavaScript from performing any potentially risky tasks, like sending orders to a printer, creating or editing files, running other programs, reformatting a hard drive, and so on. In fact, about the only thing JavaScript *can* do is modify the appearance of a Web page.

Server-Side and Client-Side Programming

To understand how JavaScript fits into the Web universe, it's important to understand the two types of programming on the Web.

When you use a search engine like Google or go to an e-commerce site like Amazon, you're actually connecting to a high-powered piece of software, known as a *server-side application*, which runs on a Web server. When you visit one of these sites, you send the server-side program information, like the keywords you want to search for or the book you want to buy. The program, in turn, consults a massive database and spits out some XHTML that creates the page you see in your browser.

Server-side applications rule the Web world, because there's virtually nothing they can't do. However, they're insanely difficult to program. Not only do developers need to worry about getting the program to generate XHTML for a browser, they also need to make sure the program can run all kinds of complex routines and consult giant databases—and they need to do it all in a way that performs just as well when millions of people are clamoring for attention as it does when there's only one person visiting a site. This is hard work, and it's best handled by the poor souls we call programmers.

Client-side applications, on the other hand, use a completely different model. They embed small, lightweight programs inside an ordinary XHTML page. When a browser downloads the page, the browser itself runs the program (assuming security settings or compatibility issues haven't disabled it). Client-side programs are much less powerful than those on the server side—they can't reliably access the huge databases stored on Web servers, for example, and for security reasons they can't directly change most things on your home computer. However, they're much simpler to create. If you've ever played a game of Java checkers in your browser (see Figure 14-1), you've used a client-side program.

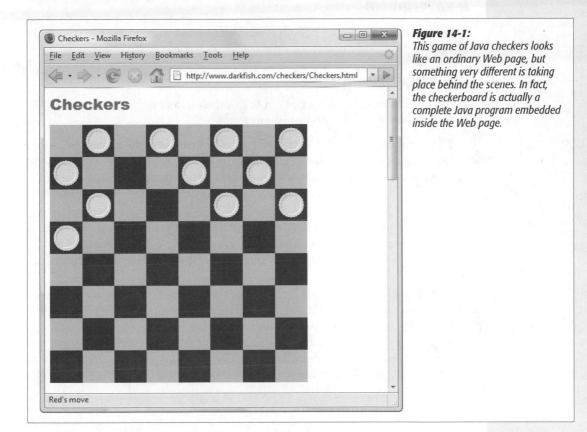

Figure 14-1:
This game of Java checkers looks like an ordinary Web page, but something very different is taking place behind the scenes. In fact, the checkerboard is actually a complete Java program embedded inside the Web page.

Scripting Languages

Even client-side programs can be a challenge for non-technogeeks. For example, to build the checkers game shown in Figure 14-1, you need to know your way around the highly sophisticated Java programming language. However, a whole class of client-side programs exist that aren't nearly as ambitious. They're called *scripts*, and their purpose in life is to give a browser a list of instructions, like "scroll that heading from left to right" or "pop up an ad for fudge-flavored toothpicks in a new window."

Scripts are written in a simplified *scripting language*, and even if you don't know all the ins and outs of a language, you can often copy and paste a cool script from a free Web site to get instant gratification. Two examples of scripting languages are JavaScript and VBScript (the latter a scripting language that uses syntax resembling Visual Basic).

This chapter focuses exclusively on scripts you create with JavaScript, the only scripting language that's reliably supported on most browsers.

JavaScript 101

Now that you've learned a bit about JavaScript and why it exists, it's time to dive in and start creating your first real script.

The <script> Element

Every script starts with a <script> block you slot somewhere into an XHTML document. Really, you have only two options:

- **The <body> section.** Put scripts you want your browser to run right away in the <body> section of your XHTML. The browser launches your script as soon as it reaches the <script> element. If you put your script at the beginning of the <body> section, your browser fires up the script before it displays the page.

Tip: Usually, JavaScript fans put their scripts at the *end* of the <body> section. That way, you avoid errors that might occur if you use a script that relies on another part of the page, and the browser hasn't read that other section yet. Because browsers read an entire page quickly, these scripts execute almost immediately.

- **The <head> section.** If you place an ordinary script in the <head> section of your XHTML document, it runs immediately, before the browser processes any part of the XHTML markup. However, it's more common to use the <head> section for scripts that contain *functions* (see page 414). Functions don't run immediately—instead, you summon them when your visitor takes some kind of action on a page, like moving a mouse.

Note: You can place as many <script> blocks in a Web page as you want.

A typical script block consists of a series of programming instructions. To get a handle on how these instructions work, consider the following example, which makes your browser display a JavaScript alert box:

```
<!DOCTYPE html PUBLIC "-//W3C//DTD XHTML 1.0 Strict//EN"
"http://www.w3.org/TR/xhtml1/DTD/xhtml1-strict.dtd">

<html xmlns="http://www.w3.org/1999/xhtml">

<head>
```

```
    <title>JavaScript Test</title>
  </head>

  <body>
    <h1>You Will Be Wowed</h1>
    <p>This page uses JavaScript.</p>
    <script type="text/javascript">
      alert("Welcome, JavaScript coder.")
    </script>
  </body>

</html>
```

This script pops up a window with a message, as shown in Figure 14-2. When you click OK, the message disappears, and it's back to life as usual for your Web page.

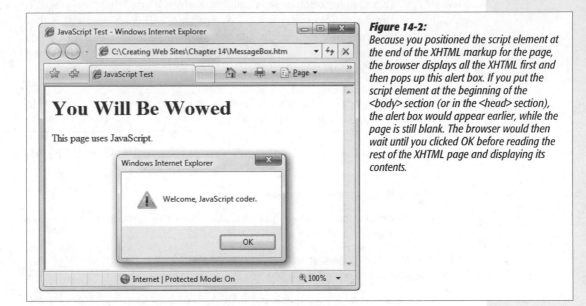

Figure 14-2:
Because you positioned the script element at the end of the XHTML markup for the page, the browser displays all the XHTML first and then pops up this alert box. If you put the script element at the beginning of the <body> section (or in the <head> section), the alert box would appear earlier, while the page is still blank. The browser would then wait until you clicked OK before reading the rest of the XHTML page and displaying its contents.

Like all scripts, the script in this example is wrapped inside a <script> element. The *type* attribute tells the browser that the script holds JavaScript code, which is an essential detail:

```
<script type="text/javascript">
  ...
</script>
```

You're probably wondering exactly how this script works its magic. When a browser processes the script, it runs all the code, going one line at a time. In this case, there's only one line:

```
alert("Welcome, JavaScript coder.")
```

This line uses a built-in JavaScript function called *alert*. A *function* is a programming routine consisting of one or more lines of code that performs a certain task. JavaScript has many built-in functions, but you can also build your own.

JavaScript's alert( ) function requires one piece of information, otherwise known as an *argument* in programmer-speak. In this case, that piece of information is the text you want to display in the alert box. If you want to display an ordinary number, say 6, you could type it in as is—that is, you don't need to put it in quotes. But with text, there's no way for a browser to tell where text starts and stops. To handle this problem in JavaScript, you put text inside single apostrophe quotes (') or double quotation marks ("), as in the example above.

Note: In programmer-speak, a distinct piece of text used in a program is called a *string*. "The friendly fox," "a," and "Rumpelstiltskin" all qualify as strings.

That's it. All this simple script does is call JavaScript's alert( ) function. (Spend enough time around programmers and JavaScript fans, and you'll soon learn that "call" is the preferred way to describe the action of triggering a function.) The alert( ) function does the rest, popping up the correct-sized window and waiting for your visitor to click OK.

Note: To write this script, you need to know that there's an alert( ) function ready for you to use—a fact you can find out on one of the many JavaScript tutorial sites.

Based on what you now know, you should be able to change this script in the following ways:

- Display a different message (by changing the argument).

- Display more than one message box, one after the other (by adding more lines in your <script> block).

- Display the message box before your browser displays the Web page (by changing the position of the <script> block).

It's not much to keep you occupied, but it does show how easy it is to get started using and changing a simple script.

Scripts and XHTML

As you've seen, XHTML uses the <script> block to hold JavaScript code. But it's important to understand that <script> is just one more XHTML element, and like all XHTML elements, it needs to follow the rules. One of those rules limits the characters allowed inside the <script> block. XHTML forbids certain characters, like the infamous angle brackets, because they have a special meaning in the XHTML language.

GEM IN THE ROUGH

Dealing with Internet Explorer's Paranoia

If you run the alert example in Firefox, you'll find that everything works seamlessly. If you run it in Internet Explorer, you won't get the same satisfaction. Instead, you'll see a security warning appear in a yellow bar at the top of the page. Until you click the yellow bar, and then choose Allow Blocked Content, your JavaScript code won't run.

At first glance, IE's security warning seems like a surefire way to scare off the bravest Web visitor. However, there's no need to worry. In fact, the message is just part of the quirky way Internet Explorer deals with Web pages that you store on your hard drive. When you access the same page over the Web, Internet Explorer won't raise the slightest objection.

That said, the security warning is still an annoyance while you're testing your Web page, because it forces you to keep explicitly telling the browser to allow the page to run JavaScript. To remove the security warning altogether, you can tell Internet Explorer to pretend you downloaded your Web page from a Web server. You do this by adding a special comment called the *Mark of the Web*. You place this comment immediately after the <html> element that begins your page:

```
<html xmlns="http://www.w3.org/1999/xhtml">
<!-- saved from url=(0014)about:internet -->
```

When IE sees the Mark of the Web, it treats the page as though it came from a Web server, skipping the security warning, and running your JavaScript code without hesitation. To all other browsers, the Mark of the Web just looks like an ordinary XHTML comment.

Unfortunately, special characters *do* sometimes crop up in code. You could replace them with character entities (page 132), but that makes it far more difficult for other people to read, understand, and edit your code. A better solution is to wrap the entire script in something called a *CDATA section*—a specialized region of your XHTML document that suspends the usual XHTML rules. Here's how:

```
<script type="text/javascript">
//<![CDATA[
  alert("Welcome, JavaScript coder.")
//]]>
</script>
```

This technique is a bit ugly, but it does the trick. It's best not to think about it too deeply and just get into the habit of wrapping any lengthy block of script code in a CDATA section. The one exception is script code you put in a separate file (page 418)—your browser won't interpret it as XHTML, so you don't need to wrap it in a CDATA section.

Note: For simplicity, this chapter uses a CDATA section only when absolutely necessary—in other words, when the script contains special characters that XHTML ordinarily wouldn't allow.

Browsers that don't support JavaScript

Some browsers will recognize the <script> element but refuse to execute your code. This can happen if a browser doesn't support JavaScript, or if JavaScript has been switched off. To deal with this situation, you can use the <noscript> element, which lets you supply alternate XHTML content.

You place the <noscript> element immediately after the <script> element. Here's an example that displays a paragraph of text for browsers that lack JavaScript support:

```
<script type="text/javascript">
  alert("Welcome, JavaScript coder.")
</script>
<noscript>
  <p>Welcome, non-JavaScript-enabled browser.</p>
</noscript>
```

UP TO SPEED

Spaces and Line Breaks in JavaScript

JavaScript code is quite tolerant of extra spaces. In this chapter, most of the examples use some sort of indenting to help you see the structure of the code. But as with XHTML, you don't absolutely have to add these spaces.

The only rule in JavaScript is that every code statement needs to be on a separate line. You can get around this limitation by using the line-termination character, which is a semicolon (;). For example, here's how you can compress three code statements onto one line:

```
alert("Hi"); alert("There"); alert("Dude");
```

Each semicolon designates the end of a code statement. This strange convention comes from the Bizarro world of C and Java.

If you don't want to put more than one code statement on the same line, you don't need the semicolons. However, you're still free to add them at the end of each line if you want. In fact, if you download a script from the Web, you just might find these optional semicolons, which is often a tip-off that a C or Java programmer wrote the script.

Variables

Every programming language includes the concept of *variables*, which are temporary containers that store important information. Variables can store numbers, objects, or pieces of text. As you'll see throughout this chapter, variables play a key role in many scripts, and they're a powerful tool in any programmer's arsenal.

Declaring variables

To create a variable in JavaScript, you use the *var* keyword, followed by the name of the variable. You can choose any name that makes sense to you, as long as you're consistent (and avoid spaces or special characters). Here's an example that creates a variable named *myMessage*:

```
var myMessage
```

To store information in a variable, you use the equal sign (=), which copies the data on the right side of the equal sign into the variable on its left. Here's an example that puts some text into myMessage:

```
myMessage = "Everybody loves variables"
```

Remember, you need to use quotation marks whenever you've got a text string. In contrast, if you want to copy a *number* into a variable, you don't need quotation marks:

```
myNumber = 27.3
```

Note: JavaScript variables are case-sensitive, which means a variable named myMessage is different from one named MyMessage. If you try to use them interchangeably, you'll wind up with a scripting error (if your browser is nice) or a bizarre mistake in the page (which is usually what happens).

You'll often want to create a variable and fill it with useful content, all in the same step. JavaScript lets you do so if you put an equal sign immediately after the variable name when you declare it:

```
var myMessage = "Everybody loves variables"
```

To make matters a little confusing, JavaScript lets you refer to variables you haven't yet declared. Doing so is considered extremely bad form and is likely to cause all sorts of problems. However, it's worth knowing that these undeclared variables are permissible, because they're the source of many an unexpected error.

Modifying variables

One of the most useful things you can do with numeric variables is perform *operations* on them to change your data. For example, you can use arithmetic operators to perform mathematical calculations:

```
var myNumber = (10 + 5) * 2 / 5
```

These calculations follow the standard order of operations (parentheses first, then addition and subtraction, then multiplication and division). The result of this calculation is 6.

You can also use operations to join together multiple pieces of text into one long string. In this case, you use the plus (+) operator:

```
var firstName = "Sarah"
var lastName = "Smithers"
var fullName = firstName + " " + lastName
```

Now the fullName variable holds the text Sarah Smithers. (The " " tells JavaScript to leave a space between the two names).

An example with variables

Although you'd need to read a thick volume to learn everything there is to know about variables, you can pick up a lot from a simple example. The following script inserts the current date into a Web page. The example on the next page numbers each line of code to make it easy to reference.

```
       <!DOCTYPE html PUBLIC "-//W3C//DTD XHTML 1.0 Strict//EN"
       "http://www.w3.org/TR/xhtml1/DTD/xhtml1-strict.dtd">

       <html xmlns="http://www.w3.org/1999/xhtml">

       <head>
         <title>JavaScript Test</title>
       </head>

       <body>
         <h1>What Day Is It?</h1>
         <p>This page uses JavaScript.</p>
         <p>
         <script type="text/javascript">
1                    var currentDate = new Date( )
2                    var message = "The current date is: "
3                    message = message + currentDate.toDateString( )
4                    document.write(message)
         </script>
         </p>
       </body>
       </html>
```

Here's what's happening, line by line:

1. This line creates a new variable named *currentDate*. It fills the currentDate variable (see number 3 below) with a new Date object. You'll know JavaScript is creating an object when you see the keyword *new*. (You'll learn more about objects on page 420; for now, it's enough to know that objects come with built-in functions that work more or less the same way as the functions you learned about earlier.)

2. This line creates a new variable named *message*, and fills it with the beginning of a sentence that announces the date.

3. This line adds some new text to the end of the message you created in line 2. The new text comes from the currentDate object. The tricky part is understanding that the currentDate object comes with a built-in toDateString( ) function that converts the date information it gets from your PC into a piece of text suitable for displaying in a browser (see Figure 14-3). Once again, this is the kind of detail you can only pick up by studying a good JavaScript reference.

4. This line uses JavaScript's *document* object, which has a function named *write( )*. The write( ) function copies a piece of text onto a Web page at the current location. The final result is a page that shows your welcome message (see Figure 14-4).

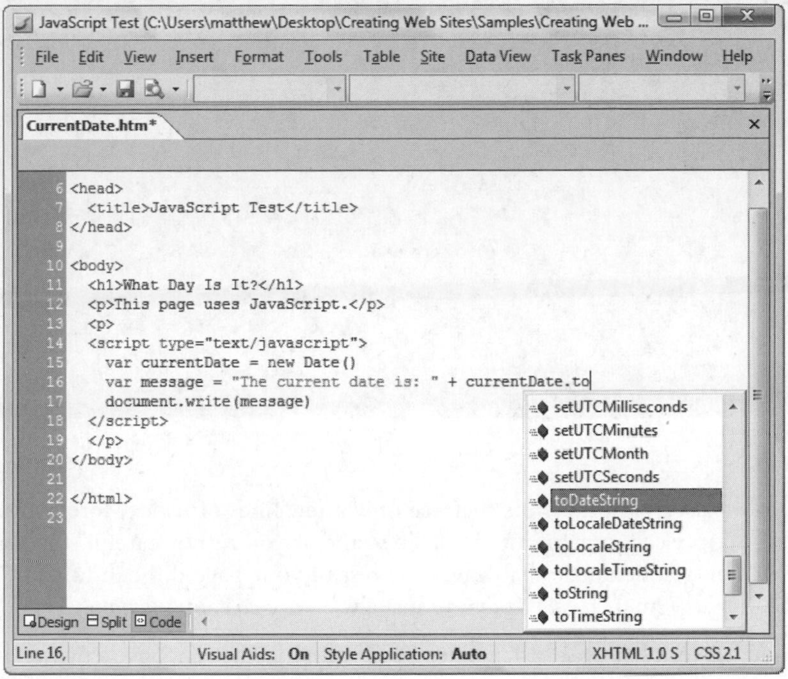

Figure 14-3:
Some Web page editors help you out when you write JavaScript code. For example, Expression Web displays a drop-down menu that shows you all the functions an object provides. Although this probably isn't enough for you to figure out how to use the Date object the first time out, it's a great way to refresh your memory later on.

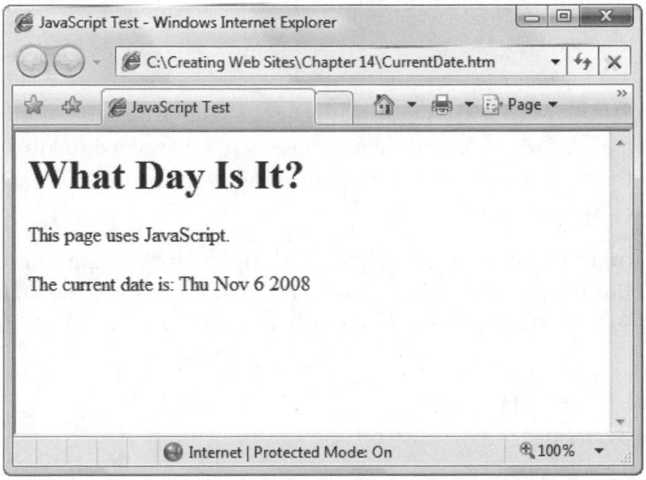

```
 6 <head>
 7   <title>JavaScript Test</title>
 8 </head>
 9
10 <body>
11   <h1>What Day Is It?</h1>
12   <p>This page uses JavaScript.</p>
13   <p>
14   <script type="text/javascript">
15     var currentDate = new Date()
16     var message = "The current date is: " + currentDate.to
17     document.write(message)
18   </script>
19   </p>
20 </body>
21
22 </html>
23
```

Drop-down menu options:
- setUTCMilliseconds
- setUTCMinutes
- setUTCMonth
- setUTCSeconds
- toDateString
- toLocaleDateString
- toLocaleString
- toLocaleTimeString
- toString
- toTimeString

Figure 14-4:
The document.write( ) command inserts text directly into a page, wherever you position the script block. In this case, the command displays the current date.

What Day Is It?

This page uses JavaScript.

The current date is: Thu Nov 6 2008

Scripts can get much more complex than this. For example, they can use loops to repeat a single action several times, or make decisions using conditional logic. You'll see examples of some of these techniques in this chapter, but you won't get a blow-by-blow exploration of the JavaScript language—in fact, that would require a small book of its own. If you want to learn more, check out the box on page 414.

Functions

So far, you've seen simple scripts that use only a few lines of code. More realistic JavaScript scripts can run to dozens of lines and if you're not careful, they can grow into a grotesque tangle that leaves the rest of your page difficult to edit. To control the chaos, smart JavaScripters almost always use *custom functions*.

A function is a series of code instructions you group together and give a name. In a way, functions are like miniature programs, because they can perform a series of operations. The neat thing about functions is that you only need to create them once, and you can reuse them over and over again.

Declaring a function

To create a JavaScript function, start by deciding what your function is going to do (like display an alert message), and then choose a suitable name for it (like *ShowAlertBox*). As with most things in the programming world, function names can't have any spaces or special characters.

Armed with this information, you're ready to put a <script> block in the <head> section of your page. But this <script> block looks a little different from the examples you've seen so far. Here's a complete function that shows an alert box with a predefined message:

```
<script type="text/javascript">
  function ShowAlertBox() {
  alert("I'm a function.")
  }
</script>
```

To understand what's going on here, it helps to break down this example and consider it piece by piece.

Every function declaration starts with the word *function*, which tells JavaScript what you're up to.

```
function
```

Then, you want to name your function and add two parentheses. You use the parentheses to send extra information to your function, as you'll see on page 416.

```
function ShowAlertBox( )
```

At this point, you've finished *declaring* the function. All that remains is to add the code inside the function that actually makes it work. To do this, you need the funny curly braces shown in the alert box function above. The { brace indicates the start of your function code and the } brace indicates the end of it. You can put as many lines of code as you want in between.

One tricky part of function writing is the fact that JavaScript sets notoriously loose standards for line breaks. That means you can create an equivalent JavaScript function and put the curly braces on their own line, like this:

```
<script type="text/javascript">
  function ShowAlertBox( )
  {
    alert("I'm a function.")
  }
</script>
```

But don't worry—both functions work exactly the same way.

Tip: You can put as many functions as you want in a single <script> block. Just add them one after the other.

Calling a function

Creating a function is only half the battle. On their own, functions don't do anything. You have to *call* the function somewhere in your page to actually run the code. To call a function, you use the function name, followed by parentheses:

```
ShowAlertBox( )
```

Note: Don't leave out the parentheses after the function name. Otherwise, browsers will assume you're trying to use a variable rather than call a function.

You can call ShowAlertBox( ) anywhere you'd write ordinary JavaScript code. For example, here's a script that shows the alert message three times in a row to really hassle your visitors:

```
<script type="text/javascript">
  ShowAlert( )
  ShowAlert( )
  ShowAlert( )
</script>
```

This is the same technique that, earlier, you saw used to call the alert( ) function. The difference is that alert() is built into JavaScript, while ShowAlertBox( ) is something you created yourself. Also, the alert( ) function requires one argument, while ShowAlertBox( ) doesn't use any.

Functions that receive information

The ShowAlertBox( ) function is beautifully simple. You simply call it, and it displays an alert box with the built-in message. Most functions don't work this easily. That's because in many cases you need to send specific information to a function, or take the results of a function and use them in another operation.

For example, imagine you want to display a welcome message with some standard information in it, like the current date. But you also want the flexibility to change part of the message by substituting your own witty words each time you call the function. To do so, you need a way to call a function *and* to supply a text string with your message in it.

To solve this problem, you can create a ShowAlertBox( ) function that accepts a single argument. This argument represents the customized text you want to incorporate into your greeting. Choose a name for your customized text, say *customMessage*, and put it between the parentheses after the function name, like so:

```
function ShowAlertBox(customMessage) {
    ...
}
```

There's no limit to how many pieces of information a function can accept. You just need to separate each argument with a comma. Here's an example of the ShowAlertBox() function with three arguments named messageLine1, messageLine2, and messageLine3.:

```
function ShowAlertBox(messageLine1, messageLine2, messageLine3) {
    ...
}
```

Here's another example that shows a finished ShowAlertBox( ) function. It accepts a single argument named customMessage, and uses the customMessage argument to generate the text it displays in the alert box:

```
<script type="text/javascript">
1    function ShowAlertBox(customMessage)
2    {
3        // Get the date.
4        var currentDate = new Date( )
5
6        // Build the full message.
7        var fullMessage = "** IMPORTANT BULLETIN **\n\n"
8        fullMessage += customMessage + "\n\n"
9        fullMessage += "Generated at: " + currentDate.toTimeString( ) + "\n"
```

```
10        fullMessage += "This message courtesy of MagicMedia Inc."
11
12        // Show the message.
13        alert(fullMessage)
14    }
</script>
```

Here are some helpful notes to help you wade through the code:

- Any line that starts with // is a comment (see lines 3 and 6). Good programmers include lots of comments to help others understand how a function works (and help themselves remember what they did during a late-night coding binge). The browser ignores them.

- To put line breaks into an alert box, use the code \n (lines 7, 8, and 9). Each \n is equivalent to one line break. (This rule is for message boxes only. When writing XHTML, you add the familiar <br /> element to create a line break.)

- To build the text for the fullMessage variable (lines 7 to 10), the code uses a shortcut in the form of the += operator. This operator automatically takes whatever's on the *right* side of the equal sign and pastes it onto the end of the variable on the *left* side. In other words, this…

```
8         fullMessage += customMessage + "\n\n"
```

… is equivalent to this longer line:

```
8         fullMessage = fullMessage + customMessage + "\n\n"
```

Using this function is easy. You just need to remember that when you call the function, you have to supply the same number of arguments as you defined for the function, separating each one with a comma. In the case of the ShowAlertBox( ) function above, you only need to supply a single value for the customMessage variable. Here's an example:

```
<script type="text/javascript">
  ShowAlertBox("This Web page includes JavaScript functions.")
</script>
```

Figure 14-5 shows the result of this script.

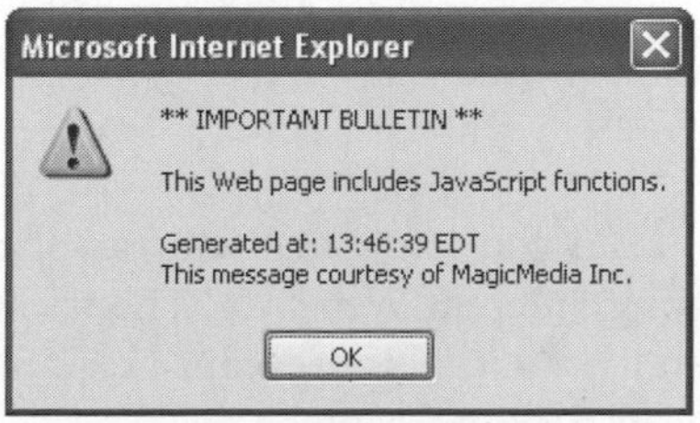

Figure 14-5:
This message is built out of several pieces of text, one of which you supplied as an argument to the ShowAlertBox( ) function.

Functions that return information

Arguments let you send information *to* a function. You can also create functions that send information *back* to the script code that called them. The trick to doing this is the *return* command, which you put right at the end of your function. The return command ends the function immediately, and spits out whatever information you want your function to generate.

Of course, a sophisticated function can accept *and* return information. For example, here's a function that multiplies two numbers (supplied as arguments) and returns the result to anyone who's interested:

```
<script type="text/javascript">
  function MultiplyNumbers(numberA, numberB)
  {
    return numberA * numberB
  }
</script>
```

Here's how you use this function elsewhere on your Web page:

```
<p>The product of 3202 and 23405 is
<script type="text/javascript">
  var product = MultiplyNumbers(3202, 23405)
  document.write(product)
</script>
</p>
```

This XHTML shows a single line of text, followed by a block of script code. The script code calls the MultiplyNumbers( ) function, gets the result (the number 74942810), and stuffs it in a variable named *product* for later use. The code then uses the document.write( ) command to display the contents of the product variable on the page. The final result is a paragraph with this text:

```
The product of 3202 and 23405 is 74942810
```

To use a typical script you get from the Web, you need to copy one or more functions into your page. These functions are likely to look a lot more complex than what you've seen so far. However, now that you understand the basic structure of a function, you'll be able to wade through the code to get a fundamental understanding of what's taking place (or to at least pinpoint where the action is going down).

External Script Files

Reusing scripts inside a Web page is neat, but did you know that you can share scripts *between* individual pages and even among different Web sites? The trick is to put your script into an external file and then link to it. This procedure is similar to the way you learned to link external style sheets back in Chapter 6.

For example, imagine you perfect the ShowAlertBox( ) routine so that it performs a complex task exactly the way you want it to, but it requires a couple of dozen lines of code to do so. To simplify your life and your XHTML document, you create a new file to store that script.

Script files are always plain text files. Usually, they have the extension *.js* (for Java-Script). You put all your code inside a script file, but you don't include the <script> element. For example, you could create this JavaScript file named *ShowAlert.js*:

```
function ShowAlertBox( )
{
  alert("This function is in an external file.")
}
```

Now save the file, and put it in the same folder as your Web page. In your Web page, define a script block, but don't supply any code. Instead, add the *src* attribute and indicate the script file you want to link to:

```
<script type="text/javascript" src="ShowAlert.js">
</script>
```

When a browser comes across this script block, it requests the ShowAlert.js file and treats it as though the code were right inside the page. Here's a complete XHTML test page that uses the ShowAlert.js file. The script in the body of the page calls the ShowAlertBox( ) function:

```
<!DOCTYPE html PUBLIC "-//W3C//DTD XHTML 1.0 Strict//EN"
"http://www.w3.org/TR/xhtml1/DTD/xhtml1-strict.dtd">

<html xmlns="http://www.w3.org/1999/xhtml">

<head>
  <title>Show Alert</title>
  <!-- Make all the functions in the ShowAlert.js file
    available in this page. Notice there's no actual content here. -->
  <script type="text/javascript" src="ShowAlert.js">
  </script>
</head>

<body>
  <!-- Test out one of the functions. -->
  <script type="text/javascript">
    ShowAlertBox( )
  </script>
</body>

</html>
```

There's no difference in the way an embedded or external script works. However, storing your scripts in separate files helps keep your Web site organized and makes it easy to reuse scripts across several pages. In fact, you can even link to JavaScript functions on another Web site—just remember that the src attribute in the <script> block needs to point to a full URL (like *http://SuperScriptSite.com/ShowAlert.js*) instead of just a file name. Of course, this technique is risky because the Web site owner might rename, move, or modify the JavaScript file. If you really want to use the code, it's far better to copy it to your own Web server so that that can't happen.

Note: Using separate script files doesn't improve your security one iota. Because anyone can request your script file, a savvy Web visitor can figure out what scripts your page uses and take a look at them. So never include any code or secret details in a script that you don't want the world to know about.

Dynamic XHTML

JavaScript underwent a minor revolution in the late 1990s, adding support for a set of features called *Dynamic XHTML* (also referred to as Dynamic HTML, or shortened to DHTML). Dynamic XHTML isn't a new technology—instead, it's a fusion of three distinct ingredients:

- Scripting languages like JavaScript, which let you write code.

- The CSS (Cascading Style Sheet) standard, which lets you control how to position an XHTML element and how it appears.

- The XHTML *document object model* (or DOM), which lets you treat an XHTML page as a collection of *objects*.

The last point is the most important. Dynamic XHTML extends scripting languages like JavaScript so they can interact with a page as a collection of *objects*. This is a radical shift in Web programming. Dynamic XHTML treats each XHTML element, including images, links, and even the lowly paragraph, as a separate programming ingredient that your JavaScript code can play with. Using these objects, you can change what each element looks like or even where your browser places them on a page.

XHTML Objects

Clearly, Dynamic XHTML requires a whole new way of thinking about Web page design. Your scripts no longer look at your Web page as a static block of XHTML. Instead, they see a combination of *objects*.

Before you can manipulate an object on your Web page, you need a way to uniquely identify it. That way, your code can find the object it needs. The best choice for identifying objects is the *id* attribute. Add this attribute to the start tag for the element you want to manipulate, and choose a unique name, as shown here:

```
<h1 id="PageTitle">Welcome to My Page</h1>
```

Understanding Objects

In many programming languages, including JavaScript, everything revolves around objects. So what, exactly, is an object?

In the programming world, an object is nothing more than a convenient way to group some related features or information. For example, say you want to change the picture shown in an <img> element on a Web page (which is useful if you want to write a script that flashes a series of images). The easiest way to interact with an <img> element in JavaScript is to use the corresponding *image* object. In effect, the image object is a container holding all sorts of potentially useful information about what's happening inside an <img> element (including its dimensions, its position, the name of the image file associated with it, and so on). The image object also gives you a way to manipulate the <img> element—that is, to change some or all of these details.

For example, you can use an image object to get information about the image, like this:

```
document.write("The tooltip says" + image.title)
```

You can even change one of these details. For example, you can modify the actual image that an <img> element shows by using this code:

```
image.src = "newpic.jpg"
```

You'll know an object's at work by the presence of a dot (.) in your code line. The dot separates the name of the variable (the first part) from one of the built-in functions it provides (called *methods*), or one of the related variables (called *properties*). You always put methods and properties after a period.

In the previous examples, *src* and *title* are two of the image object's properties. In other words, the code *image.src = "newpic.jpg"* is the equivalent of saying "Hey, Mr. Object named Image: I have a new picture for you. Change your src to point to *newpic.jpg*."

Programmers embraced objects long ago because they're a great way to organize code conceptually (not to mention a great way to share and reuse it). You might not realize it at first, but working with the image object is actually easier than memorizing a few dozen different commands that manipulate an image.

Once you give your element a unique ID, you can easily locate that object in your code, and have JavaScript act on it. JavaScript has a handy trick for locating an object: the document.getElementById( ) method. Basically, *document* is an object that represents your whole XHTML document. It's always available and you can use it any time you want. This document object, like any object worthy of its name, gives you some handy properties and methods. The getElementById( ) method is one of the coolest—it scans a page looking for a specific XHTML element.

Note: In the example on page 412, you saw the document object working on a different task—displaying information in a Web page. To accomplish this feat, the script used the write( ) method of the document object.

When you call the document.getElementById( ) method, you supply the ID of the XHTML element you're looking for. Here's an example that digs up the object for an XHTML element with the ID *PageTitle*:

```
var titleObject = document.getElementById("PageTitle")
```

This code gets the object for the <h1> element shown earlier and stores it in a variable named titleObject. By storing the object in a variable (titleObject), you can perform a series of operations on it without having to look it up more than once.

So what, exactly, can you do with XHTML objects? To a certain extent, the answer depends on the type of element you're working with. For example, if you have a hyperlink, you can change its URL. If you have an image, you can change its source. And there are some actions you can take with almost all XHTML elements, like changing their style details or modifying the text that appears between the beginning and ending tags. As you'll see, you'll find these tricks useful in making your pages more dynamic—for example, you can change a page when a visitor takes an action, like clicking a link. Interactions like these make visitors feel as though they're using an intelligent, responsive program instead of a plain, inert Web page.

Here's how you modify the text inside the just-mentioned <h1> element, for example:

```
titleObject.innerHTML = "This Page Is Dynamic"
```

If you run this code in a script, the header's text changes as soon as your browser runs this script.

The trick that makes this script work is the innerHTML *property*, which sets the content that's nested inside an element (in this case, the <title> element). Like all properties, innerHTML is just one aspect of an XHTML object you can alter. To write code statements like this, you need to know what properties are available for you to play with. Obviously, some properties apply to specific XHTML elements only, like the *src* attribute of an image. But modern browsers boast a huge catalog of DOM properties you can use with just about any XHTML element. Table 14-1 lists some of the most useful.

Tip: To get the properties that a specific XHTML element supports, check out the reference at *www. w3schools.com/htmldom/dom_reference.asp*.

Currently, the above example works in two steps (getting the object, and then manipulating it). Although this two-step maneuver is probably the clearest approach, it's possible to combine these two steps into one line, which scripts often do. Here's an example:

```
document.getElementById("PageTitle").innerHTML = "This Page Is Dynamic"
```

Remember, the advantage to getting an object first is that you can change several properties one after the other, without needing to look up the XHTML object using getElementById( ) each time.

Table 14-1. *Common XHTML object properties*

Property	Description
className	Lets you retrieve or set the class attribute (see page 173). In other words, this property determines what style (if any) this element uses. Of course, you need to define this style in an embedded or linked style sheet, or you'll end up with the plain-Jane default formatting.
innerHTML	Lets you read or change the HTML inside an element. innerHTML is insanely useful, but it has two quirks. First, it allows all XHTML content, including text and tags. So if you want to put bold text inside a paragraph, you can set innerHTML to <b>Hi</b>. Special characters aren't welcome—you need to replace them with the character entities described on page 132.
	Second, when you set innerHTML, you replace all the content inside this element, including any other HTML elements. So if you set the innerHTML of a <div> element that contains several paragraphs and images, all these items disappear, to be replaced by your new content. If you want to modify a specific piece of a paragraph, wrap that piece in a <span> element.
parentElement	Provides the XHTML object for the element that contains this element. For example, if the current element is a <b> element in a paragraph, this gets the object for the <p> element. Once you have this object, you can modify the paragraph. Using this technique (and other similar techniques in Dynamic XHTML), you can jump from one element to another.
style	Bundles together all the CSS attributes that determine the appearance of the XHTML element. Technically, the style property returns a full-fledged style object, and you need to add another dot (.) and the name of the style attribute you want to change, as in myObject.style.fontSize. You can use the style object to set colors, borders, fonts, and even positioning.
tagName	Provides the name of the XHTML element for this object, without the angle brackets. For example, if the current object represents an <img> element, this returns the text "img".

Using XHTML objects in a script

The easiest way to come to grips with how XHTML objects work is to look at an example. The Web pages shown in Figure 14-6 include a paragraph that continuously grows and then shrinks, as your code periodically tweaks the font size.

The way this example works is quite interesting. First of all, you define two variables in the <head> section of the underlying XHTML document. The *size* variable keeps track of the current size of the text (which starts at 10 pixels). The *growIncrement* variable determines how much the text size changes each time your browser runs the code (initially, it grows by two pixels at a time):

```
<!DOCTYPE html PUBLIC "-//W3C//DTD XHTML 1.0 Strict//EN"
"http://www.w3.org/TR/xhtml1/DTD/xhtml1-strict.dtd">

<html xmlns="http://www.w3.org/1999/xhtml">
```

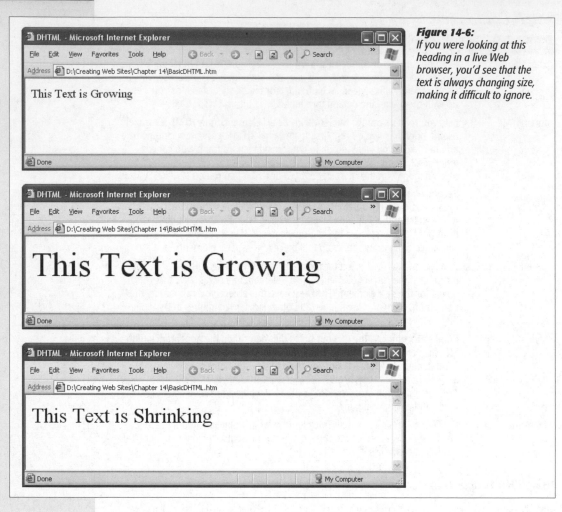

Figure 14-6:
If you were looking at this heading in a live Web browser, you'd see that the text is always changing size, making it difficult to ignore.

```
<head>
  <title>Dynamic XHTML</title>
  <script type="text/javascript">
//<![CDATA[
    // The current font size.
    var size = 10
    // The amount the font size is changing.
    var growIncrement = 2
```

Note: This script example is wrapped in a CDATA block because it uses the angle brackets to perform a numeric comparison.

Next, the script defines a function named ChangeFont( ). This function retrieves the XHTML object, here the <p> element holding the text that will grow and shrink. Once again, the getElementById( ) function does the job:

```
function ChangeFont( ) {
    // Find object that represents the paragraph
    // whose text size you want to change.
    var paragraph = document.getElementById("animatedParagraph")
```

Now, using the size and growIncrement variables, you define a variable that performs a calculation to determine the new size for the paragraph:

```
size = size + growIncrement
```

In this example, the + performs a numeric addition, because both the size and growIncrement variables store a number.

It's just as easy to set the new size using the paragraph.style.fontSize property. Just tack the letters *px* on the end to indicate that your style setting is measured in pixels:

```
paragraph.style.fontSize = size + "px"
```

If this code runs perpetually, you'll eventually end up with text so ridiculously huge you can't see any of it on the page. To prevent this from happening, you add a safety valve to the code.

Say you decide that, when the text size hits 100, you want to stop enlarging it and start shrinking it. To do this, you write the script so that it sets the growIncrement variable to −2 when the text size reaches 100. This way, the text will start shrinking from this point on, two pixels at a time. To detect when the message has grown too big, you use conditional logic courtesy of the *if* statement. Here's what it looks like:

```
// Decide whether to reverse direction from
// growing to shrinking (or vice versa).
if (size > 100) {
    paragraph.innerHTML = "This Text is Shrinking"
    growIncrement = -2
}
```

Of course, you don't want the shrinking to go on forever, either. So it makes sense to add one last check that determines whether the text has shrunk to 10 pixels or less, in which case the script goes back to enlarging the text by setting growIncrement back to 2:

```
if (size < 10) {
    paragraph.innerHTML = "This Text is Growing"
    growIncrement = 2
}
```

Now here comes the really crafty bit. JavaScript includes a setTimeout( ) function, which lets you give the browser an instruction that says "call this function, but wait a bit before you do." The setTimeout( ) function is handy when you want to create an interactive page. In this example, the setTimeout( ) function instructs the browser to call the ChangeFont( ) method again in 100 milliseconds (0.10 seconds):

```
    setTimeout("ChangeFont( )", 100)
  }
//]]>
  </script>
</head>
```

Because the ChangeFont() function always uses setTimeout( ) to call itself again, the shrinking and resizing never stops. However, you can alter this behavior. You could, for example, add conditional logic so that JavaScript calls the setTimeout( ) method only a certain number of times.

The last detail is the <body> section, which contains the actual paragraph that you resize and a script that calls ChangeFont( ) for the first time, starting the whole process off:

```
<body>
  <p id="animatedParagraph">This Text is Growing</p>
  <script type="text/javascript">
    ChangeFont( )
  </script>
</body>

</html>
```

Although the resizing paragraph trick is absurdly impractical, the technique is the basis for many much more impressive scripts (to get the whole script and play around with it, download it from the Missing CD page at *www.missingmanuals.com*). For example, you can easily find scripts that animate text in various ways, making it fly in from the side of the page (see *www.codejunction.com/detailed/sequential-fly-in-text-effect.html*); showing words appear one letter at a time, typewriter-style (*www.javascript-page.com/tickert.html*); or making a sparkle float over a title (*www.flooble.com/scripts/animate.php*). Each of these examples uses the same basic approach, but adds significantly more code and gives you a much slicker effect.

Events

The most exciting JavaScript-powered pages are *dynamic*, which means they perform various actions as your visitor interacts with them (moving his mouse, typing in text, clicking things, and so on). A dynamic page is far more exciting than an ordinary XHTML page, which appears in the browser in one shot and sits there, immobile.

To make dynamic pages, you program them to react to JavaScript *events*. Events are notifications that an XHTML element sends out when specific things happen.

For example, JavaScript gives every <a> hyperlink element an event named onmouseover (a compressed version of "on mouse over"). As the name suggests, this event takes place (or *fires*, to use programmer-speak) when a visitor moves his mouse pointer over an XHTML element like a paragraph, link, image, table cell, or text box. That action triggers the onmouseover event and your code flies into action.

Here's an example that displays an alert message when a visitor moves his mouse pointer over a link:

```
<!DOCTYPE html PUBLIC "-//W3C//DTD XHTML 1.0 Strict//EN"
"http://www.w3.org/TR/xhtml1/DTD/xhtml1-strict.dtd">

<html xmlns="http://www.w3.org/1999/xhtml">

<head>
  <title>JavaScript Test</title>
  <meta http-equiv="Content-Script-Type" content="text/javascript" />
</head>

<body>
  <h1>You Will Be Wowed (Again)</h1>
  <p>When you hover over <a href="SomePage.htm"
  onmouseover="alert('Colorless green ideas sleep furiously.')">
this link</a>
  you'll see a secret message.
  </p>
</body>
</html>
```

When you write code to react to an event, you don't absolutely need a script block (although it's a good idea to use one anyway, as shown in the next section). Instead, you can just put your code between quotation marks next to the event attribute:

```
<a onmouseover="[Code goes here]">...</a>
```

There's one detail to keep in mind. In this example, the text argument ('Colorless green…') uses single quotation marks instead of double quotes. That's because the event attribute itself uses double quotes, and using double quotes for two different purposes at the same time will horribly confuse your browser.

When you attach code to an event, your browser assumes you're using JavaScript, which is by far the most popular scripting language. However, to meet the strictest rules of XHTML, you need to explicitly indicate your language choice by adding the following <meta> element to the <head> section of your page:

```
<meta http-equiv="Content-Script-Type" content="text/javascript" />
```

Figure 14-7 shows the result of running this script and moving your mouse pointer over the link.

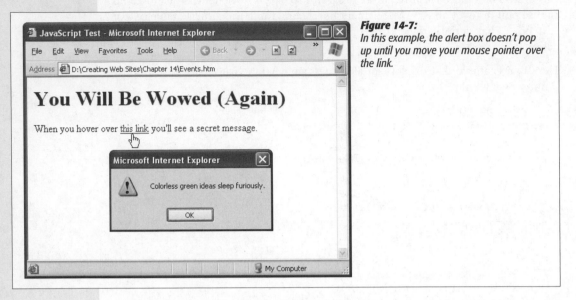

Figure 14-7:
In this example, the alert box doesn't pop up until you move your mouse pointer over the link.

To use events effectively, you need to know what events JavaScript supports. In addition, you need to know which events work on which XHTML elements. Table 14-2 provides a list of commonly used events and the XHTML elements that they apply to (and you can find a more complete reference at *www.w3schools.com/htmldom/dom_reference.asp*).

In the following sections, you'll see two common scenarios that use some of these events.

Note: XHTML requires that events use all-lowercase names, which is dreadfully unreadable. The event list in Table 14-2 breaks that rule so that you can review the event names more easily. However, when you use these events in your Web pages, you need to replace the mixed-case name (like onMouseOver) with all lowercase letters (like onmouseover) to satisfy the laws of XHTML.

***Table 14-2.** Common XHTML object properties*

Event Name (with uppercase letters)	Description	Applies To Which XHTML Elements
onClick	Triggered when you click an element.	Almost all
onMouseOver	Triggered when you move your mouse pointer over an element.	Almost all
onMouseOut	Triggered when you move your mouse pointer away from an element.	Almost all

Table 14-2. *Common XHTML object properties (continued)*

Event Name (with uppercase letters)	Description	Applies To Which XHTML Elements
onKeyDown	Triggered when you press a key.	<select>, <input>, <textarea>, <a>, <button>
onKeyUp	Triggered when you release a pressed key.	<select>, <input>, <textarea>, <a>, <button>
onFocus	Triggered when a control receives focus (in other words, when the cursor appears there so you can type something in). Controls include text boxes, checkboxes, and so on—see page 343 in Chapter 12 for a refresher.	<select>, <input>, <textarea>, <a>, <button>
onBlur	Triggered when focus leaves a control.	<select>, <input>, <textarea>, <a>, <button>
onChange	Triggered when you change a value in an input control. In a text box, this event doesn't fire until you move to another control.	<select>, <input type="text">, <textarea>
onSelect	Triggered when you select a portion of text in an input control.	<input type="text">, <textarea>
onError	Triggered when your browser fails to download an image (usually due to an incorrect URL).	<img>
onLoad	Triggered when your browser finishes downloading a new page or finishes loading an object, like an image.	<img>, <body>, <frame>, <frameset>
onUnload	Triggered when a browser unloads a page. (This typically happens after you enter a new URL or when you click a link. It fires just *before* the browser downloads the new page.)	<body>, <frameset>

Image Rollovers

One of the most popular mouse events is the *image rollover* event. To write one, you start by creating an <img> element that displays a specific picture. Then, when a visitor's mouse pointer moves over the image, your browser displays a new picture, thanks to the onmouseover event. Creating an image rollover is fairly easy. All you do is get the XHTML object for the <img> element, and then modify the *src* property.

In this situation, you can't get everything done with a single line of code. You could pile your entire script into the event attribute (using semicolons to separate each line), but that would be dreadfully confusing. A better choice is to write the code as a function. You can then hook the element up to the function using the event attribute.

For example, here's the function to swap an image. This example writes the function in a very generic way using parameters, so you can reuse it over and over, as you'll see in a moment. Every time you call the function, you indicate which image you want to change (by supplying the corresponding ID) and what new image file you want to use. That way, you can call the same function for any image rollover, anywhere on your page.

```
<script type="text/javascript">
   function ChangeImage(imageName, newImageFile) {
      // Find the object that represents the img element.
      var image = document.getElementById(imageName)

      // Change the picture.
      image.src = newImageFile
   }
</script>
```

When you create an image rollover, you need to use two events. The onmouseover event switches to the rollover picture, and the onmouseout event (triggered when your visitor moves her mouse pointer *off* the XHTML element) switches back to the original picture.

```
<img id="SwappableImage" src="pic1.gif" alt=""
onmouseover="ChangeImage('SwappableImage', 'LostInterestMessage.gif')"
onmouseout="ChangeImage('SwappableImage', 'ClickMe.gif')" />
```

Figure 14-8 shows the result.

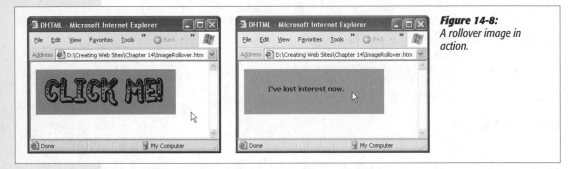

Figure 14-8:
A rollover image in action.

If you want to add more rollover images, just add a new <img> element with a different name. The following element uses the same initial image, but shows a different rollover image each time a visitor moves her mouse pointer on and off the image:

```
<img id="SwappableImage2" src="pic1.gif" alt=""
onmouseover="ChangeImage('SwappableImage2', 'MouseOverPicture.gif')"
onmouseout="ChangeImage('SwappableImage2', 'InitialPicture.gif')" />
```

If you want to get really fancy, you can even use the onclick event (which occurs when you click an element) to throw yet another picture into the mix.

Note: You'll get your hands dirty with more image rollovers when you create fancy buttons in Chapter 15.

Collapsible Text

Another nifty way to use events is to create *collapsible pages*. The basic idea behind a collapsible page is this: If you've got a lot of information to show your viewers but don't want to overload them with a lengthy page, you hide (or collapse) chunks of text behind headlines that viewers can click when they want to see the details (see Figure 14-9).

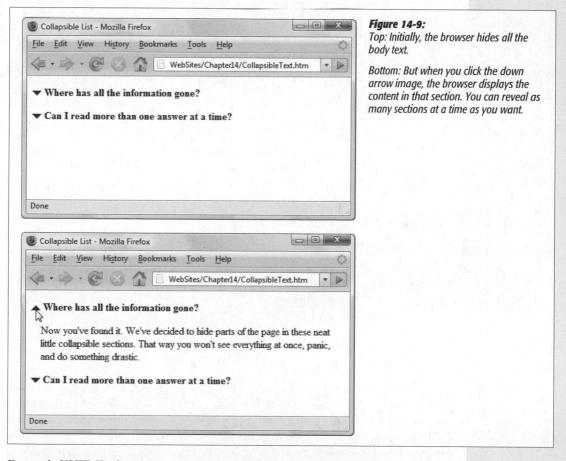

Figure 14-9:
Top: Initially, the browser hides all the body text.

Bottom: But when you click the down arrow image, the browser displays the content in that section. You can reveal as many sections at a time as you want.

Dynamic XHTML gives you many ways to trick browsers into hiding text to create a collapsible page, and the next example shows one of the best. The technique revolves around the CSS *display* property. When you set this property to *block*, an item appears in the XHTML page in the normal way. But when you set it to *none*, the element disappears, along with everything inside it.

The first ingredient in making a collapsible page is to create the function that performs the hiding and the showing. The function requires two parameters: the name of the open/close image, and the name of the element you want to hide or show. The function actually does double duty. It checks the current state of the section, and then it changes that state. That means that it automatically shows a hidden section and automatically hides a displayed section, thanks to conditional logic. At the same time, the function changes the open/close image to display a different type of arrow.

Note: This practice, where you always reverse the current state of an item, is called *toggling* by jargon-happy programmers.

```
<script type="text/javascript">
  function ToggleVisibility(image, element){
    // Find the image.
    var image = document.getElementById(image)

    // Find the element to hide/unhide.
    var element = document.getElementById(element)

    // Check the element's current state.
    if (element.style.display == "none"){
      // If hidden, unhide it.
      element.style.display = "block"
      image.src = "open.png"
    }
    else
    {
      // If not hidden, hide it.
      element.style.display = "none"
      image.src = "closed.png"
    }
  }
</script>
```

The code starts out by looking up the two objects you need and storing them in the variables *image* and *element*. Then it gets to work. It looks at the current state of the paragraph and makes a decision (using an *if* statement) about whether it needs to show the paragraph or hide it. Only one part of this conditional code runs. For example, if the browser is currently hiding the image (if the display style is *none*), the function runs just these two lines of code, then skips to the bottom of the function and ends:

```
element.style.display = "block"
image.src = "open.png"
```

On the other hand, if the browser is displaying the image, this code gets a chance to prove itself:

```
element.style.display = "none"
image.src = "closed.png"
```

To use this function, you need to add the <img> element that performs the toggling to your Web page. You also need to add the XHTML section that contains the hidden content. You can show or hide virtually any XHTML element, but a good all-purpose choice is a <div> element because you can stuff whatever you want to hide inside it. Here's an example:

```
<p>
  <img id="Question1Image" src="closed.png" alt=""
  onclick="ToggleVisibility('Question1Image','HiddenAnswer1')" />
  <b>Where has all the information gone?</b>
</p>

<div id="HiddenAnswer1">
  <p>Now you've found it. We've decided to hide parts of the
  page in these neat little collapsible sections. That way you won't
  see everything at once, panic, and do something drastic.</p>
</div>
```

The first part of the page markup (between the first <p> elements) defines the question heading, which visitors always see. It contains the image and the question (in bold). The second part (in the <div> element) is the answer, which your code alternately shows or hides.

Best of all, because you put all the complicated stuff into a function, you can reuse the function to make additional collapsible sections. These sections have the same structure, but different contents:

```
<p>
  <img id="Question2Image" src="closed.png" alt=""
  onclick="ToggleVisibility('Question2Image','HiddenAnswer2')" />
  <b>Can I read more than one answer at a time?</b>
</p>

<div id="HiddenAnswer2" style="display:none">
  <p>You can expand as many or as few sections as you want.
  Once you've expanded a section, just click again to collapse it back up
  out of sight. The only rule is that when you leave this page and come back
  later, everthing will be hidden all over again. That's just the way
  JavaScript and Dynamic XHTML work.</p>
</div>
```

Notice that you have to give each <img> and <div> element a unique id or your function won't know which picture to change and which section to hide.

Optionally, you can change this page to give it a different feel but keep the same collapsing behavior. For example, you can make the page easier to use by letting your visitor expand and collapse sections by clicking the heading text (instead of just the image). The easiest way to do this is to pop the image and the bold heading into a <div> element, and then add the onclick event attribute to that <div> element. Here's the change you need:

```
<div onclick="ToggleVisibility('Question1Image','HiddenAnswer1')">
  <p>
  <img id="Question1Image" src="closed.png">
  <b>Where has all the information gone?</b>
  </p>
</div>
```

You could even underline the heading text so it looks like a link, which lets viewers know something will happen if they click it. Use the *text-decoration* style sheet property to underline the heading (page 155).

Finally, if you want all your collapsible sections to start off as collapsed, you need to add another script that performs this service. Here's the <script> block you need, which you can position at the end of your page, just before the closing </body> tag:

```
<script type="text/javascript">
  // Hide all sections, one by one.
  ToggleVisibility('Question1Image','HiddenAnswer1')
  ToggleVisibility('Question2Image','HiddenAnswer2')
  ...
</script>
```

You could hide your collapsible sections more easily by setting the *display* style property on each <div> element with an inline style rule (page 146). However, this approach runs into trouble if a visitor turns off JavaScript, in which case every section will remain permanently hidden. By using the code approach shown here, you ensure that JavaScript-challenged browsers will simply display all the content, including the collapsible sections. The page won't be as impressive, but at least nothing goes missing.

Note: You'll see more collapsible text effects when you tackle collapsible menus in Chapter 15.

An Interactive Form

You see some of the most powerful examples of JavaScript when you combine it with XHTML forms. As you learned in Chapter 12 (page 339), XHTML forms let you create graphical widgets like text boxes, checkboxes, buttons, and more. Without using a client-side programming language like JavaScript or a more powerful server-side programming language, forms are quite limited. However, if you use JavaScript and add a dash of programming savvy, you can create pages that have their own intelligence.

For example, consider the page shown in Figure 14-10. It provides several text boxes where visitors type in numbers, and then it performs a calculation when visitors click a button.

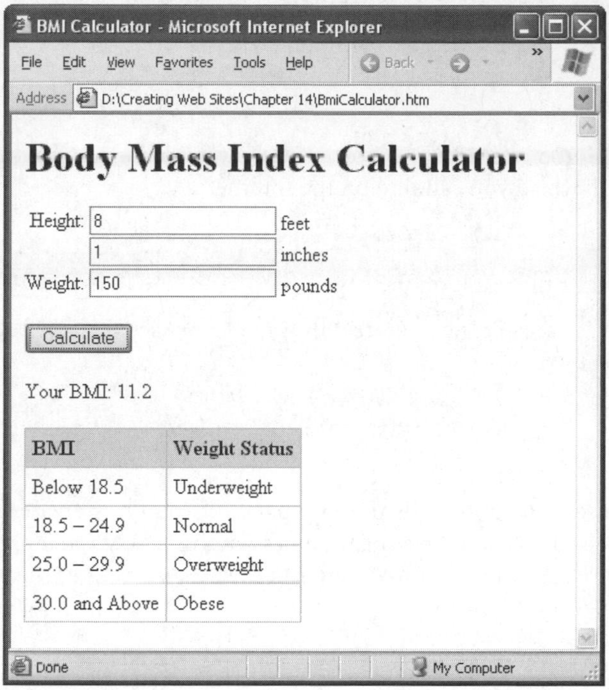

Figure 14-10:
BMI, or Body Mass Index, is a popular way to calculate a person's overall health by taking their height and weight into consideration. It produces a single number that you can compare against a few standard values. The BMI calculation is thought to be accurate for most people, but there are always exceptions.

Building this example is surprisingly easy. The trickiest part is creating the function that powers the underlying calculations. This function needs several pieces of information, corresponding to the values in the three text boxes (feet, inches, and pounds). The function also needs the name of the element where it should display the results. Here's what the function looks like to start with:

```
<script type="text/javascript">
   function CalculateBMI(feet, inches, pounds, resultElementName) {
```

Tip: *You could create a CalculateBMI( ) function that doesn't take any arguments. Instead, the function could just search for all the controls on the page by name. However, using arguments is always a good idea, because it makes your code more flexible. Now you can use the CalculateBMI( ) function on all kinds of different pages, with or without a form.*

The function code that follows isn't much different from what you've seen before. One trick is that it begins by using a Number( ) function that's hardwired into JavaScript. This function converts the text a visitor types in to numbers that the function can use in its calculations. If you don't take this step, you might still get the right answer (sometimes), because JavaScript can automatically convert textual strings into numbers as needed. However, there's a catch—if you try to *add* two numbers and JavaScript thinks they're strings, it will just join the two strings into one piece of text, so 1+1 would get you 11. This mistake can really scramble your calculations, so it's best to always use the Number( ) function, like so:

```
inches = Number(inches)
pounds = Number(pounds)
feet = Number(feet)
```

The actual calculation isn't too interesting. It's taken straight from the definition of Body Mass Index, or BMI, which you can find on the Internet.

```
var totalInches = (feet * 12) + inches
```

Finally, the function displays the result on the page:

```
var resultElement = document.getElementById(resultElementName)
resultElement.innerHTML =
Math.round(pounds * 703 * 10 / totalInches / totalInches) / 10
}
</script>
```

Creating the form that uses this function is the easy part. All you do is create the text boxes with <input> elements and give them names you can easily remember. In this example, the form uses a table to make sure the text boxes line up neatly next to each other:

```
<form action="">
  <table>
    <tr>
    <td>Height: </td>
    <td><input type="text" name="feet" /> feet</td>
    </tr>
    <tr>
    <td> </td>
    <td><input type="text" name="inches" /> inches</td>
    </tr>
    <tr>
    <td>Weight: </td>
    <td><input type="text" name="pounds" /> pounds</td>
    </tr>
  </table>
```

Finally, at the bottom of the form, you create a button that calls the CalculateBMI( ) function using the form's values. To have the button make this call, you need to program your page to react to the onclick event. To look up a value in a form, you don't need the getElementById( ) function. Instead, you access it by name through the *this.form* object, which represents the current form:

```
<p>
    <input type="button" name="calc" value="Calculate"
    onclick="CalculateBMI(this.form.feet.value, this.form.inches.value,
this.form.pounds.value, 'result')" />
    </p>
</form>
```

The final ingredient is the element that displays the result. In this case, because you want it to appear inside another paragraph, the <span> element makes more sense than the <div> element (see page 122 to review the difference).

```
<p>
    Your BMI: <span id="result"></span>
</p>
```

You can use all sorts of other form-related scripts. For example, you can check the information that people enter into forms for errors before letting them continue from one page to another. To learn more about these tricks, you need to take your search to the Web, as described in the next section.

Scripts on the Web

JavaScript is a truly powerful tool. If you're a die-hard alpha nerd who likes to program your TiVo to talk to your BlackBerry, you'll enjoy long nights of Java-Script coding. However, if you don't like to lie awake at night wondering what *var howMany = (trueTop>1?"s" : "");* really means, you'll probably be happier letting someone else do the heavy lifting.

If you fall into the nonprogrammer camp, this chapter has some very good news. The Web is flooded with free JavaScript. In fact, it's easier to find free scripts on the Web than free clip art, style sheets, or MIDI music. Most of the time, these scripts include step-by-step instructions that explain where to put the functions, what elements to use in your page, and how to hook your elements up to functions using events.

Although the list of JavaScript sites is too long to print, here are some good starting points:

- *http://webdeveloper.earthweb.com/webjs*

  Offers a huge collection of JavaScript standards.

- *http://javascript.internet.com*

  Provides a solid catalog of 2,000 bread-and-butter scripts.

- *www.javascript-2.com*

  Tips the scales with a staggering 9,000 scripts.

- *www.dynamicdrive.com*

  Provides a smaller set of scripts that emphasize modern programming techniques based on Dynamic XHTML. Includes exotic scripts like glowing green letters that tumble down the page, Matrix-style. Offers many scripts that are IE-only, but clearly indicates browser support for each script.

- *www.javascripter.net/faq*

  Unlike the other sites, this one doesn't offer a catalog of complete downloadable scripts. Instead, it's organized as a set of frequently asked JavaScript questions, with the relevant code for each answer.

- *www.webmonkey.com/tutorial/JavaScript_Tutorial*

  Unlike the other sites, this one offers a smaller set of detailed JavaScript tutorials instead of a huge variety of standalone scripts. Useful if you want to learn more about some of the core JavaScript techniques.

UP TO SPEED

Script Categories

To get a handle on the types of Dynamic HTML scripts available, look through the different categories at Dynamic Drive (*www.dynamicdrive.com*). Here's a sampling of what you'll find:

The Calendars category has scripts that produce nifty XHTML that looks like calendars—great for displaying important dates or letting visitors plan in advance.

The Date & Time category has live clocks and countdowns to a specific date.

The Document Effects category has page transitions and background effects (like fireworks or floating stars).

The Dynamic Content category has menus that slide out, sticky notes, and scrollable panels.

The Form Effects category has scripts for managing forms (see page 339). You can use them to make sure visitors submit forms only once, check for invalid entries, and more.

The Games category has complete miniature games, like tic-tac-toe and Tetris. These games stretch the capabilities of JavaScript and Dynamic XHTML as far as they can go.

The Image Effects category has slideshow and image gallery scripts, along with dynamic images that change pictures when you move your mouse.

The Links & Tooltips category has fancy links that flash, button tricks, and pop-up text boxes that capture your visitors' attention.

The Menus & Navigation category has handy collapsible menus and navigation bars that let visitors move through your site, like the ones you'll see in Chapter 15.

The Mouse and Cursor category has scripts that change the mouse pointer and add those annoying mouse trails (pictures that follow the mouse pointer wherever it goes).

The Scrollers category has marquee-style scrolling text, like you might see in a news ticker.

The Text Animations category has scripts that bring text to life, making it shake, fly, glow, or take on even more bizarre characteristics.

The User/System Preference category has scripts that dig up information about the browser that's currently displaying your page.

The Window and Frames category has scripts for a dozen different types of pop-up windows.

Using this list, you can dig up everything from little frills to complete, functioning Tetris clones. But keep in mind that a script is only as good as the coder who created it. Even on sites with good quality control, you could stumble across a script that doesn't work on all browsers or slows your page down to a sluggish crawl. As a rule of thumb, always try out each script thoroughly before you start using it on your site.

Tip: The hallmark of a good script site is that it's easy to navigate. You'll know you've found a bad script site if it's so swamped with ads and pop-ups that you can't find the scripts themselves.

Finding a Cool Script

Ready to hunt for scripts online? The next series of steps takes you through the process from beginning to end.

1. **Fire up your browser and choose your site.**

   In this example, use *www.dynamicdrive.com*.

2. **Choose the category you want from the site's home page (Figure 14-11).**

   In this case, use the Documents Effects category. For a sample of what else you can find, see the box on page 438.

Figure 14-11:
The Dynamic Drive site organizes its scripts into clearly defined categories. If you're looking for something new, scroll down the page and you'll find links to the most recently added scripts. Some sites also provide quick links to reader favorites.

3. **Scroll through the list of scripts in your category (Figure 14-12), and then click one.**

   In this case, use the Top-Down Stripy Curtain Script.

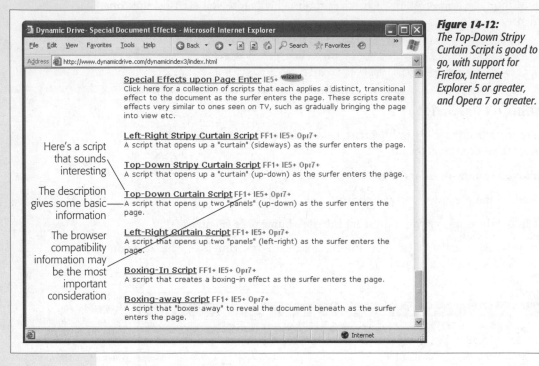

Figure 14-12:
The Top-Down Stripy Curtain Script is good to go, with support for Firefox, Internet Explorer 5 or greater, and Opera 7 or greater.

4. **The next page shows an example of the script (Figure 14-13).**

   Once the page loads, you find a script description, the author's name, and a link to try the script out (if it isn't already being displayed on the page). Underneath all this information are the step-by-step instructions you need to use the script.

5. **Follow the instructions to copy and paste the different parts of the script into your page (Figure 14-14).**

   Often, you get a set of functions you need to put in the <head> portion of your page and then some XHTML elements you need to place in the <body> section. In some cases, you can customize the scripts—for example, you might modify numbers and other values to tweak the script code, or change the XHTML elements to provide different content.

Note: Many scripts include a set of comments with author information. If they do, the rule usually is that you need to keep these comments in your script file, so other developers who check out your site will know where the code originally came from. This practice is just part of giving credit where credit's due. Ordinary Web visitors won't even think to look at the script code, so they won't have any idea whether or not you wrote the script from scratch.

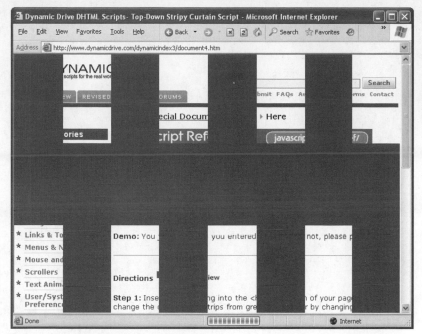

Figure 14-13:
Here's the Top-Down Stripy Curtain Script in action. It fills in the page by drawing alternating black strips, some from top to bottom and others from bottom to top. It all happens in a flash.

Figure 14-14:
The Top-Down Stripy Curtain Script has two components. The first part is a style definition that produces the solid background curtain that's wiped away with the page content. The second part creates the background curtain (as a <div> element) and includes the script code that performs the transition. Copy both of these components to any page, and you're set. (For even better organization, consider placing the code in a separate JavaScript file, as described on page 418.)

★ Links & Tooltips
★ Menus & Navigation
★ Mouse and Cursor
★ Scrollers
★ Text Animations
★ User/System Preference
★ Window and Frames
★ Other

Other Sections
> Script Forums
> Recommend Us
> Usage Terms
> Free JavaScripts

Compatibility
▶ **IE5+:** IE 5 and above
▶ **FF1+:** Firefox 1.0+. NS6+ and FF beta are assumed as well.
▶ **Opr7+:** Opera 7 and above.

Directions ⬛ Developer's View

Step 1: Insert the following into the <head> section of your page. You can change the color of the strips from green to another by changing all three instances of the word "green" to another color name:

Select All

```
<style>
<!--
.intro{
position:absolute;
left:0;
top:0;
layer-background-color:green;
background-color:green;
border:0.1px solid green;
```

Step 2: Finally, insert the below **right after** the <body> tags, before anything else. You can adjust the speed in which the curtain "draws' by changing "speed=20" in the second line to another number (greater is faster):

Select All

```
<div id="i1" class="intro"></div><div id="i2"
class="intro"></div><div id="i3"
class="intro"></div><div id="i4" class="intro"></div><div
id="i5" class="intro"></div><div
id="i6" class="intro"></div><div id="i7"
class="intro"></div><div id="i8" class="intro"></div>
<script language="JavaScript1.2">

/*
```

Fancy Buttons and Menus

Chapter 14 gave you a crash course in JavaScript, the secret ingredient you need to add slick features and frills to ordinary Web pages. Although JavaScript is quirky, arcane, and sometimes frustrating, learning its basics pays off. In this chapter, you'll use that knowledge to create fancy buttons and menus that liven up any Web site.

Although buttons and menus that pulse, swirl, and unfurl may seem like small potatoes, they're actually a hallmark of contemporary Web design. In fact, a stylized button or well-designed collapsible menu is sometimes all the polish you need to make your pages stand out.

Fortunately, you don't need to be a JavaScript whiz to add these sophisticated touches to your site. As you'll see in this chapter, there are plenty of great tools (both in Web editing programs like Expression Web and Dreamweaver and in free online scripts) that can help you get the results you want without all-night JavaScript coding sessions.

Creating Fancy Buttons

In Chapter 8, you learned to use links to let site visitors travel from one page to another. Although ordinary links work perfectly well, they just aren't showy enough for creative Web masters. Modern Web sites guide visitors through their pages with graphical buttons. Figure 15-1 shows an example.

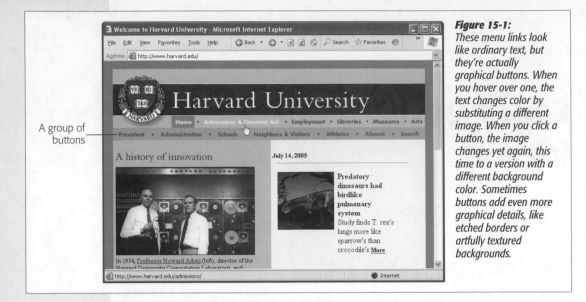

Figure 15-1:
These menu links look like ordinary text, but they're actually graphical buttons. When you hover over one, the text changes color by substituting a different image. When you click a button, the image changes yet again, this time to a version with a different background color. Sometimes buttons add even more graphical details, like etched borders or artfully textured backgrounds.

A group of buttons

A graphical button is really just an image you turn into a link. (In fact, your XHTML refers to these buttons with the familiar <img> element.) You perform this transformation in one of two ways. You can put the image inside an anchor element, as described in Chapter 8. Here's what that looks like:

```
<a href="targetPage.html"><img src="DoItButton.jpeg" alt="Do It" /></a>
```

Unfortunately, when you use this method, XHTML adds an ugly blue border around the image to indicate that it's a link. To get rid of the border, you set CSS's *border-style* attribute (see page 168) to *none*.

Alternatively, you can use the <img> element in conjunction with JavaScript's onclick event attribute (as described on page 428). This is a good approach if you want to animate your page with interactive elements instead of just redirecting visitors with plain-Jane URLs. You used this same approach in Chapter 14 with the BMI calculator (page 434)—visitors clicked a button to have the calculator perform an arithmetic operation and display the result.

Going the JavaScript route has another advantage: It lets you plumb JavaScript's vast library of features to create interactive effects that go beyond simple one-button links. For that reason, this chapter focuses on JavaScript; you'll use it as the core for your site's interactive components.

Here's an example of the JavaScript onclick technique:

```
<img onclick="DoSomething( )" src="DoItButton.jpeg" alt="Do It" />
```

This method doesn't generate an ugly blue border, so you don't need the border-style attribute. However, you do need to create a function named DoSomething( ) with code that does what you need.

Neither of these techniques is new. However, things get a little more interesting if you decide to add *dynamic* buttons to your pages. Dynamic buttons (also known as *rollover buttons*) change subtly but noticeably when a visitor hovers her mouse pointer over them. This change lets the visitor know that she's poised over a real, live button, and all she needs to do is click the button to complete the deal.

To create a dynamic button, you use the image rollover technique described on page 429. Here's a quick overview of how it works: When you mouse over a dynamic button, JavaScript swaps one button image for another. The second image looks similar to the first, yet it's slightly different. And if you click this swapped-in button, off you go to whatever link's associated with it.

Really slick dynamic buttons use *three* pictures—one for the initial state, one for when you hover your mouse pointer over it, and the third for when you click the button (just before the new page appears).

Creating a dynamic button presents two challenges:

- **Creating the button pictures.** Not only should you make these buttons look eye-catchingly cool, the different versions you use (the normal version and the mouseover version) need to line up exactly. If one has text a slightly different size or in a slightly different place, it makes for a jarring effect when your browser swaps the images.

- **Loading the images.** Every dynamic button on your site can use up to three images. For best performance, your browser should download all the images the buttons use as it loads the page. That way, when a visitor moves her mouse pointer over a button, she won't experience a delay as the browser downloads the appropriate mouse-over image.

In the next two sections, you'll learn to create button images and make them dynamic using a dash of JavaScript.

Generating Button Pictures

If you're graphically inclined, you can create button pictures by hand using just about any graphics program (Adobe Illustrator and Macromedia Fireworks are two popular choices). However, getting buttons to look good isn't always easy. It's also hard to mass-produce them, because you need to make sure every button has the text in the same place and a consistent size, color palette, and background.

Fortunately, if you need a bunch of buttons in a hurry, or if your artistic abilities are feebler than those of Koko the painting Gorilla, there's an easier option. You can use a specialized *button creation* program. These programs have no purpose in life other than to help you create attractive buttons with the text, colors, and backgrounds you choose.

The Web's teeming with a range of these tools (see the box on page 446). The following example shows you how to use one of them, ButtonGenerator, to get what you need.

Free Button Makers

Creating a cool rollover button is an age-old problem with plenty of solutions.

On the Web, you'll find a range of online button-making tools. These tools usually start by asking you to specify button details (like the text, color, background, and so on). Once you finish, you simply click a button and the program creates the button image (or images) and displays them in a new page. All you need to do is download the images and start using them in your own pages.

Some examples of online button-making tools include *www.buttongenerator.com* (which you'll see demonstrated in this chapter) and *www.grsites.com/button*. Not all these button makers can create images for each button "state." However, you can usually run the button generator multiple times and choose a slightly different color scheme to create the highlighted button image. For a change of pace, try *www.flashbuttons.com*, which lets you create animated buttons—miniature animations that run using a browser add-in called Adobe Flash (which is described on page 474).

Although these types of buttons are impressive, few Web sites use them because only browsers with Flash installed can display them.

The most powerful button-making tools aren't Web-based at all. They're separate programs you can download and install on your computer. They often give you a richer range of button choices, more configurable options, and features that let you create a pile of buttons at once. Unlike online button-makers, if you go this route you'll need to shop around a bit before you find a program that runs on your operating system (for example, Windows or Mac) and has the right price (free or close to it).

The best place to find free button-making software is a high-quality shareware site like *www.download.com*. Windows fans might be interested in trying out the free *http://freebuttons.org*. And if you have Expression Web, skip ahead to page 458 to find out about its integrated button generator.

1. **Go to *www.buttongenerator.com*.**

   The ButtonGenerator Web site provides separate tools for creating buttons and menus.

2. **To make sure you're using the right tool, start by clicking the Web Button Generator link.**

   Now, scroll down the page until you see the section "Select the web button you wish to edit."

3. **In the Show list, choose Only Free Buttons. Figure 15-2 shows you the list you'll see.**

   ButtonGenerator has a large catalog of button styles, and it offers a rotating selection of them for free. For a small yearly fee, you can join ButtonGenerator.com and access more powerful ButtonGenerator features and its full catalog of buttons.

   If you want to stick with the free option but find something you like in the full catalog, look for the "Will be FREE in" message underneath the button, which tells you when the site will offer this style for free (typically in less than a week from the current date).

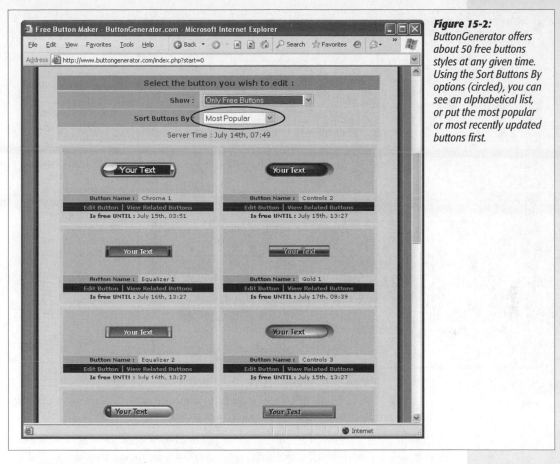

Figure 15-2:
ButtonGenerator offers about 50 free buttons styles at any given time. Using the Sort Buttons By options (circled), you can see an alphabetical list, or put the most popular or most recently updated buttons first.

4. **Once you find a button you like, click to select it.**

   Now you see a page that lets you customize the button.

5. **In the "Choose a mode" list, select Advanced Form.**

   The Advanced Form lets you create an ordinary button image *and* the rollover image at the same time. It also lets you create several buttons at once. The plain-vanilla Easy Form lacks both these valuable features.

6. **Choose a different picture or a different background for the mouse-over version of your button (see Figure 15-3).**

   To create a good dynamic button, you need to differentiate your ordinary button image (called the *initial state* button) from the image that appears when someone mouses over the button (called the *mouse-over state* button). The difference should be noticeable yet subtle.

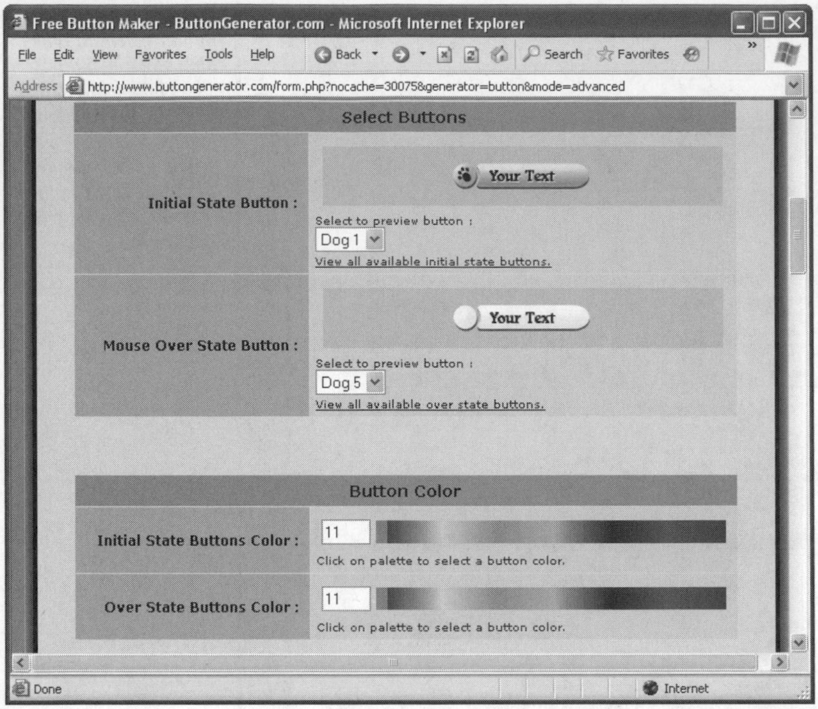

Figure 15-3:
The best way for you to distinguish a normal-state button from a selected one is by choosing different state images, as in this example. The ordinary button uses the Dog 1 state, while the selected button uses Dog 5, which is lighter and doesn't have the paw-print icon. If your button doesn't provide multiple state choices, you'll need to choose different background colors to make the distinction.

7. **In the Background Transparency section, choose Light Background or Dark Background, depending on your page background.**

   Button images often need to use some transparency because they aren't exact rectangles. The Light Background option creates an image that tends to look better when you put it on a white, gray, yellow, or similar background. The Dark Background is a better choice if your pages use a black background.

8. **In the Text Labels section, enter the text you want to appear on the button (see Figure 15-4).**

   If you enter multiple lines of text, each line creates a separate button. This is a great trick for generating a pile of buttons in one go.

9. **In the Text Font section, choose a font for the button text, the font size, and whether or not you want to use anti-aliasing.**

   ButtonGenerator limits you to a relatively small number of fonts. The good news is that you don't need to worry about what fonts your visitors have on their computers because the program generates complete button images (which include the button text), not ordinary XHTML markup.

   Anti-aliasing is a feature that smoothes the edges of a font by blending them in with the background. Usually, this makes the button look more professional.

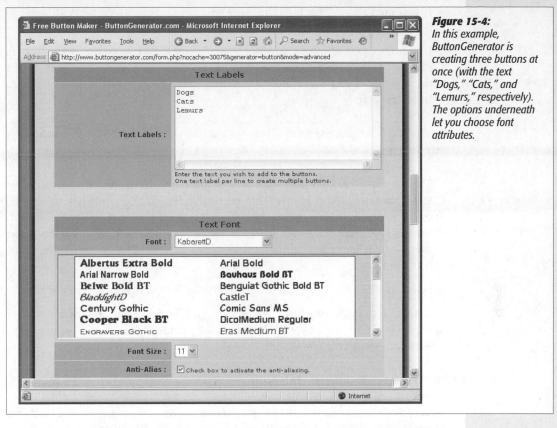

10. In the Text Alignment section, choose left, right, or center alignment, depending on whether you want your text flush with the left edge, lined up on the right, or centered in the middle.

You can also use the X and Y text boxes to offset the text slightly in either direction. Use these settings only if you find that your button text isn't aligned perfectly after you generate it. For example, if you create a button with lowercase text, you might find that the text is positioned too low on the button. You can correct this by using a negative number for the Y value.

11. **Optionally, tweak the colors for various parts of the button in the Text Color and Mouse Over Buttons Text Color sections.**

The Text Color section corresponds to the initial button image. The Mouse Over Buttons Text Color section corresponds to the image that appears when you hover over the button. If you like the current colors, you don't need to change anything.

12. **Optionally, choose an image from the list in the Icon Insertion section.**

If you want, you can embed a small image *inside* your button, like an arrow or a flag. However, you're limited to the options that ButtonGenerator gives you. Usually, you don't need a button icon—it's overkill.

13. **If you want all your buttons the same size, turn on the All Same Width check-box in the Buttons Width section.**

   If you choose this option, ButtonGenerator uses your longest piece of text to calculate the width of the largest button, then makes all the other buttons the same width. If you don't choose this option, the program sizes each button to fit its text exactly.

Tip: If you plan to stack more than one button in a column (for example, to create a navigation bar), make sure you use the All Same Width option. Otherwise, your buttons won't line up.

   There's one other option. If you have a specific width in mind, you can enter that value (in pixels) in the Buttons Width text box. ButtonGenerator then draws all the buttons at that width. This is a good choice if you're fitting buttons to a specific layout and you know exactly how much space you have. However, ButtonGenerator ignores your size setting if it isn't big enough to fit all the text you enter.

14. **Select the Click Here to Generate Your Button link at the bottom of the page.**

   ButtonGenerator creates all your buttons and displays them in a new page (see Figure 15-5). Now it's time to download the pictures (or to click your browser's Back button and try again).

Tip: Once you create your button images, you can't edit them in ButtonGenerator. For that reason, it's a good idea to keep track of the settings you used (like colors, font, text size, and button width). That way, you can generate replacement buttons later on if you need to change the wording or color of your existing buttons. Or, you can create additional buttons that match those you already have.

---

15. **You need to download the pictures one at a time. To save a picture on a Windows PC, right-click the button, and then choose Save As (the actual wording depends on your browser). If you've got a Mac, Control-click the button to access your Save As option.**

   The Save Picture dialog box appears.

16. **In the Save Picture dialog box, browse to your Web site folder, type in a button name, and then click Save. Return to step 14 to save the next picture, and continue until you've saved every image.**

   It's important to use a good naming convention for your button pictures so you don't get lost in a tangle of picture files. One approach is to give each button a descriptive name, followed by an underscore and then the button state. For example, you could name the two pictures for the Dogs button DogsButton_ Normal.png and DogsButton_MouseOver.png.

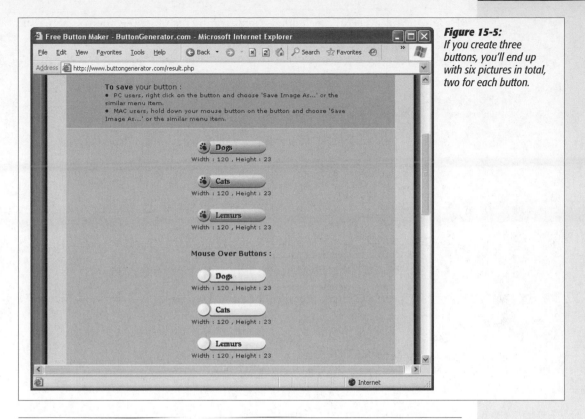

Figure 15-5:
If you create three buttons, you'll end up with six pictures in total, two for each button.

Note: All unregistered ButtonGenerator fanatics are kindly asked to include a link to the ButtonGenerator site somewhere on their Web page. It's completely kosher to bury this detail on an About Us or Credits page. ButtonGenerator provides the XHTML it wants you to include—it's below the button pictures it generates.

Building a Rollover Button

Now that you have the button images you need, you're ready to incorporate them into a Web page. You can use the exact same ChangeImage( ) function you used in Chapter 14 (page 430).

Note: If you use Dreamweaver, you don't need to write the JavaScript on your own. Instead, skip ahead to page 458 (or keep reading if you're curious to learn how rollover buttons really work).

The following example shows a Web page that includes the ChangeImage( ) script and a single <img> element, which represents one button. (This <img> element will show one of two pictures depending on whether a mouse pointer is hovering over the button.) This example puts the button inside an anchor element so that, when visitors click it, they move to another page. This example also includes a style sheet rule that removes the standard blue border that the anchor element adds around its nested image.

Here's the full XHTML, including several comments to help guide you along the way:

```
<html>

<head>
  <title>Fancy Buttons</title>
  <style type="text/css">
    /* Hide the blue link border on all images. */
    img {
      border-style: none;
    }
  </style>
  <meta http-equiv="Content-Script-Type" content="text/javascript" />

  <script type="text/javascript">
  // This is the script for swapping button pictures.
  function ChangeImage(imageID, newImageFile) {
    // Find the object that represents the img element.
    var image = document.getElementById(imageID)

    // Change the picture.
    image.src = newImageFile
  }
  </script>
</head>

<body>
  <p>
    <!-- Create the link with the dynamic button inside. -->
    <a href="Dogs.html">
      <img id="Dogs" src="DogsButton_Normal.png" alt="Dogs"
      onmouseover="ChangeImage('Dogs', 'DogsButton_MouseOver.png')"
      onmouseout="ChangeImage('Dogs', 'DogsButton_Normal.png')" />
    </a>
  </p>

</body>

</html>
```

Figure 15-6 shows the result.

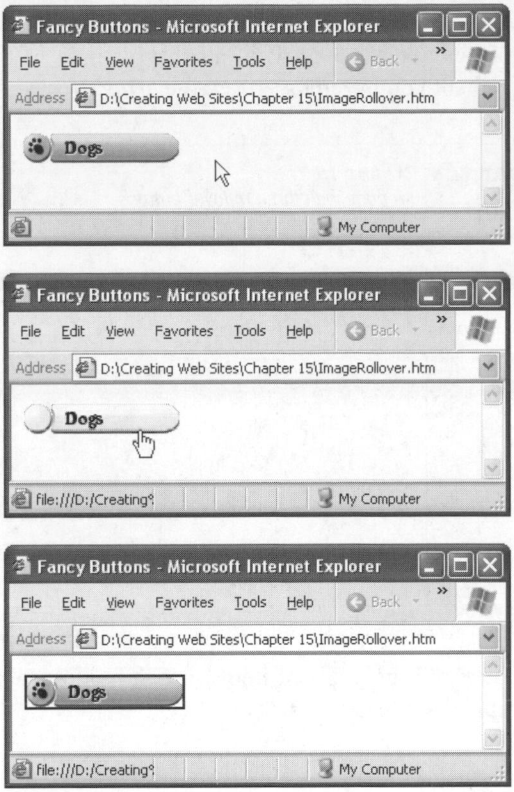

Figure 15-6:
Top: The rollover button in its initial state.

Middle: The rollover button when a mouse pointer hovers over it.

Bottom: The rollover button without the style rule that hides the border. Without this ever-important style rule, a blue rectangle appears as a clumsy indication that the button's a link.

Using image lists

Although this page gets the job done, it's a little more complicated than it needs to be. First, the declaration for the <img> element is quite long. Worse, if you make a slight mistake when you type in the image IDs or picture URLs, the code won't work. In a page with dozens of buttons, keeping all this information straight becomes a headache, especially if you store your pictures in a subfolder, which makes the URLs much longer. And if you add the image preloading technique discussed a bit later (on page 457), you're in even more danger of derailing your code with a minor mistake in the picture URL.

To minimize the chance of error, pages with rollover buttons commonly use another JavaScript technique. They declare all of the picture URLs in a single list, and put this list in a script block at the start of the page. The list assigns each picture URL a number, like 1 for the first button picture, 2 for the second, and so on. From that point onward, the rest of your page refers to each picture by number, which shortens your XHTML and simplifies life considerably.

To see the advantage of this approach, it helps to consider an example with more buttons. Consider Figure 15-7, which uses three similar buttons that all have images from *www.buttongenerator.com*. To keep track of all the pictures in this example, you use a JavaScript ingredient you haven't seen yet: the *array*.

Figure 15-7:
A page with three rollover buttons.

An array is a JavaScript object that represents a list of items. It can hold as many items as you want. Here's an example that creates an array:

```
var myArray = new Array()
```

Initially, this array is empty. To put information into it, you use square brackets to indicate an *index number*. This is where arrays get a little wonky, because they use *zero-based numbering*. This is a fancy way of saying that an array assigns the first item in a list the index number 0, the second item in the list the index number 1, and so on. Strange as it seems, programmers always start counting at 0.

Here's an example that puts a text string into the first slot of the array:

```
myArray[0] = "This is the first item"
```

In the example shown in Figure 15-7, you're dealing with three buttons. Each one has an initial image and a mouse-over image. To track these two sets of images, it makes sense to create two arrays, one for normal-state images (which you can name imgN) and one for selected buttons (imgS). Here's the code that creates the arrays and stores all the image URLs:

```
<script type="text/javascript">
  // The image lists.
  var imgN = new Array()
  imgN[0] = "DogsButton_Normal.png"
  imgN[1] = "CatsButton_Normal.png"
  imgN[2] = "LemursButton_Normal.png"
```

```
      var imgS = new Array( )
      imgS[0] = "DogsButton_MouseOver.png"
      imgS[1] = "CatsButton_MouseOver.png"
      imgS[2] = "LemursButton_MouseOver.png"
      ...
```

Now you can rewrite the button code so that it retrieves the button names from the array:

```
   <a href="Dogs.html">
     <img id="Dogs" src="DogsButton_Normal.png"
     onMouseOver="ChangeImage('Dogs', imgS[0])"
     onMouseOut="ChangeImage('Dogs', imgN[0])">
   </a>
```

There's another change you can make to streamline the code and make the ChangeImage( ) function easier to use. Right now, the current version of ChangeImage( ) uses two arguments—one for the ID of the <img> element, the other for the file name of the new image. Check it out:

```
   function ChangeImage(imageID, newImageFile) {
```

You can simplify life by modifying the ChangeImage( ) function so that it accepts an *object* that represents the <img> element, instead of the *name* of the <img> element itself. Here's the modified version:

```
      // This is the script for swapping button pictures.
      function ChangeImage(image, newImageFile) {
        image.src = newImageFile
      }
   </script>
```

As you can see, this means that you no longer need to have your script go hunting for an image object with the document.getElementById( ) method. This change also gives you a handy shortcut. When you call ChangeImage( ), you can specify the *current* element using a special keyword named *this*. The *this* keyword always refers to the object for the current element—in this case, that current object is the <img> element. Here's how it works:

```
   <a href="Dogs.html">
     <img src="DogsButton_Normal.png" alt="Dogs"
     onmouseover="ChangeImage(this, imgS[0])"
     onmouseout="ChangeImage(this, imgN[0])" />
   </a>
```

Take a moment to compare this code to the more painful version on page 452. With the above script, you no longer need to give each <img> element a unique ID to keep track of it. You also don't need to type in the picture URLs every time you call ChangeImage( ). Instead, imgS[0] refers to the first selected button image, and imgN[0] refers to the first normal button image.

Note: Keen eyes may notice that the initial image URL still appears in the *src* attribute of the <img> element. You might wonder if there's a way to set this detail through JavaScript code using the imgN array. Although it's possible, it's not a good idea. That's because the current approach works even when a browser doesn't support JavaScript. In that situation, the fancy rollover effect doesn't work, but the browser still displays the ordinary button image. If you relied entirely on JavaScript, the buttons wouldn't appear at all on feebler browsers.

To complete this example, you need an <img> element for each button. The following code groups all the buttons into a <div> element so that, using a style rule, you can position all the buttons together along the left-hand side of your Web page:

```
<div class="Menu">
  <p>
    <a href="Dogs.html">
      <img src="DogsButton_Normal.png" alt="Dogs"
      onmouseover="ChangeImage(this, imgS[0])"
      onmouseout="ChangeImage(this, imgN[0])" />
    </a>
  </p>
  <p>
    <a href="Cats.html">
      <img src="CatsButton_Normal.png" alt="Cats"
      onmouseover="ChangeImage(this, imgS[1])"
      onmouseout="ChangeImage(this, imgN[1])" />
    </a>
  </p>
  <p>
    <a href="Lemurs.html">
      <img src="LemursButton_Normal.png" alt="Lemurs"
      onmouseover="ChangeImage(this, imgS[2])"
      onmouseout="ChangeImage(this, imgN[2])" />
    </a>
  </p>
</div>
```

Here's the style rule that formats this <div> element, lining it up neatly on the left side of the page:

```
div.Menu {
  float: left;
  margin-right: 20px;
  margin-top: 20px;
  height: 1000px;
}
```

For a quick refresher on style sheet-based layout, pop back to page 247.

Preloading images

With the current example, it's only a little bit more work to use *image preloading*. This technique ensures that a browser downloads the mouse-over images when it processes the page for the first time, instead of waiting until a visitor moves his mouse pointer over a button. Although you won't notice the difference when you run the page from your computer's hard drive, preloading images makes the buttons more responsive when visitors interact with them over the Internet, particularly if they've got a slow connection.

The technique for preloading images requires a bit of a quirky workaround. Basically, you need to trick your browser into thinking that you're using the rollover pictures right away. This convinces it to download the images without delay.

Then, later on, when you hover over a button and the ChangeImage( ) method runs, your browser gets ready to download the mouse-over image. However, being a relatively clever program, the browser immediately realizes that it *already has* the image stored away in its *cache* (a temporary location in memory or on disk for storing recently visited pages and other recently downloaded files). As a result, the browser abandons its download plans and uses the image it already has.

To preload images, you need to add a function that downloads the rollover pictures. The first step is to create a dummy image object in memory. You won't actually use this image object to do anything but download your button images, but the browser doesn't know that.

```
function PreloadImages( ) {
  // Create a "dummy" image.
  var preloadedImage = new Image( )
  ...
```

Next, the script reads through the entire imgS list of rollover images, using a programming construct called a *for loop*. Each time it finds an image, it stuffs it into the image object, which convinces the browser to download it.

```
  ...
  // Load all the pictures into this image object, one after another.
  for (var j = 0; j < imgS.length; j++) {
    preloadedImage.src = imgS[j]
  }
}
```

A for loop repeats code a certain number of times using a built-in counter. In this case, the counter is a variable named *j* that starts at 0, and keeps increasing the variable number until it matches imgS.length—in other words, until it gets to the last item in the imgS array. Assuming the imgS array has three items, your browser executes this statement three times:

```
  preloadedImage.src = imgS[j]
```

The first time, j is 0, and the code loads up the first image in the list. The second time, j is 1, and it digs up the second image. You can guess what happens the third time.

Strangely enough, that's all you need to do. Even though you're not using the images, the browser still obligingly fetches them from your Web server and stores them in its cache.

The only remaining step is to make sure you call the PreloadImages( ) function when your browser first loads the page. You do this by adding the onload event attribute to the <body> element, as shown here:

```
<body onload="PreloadImages( )">
```

That's it. Your rollover buttons are now Web-ready!

Creating Rollover Buttons in Dreamweaver and Expression Web

If you're using a Web page editor like Dreamweaver or Expression Web, you don't need to write your own JavaScript code. Both programs provide a built-in way to quickly create rollover buttons.

In Dreamweaver, select Insert → Image Objects → Rollover Image. You see an Insert Rollover Image dialog box, which you can use to set all the important details (Figure 15-8). Click OK, and Dreamweaver creates the <a> and <img> elements and adds the JavaScript code for swapping images.

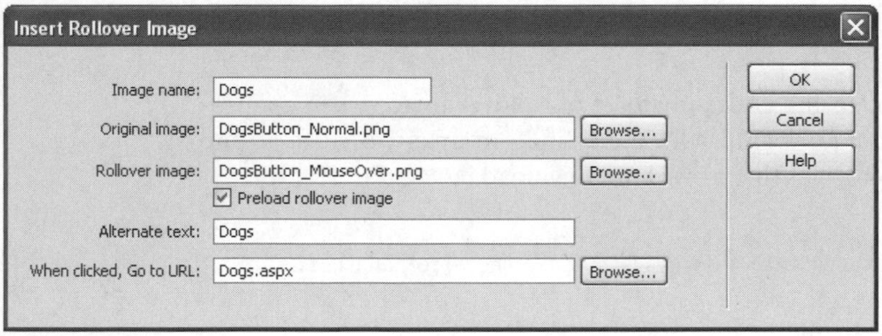

Figure 15-8:
To create a rollover button in Dreamweaver, you supply a unique button name, the normal-state and mouse-over images, any alternate text you want to appear if a browser can't display the image, and the target URL. You can also check the "Preload rollover images" option to insert JavaScript code that downloads the images for the rollover buttons when the browser first loads the page.

The only way to improve on this feature is with a tool that not only inserts a rollover button, but also creates the button images you need, based on the text and style options you choose. Expression Web provides the goods with a feature it calls *interactive buttons*.

To create an interactive button in Expression Web, select Insert → Interactive But-ton. Expression Web presents you with an impressively featured button generator (see Figure 15-9).

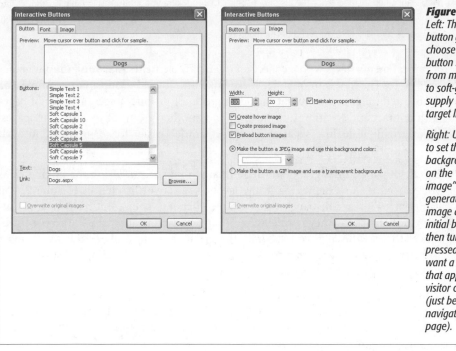

Figure 15-9:
Left: The Expression Web button generator lets you choose from a long list of button styles, ranging from metallic rectangles to soft-glow tabs. You supply the text and the target link.

Right: Use the Image tab to set the button size and background color. Turn on the "Create hover image" checkbox to generate a mouse-over image along with the initial button image, and then turn on "Create pressed image" if you want a third image, one that appears when a site visitor clicks the button (just before the browser navigates to the new page).

When you save your Web page, Expression Web prompts you to choose file names for all the button pictures you created using the Interactive Buttons dialog box.

The best part about the Expression Web button generator is that it's easy to modify your button settings and regenerate the button pictures later on. Just open the page that has the button, double-click the button in the editor, modify the settings in the Interactive Buttons dialog box, and then click OK to generate the new images.

Creating Fancy Menus

Rollover buttons are wildly popular on the Web, and it's easy to see why. There's something irresistible about a button that lights up when you mouse over it. You can, however, have too much of a good thing, and stuffing too many rollover but-tons on a page is a surefire way to create an overdone turkey of a Web site.

More recently, the Web's seen a small renaissance in simplicity and a trend away from excessive rollover buttons. Part of the reason is the increasing complexity of Web sites—quite simply, a handful of rollover buttons no longer offers enough navigational aid for today's typically complex sites. Instead, these sites use more detailed multilevel menus, replacing dozens of rollover buttons with a clearer, more streamlined set of hierarchical links.

Tip: Fancy buttons and fancy menus play a similar role in taking visitors from one page to another in a Web site. If you have a relatively small site, you may choose to use buttons exclusively. If you have a large site, you're more likely to use a combination of menus and buttons.

A typical menu starts with a collection of anchor elements that you group together on a page. The key is to organize these links into logical groups. For example, the Web site for a company might include a group of product pages, a group of pages with contact and location information, and another group of tech support pages. By arranging links into separate groups, it's much easier for visitors to find what they're looking for.

So far, this menu design doesn't require anything special. Using the linking skills you picked up in Chapter 8 and the layout smarts you gained in Chapter 9, you can easily create a side panel with a grouped list of anchors. But really neat menus add another trick—they're *collapsible*. That means you don't see the whole list of links at once. Initially, you see only the group headings, like Products, Contact Information, and Tech Support. When you click a group heading, a list of related links pops open just underneath.

You can create collapsible menus in a variety of ways. Some are easy, while others are dizzyingly complicated. In the following sections, you'll learn how to build a simple collapsible menu of your own, and then use a more complicated menu courtesy of a free JavaScript site.

Do-It-Yourself Collapsible Menus

You can create a respectable menu of your own using the collapsible Dynamic XHTML trick described in Chapter 14 (page 431). The basic idea is to use Java-Script to hide and show specific XHTML elements by changing the CSS *display* property.

Imagine you want to create the cool two-level tabbed menu shown in Figure 15-10. This page splits its links into three separate groups, each of which it represents on-screen by a tab. Only one tab shows its sublinks at a time.

This design might seem a little intimidating, but it consists of only two parts: the tabs at the top of the page, and the link boxes (menus) that appear dynamically underneath them. To make these regions easy to deal with, it makes sense to wrap them in <div> and <span> elements, as you've seen throughout this book.

Note: In the rest of this section, you'll get a chance to look at the solution piece by piece. To see the complete page, check out the downloadable content for this chapter, available from the Missing CD page at *www.missingmanuals.com*.

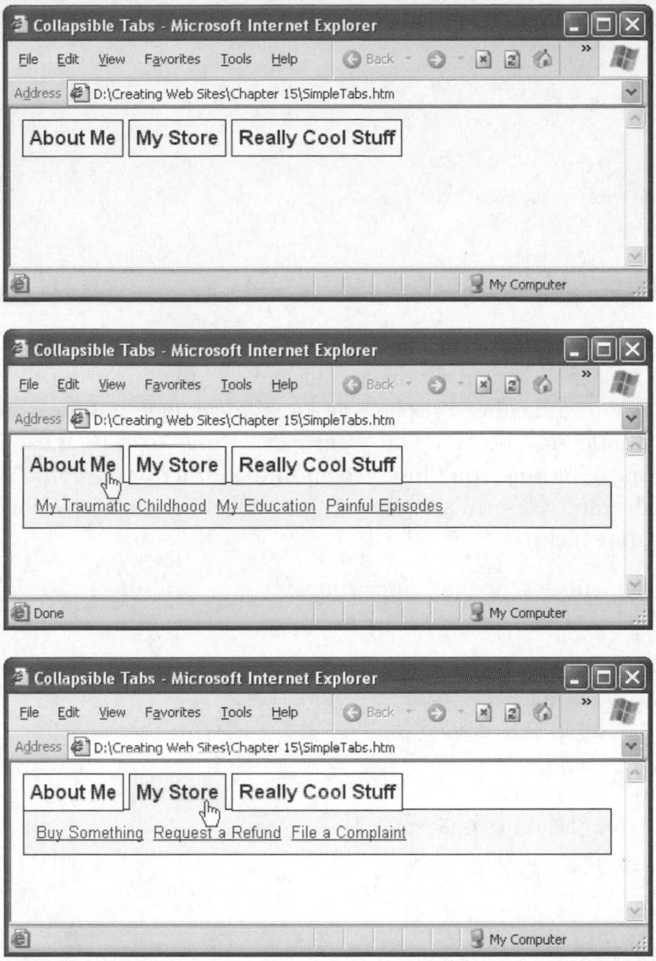

Figure 15-10:
Top: When this page first loads, it presents visitors with three tabs.

Middle and bottom: As a visitor moves the mouse pointer over a tab box, a set of related links appears underneath.

Because the three tabs appear next to each other on the same line, the <span> element is the best choice. Remember, the <div> element adds a line break and some space between each element. The <span> element is an inline element, which means you can fit it inside an existing paragraph and put more than one <span> element side by side.

Here's the XHTML you start with:

```
<span class="Tab">About Me</span>
<span class="Tab">My Store</span>
<span class="Tab">Really Cool Stuff</span>
```

These <span> elements have the descriptive class name Tab. That associates them with the following style sheet rule, which gives the tabs the correct font and borders:

```
.Tab {
  font-weight: bold;
  padding: 5px;
  border-style: solid;
  border-width: 1px;
}
body {
  font-family: Veranda, sans-serif;
}
```

After you declare the <span> elements, it makes sense to add the link groups. You can write each link group with either a <span> or a <div> element, but the <div> element makes the most sense because you want each group to exist independently on the page (meaning you won't insert them into another paragraph). You also need to give each <div> element a unique ID, so you can change its visibility based on the tab a visitor clicks.

Here are the <div> elements for the three link groups:

```
<div id="AboutMe" class="Links">
  <a href="...">My Traumatic Childhood</a> 
  <a href="...">My Education</a> 
  <a href="...">Painful Episodes</a>
</div>
<div id="MyStore" class="Links">
  <a href="...">Buy Something</a> 
  <a href="...">Request a Refund</a> 
  <a href="...">File a Complaint</a>
</div>
<div id="ReallyCoolStuff" class="Links">
  Just kidding.
</div>
```

Even though this example stacks these <div> elements one on top of the other, you won't ever see them this way on a page. When a page first loads, your browser hides all the menus, thanks to the style rule for the Links class:

```
.Links {
  display: none;
  border-width: 1px;
  border-style: solid;
  padding: 10px;
  background-color: lightyellow;
  font-size: small;
}
```

These style sheet rules, <span> elements, and <div> elements create the basic framework for your page. The final step is to create a script that displays one of the hidden <div> elements, depending on which tab your visitor selects.

The code you need is similar to that used in the ToggleVisibility( ) function demonstrated in Chapter 14 (page 432). The difference is that in this case, you're not interested in hiding and showing individual sections. Instead, you want to show a single section (depending on the tab selected) and hide everything else. A custom function named MakeVisible( ) handles this task.

Here's a simplified version of the MakeVisible( ) function. As you can see, it takes an element name, finds the element, and changes its style settings to make it appear on the page.

```
function MakeVisible(element){
   // Find the element and unhide it.
   var element = document.getElementById(element)
   element.style.display = "block"
}
```

Now you can hook this function up to all the tab buttons. You have a choice here—MakeVisible( ) could react to either a click using the onclick event, or to a mouse pointer hovering over the tab using the onmouseover event. This example uses the latter approach.

```
<span class-"Tab" onmouseover="MakeVisible('AboutMe')">About Me</span>
<span class="Tab" onmouseover="MakeVisible('MyStore')">My Store</span>
<span class="Tab" onmouseover="MakeVisible('ReallyCoolStuff')">Really Cool
      Stuff</span>
```

The page still isn't quite right. Although the MakeVisible( ) function shows the correct tabs, it doesn't hide anything. That means that if you pass your mouse pointer over all three tabs, you'll see all three groups of links at the same time, one above the other.

To hide the other tabs, you need to get a little craftier. The problem is that MakeVisible( ) knows what tab it's supposed to show, but it doesn't know the status of the other tabs. To find these tabs, your code needs to search through the rest of the page. In this example, the basic approach is to look for any <div> element that has the class name Links and hide it. You can perform this step at the beginning of the MakeVisible( ) function, so that it hides *all* the menus. Then, you need the code you saw before to display just the menu you want.

Here's the corrected MakeVisible( ) function:

```
function MakeVisible(tab, element) {
   // Get an array with div elements.
   var links = document.getElementsByTagName("div")

   // Search the array for link boxes, and hide them.
```

```
      for (var j = 0; j < tabs.length; j++) {
        if (links[j].className == 'Links') links[j].style.display = "none"
      }

      // Find the element and unhide it.
      var element = document.getElementById(element)
      element.style.display = "block"
    }
```

This code is a little tricky. As with the rollover example earlier in this chapter (page 457), it uses an array and a for loop. In this case, the array has a list of all the <div> objects on your page. As the code moves through this list, it checks the class name of each <div> element. If the class name indicates that you've found a link box, the code makes it disappear from the page by changing the display style.

The code in the downloadable example gets slightly fancier—it also fiddles with the tab to change the background border color and hide the border for the selected tab. However, the basic approach is the same.

Note: If the stranger aspects of JavaScript still look like Danish, don't worry. If you're inclined, you can learn about JavaScript programming features like arrays, loops, and if statements from a dedicated book or Web site (see page 414 for some good resources). Or, you can keep your sanity and rely on the examples provided with this book and find great free scripts online.

Third-Party Menus

If you've had enough fun writing your own JavaScript code, you'll be happy to hear that the Web is chock-full of free menu scripts. Many of these have more dazzle than the tabbed menu shown in the previous example. Some of the extra features you might find include:

• Multilevel menus that let your visitors drill down into specific subcategories.

• Pop-up menus that appear "above" your Web page when you click them.

• Ridiculously showy effects, like shaded highlighting and transparent backgrounds.

To find a good menu, you can use any of the JavaScript sample sites described in Chapter 14 (see page 437). You'll find that there's quite a bit more diversity in menus than in rollover buttons. Every menu looks and behaves a little differently. Some pop up, others slide out, and others try to emulate the look and feel of popular programs like Microsoft Outlook.

To get a glimpse of what's out there, head over to Dynamic Drive, which has a nifty set of menus at *www.dynamicdrive.com/dynamicindex1* and a particularly interesting specimen (called, rather unimaginatively, Top Navigational Bar III) at *www.dynamicdrive.com/dynamicindex1/topmen3*. Figure 15-11 shows this menu with the menu structure used in the tabbed menu example earlier in this chapter.

Tip: Before you choose a navigation bar for your own Web site, you'll want to test drive quite a few. This section walks you through the process, but you'll want to compare the results with other navigation bars before you commit to one.

In the following sections, you download the script code for Top Navigation Bar III and use it to create your menu.

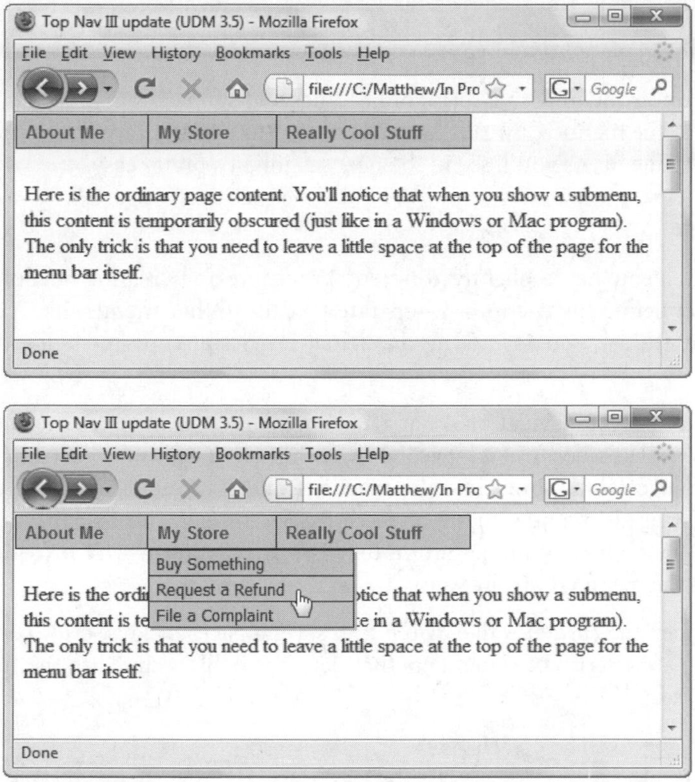

Figure 15-11:
Top Navigational Bar III is a lot like the menus in Windows and Mac programs. When you pop open a menu, it appears on top of the existing Web page content.

Getting the script

To download Top Navigational Bar III, follow these steps:

1. **Go to** *www.dynamicdrive.com/dynamicindex1/topmen3*.

   You'll see a page that displays the navigation bar, and provides step-by-step instructions for using it. A detailed table describes the browser support for Top Navigational Bar III, and the news is good—it works in every mainstream browser.

2. **Look for the download link for the** *topmenu3.zip* **file. Click it, and then save the ZIP file somewhere on your computer.**

   To use Top Navigational Bar III, you need a whole bunch of JavaScript files. To make life easy, they're all included in a single ZIP file.

3. **Unzip the contents of *topmenu3.zip*. Put them in the folder on your PC where you store all your site pages.**

   Unzipping a file is pretty easy. Just double-click *topmenu3.zip* to open it up, and then drag all the files to their new destination folder.

   Altogether, *topmenu3.zip* contains a text file with instructions (*readme.txt*), a sample page that shows the menu (*template.html*), a JavaScript file that defines the menu shown in the sample page (*custom.js*), and nine more JavaScript files that contain the behind-the-scenes code that powers the menu.

4. **Open the page *template.html* in your Web browser.**

   You'll see a sample menu with a series of headings and subheadings. To change this menu into the menu you really want, you need to edit the JavaScript code that defines the menu. As you'll see in the next section, it's pretty easy.

Creating the menu

Every JavaScript menu has a slightly different procedure for creating it. Some menus make you define the menu in a separate text file. Other menus, like Top Navigational Bar III, ask you to modify the actual JavaScript code to define the links you want.

Defining a menu for Top Navigational Bar III is fairly easy, but at times the code looks a bit wacky. That's because it's packed full of different options you can set, which let you change colors, fonts, and the exact size and placement of every submenu. You won't need to adjust many of these details. In fact, most of the time you'll start with the sample menu definition that Top Navigation Bar III provides, and edit it to get the menu you really want.

To get started, open the *custom.js* file. You'll find several pages of JavaScript code. At the beginning are a series of statements that define variables. Here are the first three lines you'll see:

```
var menuALIGN = "left"; // alignment
var absLEFT = 1;        // absolute left position (if menu is left aligned)
var absTOP  = 1;        // absolute top position
```

Note: The code in this example looks a little different because every statement ends with a semicolon (;). This is a C programming convention that's supported (but optional) in JavaScript. Programming types like the convention because it clearly indicates where each line ends. This section uses it because the developers of Top Navigational Bar III used it.

Next to each variable is a terse comment that gives you a clue about its purpose. For example, the first line defines a variable named *menuALIGN*. The comment informs you, rather unhelpfully, that this detail sets the "alignment." In fact, *menuALIGN* controls the alignment of the text in the menu, and a value of *left*, used here, lines the menu captions up with the left edge of the menu. (You could replace this with the value *center* to center each caption in each menu box.) And while *menuALIGN* may not seem that interesting, there are dozens of similar details ready for your tweaking. Table 15-1 lists a few of the most useful ones.

***Table 15-1.** Useful variables for Top Navigation Bar III*

Variable Name	Description	Sample Value
absLEFT and absTOP	Places the menu on your page using absolute positioning (page 253).	Set both to *10* to put the top-left corner of the menu 10 pixels from the top-left corner of your page. Set them to *0* to create a menu fused right to the top-left edge.
fFONT and fSIZE	Sets the font and font size for the first level of menu captions (those that appear without any clicking). Remember to use the Web-friendly fonts that every browser has (page 157).	Set fFONT to "Arial" and fSIZE to *13* if you want 13-pixel Arial text.
sfFONT and sfSIZE	Works the same magic as fFONT and fSIZE, but only applies to submenus.	See above.
mCOLOR and rCOLOR	Sets the background color for top-level menu items, both initially (mCOLOR) and when a mouse hovers over them (rCOLOR, where *r* stands for *rollover*).	Use CSS color names (like *"blue"*) or more fine-tunable color codes (like *#ffddaa*). Page 152 has more about Web page colors.
smCOLOR and srCOLOR	Does the same color-changing feat as mCOLOR and rCOLOR, but for submenus.	See above.
stretchMENU and showBORDERS	Lets you create an interesting effect: padding the right side of the menu so it stretches to the edge of a browser window.	Set both to *true* to make your menu look like an uninterrupted menu bar that continues all the way to the right side of a browser window, no matter what its size.

For now, ignore the long list of variables, and scroll down to the code that actually defines the menu. Top Menu Navigational Bar III uses three commands to create every menu:

- **addMainItem( )** creates a top-level menu heading. The example in Figure 15-11 has three such headings (About Me, My Store, and Really Cool Stuff).

- **defineSubmenuProperties( )** sets up a submenu. You use it immediately after addMainItem( ). Here's where you set the submenu width.

- **addSubmenuItem( )** inserts an item into a submenu. You use this after you set up the submenu with defineSubmenuProperties( ).

To create a menu, use these commands in the same, unwavering order, until you fill in the whole menu structure that you want. For example, to start the menu shown in Figure 15-11, you use this line of code:

```
addMainItem("", "About Me", 100, "", "", "", 0, 0, "", "", "", "", "");
```

This statement looks a fair bit more complex than it should. The problem is that addMainItem is ridiculously flexible—it lets you supply numerous arguments (13 in all) that fine-tune details like placement and colors. Many of these are the same details you saw in the variables section, but their presence here lets you fine-tune each and every menu command in a different way (which is usually a bad idea). If you're interested in unleashing your inner designer, read the comments in the code to find out what you can use. Otherwise, stick to the barebones format shown above, which includes only two essential details: the menu text ("About Me") and the menu width (100 pixels). Keep the zeroes and blank text strings for every other argument.

After creating a top-level menu item, you need to use defineSubmenuProperties( ) to configure it. Once again, you have a ridiculous number of options. The only argument that's essential is the submenu width. Here, it's set to 160 pixels:

```
defineSubmenuProperties(160, "", "", 0, 0, "", "", "", "", "", "", "");
```

Now, you fill in the submenu by calling addSubmenuItem( ) once for each menu item. You also need two essential arguments. First, you need an absolute or relative link that tells the browser where to go when a visitor clicks this menu item (in this example, it's a page named *Childhood.htm*). Second, you need the descriptive menu text (in this case, it's the words "My Traumatic Childhood." Here's the code that fills in the About Me submenu:

```
addSubmenuItem("Childhood.htm", "My Traumatic Childhood", "", "");
```

Note: Remember, you don't need to understand how this code works (or why the syntax is the way it is) to use it. You simply need to copy the sample code exactly, and replace the menu captions and page links with yours. (You should also test your page with a range of different browsers and on different operating systems.)

Now you know just about everything you need to know to create fancy menus for your site's navigation menu. You just need to repeat the previous step to create each menu item.

Here's the complete code that creates the My Store submenu:

```
addMainItem("", "My Store", 100, "", "", "", 0, 0, "", "", "", "", "");

defineSubmenuProperties(160,"","",0,0,"","","","","","","");

addSubmenuItem("Buy.htm", "Buy Something", "", "");
addSubmenuItem("Refund.htm", "Request a Refund", "", "");
addSubmenuItem("Complaint.htm", "File a Complaint", "", "");
```

Continue this process of defining submenus until you create all the menus you want. The only rule you need to keep in mind is that you create the menu items in the same order in which you want them to appear on the page.

Placing the menu on a page

All the work you've done editing the custom.js file prepares the menu you want to display on your Web site. To make it actually appear, you need to insert it into a Web page. Fortunately, this process is easy. In fact, the *template.html* file included with Top Navigational Bar III shows you exactly how to do it. You can copy this file and insert your own Web page content. Or, you can study it and copy the essential details into another file to add the menu to an existing page.

Here's a bare-bones Web page that highlights the details you need:

```
<!DOCTYPE html PUBLIC "-//W3C//DTD XHTML 1.0 Strict//EN"
"http://www.w3.org/TR/xhtml1/DTD/xhtml1-strict.dtd">

<html xmlns="http://www.w3.org/1999/xhtml">
<head>
  <title>...</title>
  <script type="text/javascript" language="javascript" src="sniffer.js">
  </script>
  <script type="text/javascript" language="javascript1.2" src="custom.js">
  </script>
  <script type="text/javascript" language="javascript1.2" src="style.js">
  </script>
</head>

<body>
  <p>Here is the ordinary page content...</p>

  <script type="text/javascript" language="javascript1.2" src="menu.js">
  </script>
</body>
</html>
```

As you can see, you can give any page a menu with Top Navigational Bar III simply by adding four <script> elements. If you want to use different menus in different pages, just edit the <script> element, and then replace the file name *custom.js* with the file that contains your menu.

Note: Once you perfect your Web site and you're ready to take it live, remember to upload *all* the Java-Script files that come with Top Navigational Bar III.

CHAPTER 16

Audio and Video

In the early days of the Internet, Web sites were about as jazzy as an IRS form. You'd see pages filled with an assortment of plain text, links, and more plain text. Over time, the Web matured, and Web pages started to change as designers embraced the joys of color, pictures, and tacky clip-art. But when that excitement started to wear off, it was time for a new trick—multimedia.

Multimedia is a catchall term for a variety of technologies and file types, all of which have dramatically different PC requirements and pose different Web design challenges. Multimedia includes everything from the irritating jingle that plays in the background of your best friend's homepage to the wildly popular movie clip of a cat playing the piano. (Depressing fact: with over 10 million views, it's unlikely you'll ever create a Web page that's half as popular.)

In this chapter, you'll consider how to use several types of multimedia. First, you'll learn to play background music and sound effects. Then you'll learn to use Flash to put a real music player in your Web page. Finally, you'll see how to use YouTube to popularize your own movie clips, and take a shot at becoming the center of attention.

Note: Before you go any further, take a moment to consider the worst examples of multimedia abuse. These include flashing banner ads, irritating background music, time-wasting intro pages, and bandwidth-sucking commercials. Before you jump on the multimedia bandwagon, think about what you want to do. Are you planning to showcase your musical compositions or provide downloadable recordings of Junior's first moments? If so, multimedia probably makes sense. But if you're just looking for a way to dazzle visitors with an animated logo, think twice. It's probably not worth the considerable effort to design something that will only aggravate most of your readers.

Understanding Multimedia

There comes a point when every new Web designer wants more than mere text and pictures. Even spruced-up fonts and elegant page layouts don't satisfy the design envy many newcomers feel when they spot a site loaded with sound and motion. That's understandable: You, too, want to trick out your pages with audio and video. But before you can jazz up your site, you need to understand a few basics.

Linking, Embedding, and Hosting

One of the key choices you make when you outfit your pages with multimedia is whether to link to or embed the files you're adding.

Linking to multimedia content is the simplest but least glamorous approach. It lets you create a link that *points to* an audio or video file you've stored along with all your other XHTML pages and files. There's really nothing to creating linked multimedia. You use the same lowly anchor element and *href* attribute you used in Chapter 8. Here's an example:

```
Would you like to hear <a href="IndustrialNoiseBand.mp3">Industrial Noise</a>?
```

Figure 16-1 shows what happens when you click one of these babies.

Note: It makes absolutely no difference what kind of software your Web host's server runs when you add audio to your site. When someone clicks a link to an audio file, the browser downloads the file to the visitor's PC and plays it there, not from the server.

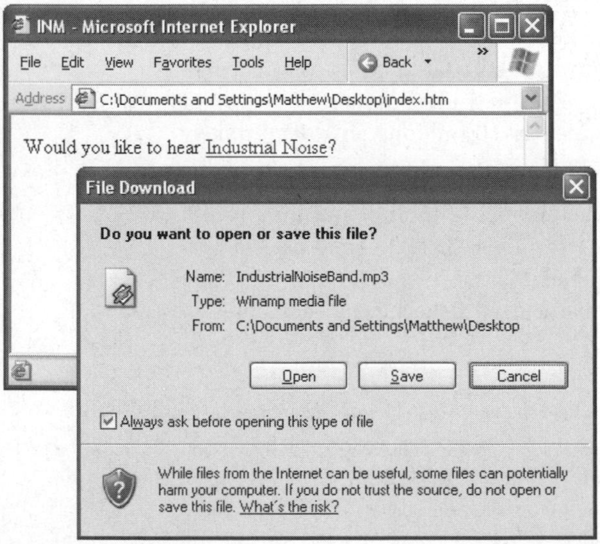

Figure 16-1:
When you click a link to a multimedia file, your browser asks whether you want to save the multimedia file or open it straightaway. If you choose the latter, your browser first downloads the file, and then launches it using a separate program. The actual program your browser uses to play the file depends on the software installed on your PC. For example, if you use the popular Winamp program (www.winamp.com) to play MP3 files, the downloaded song heads straight to your Winamp play list. Other common players include Apple QuickTime Player and Windows Media Player.

Embedding multimedia is a more advanced approach. It *integrates* music or video into your XHTML page. As a result, you can create rich combinations of text, sound, and video.

But embedding multimedia can be a challenge. Multimedia files come in many different formats, as you'll see in the next section. Some browsers support some of these formats, but few, if any, support all of them. Other browsers have no native multimedia compatibility at all. While visitors can add multimedia support with browser plug-ins (small programs that extends a browser's capabilities), you have no way of knowing which plug-in your visitors have. The bottom line? There's no guarantee that your visitors can see any particular type of multimedia content you embed on a page.

The Web offers a couple of solutions to embedded multimedia, neither of them ideal. One exists in the form of the slightly disreputable <embed> element, which you'll learn to use on page 476.

Note: The distinction between linking and embedding multimedia is the same as the distinction between linking to a picture (with the <a> element), and embedding it right in your page (with the <img> element). The only difference is that images are a basic, well-supported part of the XHTML standard, so embedding pictures never causes much concern. However, embedding audio and video takes you into less-well-charted waters.

But there's one other option for managing multimedia. That solution is *hosted multimedia*—multimedia files stored on someone else's server but displayed (or linked to) on your Web page. The best-known example of hosted multimedia is YouTube, a ridiculously popular site that plays back more than 100 million video clips every day.

Hosted multimedia is an excellent choice if you want to display really large files, particularly movie clips. It won't tap out your Web site's bandwidth (page 69), and it works with virtually all browsers and operating systems. Its only drawback is that you give up a fair bit of control. For example, if you use YouTube to host your videos, you can't show movies that are longer than 10 minutes, and YouTube ratchets down your movie's quality to make sure it performs well. (Technically, YouTube reduces the video's file size so browsers can download them more quickly—that way, visitors experience no delay in playback when they push the play button.) You'll learn to use YouTube on page 494.

Types of Multimedia Files

Your decision to link or embed files depends, at least in part, on the type of multimedia content you want to showcase. Because XHTML has no multimedia standard of its own, other companies have innovated to fill the gap. Today, there's a slightly bewildering field of choices.

Here are the types of multimedia files you can add to your pages:

- **Synthesized music (MIDI).** MIDI files store notes that your PC's sound card generate on playback, rather than playing back a recording of a musical instrument. As a result, MIDI files are small but of questionable quality. Although the actual audio quality depends on your visitor's sound card, the results most commonly resemble a cheesy Casio keyboard. But because MIDI files are lightweight, and since almost all browsers support them, they're commonly used for Web page background music. (MIDI stands for Musical Instrument Digital Interface.)

- **Digital audio (WAV and MP3).** These file types store recorded audio, which means they're of higher quality than MIDI files. But WAV files are enormous, making them unsuitable for all but the most bloated Web sites. MP3 files are one-tenth the size of WAVs, but browsers often require a plug-in to play them, which means you can't embed them with impunity.

- **Digital video (MPEG, AVI, MOV, and WMV).** These file types are multimedia's heavy hitters. They let you play back video that ranges in quality from thumbnail-sized windows with jerky playback to DVD-quality movies. Digital video files are a challenge for any Web page creator because they're ridiculously large. To have even a chance of making digital video perform acceptably, you need to compress, shrink, and reduce your clip's size and quality using video editing software.

- **Animated GIFs.** Animated GIFs consist of a series of small, still images displayed one after the other in rapid succession, like a flipbook. If you see a Web site with dancing cartoon characters, spinning text, or a pulsing globe (don't ask), you're probably looking at an animated GIF. Most Web-heads dismiss animated GIFs as not being "real" multimedia because they're so simple. But they're small, pretty easy to create, and widely supported.

- **Flash.** Flash is a versatile playback standard designed especially for the Web. It supports video files, animation, and interactivity. Flash also supports *vector-based* animation, which uses mathematically rendered images—shapes built on the fly as a result of complex calculations—rather than pixel-based graphics. As a result, even intricate animations boast small, quick-to-download files, making Flash the perfect medium for animated logos, commercials, and dazzling intro screens (see Figure 16-2). Finally, Flash supports interactivity, so Flash experts can build lightweight but slick menus and embedded games that really enliven sites.

Despite these impressive pluses, Flash has three drawbacks: First, to create Flash content you need specialized software from Adobe, which runs into the hundreds of dollars. Second, even if you shell out the Flash cash, creating professional animations requires the skill of a talented Flash *artiste*. Finally, visitors won't be able to see Flash movies unless they have a Flash plug-in installed. (That said, good estimates suggest that over 90 percent of Web-connected computers have the Flash plug-in.)

Note: Multimedia hosters, like YouTube, use Flash to show their movies. That's because Flash gives the best combination of customizability, performance, and compatibility. Of course, these high-powered companies also have plenty of cash to pay their programming teams.

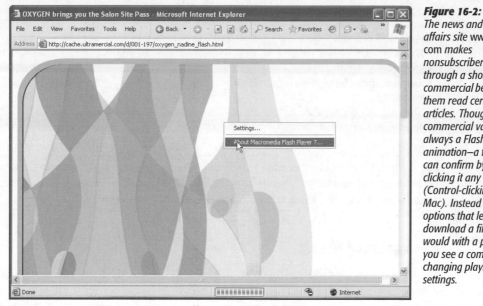

Figure 16-2:
The news and current affairs site www.salon. com makes nonsubscribers sit through a short commercial before letting them read certain articles. Though the commercial varies, it's always a Flash animation—a fact you can confirm by right-clicking it any time (Control-clicking on a Mac). Instead of seeing options that let you download a file (as you would with a picture), you see a command for changing playback settings.

It's difficult to digest all this information at once. If you're still mulling over your choices, take a look at the scenarios in Table 16-1 to help you sort out the roles different multimedia types play.

Table 16-1. Multimedia scenarios

If You Want To:	Then Use:	Embedded, Linked, or Hosted
Play a synthesized version of your favorite pop tune in the background	MIDI files	Embedded
Play a short loop of digital audio continuously in the background	Flash. (You can use the MP3 format instead, but not all browsers support it, and the looping is less precise.)	Embedded
Let visitors download your band's newest indie recordings	MP3 files (record your music using WAV files, then covert them to MP3 format to save space).	Linked

Table 16-1. *Multimedia scenarios (continued)*

If You Want To:	Then Use:	Embedded, Linked, or Hosted
Let visitors see your favorite home movie	MPEG, AVI, WMV, or MOV files (but make sure you use video-editing software to dramatically reduce file size).	Hosted (on a service like YouTube)
Show a stock animation effect, like clapping hands, a flashing star, or a dancing bean	Animated GIFs or Flash (for more features and a slicker animation).	Embedded
Show an animated intro screen or commercial	Flash	Embedded
Show a humorous animated story you've created	Flash	Embedded

Tip: If you plan to create a Web site with a lot of digital audio and video, you'll need to reconsider its space and bandwidth requirements (see page 71). Unlike ordinary XHTML pages and Web graphics, multimedia files can grow quite large, threatening to overwhelm your Web host's space and bandwidth allotment.

Background Music

Most people like to browse the Web in peaceful silence. That means no trance-hypno-ambient background tracks, no strange disco beats, and no sudden cymbal crashes. This aversion to noise may be due to the fact that something like 98 percent of all Web browsing takes place on company time.

But if you like to startle and annoy people, or if you're absolutely convinced that your Web audience really *does* want some funky beats, keep reading to bring on the background music.

The <embed> Element

Although the XHTML standard doesn't support background music, almost all browsers support the <embed> element, first pioneered by Netscape in the early days of the Web. You can put the <embed> element anywhere on your page. Here's a basic page that uses it to play background music:

```
<!DOCTYPE html PUBLIC "-//W3C//DTD XHTML 1.0 Transitional//EN"
"http://www.w3.org/TR/xhtml1/DTD/xhtml1-transitional.dtd">

<html xmlns="http://www.w3.org/1999/xhtml">
<head>
  <title>Background Music</title>
</head>
```

```
<body>
<h1>Automatic, Unsolicited Music</h1>
<p>The music now blaring from your speakers is
Scarlatti's first sonata (K. 500).
I hope you didn't tell your colleagues you were working!</p>

<embed src="soundfile.mid" />
</body>
</html>
```

The <embed> element gives you a slew of options for playback control. If you use the element without specifying any of them (as in the previous example), your visitors see a page like the one shown in Figure 16-3 and hear its audio file automatically.

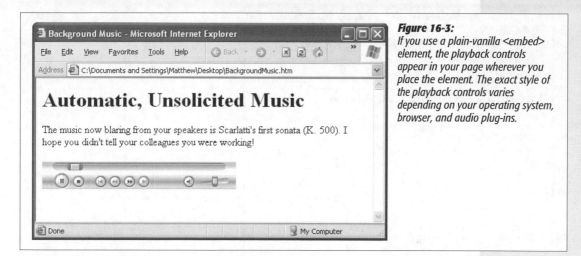

Figure 16-3:
If you use a plain-vanilla <embed> element, the playback controls appear in your page wherever you place the element. The exact style of the playback controls varies depending on your operating system, browser, and audio plug-ins.

Music playback isn't always this seamless, however. Because every browser handles embedded music a little differently, you can run into problems like the ones shown in Figure 16-4. The best advice is to test your page on at least the three main browsers (Internet Explorer, Firefox, and Safari).

The <embed> element harbors an ugly secret—it's not valid XHTML. In fact, it's not even a recognized part of the HTML language. Despite its poor pedigree, it works seamlessly in all modern browsers. But there's still a price to pay. Once you put the <embed> element in your Web page, you can no longer validate your page using an XHTML checker (like the one described on page 49). If you've sworn to uphold the standards of XHTML, this may weigh heavily on your heart. Or perhaps not—many rogue Web designers think nothing of using <embed> and retaining the XHTML doctype, which is necessary to avoid the browser inconsistencies of quirks mode (see page 31). It's up to you whether you're ready to violate the spirit of XHTML to get what you want.

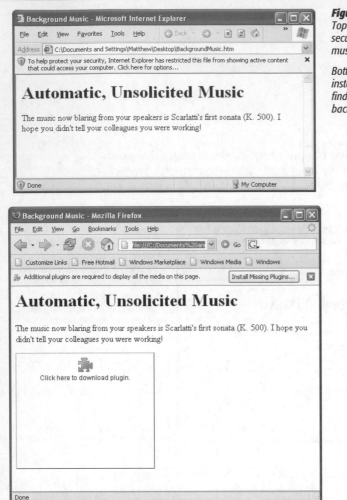

Figure 16-4:
Top: Paranoid visitors sometimes step up their security settings, which can lock out your music.

Bottom: Depending on what a Web visitor has installed or uninstalled, a browser might not find the components it needs to play your background music.

Note: There's one alternative to the <embed> element. You can use the <object> element, which lets you insert audio, video, and other types of plug-in content in a Web page. (Later in this chapter, you'll use the <object> element with Flash files.) Even thought the <object> element is more standardized, it actually suffers from more browser quirks. When you use the <object> element to play sound, it's surprisingly difficult to make sure your Web page works in different browsers.

Embedded audio options

Ordinarily, the <embed> element starts playing music as soon as your browser downloads the specified music file. Visitors can kill the sound with a quick click of the stop button (assuming you display the playback controls), but if they're not expecting to hear a burst of music it's enough to frazzle some nerves.

A more polite way to handle background audio is to display the playback controls and let your visitors decide when to click the play button. This design is easy—just use the *autoplay* attribute:

```
<p>If you'd like some soft music to browse by, click the play button.</p>
<embed src="soundfile.mid" autoplay="false" />
```

Turning off autoplay is considered good Web etiquette. A much poorer idea is the *hidden* attribute, which lets you hide the playback controls altogether. All too often, you'll find Web pages that use <embed> elements like this:

```
<embed src="soundfile.mid" hidden="true" />
```

In this example, the sound file plays automatically. Because the playback controls are hidden, the only way someone can stop it is to lunge for the volume control. Web sites that put their visitors through this ordeal rarely see a return visit.

Note: Unfortunately, autoplay and hidden playback controls are all too common on the Web. Some Web designers become intoxicated with their newfound multimedia abilities, and decide it's not enough to let visitors listen to music—they force them to. Resist the urge.

The <embed> element offers quite a few more frills. Table 16-2 has the lowdown.

Table 16-2. Attributes for the <embed> element

Attribute	Description
src	The URL that points to an audio file.
autoplay	A true or false value that indicates whether the audio should start playing immediately (true) or wait for your visitor to click the play button (false).
hidden	A true or false value that indicates whether the playback controls are visible.
loop	A true or false value that indicates whether the audio should be played once (from start to finish), or repeated endlessly. When looping audio, you'll notice a distinct pause before the audio restarts.
volume	A value between 1 and 100 that specifies playback volume as a percentage of maximum volume. 100 percent is the loudest you can get. 50 percent tends to produce the standard volume on a Windows computer; on Macs, you get that effect at 75 percent. If you set your volume to 100 percent, you can be sure you won't get any repeat visitors. When you use the volume attribute, supply a number only (leave out the % sign).
border, width, and height	These attributes let you set the dimensions of the playback controls and the border around them, in pixels. You can achieve greater customization by applying a style sheet rule (see Chapter 6).

Other audio formats

As you learned earlier, MIDI files are remarkably small because they store digitally generated notes. Because of that, they don't usually sound that great, and they don't sound the same on everyone's computer. MIDI files are fun, but they often make a site seem amateurish.

GEM IN THE ROUGH

Finding MIDI Files

Although MIDI files usually sound cheesy, you can't complain about the number of tunes available online. With a simple Google search, you can usually dig up MIDI files for your favorite band, movie, computer game, or classical composer.

Technically, it's against copyright rules to use a MIDI file of another artist's work on your Web site. However, there's a fairly large gray area. First of all, fans or amateur musicians usually sequence (transcribe onto the computer) MIDI files. So not only do they lack real instruments and vocals, they may also contain outright errors. In that respect, putting a

cheap MIDI file on your Web site is a little bit like listening to a Led Zeppelin cover band—it's a tribute to the original, not a competitive threat. That's why music companies haven't made any effort to crack down on MIDI files.

If you want to steer clear of copyright issues altogether, stick to music that's in the public domain. Music created before 1923 falls into this category, which means you're free to draw from a huge catalog of classical pieces. To download your favorites, try the Classical MIDI Archives (*www.classicalarchives.com*).

What if you want something a little more upmarket? You could use a WAV file, which are audio files recorded in an uncompressed digital file format first introduced by Microsoft but now supported everywhere. Most computers have software for recording WAV files—for example, on Windows PCs you can usually find a program called Sound Recorder lurking in the Programs → Accessories → Entertainment section of the Start menu (in Windows XP) or All Programs → Accessories → Sound Record (in Windows Vista). Mac fans may want to use the free program Audacity (*http://audacity.sourceforge.net*), which is also available in a Windows version.

You can use the <embed> element to play a WAV file in exactly the same way you did to play a MIDI file above:

```
<embed src="soundfile.wav" autoplay="false" />
```

The problem with WAV files is that they're really, *really* big. In fact, they're enormous. Think of the file size of an MP3 file, and then multiply it by 10. As a result, it rarely makes sense to use WAV files on Web pages. With a typical mid-speed Internet connection, your visitor will wait a long time before the complete music file trickles down and starts playing.

Note: A typical MIDI file is even smaller than a typical image. A 100 kilobyte (KB) MIDI file could handle the first movement of a detailed symphony.

Alternatively, you can use MP3 files. This approach works great in modern browsers, but older ones may ignore your playback attempt or they may launch an MP3 player (like Windows Media Player) to play the file:

```
<embed src="soundfile.mp3" autoplay="false" />
```

If you want to try this option, keep your file small and try it out on all the browsers your visitors might use. A 10-second MP3 file takes a modest 170 KB. (As a rule of thumb, most Web authors suggest you limit autoplay clips to 30 seconds.)

Sadly, the <embed> element won't help you create those nifty looping soundtracks you may have heard on some Web sites. Even though <embed> supports a loop attribute, the results aren't good because it doesn't loop cleanly. It pauses each time it reaches the end of your audio file. If you want a slick looping soundtrack, you need to use Flash, as described on page 483.

Tip: There's lots of great shareware available for recording WAV files and converting them into the more compact MP3 format. Two bargain-basement choices that are free to try are GoldWave (*www.goldwave. com*) and FlexiMusic (*www.fleximusic.com*). If all you want to do is convert existing WAV files to MP3 format, you can use Apple's iTunes software, available free for both Windows and the Mac (*www.apple.com/ itunes*). You can get the job done by right-clicking (Control-clicking on a Mac) any song name and choosing "Convert Selection to MP3" from the pop-up menu.

Sound Effects

Ever wanted to create one of those Web pages where every mouse movement unleashes a sound? For example, maybe you want a whoosh sound when visitors move over a button or you want them to hear an audible click when they select a link.

Sadly, there's no perfect solution that works with every browser. But there are two compromises:

- Use Flash, which lets you create pages that run rampant with sound effects. But to enjoy your creativity, your visitors need the Flash browser plug-in.

- Use the <bgsound> element (short for background sound) along with a Java-Script technique you'll learn about next. The key limitation with this trick is that it works only with Internet Explorer 5 and later—most other browsers and older versions of IE ignore the background effects altogether. And like <embed>, XHTML doesn't officially welcome the <bgsound> element.

You can find several versions of the background sound script online. The one you'll see in the next example (and available via the Missing CD page at *www. missingmanuals.com*) is one of the simplest. If you dig around on the Internet, you can find similar versions that preload an audio file, which delivers better performance. If you don't use preloading, visitors may experience a slight delay the first time you play a given sound, because the browser needs to download the audio file.

To use JavaScript-powered sounds, start by adding a <bgsound> element in the <head> section of your Web page. The <bgsound> element is an IE-specific version of the <embed> element:

```
<bgsound src="" id="SoundEffect" autostart="true" loop="1" />
```

The trick in this example is that you don't supply any source file at first. Instead, you set the *src* attribute when something actually happens on the page, at which point the sound begins playing.

Notice that you assign the name SoundEffect to the <bgsound> element. (The *id* attribute uniquely identifies an element in your document—for a refresher, see page 420.) The last two attributes in the element instruct it to play audio files immediately (*autostart="true"*) and play them exactly once (*loop="1"*).

The next step is to add the script that includes the PlaySound( ) function to the <head> portion of your page. The PlaySound( ) function has one role—to point the <bgsound> element to the audio file you want to play:

```
<script type="text/javascript">
function PlaySound(soundfile) {
  if (document.all && document.getElementById)
  {
    document.getElementById("SoundEffect").src = soundfile
  }
}
</script>
```

In other words, to play a sound, you need to call the PlaySound( ) function. PlaySound( ) finds the <bgsound> element, and then sets its *src* attribute to point to the audio file. This change causes the <bgsound> element to play the sound immediately.

Remember, functions just hang around idly until you call them. Your Web page won't make a peep until a visitor triggers a JavaScript event that calls the PlaySound( ) function.

Here's how you use the PlaySound( ) function to play a file named *soundeffect.wav* when a visitor moves her mouse pointer over a link:

```
<a href="http://www.somesite.com"
onmouseover="PlaySound('ding.wav')">Click Me</a>
```

The only problem here is that if you want to add sound effects like this to several links, you need to add every single link *separately*, even if they all use the same audio file. But don't despair. There's a solution courtesy of *www.dynamicdrive.com*. There, you can download a second JavaScript function named BindSound( ) that lets you add a sound effect to *all* the elements of a certain type in a certain container.

For example, if you want to add a sound effect to a group of links, pop them into a <div> element, like this:

```
<div>
  <a href="http://www.somewhere.com">Click Me</a>
  <a href="http://www.somewhere.com">Click Me</a>
  ...
</div>
```

Now, instead of adding the onmouseover attribute to every <a> element, you can attach it to a <div> container using the BindSound() function. The BindSound( ) function takes three arguments—the type of element you want to call, the sound effect file name, and the container that holds the elements you want to effect. Here's an example:

```
<div onmouseover="BindSound('a', ding.wav', this)">
  <a href="http://www.somewhere.com">Click Me</a>
  <a href="http://www.somewhere.com">Click Me</a>
  ...
</div>
```

Notice that in the first argument, it's important to leave out the angle brackets (for example, you use "a" to apply the function to every <a> anchor element). For the third argument, you can always use the keyword *this*, which refers to the current element (in this case, that's the <div> container). The end result of this is that you link every anchor in the <div> section to the *ding.wav* audio file.

You can use this trick to put sounds on your entire page—just add the onmouseover attribute to the <body> element that contains the page.

Tip: Looking for some free sound effects to use with this script? Try out *www.grsites.com/sounds* and *www.freeaudioclips.com*.

Flash MP3 Players

As you already learned, Flash is a browser plug-in that lets you add videos, animations, and even whole miniature programs, like games, to a Web page. Although it takes a fair amount of work (and some pricey software) to create a Flash program from scratch, it's not nearly as difficult to add a Flash-based music player to your page. That's because plenty of people have already done the work for you. The Web is awash in free Flash music players.

Note: You can download the Flash plug-in at *http://get.adobe.com/flashplayer*.

Search on Google for "flash mp3 player" to find a few free players. Most of them are surprisingly polished, with scrolling song lists, slick playback buttons, and even tiny animations that play in sync to your music.

The E-Phonic Player

One more-than-decent choice is E-Phonic (available at *www.e-phonic.com/mp3player*). It's easy to use, looks good, and you can style it in endlessly different ways (see Figure 16-5). And if you're a budding JavaScript geek, you can use script code to add some cool features. For example, you can have E-Phonic start playback or switch songs when certain JavaScript events take place, like when a visitor mouses over a picture.

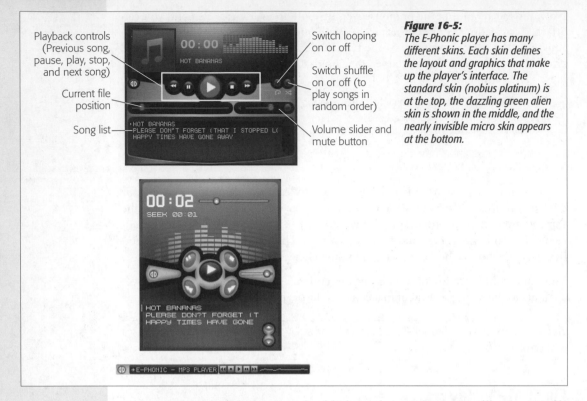

Playback controls (Previous song, pause, play, stop, and next song)

Current file position

Song list

Switch looping on or off

Switch shuffle on or off (to play songs in random order)

Volume slider and mute button

Figure 16-5:
The E-Phonic player has many different skins. Each skin defines the layout and graphics that make up the player's interface. The standard skin (nobius platinum) is at the top, the dazzling green alien skin is shown in the middle, and the nearly invisible micro skin appears at the bottom.

To get E-Phonic, click the Download link on their Web site. You'll get a ZIP file with a whole package of sample skins, including the three shown in Figure 16-5.

To use E-Phonic on your Web site, you need the following ingredients:

- **The Flash file *ep_player.swf*.** This miniature Flash program runs in your Web page. It's the heart of the E-Phonic player.

- **The JavaScript files *ep_player.js* and *swfobject.js*.** These files set up the Flash player and give you the ability to interact with it using JavaScript. Although you won't learn how to do that in this chapter, you can get all the details at *www.e-phonic.com/mp3player/documentation*.

- **Your skin folder.** As Figure 16-5 shows, you can deck out the E-Phonic player with a thousand faces. Once you choose a skin, copy it to your Web site. For example, to use the luminous green alien skin, add the alien_green folder and all its contents to your site. (Skin folders consist of one XML file, which defines the player's layout, and a whole bunch of images, one for each of the player's buttons and components.)

- **Your music.** If you want to play some music, you probably want to add the MP3 files to your site. If you have several songs, put them in a subfolder (for example, a folder named MP3).

- **The playlist file *playlist.xml*.** This lists all the files you want to load into the player, in order. You'll see how to edit this file shortly.

- **The XHTML page that includes the player.** You can add the player to any page on your site. All you need to do is add the right markup. The easiest way to get it is to copy it from one of the example files included with the E-Phonic download. You'll find one example file for each skin.

Figure 16-6 shows how these files are arranged.

The following sections show you how to get the E-Phonic player up and running in one of your pages.

Create a playlist

The playlist tells the E-Phonic player what songs to load. To create a track list with your garage band's best tunes, for example, copy your MP3 files into a subfolder named MP3 (see Figure 16-6). Then create a playlist and tweak it to play your songs. To make a playlist, start with the following skeleton:

```
<playlist version="1" xmlns="http://xspf.org/ns/0/">
  <trackList>

  </trackList>
</playlist>
```

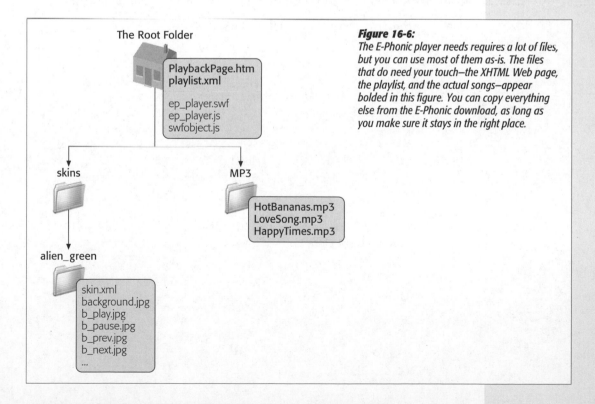

Figure 16-6:
The E-Phonic player needs requires a lot of files, but you can use most of them as-is. The files that do need your touch—the XHTML Web page, the playlist, and the actual songs—appear bolded in this figure. You can copy everything else from the E-Phonic download, as long as you make sure it stays in the right place.

This looks a lot like an XHTML page because it uses a combination of XML elements. But unlike XHTML, a browser can't display this content—instead, this format exists solely to provide information to the E-Phonics player.

In the <trackList> element, add one <track> element for each song in your playlist. You need to add two other elements inside the <track> element—a <location> element, which indicates the song's file name, and a <title> element, which identifies the song title that the player will display during playback:

```
<track>
  <location>MP3/HotBananas.mp3</location>
  <title>Hot Bananas</title>
</track>
```

Notice that the <location> element uses the same relative link system you used earlier for anchors and images (page 212). That means the link is always relative to the location of the XHTML page that displays the player. In the example above, the location points to a file named *HotBananas.mp3* in a folder named *MP3*.

You can add two optional elements to the <track> element (not shown in the example above)—a <creator> element and an <image> element. The <creator> element records the artist who made the song, which is shown in the song list next to the title. The <image> element points to an image file, which some skins show while playing a song. (For example, in the topmost skin in Figure 16-5, there's a spot in the top-left corner for song images, where the music note appears.)

Here's the complete playlist with all three songs:

```
<playlist version="1" xmlns="http://xspf.org/ns/0/">
  <trackList>
    <track>
      <location>MP3/HotBananas.mp3</location>
      <title>Hot Bananas</title>
    </track>
    <track>
      <location>MP3/LoveSong.mp3</location>
      <title>Please Don't Forget (That I Stopped Loving You)</title>
    </track>
    <track>
      <location>MP3/HappyTimes.mp3</location>
      <title>Happy Times Have Gone Away</title>
    </track>
  </trackList>
</playlist>
```

Adding the player to a Web page

Your final step is to embed the E-Phonic player and your customized playlist in your Web page. The easiest way to do this is to start with one of the sample files included with the E-Phonic download. Choose the file based on the skin you want. For the alien skin, open *example_alien.html*.

To use the E-Phonic player, your page needs three ingredients. First, you need a <script> block in the <head> section of your page that references the E-Phonics JavaScript file:

```
<script type="text/javascript" src="swfobject.js"></script>
```

This gives your Web page access to the JavaScript code you used to create the player.

Next, you need a <div> element with the *id="flashcontent"* attribute. The E-Phonics player will appear on your page at the location of the <div> element:

```
<div id="flashcontent"></div>
```

You don't actually need to put anything in the <div> element, because the magic of JavaScript will create the player for you. But it's a good idea to supply some *alternate content*. The browser displays this alternate content if it can't create the E-Phonics player, which usually means that it doesn't have the required version of Flash:

```
<div id="flashcontent">
    To view the E-Phonic MP3 Player, you need to have Javascript turned on and
    you must have Flash Player 9 or better installed. Download it (for free)
    <a href="http://www.adobe.com/go/getflashplayer/">here</a>.
</div>
```

Lastly, after the <div> element, you need to add a <script> block with the code that actually creates the player. This script also configures the player using several JavaScript variables (page 410). The variables shown here are the ones included with the samples in the E-Phonic download. To keep life simple, you can copy this whole <script> section from the E-Phonic sample Web page (like *example_alien. html*) into your own Web pages:

```
<script type="text/javascript">
    var so = new SWFObject("ep_player.swf", "ep_player", "220", "265", "9",
"#000000");
    so.addVariable("skin", "skins/alien_green/skin.xml");
    so.addVariable("playlist", "playlist.xml");
    so.addVariable("autoplay", "false");
    so.addVariable("shuffle", "false");
    so.addVariable("repeat", "true");
    so.addVariable("buffertime", "1");
    so.addParam("allowscriptaccess", "always");
    so.write("flashcontent");
</script>
```

You can tweak these variables to change the player's behavior. For example, to change song lists, point the *playlist* variable to a different file. You can make the player start the moment a browser creates it by changing the *autoplay* value from *false* to *true*. You can modify similar values to turn song shuffle and automatic repeat on or off.

Whatever you do, don't touch the skin setting. If you want to change skins, find the matching XHTML sample page and copy the <script> block from it. That's because the very first line of code in the skin script sets the size of the player, and the player size has to match the skin graphics or it won't work properly.

Here's a complete sample page that uses the alien skin and the playlist you developed:

```
<!DOCTYPE html PUBLIC "-//W3C//DTD XHTML 1.0 Transitional//EN"
"http://www.w3.org/TR/xhtml1/DTD/xhtml1-transitional.dtd">

<html xmlns="http://www.w3.org/1999/xhtml">
<head>
  <title>Page with a Player </title>
  <script type="text/javascript" src="swfobject.js"></script>
</head>

<body>
  <h1>You'll Love E-Phonic</h1>
  <p>This page has its own MP3 player built in. It's right here:</p>

  <div id="flashcontent">
    To view the E-Phonic Player, you need to have Javascript turned on and
    you must have Flash Player 9 or better installed. Download it (for free)
    <a href="http://www.adobe.com/go/getflashplayer/">here</a>.
  </div>

  <script type="text/javascript">
    var so = new SWFObject("ep_player.swf", "ep_player", "220", "265", "9",
"#000000");
    so.addVariable("skin", "skins/alien_green/skin.xml");
    so.addVariable("playlist", "playlist.xml");
    so.addVariable("autoplay", "false");
    so.addVariable("shuffle", "false");
    so.addVariable("repeat", "true");
    so.addVariable("buffertime", "1");
    so.addParam("allowscriptaccess", "always");
    so.write("flashcontent");
  </script>

  <p>(And this text is under the player.)</p>
</body>
</html>
```

Flashtrak Loops

The E-Phonic player is a great option if you want a full-featured MP3 player in your Web page. But sometimes, you're after a simpler goal. Rather than give your visitors the ability to shuffle through a collection of songs, you might just want to keep them happy with endlessly looping background music.

Although many Web sites sell audio loops, you can download free ones at Flash Kit, *www.flashkit.com/loops* (see Figure 16-7). Flash Kit offers a large and excellent catalogue of nearly 10,000 loops ranging in style from ambient to urban.

Note: Loops are the audio equivalent of a wallpaper tile. They're short snippets of music specially designed so the beginning picks up where the end leaves off. That means you can play an audio loop over and over again, and the result is a seamless background track. In a first-rate loop, the repetition isn't immediately obvious, and you can happily listen to it for several minutes.

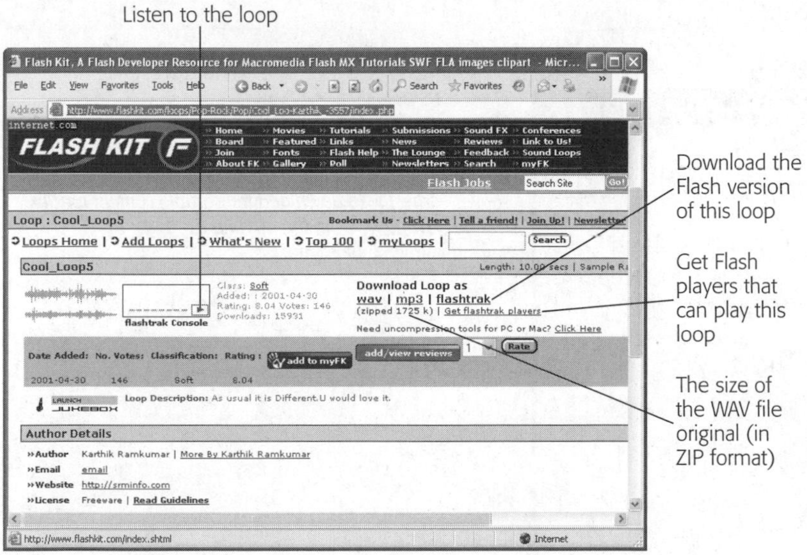

Listen to the loop

Download the Flash version of this loop

Get Flash players that can play this loop

The size of the WAV file original (in ZIP format)

Figure 16-7:
You can preview Flash Kit's loops right in your browser, without downloading them. Once you find what you want, click the "flashtrak" link to download the audio in one of three formats: MP3 (the usual), WAV (good if you want to edit it), or in Flashtrak format, which works with the specialized players available on the site. In this example, a high-quality 10-second WAV file weighs in at almost 2 MB, but the MP3 version is a more respectable 700 KB. The Flashtrak format is even smaller, requiring just 200 KB.

If you download one of these loops as an MP3 file, you can use it with a free Flash MP3 player, like the E-Phonic player discussed above. But there's another alternative, one that uses a slimmed-down audio format called Flashtrak. Flashtrak files download in a jiffy, so your visitors never have to wait to experience your site's ambience. Flashtrak files require a Flashtrak player, which you can also download at the Flash Kit Web site. (The Flashtrak player is a Flash program, just like E-Phonic is, but it doesn't support MP3 files.)

To download the Flashtrak player, look for the "Get flashtrak players" link just under the links for loops (see Figure 16-7). You can choose from more than a dozen player styles. Most have snazzy effects as they play music, like pulsing lines or expanding circles.

Note: When you download the Flashtrak player, you may end up with more files than you actually need. For example, you don't need any files that end with ".fla" (these are Flash source files that you can only edit in the Flash software). You can delete these files. Also, when you download a player, you'll probably find yourself with a pile of extra song files. Delete the ones you don't want, or your player will cycle through all of them.

Once you download a player, you're ready to embed it in your Web page. You can take care of that with a simple <embed> element that points to the player file:

```
<embed src="StarPlayerMultiTrackWithAutoStart.swf" />
```

Figure 16-8 shows you what you'll see when you run the page that contains this element.

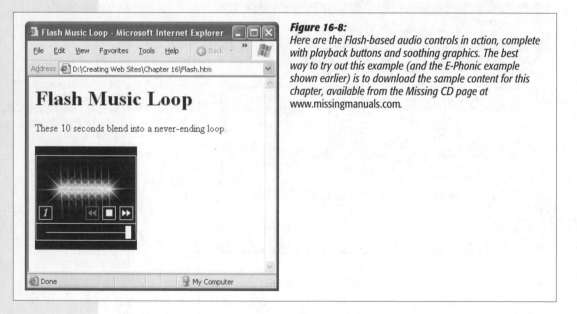

Figure 16-8:
Here are the Flash-based audio controls in action, complete with playback buttons and soothing graphics. The best way to try out this example (and the E-Phonic example shown earlier) is to download the sample content for this chapter, available from the Missing CD page at www.missingmanuals.com.

Flash content is notoriously difficult to patch into a page without breaking XHTML validation rules. The following markup provides a nice, clean solution that works in most browsers without requiring the pesky <embed> element:

```
<object data="StarPlayerMultiTrackWithAutoStart.swf"
  type="application/x-shockwave-flash">
    <param name="movie" value="StarPlayerMultiTrackWithAutoStart.swf" />
</object>
```

Notice that this technique forces you to put the Flash file name in two places.

Unlocking the Power of Flash

Flash files are utterly unlike ordinary multimedia content.

First, Flash stores animations as a series of instructions. So instead of, say, saving three dozen pictures of a circle in slightly different positions to simulate a ball in flight (as you would with an animated GIF or a video clip), you simply instruct Flash to "move this shape from here to there, at this speed." That makes complex animations much easier to create and edit.

Second, Flash uses programming code. That means you can program all kinds of devious logic into a Flash program, like making shapes move and sounds play when a Web visitor moves his mouse or clicks a portion of an animation. This ability brings all the tricks of client-side programming (Chapter 14) together with all the tools of graphic design to make really slick animations. Best of all, your Web server doesn't need any special software because the Flash browser plug-in does it all.

If you're an ambitious sort, the Flash music players you learn about in this chapter just might have you dreaming big about building your own Flash animations or programs. You can certainly do that, but it's a major undertaking. Before you start, you need to plunk down about $700 for the premier design tool Adobe Flash CS4 Professional. Then, you face a steep learning curve. Everything you've learned so far (XHTML, styles, and so on), won't help you much in the world of Flash. And once you have the right software and you've fought your way through all the new concepts, you'll find it takes more than a modicum of artistic skill to create a professional Flash animation.

To dip your toe into the fascinating world of Flash, check out the basic online tutorials at *www.w3schools.com/flash*, or read a dedicated book on the subject, like *Flash CS4: The Missing Manual*. To get a sense of what's possible with Flash, check out the gorgeous graphics in the free Flash games at *www.ferryhalim.com/orisinal*, or take on the detailed negotiation simulations at *www.zapdramatic.com*, which pit you against a host of unsavory characters.

Video Clips

Now that you've conquered the challenges of audio and learned to put everything from sound effects to looping background music into your Web pages, it's time to move on to one more challenge—*video content*.

Although browsers use many of the same tools to play video as they do to play audio (plug-ins like Windows Media Player, QuickTime, and Flash), there are some hefty differences. Most importantly, video files are big. Even the smallest of them is many times the size of an audio recording of a full-length Mahler symphony. Handling this data without trying your visitors' patience is a true test. In the following sections, you'll learn how to prepare your video content for the Web, and consider two ways to let visitors view it.

Preparing Video

Putting personal video on a Web site is a task meant for ambitious multimedia mavens. The key stumbling block is the sheer size of digital video. Consider the popular MiniDV camcorder. It stores an hour of video on a single tape. You can download that video to your computer—but only if you have a spare 13 GB of drive space handy. The ugly truth is that every second of raw, high-quality video chews through a sizeable 3.5 MB of storage. Not only is this enough to take a bite out of any Web master's server and bandwidth allocations, it's too big for even the speediest browser to download.

What can you do to make a Web video both look good and perform well? You can always use someone else's Web-ready video (or pay a video editing company lots of money to trim yours down to Web proportions). Assuming that's not what you want, you have two choices.

- **Record at lower quality.** Some video cameras let you record video using lower quality settings for the sole purpose of putting video on a Web site. Cellphones, tiny computer spy cams, and digital still cameras all create low-quality movies, letting you both dodge conversion headaches and send video straight to your site. In fact, some video fans find the best solution is to have two cameras, one for ordinary home movies and one for lower-quality Web movies.

- **Lower the quality afterward.** More commonly, you'll need to start with your high-quality video and go through a long process of *re-encoding* it to convert it to a size suitable for the Web. To do this, you need a video-editing program. Video cameras generally include some sort of tool to help you out, although you may want to pony up for more powerful software. Two popular choices are iMovie for the Mac (included with OS X) and Windows Movie Maker, included with Windows XP and Windows Vista. In addition, some video editing programs have a feature that automatically picks suitably scaled-down quality settings for videos you want to upload to a Web site.

Note: For full details on how to operate Windows Movie Maker, check out *Windows Vista: The Missing Manual*. If you're using iMovie, take a look at *iMovie HD & iDVD: The Missing Manual*.

Here are the steps to follow to get your video ready for the Web:

1. **First, film your movie.**

   Take a couple of lessons from video aficionados and film your video in a way that makes it easier to compress and introduces less distortion. Keep camera movements smooth and gradual, and don't film complex patterns. Your compressed video will be smaller and look better.

2. **Fire up the video capture program included with your video camera. Use it to download your movie to your computer's hard drive.**

   Typically, this step involves connecting your camera to your computer using a *FireWire* cable. Although USB cables aren't fast enough to keep up with huge chunks of raw video data, you might use one if you transfer video from less powerful devices, like a camera or cellphone that records short video clips.

3. **Now you need to use a video-editing program to snip out just the video segment you want to post to your Web site.**

   Some programs let you add music or special effects at this point, too.

4. **Next, re-encode that piece of video in a highly compressed format. If all the format information in your program sounds like gobbledy-gook, look for an option that clearly says "Web video" when you save your clip.**

   Technically, you make three choices in this step—you specify a video format (the algorithm your editing program uses to encode your video), the dimensions of the playback window (Web pages usually use 320×240 pixels), and the video quality (as with JPEGs, the greater the compression, the more detail you lose).

Note: There is a range of competing Web video formats, but the most common is MPEG-4. Just to make life more interesting, MPEG-4 has all kinds of quality settings, so you can use it to create DVD-quality movies or Web-friendly video clips. If in doubt, double-check the final file size of your movie. If 60 seconds of video take up 1 MB on your hard drive, you're doing well.

Re-encoding video is a time-consuming operation—even the speediest computer can take five times as long as the length of the original clip. The good news is that at the end of the process, you'll have a more manageable Web-ready video file— say, 2 MB for a full 90-second clip.

Linking to and Embedding Video

Surprisingly, you can pop a video into your Web page using the same techniques you used with digital audio (see Figure 16-1). That means you can link to a video so that it opens up in another browser window:

```
Click to download or open my home movie
<a href="ouch.mpg">Ouch, That Hurts</a>.
```

Or, you can use the <embed> element to put a video window right inside your Web page.

```
<embed src="ouch.mpg" autoplay="false" />
```

If you use the <embed> element, make sure you turn *off* autoplay. Otherwise, visitors with feeble dial-up connections will see their Web pages slow to a crawl while your video downloads.

The video window shows up wherever you place the <embed> element (see Figure 16-9).

If this seems too easy to be true, that's because it is. Although this simple test page works well most of the time, it's not entirely reliable. Depending on your movie's encoding format and your browser's settings, visitors may be forced to download the entire movie before they can start watching it. And if their browsers don't have the right plug-in or it's incorrectly installed, your video might not play at all.

Heavyweight companies that show videos on their Web sites use special Web server software to ensure good performance. Budget Web hosting companies can't compete. However, if you want to get serious about video but avoid the hosting

---

Figure 16-9:
You can add a video window to your Web pages almost as easily as adding basic audio playback controls. If you don't specify a fixed size, the window automatically adjusts to the dimensions of your video.

and compatibility headaches, there's an easy solution. You can use a video hosting service like the insanely popular YouTube.

Uploading Your Videos to YouTube

Before YouTube hit the scene, video clips hadn't really taken off on the Web. Movie clips were all-around inconvenient. They were slow to download, and playback was often jerky and sporadic. But in a mere 5 years, the landscape has shifted. Web connections are faster and browser plug-ins that support movie playback (like Flash and Microsoft's new Flash competitor, Silverlight) are more common. Ordinary people own all sorts of digital video gadgets that can shoot short movies, from true video cameras to digital cameras, cellphones, and Webcams. Popular clips rocket around the world, going from unknown to Internet sensation in a matter of hours. Family members, adventurers, and wannabe political commentators all regularly use video to keep in touch, show their skills, and dish the dirt.

YouTube (*www.YouTube.com*) is at the forefront of this revolution. Despite being a Web newcomer (YouTube was created in 2005, after the first edition of this book was printed), it currently ranks as the world's second-most popular Web site. And YouTube's range of content is staggering. With a quick search, you can turn up a range of both amateur and professional content, including funny home videos, product reviews and announcements, homemade music videos, clips from movies and television shows, and ordinary people spouting off on just about any topic (a trend called *video blogging*).

If you're still considering options for putting your video content online, there are two great reasons to use YouTube:

- **It performs well.** YouTube uses Flash to ensure that virtually all browsers can play back its videos. In addition, its videos support *progressive downloading*, which means you can watch a video as your browser downloads it, rather than waiting for the whole enchilada.

- **YouTube extends the reach of your Web site.** YouTube is one of the most popular sites on the Web. Videos that get lucky can increase their audience size from a few people to millions of eager clip-watchers. By putting your movies on YouTube, you increase the odds that someone will discover it and possibly visit your site afterward. For example, many of the most popular clip-makers capitalize on their YouTube popularity by selling themed merchandise on their sites.

One disadvantage with YouTube is that you lose control over video quality. YouTube is notorious for applying a heavy dose of compression to shrink video size, making some clips look terrible.

In the following sections, you'll see how to upload your first YouTube video, and even learn how to embed it in a window on one of your own pages.

Signing up with YouTube

Anyone can browse and view YouTube's full catalog of videos (six million clips at the time of this writing). But to upload your own, you need a YouTube account. Here's how to create one:

1. **Go to *www.YouTube.com*. Click the Sign Up link (you can find it in the top right-hand corner of the page).**

2. **Fill in your account information.**

   You need to supply the usual information, including your email address, password, location, and date of birth. Unlike some Web sites, which identify you solely by your email address, YouTube requires a *user name*, which is a string of letters and numbers like *JoeTheMovieMaker403*. Given the site's popularity, it may take a few tries to find an available name. To find out if a potential name is taken, click the Check Availability link after you type it in.

Tip: If you already have a Google Account, you can use that with YouTube. Scroll down to the bottom-left of the Sign Up page, and then click the "Sign in with your Google Account" link. You'll still need to pick a YouTube user name and supply your address, but you'll be able to log in to all the Google services you use with the same email and password combination.

3. **Click Create My Account.**

YouTube sends a confirmation message to your email address. When you get this email, click the link inside it to confirm your account.

Preparing a video

Now you're ready to post a video. But before you do, it's time to double-check your video format to make sure YouTube supports it.

YouTube helps out quite a bit in this regard. You can upload a video in just about any popular video format, including AVI, MOV, WMV, MPG, DivX, FLV, OGG, and 3GP. Best of all, YouTube automatically re-encodes your video with the right quality settings so Web visitors can download it without teeth-gnashing delays. This doesn't mean you can upload a video straight out of your camcorder, however. YouTube limits uploads to files that are less than 1 GB (1,000 MB) in size, and even a movie file that's half that size is still too large for many people to upload in a reasonable amount of time. Best-case scenario, it takes hours. Worst-case, your browser conks out halfway through the process.

With that in mind, you need to use the re-encoding process described on page 492. Although it may take a bit of trial and error to get the best settings for your video, here are some guidelines:

- YouTube supports standard and widescreen video formats. The device you use to make your video usually determines which format you choose. If you record video in standard size, use a resolution of 480×360 pixels. For slightly lower-quality content with standard video, you can use the original YouTube playback window size, which is 320×240. Either way, YouTube uses a widescreen video window to play back your standard video content, which means you'll see a black bar of empty space on the sides of your video. For widescreen video, use a resolution of 640×360 pixels for best results.

- Although YouTube supports a kitchen sink of video formats, it recommends you use the MPEG-4 or H.263 codecs when preparing your video.

- Ordinarily, you should encode your videos at 30 frames per second. However, you can sometimes cut this down to 15 frames per second to save space, and still get good results.

- The longer your video, the more compression you'll need to get the file size down to manageable proportions.

- Aim to create a file that's less than 100 MB in size. You may need to fiddle with your settings and re-encode your video several times to get the right balance of size and quality.

UP TO SPEED

Understanding Bit Rates

The main way you control video quality settings is by adjusting the *bit rate*. The bit rate determines how much raw information each frame of your movie includes. For example, a mid-range bit rate of 400 kbps means there are 400 KB of data in every second of video. If your movie is about 4 minutes long, it will total about 96 MB in size.

Life isn't quite that simple however, because many encoding programs use variable bit-rate encoding. That means they use a higher bit rate to encode more complex sections (like fast-moving action), and a lower bit rate to save space during simpler scenes. No matter what encoding rate you use, you'll always run into the same trade-off. Bigger files have the potential for better quality video after YouTube converts them. But the smaller the file, the faster you can upload it.

Because every encoding program works a bit differently, you need to experiment (and sit through a few YouTube uploads to find out how fast your Internet connection *really* is). You might also want to try scouring the Web for tips on using your video editor to prepare YouTube videos. You can even hunt down one of free program that are designed to streamline YouTube uploads.

Uploading a video

Once your video's ready, it's time to put it online. The process is refreshingly straightforward:

1. **Head back to YouTube and sign in.**

   You'll see that YouTube offers plenty of features to help you track down the videos you like. It keeps track of the videos you watch, recommends related videos for you to check out, and lets you subscribe to specific video groups. But right now, ignore these features and concentrate on adding your own video creation to the mix.

2. **Click the yellow Upload button at the top right-hand side of the page.**

   This takes you to the upload page shown in Figure 16-10.

3. **Fill in the information for your video.**

   You need to supply a title and description, which YouTube displays on your video page and when your video appears in the YouTube search results. You also need to specify a category for your video, and add one or more *tags*. When other people search YouTube using keywords that match your tags, there's a better chance that your video will turn up in the search results.

   Along with this required information, YouTube offers several sections of optional settings. You can click the "choose options" link in any of these sections to change your options.

   Use Broadcast Options to switch your video from public to private. Public videos turn up in YouTube search results, while you share private videos only with YouTubers you explicitly identify.

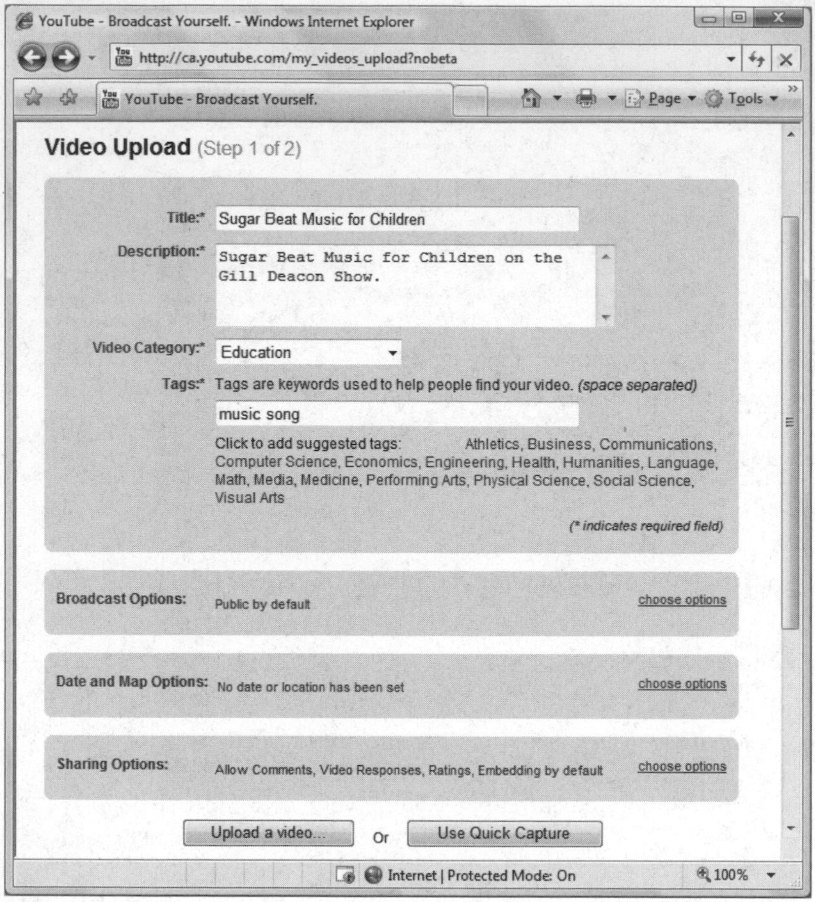

Figure 16-10:
YouTube uses just a single page to collect all the necessary information about your video and let you configure options like comment support. (Click the "choose options" links to expand these sections.)

Use Date and Map Options to identify when and where you recorded your video.

Use Sharing Options to control how other people can offer feedback or use your video. For example, you can ban people from commenting on your video, or allow only comments that you approve. You can also specify whether people can rate your videos, post a video response (a video linked to yours), and play your video on their Web page. YouTube allows all these options automatically, giving the site a somewhat raucous community atmosphere.

Note: You can prevent other people from embedding your video by choosing the "External sites may not embed this video" option. If you do this, however, it not only stops *other* people from showcasing your video, it prevents *you* from embedding your own video on your Web pages.

Don't worry if you can't decide on all your options right now. You can change them (along with the descriptive video information) any time.

4. **Click the "Upload a video" button.**

This is the simplest way to submit your video. However, YouTube offers other options.

Click the Use Quick Capture button to record and upload your video on the spot. You need to have a Webcam connected to your PC.

Click the "Use multi-video uploader" button on the right side of the page to use a special uploading interface. The multi-video uploader makes it easy to upload several files at once. This way, if you have a bunch of videos you want to put online, you can queue them all up and walk away from your computer for the day. The multi-video uploader also lets you upload files larger than 100 MB, up to the 1,000 MB maximum. If you click this button, YouTube prompts you to install the free Google Gears Web browser extension (*http://gears.google.com*), which YouTube requires to make the multi-video uploader work.

5. **It's time to upload your file. Click Browse, find your video file on your PC, and then click OK. Finally, click Upload Video to start the transfer process.**

As YouTube uploads your video, it displays a status message that counts the number of bytes copied and displays the percent of the entire process it's completed.

YouTube says it typically takes 1 to 5 minutes to upload each megabyte of video if you have a high-speed connection, so this is a good time to get a second cup of coffee.

6. **When YouTube finishes the upload, it displays a confirmation message.**

The process isn't really finished yet, however. YouTube still needs to convert your video to the streamlined Flash format, and that process could take minutes or hours depending on the number of requests ahead of yours.

As long as you didn't switch off video embedding in step 3, YouTube gives you the block of XHTML you need to embed the video on your own site (see Figure 16-11).

Watching a video

Once your video is ready, you can watch it in several ways:

- You can search for it on YouTube.

- You can browse through the videos in your account. Log into YouTube, click the Account link (at the top right-hand side of the page), scroll down to the My Videos section, and then click the Uploaded Videos link.

Tip: You can handle other management tasks in the Uploaded Videos page as well. For example, click Delete to remove a video, Edit to change the video information and options you specified when you uploaded your video, and Insight to get some fascinating statistics on the people who've seen your video.

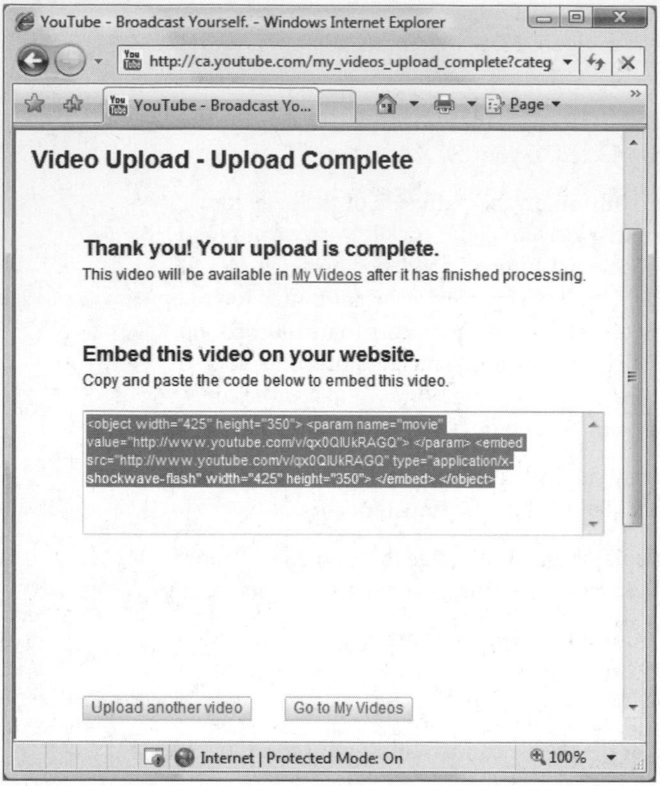

Figure 16-11:
Even though your video isn't ready yet, you can already copy the markup needed to display it on a Web page. At the moment, that markup won't have much effect—it'll just create a blank YouTube window. But once your video goes live on YouTube, you'll see it in your page.

- You can play it back in a YouTube window on one of your Web pages. To do so, copy the markup shown in Figure 16-11 into your page. If you neglected to copy this markup when you uploaded your video, go to the YouTube page for your video, where you'll find these details (see Figure 16-12).

- You can put a link on your Web page that leads to the YouTube video page. Figure 16-12 shows the information you need to create this link.

Of all these options, embedding your video in a YouTube window on your Web page is the most interesting. It lets you combine the look and feel of a self-hosted video with YouTube's high performance and solid browser support. Best of all, embedding videos is as easy as copying a snippet of XHTML markup into your page. You simply put this markup where you want the video window to appear. Often, you'll put it in a <div> element, and use style rules to position the <div> element (as described in Chapter 9).

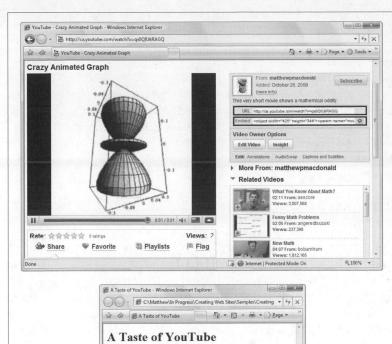

Figure 16-12:
Top: You can watch your video at its YouTube home. The page provides two useful text boxes (circled here): a URL box with the address you need to link to this page, and an Embed box with the markup you need to embed this video window in another Web page.

Bottom: Embedding lets you watch your video in a page of your own devising.

Here's the complete markup that creates the page from Figure 16-12:

```
<!DOCTYPE html PUBLIC "-//W3C//DTD XHTML 1.0 Transitional//EN"
"http://www.w3.org/TR/xhtml1/DTD/xhtml1-transitional.dtd">

<html xmlns="http://www.w3.org/1999/xhtml">
<head>
  <title>A Taste of YouTube</title>
</head>

<body>
  <h1>A Taste of YouTube</h1>
```

```
<p>The following video window is brought to you by the fine people
 at YouTube.</p>

<object width="425" height="344">
  <param name="movie"
  value="http://www.youtube.com/v/qxoOQIUkRAGQ&hl=en&fs=1"></param>
  <embed src="http://www.youtube.com/v/qxoOQIUkRAGQ&hl=en&fs=1"
  type="application/x-shockwave-flash" allowfullscreen="true"
  width="425" height="344">
  </embed>
</object>


<p>Click it to start playing.</p>
</body>
</html>
```

Keen eyes will notice that this video window consists of an <embed> element
wrapped in an <object> element. This messy markup is great for browser compatibility, because browsers that support the <object> element will ignore the content
inside, and browsers that don't recognize the <object> element will use the
<embed> element instead. However, like all uses of the <embed> element, it has
the unhappy side effect of breaking the rules of XHTML. This simply goes to show
that making a page work perfectly still trumps any standard—at least for the Web's
hottest video-sharing site.

Tip: To change the color of the border around your video window, make it start playing automatically,
give it support for fullscreen mode, or tweak one of several other details, you need to adjust the parameters inside the markup. For the complete scoop, check out *http://code.google.com/apis/youtube/player_
parameters.html*.

5

Part Five:
Blogs

Chapter 17: Blogs

Blogs

Throughout this book, you learned how to craft a Web site using basic site-building ingredients: XHTML, style sheets, and JavaScript. Armed with this know-how, you can build a fairly impressive site.

Maintaining a Web site, however, requires a significant investment of your time. You need to regularly review what you have, add fresh material, keep site navigation menus up to date, check old links, and periodically update your pages to incorporate the latest Web design trends. For some people, this constant grooming is fun—after all, you get to tweak and fiddle with the most minute details of your site until you get everything exactly the way you want it. But not everyone's that ambitious. Some people prefer to spend less time managing their sites and more time creating content.

In this chapter, you'll learn about *blogs*, a self-publishing format that can help you avoid the headaches of Web site management. Blogs are a fresh, straightforward, and slightly chaotic way to communicate on the Web. To maintain a blog, you publish short entries whenever the impulse hits you. Your blog posts are collected, chronologically organized, and presented in Web pages by high-powered blogging software. That means that if you don't want to fuss with the fine details of Web site management, you don't need to. All you need to worry about is sending in postings— and with some blogging software, that's as easy as firing off an email.

In this chapter you'll learn how blogs work, and you'll see how to create your own blog with Blogger, one of the Web's leading free blogging services.

Understanding Blogs

The word "blog" is a nerdy abbreviation of *Web log*, which makes sense because blogs are logs of a sort—regular, dated blurbs, like a cross between a diary entry and a posting in a discussion forum. "Blog" is also a verb, as in "I just ate at a terrible restaurant; when I get home I'm going to blog about it." Figure 17-1 dissects the anatomy of a basic blog.

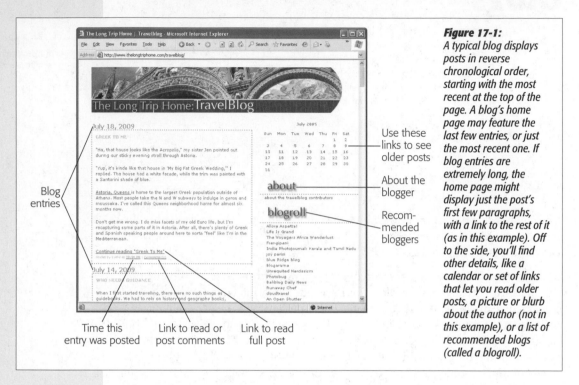

Figure 17-1:
A typical blog displays posts in reverse chronological order, starting with the most recent at the top of the page. A blog's home page may feature the last few entries, or just the most recent one. If blog entries are extremely long, the home page might display just the post's first few paragraphs, with a link to the rest of it (as in this example). Off to the side, you'll find other details, like a calendar or set of links that let you read older posts, a picture or blurb about the author (not in this example), or a list of recommended blogs (called a blogroll).

Although blogs simplify Web posting, it's unfair to say that they're just a simplified way to work the Web. Rather, blogs are a wholly different form of online communication. And although there's no definitive test to determine what is or isn't a blog, most blogs share several characteristics:

• **Blogs are personal.** You can find topic-based blogs, work-based blogs, political blogs, and great numbers of blogs filled with random, offbeat musings. No matter what their mission, however, blogs always emphasize the author's point of view. They rarely attempt to be objective—instead, they're unapologetically idiosyncratic *opinions*. Blogs are always written in the first person.

• **Blogs are organized chronologically.** When you design a Web site, you spend a lot of time deciding how best to organize your material, often using menus or links to guide visitors through an assortment of topics. Blogs take a radically different approach. They have no organization other than ordering your postings chronologically. Anything else would just slow down restless bloggers.

- **Blogs are updated regularly.** Blogs emphasize fast, freewheeling communication rather than painstakingly crafted Web pages. Bloggers are known to add content obsessively (sometimes as often as hourly). Because blog entries are dated, it's glaringly obvious if you don't keep your blog up to date. If you can't commit to blogging regularly, don't start a blog—set up a simple Web page instead.

- **Blogs are flexible.** There's a bit of blog wisdom that says no thought's too small for a blog. And it's true—whether you write a detailed discussion on the viability of peanut-butter Oreos or a three-sentence summary of an uneventful day, a blog post works equally well.

- **Blogs create a broader conversation.** Blogs form communities more readily than Web sites do. Not only are blogs more conversational in nature, they also support comments and links that can tie different blogs together in a conversation. If someone posts an interesting item on a blog, a legion of fellow bloggers often links to it within hours. Scandalous blog gossip can rocket around the globe in a heartbeat.

Note: When a large amount of activity, information, and opinion erupts around a particular subject or controversy in the *blogosphere*, it's sometimes called a *blogstorm*, or blog swarm. You can find more blogtastic jargon at *http://en.wikipedia.org/wiki/Blog*.

The actual content of a blog isn't fixed—it can range widely, from political commentary to personal travelogues. There are millions of blogs online today; Google's Blogger service alone hosts several million blogs, many thousands of which are considered active.

The best way to get a feel for the blogosphere is to check out some popular examples. For widely read political commentary, head over to arch-conservative Andrew Sullivan's blog at *www.andrewsullivan.com*. Or check out a frank, gripping account of life in war-torn Baghdad on Salam Pax's (now-abandoned) blog at *http://dear_raed.blogspot.com*. For somewhat lighter fare, visit the curiously popular *http://wilwheaton.typepad.com*, a blog by Wil Wheaton, the actor who played the nerdy upstart Wesley Crusher on *Star Trek*. Computer security whiz Bruce Schneier provides expertise and observations at *www.schneier.com/blog*. The list goes on—from journalists to hobbyists to sports heroes to porn stars, it seems that almost everyone's willing to psychoanalyze their life or chat about water-cooler topics with an audience of millions via a blog.

Tip: Blogs occupy a specialized Web niche distinct from a lot of the other types of sites you've seen. For example, you can't effectively sell a line of trench coats for dogs on a blog. But many people start blogs *in addition* to ordinary Web sites. This is a great combination. Visitors love blogs because they crave a glimpse behind the scenes. They're also sure to visit again and again if they can count on a regularly updated blog that offers a steady stream of news, gossip, and insight.

The Hazards of Blogging

There's something about the first-person nature of a blog that sometimes lures people into revealing much more information than they should. Thanks to reckless moments of blogging, lovers have discovered their cheating spouses, grandmothers have read memorable accounts of their daughter's sexual conquests, and well-meaning employees have lost their jobs.

The dangers of impulse blogging are particularly great in the working world. In most countries, companies have the ability to fire employees who make damaging claims about a business (even if they're true). Even famously open-minded Google ditched Mark Jen (*http://roseandsnail. com*) after he blogged a few choice words about a Google sales conference that he claimed resembled a drunken frat party. The notable part of his story is that he didn't set out to undermine Google or make his blog widely available. In fact, only his close friends and family even knew he had a blog. Unfortunately, a few Google-watching sites picked up on the blog post and sent the link around the Internet. There are many more stories like these, where employees lose their jobs after revealing trade secrets, admitting to inappropriate on-the-job conduct (for example, posting risqué at-work photos or bragging about time-wasting games of computer solitaire), or just complaining about the boss.

To protect yourself from the hazards of blogging, remember these rules:

- "Anonymous" never is.

- If you plan to hide your identity, adopt a pseudonym, or conceal personal details, remember the first rule.

- Funny is in the mind of the beholder. Your humorous work-related stories will be seen in a different light when read by high-powered executives who lack your finely developed sense of irony.

- Think before you write. There's a fine line between company secrets and information in the public domain.

- There's no going back. Although many blogging tools let you edit or remove old posts, the original versions can stick around in search-engine caches for eternity.

Syndication

One of neatest features of blogs is *syndication*, which lets avid blog readers monitor their favorite blogs using a program called a *feed reader* or *news aggregator*. To use a feed reader, you enter links to all your favorite blogs, and then keep an eye out for updates. The feed reader periodically checks these blogs and alerts you to new postings, saving you from having to check every blog 94 times a day to see if there's fresh content. If you follow blogs regularly, feed readers are the most practical way to stay current with all your friends in the blogosphere.

Note: Feed readers are a little like email programs, which, of course, let you regularly check to see if you have new messages from any of your friends. This is a lot more efficient than contacting each of them and asking if they have anything new to say. Similarly, you can use a feed reader whenever you want to check up on blog activity. If there's nothing new, you find out in an instant.

Although most blogs work with feed readers, some don't. To work with a reader, blogs need to provide a *feed* (Figure 17-2), a computer-friendly format of recent blog postings. Feed readers interpret blog feeds to get important information, like the post's title, description, date, and text. They display that information for your reading pleasure, without forcing you to make a separate trip to the blog Web site.

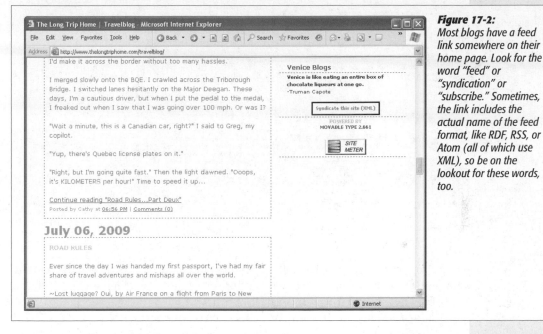

Figure 17-2:
Most blogs have a feed link somewhere on their home page. Look for the word "feed" or "syndication" or "subscribe." Sometimes, the link includes the actual name of the feed format, like RDF, RSS, or Atom (all of which use XML), so be on the lookout for these words, too.

If you want to try a feed reader, you've got lots of choices:

- Online feed readers require that you sign up and create a free account, but you don't need to install anything on your computer. You just go to the feed reader Web site and read the feeds right in your browser window. Popular examples include Google Reader (*www.google.com/reader*), Bloglines (*www.bloglines.com*), and NewsGator (*www.newsgator.com*).

- Desktop feed readers run on your PC. You can check out and download many of them on popular shareware sites like *www.download.com*. If you're using a Windows computer, you can download the excellent FeedDemon (see Figure 17-3) at *www.newsgator.com/Individuals/FeedDemon*. Mac fans might like the highly touted NetNewsWire at *http://ranchero.com/netnewswire*. Both programs are free.

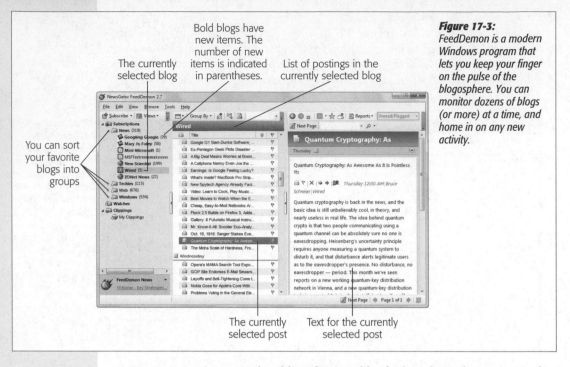

The currently selected blog

Bold blogs have new items. The number of new items is indicated in parentheses.

List of postings in the currently selected blog

Figure 17-3:
FeedDemon is a modern Windows program that lets you keep your finger on the pulse of the blogosphere. You can monitor dozens of blogs (or more) at a time, and home in on any new activity.

You can sort your favorite blogs into groups

The currently selected post

Text for the currently selected post

- Browsers are increasingly adding features like feed readers. If you use Firefox, for example, its *live bookmarks* feature tracks feeds (see Figure 17-4). Internet Explorer 7 (and later) and Safari also have built-in feed readers. (For more information about IE's support, check out *www.microsoft.com/windows/IE/ie7/ tour/rss.* For Safari, read the article series at *www.macdevcenter.com/pub/a/mac/ 2005/05/31/safari_rss.html.*) However, no browser offers feed-reading features as slick or convenient as dedicated programs like FeedDemon.

Blog Hosting and Software

Before you can set up your own blog, it helps to understand the different kinds of blogmaking options out there. There are really two types of blogs:

- **Self-hosted blogs.** If you're a hardcore high-tech geek with a Web server in your basement, you might be interested in hosting a blog entirely on your own. To do this, you need to find some blog hosting software that works on your server platform, install it, and then configure everything. This approach gives you unlimited flexibility (and maybe better performance), but, unless you enjoy do-it-yourself challenges like making your laptop talk to your coffee maker, it's probably not for you.

  Examples of blogging software include Movable Type (*www.movabletype.org*), Blosxsom (*www.blosxom.com*), and WordPress (*http://wordpress.org*).

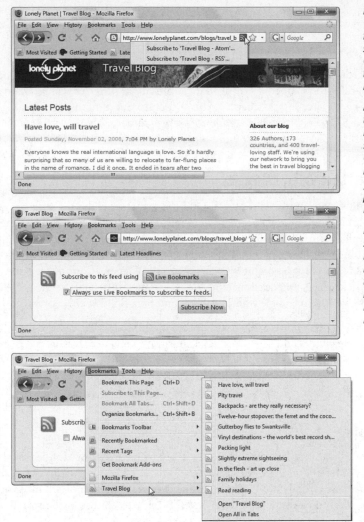

Figure 17-4:

Top: When Firefox detects a link to a feed in the current page, it displays a special orange icon in the address bar. Click this icon, and then choose one of the "Subscribe" options to add a live bookmark.

Middle: Firefox asks you how you want to store your bookmark. You can use Firefox's live bookmarks feature, or a separate feed reading service like Google Reader (just pick it from the list). Click the "Always use" setting if you don't want to see this feed options page again. Then, click the Subscribe Now button.

Bottom: Live bookmarks provide a submenu of current blog posts, which Firefox updates automatically. You still need to check the bookmark to see if there's a new post (which requires more effort than a feed reader like FeedDemon), but you don't need to keep visiting the original site.

- **Hosted blogs.** With a hosted blog, you simply sign up with a blog provider and start blogging away. Adding a blog entry is as simple as filling out a form in your Web browser. You never need to hassle with a separate program or figure out how to upload content files, because the blog provider stores all your files for you. You don't even need to have a Web site. Hosted blogs are the best bet for new bloggers, because they're completely painless and remarkably flexible.

Examples of hosted blog providers include Windows Live Spaces (*http://spaces.msn.com*), TypePad (*www.typepad.com*), WordPress (*http://wordpress.com*), and Blogger (*www.blogger.com*).

Tip: Some blog services let you store your blog files on your own Web server. This model gives you the ease of hosted blogs without forcing you to give up your domain name. On page 533, you'll learn how to pull off this feat with Blogger.

If you're interested in researching the many different blogging products and blog hosts available, refer to Wikipedia's up-to-date summary at *http://en.wikipedia.org/wiki/Blog_hosting_service*. In this chapter, you'll spend your time using one blogging tool, called Blogger. Blogger is simple to use yet remarkably powerful, which makes it the best candidate for all-around blogging champ.

Getting Started with Blogger

Blogger is the most commonly used blogging tool today. It provides the easiest way to start a blog, and it's chock-full of nifty blog management tools. Once upon a time, Blogger was available in a basic free version (supported by ads) and a more full-featured premium version, which required a small yearly contribution. In early 2003, all that changed when Google bought Blogger. Now, all Blogger's features are part of the same free package. As an added benefit, Blogger's once-unreliable services are a thing of the past, thanks to Google's stacks of cash and rock-solid Web servers.

Creating a blog with Blogger is ridiculously easy. In the following sections, you'll learn how to create a blog, add posts, and take charge of a few neat features.

Tip: You can also check out the official catalog of Blogger help at *http://help.blogger.com* and the discussion boards at *www.bloggerforum.com*, where bloggers share tips, ask questions, and vent their frustrations.

Creating a Blog

Before you create your blog, it's a good idea to assess your goals and decide exactly what type of content you plan to showcase. Will your blog contain random thoughts, a chronicle of daily life, or more targeted, topic-specific posts? Once you know how you want to position your blog, you'll be able to choose a snappy name and a suitable URL. Start with these steps:

1. Go to *www.blogger.com*.

   This is the home page for the Blogger service.

2. **Click the Create Your Blog button.**

   Creating a blog is a three-step process. First, you create a Google account (see Figure 17-5).

   If you use other Google services (like Gmail, Google AdSense, or Google Analytics), you can use that account to create your blog. Click the Sign In link, and then skip to step 5. If you don't have a Google account, continue to step 2 to provide some basic information about yourself.

3. **Type in your account information, which consists of an email address, a password, and your display name (the name your blog will display to the world).**

   You also need to type in a string of letters to prove you're not a computer program, and turn on a checkbox at the bottom of the page to officially accept Blogger's rules.

Note: You only need to create an account once. However, you can create multiple blogs for the same account.

4. **Click Continue to move to the next step.**

   You actually create your blog in this step (see Figure 17-6).

5. **Supply the title and URL you want your blog to have.**

   A blog title is just like a Web page title—it's the descriptive bit of text that appears in the browser title bar.

   The URL is the really important part, because you don't want to change this later on and risk losing your loyal readers. It's the address that eager Web followers use to find your blog. Blogger is surprisingly generous with URLs—unlike free Web

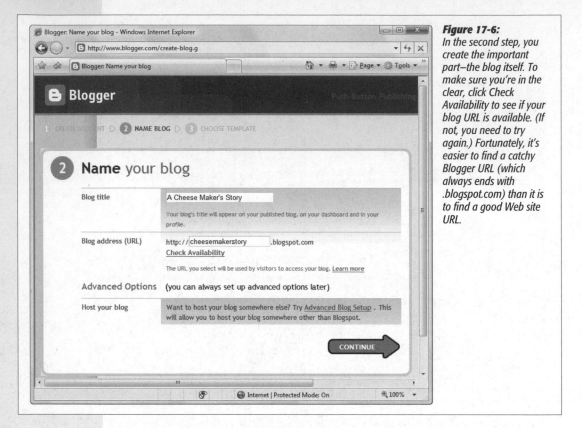

Figure 17-6:
In the second step, you create the important part—the blog itself. To make sure you're in the clear, click Check Availability to see if your blog URL is available. (If not, you need to try again.) Fortunately, it's easier to find a catchy Blogger URL (which always ends with .blogspot.com) than it is to find a good Web site URL.

hosting providers, Blogger lets you use just about any URL, so long as it ends with *.blogspot.com*. Although other bloggers have already taken some of the most obvious names, it's still reasonably easy to create short-and-sweet blog names like *http://secretideas.blogspot.com* or *http://richwildman.blogspot.com*.

If you want a customized domain name, you have two choices. You can use the domain-forwarding technique described in Chapter 3 (page 62) to forward visitors from a domain name of your choice to your blog's actual URL. Or you can use a more seamless but more complex approach, and tell Blogger you'll host your blog on another Web server (page 533).

Tip: Even though there's nothing wrong with a *.blogspot.com* URL, there's a good reason to get a domain name of your own. No matter how much you love Blogger right now, someday you might move on to a different service. It's always easier to make this transition if you don't need to tell all your readers to update their bookmarks and head to a completely new Web address.

Just under the section where you choose your URL is an option that lets you use advanced setup if you want to host your blog elsewhere. You don't need to set this up right now. You can choose ordinary hosting to start with, and then change your settings if you move your blog to another server (as described on page 534).

6. **Click Continue to move to the next step.**

   In this third step of the setup process, you choose a template for your blog (see Figure 17-7).

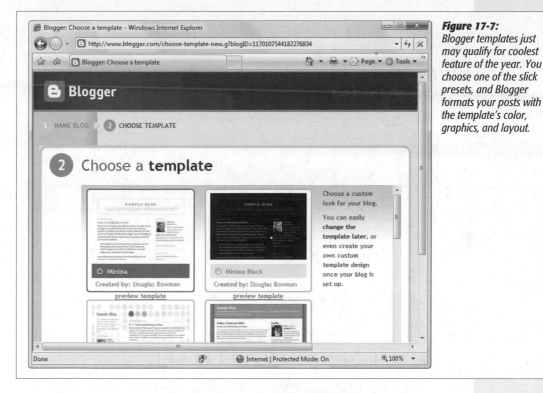

Figure 17-7:
Blogger templates just may qualify for coolest feature of the year. You choose one of the slick presets, and Blogger formats your posts with the template's color, graphics, and layout.

7. **Scroll down through the list of templates, and then select the one you want.**

   Click the "preview template" link to get a sneak peek at what your blog would look like. Don't worry too much about your decision right now—you can choose a different template any time (page 525).

8. **Click Continue to finalize your blog.**

   The page displays a "Creating your blog" message for a few seconds, followed by a confirmation message.

9. **Click Start Blogging to create your first blog post.**

   You can return to manage your blog any time by going to *www.blogger.com* (page 519). For now, continue with the next step to create your first blog entry.

10. **Enter the title for your entry, and then type the content of your post into the large text box, which acts like a miniature word processor (see Figure 17-8).**

    Don't worry about all the fancy frills in the editing window just yet—you'll learn about those in the next section.

Note: A blog entry can be as long or as short as you want. Some people blog lengthy stories, while others post one- or two-sentences that simply provide a link to an interesting news item (or, more commonly, to a post from another blogger).

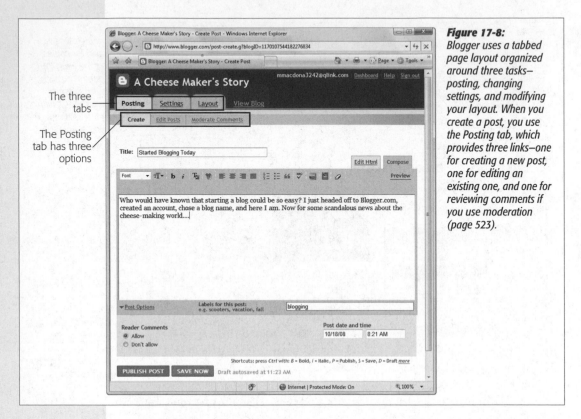

Figure 17-8:
Blogger uses a tabbed page layout organized around three tasks—posting, changing settings, and modifying your layout. When you create a post, you use the Posting tab, which provides three links—one for creating a new post, one for editing an existing one, and one for reviewing comments if you use moderation (page 523).

The three tabs

The Posting tab has three options

11. **Click the Post Options link at the bottom of the page to set a few more options.**

You can categorize your post by filling in a word (or a list of words separated by commas) in the "Labels for this post" box. When people run a search on your blog, they can look for posts with specific labels. For best results, always use the same labels to identify the same things. For example, every time you talk about your pet hogs, add the label *pig*.

You can let people add comments to your blog post (choose Allow, the automatic setting), or you can prevent them from doing so (choose "Don't allow").

You can set the post date and post time, which will appear at the bottom of your post. Blogger fills these text boxes in automatically, but the time probably isn't correct right now because you haven't set the time zone for your blog. (You'll learn how to do that on page 532.) For now, change the date by hand so readers know when you created your entry.

12. **Click Publish Post to create your blog entry.**

Blogger displays a confirmation message, informing you that it's posted your new entry online.

If, instead of publishing right away, you want to take some time to think over your post, click Save Now. That way, Blogger saves the text you just entered, and keeps it waiting for you the next time you return to your blog. (Page 520 explains how you can find an un-posted entry and edit it.)

Tip: Blogger automatically saves a draft of your post as you type, just in case you run into Internet troubles (or you accidentally close the browser window). However, it only saves your entry every few minutes. Clicking Save Now saves an updated draft immediately.

Now's a great time to check out what your post looks like. Click the View Blog link, or type your blog URL into a browser by hand. Figure 17-9 shows an example of what you'll see.

Figure 17-9:
This blog shows two recent posts (placed in reverse chronological order, so the most recent appears first). On the right, a sidebar provides sections of information about the author and other Web sites of interest (neither of which has been filled in yet), along with links to recent posts.

Creating Formatted Posts

So far, you've seen how to post text-only content in a blog. But Blogger's pretty flexible when it comes to customizing your blog. You can implement all sorts of fancy design maneuvers, from highlighting text to inserting graphics. Best of all,

Blogger lets you run rampant with the XHTML markup. You just need to know your way around the editor.

To do some customizing, start a new post by clicking the Posting tab, and then choosing Create. Type something in the Compose box in the middle of the page. Next, select some text and try out some of the buttons in the toolbar to format your post (see Figure 17-10).

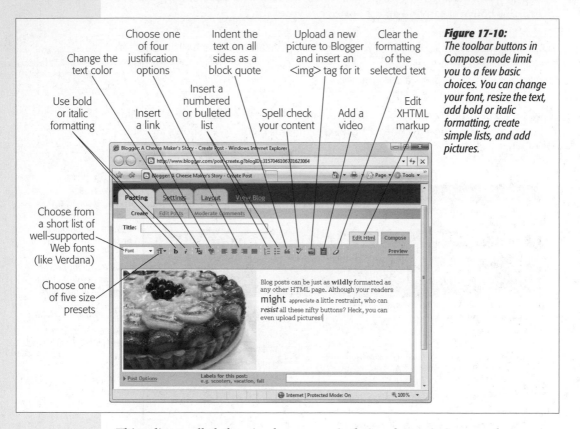

Choose one of four justification options

Indent the text on all sides as a block quote

Upload a new picture to Blogger and insert an <img> tag for it

Clear the formatting of the selected text

Change the text color

Insert a numbered or bulleted list

Use bold or italic formatting

Insert a link

Spell check your content

Add a video

Edit XHTML markup

Choose from a short list of well-supported Web fonts (like Verdana)

Choose one of five size presets

Figure 17-10:
The toolbar buttons in Compose mode limit you to a few basic choices. You can change your font, resize the text, add bold or italic formatting, create simple lists, and add pictures.

This editor, called the *visual composer*, is designed to mimic a word processor. However, if you're itching for some XHTML action, click the Edit HTML link at the top right of the edit window. Now you can add elements and other XHTML goodies directly.

Managing a Blog

Once you create your blog, you can do exactly two things when any kind of blog-related urge strikes:

- Read all your blog entries and review the comments left by other people. To do this, go to your blog, using whatever URL you picked when you created it.

Emailing a Blog Entry

To take advantage of all of Blogger's features, it makes sense to use the editor on the Blogger Web site. However, if you find yourself on the go with only limited time to spare, you might appreciate Blogger's ability to accept emails and turn them into posts automatically. It really comes in handy if you want to email a post from a mobile phone, or if you've got a sporadic Internet connection. In the latter case, you can prepare a post in your email program, and then connect to the Internet just long enough to send in the posting.

To use Blogger's email posting features, you first need to turn them on. Click the Settings tab and choose "email." In

the Mail-To-Blogger section, enter a secret word to use in your email address, and then turn on the Publish checkbox.

The secret word prevents other people from sneaking their posts onto your blog, because they won't know the exact address. For example, if your user name is lisajones and your secret word is antelope12, you need to send a message to *lisajones.antelope12@blogger.com*.

When you send an email, the subject line immediately becomes the title of your blog entry, and the message text becomes the body of the post. Blogger inserts the date automatically, based on your time zone (page 523).

• Add new posts and manage your blog. To do this, go to *www.blogger.com* and sign in.

When you try out this second option, you'll see a page called the Dashboard (see Figure 17-11). This is the starting point for Blogger management. It lists all your blogs (which, initially, includes just one), and provides a set of management links under each blog.

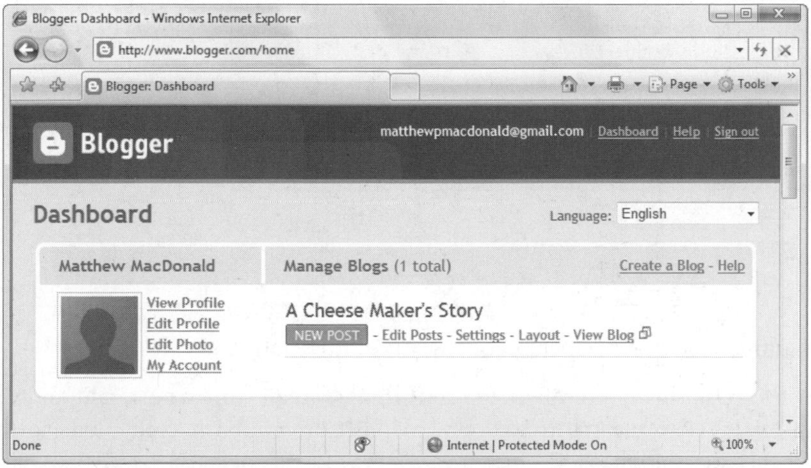

Figure 17-11:
When you log in to Blogger, you start out in a section called the Dashboard, where you see all your blogs and how many posts they have. Click the New Post button to add a new blog entry (Figure 17-9), or click Edit Posts to review earlier entries (Figure 17-12).

Although the Dashboard is the starting point for blog management, as soon as you get to work you'll return to the multi-tabbed Blogger page you used when you created your first post. This page is the core of the Blogger service—depending on the tab you choose, you can do anything from adding and editing posts to changing the way your blog works.

For example, if you click Edit Posts, you'll end up back on Blogger's multi-tabbed management page, but with the Edit Posts tab selected (see Figure 17-12). This tab lets you review and edit the posts you've published. It's the perfect tool for correcting a blunder—if you're fast enough to catch it before anyone else does.

Tip: If you haven't yet posted your blog entry, you'll see it listed with the word "Draft" next to it. This handy feature lets you pick up your blog posting where you left off.

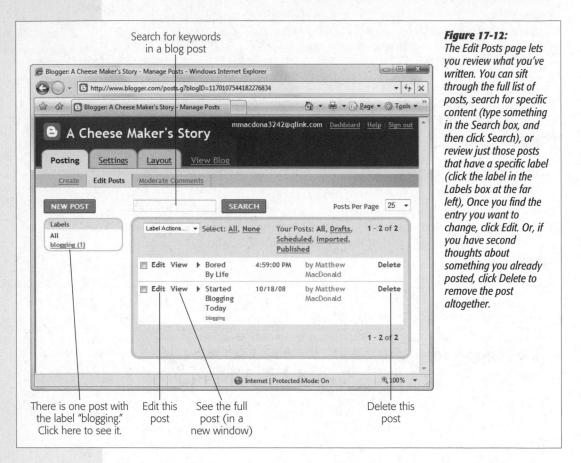

Search for keywords
in a blog post

There is one post with
the label "blogging."
Click here to see it.

Edit this
post

See the full
post (in a
new window)

Delete this
post

Figure 17-12:
The Edit Posts page lets you review what you've written. You can sift through the full list of posts, search for specific content (type something in the Search box, and then click Search), or review just those posts that have a specific label (click the label in the Labels box at the far left), Once you find the entry you want to change, click Edit. Or, if you have second thoughts about something you already posted, click Delete to remove the post altogether.

The multi-tabbed management page consists of three tabs and one link:

- **Posting.** Use this tab to do one of four things: create a new post, edit an existing one, review the status of your last post, or republish your blog (so that recent changes appear).

- **Settings.** This tab groups a dizzying number of options into several subgroups. You can set everything from basic information about you and your blog to options for managing reader comments and Web hosting.

- **Layout.** This tab lets you rearrange the content on your page or choose a new template. If you aren't happy with your blog's look and feel, come here to give your blog an effortless makeover.

- **View Blog.** This link opens a separate browser window that calls up your blog. After you make changes to your blog, use this link to take a look at the results.

Tweaking a Few Common Settings

To add a few more details to your blog, follow the steps below. You'll add a description, choose how many posts you want to display on your front page, and set the time zone to make sure your posts get the right date stamp.

1. **If you're at the Dashboard, click the Settings link next to your blog. If you're already working in the multi-tabbed management page, click the Settings tab.**

   The Settings tab gives you eight options. Initially, Blogger displays the Basic section.

2. **Add a description for your blog.**

   This description appears on your home page. Typically, you'll find it just under the blog title, although the exact spot depends on your template. Try to keep the description to a sentence or two that hints at the flavor of your blog. Two good descriptions are "The sober confessions of an unlicensed meat handler," and "An on-again, off-again look at my life and adventures."

3. **Scroll down, and then click Save Settings.**

   When you save your settings, your changes take effect immediately. But before you check out your blog, there's still more work to do.

4. **Under the Settings tab, click the Archiving link.**

   Archiving is the process Blogger uses to group together old posts and shuffle them out of sight. Every archive gets a link on your home page. For example, if you have Blogger create monthly archives, it adds links like "January 2009," "February 2009," and so on. If a visitor clicks one of these links, Blogger displays the posts from that period.

5. **Set the Archive Frequency, and choose whether or not you want each post to have its own page.**

   You can have Blogger archive your posts monthly, weekly, or daily. Casual bloggers usually find monthly the best choice. If you blog every day, you might split posts into weekly groups, but you'll end up cluttering your index page with a lot of extra links (one for every week you've blogged).

   The Enable Post Pages option determines whether or not each post gets its own page. Usually, you want posts to have their own dedicated pages. That way, a reader can blog in response to your posting, and provide the exact link to your post to friends and other bloggers. You also need to use the Enable Post Pages option if you want to support blog comments.

Note: Even though each blog posting has its own page, Blogger still shows multiple entries on your home and archive pages.

6. **Click Save Settings.**

   You're still not quite finished.

7. **Click the Formatting link (under the Settings tab).**

   The Formatting options let you choose how many postings Blogger displays on your home page and how it formats dates (see Figure 17-13).

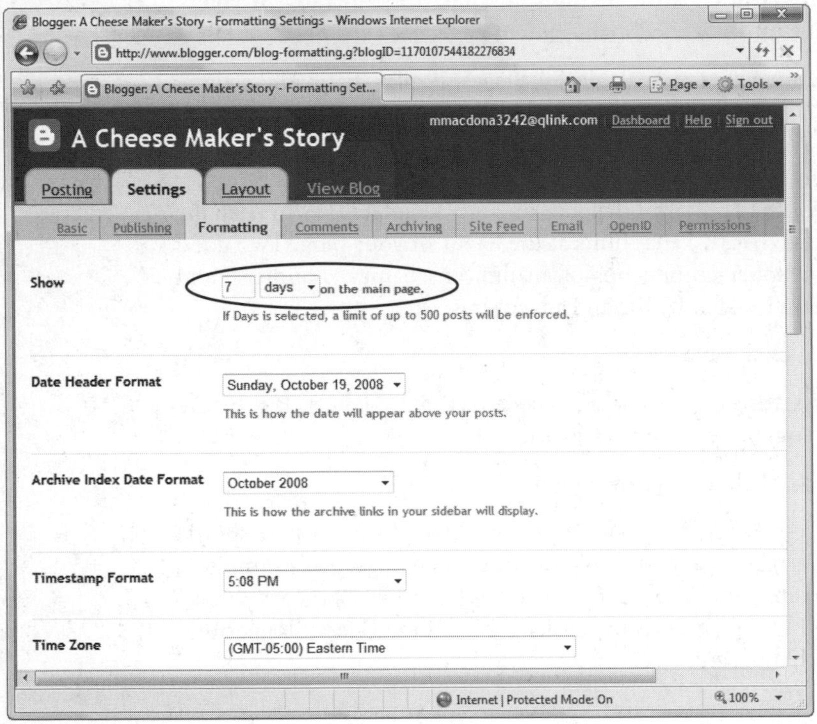

Figure 17-13:
Here's how you configure your blog to show a week's worth of posts.

8. **Choose the number of posts you want to appear on your first page.**

   You can ask Blogger to show a specific number of posts or number of days. For example, you could ask Blogger to show your last 14 days' worth of posts, or you could tell it to display just your three most recent posts, no matter when you published them. For best results, don't crowd your front page with too many entries. If you post daily, stick to a small number of posts or just topics from the current week.

9. **Set the date format you want to use, and specify your time zone.**

Blogger dates every blog post at the beginning or end of your entry, depending on your template. By setting the time zone, you won't need to manually set the date every time you create a post.

10. **Click Save Settings.**

Whenever you create a new post, Blogger saves your content letter for letter. When you change the settings for your blog, and then click Save Settings, Blogger doesn't touch this saved content—instead, it changes your blog setup. This way, when you visit your blog, you see the same entries but they reflect your new options. To see the results, click View Blog.

Configuring Your Blogger Profile

Interested in customizing the information that appears beside your posts on the home page? Blogger pulls this information from your user profile, and it's easy to customize it. Follow these steps:

1. **Head to the Dashboard on Blogger's main page.**

If you're in the tabbed view, click the Dashboard link at the top right-hand side of the page. Otherwise, go to *www.blogger.com* and sign in.

2. **Click the Edit Profile link (which appears next to the head-and-shoulders silhouette).**

Your profile page appears.

3. **Edit your profile (see Figure 17-14). Pay special attention to the Display Name, Photo URL, City, State, Country, and About Me sections.**

The profile page lets you supply a range of information about yourself. Only some of these details will appear on your blog home page. The most important include your name (Display Name), an optional photo (Photo URL), your location (City, State, and Country), and the descriptive text in the About Me box.

4. **Once you enter all the profile information you want to supply, click Save Profile.**

Head back to Blogger's main page (click Dashboard) and click View Blog to see the results of your changes. Figure 17-15 shows an example.

Templates

Templates are keenly important in Blogger. They not only reflect your blog's visual style (irreverent, serious, technical, breezy, and so on), they also determine its ingredients and how those ingredients appear on the page. Fortunately, Blogger lets you change many of your template's components. For example, you can move the About Me box to a new position, modify its appearance, or remove it entirely.

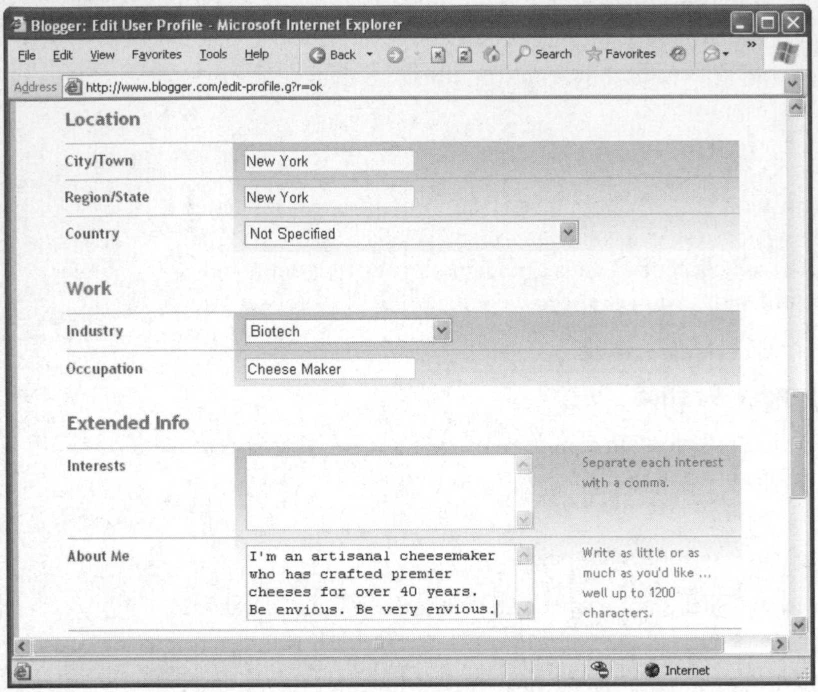

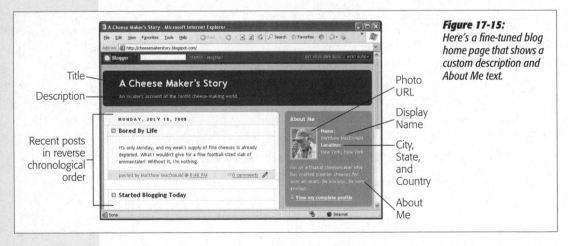

Figure 17-14:
The About Me section is one of the most important parts of your profile, because it appears prominently on your blog home page. Other sections, like Interests, Occupation, and Favorite Movies, don't show up on your home page, but readers can find them by clicking the View My Complete Profile link at the bottom of the About Me box.

Figure 17-15:
Here's a fine-tuned blog home page that shows a custom description and About Me text.

You can also add new sections, like a set of links that point to your favorite fellow bloggers, or a sidebar of targeted Google ads (page 528). You can even get more radical and replace your template entirely, even if you've been posting for years. Blogger retrofits all your old posts to the new template, so your thoughts, both old and new, remain available for eager readers.

To take control of these details, use the Layout tab.

Team Blogs

Having trouble keeping your blog up to date? If you want to be part of the blogosphere but just can't manage to update more than once a month, consider sharing the effort with some friends. Look for a natural reason to band together—for example, colleagues often create blogs to discuss specific work projects, and families create them to keep in touch.

Creating a team blog in Blogger is easy. You take your ordinary blog, choose the Settings tab, click Permissions, and then click the Add Authors button to add fellow bloggers.

You need to supply just one piece of information—the email address of the blogger you want to enlist. Blogger sends an email invitation to each potential blogger. To accept the invitation, the recipient clicks a link in the email message (and creates a Gmail account, if the blogger-to-be doesn't have one).

All bloggers have the ability to post entries. Additionally, you can give some bloggers administrator status, which means they can add more bloggers (and delete existing ones).

Applying a new template

When you first create a blog, you choose a template. Over time (or even right away), you may decide that the template no longer suits your content. If that happens, follow these steps to pick something different:

1. **If you're at the Dashboard, click the Layout link under your blog name. If you're already working in the multi-tabbed management page, click the Layout tab.**

   The Layout tab lets you either modify your existing template or switch to a new one.

2. **Under the Layout tab, click Choose New Template.**

   This page displays the same set of templates you saw when you created your blog (page 515). Look through the thumbnails, and then click "preview template" to take a closer look when you find a promising candidate. When you do, Blogger displays a full-screen rendering of your blog, current content and all, in the new template. When you're satisfied, click the Save Template button.

   When you select a template, you may see a warning message informing you that any customization you made to the current template will be lost. Since you haven't invested any effort in changing your template yet (a process described in the next section), you can safely ignore this message.

3. **Click View Blog to take a look at your changes (see Figure 17-16 for an example).**

   Blogger confirms the template save and offers a "View Blog" link. Click it to open a new window with your blog outfitted in its new clothes. If you don't like what you see, head back to step 1, and then pick a new template.

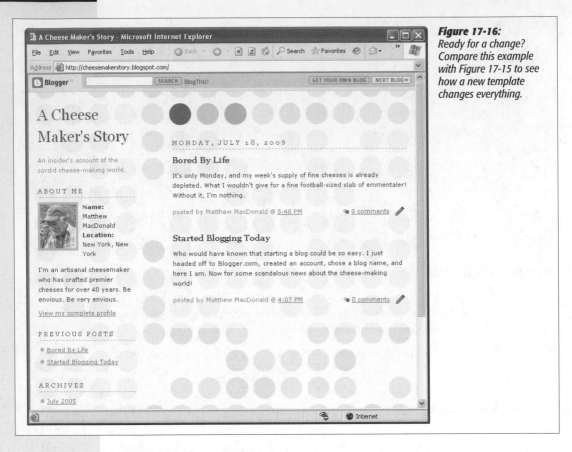

Figure 17-16:
Ready for a change? Compare this example with Figure 17-15 to see how a new template changes everything.

Customizing your template

Replacing your template altogether may seem like a drastic move. If you have a template that's almost right, you can tweak it to perfection by changing its fonts, colors, and layout. Here's how:

1. **If you're at the Dashboard, click the Layout link next to your blog. If you're already working in the multi-tabbed management page, click the Layout tab.**

2. **Under the Layout tab, click Fonts and Colors.**

   Blogger gives you an exceedingly easy way to adjust every font and color in your template. Start by picking the detail you want to change using Blogger's scrolling list (Text Color, Blog Title Color, Sidebar Title Font, and so on). Then make your adjustments.

3. **Customize to your heart's content.**

If you want to customize a color, you can use one of Blogger's three color palettes. The first displays the colors your blog already uses, the second palette shows complimentary colors, and the third offers a group of standard colors. If you can't find a suitable color in any of these palettes, specify a custom color by typing in a color code (page 151).

To change your text, Blogger has six standard Web fonts (Arial, Georgia, Trebuchet, Courier, Times, and Verdana, all of which are shown on page 158), and lets you either shrink or enlarge your text size. Best of all, Blogger previews all these changes as you make them (Figure 17-17).

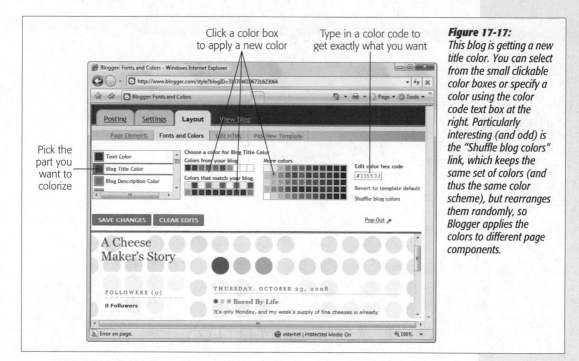

Figure 17-17:
This blog is getting a new title color. You can select from the small clickable color boxes or specify a color using the color code text box at the right. Particularly interesting (and odd) is the "Shuffle blog colors" link, which keeps the same set of colors (and thus the same color scheme), but rearranges them randomly, so Blogger applies the colors to different page components.

4. **When you finish, click Save Changes.**

This stores your color and font selections.

5. **Click Page Elements (under the Layout tab).**

Page Elements is a powerful blog-editing feature that lets you choose what content blocks your blog displays and where it displays them on the page. Blogger calls these content blocks *gadgets*. To help you move, add, and remove gadgets, Blogger displays an outline of your blog's current structure and shows you the location of your gadgets (Figure 17-18).

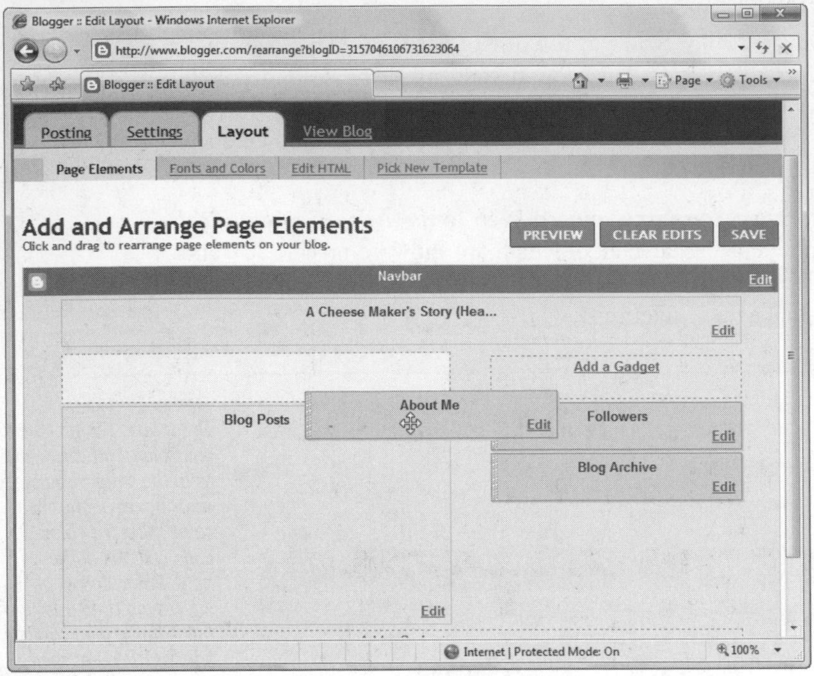

Figure 17-18:
You can drag any gadget to one of the carved-out regions of a page. Your possibilities depend on the template, but you'll usually be able to choose from a left or right sidebar, a top header region, and a bottom footer region. Here, the About Me section is being relocated to a more prominent place.

6. **Add, change, move, or remove the gadgets on your blog.**

Initially, your page displays whatever content blocks your template defines. However, you have plenty of options to mix things up:

To move a gadget, simply drag it to a new place (Figure 17-18).

To add a new gadget, click one of the Add a Gadget links in the Page Elements preview. You see a pop-up list with Blogger's wide choice of handy gadgets. Some are plain—blocks of ordinary text, lists, pictures, and links, for example. But others are much more interesting, like Blog List, a catalog of blogs you follow or admire; AdSense, which displays the money-making Google ads you learned about on page 363; and Poll, which lets you survey your readers and tally their votes. Once you find a gadget you like, click the plus (+) button to pop it into your page, and then drag it to any spot you want (Figure 17-19).

To change a gadget's settings, click the Edit link in the gadget box. Your edit options depend on the gadget. For example, the Blog Archive gadget displays a calendar of previous blog entries. You can change the order of the entries, the way Blogger groups the posts, or the way it formats the dates. If you edit the Blog List gadget, you can supply the list of blogs you want to link to.

To remove a gadget, click the Edit link, and then click Remove. One detail you can't remove is the *NavBar*, the thin strip that appears at the top of your blog.

Visitors who view your blog can use the NavBar to travel from one blog to another, sign up for their own blog, or (most usefully) search your blog for keywords. The good news is that, although you can't remove the NavBar, you can assign it a color so that it matches your template and blends in with the scenery.

Note: If you really, really want to remove the NavBar, you have two choices. You can host your blog on your own Web site (page 533), in which case the NavBar isn't required. Or, you can use a bit of style sheet trickery to hide it. For more information about this workaround, search for "hide blogger navbar" on Google.

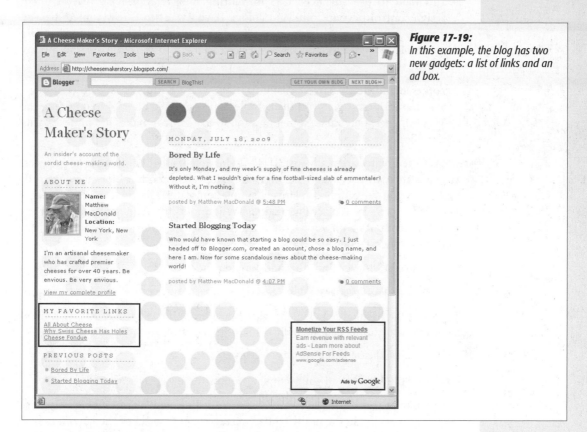

Figure 17-19:
In this example, the blog has two new gadgets: a list of links and an ad box.

7. **When you finish adding and arranging gadgets, click Save.**

Alternatively, you can click Preview to see what your blog will look like when you commit the changes, or click Clear Edits to abandon your changes and go back to the way things were.

Customizing the XHTML in a template

The tools you've used so far give you a lot of control over your blog's appearance. But there's one more frontier for die-hard bloggers who want unrestricted control over their pages—your template's XHTML markup. Using the skills you learned throughout this book, you can change virtually anything there.

This is obviously more work than using the editing controls in Fonts and Colors and Page Elements. So why take this extra step? There are a few good reasons:

- **You want to use an entirely new template.** Blogger includes only a small set of templates for you to choose from. You can find more online (use a search engine like Google, and search for "blogger template"). But before you download a template, read the box on page 531 to understand the difference between classic templates and dynamic templates.

- **You want to use advanced CSS formatting.** Blogger doesn't give you much design control beyond fonts and colors. If you want to throw something else into the mix—tweaking margins and padding, for example, or adding borders or setting background pictures—you need to dig into the template and modify its style sheet.

- **You want no-holds-barred customization.** Adding gadgets is a powerful system, but it doesn't give you the complete, fine-grained control that editing the XHTML does. Of course, sometimes too much control makes life unnecessarily complicated.

Blogger's templates are really just XHTML documents that define your blog pages. At first glance, this seems a little unusual—after all, a modest blog has dozens of pages, and you have only a relatively simple template! The trick is that the template defines special replaceable regions. When a visitor requests a page in your blog, Blogger starts with your template and fills in the appropriate content wherever it finds special codes.

For example, if Blogger finds this odd-looking code:

```
<title><data:blog.pageTitle /></title>
```

It replaces the highlighted element with your blog's title. The final XHTML file it creates for your home page actually contains this text:

```
<title>A Cheese Maker's Story</title>
```

To change the XHTML in your template, follow these steps:

1. **If you're at the Dashboard, click the Layout link next to your blog. If you're already working in the multi-tabbed management page, click the Layout tab.**

2. **Click Edit HTML.**

   You see a text box with the full XHTML for your template, codes and all. You can change some details right away, like the formatting rules in the inline style sheet. But if you want to add new content or rearrange the page, you need to understand Blogger's template codes. You can get that information at *http://help.blogger.com/bin/answer.py?answer=46870.*

Tip: Once you perfect your template, it's a good idea to back it up before you make any more changes. Otherwise, you could muck it up and have no way to get back to the right version. To make a backup, head to the "Backup / Restore Template" section, click the Download Full Template link, and then pick a place to save it on your computer. To restore a template, click Browse to find it on your computer, and then click Upload to transfer it to Blogger.

3. **When you finish making your changes, click Save Template.**

   Blogger updates your blog to use the new template immediately.

Classic Templates

Most of the Blogger templates available on the Web are *classic templates*. Classic templates use an older template system than dynamic templates, and a completely different set of codes. They lack support for the layout features described in the previous section, which means you can't add or rearrange gadgets. Instead, the only way to change the content in a classic template is to edit the template XHTML by hand.

That said, classic templates work perfectly well, and there are many beautifully designed classic templates to choose from on the Web. Classic templates are also required if you plan to use the self-hosting option described on page 533.

If you want to use a classic template, you have to click the "Revert to Classic Template" link at the bottom of the Edit HTML page. Only then can you copy the template into the text box. If you click Save Template and you get a cryptic error about misbehaving XHTML, you're probably using a classic template but haven't yet clicked the "Revert to Classic Template" link.

Incidentally, you can easily get back to a dynamic template if you decide you need the layout features. To do so, click the Template tab, then the Customize Design link underneath, and then the Upgrade Your Template button. Finally, pick a new template, and then click Save Template.

Moderating Comments

Ordinarily, Blogger lets visitors leave comments on your blog. That means your readers can post their own thoughts and follow-ups, and Blogger displays them along with your posts.

To leave a comment, readers have to have a Google account or an OpenID account (which is a standard that many blogging services and Web sites support). Blogger imposes this restriction to reduce *comment spam*—distracting comments, usually posted by automated programs, that advertise the spammer's products. Despite Blogger's best efforts, this restriction often isn't enough. If you're unlucky, you might find your blog entries swamped by offensive or annoying messages.

If that happens, you have a few options. You can turn off comments altogether, but that breaks the back-and-forth interaction that characterizes the blogosphere. You can delete objectionable comments, which is pretty easy—each comment has a trash can next to it, and a simple click banishes unwanted posts. The only problem with this approach is that you have to log on regularly to check for comment spam, and your edits take place after the fact. If you don't have the time to keep checking your blog, or you're dealing with a controversial issue and you want to make sure no one gets a chance to post inflammatory remarks for even a brief period of time, you need a different approach.

Your third option is to *moderate* the comments, only allowing them on your blog after you've given them your personal thumbs up. Moderating comments imposes extra work, but in some situations it's the only way to lock out undesirable comments—particularly if you have a popular blog on a hot topic. Here's how you moderate comments:

1. **If you're at the Dashboard, click the Settings link next to your blog. If you're already working in the multi-tabbed management page, click the Settings tab.**

2. **Click Comments (under the Settings tab).**

   Blogger gives you a surprisingly thorough set of options to control how comments work. For example, you can control whether anonymous readers can post comments (ordinarily, they can't), or you can switch off comments entirely. But right now, the most interesting option is the one that controls moderation.

Tip: Regardless of whether you allow anonymous readers and whether you use comment moderation, you should always keep the "Show word verification" option switched on. This forces readers to copy a word out of a picture before they can post their comments. Annoying as it sometimes is, this technique cripples automated comment-posting software that leaves the worst comment spam.

---

3. **Change the "Comment moderation" setting from Never to Always or "Only on posts older than 14 days."**

   The "Only on posts older than 14 days" option is an interesting compromise. It lets readers post comments when your blog entry is new, which is when most comments come in, but it switches to moderated comments after a certain number of days. This model works well because spammers are far more likely to comment on old postings than your readers are. Although Blogger suggests a timeframe of 14 days, you can reduce that number to fight comment spam more aggressively, or increase it to give your readers more time to speak their mind without hassle.

   Optionally, supply your email address so Blogger can notify you when someone posts a comment. However, this step isn't necessary, because you can moderate comments from Blogger's Posting tab.

4. **Click Save Settings to store your new comment settings.**

   Now you're ready to try the system out. First, log out of Blogger. To test the moderating system, sign back in with a different Google account or as an anonymous visitor (if your blog lets anonymous readers leave comments). You could leave a comment while you're logged in as the blog owner, but in this case Blogger assumes you don't need to second-guess yourself, and it skips the moderation step altogether.

5. **Post a new comment.**

To leave a comment, click the comment link at the end of a blog entry. Add a comment and your ID information, if required, and then click Publish Your Comment to make it official. Blogger is smart enough to know that the blog uses moderation, so it displays a message explaining that the comment won't appear until the blog's owner (that's you) approves it.

6. **Review your comments.**

To look at new comments, log in as the blog owner again, click the Posting tab, and then the Moderate Comments link underneath. You'll see the comments that await your approval (Figure 17-20).

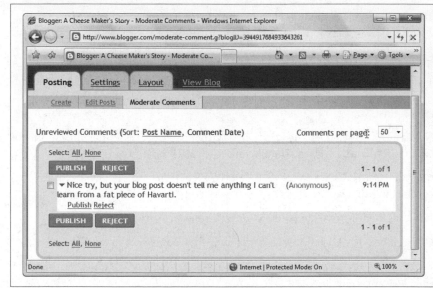

Figure 17-20:
This blog has just a single unreviewed comment. Click Publish to allow it into the blog alongside the relevant post, or Reject to toss it out. If you want to approve or reject multiple comments at once, just tick the checkbox next to each one, and then click Publish or Reject.

Hosting Your Blog on Your Web Site

In the past, cutting-edge bloggers often chose to host their own blogs because services like Blogger were unreliable—all too often, blog messages would disappear or blog tools would temporarily become unresponsive. Fortunately, Blogger has evolved into a remarkably reliable host. Even so, you still might want to host a blog on your own Web site for different reasons. One of the most obvious is because you already have a domain, and you want to use it for your blog. For example, if you have the site *www.CheeseMaker.com*, you could put your blog at *www. CheeseMaker.com/blog*.

Hosting your own blog doesn't mean foregoing Blogger's cool tools, however. You can still use the Blogger service to create your blog's XHTML pages. But instead of saving those pages to Blogger's Web servers, you'll get Blogger to upload them directly to your site.

To set this up, you need a few pieces of information at your fingertips, including the FTP address for your Web site's host, and the user name and password you use to log in to the FTP server. You then need to provide this information to Blogger. That way, every time you add a post, Blogger will connect to your Web host's FTP server and transmit the newly generated files to your Web site.

Here's how you set this up:

1. **Switch to a classic template.**

   Before you can configure your blog to use your own site, you need to switch to a classic template (page 531). That's because dynamic templates work in concert with specialized software that runs on Blogger's servers. Your Web server doesn't have the same software, so it can't use dynamic templates.

   To revert to a classic template, click the Layout tab, click Edit HTML, and then click "Revert to Classic Template".

2. **Click the Settings tab. Then click the Publishing link under the Settings tab.**

   The first line on this page tells you who's hosting your blog. You'll see the line "You're publishing on blogspot.com" unless you already followed these steps to switch hosts.

3. **Next to the "Switch to" heading, click either FTP or SFTP, depending on the type of publishing system you use with your Web hosting provider.**

   Most hosts use FTP servers; SFTP servers encrypt your password when they connect to other servers.

4. **Enter all the information about your FTP server.**

   FTP Server is the URL for your server (like *ftp.website.com*).

   Blog URL is the address on your Web domain where you can view your blog (like *http://www.website.com/blog*).

   FTP Path is the subfolder of your Web site where you store your blog. Usually, you don't want the blog in the root (main) folder, because that's where your Web site goes. Instead, you can use a path like *blog/* to tell Blogger to drop files in a blog subfolder. Make sure you include the trailing forward slash character.

   Blog Filename is the file name you want Blogger to use when it creates your blog home page. For example, you might use *index.html*. Don't use the name of a page that already exists or Blogger will overwrite it when it transfers your blog.

   FTP Username and FTP Password make up the user information you supply to connect to the FTP server. You can leave these values blank, in which case you'll have to supply them every time you publish your blog.

5. **Click Save Settings to abandon your blogspot.com-based blog and switch over to your own server.**

   From this point on, any time you publish your blog, Blogger will connect to your FTP server and transfer all your blog files.

6. **Republish your blog.**

Whenever you make sweeping changes to your blog (for example, when you modify your template), it's up to you to make sure Blogger updates and copies all your pages to your Web server. To do so, click the Posting tab, click the Status link just underneath it, and then click the Republish Entire Blog button.

GEM IN THE ROUGH

Promoting Your Blog

You need to promote your blog just as you do any other Web site. Although you can use all the techniques you learned in Chapter 11, there are some others unique to the blogosphere. Here are some important tips to get you started:

- **Add a blogroll to your site**. A blogroll is really just a set of links that lead to blogs you like. But blogrolls also make a statement. They say, "these are the people I like" or "this is the crowd I want to be associated with." In other words, blogrolls represent social networking at its best. The easiest way to create one is to use the Blog List gadget described on page 528.

- **Participate with others**. Bloggers are an open-minded bunch. If you leave an insightful comment in response to someone else's blog entry, odds are good that at least some readers will head over to your blog to see what else you have to say. If you let them comment on your posts, they're even more likely to come back for more.

- **Use the Email This Post feature**. You need to capitalize on the enthusiasm of your visitors. If you blog about a truly fascinating piece of gossip or news, readers might just decide to tell all their friends about it—if you make it easy enough. To encourage this impulse, add a link that lets readers email your posts. Choose the Settings tab, click the Basic link, and then set "Show Email Post links" to Yes.

- **Make sure you're in Blogger's listings**. You're probably already there, but it's a good idea to double-check. Choose the Settings tab, click the Basic section,

and then make sure "Add your blog to our listings" and "Let search engines find your blog" are both set to Yes. If not, you're hiding from the world.

- **Promote your feed**. Feeds, discussed on page 508, work with feed readers. True blog aficionados love them because they can track dozens or even hundreds of blogs at a time. Blogger's software lets you create a feed, and it's worth promoting your feed to your regular readers. To see your feed, click the "Subscribe to Posts (Atom)" link on your blog home-page. Or, if you don't see the link or you've removed it from your template, tack /feeds/posts/ default onto the end of your blog URL. For example, if your blog is http://cheesemakerstory.blogspot. com, odds are you'll find the feed at http://cheese-makerstory.blogspot.com/feeds/posts/default.

- **Use BlogThis**. A huge number of blog postings simply call attention to interesting news stories, scandalous gossip, or funny pictures that appear online. If you're an infrequent blogger, referencing these stories is a great way to beef up your blog. Using a nifty tool called BlogThis, you can create a new blog entry that links to an existing Web page with a single click. There are two ways to use BlogThis—you can use the Google Toolbar for Internet Explorer or Firefox, which has a button for just this purpose, or you can add a link to your Bookmark or Favorites menu that does the same thing. For the full details, check out http://help.blogger.com/bin/answer.py?hl=en& answer=41469.

Part Six:
Appendixes

XHTML Quick Reference

XHTML is the modern language of the Web. You can use it to create any Web page, whether you're promoting a local bake sale or running a Fortune 500 company. Chapter 2 introduced XHTML in detail, and since that point you've steadily added to your arsenal of XHTML elements.

This appendix provides a quick reference of all the XHTML elements you've seen in this book (and a few more). Each entry features a brief description of what the element does, and many entries provide cross-references to more detailed examples in the book. You'll also get a quick refresher of XHTML character entities, which let you display special characters on a Web page.

XHTML Elements

As you already know, the essential idea behind the XHTML standard is *elements*— specialized codes in angle brackets that tell a browser how to format text, when to insert images, and how to link different documents together. Throughout this book, you've examined just about every important XHTML element in use today. The elements in this reference are arranged in alphabetical order. At the beginning of each section are two key details about the element:

- **Block or inline.** You can put a block element directly in the <body> of a Web page. You can't do that with an inline element—you need to put it *inside* another block element. Some elements are even more restricted, and make sense only in certain types of containers. For example, the <area> element, which defines an image-map hotspot, is restricted to the <map> element that defines an image map (page 552).

- **Container or standalone.** A container element can hold text or other elements inside it. A standalone element has to remain empty, so you usually write it as one tag with the empty element syntax (page 33).

This reference also includes a few elements that are limited to XHTML 1.0 transitional (page 30). When that's the case, you'll see a special message in italics that alerts you to this restriction.

<a> (Anchor Element)
Inline Element, Container Element

The anchor element (<a>) has two roles. The most common is to create a link that, when you click it, takes you from one page to another. To insert this type of link, you supply the destination URL using the *href* attribute and put the clickable link text between the opening and closing tags:

```
<a href="LinkedPage.htm">Click Me</a>
```

When setting the *href* attribute, you can use a *relative* URL, which points to a page on your own Web site, or an *absolute* URL, which starts with *http://* and can point to any page on the Web. For a review of the differences between relative and absolute links and when to use each, see page 210.

Creating clickable image links is just as easy as creating clickable text links. The trick is to put an <img> element inside an <a> element, like this:

```
<a href="LinkedPage.htm"><img src="MyPic.gif" alt="My Pic" /></a>
```

Finally, you can create a link that, instead of sending a visitor to a new page, pops up an email message with the address information filled in. You do this by creating a mailto link, as shown here:

```
<a href="mailto:me@myplace.com">Email Me</a>
```

For more information about the ins and outs of the mailto link, see page 337.

You can also apply the *target* attribute to an anchor, which instructs a browser to open the destination page in a specific frame, or in a new window. Only XHTML 1.0 transitional allows this attribute.

```
<a href="LinkedPage.htm" target="_blank">Click Me</a>
```

You can learn about this technique on page 274.

The anchor element also lets you create a *bookmark* in a specific spot on a Web page. Once you create a bookmark, you can create a link that takes visitors straight to that spot.

To create a bookmark, you use the <a> anchor element, but with a difference. You don't supply the href attribute, because the anchor doesn't lead anywhere. You don't put any text inside the anchor, either, because it's not clickable. Instead, all you supply is a *name* attribute that gives your bookmark a descriptive name. Here's an example:

```
<a name="Canaries">Pet Canaries</a>
```

Once you create a bookmark, you can write a URL that points to that bookmark. The trick is that you need to add the bookmark information to the end of the URL. To do this, add the number sign symbol (#) followed by the bookmark name, as shown here:

```
Learn about recent developments in <a href="sales.htm#Canaries">canary
sales</a>.
```

You can learn more about bookmarks and ordinary links in Chapter 8.

<acronym>

Inline Element, Container Element

The acronym element displays the full version of an abbreviation. For example, wouldn't your visitors like to know that the hipster slang AFAIK stands for "as far as I know"? You can tell them using this markup:

```
<acronym title="As Far As I Know">AFAIK</acronym>
```

On your Web page, the information in the *title* attribute doesn't appear right away. But it's available for automated programs that scan Web pages and, more interestingly, many Web browsers (including Internet Explorer and Firefox) show the full title text in a pop-up text box if you hover over the acronym.

If you use the <acronym> element, consider applying some style sheet formatting to make sure your acronym looks different from the rest of your body text (perhaps with a different background color). That way, a visitor will know there's some extra information waiting to be uncovered with a mouseover.

<address>

Block Element, Container Element

The address element is an occasionally used element that identifies contact information (like a Web or postal address). Here's an example:

```
<address>If you have any questions about the content of this site,
  phone our offices at 555-5555.
</address>
```

Most browsers format addresses in italics, just as though you had used the <i> element. The only value in using the <address> element is that it lets automated programs that scan Web pages extract useful address information.

<area> (Image Map)

Only Allowed in <map>, Standalone Element

The area element defines a clickable region (known as a *hotspot*) inside an image map (which you generate with the <map> element; see page 552). When defining an area, you need to supply the target URL (using the *href* attribute), the type of shape (using the *shape* attribute), and the coordinates of that shape (using the *coords* attribute). For *shape*, you can specify a circle, square, or polygon.

For a circle, you specify the coordinates in this order: center point (x-coordinate), center point (y-coordinate), radius. For any other shape, you supply the corners in order as a series of x-y coordinates, like this: x1, y1, x2, y2, and so on. Here's an example that creates a square-shaped hotspot:

```
<area href="page1.htm" shape="square" coords="5,5,95,195" alt="A clickable
square" />
```

The square is invisible. If you click anywhere inside this square, you'll go to *page1. htm*. For more information, see the <map> element on page 552. For a full-fledged image map example, see page 218.

<b> (Bold Text)

Inline Element, Container Element

The bold text element displays text in boldface. XHTML experts suggest using <strong> instead of <b>, because <strong> more clearly indicates the relative importance of your text, rather than giving a strictly typographic instruction about how to format it. However, the <b> element is still more common.

```
Here is some <b>bold</b> text.
```

You can get much more control over every aspect of formatting using style sheet rules (see Chapter 6).

<base> (Base URL)

Only Allowed in <head>, Standalone Element

The base element defines a document's *base URL*, which is a Web address used to interpret all relative paths. You have to place the <base> element in the <head> section of a page, and you can use two attributes—*href* (which supplies the base URL) and *target* (which supplies a target frame for links).

For example, if you have a link that points to a file named *MySuperSunday.htm* and the base URL is *http://www.SundaysForever.com/Current*, the browser interprets the link as *http://www.SundaysForever.com/Current/MySuperSunday.htm*.

Web-heads rarely use the base URL this way because it almost always makes more sense for the browser to use the current page as a starting point for all relative URLs. In other words, if you're looking at *http://www.SundaysForever.com/ Current/Intro.htm*, the browser already knows that the base URL is *http://www. SundaysForever.com/Current*. For more information about the difference between absolute and relative links, see page 208.

The <base> element does have one useful purpose—you can use it to set the target frame used for all links on a page (unless otherwise indicated). Here's an example:

```
<base target="Main" />
```

You can only use the target attribute in XHTML 1.0 transitional. You can learn much more about frames in Chapter 10.

<big> (Large Text)
Inline Element, Container Element

The <big> element steps the text size up a notch to create larger text. The <big> element is out of vogue, and you're better off using style sheets to control text formatting.

<blockquote> (Block Quotation)
Block Element, Container Element

The <blockquote> element identifies a long quotation (which stands on its own, separate from other paragraphs) as a block element:

```
<blockquote><p>It was the best of times, it was the worst of times.</p>
</blockquote>
```

Usually, browsers indent the <blockquote> element on the left and right side. However, you shouldn't use the <blockquote> for formatting alone. Instead, use the <blockquote> element where it makes sense—to highlight a passage quoted from a book. As with any element, you can use a style sheet rule to change the way the browser formats <blockquote> text.

If you want to put a brief quotation inside a block element (like a paragraph), use the <q> element instead (see below).

<body> (Document Body)
Only Allowed in <html>, Container Element

The <body> element is a basic part of the structure of any XHTML document. You put it immediately after the <head> section ends, and it contains all the content of your Web page, including its text, image URLs, tables, and links.

 (Line Break)

Inline Element, Standalone Element

The line break element (<br />) is an inline element that forces the text following it onto a new line, with no extra spacing. For example, you can use the <br /> element to split address information in a paragraph:

```
<p>Johny The Fever<br />
200 Easy Street<br />
Akimbo, Madagascar</p>
```

<button> (Button)

Inline Element, Container Element

The <button> element lets you create a clickable button within a form, with any content you want inside of it (for example, you can put a phrase or an image between the <button> element's start and end tags). As with any other form control, you need to supply a unique name and a value that the form will submit when a visitor clicks the button. You put the button content between the opening and closing tags:

```
<button name="submit" value="order" type="button">Place Order</button>
```

You can create three types of button, depending on the value you choose for the *type* attribute. A value of *button* creates an ordinary button with no built-in smarts (add JavaScript code to make it do something). A *reset* button clears the input controls in a form, and a *submit* button sends the form data back to the Web server, which is useful if you create a Web application that runs on a Web server.

The <button> element is more powerful than the <input> element for creating buttons, because it puts whatever content you want on the face of a button, including images.

```
<button name="submit" value="order" type="button">
  <img src="Order.gif" alt="Place Order" />
</button>
```

<caption> (Table Caption)

Only Allowed in <table>, Container Element

The <caption> element defines the title text for a table. If you use it, you have to make it the first element in a <table> element:

```
<table>
  <caption>Least Popular Vacation Destinations</caption>
  ...
</table>
```

XHTML applies no automatic formatting to the caption—it simply positions it at the top of a table as ordinary text (and wraps it to fit the width of the table). You can apply whatever formatting you want through style sheet rules.

`<cite>` (Citation)

Inline Element, Container Element

The `<cite>` element identifies a *citation*, which is a reference to a book, print article, or other published resource.

```
<p>Charles Dickens wrote <cite>A Tale of Two Cities</cite>.</p>
```

Usually, browsers render the `<cite>` element as italic text. But you shouldn't use the `<cite>` element for formatting alone. Instead, use it when it makes sense (for example, when you refer to a published work you quote) and add style sheet rules that apply the specific formatting you want.

`<dd>` (Dictionary Description)

Only Allowed in `<dl>`, Container Element

The `<dd>` element identifies the description in a dictionary list. For more information, see the simple example under the `<dl>` element description below, or refer to page 127.

`<del>` (Deleted Text)

Block Element or Inline Element, Container Element

The `<del>` element is rarely used and identifies text that was present but has now been removed. Browsers that support this element display crossed-out text to represent the deleted material. Another element Web-heads sometimes use to indicate a revision trail is `<ins>`.

`<dfn>` (Defined Term)

Inline Element, Container Element

The `<dfn>` element is rarely used and indicates the defining instance of a term. For example, the first time you learn about a new term in this book, like *froopy*, it's italicized. That's because it's the defining instance, and a definition usually follows. Browsers render the `<dfn>` element in italics.

`<div>` (Generic Block Container)

Block Element, Container Element

The division element groups together one or more block elements. For example, you could group together several paragraphs, a paragraph and a heading, and so on. Here's an example:

```
<div>
  <p>...</p>
  <p>...</p>
</div>
```

On its own, the <div> element doesn't do anything. However, it's a powerful way to apply style sheet formatting. In the example above, you can apply formatting to the <div> element and the browser passes that formatting along to the two nested paragraphs (assuming the style properties you're using support inheritance, as described on page 148).

To learn more about how to use the <div> element to apply style rules, see page 175. You should also refer to the <span> element (page 123), which applies formatting inside a block element.

<dl> (Dictionary List)

Block Element, Container Element

The <dl> element defines a definition list (also known as a dictionary list), which is a series of terms, each one followed by a definition in an indented block of text that appears immediately below it. In theory, you could put any type of content in a dictionary list, but it's recommended that you follow its intended use and include a list of points and explanations. Here's an example:

```
<dl>
  <dt>tasseomancy</dt>
  <dd>Divination by reading tea leaves.</dd>
  <dt>tyromancy</dt>
  <dd>Divination by studying how cheese curds form during cheese making.</dd>
</dl>
```

<dt> (Dictionary Term)

Only Allowed in <dl>, Container Element

The <dt> element identifies the term in a dictionary list. For more information, see the simple example under the <dl> element description above, or refer to page 127.

<em> (Emphasis)

Inline Element, Container Element

The <em> element has the same effect as the <i> (italic text) element, but many XHTML experts prefer it because it indicates the relative importance of your text, not just the way your browser should format it. After all, you might use style sheet rules to change the formatting of this element to emphasize its content in a way that doesn't use italic formatting, like coloring text red.

<form> (Interactive Form)

Block Element, Container Element

The <form> element creates an interactive form, where you can put graphical widgets like text boxes, checkboxes, selectable lists, and so on (represented by the

<input>, <textarea>, <button>, and <select> elements, respectively). By putting these widgets in a <form> element, you can create pages that collect information from visitors and submit this information to a Web application. Web applications are outside the scope of this book, but you can learn how to create a basic form that emails you the relevant information in Chapter 12.

<frame> (Frame)

Only Allowed in <frameset>, Standalone Element

This element is restricted to frameset documents.

The <frame> element defines a *frame*—a rectangular subset of a browser window—inside a <frameset> element. Each frame can display a different Web page. When defining a frame, you can supply a frame name with the *name* attribute (which you use to identify the frame in your links) and the page that your browser should display with the *src* attribute.

```
<frame name="Menu" src="menu.htm" />
```

You can also create a fixed, non-resizable frame by adding the *noresize="noresize"* attribute to the frame element. You can hide the border between frames by adding the *frameborder="0"* attribute, and you can prevent scrolling the frame by adding *scrolling="no"*.

For much more information about frames and how to use them, refer to Chapter 10.

<frameset> (Frameset)

Only Allowed in <html>, Container Element

This element is restricted to frameset documents.

The <frameset> element defines a frameset page—a page that contains one or more frames. Each frame is a rectangular region in a browser window that can show a different Web page. The <frameset> element also sets the size of each frame (using absolute pixel sizes or a percentage of the current browser window). If you split a page horizontally, you use the *rows* attribute. If you split it vertically, you use the *cols* attribute.

Here's an example with two frames split vertically. The first frame is 100 pixels wide, and the second frame occupies the remaining space:

```
<frameset cols="100,*">
  <frame name="Menu" src="menu.htm" />
  <frame name="Main" src="welcome.htm" />
</frameset>
```

For more information about frames and how to use them, refer to Chapter 10.

\<h1>, \<h2>, \<h3>, \<h4>, \<h5>, \<h6> (Headings)

Block Element, Container Element

Headings are section titles. They display in bold lettering, at various sizes. The size of the heading depends on the heading level. There are six heading levels, starting at \<h1> (the biggest), and moving down to \<h6> (the smallest). Both \<h5> and \<6> are actually smaller than regularly sized text. Here's an \<h1> element in action:

```
<h1>Important Information</h1>
```

When you use headings, always make sure your page follows a logical structure that starts with \<h1> and gradually works its way down to lower heading levels. Don't start with \<h3> just because the formatting looks nicer. Instead, use style sheets to change the formatting of each heading to suit you, and use the heading levels to delineate the structure of your document.

\<head> (Document Head)

Only Allowed in \<html>, Container Element

The \<head> element defines the header portion of an XHTML document. Put the \<head> section before the \<body> section of a page. While the \<body> element contains the Web page content, the \<head> element includes other information, like the Web page title (the \<title> element), descriptive metadata (one or more \<meta> elements), and styles (the \<style> or \<link> elements).

\<hr> (Horizontal Rule)

Block Element, Standalone Element

The \<hr> element defines a horizontal rule (a solid line) that you use to separate block elements:

```
<p>...</p>
<hr />
<p>...</p>
```

Although the \<hr> element still works perfectly well, XHTML whizzes prefer using border settings in a style sheet rule to get much more control over the line style and its color. Here's an example that defines a style sheet rule for a solid blue line:

```
.border { border-top: solid medium navy }
```

And here's how you could apply it:

```
<p>...</p>
<div class="border"></div>
<p>...</p>
```

For more information about the style sheet border settings, refer to page 167.

\<html\> (Document)

The \<html\> element is the first element in any XHTML document. It wraps the rest of the document. If you create an ordinary Web page, the \<html\> element contains two other essential ingredients—the \<head\> element, which defines the title, metadata, and linked style sheets; and the \<body\> element, which contains the actual content. If you create a frames page, the \<html\> element contains a \<head\> element, a \<frameset\> element, and a \<noframes\> region.

\<i\> (Italic Text)

Inline Element, Container Element

The \<i\> element displays text in italics. XHTML experts suggest using \<em\> (emphasis) instead of \<i\>, because it more clearly indicates the relative importance of your text, rather than giving a strictly typographic instruction about how to format it. However, the \<i\> element is still more common:

```
Here is some <i>italicized</i> text.
```

You can get much more control over every aspect of formatting using style sheet rules.

\<iframe\> (Inline Frame)

Inline Element, Container Element

This element works in XHTML 1.0 transitional only.

The \<iframe\> element creates an *inline frame*—an embedded, scrollable window that displays a Web page inside another one. You supply the attributes *src* (the page you want your browser to display in the frame), *name* (the unique name of the frame), and *width* and *height* (the dimensions of the frame in pixels). You can also turn off the border by setting the *frameborder="0"* attribute, or turn off scrolling by adding the *scrolling="no"* attribute. Here's one use of the \<iframe\> element:

```
<iframe src="MyPage.html" width="100" height="250"></iframe>
```

You can put content inside the \<iframe\> element that a browser will display if it doesn't support the \<iframe\> element:

```
<iframe src="MyPage.html" width="100" height="250">
  <p>To see more details, check out <a href="MyPage.html">this page</a>.</p>
</iframe>
```

\<img\> (Image)

Inline Element, Standalone Element

The \<img\> element points to a picture file you want to display in a page. The *src* attribute identifies the picture using a relative or absolute link—see page 210. The *alt* attribute supplies text that a browser displays if it can't display the picture.

```
<img src="OrderButton.gir" alt="Place Order" />
```

Internet Explorer displays alternate text in a pop-up text box, while some more standards-aware browsers (namely Firefox) don't. In either case, you can supply a pop-up text box in just about any browser using the *title* attribute. This is the best way to add pop-up text to an image.

The <img> element also supports *height* and *width* attributes you can use to explicitly size a picture:

```
<img src="photo01.jpg" alt="A photo" width="100" height="150" />
```

In this example, the picture has a width of 100 pixels and a height of 150 pixels. If these dimensions don't match the actual size of the source picture, your browser stretches and otherwise mangles the picture to match the dimensions.

Never use the width and height attributes to resize an image; instead, make those kinds of edits in a proper image-editing program. You can use the width and height attributes to tell a browser how big your picture is so it can lay out the page before it downloads the whole image, and so your layout is preserved even if the browser can't find your picture file.

To learn more about supported image types, how to organize pictures on a page, and where to find the best material, refer to Chapter 7. To learn how to create images that serve as fancy clickable buttons, check out Chapter 15.

Finally, you can create clickable regions on an image by defining an image map, and then link that image map to your image with the *usemap* attribute of the <img> element. For more information, see the <map> section (page 552).

<input> (Input Control)

Only Allowed in <form>, Standalone Element

The input element is the most common ingredient in an XHTML form (which is itself represented by the <form> element). The input element can represent different onscreen widgets (called *controls*) that collect information from a Web visitor.

The *type* attribute specifies the kind of control you want to create. Table A-1 lists the most common types. Additionally, you should give every control a unique name using the *name* attribute.

Table A-1. *XHTML form controls*

Control	XHTML Element	Description
Single-line text box	`<input type="text" />`	Shows a text box where a visitor can type in any text.
Password text box	`<input type="password" />`	Shows a text box where a visitor can type in any text. However, the browser doesn't display the text. Instead, it displays an asterisk (*) in place of every letter, to hide the text from prying eyes.

Table A-1. *XHTML form controls (continued)*

Control	XHTML Element	Description
Checkbox	`<input type="checkbox" />`	Shows a checkbox you can set as turned on or off.
Radio button	`<input type="radio" />`	Shows a radio button (a circle you can set as turned on or off). Usually, you have a group of radio buttons next to each other, in which case a visitor selects exactly one.
Submit button	`<input type="submit" />`	Shows a standard push button that submits a form and all its data.
Reset button	`<input type="reset" />`	Shows a standard push button that clears visitor selections and entered text in all the input controls of the form.
Image button	`<input type="image" />`	Shows a submit button with a difference—you supply its visuals as a picture. To specify the file you want, set the *src* attribute.
Ordinary button	`<input type="button" />`	Shows a standard push button that doesn't do anything unless you hook it up to some JavaScript code (Chapter 14).

Here's an `<input>` element that creates a text box. When a visitor submits the page, whatever they typed into the box will be sent along, with the descriptive identifier "LastName":

```
<input type="text" name="LastName" />
```

For more information about forms and how you can use them to collect data, refer to page 339.

<ins> (Inserted Text)

Block Element or Inline Element, Container Element

The `<ins>` element is rarely used and identifies newly inserted text. It lets you create an XHTML Web page with limited change-tracking. (Of course, you don't really want too much change-tracking information in a page, because you want to keep your page sizes as small as possible so they can sail across the Internet without a care.)

You can use the `<ins>` element around block elements or inside a block element. The `<del>` element is another revision element, and you might want to use it in conjunction with `<ins>`.

<li> (List Item)

Only Allowed in <ol> and <ul>, Container Element

The <li> element represents a single item in an ordered (numbered) or unordered (bulleted) list. For more information, see the <ol> element for ordered lists and the <ul> element for unordered lists.

<link> (Document Relationship)

Only Allowed in <head>, Standalone Element

The <link> element describes a relationship between the current document and another document. For example, you might use it to point to the previous version of the current document. More commonly, you use it to point to an *external style sheet* that provides formatting instructions for the current page. You always put the <link> element in the <head> section of a page. Here's one possible use:

```
<link rel="stylesheet" href="MyStyles.css" type="text/css" />
```

By using external style sheets, you can define your styles in one file and use them in multiple pages. Chapter 6 has much more on style sheets and how to use them.

<map> (Image Map)

Inline Element, Container Element

The <map> element defines an *image map*—a picture with one or more clickable regions. When you create an image map, you assign a unique name that identifies the map using the *name* attribute. You then add one <area> element inside the <map> element for each clickable region, specifying the coordinates of the clickable area and the destination URL. (See the <area> element on page 542 for more on how the *coords* attribute works.) Here's an example of an image map with three clickable regions:

```
<map id="Three Squares" name="ThreeSquares">
  <area href="page1.htm" shape="square" coords="5,5,95,195"
  alt="Square #1" />
  <area href="page2.htm" shape="square" coords="105,5,195,195"
  alt="Square #2" />
  <area href="page3.htm" shape="square" coords="205,5,295,195"
  alt="Square #3" />
</map>
```

Finally, to use your image map, you need to apply it to an image using the *usemap* attribute. The usemap attribute matches the name of the map, but starts with a number sign (#), which tells a browser that the image map is on the current page:

```
<img src="image.gif" usemap="#ThreeSquares" alt="Image with Hotspots" />
```

You can't see the clickable regions of an image map (unless you outline them in the image). However, when you hover over a hotspot, your mouse pointer changes to a hand. Clicking a hotspot has the same effect as clicking an ordinary <a> link—you immediately go to the new URL address. For a full-fledged image map example, see page 218.

<meta> (Metadata)
Only Allowed in <head>, Standalone Element

Meta elements let you embed descriptive information in your Web pages. Your visitors never see this information, but automated programs like Web search engines can find it as they scan your site. You add metadata by placing <meta> elements in the <head> section of your page.

Every <meta> element includes a *name* attribute (which identifies the type of information you're adding) and a *content* attribute (which supplies the information itself). Although you can have an unlimited number of potential <meta> elements, the two most common are description and keywords, because some search engines use them:

```
<meta name="description" content="Sugar Beat Music for Children offers age-
appropriate music classes for children 4 months to 5 years old" />
```

Page 309 describes meta elements in more detail, and explains how search engines use them.

<noframes> (Frames Alternate Content)
Only Allowed in <frameset>, Container Element

This element is restricted to frameset documents.

The <noframes> element defines the content that browsers should display instead of a frames page if the browser doesn't support frames. The <noframes> element has to immediately follow the <frameset> element on a frames page.

It's incredibly rare to stumble across a browser that's too old to support frames (Netscape has supported frames since version 2). Today, the only browsers you're likely to find that don't support frames are mobile browsers for small devices like cellphones, and screen reading programs (typically used by viewing-impaired visitors).

For more information about frames and how to use them, refer to Chapter 10.

<noscript> (Alternate Script Content)
Block Element, Container Element

The <noscript> element defines the content a browser should display if it can't run a script. The <noscript> element should immediately follow the <script> element. The most common reason a browser can't run a script is because a Web visitor has specifically turned off that feature through browser settings.

For more information about scripts, refer to Chapter 14.

<object> (Embedded Object)
Inline Element, Container Element

The <object> element embeds specialized objects in your page, like audio, video, and even *applets* (miniature programs that run inside a Web page). For example, you might use an <object> element to place a Flash movie inside a Web page, as described in Chapter 16.

<ol> (Ordered List)
Block Element, Container Element

An ordered list starts with the <ol> element and contains multiple list items, each of which you represent with an <li> element. In an ordered list, your browser numbers each item in a list consecutively, using your choice of numbers, letters, or roman numerals.

Here's a simple ordered list that numbers items from 1 to 3:

```
<ol>
  <li>Buy bread</li>
  <li>Soak stamps off letters</li>
  <li>Defraud government with offshore investment scheme</li>
</ol>
```

To start at a number other than 1, use the *start* attribute and supply the starting number. To change the list formatting, use the *type* attribute with one of these values: *1* (numbers), *a* (lowercase letters), *A* (uppercase letters), *i* (lowercase roman numerals), *I* (uppercase roman numerals). Both the start and type attributes are restricted to XHTML 1.0 transitional. If you use strict XHTML, you can substitute the style sheet property *list-style-type* for the type attribute, but there's no equivalent for the start attribute.

For more information about ordered lists, see page 124.

<option> (Menu Option)
Only Allowed in <select>, Container Element

The <option> element defines an item in a selectable list control, inside a <select> element. For example, if you want to create a drop-down menu that lets visitors choose a color from a list of options including the entries Blue, Red, and Green, you need one <select> element with three <option> elements inside it.

When you define the <option> element, you can use the *selected="selected"* attribute to tell a browser to select this item when it shows the page for the first time. You can also use the *value* attribute to associate a uniquely identifying piece of information with an option, which is included with the form data when a visitor submits the form.

For a basic example, see the description of the <select> element.

<p> (Paragraph)

Block Element, Container Element

The paragraph element contains a paragraph of text:

```
<p>It was the best of times, it was the worst of times ...</p>
```

Because paragraphs are block elements, a browser automatically adds a line break and a little extra space between two paragraphs, or between a paragraph and another block element, like a list or heading.

Browsers ignore empty paragraphs. To create a blank paragraph that takes up the normal amount of space, use a nonbreaking space like this:

```
<p> </p>
```

<param> (Object Parameter)

Only Allowed in <object>, Standalone Element

The <param> element defines extra information in an <object> element, which the browser sends to an applet or plug-in.

<pre> (Preformatted Text)

Block Element, Container Element

Preformatted text breaks the normal rules of XHTML formatting. Inside a <pre> element, a browser pays close attention to every space and line break you use, and it duplicates that format exactly in the resulting Web page. Additionally, the browser puts all the content in a monospaced font (typically Courier), which means the results aren't always pretty. The <pre> element is an easy and quick way to get text to appear exactly the way you want it to, which is useful if you want to represent visual poetry or display a snippet of programming code. However, you shouldn't use it to align large sections of ordinary text—use tables and CSS positioning rules (see Chapter 9) for those tasks.

```
<pre>
Tumbling-hair
                    picker of buttercups
                                         violets
     dandelions
And the big bullying daisies
                              through the field wonderful
     with eyes a little sorry
Another comes
                    also picking flowers
</pre>
```

<q> (Short Quotation)

Inline Element, Container Element

The <q> element defines a short quotation inside another block element, like a paragraph.

```
<p>As Charles Dickens once wrote, <q>It was the best of times, it was the
worst of times</q>.</p>
```

Usually, browsers render the <q> element as italic text and some browsers, like Firefox, add quotation marks around the text inside. However, don't use the <q> element for formatting alone. Instead, use it to identify quotations in your text, and then add style sheet rules to apply the formatting you want.

If you want a longer quotation that stands on its own as a block element, use the <blockquote> element instead.

<script> (Client-Side Script)

Block Element, Container Element

The <script> element includes a client-side script inside your Web page. A script is a set of instructions written in a simplified programming language like JavaScript. Web designers use scripts to create more interactive Web pages by adding effects like buttons that change color when you mouse over them. To learn some of the basics of JavaScript and see scripts in action, check out Chapter 14.

<select> (Selectable List)

Only Allowed in <form>, Container Element

The <select> element defines a list control inside a form. Your visitor can select a single item from the list (or multiple items, if you add the *multiple="multiple"* attribute). You use the *name* attribute to uniquely identify this control, as in the following example:

```
<select name="PromoSource">
  <option value="Ad">Google Ad</option>
  <option value="Search">Google Search</option>
  <option value="Psychic">Uncanny Psychic Intuition</option>
  <option value="Luck">Bad Luck</option>
</select>
```

Ordinarily, controls create selection lists as drop-down menus. However, you can create a scrollable list box using the *size* attribute. Just specify the number of rows you want to show at once:

```
<select name="PromoSource" size="3">
  ...
</select>
```

For an example of a form, refer to page 339.

<small> (Small Text)

Inline Element, Container Element

The <small> element steps text size down one notch to create smaller text. The <small> element is out of vogue, and you're better off using style sheets to control text formatting.

<span> (Generic Inline Container)

Inline Element, Container Element

Use the <span> element to identify text you want to format inside a block element. For example, you could format a single word in a paragraph, a whole sentence, and so on. Here's an example:

```
<p>In this paragraph, some of the text is wrapped in a span element.
That <span>gives you the ability</span> to format it in some fancy
way later on.</p>
```

On its own, the <span> element doesn't do anything. However, it's a powerful way to apply style sheet formatting in a flexible, reusable way.

You should also refer to the <div> element (page 122), which can apply formatting to several block elements at once.

<strong> (Strong Emphasis)

Inline Element, Container Element

The <strong> element has the same effect as the <b> (bold text) element, but some XHTML experts prefer it because it indicates the relative importance of your text, not just the way your browser should format it. After all, you might use style sheet rules to change the <strong> format so it's emphasized in some other way, without necessarily using boldface.

<style> (Internal Style Sheet)

Only Allowed in <head>, Container Element

Use the <style> element to supply CSS (Cascading Style Sheet) rules that format a Web page. Always put the <style> element inside the <head> section of a Web page.

The <style> element lets you define a style right inside a Web page. This is known as an *internal style sheet*. Here's an example that gives <h1> headings fuchsia text:

```
<style type="text/css">
  h1 { color: fuchsia }
</style>
```

More commonly, you'll use the <link> element instead of the <style> element, so that you can link to a separate file that defines your styles. That way, you can apply the same styles to multiple pages without cluttering up your XHTML. Chapter 6 has much more about style sheets and how to use them.

<sub> (Subscript)

Inline Element, Container Element

The <sub> element formats text so that it appears smaller and lower (the middle of the text lines up with the bottom of the current line). It's best not to rely on this trick for formatting (use style sheets instead), but it's a handy way to deal with scientific terms like H_2O. Here's how you use it:

```
Water is H<sub>2</sub>0
```

<sup> (Superscript)

Inline Element, Container Element

The <sup> element formats text so that it appears smaller and higher (the middle of the text lines up with the top of the current line). It's best not to rely on this trick for formatting (use style sheets instead), but it's a handy way to deal with exponents like 3^3. Here's the <sup> element in action:

```
3<sup>3</sup> is 27
```

<table> (Table)

Block Element, Container Element

The <table> element is the outermost element that defines a table. Inside the <table> element, you define rows with the <tr> element, and inside each row, you use the <td> element to define individual cells and specify the content they hold. Here's a basic table:

```
<table>
  <tr>
    <td>Row 1, Column 1</td>
    <td>Row 1, Column 2</td>
  </tr>
  <tr>
    <td>Row 2, Column 1</td>
    <td>Row 2, Column 2</td>
  </tr>
</table>
```

It looks like this:

Row 1, Column 1	Row 1, Column 2
Row 2, Column 1	Row 2, Column 2

For more information about creating exotic tables and sizing them perfectly, refer to Chapter 9.

<td> (Table Data Cell)
Only Allowed in <tr>, Container Element

The <td> element represents an individual cell inside a table row (a <tr> element). Each time you add a <td> element, you create a column. However, it's perfectly valid to have different numbers of columns in subsequent rows (although it might look a little wacky). For a basic table example, see the <table> element definition above, and for a detailed table explanation, check out Chapter 9.

<textarea> (Multiline Text Input)
Only Allowed in <form>, Container Element

The <textarea> element displays a large text box in a <form> that can fit multiple lines of text. As with all input controls, you need to identify the control by giving it a unique name. Additionally, you can set the size of the text box using the *rows* and *cols* attributes.

If you want text to appear in the <textarea> element initially, put it in between the start and end tags, like so:

```
<textarea name="Comments">Enter your comments here.</textarea>
```

<th> (Table Header Cell)
Only Allowed in <tr>, Container Element

The <th> element represents an individual cell with table heading text. Use the <th> element in the same way you use the <td> element—the difference is that you usually reserve the <th> element for the first row of a table (because it represents column headings), and <th> text appears boldfaced and centered (which you can tailor using style sheets).

<title> (Document Title)
Only Allowed in <head>, Container Element

The <title> element specifies the title of a Web page. The browser displays this text in its title bar and uses it as the bookmark text if a visitor bookmarks the page. You have to put the <title> element in the <head> section of a page.

```
<title>Truly Honest Car Mechanics</title>
```

<tr> (Table Row)

Only Allowed in <table>, Container Element

The <tr> element represents an individual row inside a table (a <table> element). To add cells of information, you need to add the <td> element inside the <tr> element. For a basic table example, see the <table> element definition above, and for a detailed explanation of tables, check out Chapter 9.

<tt> (Teletype Text)

Inline Element, Container Element

The teletype element displays text in a fixed-width (monospaced) font, like Courier. Programmers sometimes use it for snippets of code in a paragraph:

```
<p>To solve your problem, use the <tt>Fizzle()</tt> function.</p>
```

Teletype text is designed for use inside a block element, like a paragraph (because it's an inline element). For a similar effect in a block element, check out the <pre> element.

<u> (Underlined Text)

Inline Element, Container Element

This element works in XHTML 1.0 transitional only.

The <u> element displays text as underlined. Be careful about using this element, because it's all too easy for Web visitors to mistake underlined text for links.

```
Here is some <u>underlined</u> text.
```

To create underlined text in Web pages that use XHTML strict, you can use a style sheet rule that applies the *text-decoration* style property (page 155).

<ul> (Unordered List)

Block Element, Container Element

An unordered list starts with the <ul> element, and includes multiple list items, each of which you represent with a <li> element. The browser indents each item in the list, and draws a bullet next to it.

Here's a simple unordered list:

```
<ul>
  <li>Buy bread</li>
  <li>Soak stamps off letters</li>
  <li>Defraud government with offshore investment scheme</li>
</ul>
```

If you use XHTML 1.0 transitional, you can change the bullet style in an unordered list with the *type* attribute (allowed values are *disc*, *circle*, and *square*). If you use strict XHTML, you can substitute the style sheet property *list-style-type* instead. Or you can use an image for a bullet, as shown on page 204.

XHTML Character Entities

XHTML character entities are codes that a browser translates into other characters when the browser displays the page. All XHTML character entities start with the ampersand (&) and end with the semicolon (;).

There are two reasons you might want to use XHTML character entities. First of all, you might want to use a character that has a special meaning in the XHTML standard. For example, if you type < in an XHTML document, a browser assumes you're starting to define an element, which makes it difficult to write a pithy bit of logic like "2 < 3." To get around this, you can replace the < symbol with a character entity that *represents* the less-than symbol. The browser then inserts the actual < character you want when it displays the page.

The other reason you might use XHTML character entities is because you want to use a special character that's not easy to type, like an accented letter or a currency symbol. In fact, characters like this are quite possibly not on your keyboard at all.

Table A-2 has the most commonly used XHTML entities. For the complete list, which includes many more international language characters, see *http://www.webmonkey.com/reference/Special_Characters*. You can also type in certain special characters using a non-English keyboard, or pick international language characters from a utility program. See page 134 for more information about these options.

Table A-2. XHTML character entities

Character	Name of Character	What to Type
<	Less than	<
>	Greater than	>
&	Ampersand	&
"	Quotation mark	"
©	Copyright	©
®	Registered trademark	®
¢	Cent sign	¢
£	Pound sterling	£
¥	Yen sign	¥
€	Euro sign	€ (but € is better supported)
°	Degree sign	°
±	Plus or minus	±
÷	Division sign	÷
×	Multiply sign	×
μ	Micro sign	µ
¼	Fraction one-quarter	¼
½	Fraction one-half	½
¾	Fraction three-quarters	¾

Table A-2. XHTML character entities (continued)

Character	Name of Character	What to Type
¶	Paragraph sign	&para;
§	Section sign	&sect;
«	Left angle quote, guillemotleft	&laquo;
»	Right angle quote, guillemotright	&raquo;
¡	Inverted exclamation	&iexcl;
¿	Inverted question mark	&iquest;
æ	Small ae diphthong (ligature)	&aelig;
ç	Small c, cedilla	&ccedil;
è	Small e, grave accent	&egrave;
é	Small e, acute accent	&eacute;
ê	Small e, circumflex accent	&ecirc;
ë	Small e, dieresis or umlaut mark	&euml;
ö	Small o, dieresis or umlaut mark	&ouml;
É	Capital E, acute accent	&Eacute;

XHTML Color Names

The XHTML standard officially recognizes only 16 color names. They're listed in Table A-3.

Table A-3. XHTML color names

Aqua	Navy
Black	Olive
Blue	Purple
Fuchsia	Red
Gray	Silver
Green	Teal
Lime	White
Maroon	Yellow

Although many browsers recognize more names, the safest option to get better colors is to use a *color code* (see page 152).

CREATING A WEB SITE: THE MISSING MANUAL

Useful Web Sites

Throughout this book, you learned about a number of great Web sites where you can download handy software or get valuable information. Odds are, you'll want to revisit some of these sites to keep honing your Web skills (or just to get free stuff). To save you the effort of leafing through hundreds of pages, this appendix provides those links, grouped by chapter.

To avoid carpal tunnel syndrome, you don't need to painstakingly type these URLs into your browser. Instead, use the online version of this appendix located, on the Missing CD page at *www.missingmanuals.com*. That way, once you find a site you want to visit, you're just a click away. In addition, check this page for late-breaking changes (like URLs that have moved to another location).

Chapter Links

The following tables list the links found in each chapter. Each table lists the links in the same order they occurred in the text. You'll find all kinds of links here. Some point to useful tutorial sites and articles, others to Web curiosities, and still more to handy free tools or downloadable pictures and media. Particularly important or noteworthy links appear in bold.

Chapter 1. Preparing for the Web

Description	URL
The history of the Internet	www.isoc.org/internet/history
	www.walthowe.com/navnet/history.html
Internet Explorer (browser)	www.microsoft.com/windows/ie
Firefox (browser)	www.mozilla.org/products/firefox
Safari (browser)	www.apple.com/safari
Summary of Mac browsers	http://darrel.knutson.com/mac/www/browsers.html
Opera (browser)	www.opera.com
Google Chrome (browser)	www.google.com/chrome
Netscape (browser)	http://browser.netscape.com/releases
Browser usage statistics	http://en.wikipedia.org/wiki/Usage_share_of_web_browsers
Spybot Search & Destroy (spyware removal tool)	www.safer-networking.org
Windows Defender (for Windows XP)	www.microsoft.com/defender
Lavasoft Ad-Aware (spyware removal tool)	www.lavasoftusa.com/software/adaware
One of many free blogging services (see the Chapter 17 link list for more)	www.blogger.com
What not to do in a Web page	www.angelfire.com/super/badwebs
The ultimate examples of bad Web design	www.worstoftheweb.com

Chapter 2. Creating Your First Page

Description	URL
Java checkers	http://thinks.com/java/checkers/checkers.htm
Flash games	www.ferryhalim.com/orisinal
XHTML validator	www.validome.org

Chapter 3. Putting Your Page on the Web

Description	URL
Smartdots (free subdomain names)	www.smartdots.com
Domain Direct (Web host)	www.domaindirect.com
Brinkster (Web host)	www.brinkster.com
DreamHost (Web host)	www.dreamhost.com
GoDaddy (Web host)	www.godaddy.com
HostGo (Web host)	www.hostgo.com
Insider Hosting (Web host)	www.insiderhosting.com

Description	URL
Pair Networks (Web host)	www.pair.com
Sonic.net (Web host)	www.sonic.net
WebHostingTalk (discussion board)	http://tinyurl.com/5zffwp
Web host research	www.consumersearch.com/www/internet/web-hosting/review.html
TinyURL (URL-shrinking service)	http://tinyurl.com
Directory of free Web hosts	www.free-webhosts.com/user_reviews.php

Chapter 4. Power Tools

Description	URL
Shareware programs	www.download.com
List of Web page editors	http://en.wikipedia.org/wiki/Comparison_of_HTML_editors
Nvu/KompoZer (Web page editor)	www.kompozer.net
Amaya (Web page editor)	www.w3.org/Amaya
HTML-Kit (Web page editor)	www.html-kit.com
CoffeeCup (Web page editor)	www.coffeecup.com/free-editor
Expression Web (trial software)	www.microsoft.com/Expression/try-it
Dreamweaver (trial software)	www.adobe.com/products/dreamweaver

Chapter 5. XHTML Text Elements

Description	URL
Firefox Web Developer add-on	http://addons.mozilla.org/en-US/firefox/addon/60
Learn about the semantic Web	http://logicerror.com/semanticWeb
Special characters in XHTML	http://www.webmonkey.com/reference/Special_Characters

Chapter 6. Style Sheets

Description	URL
CSS compatibility tables for different browsers	www.webdevout.net/browser-support-css www.quirksmode.org/css/contents.html
Online color pickers	www.colorpicker.com www.colorschemer.com/online.html
Information about font support on different operating systems	http://web.mit.edu/jmorzins/www/fonts.html www.upsdell.com/BrowserNews/res_fontsamp.htm

Chapter 7. Adding Graphics

Description	URL
Free image editors	www.gimp.org (all platforms)
	www.getpaint.net (Windows-only)
Free backgrounds	www.grsites.com/textures
	www.backgroundcity.com
	www.backgroundsarchive.com
Google image search (pictures aren't necessarily free to use)	http://images.google.com
Stock.XCHNG (free pictures)	http://sxc.hu
Overview of places to find free pictures	www.masternewmedia.org/where_to_find_free_images_and_visuals
Commercial picture sites	www.istockphoto.com
	www.fotolia.com
	www.dreamstime.com
Microsoft Office clip art	http://office.microsoft.com/clipart

Chapter 8. Linking Pages

Description	URL
Link checker	http://validator.w3.org/checklink

Chapter 9. Page Layout Tools

Description	URL
A huge catalog of style sheet layout examples	www.csszengarden.com
CSS tutorial	www.w3schools.com/css
CSS validator	http://jigsaw.w3.org/css-validator
Style sheet templates	www.bluerobot.com/web/layouts
	http://glish.com/css
CSS resources	www.westciv.com/style_master/house

Chapter 10. Multipart Pages

Description	URL
How to force frames with JavaScript	http://javascript.about.com/library/blframe.htm
EBook about Expression Web page templates	http://any-expression.com/expression-web/ebooks/expression-web-dwt-ebook.htm

Chapter 11. Attracting Visitors

Description	URL
The Open Directory Project	*http://dmoz.org*
	http://dmoz.org/add.html (submission rules)
	http://dmoz.org/guidelines (editor guidelines)
Google Directory	*http://directory.google.com*
Yahoo Directory submission guidelines	*http://help.yahoo.com/l/us/yahoo/directory/suggest/listings-03.html*
	www.apromotionguide.com/yahoo.html (unofficial)
	https://ecom.yahoo.com/dir/submit/intro (Yahoo Directory Submit)
How Google works	*www.akamarketing.com/google-ranking-tips.html*
	www.markhorrell.com/seo/pagerank.html
	http://infolab.stanford.edu/~backrub/google.html
Google site submission guidelines	*http://www.google.com/addurl* (submit a site)
	www.google.com/webmasters/tools/removals (remove a site)
Search Engine Land (industry news)	*http://searchengineland.com*
Webmaster World (industry news)	*www.webmasterworld.com*
Google AdWords	*http://adwords.google.com*
AdWords poetry	*www.iterature.com/adwords*
Wayback Machine (archived Web pages)	*www.archive.org*
List of Web robots	*www.robotstxt.org*
Google Analytics	*www.google.com/analytics*

Chapter 12. Letting Your Visitors Talk to You (and Each Other)

Description	URL
A tool for encoding mail-to message text	*http://meyerweb.com/eric/tools/dencoder*
Introduction to CGI	*www.cgi101.com/book*
ASP and ASP.NET introductions	*www.w3schools.com/asp*
	www.w3schools.com/aspnet
HTML forms tutorial	*www.w3schools.com/html/html_forms.asp*
Generate server scripts for form submission	*www.tele-pro.co.uk/scripts/contact_form*
Form submission services	*www.emailmeform.com*
	www.response-o-matic.com

Description	URL
Examples of discussion groups on the Web	www.microsoft.com/office/community/en-us/ flyoutoverview.mspx
	http://survivorsucks.yuku.com
	www.officefrustration.com
	http://forums.delphiforums.com/JLTechSupport
Google Groups	http://groups.google.com
	http://groups.google.com/googlegroups/ overview.html

Chapter 13. Making Money with Your Site

Description	URL
Google AdSense	www.google.com/adsense (sign up)
	www.google.com/services/adsense_tour
	www.google.com/adsense/taxinfo
	www.google.com/adsense/policies
Amazon Associates	http://affiliate-program.amazon.com
	http://associates.amazon.com/gp/associates/ network/build-links/banner/main.html (banners)
PayPal	www.paypal.com
	www.paypal.com/chargeback
	www.paypal.com/SellerProtection
	www.paypal.com/fees

Chapter 14. JavaScript: Adding Interactivity

Description	URL
JavaScript tutorials	www.w3schools.com/js
	www.echoecho.com/javascript.htm
	www.htmlgoodies.com/primers/jsp
	www.webmonkey.com/tutorial/JavaScript_ Tutorial
Text effect examples	www.codejunction.com/detailed/sequential-fly- in-text-effect.html
	www.javascript-page.com/tickert.html
	www.flooble.com/scripts/animate.php
JavaScript events	www.w3schools.com/htmldom/dom_reference. asp
EarthWeb (JavaScript samples)	http://webdeveloper.earthweb.com/webjs
The JavaScript Source (JavaScript samples)	http://javascript.internet.com
JavaScript 2 (JavaScript samples)	www.javascript-2.com

Description	URL
Dynamic Drive (JavaScript samples)	www.dynamicdrive.com
JavaScript FAQ	www.javascripter.net/faq

Chapter 15. Fancy Buttons and Menus

Description	URL
Button image generator	www.buttongenerator.com
	www.grsites.com/button
Flash button generator	www.flashbuttons.com
Button-making software (Windows)	http://free-buttons.org
Navigation bars	www.dynamicdrive.com/dynamicindex1
	www.dynamicdrive.com/dynamicindex1/topnavbar.htm
	www.dynamicdrive.com/dynamicindex1/topmen3

Chapter 16. Audio and Video

Description	URL
Winamp (MP3 player)	www.winamp.com
Classical MIDI Archives	www.classicalarchives.com
Audacity (sound editor)	http://audacity.sourceforge.net
WAV/MP3 editors	www.goldwave.com
	www.fleximusic.com
iTunes	www.apple.com/itunes
Sound effects	www.grsites.com/sounds
	www.freeaudioclips.com
Flash player	http://get.adobe.com/flashplayer
E-Phonic	www.e-phonic.com/mp3player
	www.e-phonic.com/mp3player/documentation
Flash background music loops	www.flashkit.com/loops
Impressive Flash examples	www.ferryhalim.com/orisinal
	www.zapdramatic.com
Flash tutorials	www.w3schools.com/flash
YouTube	www.youtube.com
	http://code.google.com/apis/youtube/player_parameters.html (configuring a video window)

Chapter 17. Blogs

Description	URL
Definition of "blog"	*http://en.wikipedia.org/wiki/Blog*
Examples of popular blogs	*www.andrewsullivan.com*
	http://dear_raed.blogspot.com
	http://wilwheaton.typepad.com
	www.schneier.com/blog
	http://roseandsnail.com
Online feed readers	*www.google.com/reader*
	www.bloglines.com
	www.newsgator.com
Windows feed reader	*www.newsgator.com/Individuals/FeedDemon*
Mac feed reader	*http://ranchero.com/netnewswire*
Browser feed readers	*www.microsoft.com/windows/IE/ie7/tour/rss* (IE)
	www.macdevcenter.com/pub/a/mac/2005/05/31/ safari_rss.html (Safari)
List of blog software and blog hosts	*http://en.wikipedia.org/wiki/Blog_hosting_service*
Movable Type (blogging software)	*www.movabletype.org*
Bloxsom (blogging software)	*www.blosxom.com*
WordPress	*http://wordpress.org (blogging software)*
	http://wordpress.com (hosted blogs)
Windows Live Spaces (hosted blogs)	*http://spaces.msn.com*
TypePad (hosted blogs)	*www.typepad.com*
Blogger (hosted blogs)	*www.blogger.com*
	http://help.blogger.com (information)
	http://help.blogger.com/bin/answer. py?answer=46870 (template tag reference)
	http://help.blogger.com/bin/answer. py?hl=en&answer=41469 (create a BlogThis book-mark)
Blogger discussion forum	*www.bloggerforum.com*

Index

Symbols

 # (number symbol) in URLs, 222
& (ampersand) in XHTML, 133
* (asterisk) in frame sizing, 269
+= operator in JavaScript, 417
/ (forward slash) in URLs, 217
// (forward slashes) for code comments, 417
:active pseudo-selector, 209
:hover pseudo-selector, 209
:link pseudo-selector, 209
:visited pseudo-selector, 209
; (semicolon) as line-termination character (JavaScript), 410, 466
= (equals sign) to store variable information, 410
\ (backslash) in file paths, 217
{ } (curly braces) for style rules, 141
" " (quotation marks) for text strings, 411

A

absolute positioning
    combining with relative positioning, 258–260
    style-based layouts and, 253–254
absolute sizing
    tables, 240
    text, 159
absolute URLs, defined, 210
acronym element, XHTML, 541

ActiveX controls, defined, 28
ad units (AdSense), 369
address element, XHTML, 541
Adobe Photoshop, 189
ads (Google AdSense)
    creating, 366–373
    creating targeted, 377
    placing in Web pages, 373–376
advertisements overview, 362
AdWords, Google, 320–321
affiliate programs, 361, 362
alert function (JavaScript), 408
aligning
    images, 190–191
    tables, 239–243
    text (CSS), 163–168
    vertical text, 244
alt (alternate text) attribute, 44, 181–182, 311
alternate image text in site promotion, 311
Amaya page editor, 87
Amazon Associates
    generating associate links, 382–387
    overview of, 380–381
    signing up as associate, 381–382
ampersand (&) in XHTML, 133
anchor (a) element, XHTML, 207–208, 540–541
angle brackets in XHTML, 133
animated GIFs, 474
anti-aliasing, defined, 448

CREATING A WEB SITE: THE MISSING MANUAL

J

Java
    applets, defined, 28
    Checkers, 28
JavaScript
    browsers not supporting, 409
    Dynamic XHTML (DHTML) support. *See*
        Dynamic XHTML (DHTML)
    external script files, 418–420
    framesets and, 282
    functions, 414–418
    overview of, 403–404
    programming with, 341
    references online, 414
    script element, 406–410
    script resources online, 437–439
    scripts and scripting languages, 405
    spaces and line breaks in, 410
    variables, 410–413
Jen, Mark, 508
JPEG format
    compression in, 187
    defined, 184
    linking to, 216
    when to choose, 188
justify setting, text, 164

K

keyword meta element, 311–312
keyword sizing (fonts), 159
keyword tricks, 312

L

large text, defined, 159
layering (style-based layouts), 255–257
layouts, ad (AdSense), 370
layouts, page
    floating, 251
    invisible tables, defined, 229
    overview of, 229–230
    pages sizes, testing, 232
    resolution basics, 232
    screen space and sizing, 230–231
    style-based. *See* style-based layouts
    tables. *See* tables
Liberty, Jesse, 349
line breaks
    element (br), XHTML, 116–117, 544
    in JavaScript, 410
lines, horizontal, 119
linking
    to fragments with bookmarks, 221–222

    to multimedia, 472
    to non-XHTML content, 216–217
    to video clips, 493–494
links (hyperlinks)
    anchor (a) element, 207–208
    broken, 222
    browser redirects, 227–228
    changing colors with style sheets, 209
    checkers, 225–227
    document-relative, 215
    for useful web sites by chapter, 563
    generating Amazon Associates, 382–387
    internal and external, 208–211
    link (document relationship) element,
        XHTML, 552
    link-building tools (Amazon), 384
    mailto, 337–339
    navigation and frames, 211
    product (Amazon), 383–384
    reciprocal, 303–304
    relative links and folders, 212–216
    relative URLs, rules for, 217
    root-relative, 215
    rot, 223
    site management to review, 223–225
    turning images into, 217–220
    units (AdSense), 370
    validators, 223
lists
    graphical bullets in, 204
    list item (li) element, XHTML, 123, 552
    list-style-image property, 204
    list-style-type style property, 126
    nesting, 128
    ordered (text), 123, 124–127
    unordered (text), 123, 126
live bookmarks feature (Firefox), 510
logical elements (XHTML), 110
logs, Web server, 323
loops, Flashtrak audio, 489–490
lossy/lossless compression, 184, 187
Lynx browser, 13

M

Macromedia Fireworks, 189
mailto links, 337–339, 344
maps
    element (image map), XHTML, 218, 552–
        553
    image, 218
    Map Overlay (Google Analytics), 330
margins
    for td and tr elements, 240
    property, 165

Colophon

Sumita Mukherji and Adam Witwer provided quality control for *Creating a Web Site: The Missing Manual*, Second Edition.

The cover of this book is based on a series design originally created by David Freedman and modified by Mike Kohnke, Karen Montgomery, and Fitch (*www.fitch.com*). Back cover design, dog illustration, and color selection by Fitch.

David Futato designed the interior layout, based on a series design by Phil Simpson. This book was converted by Abby Fox to FrameMaker 5.5.6. The text font is Adobe Minion; the heading font is Adobe Formata Condensed; and the code font is LucasFont's TheSansMonoCondensed. The illustrations that appear in the book were produced by Robert Romano and Jessamyn Read using Macromedia Free-Hand MX and Adobe Photoshop CS.

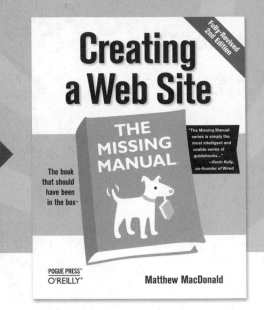